Earth, Man, & DEvolution

By R. Pilotte

Order this book online at www.trafford.com
or email orders@trafford.com

Most Trafford titles are also available at major online book retailers.

Print information available on the last page.

ISBN: 978-1-4251-5894-1 (sc)
ISBN: 978-1-4907-6899-1 (e)

Trafford rev. 03/23/2017

North America & international
toll-free: 1 888 232 4444 (USA & Canada)
fax: 812 355 4082

Trying to sell you the book you probably already bought online

I was told to make an intro that sells the book rather than making one that might scare people away by apologizing for some minor flaws that might still exist in the work. Ok so here's an ad I placed in a magazine that seems to "sell" the book and it probably gives you a good idea of where this book is heading.

ANCIENT ADVANCED TECHNOLGY CHANGES EVERYTHING!
If the ancients were physiologically, mentally, and technologically, superior: current theories have to change.

Years ago, out of the blue someone told me that ancient man had a 1000 IQ, and that they were more advanced than us. This was news to me and of course I argued the point. I had thought we were always this way. But I did remember an old movie showing a turquoise bead that was supposedly impossible for the people of the period to have been able to make. Asking around I found out the name of the movie was "Chariot of the Gods" based on the book of the same title by Erick Von Daniken. It wasn't much to go on but it turned out to lead to some extensive research and writing that spanned 19 years.

It slowly became apparent that man was indeed originally far beyond us in many ways, and not just technologically, but physically and physiologically as well.

These ideas are NEVER suggested to the kids in school. But the evidence is undeniable. All the same, people who promote this view of ancient history are shoved aside and said to be part of the lunatic fringe, mainly because this could seriously challenge some very ingrained theories.

For example, this challenges the theory of evolution. If man was more advanced physiologically in the ancient past, this means man isn't evolving, but devolving! This actually stands to reason, [because] Entropy and the laws of thermodynamic are well proven! And that's only the scratching the surface!!! Once evolution is disproved a lot of the evidence takes on new meaning and when looked at in a new light, things that were a mystery before suddenly become incredibly plain! The theory of evolution is like a pair of blinders that once removed, allows one to see the world as if for the first time.

This book takes these ancient mysteries and deciphers them based on the devolutionary principal and handily explains them so satisfactorily, that one wonders why no one saw it before.

This work could disrupt almost every school and science building around the world and could be the most attacked book since the Velikovsky trilogy.

Curiously I was not trying to cook any sacred cows, but merely looking at the evidence to see what picture developed out of the clues, but the results have far reaching ramifications.

I wasn't initially even interested in the pyramids or UFO's. But my curiosity was piqued when they kept cropping up in the research material. So thinking I was taking a break from the research at hand to read about UFO's and Pyramids, I was stunned to find they fit right in! The conclusions are frightening and mind blowing, but unmistakable. I had to wonder why no one came to the same conclusions. It has to be the prevalence of evolutionary thinking.

To be sure some researchers do get close on some of the theories presented in this work. Some may have come to the same conclusions, but this book takes them all and fits them together to give a completely compelling overview that has you stunned with the visualizations you inevitable find yourself doing.

Though this book had only been out a few months [Since Feb 6, 08] immediately new evidence found on Mars confirmed some of the startling theories present in this work. I won't spoil the surprise or tell you what Mars has to do with anything. But I will say that once again Velikovsky is at least partially vindicated.

The ancient mysteries sorted out in this book are legion, and at first one might wonder how a single book could decipher so many mysteries in one go. Well to start with, this is a huge book with the word count of about 5-7 normal paperbacks (over 340,000 words); but the key of course is the Devolution theory.

Once that is accepted the answers just fall into place. Well not quite. There was a lot of head scratching going on at first, but proofread after proofread made the evidence slowly organize itself in such a way that more mysteries sorted themselves out.

Though this book will seemingly fly in the face of almost all accepted earth sciences and established theories, we can thank archaeologists, paleontologists, geologists, anthropologists, and many other scientific branches for unearthing so many curious discoveries and clues. For without these discoveries we wouldn't know what questions to ask and what mysteries needed solving.

Rest assured this book will change forever how you view the earth and ancient history, and you will never again see the past in the same light. But it will challenge you too, as it did myself, and some will fight like mad against the conclusions. In some areas I had a hard time too, until I finally admitted there was just no way to avoid the conclusions. But if you agree with these findings then you will be changed forever and the world will seem like a different place to you.

It will also make you very aware of just how fragile this planet and we are, and how much we can and have affected our planet [in the past]. No doubt, if this book is ever fully accepted it will even change how we live, for suddenly major reforms seem entirely necessary and we'll look at our forefathers with a renewed respect. You will see how man has continued over and over again to destroy his environment, which in turn destroys earth's livability and consequently disintegrates our own viability. Will we be able to face the music? Or will we steadfastly cling to the flimsy theories that make life here seem so stable?

Mysteries solved in this work include: The original purpose of the pyramids. The identity of the UFO's and their origins. The mysterious "Planet X" is identified. Why the moon is so cratered and the earth is not. What caused the asteroids to come into being. What caused the flood of Noah; where the water came from and where it went. The origin of the other large floods in the ancient past that changed the face of the earth. The origin of the "erratics" seen all around the earth. The origin of the earth's fault-lines and what started the continents to drift. Origin of the races, the plague of the river of blood, and the cause of mass extinction sites around the globe, including the dinosaurs. This book even solves many, if not all the disappearances of the Bermuda Triangle. The purpose of the Tower of Babel is even opened to us. We'll even find out just who those gods in their chariots were.

I hope you'll read "Earth, Man, & Devolution"

R. Pilotte

Before you do get into the book one thing I have to mention is, that it is difficult to know which order to present the material in. Each chapter supports the evidence in each of the other chapters and sometimes it's difficult to know what order to present the material because no matter what you read first it will appear that I'm might be jumping to conclusions in some part of that chapter. But no matter how you read this book, eventually you will see that all the material eventually becomes substantiated. Well enjoy the book no matter order you decide to read it in.

PREFACE TO THE THIRD EDITION

But before I start…. I would still like to apologize at this time. I'm on income assistance, so professional editing of this work is out of my ability to afford, so I'm left to my own limited ability. I was the second worst speller in school and always sat down right after another guy …who usually sat down on the first word. I might get one or two right then down I went. I met a person with a 177 IQ and she was the worst speller I ever saw…couldn't even spell 'house'! So maybe I'm in good company. Thankfully there's spell check but even that can mess you up if you spell 'bee' and mean 'be'. Though I think I've read this book 16 times before publishing it was despairing to show it to people and in seconds they would find typos…not to mention brutal grammar. So please forgive my possibly even dismal writing ability as I can read it over and over and just not see it. I felt though that the information and solutions to so many mysteries in this book was just too good to let these inadequacies stop me from publishing. So please bear with me. There are times when it's even fun to read. This is my third edition and I hope to get it more tolerable. One chap, Cornelius, read my book and marked as many typos as he could find (about 400 or so) so that should help. (Thanks Cornelius!) And there will be pictures! Mental resting spots! You can't spell *them* wrong!

Ok... Since originally publishing in 2007 (with a few fixes, typos fixed and some new info added a few months later in early 2008) I kept finding more neat stuff that just adds weight to the material presented here. So in this edition throughout the book as I find more things pertinent to each section and chapter I will add them as (3rd ed. Insert 2016) (I've also noted where 2nd edition inserts are so you can see that too) With 3rd editions, rest assured if I find things that present problems to the theories presented here I will also present them. But by and large virtually everything I found just seems to confirm my solutions, deductions and conclusions.

Contents

Chapter 1

EVOLUTION ASSESSMENT

The basic work of this book is to explain and show the origins of what so far has been considered inexplicable. It would appear the reason so many mysteries go on unexplained is because people attempt to explain them in the light of established theories. One theory is built upon another. But if other theories are flawed and wrong eventually no matter how elaborately they are constructed they will eventually fail to explain something, which the theory should in fact explain. For example what started the continents drifting. Current theories are unable to come up with a working hypothesis to explain the origin of the continental drift. To make it less bothersome they simply say it took millions of years to happen, and leave it at that. Furthermore the current dating theories which say Continental drift took 200 million years do not account for the evidence, which suggest the continents drifted faster, much faster.

Another example. Many ancient structures are beyond comprehension. How did the ancients build them? No current accepted theory explains them sufficiently. Archaeologists assume extremely long building periods for some of these structures and then ignore them and go on to things they feel more comfortable explaining. But how did they move dressed stones that were 2000 tons to great heights? Current theories insist man was a backward savage and slowly advanced and seemed to have this bizarre penchant for moving huge stones to create inexplicable buildings. We don't for a minute impute great advancement to the ancients because the theory of evolution says we are advancing from what the ancients were back then and they were advancing from some caveman and monkey before that. This evolution theory does not explain these mysteries.

Other problems arise, like how can a city be built a few thousand years ago on the shore, yet now be in the mountains 12 thousand years old? Or where did the asteroid belt come from. Or what caused the flood or where did the water come from and where did the water go after the flood...and who or what are UFO's? Many unanswered questions. I maintain that the reason they go unanswered is because the established theories are inadequate to explain them and the theories therefore have to be refuted, overturned, and replaced with theories that explain more. Popular accepted theories do not explain these mysteries, or if they try to, they appear contrived or fall short of real logic.

Yet the theories are so ingrained that before I can explain, say what caused the continental drift and how fast it occurred, I have to rebuild or replace the theories from the ground up.

The largest hurdle to explaining the mysteries correctly is the theory of evolution. However to dispute the theory of evolution properly a whole series of books could be written on this subject alone. Originally this part was 80 pages long! But that's boring and I want to get to the good stuff so, for the purposes of this book, this part is reduced to a mere chapter. Hopefully this will be convincing enough to lay the groundwork for the rest of the theories presented in this work. If this only succeeds in making you admit there are problems with evolution theory, you can follow that up with more research if you so desire. Once one sees there are problems with the evolution theory, the theory becomes less and less sustainable as you read further on.

This chapter will attack the theory directly, and subsequent chapters to some degree do it as a by-product of the evidence presented. For now, humour me and allow me to continue on with my theories. The theories will in turn support this chapter simply by the evidence presented. Actually each chapter supports the other as I feel all these theories are intertwined and mutually supportive. For example when I started the research I wasn't even interested in the pyramids or UFO's but the research in other areas ended up deciphering what they were all about.

EVOLUTION IS A PROBLEM

Evolution is a problem, because it doesn't account for and explain all the evidence, and indeed it often contradicts the evidence. My original purpose for this work was to prove that man was MORE advanced in the past then we give the men of the past credit for. But this is a problem. Well the evidence isn't a problem, it's there, but it doesn't work if you try and combine it with evolution. The theories are mutually exclusive and diametrically opposed. Either evolution is correct and man was very primitive in the past or man was superior and more advanced in the past. Why is this a problem? Because Evolution says we are evolving in an upward trend and we are getting smarter, wiser, and as a species we are becoming more perfect. But if man was more advanced in the past than we are now, then this contradicts the theory of evolution. So either we were inferior and less advanced in the past than we are now or there is a problem with evolution. Since the evidence points to man being more advanced in the past, we need to take a more critical look at evolution. (For those of you one step ahead, don't worry, we will deal with panspermia too.)

Ok some of you are saying but there *were* cave men in the past. I don't refute this, but this can also be seen from a different perspective. The existence of cave men is allowable in both theories. But the nature of the cave men and the point in time they existed is a problem. Evolution says we advanced slowly for about 2 million years from cave men, whereas my theory shows speedy decline in the order of a few hundred to a thousand years to a point in time when the cave men appeared. So we can see that dating also becomes a problem. Therefore dating methods also have to be scrutinized, and a chapter is dedicated to that too. We will show that pockets of disorganization happened after great organization, that is to say the cave men came AFTER great order and not before, and then slow reorganization upward from cave man status took place. If 10 be perfect organization and 1 be cave men then originally we were at 10 then 1 then 7 then 1 then 5 then 1 and so on. Also peace and war determines the amount of organization allowable in any given period. Don't worry I'm not going to bore you with endless war tales, because we are not necessarily trying to prove organization in the past but genetic and mental superiority. This is the essence of the problem. Evolution says the exact opposite, so to give the upcoming theories a solid foundation evolution has to be "destroyed", at least that's what my dad said the original 80 page work did to evolution. Maybe boiled down like this it will only dismantle it.

I present here basically the original eighty legal size pages boiled down and used as a term project in English that stipulated ten 8 1/2 X 11 pages for the work. (By the way relax, this was written long after I graduated so we aren't going to be looking at a grade nine school paper here) Actually this was a fun challenge in itself, to boil down 80 pages to ten. The teacher gotz a kick out my paper because everyone else was double spacing with wide margins and I was trying to squeeze as much as I could into that ten pages with real thin margins small print and single spacing…and I left the references to an 11th page. I got an "A" and the teacher even said she understood it! That was great that she understood it, so except the odd bit added here and there and some clarifications…and maybe a few more paragraphs, I present it here as handed in to my English teacher.

MY ENGLISH PAPER.

I started reading the bible when I was 12 after some interesting discussions with my dad. When I went to grade 8, a teacher proceeded to start teaching about the evolution of the earth and monkeys and all that. This seemed interesting, as I hadn't heard about this before. I listened assuming eventually this would tie in with creation. The semester went on and I was beginning to wonder how this was supposed to tie in with the bible as I did not remember reading this bit, but I hadn't read the whole bible yet so I was assuming I hadn't got to this part. About halfway through the semester I was just too curious and went to the teacher after class and asked him when and how this would tie in with the bible, and creation. He told me it wouldn't because that was a different theory. I asked if he believed in creation and he said he did not. I was actually quite surprised by this. I asked him what class would teach the creation aspect and he said none would unless you went to university or college.

The predominant theory of today is that of evolution. However this work is based on the proven observation commonly referred to as entropy and I mainly key in on the aspect of Devolution.

Since Evolution is so accepted I find it necessary to scrutinize evolution and show it's fatal flaws so that Devolution can take its place and thus lend weight to the theories presented in this work which rest on the devolution evidence.

Evolution is called a science, yet many refute this claim, saying evolution has no true scientific foundations whatsoever. The people who make this claim are by and large creationists, and many who refute the theory of evolution are, in fact, scientists with degrees. This is quite unknown to the general populace, who are taught evolution all through school and are led to believe this is a thoroughly substantiated science. The creationist camp is quite bothered that such a 'flimsy' theory is given so much weight in school, whereas such a plausible theory as the science of creation is given no exposure to students whatsoever. Furthermore, students fail tests if they refuse to answer evolution questions with an accepted evolution theory answer rather than with a scientifically observed answer that contradicts the theory. Creation scientists feel creationism should be given equal time for students to be able to make educated choices. This too would vastly expand the scientific community and further extend knowledge in this field were students exposed to both theories. So, is evolution a 'flimsy theory', or does it actually stand up to scrutiny based on known scientific datum?

Though the theory of evolution goes back to the 19th century it has embraced the Big bang theory and so the evolution doctrine in a sense begins and rests on the Big Bang theory because the universe 'evolves' from a bang. Then life and such evolve from the result.

THE BIG BANG LOOKED AT

The Big Bang theory suggests that all matter was originally compressed into one small point in space. The size of this point varies with the theorist, from a giant star to a pea-sized object and even to an atom-sized object or even smaller. Some have even theorized this object had virtually no mass at all. This is tantamount to saying all matter came from nothing. Already this sounds a bit illogical, not to mention it break a physics law that states you can't create or destroy matter. This compressed object at some point blew up, rapidly expanded and created all atomic matter. It spread across the universe like one great nebula, swirling as gravity acted upon each particle, be it in the form of light, matter or energy. This swirling mass took on the basic structure of galaxies, forming stars with nebulous material around them from which planets were formed. Though some disagreement exist here, basically they say the heavier atoms attracted by the more intense gravity at the center of the solar system turned into the inner rocky planets while the lighter, gassy atoms accumulated further from this source of gravity and formed into the gas giants. One can quickly see flaws in this because stars are usually made of Helium and hydrogen...light atoms, thus not fitting the solar system as we know it today. And this theory breaks several observed laws, but to make it seem more plausible it's suggested it took "Billions and Billions" of years as some might put it. Time is added to explain the inexplicable…lots of time.

Einstein's lensing theory says that sources of intense gravity would bend light. This theory has been proven with the actual observation of a case of "lensing" around 1990. (someone threw out a bunch of my water damaged Discover and Astronomy magazines so in some cases with material of this sort I can't give exact dates or references. No doubt Internet and other sources can confirm these facts) Lensing occurs when a star is directly behind an intense source of gravity (as see by the viewer) like another star of immense proportions. The gravity of the immense source will bend the light of the star behind it, possibly creating a ring around the source or creating a double image of that star, one above and one below the source of gravity in front of it. The eclipsed star would appear like two stars but they would have identical 'fingerprints' proving they were the same star. The observation of an example of lensing proved that an intense enough source of gravity could bend light and by inference we could extrapolate and conclude that a large enough source of gravity would deny the escaping of light from it, in other words a "black hole".

The reason this information hurts the big bang is because all matter had to come from the initial explosion. Though black holes are still pretty much theoretical creatures, black holes are unlit sources of gravity so powerful that light cannot escape because gravity won't allow it to...are you following? If a mere little old black hole won't allow light to escape, then how is light or matter or energy going to escape a big bang? If all matter is in a ball for a big bang to escape from, how much mass is supposed to be in this ball? FAR FAR more matter then the matter of a teeny weenie little black hole. How much more? ALL!...trillions and trillions of times more mass than a big star or a black hole. If a big star can bend light and a black hole can stop light from even escaping how on earth is any matter, energy or light going to escape the big bang? Since all matter was at that point, the gravity would have been trillions of times stronger than any black hole and thus light could not escape it. Therefore if light couldn't escape it, neither could energy or matter because another law shows that matter cannot exceed the speed of light.

Matter, light or energy would have to attain multiples of the speed of light to escape the source of gravity in this object that blew up to cause this "big Bang". Ergo the big bang is not a valid theory. If and I say *if* we presume matter, energy or light did somehow exceed the velocity of light, then evidence of matter, energy and light moving at these impossible speeds would still be evident. They are not...we look for them and we theorize they could exist but they do not. The fact of the matter is, if they existed they would be the rule and not the exception because there is nothing out there to slow them down! And thus any age of the earth based or linked to this fictional theory also becomes irrelevant. This is an incredible blunder in the big bang theory. How is anything supposed to move faster than the speed of light to escape a source of gravity in the big bang when it has been proven that nothing can? (3rd ed. insert. 2016. Though this is now in doubt with some experiments which have sped up and slowed down the speed of light)

If that isn't problem enough there are other problems with the big bang theory, such as the nature of explosions and gravity. On Earth with its atmosphere, we would observe in an explosion the swirling motion needed to create swirling action observed in galaxies. Look at any explosion in a blockbuster movie and you will see billowing clouds. The clouds of the explosion billow because it interacts with the air to slow the explosion down and contain it...so to speak. The air and the gravity of the earth actually contains the explosion. However, in space, the properties of an explosion would be dramatically different, particularly with the presence of no other matter or source of gravity to affect the outcome. In such a "big bang" all matter would proceed from the center of the explosion in a **straight line!** No swirling action or billowing clouds can possibly take place because there are no other sources of gravity out in space to pull or curl the momentum of the matter into a swirling motion, and there is no atmosphere or "air" to interact with the 'matter' of the bang.

Some might suggest that the gravity needed to swirl the matter came from the other matter/ light / energy in the explosion. This cannot possibly be correct for two reasons: one, if the matter escaped the source of gravity in the initial big bang it is not going to be affected by neighboring matter which has far less mass; and two, not only is all matter moving further from the source of the big bang, but all matter is also moving further away from all other matter! If the gravity of other matter is not going to affect other matter at the beginning, it is not going to affect it later because gravity decreases with the square of the distance. Nothing can turn in space without a force or object affecting it's path. There are not supposed to be any other matter or objects out there because it was all contained in the bang, so, all matter will continue to move in a straight line forever! Because of this, this theory simply cannot account for spiral galaxies. Perhaps you say 'but the galaxies *do* swirl. True, and this is why the big bang theorists put swirling galaxies in the explosion right away, but the mechanics of a big bang cannot account for this swirling motion, so another theory has to take the place of the big bang theory. ((2nd ed. Insert 2008) Some big bang theorists' spice up the theory a bit and suggest this micro speck of nothing which was soon to explode was also spinning rapidly. I guess this is suggested to somehow account for swirling of galaxies. It doesn't work, but assuming it did, there is another law broken when comparing the expected results with what is observed. The law broken is the law of the conservation of angular momentum. What this means is that if a rapidly spinning big bang occurred the parts of the big bang would also be spinning in the same direction as the nothing that exploded. However when comparing this expectation to the observed universe we see that some galaxies are spinning in the WRONG DIRECTION! Furthermore, some of our solar system's moons are orbiting in retrograde orbits and indeed at least two planets are spinning backwards and Uranus is spinning at almost 90 degrees away from the vertical.)

Another problem with the big bang is the lack of heat. Immediately preceding the big bang all of space would be at absolute zero including the "matter" about to explode. At absolute zero, all motion ceases, and no energy exists. If this is the case, how can something with no heat, and therefore no energy (and apparently no mass) explode, create heat, raise the average temperature of the universe three degrees and create all mass? It was first thought that intense gravity would cause a big bang but it is now known that such an object would only collapse and continue collapsing! Atoms themselves would eventually collapse, and what does a collapsed atom become? In all probability it becomes what is known as "Dark Matter". It makes you wonder why the Big Bang theory still stands.

Even if there was a big bang, two more observed laws act upon the matter. What would exist after any such big bang would be matter chaos, which would eventually be followed by heat death. Both these terms are used to describe what happens when matter is scattered completely, and energy becomes unavailable for use. This is HUGE yet it is completely ignored by the big bang theorists.

They expect complete order to come from complete chaos. The big bang theory does not really stand up to scrutiny or logic and must be discarded. Another, suitable, theory is needed which encompasses all the observed laws. In fact theorists know these laws are broken and assume a time existed when other laws were in place. What laws? Laws where entropy was not the case. But as to how the laws just changed one day, no one can say. It sounds as if the theorists have changed the laws arbitrarily just to make the theory seem plausible. Actually there is a way to show how the law changed but evolutionists will have no part of that contingency. To make this all sound feasible they simply tack on a few billions years to the theory and suddenly it all comes up smelling like roses. They just say it must be so and the morning and the evening were the first day. Such faith. How did the big bang theory get off the ground?

DATING BY THE STARS

The reason the big bang theory got off the ground in the first place was because of the evidence in the universe of a red shift as seen in so many stars. It was concluded or interpreted that objects displaying a red shift were moving away from the viewer. Stars that displayed a blue shift were supposedly stars that were moving toward the viewer, similar to how the sound of a train changes the pitch when it passes the observer. It was then determined that the stars were moving away from a common center. Curiously this center by some sources appears to be the earth. I mean this seems strange to me. If all the universe is moving away from the earth maybe we are interpreting this red shift wrong…that or the big bang happened right here. Also if all the stars were moving away from the earth because of a big bang, why would any stars display a blue shift at all and why would any stars be moving toward us, if they are all supposed to be moving away from us? OK, yeah spiraling galaxies, but why are galaxies spiraling? Have you seen animation showing the big bang theory? They show immediately spiraling objects coming out of a big bang indicating they are using earth based explosions to explain something that happened in space where nothing is supposed to be in existence to cause spiraling. I say stop believing animation and ask logical questions.

Evidence that refutes this interpretation of the red shift exists, but in the interest of scientific fairness this evidence was suppressed. Ok that's sarcasm.

What about dating the age of the universe based on red shifts of stars which suggest an expanding universe and light traveling to earth for millions and even billions of years?

MAVERICK EVIDENCE SUPPRESSED

I won't go into great detail but here are some notes I've researched that show the age of the universe, as far as red shift goes, is not as proven as we are led to believe. (Red shift does not date the universe but some information extracted from red shift figures do. By calculating the speed of stars based on the amount of red shift and their distance from the center of the bang, they come up with an age of the universe)

Red shift problems. (type in "red shift" and "maverick" on the internet for some of this data) A significant body of scientists do not support the red shift seen in the galaxy as purely indicative of speed of expansion. Neighboring galaxies have differing red shifts not consistent with expectations which indicate a red shift from a source other then Doppler.

The theory also exists that as light travels distances it slows down and the red shift alters to red. In other words light is slowing down, and is called "tired light", suggesting the speed of light is not a constant. (light has been slowed down in the laboratory to the "speed of a car"! This experiment proved that light does not always move at 186,200 MPS) If some substance can slow down the speed of light temporarily this greatly alters the size and age of the universe as we know it. Several scientist now support the 'tired light' theory.

LIGHT SPEED: CAN YOU SEE IT AS FAST AS YOU READ IT?

(3rd ed. Insert 2016) I've heard reports that light has been slowed down. The February 18th 1999 issue of the Houston Chronicle states Danish Physicist Dr. Hau super cooled light and slowed it down to a slumbering speed of just 38 or 39 miles per hour by cooling it to -459.67 degrees or just a smidge above absolute zero. Soon after, by refining the process, he managed to slow light down to just one mile per hour. Other experiments with light pulses have sped up light as well. I must admit, with the average temperature of "empty" space being just 457.87 degrees or about 3 kelvin, just how fast is light travelling though that? No doubt people can jump all over that one for proving the universe is "Billions and Billions of years old"…maybe even trillions…ZILLIONZ! Unless like God, light was instantaneous at the time of creation then slowed after some …er…event.

Conversely particle physicists have shown that light pulses can be accelerated up to 300 times the normal speed of light. Dr. Lyun Wang transmitted pulses toward a chamber filled with cesium gas. I'm still mulling this over. But in light of possibilities we obviously can't date the universe positively based on the speed of light. (It is done by assuming distance from an object based on speed of light means the universe has to be at least old enough for the light from that object to reach earth)I strongly suspect in the initial creation light was instantaneous.

Stars over 100 light years away are impossible to accurately gauge distances for, because the angle to measure them via trigonometry are too small to accurately gauge. They use the position of the earth on one side of the sun and the other to get one side of the triangle, which is only 16 light minutes long, then work on distances over 100 light years away meaning the angles used are smaller than .00017th of a degree, when triangulated on distant stars.

MY, WHAT BIG FUZZY RED EYES YOU HAVE!

It has been noted that something in the gravity of bodies may actually be a determining factor in the speed of light. In fact light may not even move or have a "speed", but be instantaneous, and only appears to move based on the gravity of bodies affecting it. This is a wild theory but some are looking into it. Some indications shows mass as well as motion will display a red shift... even our own sun displays a red shift. Spiral Galaxies tend to have higher red shifts than elliptical Galaxies. Mass and luminosity also seem to alter red shift properties. Several galaxies displayed two red shifts... for the same galaxy!... and this was not due to rotational variation (IE one part of the galaxy swirling away from us and another part swirling toward us). Upon this discovery, Big Bang theorists discouraged publication of these findings! Shows how scientifically unbiased they are! Red shift 'speeds' have been shown to clump at intervals, multiples or divisors of 72Kilometeres Per Second (divisions IE 24 K.P.S.), indicating not speed of expansion, but some other factor is suggesting speed of motion if taken as 'Doppler. In other words the red shifts are not random depending on distance and speed, but clumped in specific 'speed' groups, which suggests the red shift displayed has nothing to do with Doppler speed at all.

Now you might ask how does what I just said prove that the universe is not expanding, let alone for the estimated billions of years?

OK first the big bang theory and accepted red shift interpretations are related or linked theories. The interpretation of the red shift (an expanding universe) has in fact given rise to the big bang theory. Red shift, interpreted as an expanding universe, means it must be expanding from a specific point and taken backward we get a specific date for the age of the universe and a time when it started to expand. This is presuming a constant rate of expansion which is also not the case thus the vast differences in the calculations, ranging from 4.5 to 30 billion years. But if red shift does not indicate expansion then it does not indicate a time for the expansion to have started. And thus the date of the universe which has been calculated because of the link between the two comes into question. In fact it becomes irrelevant. If light can slow down or become "tired", light is not a constant so dating by it becomes faulty.

I do admit one weakness here. Traditional reasoning says the further away a star is from the earth the longer it would take for the light from these stars to reach the earth. Since some stars are so far away they also suggest an old earth, this would appear to be a flaw in the young earth universe creation theory. I will say, like the cosmologists say, that a time existed when the laws we know now were not in place. If the earth and universe was created, as we shall see in an instant, at a time when entropy did not exists, perhaps light itself was an instant phenomena. When entropy entered the universe due to a cause, it affected the entire physical universe, causing light to slow down, from instant to a measurable speed, perhaps similar to coming out of hyper drive as seen in movies. Light from these distant stars reached the earth in that original instant, then something on the earth happened to make stars seem to be receding from it because light or the perceptions of it altered as seen from the earth. We'll explore some alternate theories and a cause for the changing of the laws later.

MORE ON RED SHIFT.

(3rd ed. Insert 2016) What's really crazy, well to my way of thinking, is they have realized that the farther the object is away from the earth, the greater the red shift. So for example, if an object is 3 times as far, the red shift will be 3times as much. So from this they conclude this means that objects are moving three times as fast! Where's the logic here? This makes no sense, even in the light of a Big Bang theory or gravitational science. Why? Because it would mean something, or rather nothing, is attracting the objects away from the central big bang area of space where all the matter (and gravity) is. Presumably the gravity of nothing (outside the universe) is supposedly speeding it all up. (Or possibly the further away mass gets from the mass of the center of the universe the faster it moves, but that's illogical too) What out there could possibly be pulling mass outward and speeding it up?! Then they further contradict themselves by saying the universe will collapse at some point, like Carl Sagan used to love to say...Billion and Billions of years from now... and have another big bang as though the cosmos is "breathing". How is the universe supposed to collapse if the outer reaches of the universe are moving away from every other part of the universe at greater and greater speeds, even approaching the speed of light? (Though a fair question could be if it's just denser dark matter out there could it's gravity be pulling?)

Clearly red shift is accumulating through distance, just as how the thicker plate glass is, the greener the glass will be. Thus there's just as good a reason for deducing that some aspect of space itself is causing this build up of "red shift", and it may simply be an accumulated effect due to the amount of space in between the objects and the observer.

An astronomer, Halton Arp, who got lots of cudos for his work and was given lots of telescope time and ranked in the top 20 astronomers in the 'Association of Astronomy professionals' discovered some problems with the red shift and wrote a book called Quazars, Redshifts and Controversies. Suddenly he ranks below the top 200 astronomers and no one will give him any telescope time. This is a constant trend in scientific circles. Disprove the prevailing theories and you are not hailed, but ostracized, and shown the door. He states Red Shift is part of a chain of theories which depend on each other. Break one link in the chain and the chain falls apart. Big Bang was invented to explain the expanding universe. The expanding universe was invented to explain why galaxies appear to be moving away from each other which was deduced from the Doppler interpretation of red shift. Red shift then, to keep the chain together, had to be interpreted as a measure of velocity and only velocity. Interpreting the red shift as anything else and the chain of theories breaks down. What Arp discovered was quasars in front of galaxies with far higher red shifts than the galaxy behind the quasar. Galaxy NCG 7319 has a red shift of 0.0225 and the quasar between the galaxy and earth has a red shift of 2.11...meaning that red shift cannot possibly be something to do with speed! He found quasars appear to be ejected out of active galaxies and he has deduced red shift has something to do with age and not speed, with higher red shift meaning a younger galaxy, quasar or star. I'm not sure I agree as I suspect it also has something to do with a build up based on distance as mentioned above, but the very fact he proved it could not be interpreted as speed once again disproves the science we are being spoon-fed by the establishment. In fact his discovery might even disprove my idea, though the two ideas could work together with high red shift objects being rich in whatever is the source of red shift in the first place standing out of the backdrop of space. (see Atlantis Rising # 75) One question: By active he meant younger, but could active by any chance mean actively self destructing?

UNEXPANDED MATTER, OR WHEN IS MATTER, MATTER?

Scientist are completely baffled by what they refer to as "dark matter", which I prefer to call unexpanded or collapsed matter, as this would seem to describe what it is, and if indeed this is what it is, this also lends itself to an explanation to the origins of the universe. Cosmologists don't know what it is so they cannot possibly understand what it does to light. This unexpanded matter is the predominant substance of the universe, it is not the exception, it is the rule! So not only is the big bang theory and the estimated age of the universe in serious doubt, these theories or conclusions do not even take into consideration the larger part of the mass of the universe. An alternative theory needs to take the place of the big bang.

ALTERNATIVE THEORY OFF THE TOP OF MY HEAD

For example perhaps matter is shrinking towards collapse thus causing some of these effects. Based on the laws of entropy, we are fairly sure this is the case but it doesn't seem to be a factor used in such theories. I do not mean for example the size of the suns and stars are expanding and shrinking, but the actual atoms that make up matter of the stars and planets are shrinking. This would keep all stars at a relatively constant specific distance from each other but the actual space taken up by all visible matter would decrease. This could easily play on light given off by matter, and give objects seen in space the appearance of motion away from the observer. I do not necessarily mean to say this should be the predominant theory, I'm not even sure it's a good theory; I just use it as an example.

The universe may in fact be something completely different then is being taught. Consider this. Matter is losing volume all the time as matter shrinks towards collapse. How is that being measured in relation to stellar distances and red shift interpretations? It's not. How is unexpanded matter being taken into the equations of stellar distances? Since we don't seem to know what it is, or how it affects normal matter, it is not used in calculations of this sort. We now know light when passed though a particular substance can be slowed down to the "speed of a car"! (Unfortunately I cannot relate what that substance is because I heard this information by chance on the TV on some sort of scientific show, and have been unable to find further information about this experiment. A woman scientists accomplished this feat) How is this news changing distances and therefore age estimates?

Unexpanded matter may be a light distorting substance, and with shrinking matter in the equation, the universe could be really different then is perceived and possibly be really small. A couple times the bible talks about the sky rolling away to reveal something startling. Are we in a fish bowl? In the past people believed that the stars were holes in the sky where heaven could be glimpsed through. Obviously I don't suggest this is the case, but the idea of something being able to completely change the face of the heavens suggest all is not taken into account in the theories that exists. Though at this point in the work this is a bit premature, but if we consider creation as an option and refer to a source that presents this theory, we see in the bible there is a time when God comes down to Moses in the darkness and in the "thick darkness". In the same verse two different types of "darkness" are spoken of. When one checks the original Hebrew, one of these words translated into "darkness" appears to have the properties of a liquid. (see Deuteronomy 4:11, and I Kings 8:12) And note in the beginning darkness was upon the face of the deep and the spirit of God moved upon the face of the waters. Again this watery property seems to be linked with this unexpanded matter. God speaks and some of this stuff expands and becomes matter as we know it. I tossed in a possible explanation or quickly theorized shrinking of matter itself that could be causing some of the signs in the universe we are not understanding and grasping. Another idea possibly similar to mine has been suggested that matter isn't speeding up, but time is slowing down and this effect is visible by the fact that light seems to move faster the farther from the center of the universe it is. (Atlantis Rising #95 page 14) …Is this simply a variant to the tired light idea?

EVOLUTION

There are three main types of evolution, Evolution through chance, Progressive, and Theistic. What is really funny is that all three types of evolution actually conclusively disprove that the other two types of evolution are not possible! Yeah! Evolution has actually gone to the trouble of disproving itself successfully! One wonders why I even need to disprove evolution. The three types of evolution already disprove themselves! But just for fun I'll put my two cents worth in. But I must say, if evolution is already disproved, why is this dead orphan still being coddled, propped up and supported as the ruling theory? There has to be some ulterior motive. Could it be to distract us from the Creation theory?

Basically the Evolution theory goes as follows: approximately 4 billion years ago in the primordial soup on the primitive earth, chance atoms and molecules formed and linked, forming proteins and amino acids, the substance of life. About 3.9 billion years ago primitive genes, or RNA and DNA about 100 links long formed, which had the ability to reproduce themselves. About a hundred thousand years later the cell formed around these genes creating bacteria. Through minute changes these bacteria changed into various forms of single and multi-celled organisms. These became more complex, developing calcium structures for bones and shells, or hair-like appendages for propulsion. Eventually, through many stages, varieties of fish formed and some that came upon land developed strong fins to navigate on land. The fins eventually formed into legs or wings, and their bodies developed fur and warm blood to adapt to the harsher weather patterns. Some developed rear legs larger than the front with the ability to support the entire body, freeing the front legs to develop further to the point they could manipulate sticks, and eventually form tools. The best creature that arose in this regard was the monkey. With developing hands came thought and the developing brain to eventually form man.

MY DAD…HE'S SOLID AS A ROCK!

(3rd ed. Insert 2016) Evolutionists get all tied up in knots when a creationists suggests that all the types of dogs in the world came from a single pair of one kind of dog, (Two of each kind (not species) on Noah's ark) yet think nothing of saying we all evolved from a rock. One evolution lady got upset at it being suggested that evolutionists believe they came from a rock. So she was asked by Kent Hovind, where do you think you came from then? She said from an ape. Continuing, she was asked 'so where did that come from?'. she said from single celled organisms, and where did they come from?. From the primordial soup! and where did that come from and she finally saw that yes they believe they came from a rock. Curiously there is a scripture that says "they will say to the rock you have begotten me"(Jeremiah 2:27)

NEW SPECIES AND VARIATIONS WILLED INTO EXISTENCE?

Actually already this has obvious problems. This theory would suggest genes can spontaneously be altered by our desire, needs, whims and will. This is like saying we, as the peak of evolution, will find that in our constant penchant for inventing will find that we could use another pair of arms and hands. And so the inventors started to grow extra limbs according to need, and then as a byproduct became superior fighters too, thus the two-limbed breed of men became extinct.

Creatures that can't use their appendages to stand on, are not going to spy an apple in a tree and then learn or will new genes to come into being in order to be able to reach that apple, but rather they will continue to find food where they can reach it.

This would suggest that need creates genetics. Though environment can cause variation, it cannot create a new species. The fact is when an offspring occurs it starts with the original genes the parent had and environment causes build up of the more used natural abilities. People in equatorial climates compared to people in polar climates actually have built in mechanisms for living comfortably in the climate they were born and raised in. So consequently someone from the equator will actually feel colder in London then an native Londoner and need to compensate with more clothing. Their systems have actually adapted to their climate. But no one in their right mind would suggest these two people are a different species. (Though it would seem at one time people thought exactly that)

REPLICATION

The late Doctor Henry Morris referred to Marcel J. E. Golay's studies when he states that the minimum number of parts a machine needs to be able to reach into a bin of parts and assemble a fully functioning replica of the machine that built it, is 1500 parts or bits of information to complete the task (book 9 P64) (1). Now granted this is a hypothetical bin of parts not necessarily meaning a living creature COULDN'T reproduce with less parts, however this 1500 bits curiously also happens to be the "Amount of structure contained in the simplest large protein molecule which, when immersed in a bath of nutrients, can induce the assembly of those nutrients into another large protein molecule like itself and then separate itself from it" (IBID.)(2). If the minimum complexity needed for a creature to reproduce itself is 1500 parts, why do evolutionists propose the first genes had only 100 parts? No such creature has ever been found. Granted this is extremely small, but we've found an abundance of 1500 part organisms, so why haven't any 1000 part creatures been found? It is because either they don't exist, or if they ever did exist they couldn't reproduce themselves and 'died' or decomposed. So we will have to presume our ancestors were these 1500-part organisms.

This 1500-part creature is a one-sided RNA, or DNA virus. (Helix spiraled, or two sided virus' start at about 11,000 parts or nucleotides.) Now of course the 1500-part creature is just the actual nucleus and not the cell. In order for this 1500 part virus to reproduce it will need the "bin of parts", that is the cell wall and the contents. It also needs the ability to find, absorb and process nutrients, and expel waste. All this needs to come together through random, spontaneous chemical reactions that occur in the primordial soup in order for evolution to be completely valid, because the 1500-part virus just cannot reproduce without it. The cell contents and wall must appear at the same time and place as the 1500 part virus, otherwise it will quickly disintegrate. This 'simple' cell needs to contain enzymes, micrvilli, microfilaments, microtubules, scavenger organelles, lysosomes, cilia, mitochondria, pinocytosis, uesicles, ribosomes, the endoplasmic reticulum, and chloroplast in plant cells in order to repair and keep alive the viral DNA or RNA structure.

Similarly if the virus isn't present the cell (the bin of parts) with its host also breaks down, so if the cell spontaneously comes into existence so too must the nucleus at the same time at the same place. Doctor Morris writes "The insuperable barrier, however is that DNA can only be replicated with the specific help of certain protein molecules (enzymes) which, in turn, can only be produced at the direction of DNA. Each depends on the other and both must be present for replication to take place."(book 9 p. 47)(3) In other words they can't live without each other, they are interdependent, and they all had to appear at exactly the same time at the same spot. If the evolutionists are not bothered with this, the biologists are. "Much to their frustration, however, biologists can still only speculate on how these simple organic molecules, emerged through the eons as proteins and genes."(Gore 1976 p. 390)(4) This of course breaks the law of entropy by assuming such a complex creature could fall together, but there is in fact another law broken in assuming such a molecule ever came into existence: the law of chemical mass action which would quickly bring the "primordial soup" to a steady state. You see, this 1500 part RNA molecule is an acid, which, if it ever did form by chance, would quickly just break down to a neutral pH level when the rest of the primordial soup reacted with it!

OOZING RED GOO

(3rd ed. Insert 2016) In the famous Miller Urey experiment where they attempt to duplicate (a theorized) primitive earth's environment to see if life can spontaneously appear from non living matter in the laboratory: they put Ammonia, methane, Hydrogen and water vapor in a chamber, circulated them with sparks (to simulate lightning). A red goo formed in the bottom which they said was "rich in amino acids". They eliminated oxygen from the experiment. Why? Because oxygen would oxidize and destroy the ammonia, one of the gasses used. This goo supposedly rich in amino acids was 85% tar, 13% Carbolic acid (both toxic to life) and 2% amino acids, which bond much quicker with tar, water or carbolic acid than to each other. One cell would need trillions of amino acids.

ONE TWISTED DUDE

(3rd ed. Insert 2016) Furthermore these little strands of combined molecules similar to RNA and DNA they called "life", in these experiments had several flaws. First as mentioned they could not add any oxygen… putting oxygen in would destroy such 'life', even though you need oxygen to make ozone. Ozone blocks UV light, and UV light destroys ammonia, so without oxygen you can't have "life" evolve, and with oxygen you destroy the theorized process…Good theory! Even supposing they could overcome that, when these random molecules bond to make "DNA" or "RNA" strands they bond randomly in left and right configurations…but for DNA and RNA to work they have to be all in one direction or the other, a statistical impossibility when you consider DNA strands are billions of links long.

A KICK-START

Let's assume now, that by some as yet unexplained incredible sequence of events, an entire cell complete with all it necessary parts in perfect working order just appeared on the primitive earth all in exactly the same spot and they grouped together and became a complete cell. What would we have? It would be a very interesting configuration of atomic particles and structures; a strangely complicated shape in an orderless world. A blob of uniquely constructed elemental material contrasting strangely against its random backdrop. It would now decompose, quickly deteriorate until all trace of it disappeared, and we would be right back where we started! Why? Because it is missing the essential ingredient: life. Heat would decompose it faster, electricity would destroy it and radiation would ruin an already perfect structure. No reasonable theory exists to explain the occurrence of life. Evolutionists presume the cell spontaneously came to life. Incredibly in regards to dead people, they suggest that not enough corpses have been watched to say with absolute certainty that none will spontaneously become alive again. (Ripkin 1980, p. 43)(5) Actually there have been dead people brought to life, but in every case, if it has not been assisted by a doctor, it has been attributed to God brought on by deliberated prayer of at least one individual, something evolutionists dismiss and ignore. That's not what they are looking for at all, because evolution is also a contradictory theory to the existence of God. The two are mutually exclusive. (Unless you count theistic evolution, but then this theory assumes an extremely weak creative force not capable of overt deliberate spontaneous creation on any large scale) So in essence if that very first perfectly formed cell that came into existence merely by pure chance didn't also come to life, then another one would have had to. It means, based on the average rate of dead people that come back to life, there would have to be billions of these randomly formed cells to have one of them come to life spontaneously. The chance of a single one coming into existence are nil, let alone billions of them.

No real credible explanation exists in the evolution theory to explain the existence of a complete cell to turn the processes of evolution on, and no satisfactory explanation is forthcoming to explain the existence of life, so we have to presume somehow it just came into being. This first spontaneous cell must also be alive, for the mechanism of evolution to go to work on it. Evolution methods are said to work by three possible ways: natural selection (choosing the best mates); survival of the fittest (the weeding out of the weak or deformed); or beneficial mutations (through radiation); or all three. If we can show that none of these methods will create a new species from our 1500 part virus, then evolution is not a valid theory.

CLIP...SNIP...YUCK...EEEWW GET IT OFF OF ME!!! OW OW OW OW...RATTLE.

The only ways to change DNA molecules are to cut and shorten, add to, or radiate causing mutation. Scientists have found surprisingly that adding or cutting length to DNA does nothing to create new species. Every part of the molecules length is needed to make the same species, and just clipping it won't make an eel into a duck, but rather just a non-reproducing mass of DNA, and adding length to the DNA only produces cancerous cells. In fact scientist are baffled as to how DNA actually changed length. The only possibility I can think of is if a virus attached to a so mutated or cancerous gene that by some fluke they worked. But this stretches even the evolutionists' mind, and none even suggest this as a possibility.

Back to our perfectly formed virus. Believe it or not, the fact that this 1500-part creature, our simplest form of life, is a virus really bothers evolutionists. Why? Because every last virus is completely parasitic! They cannot reproduce themselves unless they have a host cell to attach themselves to, and then when they do this, they actually kill the cell! Even if the virus was the first 'life', it couldn't reproduce until a more complex cell came along. Viruses don't have cells. Actually scientist argue whether a virus is even alive. They describe viruses as 'chromosomes on the loose'. Radiating a virus is no good because changing a single link destroys them, adding weight to the deduction that this is the minimum number of 'parts' needed to replicate. The fact that a 1500 (to as many as 730,000)-part virus cannot possibly procreate makes it look pretty bleak for the evolutionist's fictional 100-part creature. We are already facing insurmountable barriers for our 1500 part virus to continue its chance existence. It can't multiply unless it has a host cell and a host cell means a far more complicated cell must have come into existence first for the virus to continue, but if the virus finds this new cell it will kill it! Yet evolutionists persist, so too must we.

WHAT WAS FIRST?

The next least complicated cell on the ladder is the BACTERIA, with a minimum 1,100,000 links with approximately 75 million atoms arranged in precise order, and this must come into existence through chance in order for evolution to be even remotely feasible. Yes that's right over a million integrated multi atom parts...! all coming together by sheer chance along with the cell and cell wall and all the parts of the cell mentioned before. To go into the odds of this ever actually occurring would be a moot point for one huge reason. The evolutionist doesn't even want a bacteria because of a problem they found: "The earlier idea, that full-fledged bacteria arise from nonliving material by spontaneous generation, has been disproved by careful elimination of living bacteria from non living material"(Author, 1986? p299)(7) What does that mean? They are admitting that a bacteria cannot just spontaneously appear! So why can't they admit their 100 part or 1500 part virus can't just spontaneously appear? Because then it would mean their theory is worthless and they would have to abandon it, so they cling tenaciously to their flimsy theory simply because they do not want to accept the alternative... which logic will show means a creation, thus a creator.

TO REVIEW

Some evolutionists knowing that viruses need host cells to reproduce, stipulate that the first life on earth was a carbon-eating bacterium, which have over a million nucleotide links, and it has been proven that they can't appear spontaneously from inorganic matter. To overcome this they claim that bacteria sprung from simpler constructs of DNA. The only simpler form of DNA is a virus that cannot reproduce without a host cell. This does not stand up to true scientific scrutiny. We've seen that neither of the two simplest forms of life could be the first, and there doesn't appear to be a logical third choice. The viruses can't exist and reproduce without a host cell and the host cell, our bacteria, have been proven as something that cannot come into existence by spontaneous generation. Yet the theory still stands? WHY?

CLUTCHING AT STRAWS

I guess we have to help the theory along and suppose the third simplest sort of living organism formed in the big bang or primordial soup or something! Anything! The third least complex creature is the fungus... but they are not simple at all; they are about 47,000 times more complicated than the virus. In fact some fungi are more complex than man! In fact if man were to evolve to the next highest order based on the complexity of the cell we would become a rose, frog, or a protozoa! Not only does the evolution theory deteriorate upon scrutiny, we also uncover seemingly deliberate deception. Take this quote for example from The Encyclopaedia of Science and Technology, which suggests "simpler" organisms have less DNA.

"There are about 2×10^{-16}g of DNA in a bactieriophage, as compared to about 10^{-14}g in the bacterium escherichia coli and about 3×10^{-12}g in rat liver cells. Whereas mammalian cells contain about $2-3 \times 10^9$ nucleotide pairs of DNA. Amphibian cells vary widely, ranging from less 2×10^9 to about 1.5×10^{11} nucleotide pairs." (Author, 1971? Vol. 2 p.299)(8)

You may have noticed that they changed the scale of reference from grams of DNA to the actual number DNA nucleotide pairs. This is done purely to deceive because 10^{-16} appears to be much smaller than 10^{9-11}. Actually the reason I was looking in the Encyclopaedia in the first place was I was hoping to find this exact thing. Believe me I was surprised I found it so soon! I had remembered in grade nine science reading the same thing in a text book and I asked the teacher why they did this. After the teacher read it he agreed this was peculiar and he told me he would find out how to convert the information to the same scale for me. I asked him a few days later but he hadn't had any luck. He never did find out. To really understand the statement we are forced to convert. And I must say they did not offer the conversion table...and it was hard to find too!

There are approximately 10^{21} nucleotide pairs in one gram of DNA. Thus mammalian cells contain

2-3x10^{-12} grams of DNA, or virtually identical to the rat liver cells they describe! They try to suggest that as organisms advance along their evolutionary scale their DNA gets more advanced. This couldn't be farther from the truth. (See diagram.) To my surprise some protozoa are staggeringly complex having a thousand times more DNA than man! The evolution theory is decomposing before our eyes so to start the ball rolling lets help and try evolution by mutation.

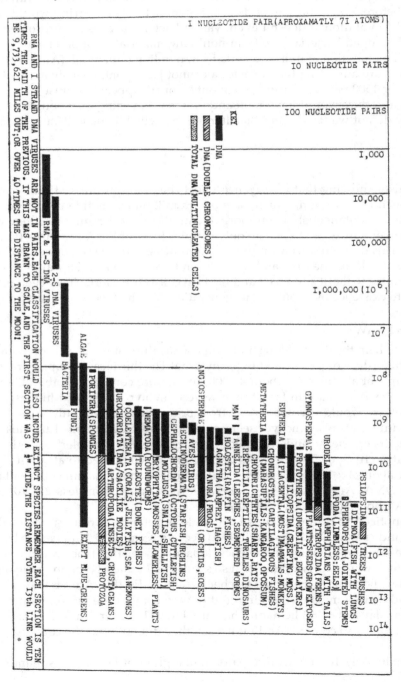

SWIMMING IN PEANUT BUTTER

(3rd ed. Insert 2016) As we've seen the idea that man is the most complex of creatures is patently false. Many microscopic organisms are staggeringly complex. But there's more. Take for example a certain bacteria with a "propeller". This propeller rotates at 100,000 rpm's! Put that in your car and it'll just blow up. It would take 8 million of these bacteria to span the width of a single human hair. Things at that size would normally have a real difficulty maneuvering in water due to the viscosity, but this propeller does the trick. If humans had one of comparable size we would be able to swim at 60 miles an hour…through peanut butter! (I know this might be a problem to some because it wasn't specifically stated if this was natural, smooth, homogenized or chunky style peanut butter.)

ONE LITTLE, TWO LITTLE, THREE LITTLE CHROMOSOMES….

(3rd ed. Insert 2016) Another way of looking at the gene pool is by counting chromosomes instead of DNA links. Man has 46 chromosomes and if we assume we evolved from something with fewer chromosomes, then we could have come from a bat (with 44chromosomes) or wheat (42) a soy bean (40) or perhaps a Cat (with 38). On the other hand, by adding chromosomes we might hope to evolve to a tobacco plant (48) which I think some people are well on their way to evolving into that exalted state in this very day and age. If we leap a step or two we can evolve to an Amoeba with 50 chromosomes, and some day waaaay down the road we can evolve to a Dog or Chicken with 78, or maybe a turkey with 82, a sweet potato with 90 and ultimately; complete nirvana as a Gold fish with 94 or even a Carp with 100chromosomes! Our future is looking pretty bright.

EVOLUTION BY MUTATION.

We'll assume some creature that could reproduce came first. What that creature could possibly have been is still undiscovered. But let's pretend some 100-part creature existed, reproduced, conglomerated with others like itself and accidentally transformed into something bigger, and the original 100-part thing became extinct. This isn't what Evolutionists suggest so we'll suggest it for them so they can save face. Voila instant placebo creature.

The very first problem we come across is there is too much time to complete the job. That's right, not too little, too much!(Or not enough time if you go into the odds of this ever occurring) My calculator could only make it to 3.33 billion years instead of the full 3.8, but that's close enough to illustrate the point. If the one species mutated after 10 million years, creating two, then after 20 million years we could expect both those species to mutate into 4 species, and so on. Perhaps one mutated in just 5 million years, but the other took 15 million, we could still average it to 10 million for any given species. The formula for this over a span of 3.8 billion years would be 1×2^{379}. (My calculator 1×2^{332} , which works out to $8.749002896 \times 10^{99}$ species on earth.) Now there are a lot of species on earth; an estimated 30 million, with a full 1,392,485 species being documented.(Author 1991 p{add insert})(9)(there might be one or two more since the source was published) With the theoretical $8.749002896 \times 10^{99}$ plus species supposedly in existence after 3.8 billion years, new species should be popping up quicker than $2.772399311 \times 10^{85}$ every second! Yeah every second! Even with the currently known number of 1,392,485 known species now existing, we should expect to gain one known new species through mutation every 7.922 years (based 365.249 days per year). New species are certainly not appearing at the rate of $2.772399311 \times 10^{85}$ plus new species per second, and not once in all the time we've been looking has a new species been observed coming from an old one. Sorry, that peppered moth doesn't count. I might add, that with the estimated 30 million species existing on earth, we might expect a new species to come into existence every 134 days. The fact is we are not gaining new species, we are losing species at the rate of 17 per hour; not what evolution predicts.(Author? 1990 p58)(10) In fact all attempts at mutating (and breeding) have failed to produce a new species, and it has been found that mutating only destroys the species.

Another problem is if new species appeared by mutation there would be so many transitional species in existence that scientists would find it impossible to agree upon a classification table. Another problem is the DNA count. Every individual of the same species has the same number of links in their DNA structure, the exact same number. No species has a volatile DNA, and the number of elements in the DNA nucleus are constant. None are even in transition, but are firmly entrenched in their uniqueness. This is why wheat will always produce straw, and bird will beget birds and not mammals or bees, "Without exception ever" (Charroux 1969 p. 54)(11). The fact is DNA and the cell are so finely tuned and fragile that the least bit of radiation or damage can kill it. "Mitochondrial DNA has been so finely tuned that nearly every base pair is essential, and a mutation of almost any kind is likely to impair its ability to produce enzymes critical to cellular respiration." (Author? 1989 p. 14)(12)

It is estimated that one in 20 million mutations would be beneficial. (Däniken 1977 P. 206)(13) If as many as one in two were beneficial it would take 10299843 creatures to find one with an upward trend.(Morris p.66)(14) The reason this number is so huge is because you need at least a million beneficial mutations in the same DNA strand to manifest a physical change. And this is just not happening! We humans on average have about 300 mutations in our genes. (Remember DNA usually has millions of parts, not just 1500 like our vagrant virus.) You need even more to break out of the species, and every one of those mutations has to be a good one. Mutations can't work toward one species in one part and toward another species in another part; all the mutations have to be in the same direction. You can't just evolve in stages either. If an amoeba is only 30% planarian it would be disoriented and a real amoeba would just eat it rather than mate with it. "Get your slimy pseudopodias away from me…you mutant!" (do amoebas even mate? Ahh… who cares… you get the idea.)

Any wrong mutations don't go away either, they are passed on with the good ones. If all this isn't enough, there has to be two occurrences of the same species at the same time, male and female on the same planet close enough to find each other. Perhaps a mutation in a flower might produce a double bloom and some might consider this "beneficial", but a two headed flower? Does this mean a two-headed fly is a beneficial mutation? Even so it would still be a fly with the ability to only engender more flies. Chances are it would be disoriented and quickly be eaten up by its descendant the bird...oh sorry they don't exist yet.

MISSING PART = NON FUNCTIONING = USELESS.

(3rd ed. Insert 2016) Scientists are starting to minutely examine and marvel at the machine like precision of the things that make life possible at the molecular level. They've closely analyzed several microscopic organisms and their parts; things with complex names like Eukaryotic Cilium, Aminoacyl-tRNA, and some we might recognize like Ribosome, Antibodies, and Bacterial Flagellum. What they've realized is these things with around 35 highly intricate genes or whatever are not only unbelievably complex, they form irreducibly complex systems, meaning if you take a single part out, the entire 'machine' stops working. They've been researching many things and eventually they realize virtually everything at a genetic and molecular level is extremely complex and stops working with just one part removed, no matter how insignificant that part might appear. Though they seem to be studying anything they can get their hands on, yet every conclusion ultimately ends with the realization that it's A) very complex and B) irreducibly so, thus they are giving evolutionists nightmares. Evolutionists are at a loss to explain or come up with any plausible method that could bring these complex things about by pure chance. One could go on and on about individual analysis and results but I thought one was rather telling: that of how we stay healthy.

ANTIBODIES AND THE ADAPTIVE IMMUNE SYSTEM.

(3rd ed. Insert 2016) Lymphocyte cells in your blood produce antibodies by mixing and matching portions of genes to create over 100 million varieties of antibodies to protect you from the harm of a viral or bacterial invader. The system has to be able to know and identify what an invader is. The system determines it is an invader, tags it, then creates the needed antibody to destroy it. The system has to know something *is* an invader and be able to create the necessary defense against that invader. So you need a way to recognize invaders, a way to tag, and a way to make the right antibodies to destroy the invaders, and ONLY the invader so the antibody can attack just it, and not then go crazy and attack you. The conclusion was not only was this system incredibly complex, it is irreducibly so. The genetics behind this system alone gives evolutionists nightmares; there's just no happenstance about it and the system simply and frustratingly speaks of being designed and not evolution at all. But this single system alone allows life to exist or at least continue on in the forms we see walking around us, not of just man, but every animal, bug and living thing. Without anti viral and anti bacterial defenses built into every living organism, life would simply be nonexistent. (See Atlantis Rising #84 and [...if you're up for a more challenging read] Darwin's Black box: the biochemical Challenge to Evolution by Michael Behe)

NATURAL SELECTION

Believe it or not, natural selection is now being abandoned by many evolutionists as a cause of evolution, because all this process does, is insure that those which go on to propagate the species are merely the 'fittest'. It does nothing to explain how they became fit in the first place. Natural selection only serves to strengthen a species. An analogy might be like using glasses to make an image sharper and take away the 'fuzzy edges'. If natural selection were a method for altering a species, then survival of the weak and the misfit would be very dominant in nature, because it is presumed that from such is what new species arose from. Evolutionists now reluctantly conclude that natural selection is a safeguard built into every species designed to maintain genetic stability; exactly the opposite of what they are looking for.

SURVIVAL OF THE FITTEST

Some have toted that a new species has occurred through survival of the fittest with the Peppered moth of England, including National Geographic. (Sisson Mar. 1980 pg. 400,401)(6) Around 1830 the white peppered moth began to disappear because the coal from the industrial revolution was soiling the trees making the white variety easy prey for birds. Thus the black and gray sort remained. This is not a true new species because the black can still mate with the white. Also since the cleaning of the air from all the coal soot, the trees have cleaned up allowing the white type to return in large numbers once again. Saying this white variety of peppered moth is a new species is like suggesting that if lions liked to catch and eat only blond haired or even light skinned humans that what would remain would be a new species of human. This is really absurd. All humans can mate with all other humans regardless of tones, just as all peppered moths can mate with other peppered moths. And once lions were eliminated or controlled then light coloured humans could return. The light and dark coloured moth varieties are inherent in the genes, which remain unchanged beyond normal species variation. Only with actual changes in the DNA is it possible to come up with a new species.

MORE ON THAT PEPPERED MOTH

(3rd ed. Insert 2016) I have found out that peppered moths don't even land on bark! They live high in the trees. The picture of peppered moths on bark is a complete fake! The person who took this picture put dead moths on the bark. Thus the entire suggestion that the peppered moths changed colours over the years to hide on sooty trees is completely false. In fact this type of moth doesn't even fly in the daytime! And even this premise, were it true, doesn't mean they changed species, only the ratio of each colour changed.

CHICKEN AND EGG STUFF

(3rd ed. Insert 2016) Flowers on plants might seem perfectly normal in an evolutionary sense. But think about it. What happens if a flower doesn't get pollinated? No seeds, no more of that plant. So the bees had to be there ready to pollinate as soon as flowers appeared. Or what about the other way around? If bees exist and eat only pollen / nectar, aren't they going to be pretty hungry ...or dead, waiting for flowers to suddenly appear? And will they know what they are when they show up? Yet bees have ultra violet vision that can spot a reflector of ultra violet rays a mile away, and what do you know...Flowers shine ultra violet light back to attract the bees. What are the odds?

One real problem with Darwinism is the repeated invention of flight. Bugs, flying reptiles, birds, Wright Brothers, all fly and they all had flight right from the start(Well maybe the Wright brothers had to evolve a bit)... No gliders, or half developed creatures that would one day fly. Not to mention flight is complicated, wings, control surfaces, fully developed feathers, ailerons or whatever they fly with. These creatures all came up with flight in different ways! leathery wings, feathers, fragile crystal clear wings, plus the muscles to use them, eyes to see from way up there, the ability to escape predators right away...on and on and on. Flight appeared all at once and did it repeatedly. (The eye did the same, much to Darwin's consternation)

MORE FUN WITH DNA.

(3rd ed. Insert 2016) Evolutionists claimed that you could tell how closely two species were related by simply looking at their DNA sequencing, so two reptiles for example would have DNA more similar than say a Bird and a crocodile. But this is not the case. The DNA of a snake and a crocodile have about 5% of DNA sequences in common whereas a crocodile and a chicken have 17.5% in common. Even more unpredictable was the fact that there was a greater variation of DNA between two different frogs than a bat and a Blue whale! No evolutionist would have predicted that! (See Atlantis Rising # 80 Page 27)

How can anyone, even an evolutionist, expect to get new species to arise from such a random and destructive mechanism as mutation? To perpetuate evolution based on this evidence appears to be more from wishful thinking rather than from genuine analysis of physical evidence. This thought really bears weight when one looks into the background of the chart of the evolution of man.

SOME FAMOUS AND INFAMOUS INDIVIDUALS

Ramapithecus (also included: Kenyapithecus, Dryopithecus, Oreopithecus, and Limnopithecus) We are told these are the common ancestors of man and ape, yet Dr. Robert Eckhardt of Pennsylvania State university concluded that Ramapithecus appeared to be, morphologically, ecologically, and behaviourally already an ape.(Morris p.172)(15) The reason these have been classified as hominid is because of the teeth size. To presume teeth size determines whether a monkey will evolve into man is purely speculation. It has been discovered that a high altitude baboon exists, Theropithecus Galada, which has similar teeth and it is not even remotely human. This whole line of pithecines may actually be just one species. Dr. Eckhardt measured the degree of dental variation from two 'species' of Dryopithecus compared to Ramapithecus. He also measured several Liberian chimpanzees to determine variation within a single species. In 14 out of 24 the measurements varied more than the fossils, and the remainder were close or only slightly less. He later measured the rest of this fossil type and concluded that based on tooth size there was little reason to classify all these as more than a single species.(Gish 1978 p100-103)(16)

Australopithecus (includes A. Afarensis (Lucy), A. Africanus, A. Robustus, A. Boisei (Zinjanthropus) 1 ¾ -3.6 million years old. The skull variation is allowable within a single species, and many suspect just that. When these skulls are lined up with human skulls (Weaver 1985 p. 568-573)(17) one wonders why they are even in the same line-up. Australopithecus Boisei is as far away from Homo Habilis, as any present day ape is from modern man. It is still argued whether this line is really a link to man or just a variety of extinct ape.

The suggestion that they walked upright has been strongly discredited by Solly Lord Zuckerman. His research team spent over 15 years studying the anatomy of modern apes, monkeys, humans, and the Australopithecine fossils. He remains totally unpersuaded of their upright status. Whenever someone claimed such a fossil had the ability to walk, his research team studied them to try to prove this, but always ended in failure. Richard Leakey found complete skeletons, which have long arms, and short legs confirming they were an extinct form of knuckle walking ape. But when it was suggested that Lucy might have walked Leakey went with this despite Zuckerman's findings. The reason Australopithecus is deemed similar to man is because the teeth are smaller compared to other apes, and the jaw is closer in shape to humans. Sound familiar? Again the modern ape, Theropithecus Galada, has teeth and jaw structure very similar to that of the Australopithecus. The 'human quality' of the teeth and jaw has been determined to be related to diet and habitat, and not because of similarity to humans.

IT'S A MIRACLE!

(3rd ed. Insert 2016) Lucy's knee was said to be evidence that she walked because the bone was angular to the joint. True it was angular, but many monkeys today have angular knee joints. However, Lucy's knee was found one and a half miles away from the rest of Lucy...and 200 feet deeper. Hmmm. It just kept walking after the train hit her?

1470 Man (Homo Habilis: 2 million years old.) Richard Leakey had some telling thing to say about his find. "Either we toss out this skull or we toss out our theories of early man." "It simply fits no previous models of human beginnings" "...leaves in ruins the notion that all early fossils can be arranged in an orderly sequence of evolutionary change."(Leakey 1973 p. 819) (18) For better or worse, 1470 Man has been put in the evolution of man chart 'line-up' even though Zinjanthropus dates at 1.8 million years old. This means '1470 Man' predates both of these supposed ancestors. (Maybe the bird DID eat the two-headed fly!) It is interesting to note that originally 1470 Man was dated at 2.8 million years old(IBID. p.819,820,824)(19), but is now dated at 2 million years (Analyzer unknown, 1985 p. 571)(20), presumably to make it a better fit, because with the older date it would predate Australopithecus, ruining half the chart!

The reason this skull is inserted in the chart is the skull cranial capacity is only 800 cc compared with modern mans 1400 cc average. Some doubt the 'humanness' of Homo Habilis and Homo Erectus with their small brain size (800-1100 c.c.s) but this is within the range of modern man at the low end. Pygmies have quite small heads where this skull was found, and the skeleton of a 12 year old boy was found in 1984 and classed as 'Homo Erectus' with a skull capacity of 800 c.c.s.(Weaver 1985 p. 629)(21) When fleshing out the 1470 skull it looked entirely human except for the nose, which appeared apelike. However the nose shape cannot be determined from the skull. It appears that human skulls are made to look as apelike as possible and ape skulls are made to look as human as possible through artist's rendering directed by evolutionists.

Java Man, Peking Man, Heidelburg Man, Piltdown Man, Nebraska Man All these have been proven to be hoaxes. Java was a gibbon skull, and a human thighbone, with three different teeth (2 orang-utan, 1 human) found 50 feet away. Peking Man was an ape killed by hunters found with the fossils of 100 other animals and ten human skulls. Heidelburg Man was built up from a human jawbone. Piltdown Man was built from a fossil human skull fragment and a recent ape jawbone made to look old, with teeth filed to appear human. It deceived for over 40 years. Nebraska Man was built up from a single tooth, which turned out to be that of an extinct pig. All this and yet two of these 'men' can still be found in modern evolutionary charts.

Neanderthal Man The skeleton of this individual is stooped. It has been determined that this stoop was caused from rickets, or arthritis, common among the local people where the skeleton was found. His brain capacity is equal or greater than modern man. There is really no doubt that this individual was fully human, yet he is still listed on the chart. (Some doubt is now cast on the rickets hypothesis and this type apparently had 50% thicker bones and a stronger human. Some had arthritis and curved bones the wrong direction for some of these deductions. Neanderthal may have been a simple race but they were interbreeding with the rest of the Europeans and that would not be possible if they were a different species.)

Cro-Magnon Man He is at least equal in physical appearance and brain capacity, and could not be distinguished from modern Europeans if he were dressed like us and walked down the street. So what's the difference? This almost seems like an excuse to justify saying some races of man are more or less advanced than other races. Poppycock.

MORE EVOLUTIONARY MEN, MORE BALONEY SANDWICHES.

(3rd ed. Insert 2016) One person in the evolutionary line up of man I hadn't heard of was "Rhodesia man" or "Broken Hill man". I guess it doesn't matter as he turned out to be a diseased man and not a link at all. But looking it up…well naturally it's still presented as evidence for evolution, from 125,000 to 300,000 years ago. Analytical eyes said the remains screamed 'diseased'.

DELIBERATION

(3rd ed. Insert 2016) Deliberate deception is often the case with so called discoveries. Take the Peking Man (discussed earlier) Ten normal Human remains were also found at the site where the "Peking Man" was discovered. It's been argued that "Peking man" was in fact just a monkey, and as it happens all the Peking Man…er…monkey skulls were smashed to pieces. So the site wasn't a discovery of a new form of man at all, it was a site where men ate monkey brains

WALKERS AND SWINGERS

(3rd ed. Insert 2016) One common bit of horse feathers the Evolutionists foist on their students and the general population is the idea of "vestigial organs". This is the idea of evolving to the point where some organs, whether from being a previous species, or as we evolve to another, are no longer needed. They have a few favorites. One is the "Whale leg bone". First, the idea that a whale walked on land then went back into the water is just plain backwards according to normal evolution doctrine. Be that as it may, scientists have studied this "leg" bone and found it has nothing to do with walking…it has to do with mating. Similarly the snake leg bone is used for the same purpose. I'd actually bought into this idea with the snake because originally the snake in the Garden of Eden appears to have walked (climbed) , or flown into the tree (winged serpent), clarifying why God said he would make snakes do what snakes do now…go on their belly. In man's "evolution", theorists continue their idea of vestigial organs saying the appendix is one. It's not. It has an important function in the immune system. When taken out, the immune system is much more susceptible to diseases. And then there's man's "tail bone", supposedly left over from our tree swinging days. Nothing could be further from the truth, but this is very important in several "bodily functions" that we…uh…won't go into here. Though I must admit I do like bananas…hmmm.

HORSE AND CART THINGS

In 1971 human bones which show very modern characteristics such as upright walking ability and similar brain shape as that of Modern man were found. These were dated 2.6 million years old. This assigned age makes these bones predate Neanderthal, Homo erectus and even Australopithecus. This makes normal ("modern") man even older than his supposed ancestors. (22) Human biped footprints have been found in lava and dated 3.6 million years old. (23) Fossilized human bones were found in an Italian mine surrounded by strata dated in the millions of years. And of course the famous shoe print that is shown to have squashed a trilobite, which was supposed to have become extinct 200 million years ago. Obviously evolution is extremely flawed and apparently dating methods are in serious need of scrutiny.

FRIENDS AND COHABITERS.

(3rd ed. Insert 2016) More and more fossils of supposed ancestors of man are continually being unearthed, supposedly filling in gaps in the evolutionary lineage of Man from lesser evolved forms. New names are given to new finds, usually, named after the discoverers, names not necessary to recite here. The point is, it's been realized there are so many now, that there is not the time needed to change from one species to the next under the supposed evolutionary processes. These are supposed to take place slowly over millions of years, but the time frame for man as we know it is maybe 2. 5 millions years. Furthermore, study shows that some of the fossils have some of the characteristics of some of the others but not all... brows, funny knees, big this, small that, and so on. But it's becoming clear these were not descendants of any of the others but cohabiters with them. Meaning they all lived in the same general time frame and lived together. What's really a fly in the ointment is some of these examples have larger brain capacity, bigger body frames, and more problematically, these examples of ancestors are contemporary with the australopithecines. Many of these men have features that are simply too modern, like brain, pelvis, noses or worse, are more advanced than modern man's examples. Furthermore, deductions have shown these people were in fact interbreeding. They don't all converge at a single ancestor, they came together to create the races, or simply diversity and not races or species at all. Other types are proving to have been dead ends with no logical progeny that could possibly be placed in the family tree of Man. There are deduced to be no stages of evolution between them, but they are all hybrids, half breeds or whatever exchanging genes... from 'day one". These observations and deductions just throw monkey wrenches in the entire Evolutionary charts right from Darwin to present date. (See Atlantis Rising # 105)

Michael Cremo has noted that there is an immense amount of skull variation in 'modern' skulls, as they vary from race to race and location to location. Some have brows, some divided broken brows, some with no chins, some with or without a ridge down the center of the skull. Often if 'scientists' find these skulls they typically classify them as something other than anatomically modern humans. Many of these features are seen on skulls classified as Australopithecus, Homo Habilis, and Neanderthals. Because of this discovery, Franz Weidenreich feels that all 'ape-men' from Homo erectus up to the Neanderthals should all be classified as modern humans. Not only do these variations exist on the same continent, they exist within the same families! Even Richard Leakey clued into this and thus felt that homo sapiens could be traced back 2 million years (far more than the supposed 150,000 to 200,000 years max for 'modern' humans.

The idea that such variance could exist within one species shouldn't be considered odd. Cremo makes the good comparison to the variableness of dogs which are all one species. If dogs were extinct, he figures scientists would consider Chihuahuas and great Danes (not to mention many dog breeds in between) as different species. (See Atlantis Rising #69)

THEM'S HOMO INFERIOR FOOTY PRINTS....CAIN'T BE OURZ...DEYS TOO OLD.

(3rd ed. Insert 2016) Apparent "modern" footprints were discovered in Kenya which were indistinguishable from the striding patterns of barefoot humans. However they were dated to 3.7 millyun yeers oooold. Wow! But the prints were in volcanic ash. (Chapter five dating section tells some problems with dating Volcano spew, but for the time being we'll say they are 3.7 million years old.) But because the prints were so old, Evolutionist can't accept this because it means normal "modern" humans were around at the same time as their supposed ancestors...and that obviously doesn't work for them...(well unless we had time machines to film these ancient ancestors for today's nature programs and accidently left some of our footprints behind while trying to fit in with the ...herd?) So because the prints are so old they simply called them footprints of a Pre-human Hominid Homo erectus. The article says "...there is no real justification for doing so, other than blind commitment to the current theories of Human evolution."

Similarly more human footprints were found in some Mexican volcanic ash thought to be 40,000 years old at the time of the find. Fine...until someone dated the ash and found it to be 1.3 million years old. Whoops! So suddenly they can't be human footprints. Evolutionists constantly filter out any evidence that contradicts their cozy little comfort zone, apparently because they can't handle the truth. (See Atlantis Rising magazine # 76)

GEOLOGIC COLUMN FUN

(3rd ed. Insert 2016) Charles Lyell a lawyer, made up the geologic column in 1830 and gave the layers really old dates because he hated the bible. Yet no place on earth does this complete column exist. 80-85% of earth's land surface does not have even three geologic periods appearing in the "correct" consecutive order, which appear in only 26 places. No place has all the strata, and if it did, it would be about 100 miles deep. Arbitrary dates have been given to various strata's, then linked with fossils found. Fossils date the rocks and the rocks date the fossils. Actually when you think about it, you can't date rock by the fossils in them. Why? The rocks and such already existed at the time the creature died, but for how long before that? There's no connection! It's like saying the rock and dirt you get buried in is the same age as you. It's nonsense.

THEY SAID THAT!? PING PONG ANYONE?

(3rd ed. Insert 2016) The strata of earth layers are dated by the fossils found in them and the fossils are dated by the strata they are found in. This is impossible to do, yet the old earth "scientists" do this all the time. Magic? It's termed "Circular reasoning".

J.E. O'rourke states in Pragmatism Versus Materialism in stratigraphy; in the American Journal of science Jan 1976 "The charge of circular reasoning, in stratigraphy can be handled in several ways. It can be ignored, as not the proper concern of the public. [none of your business] It can be denied, by calling down the law of evolution, it can be admitted as common practice…or it can be avoided, by pragmatic reasoning."

One evolutionists, Nils Eldridge, asked his fellow evolutionists "If we date rocks by the fossils, how then can we then turn around and talk about patterns of evolutionary change through time in the fossil record"

BIT-O-BUGS…COME AGAIN?

(3rd ed. Insert 2016) Coelacanths are index fossils…meaning they date rocks and visa verse, (shown as circular reasoning) but even screwier is the fact that if they find a coelacanth in fossil form they say the rock layer it's found in is 325-410 million years old. Why!? Coelacanths are still alive! So shouldn't the rock then date anywhere from 410 million years old to a few years old? (As we shall see, fossils can form a lot faster than you may realize)

Graptolites, very similar to Trilobites, are also stated to be extinct for 410 million years and considered an index fossil. Yet they are still alive in the South Pacific. and there's some debate on whether they are similar species or the same species.

MISSING LINKS AND TRANSMOGRIFICATIONS

(3rd ed. Insert 2016) Colin Patterson from the British Museum of Natural history which houses the largest fossil collection in the world, wrote a book called "Evolution". He was asked why he didn't show any missing links in his book to which he replied "I fully agree with your comment on the lack of evolutionary transitions in my book. If I knew of any, fossil or living, I certainly would have included them. I will lay it on the line, there is no such fossil."

Darwin said "…we cannot prove that a single species has changed; nor can we prove that the supposed changes are beneficial, which is the groundwork for the theory." (Book 53 page 222 quoting a letter to a Bentham) To date no such transitional links are known. *None.* Some suggest the Xiaotingiai, similar in some ways to the Archaeopteryx, is such a link but I found out, *that* fossil was completely faked! A hoax made to be sold to someone gullible enough to buy it, or willing to perpetuate the belief in evolution at any cost. And think about it. Do you really think a nice big heavy dinosaur is a logical choice to turn randomly into a light hollow boned bird? Every instance of these so-called reptile bird fossils has been seen to be two slabs put together to appear like one. Fake rock and adhesives have become very easy to make and difficult to spot. These Xiaotingiai fossils are composites meant to fool and be sold. But even if they were genuine there's no way they could be considered a transitional fossil but would have to be a completely new species previously unknown. As for the Archaeopteryx supposedly being a transitional species: no indication of a leg slowly forming into a wing is evident. No evidence of scales evolving into feathers. The feathers are completely formed. The feathers are already fully and completely feathers with hooks and eyelets for zippering. As for hooks on the wings, birds exist today with hooks on their wings.

R U SUPERIOR?

(3rd ed. Insert 2016) Do you by any chance happen to know the full complete title of Darwin's Book, more commonly referred to as the "Origin of Species"? Back then it wasn't uncommon to have long titles, and this book was no exception. The full title to Darwin's book is "The Origin of Species by Means of Natural Selection or The Preservation of Favored Races in the Struggle for Life". Darwin's Book was an attempt to justify racism. For example Darwin thought Natives were just advanced animals. But his belief in favored races spread to anyone that would have doubts about certain biblical doctrines.

Mao Tse Tung murdered 15,000 Christians a month. His two favorite authors were Darwin and Huxley. Both Hitler and Mussolini thought they were of a Superior Race. Lenin and Marx were both believers in God until they read Darwin's book. Cambodian Leader Pol Pot killed 3 million of his own people, 1/3 of his country's population; because he believed they were of an inferior sort! If fiction has caused countless people to prefer fantasy over reality, phony science has caused countless people to be murdered due to false information.

THE RELIGION OF SUPERIORITY COMPLEXES… OR FAITH IN THE BLESSED HOLY LUCY?

(3rd ed. Insert 2016) Julian Huxley in a TV interview said "I suppose the reason why we scientists all jumped at *The Origin of Species* was because the idea of God interfered with our sexual mores" Well some honesty at last. The bible says they "didn't want to retain God in their knowledge" (Romans 1:28) Dr. Michael Rose (professor of Philosophy and Zoology) admitted …well let him say it… "I must admit Evolution is a religion. This was true in the beginning and it is still true today". It is in fact a state supported religion foisted on kids in school. Look at evolution material and see how often you have to "imagine" it happened or they say it "must have happened" or you have to have "faith". They say a time "must" have existed when the laws of nature were different as they break all kinds of laws of physics to support evolution. Or take this quote from Pierre de Chardin "[Evolution] is a general postulate to which all theories must henceforth bow …Evolution is the light which illuminates all facts, which all lines of thought must follow…" See what I mean!? If you use Evolution as your basis for theories about ancient man, as this man says you must, then you tie your brain behind your back when trying to solve ancient mysteries. The rest of this book does not assume evolution is correct and I use …shall we say… "critical thinking" when examining things formerly darkened…sorry… "Illuminated" by evolution.

CRITICAL THINKING?

(3rd ed. Insert 2016) Evolutionists say to think critically, but do you dare criticize?

It's been calculated that all land above water would completely erode from hydraulic action in just 14 million years…so why are there 400 million year old fossils? And why are we here to examine them?

Some genius came up with the theory that birds evolved from dinosaurs. Seriously? Think critically!

Fossils don't even count as evidence for evolution. You can't look at a bone and say this creature had kids…let alone different kinds of kids. All you can say with any certainty is that it died. In fact when comparing fossils to the "modern' counter parts, the overwhelming conclusion could easily be that they prove devolution, as virtually every fossil is superior in size to present day examples of the same creatures. And neither does extinction of a creature prove evolution, but it indicates devolution because diversity in the flora and fauna has diminished. (Devolved)

MUTADUDE! FEEBLE THEORY?

(3rd ed. Insert 2016) Dr. Karl Raimund Popper, Philosopher of science, writes "Evolution is not a fact. Evolution does not even qualify as a theory or as a hypothesis. It is a metaphysical research program, and it's not really testable science."

Daniel Brooks in an article "A downward slope to greater diversity" (Science volume 217 Sept 24 1982 page 1240)wrote "Natural selection may have a stabilizing effect, but it does not promote speciation. It is not a creative force as many people have suggested."

Pierre Paul Grasse, in "Evolution of living organisms" (1977 pg 88) states "No matter how numerous they may be, mutations do not produce any kind of evolution." Parasitology 6th ed. by Lea & Febiger pg. 516 "Natural selection can only act on those biologic properties that already exist; It cannot create properties in order to meet adaptational needs."

In "Evolution of Living Organisms" (1977 pg 88) Pierre Paul Grasse states "Mutations do not produce any kind of Evolution"

OLDER IS BETTER THAN TRUER.

(3rd ed. Insert 2016) You may recall text books showing drawings of various creatures in embryonic stages all with a similar look to them. This similarity was touted as proof of evolution as supposedly we all looked the same at one point. The various embryonic stages of the human fetus and many other creatures were said to show signs of originally being fish with the evidence of gill slits showing up in early development stages, and they were drawn into the images and made to look as similar as possible yet drawn to look all very scientific. The text and "science" books often show the drawings of these stages to deceive kids. But these drawings were deliberately faked and proven wrong and indeed a complete hoax in a much publicized trial in 1875! But even though proven fake, these drawings are *still* in the textbooks today, despite laws that say they should be updating text books when new, more accurate, information outdates older inaccurate information. It seems 140 years isn't too long to let misinformation sit around.

BUT THE PROGRESSION OF SIZE LOOKS SO GOOD!

(3rd ed. Insert 2016) Horse evolution was proven wrong over 60 years ago. George Simpson in Science monthly Oct 1950, states,"Many examples commonly cited such as the evolution of the horse family or of saber toothed 'tigers', can be readily shown to have been unintentionally falsified and not to be really orthogenetic."

Science newsletter Aug. 25 1951 "The early classical evolutionary tree of the horse…was all wrong."… And still in 1992… "…the much repeated 'gradual' evolution of the modern horse, have not held up under close examination." (Biology the unity and diversity of life" Wadsworth.) This too is still found in text books.

Modern horse is found in layers with, and lower than "ancient" horses and the "ancient" horse is still alive today in Turkey.

MAKE NO MISTAKE…THOSE MISTAKES ARE NOT MISTAKES.

(3rd ed. Insert 2016) Roger DeHart, Burlington-Edison Science teacher, was told he could not tell the students about text book errors using current science journals. Kevin Haley, Biology teacher, in Bend Oregon lost his job for exposing text book errors. The cad!

WHY WERE YOU FIRED?

(3rd ed. Insert 2016) Once institutions and theories are thoroughly entrenched in society they become virtually impossible to change. Take this case in point. In the 1950's Thomas Lee of the National Museum of Canada found incredibly advanced stone tools in glacial deposits at Sheguiandah, on Manitoulin Island in Lake Huron. These deposits were dated at 65-125,000 years old. The Director of the Museum was fired for not firing Thomas Lee, the discoverer of these artifacts and stone tools! Tons of these artifacts just disappeared into storage bins and the discovery was swept away. Why? Because "it would have forced the rewriting of almost every book in the business". Accuracy is NOT an option!

CREATIONISTS ARE SICK AND MENTALLY UNSTABLE.

(3rd ed. Insert 2016) If you think school is a place of learning, you would be mistaken. It has turned into a place of indoctrination. Why do you think they want your kids in school even younger and not want them home schooled? Consider just a sampling of comments by various professionals…(quotes taken from scientific creationist video)

The Humanist John J. Dunphy wrote in 1983 "The battle for human kind's future must be waged and won in the public school classroom by teachers who correctly perceive their role as proselytizers of a new faith…(that will replace) the rotting corpse of Christianity"

Dr. Pierce of Harvard University in 1973 stated that "Every child who enters school at the age of five is mentally ill, because he comes to school with allegiance toward our elected officials, founding fathers, institutions, government, patriotism, nationalism, sovereignty,…All this proves the child is sick, because the 'well' individual is one who has rejected all those things and is what I call the true international child of the future." Makes you kinda queasy reading stuff like that, don't it?

Paul Brandwein in 1970 "The Social Sciences" stated "any child who believes in God is mentally ill."

Charles F. Potter : *Humanism: a New Religion* c 1938 stated "Education is the most powerful ally of Humanism, and every American Public school is a school of Humanism"

Kendrick Frazer, an Iowa professor in the fall 1983 issue of Skeptical Inquirer said they "… should be able to fail any student no matter what the grade records indicate, if they discover the student is a creationist, or take degrees away if the student becomes a creationist later".

John Paterson stated in the fall issue of the Journal of the National Center for Science Education "As a matter of fact, creationism should be discriminated against…no advocate of such propaganda should be trusted to teach science classes or administer science programs anywhere or under any circumstances. Moreover if they are now doing so they should be dismissed."

Kent Hovind, a Science teacher for 15 years, a Creationist with a sense of humour and unafraid to debate evolutionist and who reached over a billion people with his uncopywritten lecture tapes and DVD's by either sending them free (or accepting donations for them) or by others copying them to hand them out, was arrested in the middle of the night at gun point. The charges? "Structuring", meaning he took out two withdrawals from his bank in a period of 12 days that added up to $10,000. Why was he doing this horrible thing? To pay his employees, or the costs of his ministry!... which ran about $400,000 a year. The judge said what he did was "worse than rape", and asked the jury to determine if he was guilty of withdrawing funds of less than $10,000.00! We're all 'guilty' of that! But they used a screwy law to put him in jail for nearly 10 years! Why? because they didn't like his success of disproving evolution to so many people and making evolution look silly. HOW DARE HE!!!!! Check out his story on the internet.

A text book (HBJ General Science) stated, if a movie of time were in reverse with the universe contracting "until it disappeared in a flash leaving nothing. In the realm of the universe "nothing" means nothing, not only matter and energy would disappear, but also time and space."

Thus they are saying the 1st law of thermodynamics which states 'you cannot destroy or create matter' is easier to believe possible, than creation. And Creationists are mentally unstable? And then they say something like this…

"It is absolutely safe to say that if you meet someone who claims not to believe in evolution, that person is ignorant, stupid, or insane" (Richard Dawkins in an article "Put your money on Evolutions" in NY times

April 9 1999 pg 35) But it's sane to believe you can create and destroy matter and that man originated from a rock. LOOK!!! IT's a Vision of Lucy…In the sky! She's wearing Diamonds!!!

UNTHINKABLE?

(3rd ed. Insert 2016) In the 100th anniversary edition of Darwin's book 'origin of species' in the foreword by Sir Arthur Keith he says "Evolution is unproved, and unprovable. We believe it only because the only alternative is special creation, and that is unthinkable"

THE LAST ROUND-UP

It seems to me that Evolution is indeed a flimsy theory held together only by the sheer will power of the determined evolutionist. It does not even appear to be a valid theory as nothing in the theory from start to finish satisfactorily explains the evidence. In fact evidence has been falsified to continue on with this theory. It really doesn't have any scientific basis for its existence. Creationism could be shown to have great credibility and would merit teaching in normal school curriculum. However evolution is so entrenched in scientific dogma that only a presidential decree, if that, could reinstate creationism back into normal youth education. Many people don't want creationism taught in the schools. They resist creationism seemingly because it would mean the existence of a creator, meaning we suddenly become accountable to him for what we do. If we pretend God doesn't exists, we don't have to do what he says. We seem to enjoy doing whatever we want and justifying it by suggesting there is no higher authority than man to worry about. Thus laws and morality become relative and not absolute and changeable subject to whims, fads, or passing parameters. It seems we are trying to get as far away from absolutes as we possibly can. Even some so called "churches" allow immoral practices suggesting God loves all and we can do no wrong. Even our own mothers and fathers know we can do wrong in their eyes so why not a creator, the father of all? If we abandon evolution it would mean we have to clean up our act, and most people don't want to do that and "Science" is just accommodating the population making it easier to escape reality. Consequently our children are straying further and further from any semblance of morality. Were creation taught perhaps some of the kids would start to look into who the creator is and maybe realize that what they do and how they act means something in the big picture. It is amazing to see when youth get a grasp on such things how they can wilfully become nicer, more loving, caring and concerned about how they act in society and in Gods sight. When we become aware of the existence of God we start to take his opinions more seriously and allow his rules to change our actions. We become harsher critics of our own words, actions, and deeds in the attempt to do what is right. Why would we want to avoid that? It seems to me society would only benefit from this outlook.

Though few people know this as this is one of those embarrassing things evolutionists don't like to talk about, at the end Darwin abandoned the evolution theory because he just couldn't see how the complex eye could evolve in so many separate paths. He felt evolution forming even one type of eye was pushing it.

((2nd ed. Insert 2008) Is Evolution a flimsy theory or is it credible? Kent Hovind debates evolution professors around the world and had a standing offer of one quarter of a million dollars to anyone who has real evidence for evolution. No one was ever able to claim it. Each discipline of science believes another discipline has the evidence that proves evolution. Yet evolution is pushed on students as a "Fact". It's a theory and there is not a shred of evidence for it.)

Charroux Robert. 1972 The Mysterious Unknown Corgi edition 1973 London :Transworld Publishers Ltd.
Gish Duane T. Ph.D. 1978 EVOLUTION? The Fossils Say NO! Public School Edition San Diego,: Creation-Life Publishers
Gore Rick 1976 The Awesome Worlds Within a Cell National Geographic September 1976 Washington D.C.
Leakey Richard E. 1973 Skull 1470 National Geographic June 1973 Washington D.C.

Morris Henry Dr. <u>Scientific Creationism</u> 1974 Edition 1985 Green Forest Arizona :Master books
Ripkin Jeremy (with Ted Howard) 1980 <u>Entropy: A New World View</u> Bantam Edition 1981 New York N.Y. :Viking Press
Sisson Robert F. 1980 <u>Deception: Formula for Survival</u> National Geographic March 1980 Washington D.C.
Däniken Erik Von 1977 <u>Von Däniken's Proof</u> Bantam edition, Great Britain: Souvenir Press
Weaver Kenneth F. 1985 <u>The Search for Our Ancestors</u> National Geographic November 1985 Washington D.C.

1   Scientific Creationism. By Dr. Henry Morris. Pg. 64 Quoting Marcel J.E Golay
2.   IBID.
3.   IBID. page 47
4.   National Geographic September 1976 page 390
5.   Entropy: Jeremy Ripkin page 43
6.   National Geographic March 1980, page 400
7.   Encyclopaedia of Science and Technology, Volume 2, page 299, 1987 Ed.
8.   IBID., Volume 12, pg. 212.
9.   Time magazine, March 25, 1991, Special add insert.
10. Discover, April 1990, page 58
11. The Mysterious Unknown by Robert Charroux Page 54.
12. Discover, September 1989, page 14.
13. Von Danikens Proof, Erik Von Daniken. page 206.
14. Scientific Creationism, page 66
15. IBID., Page 172.
16. IBID. &, Evolution the Fossils Say No, 100-103.
17. National Geographic November 1985, Pages 568-573.
18. National Geographic June, 1973, page 819
19. IBID. Page 819, 820, 824.
20. National Geographic November 1985, page 571.
21. IBID. Page 6
22. Scientific Creationism. By Dr. Henry Morris Pg 176
23. National Geographic April 1979

I don't really like this sort of bibliography or index or whatever it's called, but it was one of the correct options given to me by the teacher and it seemed easiest. The rest of the book will take a different format. "Nat Geo" will refer to an issue of National Geographic "Book 15 page 123" will refer to a book in the order they were read (see back) and page. Other references will be spelt out in the text…unless they force me to do something more proper at the book printing place. If I have forgotten to put an exact reference it will be lost somewhere in all those books I read…usually. Biblical references will name the book chapter and verse.

Chapter 2

EARTH IN PRE FLOOD ERA

Since we see there are some serious flaws in the evolutionary doctrine, the logical thing to do right now might seem to be to prove the reverse is true, with a theory of devolution, showing where all things, including the solar system, the earth and man are going from complex to simple. Actually many evolutionists realize that if evolution is not true then creation has to be the only alternative, mainly because if things are not advancing to a point of perfection they must be declining *from* a point of perfection. And indeed the laws of thermodynamics and entropy are well established, which, in a roundabout way prove this very thing. However we will get to that.

So then we will tentatively say it is safe to continue on from a devolution standpoint and indeed we have to, because the theories presented here rest on this foundation, and what we extrapolate from this foundation explains everything. We tenatively further conclude that a creation thus a creator created all things in a state of perfection and then the creation at one point started declining from that point in time for whatever reasons.(Panspermia will be dealt with later) Obviously man and woman eating the forbidden fruit to gain the knowledge of good and evil is the point of no return and we won't deal with this aspect in any depth except for some clarifications. And don't worry, I won't antagonize you with a bunch of religion forced on you in here on some flimsy pretext. If you want that you can read a bible and go to church. You no doubt paid some pretty good money for this book and I don't want you to feel like you get snookered. I will do my best to keep it scientific, though occasionally I will climb on a soap box and then jump right back off.

Instead of starting out with proving decay, which basically has already been done by the science of entropy, it might be a good idea to show first just how complex things were to start with, and then we can begin to see how much decay has already occurred. Doing so will in part further prove the point which will become clearer and clearer, so that when we come to presenting the devolutionary aspects of the solar system, life on earth and even man himself, the material presented will fall into place. For now we'll leave the devolution aspect for a future chapter. However this chapter shows many aspects of this decay by turning the clock backwards to see what the earth was like prior to the flood, so in essence it really does the same thing anyway.

If we can show what creation and man was initially like we can then have a groundwork laid down and establish that because of this initial advanced and superior state of man, he was able to create advanced technology and consequently cause destruction (or entropy) of his environment on an incredible scale. Since so much of this work is interdependent with other sections, it's difficult to know what order to present this material. So at some point some conclusions may appear premature. But if this is the case, have patience, as how these conclusions were arrived at will be presented later on in the work.

THE MYSTERY OF 'WHAT CAUSED A WORLDWIDE GREEN HOUSE CLIMATE IN THE PAST?'

It's known the earth at one time did not have climate belts but that the entire surface of the earth was in a warm climate. This is deciphered through rocks and fossils of plant life among other things. For example Siberia is known to have at one time been in a temperate zone, and even Antarctica shows evidence of it being in a temperate zone at one time. But when one tries to rearrange the continents in such a way so that all landmasses exist in a temperate zone with no climate belts, things just don't work. Any theoretical rearranging of the continents on the earth so that all land has a temperate climate simply doesn't work. And no arrangement can explain the even climate in such a way as was known to have existed on all landmasses on earth at one time.

Geologists have now accepted that at one time all the continents were originally part of each other before continental drift started. They do not know what started continental drift but they know it happened and at one time all the landmasses of the earth were part of a single continent. But even this simply does not explain the even temperate climate that existed on the earth at one time. Clearly something has changed that is being missed.

Geologists know some other factor must have existed to give the earth a universal even climate but they can't seem to figure out what that factor is. This is probably because they are still attacking the problem from an evolution standpoint and do not believe old legends and written histories. Also they are looking at the earth in its present form not realizing some huge physical earth change occurred. It's like a bushman looking at a crushed cube of metal that was formerly a automobile and trying to decipher how it was driven before. Probably a bad analogy, but looking at things now in a devolved state and trying to figure out how it was in it's initial state is very difficult, unless you have some sort of record from before the change occurred. Believing evolution, they therefore do not believe anyone intelligent was alive before the change occurred that could tell us what happened. So by their theory they handicap themselves.

EVEN CLIMATE

(3rd ed. Insert 2016)With trees and coral and other warm environment evidences in Spitsbergen, Antarctica, Greenland, and other polar fringes of North America, the conclusion has long been "Difficult to imagine any possible condition of climate in which these plants could grow so near the pole, deprived of sunlight for many months of the year" (book 53 page 41 quoting C.O. in Dunbar Historical Geology) D.H. Campbell had similar difficulties. In noting earth's axis of rotation, the earth's orbit, with the equatorial regions receiving more sunlight than middle latitudes which got more than polar latitudes he says "…It is much more difficult to think of a cause [a condition the earth would be in] which will raise the temperature of the polar regions by some 30 degrees F [Fahrenheit] or more while leaving that of the equatorial regions almost unchanged" (Book 63 quoting C.E.P. Brooks Climate through the ages 1949) Great geologist can't get it but the answer is quite clear in historical references if they'd just read and believe.

THE ANSWER WRITTEN IN HISTORY

The ONLY way you can solve this climate riddle is with something in place that causes the atmosphere around the earth to be even in all places, not some theoretical rearranging of the land masses. Are there any records that speak of such an environment on the earth?

Ironically many creationists have known the answer to this dilemma for a long time because the answer is written in history as seen in Genesis, and this missing clue is also decipherable from some other ancient legends. Some ancient traditions say heaven and earth changed places and some say the sky fell.

The answer is there was a water canopy or shell surrounding the earth high above, containing the atmosphere and creating something of a greenhouse on the earth. The firmament or air divided the waters above and below…. Gen Chapter 1 verse 6-8 "And God said, let there be a firmament in the midst of the waters, and let it divide the waters from the waters. (7) And God made the firmament, and divided the waters which were under the firmament from waters which were above the firmament: and it was so (8) And God called the firmament heaven and the evening and the morning were the second day."

So here we see an ancient document give some clues as to what the earth was like before the flood.

When I first read this account of the physical makeup of the earth as a 12 year old I went outside and looked up at the clear sky and wondered "is there water up there?" The bible makes it so clear that this was the case that even as a 12 year old I could figure this out. So clearly this obvious information has been completely ignored by orthodox sciences. I looked at the clouds and tried to see if there was something watery about the blue sky. I then went inside and asked my dad if there was water up there but clarifying that I did not mean in the clouds. He said there used to be but it wasn't there any more as it came down in the flood.

I always found this somewhat fascinating that water could be up there originally and wondered why it wouldn't fall down, and wondering what changed to bring the water down.

This is what the water sphere originally surrounding the earth looked like, something like a very thick crystal clear bubble. As time went on I understood that the earth in the pre-flood era was a very different place compared to what it is now, and it was because of this water shell that was originally in place. Though certain clues exist in scripture they also exist in other histories as well. If we can accept that there was a water shell over, above and surrounding the earth we can start to understand that a very different earth existed before that water came down. Later on we will show what caused it to come down and what caused the water to go away. But for now we will poke our heads into the past and see what the earth was like before the flood. The following clues are from the Genesis account.

THE PHYSICAL CHANGES: NO RAINBOW

The first and most obvious clue to me that something had changed from pre-flood to post flood times was this. The rainbow was given as a sign and reminder to Noah and us that there would never be a worldwide flood again. So what this means is that the earth before the flood never had rainbows. So what sort of environment existed that such would be the case? Can we assume they did NOT have clouds because this is where rainbows are usually seen? Though I have actually seen a rainbow in a completely clear sky, I must presume there was some sort of vapor present to make the rainbow. I know I saw this because a friend also commented on this peculiar sight. I mean it is such an odd occurrence I had myself doubting I saw it! If they did have clouds as they clearly had mists something was different enough to not allow refraction of light in mists to show rainbows. I mean this is fascinating. We take refraction of light into rainbows for granted; yet this phenomenon did not exist before the flood. I have to think they could still refract light through a prism, but were certain light waves not even getting to the earth? Imagine an earth with no clouds. The sky would always be clear, but what would the sky look like?

If this idea of a water shell seems like something that is impossible then realize when water and liquids are in the zero gravity of space they form naturally into a sphere. One can poke a straw into that water sphere and force air into it and the air will gravitate toward the center creating a bubble as seen in National geographic October 1974 (Pg 446.) This water shell would have protected the earth from harmful solar radiations and kept the earth atmosphere held to the earth. Now we lose atmosphere to space, particularly during heavy solar activity.

We know that when it rained during the flood that this was in fact the first time it ever rained! Again a clue as to pre flood environment. Clouds mean moisture in the air and potential rain so there must not have been clouds in the sky. There must have been evaporation, but it just didn't form into clouds but into different levels of humidity so humidity levels must have been different too. Though some people theorize there was a mist above the earth, mist is vaporized moisture and thus it could potentially condense and again turn to rain. They also theorize this mist covered the entire earth but then we would not be able to see the moon or the stars, and it says the stars were given to tell times and the seasons, so we must have been able to see the stars before the flood, so mists above doesn't fit. So the water shell above the earth had to be clear and actual water, not mists. As hard as it is to comprehend, the earth at one time had an endless clear sky, but what did the sky look like, with all that water up there?

Looking at the sun and moon had to be different than it is now. Now we have a halo around the sun and the moon, but this halo is a rainbow. There were no rainbows before the flood and so presumably no halos. Actually the rainbows we see on earth are different when seen from the air. From the air they are complete circles, thus they are in essence haloes as well. One can see what is being illustrated here when you see motion picture scenes as cameras pan from one spot to another with the sun being panned across. A rainbow halo is seen at the moment the sun is crossed by the camera. It's almost like we are in a tube of halos, one in front of us surrounding the light sources and one behind us reflecting the light source. This just wasn't occurring before the flood.

NO RAIN

Mist came up at night from the ground to water the earth.(Genesis 2:6) This also shows how and where water came from to sustain life similar to how rain does today. This mist must have been in rather amazing proportions too. We know it came at night and this is still the case, but consider this. There were rivers in existence before the flood, some of which are named. Now it is possible that these rivers are of an underground origin, and indeed this seems to be the case for at least some of the rivers, but I don't think they all could be. Many riverbeds continue out into the sea to the edge of the continental shelves. My point being the mist that watered the ground must have been extraordinarily excessive to be enough to make rivers...this is assuming the rivers were sourced by the mist. It's also known that vegetation at this time was huge! This also speaks to the voluminous nature of this mist. This is of course not to be confused with clouds, though I suppose there might have been enough mists that they could appear like a low fog. But again this is telling because if the rainbow didn't exist before the flood, not even these mists were displaying a rainbow. Yet any water sprinkler today (which often sprays a heavy mist) will usually show a rainbow in it. I must confess my meteorological knowledge is pretty minor so no doubt my deductions are possibly pretty limited and maybe even wrong.

One wonders how much humidity there was in the earth. The entire earth had an even temperate climate so it was this way everywhere with no temperate zones except day and night variations, and even that would have been less dramatic. But of course we see in Gen 3:8 there was a "cool of the day". There was no incredibly hot equatorial climate or any frigid icy Antarctic environment. This is also borne out when one sees that at one time the entire Sahara desert was a lush tropical area. All land was equally hospitable.

TIDAL REFRESHING?

(3rd ed. Insert 2016) One thing I mentioned as a possibility was streams coming out of the ground might be flowing from the force of earth's rotation. Herodotus mentions an Ammonian spring which was tepid in the morning. Cools off by noon, and heats up by evening and in the middle of the night boils furiously repeating this process every day. (Herodotus Book 4: 181) Could it be related?

LESS WATER...MORE LAND

It also appears that there was more land above sea level. There may have been an entirely different water to land ratio before the flood. (I've seen suggestions of as much as a ten to one Land to water ratio.) We also see the waters were in one place. (Gen. 1:9) Also there appears to have been more continents or landmasses such as Lemuria, Mu and Atlantis, though they would have been all part of the single continent before the breakup of the land into the continents we know today. All these facts correlate with each other. At one time the mean average of the land was 1000 feet above sea level. Now it is about triple that...which is odd when considering a lot of the water from the flood still remains on the earth. This is evidenced by the continental shelves having rivers that continue from land to under water all the way to the edge of the continental shelves. One would think with more water on the face of the earth the average height of the land above sea level would have dropped not increased. Why this is the case will be understood as we go along. If some of that flood water was not still here, the average height of land above sea level would be considerably higher still.

HIGHER AIR PRESSURE

One thing I thought possible is the air pressure might have been higher at sea level before the flood than it is today. It may even have been constant regardless of your altitude. Whereas today the earth has a vapor trail behind it, showing we are always losing atmosphere to space and consequently the atmosphere gets thinner the higher up you get. Originally with a water canopy holding ALL the atmosphere close to earth it seems possible the atmospheric pressure would be the same at all altitudes, though this seems so odd to me I have to wonder if this was the case. But if we consider a bubble, one has to presume the air in all parts of the bubble is at a constant pressure. But it might have been a more gradual decompression as one went higher in the atmosphere.

Only gravity holds what little atmosphere we have left to the earth, whereas before the flood the water shell was the prime cause of retaining atmosphere to the earth. Nowadays the air pressure at sea level is 15 pounds per square inch. As you go higher in altitude the pressure is less and as you go deeper into the earth the air pressure is more. On Mount Everest water boils at around 189 degrees and it takes a lot longer to cook an egg. It's quite likely the atmospheric pressure on earth was several pounds heavier, and water would have had a higher boiling point. There's no reason to think this would in any way have a negative effect on life on earth and indeed it may be a factor in the longevity of man and animals. Divers often get to a few atmospheres when they go below the surface. If they rise too quickly they have to decompress but the actual higher pressure itself doesn't seem to have any ill effects on them other then the rapid decompression, which is a result of changing atmospheric pressures too suddenly and not the result of the pressure itself. (Though at extreme depth they have to breath a helium oxygen mixture)

STRONGER MAGNETIC FIELD?

When the forces were stationed on and near the island of Baltra, the soldiers noticed some peculiarities about this island. For one it never rained there. Rain would sweep over them, then as it came to the channel it would stop half way. Then after the clouds got past the island it started to rain off the island on the sea. They also noticed they felt very different or strange on the island. Watching birds fly toward the island was very weird because they would stop in mid air as if hitting a wall, and not fly over the island. Compasses went wild on the island. (Book 50 Pg 104) So possibly higher atmospheric pressure and a strong magnetic field will also assist in keeping water from falling. Whether or not this factor kept the water shell up I can't say. We can say that the magnetic field of the earth before the flood was at least sixteen times as strong as it is today based on known decay rates of the magnetic field of the earth.

The Magnetic field of the earth being so much stronger deflected far more radiation around the planet not allowing it and other cosmic forces to hit the earths surface. One wonders how a strong magnetic field would interplay with light and the water sphere surrounding the earth. The Bermuda triangle may provide some clues as the sky occasionally appears different there and this is in conjunction with the compasses of ships and planes going haywire, and this is associated with a strong magnetic field.

NO ATMOSPHERIC LIGHT SHOWS

Likely there would have been no aurora borealis, but one has to wonder how light would have played on the water sphere surrounding the earth.

MOON STOOD STILL

The moon was for the night, and the sun for the day, and the stars were for signs and navigation. (Gen. 1:16) But what's this? The moon was for the night? Does this mean it did not move from the night sky? This is a very curious scripture and we will get back to this one. The moon and the earth's orbital plane no longer coincide, suggesting some force altered the moons plane, the earth's inclinations of it's axis or both. Since both the earth and the moon" wobble", it seems logical to presume they have both been altered from some original orbital pattern.

Eskimo legends seem to suggest that the moon has done something that caused it to change its patterns though the legend is admittedly obscure and not worth going into. My guess is the moon was always stationary in the sky in some sort of heliocentric tidally locked orbit with the sun and not the earth. Tides would have been absolute clockwork and incredibly even. See other chapters to see why the moon changed and started its altered orbiting pattern.

NO EARTHQUAKES OR TSUNAMIS

There would have been no such things as tsunamis, because before the flood there were no fault lines causing earthquakes. (We'll explore this further later on.)

A BIG GREEN HOUSE

The people who do the study of the environment of the ancient earth insist that the earth was a far warmer and more temperate and evenly keeled place to live, like a big green house with very stable temperatures. They also say this affected the trees as they grew uniformly all year round. This means that the trees grew at an constant rate all year long and thus they never had tree rings as we see now. In the late 17th century there was a minimal sun spot activity and tree rings grew so evenly each year it is very difficult to tell one year from another. (Scientific American Sept. '75 pg. 50) If the earth had the uniform climate all year round like before the flood the trees would have no rings. It's even possible all trees were evergreens, losing only the leaves gradually and replacing them like other evergreens do.

NO NEED FOR DOCTOR DOOLITTLE

Possibly animals spoke. Ok that sounds pretty airy-fairy, but if we consider some clues then maybe not. Of course there's only two instances in the bible where animals spoke; the serpent in the tree and the donkey of Balaam, which occurred after the flood and God opened the donkeys mouth. But before the flood it appears this is not the case. If we consider a few things this may indeed be true. Even now your pets when you come home will make it clear they are hungry or want out. Some even seem to know the time of day because they come at that time you usually feed them. Even birds that can mimic speech of man, appear at least in some cases, are able to attach meanings to the words. We will show that man had intelligence far beyond what we have today. If before the flood, man's intelligence was so far above what it is today, it stands to reason that even the animals' intelligence was superior to their standard now. They may have had IQ's similar to a low IQ human today. Also with man being super intelligent they may have understood animal meanings enough to be able to communicate on a non-verbal level. Remember God created man a little lower than the angels, and of course this would mean pre-flood man. Some angles (sons of God) actually came to earth to take wives so we must have been something special indeed to attract angels. How smart are animals? Maybe vastly smarter that we tend to believe. Popular in the early 20th century was getting horses to count by tapping their hooves, to give their answers. But some horses had staggering abilities, able to extract 3rd and 4th roots from huge 5, 6, and 7 digit numbers, and fast, often in less than 10 seconds! And some could, at least phonetically spell names even that we would have a hard time guessing correct spellings for…well I would anyway, for whatever *that's* worth. (See Atlantis Rising #74 what do animals know)

POPULATION

Although some people say there are more people living on the earth today then all the rest of the people in history combined, this may not necessarily be true. People before the flood were fertile for possibly 6-700 years or more. Figuring based on this has come up with population figures before the flood of 5-10 billion people. (Book 38 pg. 30) Women today, have had as many as 50 children or more, without the aid of fertility drugs or whatever, so there's no reason people living this long couldn't have had hundreds and hundreds of children.

FEAR FACTOR

The animals after the flood became afraid of man. So thus they were NOT afraid of man before the flood. You could walk up to a bird and put it on your hand. Based on certain ancient manuscripts and texts it is thought that man first learned war after the flood with Nimrod, or the Sumerians. Did the pre-flood era have no war? If this is the case, and I don't say for sure it is, but if it is, it meshes very interestingly with the animals, becoming afraid and violent after the flood. (Conversely in the 1000 years of Christ's rein on the earth the child will put his hand in the hole of a asp, and the lion will lay with the lamb. It seems that the earth will once again be as it was before the flood) Although one could deduce there was some sort of war before the flood it's quite possibly the actual environment of the earth itself before the flood is the cause of the animals sedateness and lack of fear of man.

LONG LIFE SPANS

Man lived a lifespan usually in excess of 900 years. Man after the flood lived to about 600 years, and the life spans of men steadily declined after the flood. Interestingly before the flood God says that one day the lifespan of man would be 120 years, so at that point he knew something was about to change. Later on after the flood God says mans age will become 70 years, so again something changes. But we'll get to that later. Something in pre-flood period allowed man to live longer. Though many pooh-pooh the old ages spoken of in the bible there may be some corroboration from another source.

A lineage of Egyptian architects exists extending over a period of 2000 years. But the lineage only has 25 names in the line. Its felt this is only one third the needed number to constitute a continuous lineage for 2000 years. However this works if you allow similar life spans as those spoken of in the bible shortly after the flood.

Normal cells in today's world die after the 50th population doubling, which suggests a maximum age of 115 years possible. Even when cells are placed in Vitamin E they live as long as 117 population doublings equivalent to 269 years. (Book 1 pg 130) Still far short of the 900+ years. However when stuff is placed in the pyramid of Egypt things get interesting. Cell structures live longer with more doublings then the same type outside the pyramids, suggesting that some aspects of the pyramids is similar to the affect on life as evidenced in the bible where people lived 900 years. A doctor put microbes in a pyramid and found they live 64 hours longer then their average life span. Cells from humans, when placed in a Nutrient solution and then placed in the Pyramid lasted 9 times as long! So nine times 115 years equals 1035 years thus these long life spans spoken of before the flood become at least theoretically possible. Water stored in a pyramid grew plants 4 times as large and they grew faster.

People have studied inside the pyramids and felt the interior seems to clear their minds. I suppose it could be argued that the forces in the pyramid act more like a drug on the physiology of the recipient of these benefits thus in fact clouding their minds more, similar to how drugs can make a person think he has had his mind enlightened when in fact it has become deadened by the affects of the drug. However there are no actual studies of how the pyramids affect the mind and body that I am aware of.

Some clues tend to suggest some of the major pyramids are a pre-flood structures. If this is the case then the interior may be a residual pre-flood environment. Cats, dogs and rats tend to mummify if they get lost and die in the pyramids. Garbage bins are emptied when they are full of these dead animals and it's been noted that the garbage has no rotting going on in them. Curiously it's odd that creatures such as cats would get lost inside the pyramids considering cats can find their way to a owners house from tens and hundreds of miles away, suggesting something in the pyramid is messing with the normal function of their brains. (book 1 pg 147)

GRAMPA BEETLE BROW.

(3rd ed. Insert 2016)Here's more evidence that man lived far longer than most people believe. You've no doubt seen the human skulls that have bulging eyebrows…or "beetle brows" as they are called. Well it turns out that this is a part of the skull that never stops growing, so one can determine roughly the age of the person by the size of their brow. We never see large brows in the general population today because very few live to be over 200.(However some brows do exist as a normal variation in our species, so some extrapolation would be needed to figure out the cause of such a brow)

Saint Germain said he studied inside the pyramids. Though this man seems like something legends are made of; he was said to be a man that knows everything and his longevity was something of mythical proportions as well. Some indications suggest he was at as much as 161 years old when he died and possibly older than that. (He was observed to look about 50 when he first appears in history. If he looked about fifty when first met and lived this long he may have taken longer than usual to look the fifty in the first place.) (Book 11 Pgs 145-155)

HOW OLD?

(3rd ed. Insert 2016) Though not a pre-flood tale this does cast some doubt on the Guinness book of world records. Javiera Pereira was born in 1789 and though the date of his death is disputed, his birth date doesn't appear to be. His most accepted date of death is March 30 1958 making him 169 when he passed on. Doctors studied him and felt he must be over 150, (how they determined this wasn't noted) but he was fit, able to spin while standing on one foot, walk fair distances and climb up several flights of stairs without losing breath. He knew stuff about well-known historical events like the Battle of Cartagena (1815), and gave accurate details about Indian conflicts and a terrible famine that had taken place years before.

Pakistan's Hunza's when first discovered lived on average to the age of 160. After their discovery their average age dropped to about 90. They treat apricot seeds like money, and they somehow stop the signs of aging. Their 80-year-old women look fantastic. And they never get cancer. It'd be interesting to examine their brows. Bet they could brow beat the best of us.

ANOTHER BIT OF EVIDENCE SHOWING MAN LIVED FAR LONGER BEFORE THE FLOOD.

(3rd ed. Insert 2016) Atmosphere before the flood would have similar qualities to a hyperbaric chamber where people heal faster due to the higher oxygen content and the higher air pressure. Higher air pressure would be found on the earth before the flood due to the water canopy keeping air pressure constant and not allowing it to expand and escape into space as it does now. The higher air pressure and oxygen content would have let people stay healthier, heal faster, live longer with more energy and grow larger, probably proportionally as large as other creatures found. Cherry tomatoes have been grown in a hyperbaric chamber and they grow larger than normal tomatoes do now, and the plants grow to the size of trees. (Remember… those were "Cherry Tomatoes").

INSECT FOSSILS PROVE HIGHER PRESSURE AND OXYGEN CONTENT.

(3rd ed. Insert 2016) Insects in amber occasionally display bubbles in the same piece of amber. The oxygen content of these bubbles is from 35% to 50% higher than considered normal by today's standards. (since these insects in amber appear to be closer to "normal" size I would bet these were from the early post flood period when the atmosphere was still denser but beginning to escape into space after the collapse of the water canopy)

Fossils of insects have been found in gigantic proportions. Some of the finds are frightening…18 inch cockroaches, 8 ½ foot centipedes, 2 foot grasshoppers, and 3 foot tarantulas. Also found are dragon flies with 50 inch wingspans. One might suggest these were a different species. Not so…they have to be the same species as today. But why so big and why don't they grow that big now? These bugs simply cannot get this big today, because they have less surface to volume: the larger the bug the more oxygen it needs so the oxygen/atmospheric pressure limits the size that bugs can get today. Bugs breath through their skin so they have to get more air to get bigger otherwise the amount of oxygen they can absorb won't be sufficient for their needs. Thus they can only grow to a fraction of the size they grew before the flood when the oxygen content of the air was higher and the atmospheric pressure was far greater. The amount of air they can access determines the limits of the size they can grow to. Were we to grow bugs and things they eat in a large hyperbaric chamber today, the bugs would reach frightful sizes, but then once they reached larger than normal proportions they would die in our atmosphere from not being able to get enough air.

Stephen Robbins, Ph. D seems to be onto this as well. In Atlantis Rising #72 he wrote. "The garden of earth may not have been as perfect as it once was. Perhaps there was once an even greater concentration of oxygen. Why were there once dragonflies with two foot wingspans? Why enormous brontosaurus with nostrils scarcely enough to support a horse?"

DINO BREATH.

(3rd ed. Insert 2016) It's been noted that dinosaurs have a strange problem, as we've just read. Their nostrils are too small for such a large animal, and it's been wondered how on earth they could breath in enough air to live. But with the denser, more compressed atmosphere before the flood, and for a while after the flood, this answers that problem.

TOO EASY! TOO OBVIOUS! CAN'T BE!

(3rd ed. Insert 2016) Atmosphere just supported larger growth before the flood. Rhinoceros ten feet tall have been found. Donkeys 9 feet at the shoulder, 8 foot long beavers and sharks 80 feet long have all been found indicating the environment before the flood allowed larger creatures to grow. And as much as evolutionist refuse to accept the finds, giant skeletons of men have been found ranging from 10 to 13 feet tall. As we've noted insects can't get this big now for an important reason. The higher oxygen content that existed before the flood allowed bugs to grow larger. This is one of those clues that has paleontologists and geologists and the like scratching their heads because they refuse to believe the records. They can't seem to figure out what happened on the earth to allow things such as these giant bugs to have existed. They are restricted in their thinking by forcing evolution into their reckoning and refusing to allow devolution into their theory. They refuse to believe the earth isn't millions and billions of years old and thus they refuse to believe that man lived during the age when these bugs were alive. Flood? No way! And they therefore refuse to believe mankind saw and recorded what happened on the earth to change the environment so drastically and change the way these bugs, animals and man and such grew. They treat the ancient records as written by ignorant savages or religious crackpots and dismiss the very answers they supposedly are searching for…why? Because it's "unthinkable".

THE OSTRICH AIR FORCE…BOMBS AWAY!

(3rd ed. Insert 2016) One result of a denser atmosphere before the flood I hadn't thought of before was that some birds we have now that can't fly, probably flew before the flood. Chickens most certainly, but the possibilities go further. Emus and Ostriches possibly flew. Maybe even Dodos and Auks? Thus the very fact they don't fly now is evidence of a denser atmosphere in the past. By extension this is also further evidence for creation and devolution; as why make birds with feathers that don't fly? I have to think creationists in the past must have wondered about this and evolutionist must have rubbed their noses in it... "See an intermediate species!" (Actually it's funny... they never even thought of these flightless birds as missing links...or did they?) Why would God make a bird that couldn't fly? It's simply further evidence of a deteriorated earth.

DESTRUCTIONS IN THE COSMOS

If the earth, solar system, and the universe were created perfect, why do we see such randomness in asteroids and comets? We do know comets and meteors are hitting the earth less frequently because many ancient texts, myths and folklores speak of much fear of comets, and rocks coming down from heaven, and comets were far more common in the skies. Some suggest these comets and asteroids were created to bring judgments to man, but it seems they were not actually present at creation. Some have traced backwards the meteors and asteroids by their orbits and find a point in time when they were all in one spot suggesting an event in the sky happened to create the asteroids in recorded times. Thus it seems at one time there were no asteroids and comets in the sky, so even the sky was more benign.

Should a comet or meteor or asteroid hit the earth through the water canopy surrounding the earth clearly this could wreak havoc with it and life on earth. Does it make sense that there were even more meteors and asteroids and comets in antiquity? Were they created in the original perfect creation or did something happen to cause them to come into existence?

A LITTLE LOWER THAN THE ANGELS

Man before the flood was a genius in every way. This was brought to my attention and at first I didn't see it. It was stated to me that God brought all the animals to Adam to see what he would name them, but we are talking about as many as thirty million species! When man decided to invent something he probably skipped many stages of invention and advanced with inventions far in excess of what we do, and they would have understood earth sciences so well that they would have come up with stuff as easily as we dream them. They would have advanced farther and faster than us. There is NOTHING new under the sun (Ecclesiastes 1:9) ...except one thing...but I'll let you figure that one out. (don't worry I'll reveal it later)

WE HAVE MET THE MARTIANS AND THEY ARE US

Man was red skinned yet Blue skin seems to be attributed to this era as well and it's possible even Green skinned individuals existed. These colors of skin crop up in stories and they will be spoken of in later chapters. The name Adam means red earth and it's presumed this meant he had red skin, and it may have been VERY red. Hawaiian legends confirm some biblical accounts and speak of the first man being made out of red earth, and his wife name was Ivi (pronounced Eve-y) (book 16, pg 100)

A DIFFERENT SKY

Was the atmosphere luminous and twilight more gradual, lasting longer? Possibly the upper atmosphere and water sphere may, all night, have been somewhat coloured rather than a black sky like we see today. Perhaps the night sky was a different colour like a dark green with light reflecting inside the water sphere, similar to how some plastics and fiber optics hold light inside them. Maybe the day sky was a light green.

Mexican legends speak of a world age that came to an end when the sky collapsed and darkness enshrouded the earth. This gives credibility to the thought that the sky might have been a colour in the nighttime sky rather than just black. (Book 14 pg. 103-104) It's been noted that the sun when on the horizon shining through more atmosphere turns the sky a more greenish hue.

EMERALD SKY

(3rd ed. Insert 2016) As noted the Sky before the flood was probably Green. It's been observed that from Antarctica the sun can look green when it sets.

IT'S GONE

But obviously this era of earth history ended. Other ancient legends and histories also allude to a different sky and some great disaster or many disasters. Chinese legends refer to a sky that collapsed when the mountains fell, which led to beliefs that the mountains held up the sky. Though this appears to be in reference to further earth upheavals, mountains might have crumbled when the flood occurred from excessive water and the fountains of the deep breaking forth. Samoan legends say the heavens fell down, and African legends speak of the collapse of the sky.

Ovaherero tribes tribesmen say that long ago "the greats of the sky' let the sky fall on the earth." An enigmatic statement to be sure. Later on I will repeat that sentence and it will make perfect sense. Many other ancient legends speak of a collapsed or fallen sky and speak of there being anywhere from four to seven different skies in the past, but with there being 7 skies or "heavens", it is not always discernable which sky is being referred to, and most appear to be referring to how the sky acted after the flood or various earth upheavals. We will show these catastrophic upheavals happened and what caused them. The "primitive" African tribe Wanyoro in Unyoro says the sky fell and killed everybody: a god named Kagra threw the firmament upon the earth to destroy man. (Book 14 pg 104)

So what caused the flood, or 'the sky to fall' as chicken little might say? To figure this out we must first establish that man in the past was something of a superman for the explanation of the cause of the flood to make sense and be believable, for we will see that the flood occurred as a direct consequence to something man did.

Chapter 3

ADAM 900

If man was created perfect then what was he like and what could he do? What was his original state? If all things are degrading from orderly to chaotic what was the state of things at the beginning, or at least at the point when things began to break down because of entropy? We've gotten a glimpse of what the earth was like in the beginning before the flood. Now we will see what man was like in the beginning, and then we will see what he accomplished. Though a lot of this is based on post flood evidence, it is sufficient to give a good picture of what man was capable of before the flood.

Since the apple or whatever that fruit was that Adam and Eve ate, man has been in a state of decline. Originally man was not meant to die. Then after the fruit he dies 900 +years later...slow, but eventual. Compared to after the flood, where we see man's lifespan is shortened to 600 then 400 then 175, then 120 years, and now the days of man are three score and ten. So clearly his genetic soundness has diminished, and did so rapidly after the flood. However his lifespan was stable during the pre-flood period. All men with few exceptions from the start of creation to the day of the flood lived to 900 or more years, but after the flood man's lifespan, with the exception of Noah, becomes volatile in a downward trend suggesting something new about his environment after the flood was causing shorter life spans and more rapid aging. Noah was born well into the pre-flood so the earth state right after the flood was still sound enough to allow his normal pre-flood or only slightly diminished aging to continue.

Longer lives mean more time to bear children and probably many twins, as evidence suggests more twins occurred in the past. So conceivably parents could have 80 or more children in the short time after the flood to when ages started to rapidly decline, possibly before the birth of Peleg or the event at the Tower of Babel, and be great great great grandmothers in a short period.

One thing that seems to get overlooked is the fact that mans intellect might also have declined. What originally started me doing all this research was an offhand thing someone said to me that Adam was far more intelligent with an IQ of about 900 or even 1000, more than anyone we have on earth today, because he named all the creatures. (Geneses 2: 19-20) Well that didn't immediately impress me as that seemed like no big deal...until I realized that there were probably 30 million creatures to name with names that were indicative of the creatures' characteristics. Well my curiosity was peaked, though an IQ of 1000 seemed a bit of a stretch.

We on earth today only use on average about 10% of our brain and mental capacity, thus 10% equals IQ 100, or at least that is what I've been told. So if before the flood we used 100% of our brains mental capacity we would have an IQ of 1000. This does stand to reason because if we were created perfect wouldn't we be using all our intellect? But perhaps that other 90% is subliminal meant for things like instinct. However there still is the odd person with 150 and 200 IQ's. So was it possible for people in the past to use all or nearly all their brain capacity? However I've not found anything that shows certifiably that we only use 10% of our mental capacity. The average IQ of 100 is exactly that, the average of people on earth today. So if pre-flood people also took intelligence tests the average would also be "100", but 100 at a different level altogether. Deviations are either unintelligent people compared to the average or very intelligent people compared to the average, so the average may not have anything to do with the percentage of your brain actually being used, but merely the average of people that are alive at the time of the tests. Be that as it may, I.Q. variations are clearly distinguishable.

A person with an 150 IQ is not 50% smarter than an average person with a 100 IQ. The average students vocabulary is 5000 words. A person with a 148 IQ has a vocabulary of 36,250 words! This is 7 times as many as the average. People with IQ's above 200 can say their first words inside of 2 months and have learned 4 languages before their 5th birthday! So higher IQ numbers are not mathematical, but exponential! What on earth could a 900 or 1000 IQ accomplish? And it's not just mental abilities, but natural passive abilities too! Things like photographic memories and unintentional memorization would be part of the IQ package, though such abilities might not show up on normal IQ tests.

I suppose it is possible that some aspects of our minds are being fogged by our environment whereas the earth in the pre-flood environment may still have been conducive to extremely high intellect, whatever that actually was. (Actually the bible does refer to our minds being veiled, but I can't seem to find the verse) I figured if some aspect of this was true there must be some evidence of very advanced technology in the past.

It also occurred to me if man was this advanced in the past then he must have had space travel as well. But could I find evidence of such in the past? I figured if it was there it should be common knowledge and I had never heard of such a thing, so the possibility of this being true did seem in doubt to me. Though I suppose in light of the evolution theories dominance and deliberate distortions and falsification of evidences, any such evidence of vast technology in the past might be disbelieved, misinterpreted, discredited, suppressed, or even deliberately destroyed. We've seen that variant red shift evidences were suppressed and phony 'men' stuck in the evolutionary lineup so maybe other items have been distorted or hidden from the general public. For fun I decided to give it the old college try, and I decided to search for evidence of man in the past being more advanced then we give him credit for, and see what I could find, and what could be made of whatever evidence there was.

Part of understanding what we find depends on perspective. First consider this. If Adam was created perfect, then he would have been using all his mental capacity, and his children (us) would have inherited all or some of his abilities too. If Adam was a superman of sorts then some of his characteristics would continue to be inherited by his descendants. What we will see is the earth's environment has changed to such a degree as to affect man and consequently his abilities have waned...but still occasionally on earth, even today, we come across savants with abilities so far in advance of all their peers that they are said to have no peers. These people had to inherit these abilities from somewhere. If man was created perfect...then what was a perfect man like? We can safely say a genius in every way...in fact man was such a super race that were people of today to meet them they would have been considered as 'gods'. We'll see that there is much evidence to suggest such meetings have taken place in history.

So if we show that man was mentally, physiologically, and technology far superior to present day man we can virtually give evolution a devastating blow, and we lay the groundwork to understand how this plays a role in what caused the flood and the creation of the continents. As it turns out there is so much evidence of man's former heights and of physical, mental, physiological and even spiritual decline, that not all the evidence can be explored in depth. This information, so deadly to the theory of evolution, *is* often suppressed, or completely disregarded; or hoax is cried out so the evidence gets ignored. In fact many never read, or even plan to look into evidence that exists and still insist the evidence is false.

SOME OF ADAMS DESCENDANTS ABILITIES

We can presume if a person is found to have an extraordinary capabilities then this capability was inherited from a forefather somewhere in the past on the genealogical tree. Obviously that person is Adam and his immediate descendants up to the time of the flood. So we have to conclude that any advanced or superior natures and abilities were at least some of what Adam would have been capable of. Any signs of deficiency must be attributed to entropy, mutations and decline, whereas any evidence of superiority to the average must be attributed to remnants of former glories and abilities of men before the flood. We know mutations are harmful and building up in the general population so we have to conclude that the mutations are destructive elements in man's physiology, reducing man capabilities not enhancing them. Thus we have to presume the positive abilities are remnants of what was at one time normal abilities of ALL men and women.

Miss Shakuntal Devi from India in 1959 was considered the human calculator. She could do incredibly complex calculation in her head. In New South Wales she faced "UTECOM", Australia's largest computer, and was asked to find the cube root of, 697,628,098,909, and came up with the answer 8869 in 7 seconds. The computer came up with a different answer. She was certain she was right, and further recalculations proved the machine was in error and she was correct! (Book 11 pg 122 123) In 1980 she was given two random 13-digit numbers to multiply together. She got the correct answer in 28 seconds (1989 Guinness book of records)

Some people remember naturally. Though this might not seem like much, this example happened to me so I present it here. I went to a doctor's office without an appointment, as I didn't know you had to make appointments...I was young. The receptionists took my name and let me see the doctor. After eight months I needed to see a doctor again so once again I just showed up. The receptionist started making notes then asked me "one 't' or two?" in reference to my last name. She had nothing there! I had just walked into the office and went up to the window. She simply remembered my name after one brief interaction from eight months previous! Boy wouldn't we all like to have this ability! But that's nothing...

Elija Ben Soloman (1720-1797) read 2500 books once and just remembered them as though it was just natural, with no deliberate attempt. He could quote any passage at will or upon request. He was called a walking library. Heck forget remembering them, anyone that even reads 2500 hundred books has got to be a little above normal I would think.

Nicola Tesla is in my opinion one of the most fascinating people of modern history. In the last years of his life, the FBI followed him wherever he went picking up any scraps of paper he discarded in hopes that some invention would be aimlessly scribbled. When he died, FBI swooped into his apartment. He at one point said he had come up with a system of defense so inpenetratable that war would cease to be. It was a defense system very much like the system Ronald Reagan wanted to put into place...the star wars project. Tesla's mind was so sharp that there is little doubt that he would have been able to do this, but his known specialty was electricity.

He created wattages in the 19th century, that as far as I know, we still have not been able to match! He too could read a letter and memorize it at a glance. He was able to discern patterns in electrical storms with his natural abilities which we are only starting to discern with modern instruments. And of course he invented the Tesla coil, which paved the way for the Niagara Falls power station to be able to be built. He invented radio control, and illumination without wires...among other stuff. Had he forced people (Westinghouse, Niagara Falls electrical plant) to pay the royalties due from his inventions he would have had plenty of money to finance his inventions.

He later detested the idea that people were paying outrageous amounts for electricity, when he knew it was possible that we could get it for free by simply pounding a stake into the ground! He planned on doing something to the planet that would enable people to do this! More on that, later!

He was once seen in his laboratory well removed from incredibly huge machinery weighing tons, floating around as though it were weightless and lighter than air, guided by a cord that connected to something in his hand, which apparently contained silver balls. Once he pulled something out of his pocket and placed it on the side of a high-rise building during its construction. The building slowly began to shake and sway to the point everyone on the building was in a panic in fear that the building would collapse. Then he put the thing in his pocket and walked away. He was completely versed in harmonics, which is apparently what this device had something to do with. Tesla's hearing was also exceptional. He could hear thunderclaps 7-800 Kilometers away, he could hear a watch ticking three rooms away, and neighbors fire crackling next door. Train whistles 20-30 miles away were unbearable to him. He was continually aware of the ground trembling under his feet, and when he was sick these sounds were amplified even more and he could hear flies landing. (The ground does tremble constantly and occasionally I become aware of it, and it's quite unsettling if you are inside a large building when you feel it. The entire structure feels wobbly) I'm not sure this last feat is any big deal, and this may be the result of sound appearing to be louder when we relax, similar to how a radio can seem too loud even after several times of it being turned down. A fly could be heard to land under such circumstances. (I personally can verify that flies landing can be heard as I have heard them too when I was a kid. I mentioned this to someone and he thought I was imagining it. I told him to listen as the fly was still in the room. After several landings he too could hear it. Since it was daytime and I was in bed I have to think I was sick at the time too, though the ability to hear it may not be linked to being sick but being relaxed.) When Tesla invented his alternating current dynamo among other inventions, he would build it in his mind's eye piece by piece and actually watch it assemble and work. So strong was his ability to visualize that he at first thought he was able to reach out and touch his visualizations! He would have his manufactures make any individual part: he knew the exact dimensions and they would always fit perfectly. He always built the inventions in his mind first, and when the parts and inventions were made they ALWAYS worked! I've made inventions in my mind and they seem like they would work, but when I put them together often they are completely useless, because I've missed some real obvious particular. Tesla was certain there must be some way he could transfer these visualizations onto a screen or film with the right technology.

He was right! A certain **Ted Serios** after an illness found he was able to produce photographs of scenes hundreds of miles away. In a controlled test he was given a Polaroid camera just loaded with fresh film. He would point the camera at himself at arm's length, relax a minute, then click. When the film developed, instead of a picture of him staring at the camera on the film, there was a scene of a Canadian Mounted Police Airplane Hangar In Rockcliffe Ontario, but the picture was taken in Evaston Illinois! (Book 62 Pg 165)

Amadeaus Mozart is by many considered to be a genius bar none in the realms of music. At five years old, his father's string quartet was missing a person, so he filled in, not ever having seen the music and played it perfectly. In reply to their astonishment he merely said "surely you don't have to study to play second violin do you?" The Vatican had a long complex polyphonic tune played once a year, and they had the only copy of it and anyone else playing it was excommunicated. Mozart heard it once and transcribed the entire score from memory. He was able to compose his music in his head without hearing a single note. Of his ability he said "I see the whole of it in my mind at a single glance, I do not hear it in my imagination as succession the way it comes later, but all at once as it were".

Christian Frederick Heinecken. Born in 1721 by his 8th week was speaking comprehensible German. By his first birthday he had read the first five books of the bible and was familiar with the entire bible between ages 2 and 3. Before he turned 4 he had learned to read French and Latin while studying History and geography.

A man named **Helmholtz** was able to view things in total darkness by the illumination of his own eyes! (Book 55 Pg. 253-258)

Some people's vision is so acute they can see clearly some things, other people can only see in a microscope, and they can distinguish individuals from over a mile away, or see the phases of Venus with the naked eye. A friend of mine could see the phases of Venus and distinguish the four moons of Jupiter without the aid of any optical instrument. I can't even be sure I see the phases of Venus with my 15 power binoculars! Though if I got a tripod for the thing....

Some can see things clearly which have passed before their eyes in an instant. On occasion I've seen movies go by one frame at a time. Once while in a movie I saw absolutely clearly a subliminal add. One single frame was a few bags of popcorn, and a couple of ice cold drinks with condensation on the cups all on a white background. But the person sitting beside me saw nothing. Others have reported seeing these things and forced the movie theatres to stop it when they were proven correct.

The U.S. has set aside research funds for overcoming gravity, but it seems some people have long been able to do this. **Vasilov Nijinsky** could leap and hold a height longer then was considered scientifically possible. He did not know how he was able to do it, it just seemed natural and effortless.

"Saint" Francis of Paula was observed through a half open door by King Ferdinand I floating high above the floor as he meditated. A discipline called Lung-gom-pa is the mental ability to change your weight from so light you need weights to keep yourself from floating off into space, to so heavy that no amount of pressure from any number of people can budge you. One Tibetan Lama was seen bouncing so high and so fast that the observer was not able to keep up while riding a horse in pursuit! The Siddhas were able to become light as a feather, or extremely heavy, which suggest not just control over gravity, but atomic weight as well.

Nicola Tesla said in some instances he had seen the air all around him filled with tongues of living flame. This seemed to happen whenever he got inspiration for new ideas. Zoroaster Of the Chaldees also was subject to floating when in prayer and became luminous with flames resting on his head. This may be different then the account in Acts 2:3…though it could even be similar. Here we see three very different events and people all experiencing the same or similar phenomena. It may be linked in some way to the expression the "kingdom of heaven [that] is within you". Clearly if man was all he were meant to be he would experience a vastly expanded series of individual phenomena. This is also the case with luminosity. We know Moses face and Jesus' apparel shone. Tesla often when coming out of experiments was seen to be very radiant with light flaming out of every pore...but he also often shot millions of volts of electricity through him so this may be a by-product of these experiments. We know we have electrical aspects to our physiology so this may be a side effect related to something natural within. (See Ecclesiastes 8:1[wisdom makes the face to shine], Acts 6:15[face like an angel] and other verses)

A speaker (**Fay Clark**) while speaking on powers of the mind unwittingly displayed one. She felt strange as she spoke thinking she could fill the room and touch all the walls. Her chest was bothering her during this experience so she decided to cut her talk short and sat down. This is not what the audience saw. For about 2 minutes, though heard, she could not be seen! She only reappeared after she sat down! She was simply invisible! (Book 30 Pg. 215-216)

Teleportation. In 1960 Mrs. Barbara Taggart and her daughter were coming home with groceries. The door was locked and Mrs. Taggart had the keys. The daughter ran on ahead with some groceries. Suddenly the mother heard muffled cries, and had to unlock the door to find out what was wrong. Upon reaching the first landing the daughter suddenly found herself instantly inside the house. Similar events are in the bible. After Philip had baptized the Ethiopian the spirit caught away Philip to Azotus(Acts 8:39-40) A similar thing occurred to Jesus where the crowd was going to throw him over a cliff but "passing through the midst of them went on his way" (Luke 4:16-30)

People have been seen to walk through walls. More on that later.

Comparisons in the chemical makeup of lizards and certain amphibious creatures to man shows that man has all the necessary stuff to regenerate limbs. This finding startled the scientists and they were unable to explain why we don't automatically regenerate limbs when we lose them. Yet Jesus told the man with the withered hand to stretch it out and it grew back whole. So we do have the ability, but something is blocking it. There have been people that don't even believe in God or miracles that were able to heal people. So miraculous signs are not all necessarily of Godly nature, but appear to be part of Adams original physiological nature. People will say they healed in God's name, but could actually have little to do with him other then seeking the glory associated with doing miracles. (see Matt 7:21-23) So it seems that these 'latent' powers are not latent at all but all part and parcel of how we were originally created to be "in the image of God". But it seems that over the millennia the manifestations of these 'latent' powers has diminished. All these people mentioned above are Adams descendants, so we must presume Adam had all these abilities as well as many more.

ADAMS DESCENDANTS HIGHLY ADVANCED INVENTIONS

If we occasionally inherit special physiological abilities and hi IQ's then Adam must have had these physical and physiological aspects too. If some of us can do incredible calculations in our head so too must Adam have been able to. Sophisticated music…piece-of-cake for him. Makes you wonder just what music they did have! Ability to invent? no problem! "When do you want your hydraulic ramjet peanut butter spreader by? Tomorrow at noon? Done." So when all things are taken into consideration, an amazing picture forms, not only of Adam and the children of the pre flood period, it also sheds light on the society he must have lived in! So If Adam and his pre-flood descendants had super brains, then it stands to reason they had super inventions.

This sheds incredible light on the verse in Ecclesiastes where it says "there is nothing new under the sun…see this here it was of old." Folks they were not just talking about wagons and cartwheels! And I am certain this verse still stands true today…see this nuclear bomb? No big deal we had them before, see this rocket that travels to the moon, child's play bin there done that with bigger and better interplanetary vehicles! Consider that every human being on earth in the time of Adam in the pre flood period had these capabilities! What marvels they must have created! They were not living in caves, riding donkeys and banging rocks for music! That came well after the flood.

Technology diverges greatly. Germany in the 12 years it was cut off from the world had huge diversifications of technology. Doctoring took strange turns with metal bars rammed inside bone to help heal broken legs. Though they did not develop radar and nuclear weapons they did developed infra red, and anti radar devices and were far advanced in rocketry. What do we even expect to find in the past, and would we even recognize it as High tech? Many steps of invention would have been skipped. Japanese are using porcelain engine parts, because they can take higher temperatures. We wouldn't know what those were if we stumbled upon them! How did they move 20-2000 ton stones? What were the Pyramids for? We shall see! Legends exist of huge stones flying through the air controlled by a single man.

In seeking evidence of mans advanced technology in the past, what do we look for? Standard school of thought would suggest that over time, man would slowly be advancing in standards of knowledge and abilities as libraries grew and experiments expanded knowledge. Some pockets of regressions should occur when libraries or structures were demolished, but overall the timeline would show a steady upward climb. But this slow upward climb is not seen when looking at ancient knowledge, histories, ruins and technology. In the time slot that archaeologists are showing primitive man, we have to find super cities and space travel. While looking for the obvious I occasionally walked right past the subtle. A lot of what was found was long known, but interpreted in the light of evolution, but in light of this theory these objects take on new meaning.

As it turns out I am not the first to hunt for or find such material. Many archaeologists have discovered curious anomalies. Archeologist Dr. J. Manson Valentine was interviewed about ancient technologies regarding stone structures. "do you feel that this world before our own was on a par, with our technology, or would it have been farther or less advanced..." to which the Dr. replied "I think it was far beyond us" (Book 30 pg. 62)

Here are some of the evidences of incredible technology in the past. Since most of these are post flood, they only intrigue further.

Sumerians. Constantly, through various sources, the awe of the Sumerians technology is evident. The Sumerians are almost unanimously agreed upon as the first civilization, but counter to expectations, it is the most advanced! This group of people just seem to pop out of nowhere around 3000 BC fully equipped with the first written language, sophisticated mathematics, and display a knowledge of physics, chemistry and medicine, with no apparent stages that might be needed to get to this point of advancement. Some do not understand how they got all this knowledge so suddenly, some of which seems of no apparent use to them, like astronomy. The Sumerians were far beyond the people indigenous to their area. (Book 1 pg 100)

Others have noted that all languages seem to come from a common source and though some don't name that source, others indicate clearly this was the Sumerians. Yet, by some accounts, the Sumerian language seems unconnected to any other. The language and the writing are apparently not related to any other form of language or writing. Ancient translations from known languages to Sumerian exist. People like Von Daniken suggest that they got their knowledge from "spacemen". Though this conclusion seems completely off the wall, it does indicate just how fantastic their abilities were that some feel they have to attribute their abilities to spacemen. Yet oddly these Sumerians worshipped "moon gods". Whether or not there is anything to this theory we will explore later on.

The Sumerians themselves say "whatever seems beautiful, we made by the grace of the gods" the Sumerians made ziggurats (similar to pyramids) for the Gods to come down onto. It appears they expected the moon to come down and land on these ziggurats! Now if these Sumerians were so smart, what is *this* all about then?! Now we would expect that Noah and his three sons to have A) brought technology with them onto the ark, and B) to have been originally just as brilliant as pre flood folk as Noah also lived to 900+ years. But why do the Sumerians look to Moon Gods? Who were these moon gods? I think I know and will get back to them.

As mysteriously as they appear, the Sumerians disappear...and it's been shown that their language suddenly came into disuse! What could cause such sudden eradication of a language? The bible and other ancient histories have the answer...the tower of Babel! All evidence points to the Sumerians being the original language that man spoke after the flood. It would seem that along with the end of the Sumerian language came a further decline in man's abilities, for no subsequent civilization appears to be as advanced as the Sumerians were. Almost as if the very act of confusing of languages came a confusing or fogging of the minds as well.

These Sumerians can only be the people of the post flood period before the tower of Babylon incident! Though some sources suggest the Sumerians lived as long as 2000 years after the flood this doesn't seem possible, as they would be contemporaries of many civilizations that looked back on them. It seems Sumerians existence ended at the tower of Babel when their language ceased, but not the actual people, which could account for this contradiction.

The Egyptians puzzle archaeologist and anthropologists too by starting at the peak and then deteriorating over time. "The early history of Egypt, in fact, contains a strange anomaly, for its period of superior culture seemed to have evolved at once without any appreciable evidence of the usual transition stages" (book 37 pg 75,) Sounds similar to the Sumerians. The first pyramids are far more advanced than the later ones. (though that doesn't mean they were all built after the flood and during the reign of the Egyptians) They went from the Stone Age to almost modern civilization overnight. This transition is so intense that again people have suggested "supermen" or spacemen were the cause. Curiously the Egyptians speak of a reign of gods before the first dynasty, which started around 3100 BC. (book 13 pg. 54) The 'gods' of the Greeks and Romans can be traced back to the same gods of the Egyptians and the Sumerians. But it turns out these 'gods' are not 'gods' at all, but are in fact men. So why would men look to other men as though they were gods? It would seem devolved man and a more wholly intact man intellectually were at some point in contact with each other. This is odd and how could that be? We shall see.

THOSE KNOW-IT-ALLS!

(3rd ed. Insert 2016) One thing Ignatius Donnelly clues into is the fact that ancient "Egypt at the beginning appears mature, old and entirely without the mythical and heroic ages as if the country had never known youth. Its civilization has no infancy, and its art no archaic period. ...It was already mature." (quoting Winchell Alexander The Preadamites: Atlantis Pg 132) Though Donnelly attributes everything to Atlantis, this does clearly suggest man's civilization didn't need advancing right at the beginning, or right after the flood but only decline was possible. Later on Donnelly notes (quoting Lenormant and Cheval, Ancient histories of the East" Volume II pg. 208) "The Egyptians spoke of their hieroglyphic system of writing not as their own invention, but as "the language of the gods." "The gods" were, possibly, their highly civilized ancestors (which Donnelly as always concludes must be the people of Atlantis.) but it once again serves to note original people had all the knowledge right from the start. Who those gods *really* were will be shown later on.

Furthermore, Donnelly quotes "...the words of a recent writer in Blackwood" [a magazine circa 1880] "Instead of exhibiting the rise and progress of any branches of knowledge, they tend to prove that nothing had had any rise in progress, but that everything is referable to the very earliest dates. The experience of the Egyptologist must teach him to reverse the observation of Topsy, and to "'spect that nothing growed," but that as soon as men were planted on the banks of the Nile they were already the cleverest men that ever lived, endowed with more knowledge and more power than their successors for centuries and centuries could attain to. Their system of writing, also, is found to have been complete from the very first..." "As we have not yet discovered any trace of the rude, savage Egypt, but have seen her in the very earliest manifestations already skillful, erudite, and strong, it is impossible to determine the order of her inventions."... "We never find them without the ability to organize labor, or shrinking from the very boldest efforts in digging canals and irrigating, in quarrying rock, in building, and in sculpture." (Atlantis: Donelly page 360-361) The elephant in the room? No hunter gatherers, no cave men.

Originally to me the pyramids didn't seem to be any big deal. This attitude no doubt comes from originally learning about them through accepted theories put forth in school text books. But things in the research material kept pointing to them. Ok they are odd buildings or structures or ...what are they? They are apparently evidence of incredible technology, but what were they for? I didn't really care at first. But they kept cropping up in the research. I thought since they kept mystifying people, maybe I could take a stab at it and figure out what the big deal was and what they were used for. So I read a few books about them. I made many guesses. None seemed quite right. Maybe a giant puzzle like those wooden puzzles you take apart and put back together. Nah. But the answer slowly dawned and wow, it turns out that they are huge in the scheme of things! My guess as to their purpose will be presented in the chapter "Peleg". Suffice it to say these are evidence of incredible technology in the past, not only in their construction, but also in their purpose.

IF THEY COULDN'T, WHO DID?

(3rd ed. Insert 2016) One thing I thought striking as I skimmed through the research material again was that though the Babylonians [and I'll add Sumerians] possessed scientific knowledge of algebra, geometry and arithmetic, "The Egyptians on the contrary had in these subjects no real science at all. ...in that respect he was incurious as well as ignorant." (Book 34 page 143 quoting Sir Leonard Woolley and Jacquetta Hawkes book Prehistory and the Beginning of Civilization) THAT is fascinating! As some have stated the pyramids were old even to the Egyptians; this statement also shows they couldn't have built them as many have concluded the pyramids were mathematical marvels. Once again this puts their date of construction into the period of man when there was little or no devolution of his physiology…within a couple hundred years of the flood at least, or Pre-flood. (Is this really still considered true? The Egyptians had no math skills?!?)

The biblical timeline shows age of man rapidly declining after the flood. Something happened to the earth (the flood and it's side effects) that caused shorter life spans, and apparently degraded humans, because some were already looking to other men as gods. Yet there appears to have been technological intervention right near the beginning after the flood but before the first dynasty of the Egyptians. By my calculations this is a period of about 300 years.

Sumerians also had physical help and intervention from their gods and they had to be pre Tower of Babel, whenever that was. Earth's population was already high enough at this early stage to cause a fear of break-up of population into disassociated groups. This of course depends on how much time transpired between the flood and the tower of Babel. This fear of spreading out prompted the creation of the tower of Babel, and some spread is inferred to already have occurred from the base population before it was built. What *were* they building at Babel anyway? Something which would give them a 'name' or make them of renown…could this be similar to the pre-flood men of renown that is the Nephil(giants)? It was supposed to reach unto heaven. But this was just a tower of baked bricks! How would that give God cause for concern, and how could just a 'tower' of bricks assuage the tendency for migration? But this tower had to be something of such magnitude that God himself actually stopped the project. Interesting. More on that later.(chapter 9)

On Easter Island there are three cultural levels from as many eras, and the earliest were the most advanced.

South and Central Americas were more advanced in the earlier eras than the later ones, which still existed when the Spaniards discovered them. They seem to have started from a plateau and disintegrated to comparative barbarianism. In 1950 an earthquake in an ancient Incan city destroyed 90% of the modern buildings, but not a single ancient Incan building was damaged.

In Mohenjo Daro the deeper buried implements and jewelry were of higher quality and refinement then the ones found at shallower levels, though burial depths do not necessarily indicate relative age, as we shall see in chapter six.

The period from **Ptolemy to Copernicus** (14 centuries) there was no expansion of astronomical knowledge, yet the people of Ptolemy's time look backward to a golden age of science in the past. Some civilizations could predict eclipses but used ancient formulas that were not to be tampered with…often it was noted that these formulas were of Sumerian origin.

Ancient myths and histories whether verbal or written, when not understood by modern anthropologists, are often thought to be allegorical in nature. But often when taken at face value they seem to indicate incredible technology and knowledge in the past. True some were written cryptically deliberately, but some were meant to be as lucid as they could possibly record them. For example if the ancients speak of "thunderbirds" could that not be something else besides just a loud bird? (Later I realized this to be a bad example because actually it could be both. [See chapter 7] So let's go with men coming out of giant eggs, that is usually taken allegoricaly but in fact may be literal. See chapter 9)

A MYTHS CREATION AND ITS FACTUAL COUNTERPART.

In the ancient past stories get handed down that appear to present day anthropologists and historians to be myths. But if picked apart one can see they may indeed be based on actual events and technology. To show what I mean I have come across a modern day equivalent. I think this little story is important to understand how some ancient myths get started. Though this "myth" was only observed by a single man and never got "off the ground" so to speak (that is to say spoken of from generation to generation) but it still has valuable applications when considering other "myths".

An Eskimo named O'dark was brought back to New York with Peary (who was the famed chap that went to the north pole) and experienced New York life for a brief spell and then went back to his people and described what he saw. He said houses rode around filled with people, and people dwelled on top of each other like birds in a cliff. He said he had talked to Peary through a thin thread, even though Peary had been in a settlement remote from him. The Eskimos did not believe him. His peers told him to tell his stories to the women. (Book 56 pg 164, 165)

What's really interesting is that the author (Peter Freuchen) when referring to this story thought this Eskimo O'dark was a liar too! Even though he had been to civilization and should have been able to figure out what he was talking about!! When one looks more carefully at O'darks story and dissects it, it makes perfect sense as a witnessed series of events spoken of so that those of his people who had never been there could understand. Clearly what O'Dark the Eskimo described is Cars, phones, and apartment high rises.

People dwelling on top of each other like birds in a cliff is simply a reference to sky scrapers. Eskimos have very small houses and a car to them would be as big as a small house or igloo. Telephones are connected to thin thread (Wires) and one can talk to people many miles away on them even people on the other side of the earth! How else could an Eskimo describe these things in terms he and his peers would understand? I still find it fascinating that we can somehow talk through wires, and I remember holding the wire as though holding my voice as it went out, even crimping it to see if it would affect the conversation.

Ancient texts also hold such stories that have often been overlooked or thought of as flights of imagination. The North American Indians originally called rifles "Thunder sticks" and booze "fire Water". Get the idea? Or did they just call them that in the movies?

Often you'll see me refer to ancient legends, texts and histories but don't actually refer specifically to a particular text. Usually this is because I haven't actually read them as I've only been able to track down a few of them. And some that I have tracked down are incomplete, so I've had to accept other authors interpretations and references to them. Consequently I can't always give a specific reference, as often the ancient record referred to by another author may have been somewhat nebulous in the research material or not even apparent, other than in generalities. And no doubt I'm to blame in some instances as I may have only long after the reading of a tidbit realized the importance of an ancient reference but already lost it, so I'm forced to refer to a lost reference, which of course would be buried somewhere in the bibliography. I hope you'll grant me some slack in this regard as trying to find endless usually tiny lost references in some 100 or more sources is just too frustrating and time consuming. It would mean rereading each of the texts over and over again until I found each missing one referred to in this work. This would potentially mean years of rereading. So I hope you'll allow that I have remembered reasonably correctly.

Robots are alluded to in the past. Greek legends talk of Hephaestes making statues that looked like women that helped lame people walk. Chinese legends also exist that speak of the art called "Khwai shuh" which brought statues to life in order for them to serve the master. (book 11 pg. 122)

Guns way back A bison skull was found with a hole identical to a bullet hole in it...problem was the skull dated 43,000 years old. Extinct Bison (in American Falls Idaho) dating around the same period also display bullet holes. A "Neanderthal" skull was found dating "40,000 years" old with a bullet hole in one side and shattered skull on the exit side. Delaware Indians speak of the 'gods' being able to kill animals from mountain tops with thunder bolts...sounds an awful lot like Thor and Zeus...or "thunder sticks".

TV in the past. Things in the past were called "magic mirrors", but descriptions sometimes fall short of understanding to what they are referring to. The ancient book Enoch, says men were taught by Azaziel to make magic mirrors through which one could observe distant people and places. Another account in the Vera Historia speaks of a looking glass placed over a shallow well and when you go in you could see all the nations and cities of the earth...sounds like a movie theatre. Enlil, a Sumerian 'god' had "eyes that could scan all the land". When you look at a TV or computer screen when it is turned off you can see your reflection. Magic Mirror? (book 11 pg. 130)

Large stones so big as to be impossible to move even with today's cranes have seemingly been shoved around in the past as though they were feathers. A physical clue does exist. In one series of stones in a huge structure that was discovered by the Spanish in the new world, they found it to have bore holes which still had huge silver bars in them which seemed to serve no purpose. These same holes (without silver in them) have been seen in Egyptian structures and no explanation has ever been put forth as to what these holes were for. In the Egyptian display at the museum a huge carved stone cornice displays two perfectly smooth boreholes. This could only be caused by a high-speed coring drill. In the write up on the piece the holes are completely ignored! Why? They don't know what they are for, or how they were put there, so they ignore them!

MACHINE PART?

(3rd ed. Insert 2016) The Cairo Museum displays something found in 1936 called a "Schist Disc" also called a Tri-lobed disc. It still baffles experts. Supposedly a decoration or bowl, it looks more like a machine part. **(see drawing 1).**

DRAWING 1

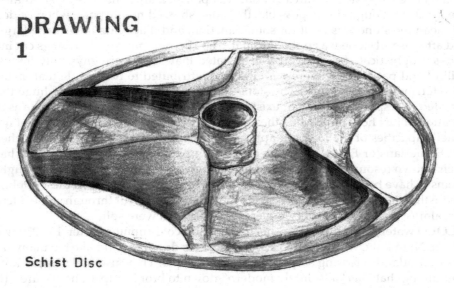

Schist Disc

Looking up what it was made out of apparently it's made of "schist", a fragile ROCK! There is NO way anyone could carve this thing…it's just too impossible. It had to be…molded? Trying to determine what it might have been used for a virtually identical item is used by Lockheed inside an oil chamber…in one of its planes? By the way this museum also holds many vases made out of diorite, a very hard composite rock similar to granite. These vases are completely hollowed out with nice thin walls. No one in their right mind would even consider making vases out of rocks today. It's just too difficult or would burn out machines and bits at such a rate as to make the cost of the vases prohibitive. (see Atlantis Rising #106 pg 14) Were they using the "John Hutchinson effect" as it's been dubbed to make these bowls? Some call his effects a hoax, but the ancients had to have used something like this. (See further on in this chapter "Rock-a-by Jello".)

Cut blocks and cores. Don't look at just the stone blocks but the tool used to make them and the civilization that must have existed to create these tools. A core from one of these Egyptian holes was found and it was perfectly smooth, and compared to a modern one it was far superior, the new one showed jumping and scraping, the Egyptian one show clean and irresistible technology. (That was 1893) I found a newer core in the lapidary society and had to do a bit of work to smooth it, as it was still fairly rough, although clearly better than one from 1893, but it was still inferior to the bore holes seen in that Egyptian cornice in the museum. In fact the holes are so smooth one wonders if they were even made by drills. Some other clues suggest they may have been able to make rock temporarily soft and a hole could be made as simply as doing it in butter. Some observers, examining ancient cut stonework blocks, deduced that a jeweled saw at least 9 feet in diameter was used to cut the blocks they made because of the direction of the cuts. Legends exist of huge stones, flying through the air and into position. I am convinced that antigravity existed in conjunction with a worldwide system which was put in place during antiquity, which is still evident today. More on that later! Legends speak of antigravity and incredible advances in the past, which are summarily dismissed as nonsense by any 'credible archeologists' worth his 'salt'. Even the hieroglyphics cut in some stonework were so precise it was felt to be impossible by ordinary carving methods, as suggested by orthodox archaeology. The evidence suggests power tools were used.

Even quarries show absolutely wild technology. Some huge carved block show no signs of chips, and large stones have been pulled out of areas showing two 90 degree corners! So wild are these sites that some have suggested glaciers did the work because the stone is so polished...but glaciers do not cut stone at right angles. Some have suggested the area cut out was polished after the rocks were pulled out. This too is just nonsense, because though this is possible, the stone showed no purpose, whereas doing something like this would mean the stone was built for some function, and it appears to be just a large bulk of stone which remained after useful stone was pulled from it. The Hieroglyphics and carvings cut into many of the stones of old are so sophisticated that Hyatt Verrill stated that these were physically impossible to do no matter how skillful and patient they were with the tools attributed to the people that made the carvings. (book 37 pg 79 referring to H.V.'s work) The stone statues on Easter Island are so huge that 'space men' have been suggested as responsible for their existence, and erection. Now as improbable as that may seem, it gives an indication of just how impossible these tasks were to accomplish in the light of normal theories, and the presumed capacities of the locals. It appears for whatever civilizations worked these marvels, be they Egyptians, Sumerians or Easter islanders it seems impossible for these peoples to have done these things given their known resources and assumed technology. Some other factor often thought to be gods or "spacemen" seems to have been in place in order for them to have accomplished these sophisticated works. Whoever did these things, in some cases, appears to have been able to cut through stone, literally like butter with a hot knife, almost as though the very molecules of the rock were split.

HOT and COLD water / big ships. Ancients had hot and cold running water. In 1920 two roman Ships were found in Lake Nimi Italy, which carried 120 people. This doesn't sound like too many people until one realizes the first transatlantic crossing ships held only 94 people. They also had Copper hot water heaters for baths and plumbing that was "absolutely modern" down to bronze pipes and fixtures. (Book 11 pg 18)

ACCURATE MAPS AND CLOCKS

Traditional history says that man thought the earth was flat until after Columbus's voyages. Yet there's reason to suspect Columbus KNEW the earth was round based on some of the maps that appear to have been in his possession. Some maps turned up in the 1300's called Portalanos, which were far in advance of the map makers abilities of the period. These maps, which were copied carefully over the years, even showed Antarctica... without ICE! These maps clearly indicate the ancients knew the earth's exact diameter and knew spherical geometry yet these mathematical formulas did not get discovered until hundreds of years later! Some people who have studied the ancient maps declare that they do not know how they could have made such accurate maps without flight. (Book 51)

Actually at the time of Columbus there was quite a bit of controversy about the roundness or flatness of the earth. In 1492 (before Columbus came back) Martin Behaim had already projected the known land onto a globe, but because the cartography of the day was so horribly primitive, and the size of the earth was unknown to any accurate degree, the globes mapping of the land masses appears so distorted that were the information correct, the earth would have been 21,600 in circumference from pole to pole but 13,200 miles around the equator.

The ancient Eratosthenes wanted to know the dimensions of the earth and using two known cartographical points obtained a figure only 80 Kilometers out (book 11 pg 60) Others have calculated earth's diameter before Columbus with varying degrees of accuracy and arrived at figures anywhere from 18,000 miles around to 23,180 miles. The Popul Vuh, an ancient book of the Quiche Mayas talks of an ancient civilization that knew about nebulas, the solar system and the round surfaces of the earth. Other ancient writings speak of a round earth hanging in the ether, or suspended in the air, and Job26:7 speaks of the earth hanging on nothing. Even Egyptian children were taught the earth was round.

Officially the Canary Islands were discovered in 1395 but 20 years earlier a Catalonian atlas was published which noted their existence based on information copied from ancient maps!

Cotton of ancient America is a crossbreed of a local type and the Mediterranean cotton and no one is certain how it came about, let alone how it came about in ancient times. Were there great shipping routes or some other factor? Birds didn't eat it so it couldn't have spread that way, and salt water destroys the seeds. Many mysteries exists about how so many things could be common to both sides of the Atlantic; chapter six will clear them up.

Piri Reis, a collector of old maps, got some maps from one of Columbus's navigators, which dated to Alexander the great! He used his collection of maps to compile a world atlas in 1513. What's odd about this atlas is that the Americas were in the maps. Why is this odd? Because people at this point in time still thought the Americas were part of Asia. The Pacific ocean was not seen until 1513 by Balboa, and not sailed until 1520 by Magellan... seven years after the Piri Reis atlas. The Atlantic coast of South America was not even partially charted until 1519.

In this 1513 atlas, the Amazon River was shown, yet it was not discovered until 1541! Interestingly, Antarctica was shown to be connected to South America, which geologists admit was the case at one time. That Antarctica was mapped at all is odd because it was not discovered until 1818! The map of Antarctica even shows mountains. At first glimpse the maps appear to be as lousy as other maps of the period because the projection is so unusual. It took 20 years to figure out why it was drawn in this manner. It was eventually discovered that the map is projected from Syene Egypt outward, rather than how we do it from the equator upward and downward. This would be like showing the North Pole in the center of a map and showing the continents...it would be a really odd looking map, with land at the extreme edges looking very distorted. Antarctica would look like a ring of land around the earth. When these unusual maps of America were plotted on the current projection it was astonishingly accurate...in fact *too* accurate! This map was superior to any map that could be drawn for the next 250 years! Arriving at the correct longitude was not yet solved, and the size of the earth was still not known (although Amerigo calculated it within 50 Miles in 1501) and spherical trig not yet been discovered.

Some ancient and medieval maps have islands that are no longer there, and people have suggested they drew these places to fill in bare spots. This is just ridiculous supposition, because the sailors lives depended on these maps! Columbus believed he could get supplies from islands drawn on his maps in areas where no islands were because he had maps depicting islands there...and nearly perished because of it! The last thing voyagers' want is maps with fake islands on them!

Constantly for hundreds of years Antarctica appears on maps before it was discovered. These maps of Antarctica apparently date prior to Alexander the Great. Captain Cook actually looked for Antarctica because so many maps existed showing the place, and had the maps of Antarctica at his disposal been correct, he should have been 700 hundred miles inland of the Antarctic coast. Instead all he found was floating ice, thus he "proved" Antarctica did NOT exist and consequently Antarctica was removed from all maps in the late 1700's.

What's odd about these Antarctic maps is everything else was accurate, even the mountains! Three different maps drawn by people around the world in 1532, 1538 and 1559 show the exact same Antarctica... pressed up against the southern tip of South America, which no doubt is why Magellan tried to squeeze into the straights that now bears his name, believing it the only way into the Pacific. But maybe it was just as well he went this way as who can say if he would have survived a trip around the horn? Not only do these maps showing Antarctica match up with each other, they match up with what we know about Antarctica now! So why did Cook not find it, if these maps of Antarctica are so accurate? The problems was the 80th parallel was confused with the Antarctic Circle thus Antarctica was drawn too large. When this error was compensated for the map was perfect! Some of these maps even show rivers and accurate topography (that is mountains), which matched up with seismic portraits! Although the actual drawing of Antarctica seems erroneous, it is because it was compiled from several pieces and spliced together only reasonable accurately. Each piece however has been determined to show an accurate depiction of the slice of Antarctica that it contained.

An accurate map also exists showing Greenland without ice dated 1380!(book 11 pg 90, book 51 pg. 154-55.) It was converted from a portalano projection to a different type of projection with an incorrect pole, and thus shows distortion, but when plotted on a correct globe it shows up very accurately.

Back to those portalanos. The first time I saw one it was immediately obvious they were FAR superior to normal maps from the period...how accurate? They were out by as much as 1/3 of a degree in 3000 miles! They could be stuck in current atlases! Yet they popped up in the 1300's! Even maps from 1500 look absolutely dismal compared to them. These appear to date back at least to the Phoenicians and Carthaginians...yet they had no means of drawing them! Antarctica should have been well frozen up by the time they came along. The only time the portalanos are in error is when people add to them later on! No one really knew what they had because when explorers came home with new charting of places, the older portalanos were abandoned as inaccurate so consequently atlases got worse as the portalanos were discarded in preference to the new material being brought in by the explorers.

Oddly these portalanos use the 360 degree circle (12 and 24 wind system), the same used by the Sumerians! This system was abandoned and replaced by the 8-wind because the 12-wind system was too difficult to use! Not even renaissance explorers used the 360-degree system, even though we know the ancients did.

In 1936 in Oslo, professor A.W. Brogger caused a real commotion when he stated that there was a golden age of navigation which was at it's height about 3000 BC which declined until about 1500 BC. This flew right in the face of conventional belief that seamanship had its beginnings then. He put the Phoenicians at the BOTTOM level in terms of navigational abilities.

In 1901 **Sponge divers** found a wreck since dated at 65BC and found on it was a shapeless lump which when cleaned turned out to be a metal geared device. In 1959 this was deciphered to be an astronomical clock to pinpoint constellations and such. It's known as the Antikythera mechanism, device or computer. It was determined to be very accurate, and skeptics said "rubbish, it's much too accurate to be as old as that... you might as well say that Percales told time by his wristwatch" Another said "finding a thing like this is like finding a jet plane in the tomb of King Tutenkhamen" (Book 22, pg 48-49) Oddly enough there are ancient pictures that exist which show people wearing what appear to be wrist watches!

BACK TO ANTIKYTHERA.

(3rd ed. Insert 2016)More examination of the Antikythera computer has people mystified. The teeth of the gears are virtually all a perfect 60 degrees which allows for a "gap tolerance" of less than five-hundredths of an inch. Two experts trying to recreate identical bronze gears failed more than once in the attempt. It was also discovered that a couple of the gears were deliberately slightly misaligned with a small pin inserted into one of the gears so it could be moved slightly out of place "...to simulate the irregular elliptical orbit of the moon around the earth, known today as the First Lunar Anomaly." Furthermore there has been found on some of the gears writing that measures eight-hundredths of an inch in size, "- far too small to have been etched with any type of ordinary metal tool." Analysts deduced that this writing must have been etched with a lazer! The device is so advanced that it cannot be a one of kind fluke created by a single very clever person who just happened to be way above his contemporaries. It has to point to a whole system and civilization of advanced technology. So mystifying and accurate is this piece no one even seems to know when to place the artifact on the historical timeline. It's deduced that originally it had at least 37 gears, and possibly as many as 70 and it was able to tell time, longitude, and acted like a perfect planarian with gears for each of the planets out to Saturn. It even took into account irregularities of the moon and the earth, and there's rumors it could clean dishes and windows! It was repaired a couple times when it was in use so it's thought to date at least 150 to 100 BC, well before the 65 BC boat it was found on. But the technology of this device clearly indicates the people who made it knew full well the planets moved around the sun making it at least as old as 400 BC, as this heliocentric idea fell out of favour with the Greeks by the time period of the Greek Boat on which it was found. (See Atlantis Rising # 76)

TELESCOPES AND FILTERS WERE IN OLD TIMES

As far back as 1616, Sir Walter Raleigh wondered how the ancients could have known about the phases of Venus, when Galileo had only 'recently' discovered them! It was clear to him the ancients knew this. Why isn't it to us? Because we cannot accept that the people before Galileo had telescopes, so this fact is ignored and not used when teaching ancient history.

When the telescope was invented it couldn't be patented because too many people knew about them! There is a drawing that dates at least as old as 1500, but possibly as early as 1200's that says it's a drawing of an area in space known as "by the navel of Pegasus, the Girdle of Andromeda and the head of Cassiopeia". Study of these drawings suggest it to be a nebula, and the person who drew it had a telescope. There was also a detailed leaf drawing that appears to have been drawn with the aid of a microscope. However these are interpretations of the drawings, as an accomplished artist did not do the drawings.

The **Maoris** of New Zealand were aware that Saturn had rings. These can't be seen with the naked eye, and can only be hinted at with a 15 power binocular as a slightly football shaped 'star'. The rings don't show up 'till about 25-30 magnification.

Democratus said there are more planets then we can see, but these need telescopes...lucky guess? Babylonian Tablets describe the location of an outer planet. (book 8 pg 21)

The Iliad and Hindu's were aware of a seventh extra planet...so all but Pluto were known. Foreknowledge of Mars' moons appears to have existed...although Velikovsky states from his research that possibly Mars at one time was close enough to earth for us to have actually seen the moons! More on that later! Evidence exists that seems to show the Babylonians were aware of seven moons of Saturn. The Efe Pigmies of central Africa were aware of nine moons of Saturn...yet you need a 20-inch telescope to see them!

The **Dogons** were aware that Sirius was accompanied by a heavier unseen star, which was proven correct in 1862 with an 18 1/2 inch telescope. They also knew the period of rotation to be 50 years. They also state that Sirius is rotated by another star bigger, yet 1/4 the weight and has a larger orbit in the same direction which also takes 50 years and is accompanied by a planet... and a third star rotates around Sirius in the opposite direction. We still have not been able to verify this! How do they know? (Book 10, pg 73-78, book 34 pg 112) The Dogons traditions have been traced back to the Egyptians and the Sumerians!

The Mayans knew the length of year and month to four decimal places.

In the first century comets were known to orbit like planets. (book 11 pg 68)

A Babylonian astronomer knew the moon affected the tides, yet this was not even suspected until the 1600's

An eclipse was predicted in 585 BC using ancient "pre Semitic Mesopotamian" (Sumerian) calculations. Eclipses are predicted using three sites around the earth in conjunction with each other!, and you need a telescope to observe the Moons wobble which is only visible for a few days once every 9.3 years. How were they able to relay information from observers to correctly predict eclipses? Slingshot relay? Carrier pigeon?

Aztec drawings depict people looking at the stars though a long tube...though that tube could not possibly be a telescope because they weren't invented yet so it must be a tube from the end of the roll from the Christmas wrapping paper.

In 1853 a crystal lens was found in Nineveh dating to about 600 BC. Lenses were not supposed to have been invented until much more recently. Other lenses have been found in Libya, Iraq, Mexico, Egypt, Jordan, Ecuador, and central Australia! A spherical lens of great precision was found in the Nile Valley. A lens found in Helwan Egypt was mechanically ground, a fact, which no one disputes! This lens is in the British museum. Concave mirrors (such are used in telescopes) have been found as well. No one has any idea how they were made. Maybe they should go to a local telescope maker and see how they are made.

An ancient Peruvian dictionary translated in 1540 has the word "Quilpi" which can be translated to mean 'optical instrument for looking in the distance'. (Book 22 pg43-44) Why do 'savages' have a word for telescope in their vocabulary at least 68 years before it was invented on a different continent?

A transit of Venus was observed Nov. 25, 416, and 2000 years ago the Chinese recorded sunspots. Either they had telescopes and filters or a lot of astronomers went blind in the old days.

ELECTRICITY IN ANCIENT TIMES

To grind lenses today we use cerium oxide, a substance only isolated through an electro chemical process. If the ancients had telescopes and lenses, did they have electricity? Maybe we didn't have it in 1608, and we used other abrasives, but they did have electricity back in ancient times.

In 1938 a German archaeologist, Wilhelm Konig found several little jars with copper cylinders and corroded iron cores near Bagdad. They were even soldered with a 60/40 lead tin alloy...the same we use today. These items were over 2000 years old, yet they were believed to be batteries. After the war William Gray of General Electric made duplicates of them, added an electrolyte, and they worked! (Book 11 pg93, Book 35 pg71-72, book 30 pg65)

An ancient document Agastya Samhita gives instructions on how to make electric batteries, and even mentions that a chain of 100 "would give a very active and effective force" (book 11 pg 95) Ancient electroplated items have also been found.

Aluminum was discovered in 1808, and could not be extracted properly until 1886, because so much electricity was needed to extract it, and was still prohibitively expensive. However a tomb in China dated 316 AD yielded a metal belt which was analyzed in 1958 and found to contain 10% copper, 5% manganese and 85% aluminum. (book 21 pg 79, book 11 pg 32) And by the way, Manganese was not "discovered" until 1774.

Platinum discovered in Columbia by the Spanish was thrown away as unripe gold and discarded as an unmeltable metal until 1788 when they improved the forges. However articles of platinum made while molten, were found in the Andes, Ecuador and Egypt. The original Americans were able to make forges with temperatures reaching 9000 degrees. Peruvian Mochicas were able to work with gold, silver, copper and alloys in ways still not duplicated.

A very old pillar exists known to be at least 1600 years old because of a Kings inscription that was placed there in 413 AD, but the pillar was already very old then. The pillar is estimated to be 4000 years old. What's odd about this pillar, which is 18 feet tall 18 inches thick, is that it's made of iron that wont rust. We were not able to make this type of pure iron, which contains no phosphorus or sulfur, until 1968 and only by electrolysis and only in tiny amounts! The pillar weighs 6 tons! Several people referred to this unusual pillar. (Book 21 pg 79, book 2 pg 92, 43, book5 pg 21, pg 22, book 31, pg 26, book 11 pg 33) Arab legends also speak of swords that would not rust. Unbreakable glass is also referred to in ancient documents. If they could make fancy metals, they were using them for a lot more then jewelry and pillars. Speaking of jewelry, a quartz bead was found on a mummy that had a hole in it so tiny that this was not duplicated until the '60's. But get your mind off the bead and imagine the tool used to drill it, as it took technology contemporary with the landing on the moon to duplicate it!

WHERE ARE THE SIGNS OF DEVELOPMENT?

(3rd ed. Insert 2016) When you research for ancient technology time and time again you read things like this quote in relation to the Steel Delhi Pillar. "This is indicative of a form of technology that had to have been the result of many centuries of experimentation by trial and error. Yet we do not find evidence of such developmental stages having existed at any point or before or since." (Atlantis Rising #75)

(This particular reference is to this pillar which is only known to be from at least the 5th century by markings on it, but probably dates from much further back in time) But statements like this are said about many civilizations, such as Egypt and Sumeria. The point is there *wasn't* any development. They just knew how to do these things because they were not devolved like we are now where we have to make many many transitional developments to get an invention of any kind up and running. They were smart enough to see the problems before building any inventions and got the bugs out before building a single prototype. They probably didn't even use the word "prototype". Thus no intermediate developmental stages will be found, or if anything, devolved or primitive copycat versions of inventions will be found. Similarly for the batteries found in 1930 by Dr. Wilhelm Konig. "Yet the mystery is that the background steps necessary for the development of the battery exist nowhere. It is as if they suddenly came out of thin air, from no known contemporary source." (Atlantis Rising #73 pg 63) (I personally think these batteries are pretty primitive and are either devolved examples of previous perfected examples or *are* the prototypes. But don't tell those archeologists that. We alternative archaeologists need all the help we can get)

In 1961 a rock collector found a geode (hollow rock with crystalline interior) in California. When cut in half, it nearly destroyed the saw, because there was something inside completely unexpected...a manmade metal and ceramic object! When the halves were x-rayed it was unmistakably a manmade object...in the interior of a rock supposedly 500,000 years old! Analyzing the object came up with the conclusion that it was likely a sparkplug! Either civilization is way older than we thought, or that geode is not 1/2 a million years old! Later on we'll deal with dating errors.

ARTIFICIAL LIGHTING

Dark passages and tunnels get black from smoke when torches or candles are used in them over long periods of time, as seen in Roman and Greek tunnels, and dark passageways. But in Egypt there are subterranean tunnels with carved and painted walls, which show no signs of smoke, strongly suggesting artificial light. (Book 2 pg 98, book 7 pg 205) Also in caves where there are paintings in Western Europe there is no sign of smoke.

The Temple of Hathor in Egypt shows giants holding what appear to be large huge glass bulbs similar to electrical tubes or clear light bulbs with snakes inside. **(See drawing 2)** The bulbs are connected to cables with what appear to be some sort of electrical transformers holding up the bulbs which might be "tet"'s, a Egyptian term used in relation to bringing Osirus back to life. (More on that later) The snakes in the bulbs could be indicative of a snakelike filament and of how electrical power "bites" like a deadly snake might.

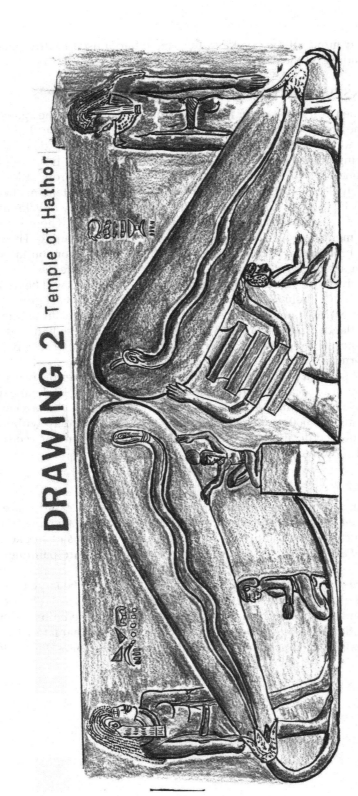

DRAWING 2 | Temple of Hathor

A Greek named Lucien (circa 120-180 AD) viewed in Heirapolis Syria a Statue with a jewel in its forehead that lit up the whole temple. (Book 11 pg 94)

In Antioch there was found in the 6th century AD a lit lamp that according to the inscription had been burning for over 500 years.[Book 11 pg 94]

In 1401 the tomb of Pallas was opened and the inside was lit up with a lamp that had to be glowing for more than 2000 years! (Book 31 pg 67)

In 1652 there were found lit lamps in an underground room in Memphis.

Lamps that burned neither oil or any other consumable product were used by Jewish and Islamic people in the middle ages, the origins of which were attributed to "watchers of the sky". We'll find out who these 'watchers' are later.

A city, cut off from civilization near Mount Wilhelmina in the western half of New Guinea was chanced upon by traders. It was described as having a system of illumination equal or superior to 20th century. Traders were quite frightened by the small mountain town's lighting. Many huge stone spheres that had been built on top of pillars, started to glow after sunset and lit up the town with an eerie neon like light. (Book 11 pg. 96-97)

Somewhere in the Brazilian Matto Grosso in the 1920's Col F.H Fawcett was trying to find a place the Indians there said existed, but were afraid of as 'haunted'. The place had structures described as "a fat tower of stones that were capped with light that never go out". He had been told of lost cities by the Matto Grosso natives, which had mysterious 'cold lights' lighting up the cities. Evidently he found the cities and he stated that he felt they were a remnant of a long gone civilization, which had retained old knowledge. These cities have never been brought to light, partly because of their remoteness, and partly because Fawcett was never heard from again after May, 29 1925. (Book 11 pg 97, Book 12 pg 27-28) When the Paraguay River was being explored in 1601 (also in the Matto Grosso) they came to a lake with an island near the source of the river. On the island there was a city that contained a 25ft pillar on top of which was a large 'moon' that lit up the entire lake. In several places around the earth there exist perfectly spherical stones (some in excess of 8 ft in diameter) in various settings. They are clearly manmade as it takes precision instruments to make them as round as they are. There are no explanations for their existence or purpose.

Interesting stories about stone with weird properties persist; some glow, some give visions as though a recorded message were being played. People have seen events happen before their eyes that happened years prior, as though some event were recorded in the environment and was being replayed as though some event or timing device set the recording to playing. Wars and battles have been heard all over again. For example near the beach of Dieppe the landing was heard 9 years later in 1951 at the same time of day. This suggests that there is something about items that can record events we appear to be unaware of. People have seen Vikings land and sack buildings that weren't there the day before, but were there hundreds of years prior, or heard troops marching in vast numbers that were not there. Stones have been heard to give off music in the sun. Genesis 31:51 speaks of a stone pillar as a witness. Habakkuk 2:11 says a stone will cry out and a beam will answer, and in Luke 19:40 Jesus suggests that the rocks would cry out.

Nikola Tesla seemed aware of some sort of living element in stones, declaring crystal was a form of life! William Gilbert in 1570 found that a number of gems, including diamond, sapphire, amethyst, opal, carbuncle, jet and even ordinary rock crystal built up and produced an electric charge when rubbed (book 63 pg 157)

One dolmen stone move downhill needed 6-40 horses to pull it and the harness broke killing some of the horses. The stone was used as a bridge, but the stone kept rolling back onto the grass during the night. Finally the villagers gave up and only one horse was needed to pull it back *uphill* to its original place. (book 13 pg. 193)

One interesting experiment done in 1880 by Professor Eric Laithwaite of London, with two stone flywheels visible in a chest weighing a total ten Kilos. The wheels were started up and then the chest weighed just 7.5 kilos!

INTERESTING CHEMISTRY

Under normal lighting conditions an Ajanta cave painting dated to 6th century is clearly not the work of "cavemen". It is a painting of women carrying gifts, which is said to be nothing special, and lacks depth... that is until the lighting is turned off! As you grow accustomed to the dark the painting glows and appears to have three-dimensional depth "as if it were made of marble" The secret of this paint has long since been lost.

In 673 AD a Kallinikos came to Constantinople with a secret formula for a new weapon... "Greek Fire" which, for example, was used to destroy 800 Arab ships in 716AD. What was special about this fire was it could burn on and under water, and could not be extinguished until it was all consumed. Kallinikos was not a chemist but appears to have found the formula while excavating a site of an ancient civilization, which dated back to ancient Ninus and Babylon.

HUGE WEIGHTS MOVED

Traditional explanations of how the pyramids in Egypt were constructed apparently do not add up. They insist that the stones were moved around by thousands of slaves. It's figured about 100,000 slaves would have been needed to do the various steps in the buildings. The stones weighed between 15 and 100 tons, (based on 600 cubic feet equaling 50 tons) and used up wooden rollers at a rate of about ten per stone over the course these stones were brought. Some of these stones came from as far away as 600 miles. An estimate of 2.6 million trees would have been used as rollers to move the stones. That's a lot of wasted trees! Not to mention economic waste of labor. No evidence exists that Egypt ever had such a forest! (Though I suppose they could have imported them from somewhere, but this would have been economic suicide.) If they cut and dressed and moved 10 stones a day it would have taken 680 years to complete the job! And these stones are so accurately laid that not even a penknife can be pushed between them.

Furthermore the 6.5 million tons of stone in the pyramids show no sign of settling! The land they are built on is within 1 inch of level over a 13-acre area. (I wonder if this "out by an inch" might even have taken into consideration the curvature of the earth? I know we have built bridges so long that the curvature of the earth needed to be taken into the calculations in order for the bridge to be sound, so it seems logical the ancients might have done this for the pyramids, though I have not seen anyone make this connection.)

The cement is so strong that after 5000 years or more, the rock will shatter before the cement gives in. Because archeologists usually believe evolution, they make up plausible guesses based on their knowledge of ways the ancients could move these stones, because they assume no advanced technology existed back then. But these explanations often do not make sense when looking at the evidence. Why would ancient civilizations move 100 ton stones hundreds of miles, tying up resources for an idol or a tomb and spending as long as 600 years to build them? It's just not workable! Some other capability had to be in place.

Admittedly some structures MAY have been built in these arduous ways. It seems the temple of Solomon was made in similar ways, and some churches in the middle ages took 40 years to build, possibly in similar ways archeologists suggest. But such churches had to be a fraction of the work compared to the pyramids. If some church took 40 years to make how long did the pyramids take to build if they used the same technology? Why would they build them if they knew they would take that long to build? But earlier and bigger structures are far beyond these suggested methods of construction. Conversely to be fair, one source says there are approximately 2.3 million blocks of stone in the Great pyramid weighing only an average 2 1/2 tons per block. Eight men could lift such a block, and some feel the pyramid could be built, with enough men, in less than 20 years (book 33 pg. pg. 24-32) But even so, in this best case scenario, why would anyone build such monuments to bury a king? It's just not in any way logical and this can't be the correct interpretation of these structures purposes. And I have to think if it took us forty years to build some churches in the middle ages, it would have taken considerably longer to build the pyramids if similar methods were employed.

Compare this to Solomon's temple which took 70,000 bearers of burdens seven years to build. This temple was 60 X 20 cubits and 30 cubits high, or about 117 X 39 feet and 58 feet high. The temple was relatively easily destroyed and little of it remains to this day. The largest costly stones used for the foundation [cut with saws], used by Solomon were 10 cubits (about 19 ½ feet), presumably cubed, though I don't know this for sure. That's 7414 cubic feet meaning even these were in the neighborhood of 617 tons. [Some were 8 cubits, or 320 tons] I don't know at present if these calculations are correct, but if they are, they were indeed pretty heavy stone blocks. Curiously no one seems to suggest aliens helped Solomon's workers move these blocks, which were presumably moved in traditionally accepted ways, with pulleys, levers, rollers and brute strength. However it would appear the blocks of the buildings and walls of Solomon's temple were not built with nearly the precision of the pyramids.

Now the cubic volume of Solomon's temple was thus 288,000 cubic feet and this took 7 years to build. (for ease of calculation I used 2 feet per cubit). The great pyramid, supposedly built by Khufu, because of some red painted graffiti found inside of it with his name (what? they didn't have people put their names on old buildings in the past? Actually this writing was a hoax done in recent days, by a shyster of an archaeologist) is a total volume of (756 x 756 x 480 divided by 3) or 91,445,760 cubic feet. This is 317.52 times the volume of Solomon's temple. If we then assume the same 70,000 people that built Solomon's temple also built the Pyramids it would have taken them a total of 2223 years to build! C'mon people let's get real! Some other form of technology was in place to build the pyramids besides brute force! (Note: some of these materials were put in the temple and some in Solomon's house, but the 'bottom line' doesn't change)

MACHINED?

(3rd ed. Insert 2016) Christopher Dunn likes to measure ancient masonry to see if there's evidence they were machined and not just cut. He was checking the Andes sites such as Ollantaytambo, Pisac (I hadn't heard of this one before) and Macchu Picchu, and soon decided to leave most of his tools behind because though most sites there are impressive, machining seemed out of the question,… until he stumbled upon a little visited site called "Puma Punku". He says "…my jaw dropped as I encountered a block of andesite with flat surfaces and near one edge a groove precisely cut along its length with small holes drilled at intervals along the length of the groove". Looking around he noticed a jumble of blocks some with perfectly square corners, flat surfaces and on and on. He had to jump in a taxi and get his instruments because all the blocks just looked like they had been machined. The flat surfaces were so flat they were within the limits of .0001 inch his instruments could measure stuff in. Some angles though not 90 degrees, appeared deliberately so. And though other blocks didn't have quite this degree of accuracy, It didn't take long to conclude they were using a "…precision high in the Andes which was produced by any pre Columbian civilizations cannot be explained in the archaeological record". Though he left the site and couldn't absolutely determine if they were all machined stones, the entire site screamed far more advanced techniques were used than any mainstream archaeologist would normally credit the ancients with. (see Atlantis Rising Magazine #103)

In Tiahuanaco stones from 50-200 tons were moved from quarries 30-90 miles away. They fit absolutely perfectly with others and no mortar is needed! Not even a chisel can be hammered in between them at the joints. Most cranes today can't lift 100 tons. Some super cranes have been built in shipyards that can move more now, but these are stationary and they could not move such blocks over 600 miles. A 200-ton block of stone was moved in Russia in 1961 to make a statue out of. It was "barely within the means of modern technology" of the day. This was a big deal back then whereas these temples often had hundreds of such stones used in their construction. I would guess Solomon used four of his ten cubit stones, and ten of his 8 cubit stones. How *did* he move them?

On the Magdalensberg near Klagemfurt stone blocks were used to build a city's walls 2500 years ago.

These stone walls were 23 feet thick. On the island of Cozo near Malta there are ruins with upright stones (no weight given) 16 feet high, and up to 26 feet long and 13 feet wide have been moved around. Assuming straight dimensions I estimate them being 5408 cubic feet and thus weighing 450 tons!

A fortress or monastery is built in Ollantayparubo (I don't make these names up) in Peru with blocks weighing from 150-200 tons which were carried over the screwiest terrain imaginable from quarries as far away as 1000 miles! The terrain is so rugged and the task so unsettling to archeologist, that *they suggest the terrain was more gentle at the time it was built,* as they are at a complete loss to explain how these structures could be built.(book 53 pg 78, book 37 pg 79)

WELL SO MUCH FOR THE SMALLER STONES...LETS GET TO THE REAL MONSTERS!

In Bamian a small half ruined town in central Asia exists between Cabul and Balkh. In front of partially artificial caves there are 5 huge statues, of which the largest is 173 feet high. By comparison, the statue of liberty is 103 feet high.(book 12pg 21) Though the statue is part of the mountain and not actually a lifted block, the statue and area it is cut out of is still *very* impressive.

In Baalbek Lebanon there are several ancient structures that stupefy modern engineers. There is an ancient 'temple' (why are they always presumed to be ancient temples or monasteries? why not shopping malls?) that has 54 pillars that are 8 feet wide and 90 feet high. (that's 4,524 cubic feet, or by my calculations 377 tons) That's the easy bit. If raising these pillars wasn't enough to make archaeologists pull out their hair while using their calculators, the roof is enough to give people heart failure. On top of the pillars are slabs so large they can't be accurately 'weighed" but they are estimated to be between 1200 and 1500 tons!!!! Modern technology can't move these slabs! How did *they* do it? Remember these slabs are 90 feet up!

In other parts of Baalbek where the original structures have been taken away and Greco-Roman structures take their place there remain the original foundations. These foundations are comprised of stones weighing from 750 to 2000 tons! The sizes of these stones are so huge that bizarre theories suggest they were space ship platforms. How did they move them? Even if that question goes unanswered they did move them and were still doing it when construction abruptly stopped. One half mile away the quarry still has a stone that was about to be moved. It's 60-80 feet wide by 13 3/4 by 15 3/4 Feet estimated to weigh 2000 tons (sources vary as to its exact size and weight [80' X 15' X 15' as Book 21 pg 33 relates making it about 1500 tons]). A clue exists in that there are holes around the edge as though something was clamped onto the terrace...possibly silver? Similar to that found in the unfinished walls of Tiahuanaco. They found silver rods weighing up to 3 tons each in drilled holes in the wall. Similar holes have been found in large stones in Egypt whose purpose is still unknown. Large blocks in the ruins of Parhaspur of Kashmer in Northern India were scanned and found to contain metal shapes in the stones...silver? (Book 10 Photo section)

Probably the most convincing evidence of extreme technology in this rock moving business is the capstone of India's black pagoda. This capstone is a 25-foot thick monster also estimated to weigh 2000 tons but it is placed on top of the pagoda 228 feet up! I mean drop that and the whole pagoda goes kablooie!

There seems to be no limit to the size of stones they could move. Off the coast of Morocco in a submerged piece of real estate lies a manmade wall that contains blocks the size of 2 story houses (book 6 pg 163)

The big daddy of them all has to be the huge stone near Sacsayhuaman Peru. This stone looks like it's been cut with a butter knife at all kinds of angles, almost as though it was a mobile quarry. This piece of masonry about the size of a four-story house is estimated to weigh 20,000 tons! (book 2 pg 37) Actually there are a couple bigger ones but they will be spoken of later.

Archaeologists are at a complete loss as to how these stone were moved and history books just ignore them. And why would they bother to fabricate such huge stones? Just to bury a single human, or house a single idol? C'mon they can make better guesses then this. They were building civilization, and this was normal building practices, not considered unusual or they wouldn't have been doing it all over the world!

HOW TO ESCAPE POPULAR OPINION.

(3rd ed. Insert 2016) As noted, there is an ongoing persistence to deny the vast capabilities utilized by the ancients in the study of old civilizations and archaeology. Consider.

The Spaniards in 1532 when they came across the Incan empire marveled and were agog at some of the structures they saw. They felt that the city of Cuzco and its buildings were the finest they had ever seen. Furthermore Cieza de Leon wrote that the Spaniards were speechless with astonishment saying "...neither the stone aqueduct of Segovia, nor the buildings of Hercules, nor the work of the Romans had the dignity with this fortress..."

OK you say these were just 16th century savages...consider someone a bit more contemporary...

Though refusing them to be called ancient or "pre Incan"... Victor Von Hagen (Realm of the Incas) admits "The immense rock masses remain to amaze us; Stonehenge's pales beside it, the tomb of Asamemnon and Argos is nothing alongside of it; even the cyclopean wals (sic?) of Asrigentum fall short in comparison with the fortress of Sacsahuaman." And he further states of this structure it's "one of the greatest single structures ever reared by ancient man" and he further marvels and inquires "How was such intricate stonework (admittedly the finest ever done) worked without the tools we think necessary for such an operation?" He insists that all these works were contemporary with the Incans known by the Spaniards because all the buildings show similar workings and pictographs, and the ever present trapezoid window which to him indicated a master plan. Master plan?...perhaps. However many archaeologists of his time concluded that Sacsahuaman *was* Pre Incan, which Hagen acknowledges, though he disputes this conclusion. All this refusal to admit Pre-Incan I don't understand, simply because of some similarities and an ever present constant design noted as a trapezoidal window?

As a counter to his refusal to accept the structure as pre Incan or Ancient...Could the Incan's not have been patterning their cities on something they saw with the gods? Would that not also explain the uniformity, or apparent "Master Plan"?

Though I have found out that at least one of these cities was being constructed while the Spaniards came upon them and the evidence of how the large stones were moved with ramps built up to the tops of walls. It doesn't come close to explaining the impossibly accurate fitting of 32 sided blocks. Some sort of incredible technology must be linked with the building of these structures.

Why the insistence to refuse the obvious by any archaeologist? Because it would mean the (apparently) unthinkable. We are *not* as smart or as advanced as the ancients were, and that would simply mean we are devolving...something that goes against the ever present theory of evolution and the ego of man in general. We just can't seem to admit that the people we've called savages for so long were more brilliant than our Einstein's.

One source says the Chaldean priests of On could conjure up storms to lift stones 1000 men could not lift. (Book 21 pg. 100.) Now this is actually quite revealing. The storm itself likely did not lift the stones but it is a result of the power used to do so. It is likely some byproduct of the technology used to overcome gravity, possibly similar to strange weather around missing boats and airplanes in the Bermuda Triangle and effects seen around UFO's. Curiously Tesla's laboratories were often the focal point of weird and wild weather storms.

ANTIGRAVITY IN THE PAST?

Maverick scientists independent from each other suggest that possibly the ancients had antigravity. Ancient texts also support this notion and offer interesting clues.

When the Spanish invaders came to the new world and saw the ruins in Peru they asked the locals how they were built. They said they were built by the gods and they caused the enormous rocks (weighing hundreds of tons) to fly into position from across mountains, rivers and valleys. Commenting on the cyclopean ruins of South America on top of cliffs such as the Ollantayparabu, (or is that Ollantayambo?)

Charles Berlitz says "they look almost as if they had flown them there as the legends have suggested". If this were the only such story, we could easily dismiss it as an explanation...but it's not.

On the island of Ponape (approx. 7 degrees N 158 E) in the Caroline Islands is another site of Megalithic walls, buildings and breakwaters. Because so few people live here it's wondered how they could have gotten enough people to push these stones around or even how these structures could have been built. But Native legends say nothing of such toil. They say god like heroes made the stones from distant quarries fly into position...apparently over 8000 miles away! Unless these islands were closer to the quarries originally... which is a very distinct possibility!

Ancient explanations get wilder. Apollonius Rhodius of the 3rd century says that the Greek megaliths were living stones that possessed a sensibility that they could be moved by mental force. (book 21, pg 32) Interestingly Jesus said if you have faith as a mustard seed you could tell a mountain to move somewhere and it would obey you, and nothing would be impossible to you. (Matthew 17: 20) Keep in mind Jesus also refered to some who do these miracles could also be workers of iniquity. Again we are back to what appear to be mans' abilities. People in the past that displayed these powers or abilities either through faith or technology or something in between were referred to as 'gods'. Anyone moving a mountain on command or however could be perceived as godly or spiritual indeed! It also seems that something of these abilities are natural.

Arab myths about the Egyptian structures say that they used rolled up Papyri with magic words on them and the blocks came flying through the air... They also say ancients understood the power of vibration and used it as a means of carving flint (book 21 pg 100) This might explain some of the impossible carvings found. (Hutchinson effect? We'll get to that in a bit)

Another source say they wrapped the stones in Papyrus and were struck with a rod and the stones flew about 50 meters. Coptic writings say they used sound and chanting to move them. Others are more specific and say the stones of the pyramids were elevated by sound produced by vibrating rods, or by chanting. Other sources say the rods were only entrusted to the priests. Furthermore these rods had to be cut at specific lengths to "produce a properly pitched vibratory sound on specific wavelengths".

Babylonian priests also moved heavy stones "which a thousand men could not have lifted" by neutralizing gravity through the use of sound frequencies (book 31 Pg. 111-112, book 11 pg 99) Others state the Babylonians moved the huge stones by using magical wands that raised storms and floated the huge stones for their temples through the air. (book 12, pg 149-150) In the Torres Straight Islands (143 E, 10 S) between New Guinea and Australia there (still?) existed three "booya" scepters in Chiefs possession that when pointed to the sky caused a flash of greenish blue that appeared to envelope all who witnessed the phenomena. (book 11 pg 97)

Alexander Hislop studied ancient texts in the 19th century and believed that the "priests of paganism" actually brought lightning down from heaven, but doesn't note the method of how this was done. (Book 41 pg 259) This power through time seems to be called "vril" and is associated with these powers, and may be why the rulers even today have scepters to symbolize power and authority.

The Egyptian book of the dead says "Homage to ye gods who dwell in the divine clouds and are exalted by reason of your scepters" (book 61 pg146-148) Strange language unless we take this to mean that men with the ability to travel in the clouds and above had power to do things tied up in a incredibly high-tech scepter. (Book 61 page 73 and 75)

It appears that these levitating devices were tuned to specific individuals electrical patterns. Cortez was given two flat discs of pure gold that were said to be used for levitation but were tuned to the original owners. One was about 10 inches and 1/4 inch thick, the other the same but thinner. (Book 23 pg 164) So stealing the rods or disc would be useless to the thief, and consequently the original owners could be perceived to be gods.

Do these 'vril' rods exist? In 1515 Francisco Alvares (secretary to the Portuguese embassy) went to a certain church in Bizan Abyssinia to verify that a floating rod existed. He took a stick and waved it all around the object and was satisfied of its genuine floating property. Dr Charles Jacques Poncet also verified it existed in 1698, 1699 and 1700. This rod was seen as late as 1863 by the French explorer Guillaune Lejean. (Book 21 pg 101, book 11 pg 101) does this rod still exist? Has it been stolen to resurface one day in the hands of a despot?

Archaeologists have been trying to find other rooms in the pyramids, which are thought to exist. Legends say priests were chosen for strong voices, as they had to utter certain words at specific pitches to open these hidden doors within the pyramids. [Open sesame?](Book 29, pg 71, book 21 pg 101) Science still sees no connection with sound and antigravity, so no one is in their trying out sounds to open the doors.

IS WEIGHTLESSNESS, ANTIGRAVITY OR LEVITATION A NATURAL PHENOMENON?

In 1859 at Nottingham England hailstones almost an inch in diameter fell slowly. (book 47 pg 89) This happened near Clement-Ferrand again in 1873, with stones over an inch wide, and no damage was sustained. What was noticed was that though they fell slowly, once they hit roofs and bounced, they then fell at regular speed, as though contact with the roofs discharged whatever force was causing them to fall slowly.

On an exceptionally calm day in Liverpool in 1842 cloth lines bolted upward then moved away slowly...what little breeze there was, blew in the opposite direction as seen by the smoke from chimneys. This occurred again less than two months later at Atcupar Fife...a loud detonation was heard just prior to this event.

Near Marbleton NY on Nov 15 1815 Men saw a stone rise up to about chest level...move along horizontally about 30 feet then drop to the earth. (Book 47 pg 90) Is this a natural phenomenon that the ancients figured out and harnessed?

People, boats and other items have been picked up and thrown, sunk and dropped as though some unseen hand held and threw them.

A satellite when launched weighed 300 lbs. When it came back on a parachute in 1960 it weighed only 125 lbs. A piece of Sputnik 4 landed on a lawn in Woodbridge. It was extraordinarily light weighing less than 1/2 its original weight. It was later placed in a jar and the jar also lost weight. (Book 62 pg 175)

There are two boulders in Shivapur India which people surround, chant a phrase at a specific pitch then they touch the stone, and it raises to above their heads, then drops...like a stone. (Book 11 pg 104. Book 13 pg 263)

An experiment exists that takes 5 people. Four of the people place their hands on the 5th persons head for 12 seconds (no pressure) alternating so your hand does not touch your other, then as quickly as possible place two index fingers under arms and knees of seated person and lift and they go up with no effort. (Book 22 pg34)

Oddly enough, physicists do still not understand gravity yet, based on some clues, it might be as simple as understanding a broken magnet, and some properties of silver.

Back to Tesla. Unfortunately Teslas' mind was so astounding in its ability to visualize inventions to perfection, he rarely wrote anything down decipherable to others, so many of his inventions died with him, partly because so many people stole them or ripped him off of his royalties. He knew electricity better than any man alive and his accomplishments are still unmatched today. He often spoke of how sound and molecular vibration would induce weightlessness and he was seen moving huge weights around his laboratory as though they were weightless. I know of no evidence that he knew of the ancient legends and must presume he came to these conclusions independently.

In 1921 Lester Hendershot literally dreamed up a motor that would run using the earth's magnetic field. It "cut the magnetic field, east west and thereby developed rotary motion" He called it a fueless motor deriving power from the earth's magnetic field. The little motor worked and powered a lamp, and a sewing machine and also put in a model Airplane and it flew for 26 hours straight. This all ties in with what Tesla also asserted in that the Earth could be used for free electricity. This even ties in with what UFO pilots say of their craft, that is if these reports are to be believed.

John Keely appears to have been aware of these phenomena. He built a second machine (refining a first) that started with a note on a violin as far away as ten feet, which ran on "the flow of magnetic currents from pole to pole" Another device he created sounded so much like a device Tesla created it made me wonder if I had confused the two. A set of three glass chambers with 6 oz spheres inside that floated up and down. Platinum and silver wires linked to a "sympathetic transmitter". This machine was connected to and was used to levitate items regardless of their weight at whatever height he desired. Items weighing many tons were moved around as light as a feather. Oddly when others were invited to use his inventions, they could not make them work unless he touched the person. However after Keelys' death some sources say that he was discovered to be something of a hoaxer, using concealed air compressors to power machines apparently run on water, so this too may have been one of his tricks to extricate funds from the starry eyed. But others defend that the compressors were simply too bulky and put down there to get them out of the way and Keely made no secret of them.

One more interesting bit that ties in with antigravity is the use of divining rods and strings. Experience diviners know that virtually any substance from water to steel can be divined for using various methods. One thing that comes out of this study is how to divine for, say steel, with a string, the diviner must determine the length of the string for it to work for the diviner. The string length will vary for the item being divined for, but when the correct length of the string is determined(with some sort of fob on the end) the string will swing, rotate or in some occasions point straight out seemingly defying gravity with it's obvious attraction to the specified substance. But what is interesting, is that the length of the string will vary not just for the item divined for, but will vary from individual to individual for the exact same item. So we see that as with the varying thickness of the Aztec gold discs, the varying length of the Vril rod or scepter, and John Keelys need to be touching the individual all corroborate that some tuning to an individual is connected with the ability to "divine" or overcome gravity.

Well when comparing recent and current inventions with regards to antigravity and comparing the technology to tales of old regarding how huge weights were lifted, we see some very substantial similarities, which give clues to overcoming gravity, and we also have to conclude that the ancients in all likelihood had power over gravity. I personally am convinced they did.

FORM FITTED ROCKS

If it was just anti gravity in regards to huge rocks I would move on, but it seems there is another aspect to the fitting of rocks that needs to be looked at.

The precision with which these stone have been fitted is beyond the realm of possibility when it comes to some of the stones set in place in the light of normal precision fitting. In the walls of the fortress of Ollantayparubo and Sacsahuaman in Peru the walls are made of far from ordinary blocks. Some of these stone 'blocks' have as many as 32 sides! and they fit so perfectly that no mortar is used! People have tried to put penknives, paper, business cards, and razor blades in the seams where the rocks join with no success.

This precision fitting is very hard to do even with just square blocks without highly perfect grinding techniques. This is more than a feat of accurate carving. If they were carved, one error would throw out the accuracy of the entire rock! It's kind of like trying to cut four legs on a chair the same length by eye. You're going to mess up and the chair will wobble. Try doing it on a 32 leg chair, and then do it to a chair with these legs facing in all directions so that it will fit perfectly into a pre-built box. One mistake and the legs wont all touch the sides of the box. Ok, It's not really a chair is it, it's more of a wooden star but you get the idea.

These rocks also exhibit an unusual magnetic field. When looking at the rocks you get the impression that they were semi liquid or soft, held in a retaining wall and then shook to fit then solidified. Others have gotten this same impression. Yet these are stone and not some form of cement. But we as yet have not been able to do this! These are not just little blocks but they weigh from 12 to 250 tons. If they were ground together back and forth even this would speak of extraordinary abilities. This might work for some of the simpler shapes but certainly not for multi-angled stones! It would appear they were able to turn the rocks into a semi fluid state and then back to a solid state, suggesting they were able to interfere with molecular properties of matter.

Well what do the legends say? One legend is that a bird places a special leaf on the rock, which softens the rock enough for the bird to peck the rock, and one Colonel P.H. Fawcett says he actually saw birds doing this. (He's the guy that disappeared in the Matto Grosso) This Fawcett heard a story of some miners stumbling onto some burial mound, one of which contained a jar of liquid. They cruelly tried to make a local native try to drink the stuff and in the scuffle some spilled on a rock which then became soft for a while then later re-hardened.(book 37 pg 80-81)

One chap while riding horseback through low plants with thick red leaves found his spurs melted and eaten away. These bushes the natives said were the one where this liquid was procured. Others have stumbled across this secret plant and it's properties, but they are seemingly ignored. Possibly the stone covered with this fluid was subjected to vibratory electrical fields making the outer edge more viscous as some similar experiments have shown, which might account for the rocks displaying a magnetic field. Whether these bushes still exist, or if deforestation destruction has made them extinct one can only guess.

WHAT HAVE WE HERE?

(3rd ed. Insert 2016) Close microscopic analysis of Incan stone masonry has revealed something no one has previously clued into. On normally worked masonry the repeated hammering and chipping of the rock to gain smooth surfaces will show microscopic fracturing, even if polished afterwards. Like a signature, the method of crafting the stone can be determined with close inspection. But hammering and chiseling the stonework is not the case for Sacsayhuaman's stony exterior. The surfaces of the stones actually look more like ceramic glaze! (See Atlantis Rising #97 Pg 70) Research finally showed that the surface exactly resembled something called "thermal disaggregation" was likely used on the rocks...something theoretically possible by focusing the suns light and heat on tiny spots of rock. It's theorized that large parabolic gold mirrors were used to obtain this finished surface. Well true the Incan's did have some gold parabolic dishes when discovered and ransacked by the conquistadors, but why the Incas would train for endless hours the focal point of the sun on the massive stone structures to achieve this sort of finish on the surface of the rocks seems beyond reason. I find this hypothesis stretching it, as the sheer volume of masonry just makes this deduction somewhat unfathomable. I have to think the stone had this type of finish, not as a result of painstaking polishing of building rocks with the sun, but as a byproduct of whatever technology they used to create the shaped stones in the first place. However this discovery once again shows the ancients were using technology we still do not yet fully grasp, or at the very least have to use highly advanced technology to recreate.

ROCK-A-BY JELLO.

(3rd ed. Insert 2016) I've long figured that the Cyclopean building sites of Sacsayhuaman and Ollantaytambo were not built with precision stone cutting methods but they were using a form of technology that softened the rocks to make them fit like they do. Some have suggested that some plant might have been used to soften the rocks, and I suppose that's possible, but close examination of these sites (pictures... I didn't go there) and in particular Ollantaytambo show they appear to have been softened from a point in front then disengaged...leaving a telltale extrusion in front of most stones. Sacsayhuaman has the appearance of the rocks being retained in a form while they were softened. (That extrusion point might be buried in the sides as they added rocks as they went...meaning one such rock on each building would display the extrusion point, but that's just a guess) I can't see a plant being used to get these particular results, as the amount of plant material it seems would be immense or prohibitive, without the plant being still extant and well known. And wouldn't there be evidence of such a plant near the structures?

I then read issue #72 of Atlantis Rising magazine and there appears to be a guy (John Hutchinson) who has stumbled on the technology that did this but he is probably completely unaware that he has partly solved the riddle of how these cyclopean sites were constructed. He not only has conquered gravity as the article suggests, but he has somehow gotten various substances, mostly metals it seems, to turn soft when near, what sounds like, vibrational electromagnetic fields, thus loosening the material to flow at an molecular level. I've seen some of his videos and he seems to have the technology that will cold "melt" metals of various kinds and they droop over and encapsulate things like wood without the wood being burned from heat, because the metal is cold when it does this, so it just swallowed the wood and wraps itself around it as the metal seeps and oozes. I suspect he has loosened the binding of molecules electrically or magnetically on the atomic level so the metals can flow at room temperature.

I'm sure with fine tuning of his device he could soften rock like he does metals to get the same results as seen at either of these two ancient building sites. (The site suggests the rocks were in contact with the technological device. So the Hutchinson's device would have to take this into account) Obviously with this technology used on building sites, you could make buildings virtually earthquake proof.

Clearly ordinary rock seems to exhibit an array of potential. Stone spheres apparently charged in a way to illuminate old cities, recording events, and even some exhibiting great superconductivity at low temperatures. Magnetic forces being still evident after thousands of years from the initial exposure to the force exerted on the stone, suggests rocks can hold energy, or a charge, if one knows what to do, and potentially one could make lamps from this power source, lasting maybe thousands of years.

The Roman Aqueduct of Nimes is a relatively recent accomplishment that is clear indication of advanced workmanship in the past. A water carrying system that had to span 31 miles and descend 13.4 inches per kilometer, over streams and through hills. Only sophisticated surveying techniques, which supposedly were not developed until the 19th century could have accomplished this. One famous section is still standing and it's the height of 16 stories! I'm led to believe, we were not able to get above 5 stories safely until the late 19th century or the early 20th. The gorge this section spans is known for ferocious winds, and many other structures built over this same gorge have been washed away. (Scientific American March 1989) It's amazing this structure still stands as such winds and earthquakes over time would have knocked something this big down. Studies show this to be extremely well engineered even to taking the wind into consideration. This is truly one of the most beautiful ancient structures still standing after 2000 years.

A drainage system in Knossos Crete is still working after 4000 years. Try and get your city hall to get systems to stay in working order that long. Also 75% of Iran's water is supplied by a aqueducts built 3000 years ago.

In the book of Ecclesiastes 1:9-10, 3:15 it says basically there is nothing new under the sun, and that which is, has already been and that what is to be has already been. Simply put, there is nothing new, what is, and is to be, has already been...but when? It must mean before the flood.

GENETICS IN THE PAST. AGRICULTURAL FEATS...WHICH LEAD TO MEDICAL FEATS

Corn is called a biological monstrosity because it has no way of spreading its seed. We have to physically remove the kernels from the cob and plant them. It is not a natural plant! The origin of corn is still a mystery. Some suggest it originated in America. Yet there was corn in Egypt that Jacobs sons went to get. Corn is called the most highly developed agricultural plant in the world. It's felt that thousands of generations of selective breeding would be needed to come up with corn, and they are not even sure it can be recreated this way. The only other way we know of altering a plant...is genetic restructuring.

Bananas also fall into this category. Bananas either have no seeds, or the seeds they have are sterile. Bananas would be extinct in a single year, because the plant only produces bananas for one year and the entire plant is cut down. You have to cut a piece of rootstalk each year to get a new banana-producing shoot. So where did the first banana shoot come from? From sophisticated breeding, and possibly genetic manipulation

Cotton The Mexican 'god' Quetzalcoatl is said to have started cotton but no one takes this seriously. Oddly he is also attributed with providing cotton of colored fibers such as blue, brown and grey, yet we only know how to make white, and have no idea how to make other colors, yet it has been *firmly established* that they did grow cotton in these other colors! Colored cotton plants are now extinct. These plants only grew during Quetzalcoatl's reign. Obviously a pretty volatile plant to go extinct as soon as this fellow left, suggesting it needed constant attendance to keep it extant. Corn is also connected with Quetzalcoatl as it grew higher during his time as well.

Wheat, Barley, Spelt, Millet,& Rye, come from wild grasses and are traced back to the near east, specifically to the Sumerians. It's believed thousands of generations were needed to come up with the grains as they are now, yet no evidence of ongoing breeding exists. This part of the world kept creating new grains, fruits and vegetables like "some kind of genetic botanical laboratory" (book 17 pg 7) In Iraq there was a cave found which was a burial place for "Neanderthal man", but buried with them were grains already fully developed. These were not developed by some primitive cave man. "Look Thag, me squish grass with butter cup and make banana." A sophisticated plant came from sophisticated men using sophisticated technology, not from so called Neanderthals. That, or Neanderthals were not the primitives we consider them to be.

Spelt is a real mystery because it is DEFINITLY the result of mixing genes from several different plants! (Book 17 pg 414) It IS a manmade concoction, so there *must* have been some genetic tinkering in the past! Even the very idea that they could alter and improve plants is a very original idea...attributed to... Neanderthal men? Cavemen? savages? Even to conceive of altering a plant speaks of high intellect and advanced civilization to know it could be done! Yet even the advanced Sumerians give credit to the 'gods' that "lived in the celestial abode lowered to earth from the twelfth planet"!!!

SPLICE-O-MATIC.

(3rd ed. Insert 2016) Being content to find the more obvious evidences of genetic tinkering in ancient times I may have missed a large piece of the picture. Conventional beliefs of ancient breeding assumes Neolithic man, 5 to 10 thousand years ago and now modified to 32,000 years ago, took wolf cubs and tamed and bred them to be the hundreds of tame breeds we have today. Similarly hundreds and thousands of generations of grain breeding supposedly brought about the plants we eat today. But Stephen Robbins (Atlantis Rising #92 From Ferocious to Fido?) brings the picture into sharper focus. He notes in the last 5000 years no useful plants have been created by this method. (I ask: Why wouldn't this legacy continue if it was obviously so successful? Answers: Devolution and the gods left.) Even deliberate attempts by Russians on transforming wild rye sine 1837 into domestic rye are even to this day a work in progress. He notes the more wild versions of grain would have required doubling to quadrupling the number of chromosomes to come up with the domestic kinds we have today; going from 7 chromosomes to 42 for wheat and oats, and sugar an 8 fold increase, peanuts by 4 and so on.

No one assumes that Neolithic man knew anything about gene-splicing, but domestication simply isn't going to come up with what we see today. He notes that in the case of many domesticated vegetables we don't even have a known starting point (ancestor plant). And the few we do know the parent plant would have been virtually useless to Neolithic man. Why would he spend countless generations experimenting and breeding when he has to eat today?

Even the difference in the genes of wild creatures to those we've supposedly tamed have a genetic difference, not large, but on the order of .2% but just this minimal difference on the genetic level means about 3 million chromosomal base pairs to adjust and breeding just isn't going to change anything on the genetic level! Clearly modern conceptions of how ancient man came up with tame dogs, cats, and edible grains needs revision. Even the lovely Cheetah appears to be the result of advanced genetic work, as Cheetahs are all genetically the same, which in modern day examples of genetic similarity has only been seen in genetically altered lab rats and other such lab animals. He finished his article with the very plain statement fostered by Zechariah Sitchen in his book The Twelfth Planet (Book 17) "This thesis, as is well known, argues that historical record of the Sumerians explicitly states this to be the case: Humans, domesticated animals and domesticated plants were the work of the "gods" in the "house of fashioning" thousands of years ago." By humans I would interject that this would be worker class of monkeys and man apes, possibly yeti types, (Which might explain the central African finds not too distant from Egypt, where worker apes were known to be common) and the half man half animal types as well as the various races and colours of people.

Ancient Medicine When explorers reached the great lakes region they found Indians that used 550 plants for food, smoking, dies, drinks, and 83 other uses, including 275 of them for medicine. Studies show many of the plants they used for medicinal purposes were correct, and many of these medicines plants were never identified.

Early medical knowledge and traditions were still in practice in the Andes, and again some of their source plants are still a mystery. People as far away as Greece sought Egyptian Medicine, yet their knowledge did not evolve slowly, but started right off with all the knowledge. Even today some or our medicine comes from Egyptian origins. They had over 700 medicines and these medicines were used all across the Mediterranean. Eventually Egyptian medicine disintegrated to a bunch of mumbo jumbo, hexes and curses that sound like a bad movie, suggesting further, that man can degrade and decline over time even when encompassed in a civilized setting. I would even dare to say that in some ways we are declining, even as we advance. As we coddle kids in school making it easier for them to learn, trying not to hurt non achievers feelings we destroy the incentives for the achievers, and they learn even less. Now we even have gender/ racial quotas which often means we accept people with inferior abilities to meet these quotas, further degrading the quality or services, products and other aspects of society.

Ancient India cured many ailments we still cannot cure today. Scholarships have been awarded to study ancient Indian manuscripts in hopes of rediscovering some of these medicinal cures they had.

Ancient Mexicans filled cavities. Crowns so well glued they were found still in place as were the fillings compared to today's, which often come out.

Ancient Chinese knew the heart moved the blood, even though we thought the liver moved it until the 17th century.

Successful heart surgery has been seen on bones "100,000" years old. The ribs showed re-growth for 3-5 years. (Book 1 pg 48) Also successful brain surgery was found in Chile and Egypt using identical instruments to the ones we use. Skulls with holes were found, which showed partial re-growth of the skull bone over the cavity. Some of the silver dollar sized holes in the skulls were over very dangerous spots, yet the patients survival rate was 85% and they lived long enough to show re-growth. But since they didn't have machinery back then I guess the holes were precisely cut with stone hammers and arrowheads. The first modern brain surgery occurred in the 1780's and it was always fatal, yet thousands of successful surgeries such as this were accomplished in ancient times.

Chinese records document successful anesthetics in 300 BC for operations. We had no anesthetic until the 19th century. Ancient India and Egypt also used anesthesia.

Ancient Mesopotamia 'removed the shadow covering a man's eye'. This can only speak of cataract surgery... that or they were good at shoving people out of shady places. (Book 17 pg 33) The Mesopotamia surgery came from Sumerians, so we can presume they had it all too. They could do C-sections; counter poisonous gas, Vaccinate and many other things you need a medical dictionary to comprehend.

The new medical practice of Gynecology was done by doctors in ancient Rome and Egypt. The tools for these skills were necessary of course...though little remains, yet some have been found, and they are identical to instruments we use today.

Pompeii yielded an instrument that had "screws as threadlike and capable of delicate manipulation as anything to be found in today's achievements" (Book 30 pg 64 quoting Scientific American Oct. 20 1900)

A car crash victim was operated on, using a tool 3000 years old! (Book 21 pg240) Some of the old tools found were far superior to ours using obsidian blades with edges as thin as 10 molecules thick!(3-4 Billionths of an inch thick!)

Something like Kirilian photography may have existed in ancient history as the 741 Acupuncture spots used by the Chinese are visible in Kirilian photography.

X-ray appears to have existed back then. Ancient India speaks of illuminating the organs of the body to know what is wrong with a patient. A certain doctor was said to have passed a "gem" in front of a patient to illuminate a body like lighting up a house. This same doctor also practiced brain surgery.

China also appears to have had x-rays. In 206 BC a "precious mirror that illuminated the bones of the body" was found in the palace of Ch'in-Chi

One of these "mirrors" may still exist. A "sun Queen" Ameterasu sent her grandson to earth to rule the land of Japan and he brought three items with him, one was a mysterious metal mirror. The ancient Japanese obtained these items and revere them highly, and they are wrapped in many protective layers and are never looked at, but they still exist. Whatever these items are they date to at least 4 generations before the first Japanese monarch. (660 BC) I suppose any piece of a machine with a shiny reflective face could be referred to as a "Magic Mirror" and 'magic mirror references are plentiful in ancient history.

Now for the good stuff. Previously we dealt with things we understand, but further descriptions exists that sound like science fiction!

In the middle of the 15th century the tomb of Tullia was opened (Cicero's daughter). Her body was intact and preserved in a clear liquid and a lamp burned at her feet...which had been burning for at least 1500 years. A cat submersed in a cryogenic fluid for a short-term of an hour was revived successfully. Could this fluid have been similar?

The Ancients were fanatically concerned with preserving soft tissue. This fanaticism is even alluded to in the bible, where they were worried about corruption of the flesh. The Egyptians and other cultures spent long periods in mummification to ensure flesh would not rot.

In April of 1485 the body of a young woman was found with her sarcophagus. She was immersed in a dark ointment which preserved the girl perfectly. Her tomb was also lit with a lamp. When the ointment was removed, she looked lifelike with red lips, dark hair and a "shapely figure". (book 11 pg94)

Only the chief of three tribes of Amazon Indians are allowed to speak of ancient traditions and stories. This is one of them... There is a room and the walls of that room emit a mysterious light. In the middle of that room are four blocks of transparent stone. Inside them are four people, 3 men and a woman and they are sleeping. They have six fingers and six toes, and they are lying in a fluid that covers them up to the chest. (is this out of a sci-fi movie or what!?!) Yet this is an ancient story handed down for thousands of years.

The ancients were deathly afraid of their bodies being decomposed and were aware of how to preserve it. They believed that they could only enter the realm of Osirus if their body remained intact. (Book 50 pg 147, book33 pg 22)

The Egyptians were certain that besides the soul there was another part of man that could rise again, and that preservation of the body was imperative to insure eternal life...without this belief mummification would be meaningless. Skin cells of large portions of mummies still remain completely intact. Another source shows them to be so intact that they were capable of living! How can a cell live again? What's even wilder is that although this was realized long ago and these references where I found them were usually in the sixties and seventies, the Authors did not appear to be aware of cloning! We can only surmise that with the ancient's fanaticism of preservation and their knowledge, they knew something about cloning...in fact they must have known a lot! When you read the ancient stuff with the idea of what they likely knew it becomes abundantly clear that they must have cloned successfully.

The legend of Osiris (who was cut into 14 pieces by Set and scattered along the Nile or sent to people) quickly shows evidence of cloning. According to sources, Osiris is in every culture with different names. Though my minimalist look at ancient history is poor I do have a sense that some of the people thought to be Osiris, may be other people or gods, and I think further looks into this are worth spending time researching, particularity in the light of the theories that are being presented in this work.

In the Bible Osirus is called Nimrod, "the hunter of men's souls" as some translate it. Yet he was lamented over greatly. Isis gathered up the pieces. Isis with Anubus restored Osirus to life...how? It would have been impossible to stitch him back together. Here's where it gets real wild. She was said to have conceived without conception. Careful this is NOT the same as the Mary who bore Jesus. The Mother and child are adored throughout the world, and they have been found in places where Christian teaching was never brought. She is also referred to as the queen of heaven, not to be worshipped. What's even wilder is that the son she bore was said to be the exact image of Osirus! This convinced people that Osirus had been born again. Again, *not to be confused* with the biblical "born again".

As I understand it, to clone, one puts a cell of the donor inside a egg shell of a woman and indeed when placed back in the womb is conception without knowing a man. This was so convincing that virtually every culture in the world seems to have some reference to this incident, and this has to be the origin of the belief in reincarnation. They would have had the technology to have snapshots or memory to remember the original Osirus, and lived long enough to compare the original Osirus to the new one, and they may even have photographs to compare with. Anyway whatever occurred was very convincing. The book of the dead also consolidates this. (book 4, 20, 61) Horus and Ra (other names for Osirus) are called the twin gods, or having a "ka" or duplicate.

WHY THERE WAS A "VIRGIN" BIRTH BEFORE MARY.

(3rd ed. Insert 2016) Isis gathering the parts of Osiris before burying them "...she managed to extract from the body of Osiris its "essence," and self-inseminated herself with his seed, thus conceiving and giving birth to the boy Horus." (book 42 page 42) Obviously this can't be Osirus seed as we know it because all authorities agree, she never found the phallus.

It even seems that we know which cells she used in order to clone him. "I am Horus and have come forth from the eye of Horus" also "and he hath made to live a million years through his eye"

Every year in Mendes Egypt a "tet" (which looks like an electrical apparatus. **See drawing 3**) is set up in memory of the resurrection of Osirus. The cloning may have taken place in a pyramid as they were considered "links with the second life".

Cloning is also alluded to in the case of Jupiter who committed his members to Apollo to be properly interred. From these members a "new regeneration" occurred (from the heart) and he emerged again to be among the number of the 'gods'. (Book 41 pg 191)

Cloning is clearly referred to in the bible. Adam had a son in his own image in his own likeness. This is the only time in the biblical genealogies an offspring is referred to in this way. Weird language. Could this speak of cloning? (see Genesis 5:3) Here we get a rare glimpse pre-flood technology, and it can only be cloning, something we still haven't duplicated! In every instance of the bible the usual reference to their conception and birth is 'so and so knew their wife and bore so and so...everyone except one... Seth. At first it's stated in the usual way, but then in Chapter 5 it's referred to AGAIN...why twice? It says he beget a son in his own likeness in his own image, like it was done deliberately. Are we descended from a clone? We know Seth was a replacement for Abel, and "Seth" means "substitute" This must have been unsettling, because Seth bore a son named "Enos" which means "mortal" or "a man", or another translation is "human". What a weird thing to call your kid, unless we consider the 'cloning' card. If Enos knew his status as the son of a clone then he may have wondered about himself, but every time he was called by name "hey Man" his humanness was reaffirmed. We still have not as yet cloned a human, but we are trying...there is nothing new under the sun! What is and is to be has been.

GENETICALLY MADE ANIMALS

We have made and patented a mouse with a gene that gives it a 50% chance of getting cancer by the time they are 300 days old. (Discover Jan '89 pg.78) As of 1988 there were 40 patented animals on file.

Although not genetic in nature, this is still worth noting. Baby chicks not yet hatched were implanted with Japanese quail brain cells. When hatched they had markings of the Japanese quail on their head and their song was somewhat quail-like. (Discover Feb '89. pg 14)

Scientists have given mice human genes to produce a growth hormone. These mice grow huge and are in some laboratory somewhere. If these got loose we would definitely need a better mousetrap!

Human cells have been fused with hamsters' chickens and even mosquitoes... eww! Big smart mosquitoes? Sounds like something out of a sci-fi horror film. Most so far have proven to be short lived... but where will it end?

Scientists in Sweden have fused human cells with a carrot, not unlike the creature in the 1951 sci-fi movie "THE THING". But fusing is not the same as splicing which is more haphazard like a bizarre lottery. Splicing introduces specific genes into a cell to create a desired end, fusing is more haphazard where different cells are turned into a single cell, then when the DNA splits there is no idea of what will transpire.

A mouse was created that cannot reject foreign tissue. To do this they took out the hair gene. If we did not know this was done we would call it a new species of mouse! A nude or hairless mouse. (Nat Geo Dec '84, pg836) Are there creatures around that are in fact genetic manipulations? How would we know?

It again would seem that such splicing has occurred in the past. If they cloned man, genetically created new plants, did they make new creatures too? The most obvious guess as to a manmade creature is the platypus. It is so unusual that when it was first introduced scientists thought it was a fake. It is also the only creature in its class. It has webbed feet and a duckbill and lives in the water, yet it also burrows in the dirt with sharp claws. The male has spurs or fangs on its hind feet. The spurs are hollow and give out poison like a snake. It is the only furred creature to have fangs. It lays eggs like a bird or a reptile. It nurses it young like an ordinary mammal, yet mammals never lay eggs, and reptiles never have milk glands. It's like every feature of this creature has nothing to do with any of the other features. Was this creature built on a bet?

The farm pig is also suspected as being an unnatural creature. Some have said they believe it to be a creation of the Atlanteans. It is said that man was used as part of the genetic material to make up the pig. Pork is said to be the most similar to man in its makeup. It may be the cross or splicing of a wild boar and some aspect of man. It is singled out as meat not to be eaten in the bible. A legend exists that on the isle of Circe there were men turned into pigs. Is there a connection?

The reverse of man being descendant from apes is now seriously being considered. (Book 9 pg. 202)

This is real odd and I don't know how people today flashed on this idea, but the ancients were certain that apes came from man! Popul Vuh says monkeys are a degenerate descendant of early man that came down to this world. The Ramayana says apes were created by the gods to aid in war. (book 11 pg. 74, book 22 pg 206 [My copy of the Ramayana does not have the Brahmin additions so I quote these sources and trust that their copies of the Ramayana are more complete])

Zacharia Sitchen also stumbled on this and suspected Homo erectus was the result of "genetic manipulation". The Sumerians 'god' Ea is said to have wanted new workers and imprinted an aspect of the 'gods' on a creature that already existed. (Book 17 pg 344) Ancient Aryan writers say at one time apes spoke. Egyptians said that apes could understand everything being said. (Book 22 pg 205, 207) Ancient Indian writings speak of apes that could write. Egyptian drawings show baboons taking care of children and picking fruit. (Origin of sasquatch?)

Whether or not any apes existing today are direct descendants of these ancient intelligent ones, or whether they died out in one generation is hard to say. Studies on apes show very different and unusable vocal chords for speech. Apes certainly don't seem this intelligent now, certainly not in the way the ancients speak of them. Have they declined into relative barbarism, just like pockets of men did after periods of war and massive destruction in local areas? More likely these apes mingled with normal apes and just degenerated into wild beasts once again. Or is it all bunk? Just the existence of these legends and beliefs of the past, particularly in the light of the rest of this work is certainly enough to make one wonder.

Interestingly, it has been found that baboon and pig hearts and organs are good temporary substitutes for people who cannot get a human organ donated in time, and they can be used for months.

CHIMERA

One could speculate about many creatures, but there also exists stories of creatures in ancient times that no longer exists. Just as we have been making new creatures today, some even with seemingly no applicable purpose in mind; it seems the ancients were doing something similar to this too, but with legendary effects.

The ancient Greeks talk of a chimera, a female fire breathing monster with a lion's head, a goats body, and serpents tail...sound rather platypus like?

Another ancient weirdo is the griffin. The front and head is that of an eagle, the back is that of a lion, and it had wings. Ancient myth? Figurative and not literal?

Then there's Pegasus, the flying horse? Fable? And Hydra the seven-headed serpent? In 1959 the head of a dog was grafted to another dog and it lived for 22 days. We know the ancients could perform transplants. A cat with two tails has been seen.

There are occasionally freaks in nature that lead one to suspect that someone has been monkeying with genes and these features occasional crop up, such as two headed men. These may even have been done on a genetic level as similar offspring have been occurring occasionally over the years. And what of Minotaur's; half bull, half man?

Two one eyes not that same as one two eyes... What about Homers Odyssey and that "mythical man the "Cyclops". Was that fiction? I'm not so sure. In 1793 a girl was born with a single eye in the middle of her forehead, but was otherwise normal. She lived to the age of 15. (Book 15 pg 104) If the gene existed to allow that girl in 1793 to be born with one eye, somewhere in the past the gene had to be manipulated or introduced.

(3rd ed. Insert 2016) Once again another Cyclops has surfaced in my research material. A one eyed individual was also found in a Mississippi backwoods community which was written about in the Boston Medical Journal. He was offered jobs with carnivals but didn't want to be a public spectacle (World of the incredible but true Charles Berlitz page 74)

Ancient India talks of a "lion man" and they placed him in the lineage of man, possibly in a similar fashion to our evolutionary charts. It wasn't even a question as to whether they existed; they just put him in the line. Did lion men exist? You know they did as they are also mentioned in the bible three times! 2nd Sam 23: 20, and (same incident is in 1st Chronicles 11:22, Also 1st Chronicles. 12:8). Egypt credits "lion gods" as living in the underworld. The sphinx also puts lion and man features together. Why? Is it reflective of the zodiac or is there some other reason?

In an Egyptian tomb thought to be that of King Udimu there was found a skeleton of completely unknown animal.

There are many half man half beast in ancient "myths"... Larkies (half women, half birds), Pan (Half man half horse), half man half goat...which is traced to the Sumerians, Half woman 1/2 snake, mermaids (1/2 women half fish), Anubis (1/2 man, 1/2 dog), men with horse feet, bulls with the heads of men, horses with dog heads, horse fronts and fish rears, men with two or four wings and two heads, male and female! It appears that in their attempt to come up with a primitive worker many weird creatures came into existence in the interim. No bladder control, no organs, infertile, diseased eyes, sick livers, and so on. Some of these genes seem to still exist and surface from time to time in the general population.

Mythter and the Mytheth (3rd ed. Insert 2016) Heracles after coming from a place beyond the Pillars of Hercules (Atlantis during the time it still was above water) came to a place called Scythia and while looking for his horses which had gotten loose while he slept came to a cave with a Woman that was Snake from the butt down. To get his horse he made a bargain with the woman and had three sons by her. (She must have been desperate to keep the horse *that* long, that or Heracles wasn't looking too hard.) Anyway this fair maiden quite likely was a result of a genetically altered offspring. (Herodotus Book 4: 9)(Interestingly this is the same Heracles that rowed a boat around the Continent of Africa.)

Oddly some bizarre creatures turn up in more modern times yet our technology isn't good enough in the times these creatures turn up to explain them. Are these misfit births that get discovered that somehow escape natures tendency to eat them, some single example of new species turning up like evolution suggests, or is someone else making these creatures? In the 1700's legends of a Loup-garou (wolf man) persist. In 1883 in Australia, a headless pig like creature surfaced that had an appendage similar to a lobster tail. In 1878 an incredibly frightening creature was obtained and led through London. It was about 2 feet long, two feet high, described as a "living cube". It had hair like wire, It had a head and a tails like a boar, but it's eyes were said to be "satanic". It had no abdomen, and its hind feet were unusually close to its front feet. It was so disturbing it caused a panic and accidents and the owner was told to get rid of it in no uncertain terms! It had been originally found in the Pyrenees in southern France.

In 1951 in Ramesgate Kent, a hedgehog like creature was found which had the tail of a rat, and the head of a cat.

In 1954 A reverend Joseph Overs found a 2 1/2 foot long creature that looked like a fish with 'staring eyes" and a big mouth. What made the creature so weird was that it had "two perfect feet each with 5 pink toes"

Ever heard of the New Jersey Devil, which the hockey team is named after? It is a horse headed creature that flies and has a devil-like tail. And they insist it is there and is often heard with its chilling scream! Some say this creature is a hoax. Is it? Or has some creature somehow survived a weird birth, or is someone letting these oddball creatures get into our world?

Quetzalcoatle's full name is Viracocha Tachyachachic, which means creator of world things. Credited with the creation of corn and colored cotton, he is also credited with creating a race of giants, and some giant skeletons have been found. When these giant remains are found they are either declared a hoax, or quickly covered up. Apparently we can't have "Giants" confirming the biblical reference to giants. And it also tends to suggest that giants are a better race of man, which would tend to confirm the idea we are declining. Hmmm...sounds familiar somehow. Giants are usually considered either abnormal or equated with features of the 'gods'. Often ancient histories speak of giants in the past, and graves in America have revealed giants, or certainly men of incredible stature.

The ancients appear to have also come up with dwarves and more than one sort. In 1938, Chinese archaeologists discovered graves in the mountain caves of Baian Kara Ula in the Sino-Tibetan Border District. These were small human skeletons but with distinctly larger skulls. By the drawings on the cave walls they appear to have come from the stars. There is a corroborating Chinese saga about the same Baian Kara Ula region which tells of spindly yellow beings that came down from the clouds and were shunned and killed by the Dropos because of their ugliness. (book 4 pg 96-98) Were these little men (about 5' 3") a tribe of odd dwarves, men from the stars, or genetic achievements, or all three. Could these be genetic men for the purpose of working on the surface so those that made them didn't have to work in the hostile environment now existing on the surface? Sounds similar to some UFO sightings.

Did any of these creatures exist? Some of these may have been allegorical, but it seems many believe they existed, and were made by the "gods". Although through time oddball creatures pop up, it seems there was a time when their existence was better known, similar to the first test tube baby's fame. They likely would have been extremely rare, likely one of a kind, and thus very difficult to substantiate with any sort of fossil evidence. But one fossil proof would certainly substantiate much.

In October 1876 a news agency of Mexico City announced an amazing find...the skeleton of a most unusual being had been found that "might possibly be the remains of an extraterrestrial creature" (over 70 years before "UFO's were all the rage!) The skeleton was never seen before or since. The skeleton had a spinal column and shoulder bone and the beginning of arms. It had a dog like head with small eye sockets, yet only a bit of a snout. (Book 10. pg 117) (Pre curser to Anubis?)

One gets the idea that the ancients were trying to create a servant sort of manlike creature with many failures, some of which were very belligerent and dangerous, and the possible success's being the orangutan or similar beings like lion man. It may even have been a thing one could order, a child with unusual things like leopard spots. Why tattoo when you could have the real thing? Why wear leopard skins if you could put a little tiger in your tank.

Colours for people and different races. I asked my dad once where different races come from and he didn't know... I asked who would know and he said "No one knows". That just amazed me! Wow what a mystery to solve! I was 12 or so. Neither the creationists nor the evolutionists have come up with a satisfactory explanation for the existence of races...yet they both agree there had to be just one race to start with. Segregation would only isolate certain physical traits, but if we are all white, red, Blue or what ever... that colour is going to remain. With just one language, segregation would never be complete. Migratory or cataclysmic division would still show similar languages like France and Quebec. We do have a scripted reason for language change and it's been assumed this also facilitated racial change, but this does not work. Scientists have isolated the gene in fireflies and kittyboos and spliced them into E-coli to create five new colors of luminous bacteria. (Discover Nov. 1989 pg.12) Could not the ancients have done similar things with man, and thus the origin of different races? This could explain it. Please understand this is not in any way meant to be some sort of negative or positive racial statement, I am merely looking at the clues to come to a plausible origin for various races which so far neither evolutionists or creationist have answered satisfactorily. It appears that the ancients were not just trying to make a servant class of men, they appear to have been trying to design men too.

Since the black race are called Cushites it stands to reason the first known black is Cush. (book 41 pgs 25-44) This is important because specific mention of this color at this time obviously indicates that various races existed prior to the creation of Babylon and the tower of Babel, which Nimrod, who we know was black (book 41 pg 43-44) helped to build! So we are forced to concede that races existed before the incident creationists have tried to attribute race to...the tower of Babel.

We can also conclude that the origin of race is during the time of the Sumerians, a time when all spoke the same language so we must assume that language was Sumerian. More about Nimrod is odd as he is shown as wearing or growing horns. He is also shown as having from the waist down legs and cloven feet of a Bull! It would seem that Nimrod himself was a composite of man and Bull. Now since he was a leader the horns have come to symbolize power.(book 41 pg 34) So if the technology existed to change man's physical traits as well as colour, who had it? As we are at the dawn of civilization after the flood. Who is Cushs' father? Ham! so Ham either brought the technology with him from pre flood period or he was able to replicate the technology himself as Ham is Noah's son and both were on the ark.

Curiously the farm pig is thought to be an artificial creature being the cross between a boar and man, but it also nicknamed "ham". Could Ham be the originator of the farm pig as well as some other genetic tinkering? But there may be another possible origin. A Sumerian text exists that states that Enlil came to earth before the "black-headed" people were created. (Book 17, Pg. 96) This term was apparently a Sumerian nickname for mankind. Could it be an allusion to the creation of various races?

All that may conceivably be taken the wrong way entirely so now for some "damage control". What few people realize is that Moses was married to an Ethiopian, that is a black woman. Though I may have stated that before, there is something else worth adding here. When God got furious with Israel for so soon abandoning the God who brought them out of Egypt, and turning to idolatry, God was going to wipe out the Israelites and make a people of promise out of Moses and his family. I find real irony in this. With the treatment of the blacks in the 19th century by slave owners, often considered justified, even on religious grounds, yet here we see the black race very nearly became fully half partner in the promises given to Abraham...the very Father of faith to which some of these religious people supposedly clung to. Even further on we see that King David was a great grandson of Ruth a Moabite woman. This is real interesting because the Moabites were cursed and not allowed to enter into the temple of God. (Deuteronomy 23:3) Here what was originally a cursed people, have become part of the most important lineage in the bible. If God was not concerned about race, why then should we be? Also for the people who don't like to take orders from people of other races, consider how Moses took advice from his father in law Jethro. (Exodus chapter 18)

Another legend shows that Viracochi (possibly another name of Quetzalcoatl) could indicate the gender of a human before it was born and even chose which it was supposed to be! Another ability credited to him is sculpting in stone designs of all the nations he intended to create. It would seem that race is a product of technology and nothing else. But it does not seem that Enlil and Virocahi are the same or came at the same time, but Enlil came in Ham's lifetime and Virocochi seems to have come when the decline of man was already visible and evident. Ancient Nascan (Peru) pottery shows people of white, yellow, brown, copper, black and shades in between. What's odd is at the time of their discovery; these colours of people were not represented on the continent!

Colors get even odder. In Egypt Ammon and Shu were Blue, Thoth (the moon 'god') was light blue and green, and Osirus was Green (Something's wrong in my sources, which say Osirus is Nimrod who was black.) Plato says that the people of Atlantis had skin color different from everyone else, and the scholars that take Plato seriously tend to think their skin color was blue. Plato used Egyptian sources where it's said that Atlantian's visited North Africa (Egypt?) in ancient times. It's said Egypt was ruled by 'gods' in the beginning. "Blue blooded" and "royal Blue" are ancient terms, which refers to rulers and royalty...which is odd because royalty is supposed to wear purple. The Picts and other European and African tribes that bordered the Atlantic Ocean used to dye their skin blue to resemble the sons of Atlas. "Blue blood" is also meant as a cross of Indian and white in South America, and the Peruvians had white 'gods'. Oddly people in the high altitudes do have a bluish tinge...possible from less oxygen.

Some have read into the ancient stories clues that suggest that the ancients were helped by UFO's with blue skin that came from a doomed planet. Well if this is the case I say that 'doomed planet' was either the earth! (pre-flood) or from the asteroid belt before it became the asteroid belt. The crediting of these 'gods' as being extraterrestrial may be sensationalism or an inability to explain things in light of things accomplished by the ancients. The persistence of these legends tends to suggest there was more to them then fable.

Guatemala, Mexico, Columbia, Peru and Bolivia have legends of "non human" races of Blue men which had pointy or flat heads. Well you and I know that does not mean they were inhuman, but only displaying features differing from the general populace. They are said to be the first race which date before the flood! It is also said that these blue people had all knowledge and were the same people whom we referred to before as having studied the four points of the horizon, the 4 quarters of the heavens, and the round surfaces of the earth!

Another color attributed to the Atlantean's is Reddish. Well why not! Red...blue...green, grey, what difference does it make...if they ever existed, they've all disappeared so how do you prove they existed other then in old legends...or have they all disappeared?

A red man showed himself to Napoleon during his years as leader of France while he was in Egypt. This red man apparently knew him as a schoolboy but did not reveal himself to him. Others saw this red man and he warned Napoleon if he did not make peace it would all be over for him.

In 1491 Facius Cardan (mathematician's Jerome Cardan's father) was visited by 7 men who appeared to be about 30 years old but said they were 40. The one in command had dark red skin. They said they lived as long as three centuries. They said they were made of air (holograms?) and were born like regular folks and although were highly technologically advanced they were not allowed to divulge any technology because of heavy penalties. They said that God did not make the world to last eternally but was created at each instant and in an instant and the world could cease to be. This red man appeared to be *very* red whereas the north American Indian (commonly referred to as "red man") is really only brown. Where are these red people coming from?

It's said a little grey man counseled King Charles XII of Sweden. He was also urged to make peace but ignored the advice and died in one of his campaigns in 1718.

In the 12th century and again in 1887 two children were found...with emerald green skin! The skin was scrutinized and the color did not rub off. Both the boys died soon after discovery; one of the girls lived 5 more years, the other married. Eventually the green skin faded (sunshine was no doubt the culprit) and they eventually appeared Caucasian. (book 5 pg 143-44, Book47 pg. 96, 97, Book 50 pg121-22) The 1887 kids said that an earthquake and a terrible noise occurred that lifted them UP and put them in the cave from which they were seen to wander out of.

In 1953 two tall blue people (supposedly from Venus) were met by the members of the press (paper not mentioned). To prove their origins, one dug a groove in a hard desk with his fingernail. The next day they did the same thing to a steel bar 1/2" deep! To do this feat 1800 lbs per square inch is needed. Later the steel was analyzed and there were found 14 elements in the grove that were not there before. It's seems as though the 'Venus" story was a cover as they had mentioned the heat of the desert, and Venus is known to be about 800 degrees, and with an atmospheric pressure from 85-100 times that of earth. So if it was hot in the desert to them, they sure as heck weren't from Venus! People viewing UFO's have seen occupants with white, reddish, grey and blue skin. Though occasionally some have seen UFO pilots wearing 'space suits', all varieties of humanoids seen in UFOs, have been seen without suits, as though they were at home in earth atmosphere. (book 47 pg 30-33) In chapter nine we'll make some sense of all these UFO's and this material.

So what was the first original color of man? The name Adam means to "be made or dyed red or rosy". By other accounts it means "red earth". This red is probably the red of a ruby, garnet or some other gem. This is oddly corroborated by a witch doctor from South Africa in possession of ancient knowledge which broke his vow of secrecy. His published story sounds familiar. He said the first people knew all about radioactivity, robots, and space travel and their skin was red. (Book 22 pg 160) Well we certainly are not red now...although some red blotchiness and high blood pressure can make for more red appearances of some. Caucasians do have a reddish orange tinge I suppose but this is due to blood color, though some people can be so pale as to appear white. The red spoken of though seems to refer to a more deep rich red. Curiously this race of very red men seems to have disappeared from off the face of the earth. Could it be that *none* of us are from the original race? If some think maybe these red people from before the flood are now pinker or "white", remember the green children. When prolonged exposure occurred the green tint faded and the girl appeared like a normal Caucasian. (book 5 pg. 144)

Flight in the past? This is one of those things I was looking for in the first place. Is there any evidence that confirms the theory that Adams race flew or went into space?

Several sources speak of ancient model aircraft found in Egypt, Columbia and other places. In 1898, an object was found near Sakkara Egypt and put in the Cairo Museum and labeled as 'bird' and sat there for 50 years until it was noticed it had straight wings and an upright tail just like a jet. In 1898 who knew?... as it was 5 years before The Wright brothers first flew. When this plane was blown on it flew from the hand. At least 15 model airplanes have been found In Egypt alone. Model planes have turned up in Mohenjo Daro and models have been found in pre-Columbian tombs. One made of gold thought to be a flying fish was shown to an experienced pilot without telling him about the object. He identified it as very similar to an F-102 fighter plane. The shape of the wings gave it away as a supersonic jet, able to fly at 60,000 feet. He also felt this form of plane would have the ability to 'fly' underwater without tearing the wings off. All this is interesting, as "UFO"s have been seen flying in and out of water. More model aircraft have been found and on January 12 1972 an exhibition of 14 ancient model aircraft was put on display in the hall of the Egyptian museum for antiquities. Some of them actually fly. (book 3 pg 171 and other sources)

I recall as a child calling planes that broke the sound barrier "thunderbirds". I even made the connection briefly to the term the Indians used and threw the idea out as lunacy. Once I saw a real cool video of a bird landing with heat waves rippling the scene. It took me a few seconds to realize this was a zoom shot and this "bird" was a British supersonic Concord being filmed nose on! Oddly the Indian "thunderbird" is a legend about a man with the ability to remove his mask!? Figure that one out! Could it be about a man with the appearance of a bird that could fly? I mean why create a legend about a man that can remove his mask?...space mask? The thunderbird is always on the top of the totem pole...certainly not a place devoted to weirdoes playing with masks and bird costumes.

Though I was looking for flight in ancient times before the flood and up to about 500 years after the flood I didn't expect to find this. Even some absolutely boggling statements are written relatively recently! It appears they mastered flight early in the previous millennia long before they told the Wright brothers it was impossible to fly!

In 13th century Roger Bacon wrote "Flying machines as these were of old, and are made even in our days"... This is in the 12 hundreds!! This statement still boggles historians!

In 1766 Emperor Chang Tang (or Cheng Tang as one source states) ordered a certain Kis Kung Shi to build a flying chariot, apparently based on old blueprints. The machine was built and when the emperor saw it work, he ordered it destroyed in case the wrong people got a hold of it and used it for evil. Chinese records show that flying machines were once common.

I guess this makes sense. Flight isn't particularly difficult. We see the birds so that puts flight into our heads, and with enough ingenuity any organized culture could come up with something. Kites have taken people into the air. A plane known as the Gossamer Albatross on June 12, 1979 was the first to make the flight across the English Channel using man-powered flight. People spoke of the design of this plane as of a person who knew nothing of the principals of flight. It's also possible someone came up with balloon flight in times where they might not be expected. One person built from scratch a balloon to get out of an oppressive country, and a dramatic escape was engineered where the prisoners made a glider to get an important scientist out of a prisoner of War camp, using material in the camp. One challenge TV Program (Junkyard Wars) shows people have made workable manpowered flying contraptions from scrap in ten hours of building time. They didn't fly very well or for very long, but they did fly.

There is a Mayan legend that speaks of a giant eagle that came down from the skies with the roar of a lion. (Book 29 pg. 51)

A Sumerian leader named Gudea referred to as a 'god' because he shone like heaven, stood with two companions beside a "divine black wind bird" (book 17 pg 138)

Ancient Indian, American and Mediterranean countries speak of "fire birds" and Easter Island has "bird men" in their prehistory.

Hawaiians remember "flying Cherubs", and African histories speak of white teachers that came down from huge birds.

An unnamed King of Egypt took refuge in a white bird that "came down from heaven in a trail of fire."(book 21.pg 192)

The Thunderbird came to the "steelheaded man" in a great crashing and rumbling of thunder" (Book 16 pg 73)

African Dogon "myths" speak of a few men that when they "climbed down from heaven that the great sea rolled like thunder and was set in motion and the mountains and hills groaned aloud"(book 10 pg 106)

An Indian legend speaks of a ape that was king of the apes who could pilot a flying vehicle, which when it took off from mountains the "tops of cliffs break" and the mountains shake, giant trees lose their branches and a shower of wood and leaves falls to the ground, and the birds and animals flee to their hiding places. (Book 10 pg 148[quoting the Ramayana. I did not come across this in my copy of the Ramayana which is missing the Brahmin additions]) This is very clear, since they are specifically saying birds fled to their hiding places; they are not confusing birds with flying vehicles

Eskimos speak of the first men, who were much bigger, who could fly in their magic houses. They made so much noise a powerful man complained about the noise as they flew through the air that he stopped them from ever doing so again, and the magic houses lost their ability to fly.(book 56 pg231, book 10 pg 111) Sounds like the laws passed to make cars quiet with good mufflers and planes not allowed to fly low with their sonic booms... I miss that sound...it was cool!

Even the Hopi's weigh in. (3rd ed. Insert 2016) There was one woman who was becoming known throughout the world for her wickedness in corrupting so many people. (Could this be Semerimas, Isis, and other names attributed to her?) "…the Bow Clan they began to use their creative power in another evil and destructive way. Perhaps this was caused by that wicked woman. But some of them made a Pa'tuwvota (Shield made with hide) and with their creative power made it fly through the air. On this many of the people flew where they came from. Soon the people of many cities and countries were making pa'tuwvotas and flying them to attack one another."

The Epic of Gilgamesh speaks of Enki that was seized by the 'sun god' with mighty wings and claws. The effect was that he felt as heavy as a boulder! This could be multiple G forces! You don't experience that on a horse, but with fast acceleration!

The Ancient Sumerian Lord of Ur (of Chaldees) had a sacred "boat of heaven"(book 17 pg 113)

Contrary to anthropologists who insist that North American Indians and Eskimos came from across the Bering Strait, the Eskimos say they were brought to the north in "great iron birds!". (Book 11 pg 111) If they wanted to know where the Eskimos came from why didn't they just ask them? Has anybody bothered to tell them? Seems kind of clear to me. But give them a break. I mean if I heard this firsthand I might roll my eyes and say "sure O'dark". But when one realizes virtually every ancient civilization on earth speaks of flight in the past, even the Sumerians which aren't here to try and impress us with the most colourful history, then one has to stop and consider that maybe there is something to this.

Ancient Indian texts credit the Ancient Greeks (Yavanas) with the ability to make Arial Chariots and wanted the Greeks to make them one as they had the knowhow, but said they wouldn't make one because they wanted to keep the secret to themselves. The ancient Greeks who were requested to make one, had no idea how to build them and had not even seen one, although they were aware of their existence, and knew the artisans who made them guarded the secret, even under torture. (book 34 pg 55-56)

Ancient descriptions of a flying chariot sounds familiar, but it's weird! It looked like a "clay roll" as high as two men and the same width...round?!! Egg shaped?

The Mahabharata speaks of an aerial chariot with the sides of iron and clad with wings. Actually in Modern India, it's common knowledge that their ancestors had flight thousands of years ago. Ancient Indian texts were translated long before flight and the translators thought the writers were loonies. The writings also contained references to bullets of iron which the translators though were inserted later to make it appear that Indians had them first.

Actually for some time Indian Scientists have been studying the ancient texts to rediscover lost secrets of SPACE flight! These ancient texts speak of "vimanas" which could go through air, on land and under water! They could go anywhere...from land to land and even "globe to globe". They were very durable, could not break, be cut or catch fire, and they could remain motionless. That's no big deal or is it referring to hovering!? ...antigravity? They could also become invisible! We seem to think "impossible" because we can't do this yet...remember... Nothing new under the sun. We'll discuss how this is possible later, in chapter nine. They could hear talking and noises in an enemy craft, and could determine the direction of another craft's approach. They could cause the pilot of another craft to become unconscious and special clothing had to be worn by the pilots... space suits? The crafts were made of 14 or 16 different metals, and pilots training included take off, forced landing and collisions with birds...yeah *real* birds...once again the distinction. (Book 11 pg 110) Even the power source is described as best as they could. It had a mercury engine that is it had an iron-heating unit that had the ability to derive power from mercury, which set a 'driving whirlwind' in motion. This is not at all farfetched! In a 1959 Paris space congress there was talk of an ion mercurial engine and in 1966 there were plans to launch a satellite with a mercury solar furnace. {book 21 pg 61} In the caves of Turkistan and in the Gobi desert were found spherical glass or porcelain objects with a cone and inside was a drop of mercury. Related? Four engines were used in tandem, they could lift a vimana as large as a temple, developed "thunder" power and could be instantly a 'pearl in the sky"...not a bird...a "pearl"(book 37 pg 39-40) again round, oval or spherical craft! Egyptian spoke of "circles of fire" that soared through the skies in the reign of Thut III. So it appears that the ancients had conventional aircraft and weird round ones without wings! But the only round ones we know of today are "unidentified"! Well whatever these machines were, here the veil is lifted far more than usual. This is not talk of giant birds and thunder sticks. This is a clear attempt to speak about what existed in the best scientific term available...clear enough to be studied by several groups searching for clues. Serious attempts are made to describe tangible mechanical flying apparatus's... and these records are thousands of years old. It may not be an actual flying machine but it's the next best thing! It also indirectly speaks of devolution, because it appears to be uneducated or devolved people describing highly advanced technology of the gods. Who were the 'gods'?

The Chinese have also been searching ancient documents to see what scientific knowledge they can glean from their pages, which is usually written in disguised terminology because such knowledge was purposely kept secret by those that held and controlled the knowledge. (Book 37 page 44-45)

The Egyptian 'god' Horus flew in a winged disc that shone in many colors. Archaeologist and ancient historians constantly confuse "Horus" as the sun, but the book of the dead speaks of Horus who "dwelleth in his divine disc". Hathor also dwelleth in a spacious disc, yet no one suggests 'Hathor' is the sun. The disc is not the sun as there are references to the disc "representing the sun" one of which was seen around 400 AD in the temple of Serapos rising of its own accord.(book 21 pg 100) The disk of Ra is also measured! It is seven cubits and the 'pupil' is three cubits...or about 16.58 feet and the pupil being about 6 1/4 feet. (Book 61 pg 305-306) They flew with the speed of wind and with a melodious sound. They were 'golden discs which were kept aloft by means of sound vibrations at a certain pitch by continuous hammer blows. So was Horus the sun, or a machine that looked like the sun, because it glowed and was in the sky? Now we have disc shaped flying craft too!? Hmmm...that shape sounds familiar.

The Ramayana describes a flaming chariot that shone like flame in the night sky, it swept by like a comet and it was as if two suns were shining because it rose up and all the heavens were brightened. We can see why the confusion of Horus being the sun, but just what were they describing? Actually tablets exist which show two suns in the sky! A rock painting shows four discs in the sky but only one is clearly the sun, and a football shaped thing is shown lifting on a cloud of smoke. (book 3 pg 70 [again, not in my copy of the Ramayana]) also shown is a man in a bizarre diving suit with antennae!

WELL IT CERTAINLY APPEARS THAT THEY HAD FLIGHT IN OLD TIMES...WHAT ABOUT SPACE TRAVEL?

In my research many other researchers referred to a Babylonian named Etana who wrote a story about his flight in the eagle. Most of the story to me is not all that convincing but one bit is interesting. Many a devolved ancient believed the sun, moon and stars rotated around the earth, but this tale does not fit this pattern. The flight is mentioned to have taken place in the daytime, but during the flight he mentions coming into the "plane of the fixed stars". Still not too convincing in my mind as some people even back then knew this. Still it is curious. Actually you can see bright stars or planets in the daytime with a telescope if you know exactly where to look. I have found Jupiter this way.

A similar story exists in the Ramayana where a "chariot abandons the closeness of the middle world" and Sita and Rama ask "how is it that even in daytime there appears... this circle of stars?" If these are not firsthand sightings they are very VERY good guesses.[more and more so I wish I had found this version of the Ramayana]

Vimanas. Indian legend speaks constantly of flying machines, which could go in the air from place to place to place, land-to-land and globe-to-globe, as we've seen. (Book 34 pg. 62.) When you think about it this is not just evidence of knowledge of flight and a round earth but a solid clue to the existence of inter planetary flight!...still beyond our capabilities or at least on a par with them, if you count the moon as one of the "globes".

In 2309 BC a certain Hou Yih decides to go to the moon in a celestial bird. He explores space by mounting the current of "luminous air". Is this a clue to a method of propulsion? Some forces such as electro-magnetism can illuminate the air, or is this just talk of rocket fuel going off illuminating the air? He gets up high enough to not be able to discern the rotary movement of the sun. If he believed the sun to rotate around the earth, then this IS an interesting statement, because this would be an account of a believer of the sun rotating around the earth not understanding why it does not appear to do so. He would have stumbled onto the fact that the sun does not move around the earth but would have appeared surprisingly stationary. But again this appears to be a mixture of unlearned men in the presence of advanced technology, suggesting a time when the two were coexistent on the earth, similar to today where backward savage tribes see our technology.

The India Surya speaks of the earth as a sphere, where above and beneath were relative and everyone on earth thinks of their position on the earth as the uppermost part but since the earth is a globe in the ether what is the upper part and what is the under part of it? (Book 14 pg. 262)

The Mayans used huge numbers like the Kinchilyun = to 23,040,000,000 days and the Alautun = to 63,123,000 years. These appear to be astronomical figures and not debt payments or grains of wheat in their silos! Actually many suggest the use of such large numbers suggest the earth really is this old, but we ourselves use similarly large numbers, but we shall see the earth is a whole lot younger then we are led to believe. Anyone can trace a planet backwards in time...well anyone well versed in gravitational mathematics anyway...for however many years you want to...it doesn't mean the planets actually existed that far back.

In a text dating to the second century which was originally considered for inclusion in the bible, but may have been rejected because authorship was uncertain. It's not certain if the Abraham the text refers to is even the same Abraham, referred to in the bible. It speaks of a voyage that this Abraham took up into a large construct, which was fixed, on the firmament. Inside he "wanted to fall downwards on the earth. The lofty place on which we stood now stands upright, now turns itself downward" (book 10 pg180) This sounds an awful lot like being inside a space craft of a spherical shape of some sort rotating high somewhere above the earth to create artificial gravity with the earth still in sight.

Twice in 1962 and in 1931 manmade metal objects fell from the sky and "disappeared" into museums or the government holds...who knows where.

The Brazilian Kayapo Indians have a very strange festival. A man is dressed up in a woven human shaped basket, and he is completely enclosed, even his head. Just looking at the man brings thoughts of robots or A deep sea diver...which may be close because the suit is suppose to represent "visitors from the cosmos"!(book 10 photo section.) If however this was a Human Cosmonaut one wonders why he would have been wearing the suit.

Almost unbelievably one of the carvings (?) at Angkor Wat is of an astronaut. I would have thought the space gear would have been completely different from what we use, but it is so similar to the ones used on the moon, that if you didn't know Angkor Wat was about a thousand years old, you'ld think they used our 1970's astronauts for a model. (see drawing 4)

DRAWING 4

Angkor Wat Astronaut

When the Sumerians went up in the "boat of heaven" they had to put on and wear a 7-piece uniform for protection. (Book 17 pg 136)

A Sumerian ruler named Gudea wrote that he could tell that a shining man was a god "by the helmet on his head". (book 17 pg.136-138) These helmets were often described as "firmaments" , similar to Ezekiel's

Vision (see Ezekiel 1: 22-26) These were probably clear helmets with radiation and ultraviolet screening capabilities, and this may have something to do with why so many artists painted haloes around heads.

The Mayans speak of a giant eagle that came down, the beak opened and four creatures came out that did not breathe the air we breath... Oxygen tanks?

10...9...8...(3rd ed. Insert 2016) There's a carved lid or cover in Palenque, Mexico. A Russian Space engineer, [and] some scientists deduced the carved lid depicts an astronaut or cosmonaut housed or seated similar to our astronauts in a capsule with numerous controls within his reach including Antenna, space directional system, Control panel, Turbo compressor, refuel tanks, and turbine and combustion chamber. (World of the Incredible but True, Charles Berlitz pg. 18)

Legends say a space ship is buried beneath a landmark that is "like a lion and yet like a man"...but try and convince the Egyptian government to burrow under the sphinx! I've not been able to find the source of this legend so for all we know it is just psychobabble hearsay.

The Sumerians built Ziggurats that meant "the house for descending from heaven" and they served as a "stairway to heaven" and they looked to moon gods. But it's also entirely possible the moon 'gods' came from a moon shaped ship that landed on the ziggurats!, or raised platforms.

In 1725 In Northern Tibet there was discovered a 3-story pyramid built by "star worshippers" called Hsing Nu. Nearby is a palace with thrones surrounded by images of the sun and moon. In 1952 some information about this pyramid was discovered. The lowest story of the pyramid meant "the ancient land when men rose up to the stars", the middle floor meant "the middle land when men came down from the stars" and the top floor means "the new land the world of distant stars"

Many nations and tribes refer to themselves as being descendants of sky people or gods from the heavens. This at the very least corroborates the biblical reference to men marrying angels ("sons of god") in the pre flood period, but these texts and ancestors are by and large post flood in origin as though after the flood people came down from the sky in what appears to be in bright moon shaped globes who seemingly existed before the flood. In Peru legends state that people of that country were originally born out of gold, silver or bronze eggs that floated down from the sky. There's that shape again.

South Sea islanders say they are descended from the gods of heaven who came down in a big gleaming egg. Many records and legends insist there were these 'gods' that took human mates and they are descendants of them. But one eventually has to ask the question...if these were extra terrestrials, then how could they mate with mankind? Simple, they were not extraterrestrial. Would they have wanted some scaly reptilian monster ruling over them!? Not likely...they would have fought them tooth and nail! There is no mention of these 'gods' having weird features...only that they gave others these features apparently through genetics... These weird chimerical creatures may possibly only be attributed to Ham, son of Noah.

Not all these 'gods' came from space! Quetzalcoatle is said to have come from and returned to the sea, and the Hopi Indians are said to have come from underground!

PRECONCEIVED IDEAS OR BIASES MEANS YOU MISS THE OBVIOUS.

(3rd ed. Insert 2016) In Gods and Spacemen in the Ancient East, Raymond Drake blows his nose in the general direction of the biblical beliefs and writings, putting in pre-eminence other ancient histories like Ancient India. Ok fine if he wants to do that, and I'll get back to this later. But in his forcing the belief that man was evolved by a push from spacemen for page after page, he makes a statement that just had me shaking my head. "If our own scientists of acknowledged genius by empirical studies are turning towards the Cosmos and wonder if planetary radiations affect matter and Man, both accretions of energy, then the Initiates in ancient days who brought astrology to such mathematical and philosophical refinement must have developed a super-science enabling them to conquer space, control the elements, defy gravity, fly faster than light, to act as Gods, as spacemen!" (book 34 page 31) So I ask the question; If man in ancient history could have done this as Drake suggests might have been done, why then does he have to assume any spacemen coming to earth spoken of in legends couldn't be of earthly origin? If they reached this state after the flood, what on earth did they attain before the flood?

Clearly there are definite indications the men of the past had flight and even space travel. Did some pre flood men still exist, caught in space at the time of the flood? But the flying vehicles that could get into space seem round, egg shaped or spherical. Well I found flight in the past, but what bizarre methods of flight indeed! But if they were more advanced than us then maybe they could make pigs fly for all we know. They had incredible weapons too.

WILDER THEN JUST CHEMISTRY... RADIATION!... AND???

In 1919 off the south end of a tiny uninhabited Greek Island a sponge fisher named Zalakhos came across a sponge that burned his hand because of the sand they grew in. His partner Gabriel went and got some of the sponges (I guess without touching them) and found a piece of iridescent metal described as neither metal nor glass. Apparently there are several jars of this stuff down there. Shortly after Zalakhos was feeling terrible and his body was burning up even with them pouring water on him to cool him, and he died that afternoon. Later that night they decided to bury him and found him glowing with a phosphorescent golden light...they decided to bury him at sea as soon as possible. Gabriel did not completely escape either. The hand that touched the 'metal' got bad, slowly swollen up and twisted. Doctors commented that it must have been in contact with something stronger than radium. Other divers have also died in this area. Did the ancients produce something radioactive stronger than anything we've come up with, which unfortunate divers have stumbled across thousands of years later? Remember, this was found in 1919, at least 25 years before the first Nuke went off!

It's been found that the Egyptians used radioactive ingredients in mummification and the wrap was also radioactive (maybe this is the source of the "curses"?) Some have suggested this was why they used the stuff, but then they would have to have known this and been able to protect themselves from it. We also know radioactivity prolongs shelf lives of Fruits and vegetables...did they, or was this a fluke?

Ancient India had a time measurement called the "Kashta" equal to 1/ 3 millionth of a second...now why do you suppose they had such a minute measurement of time? They also knew the time span of the rotation of an electron around a nucleus...or this may be the time the "Kashta" is referring to. Their smallest measurement of time was the "period taken by an atom to traverse its own unit of space" (book 7 pg. 224, book 11 pg 54)

TRANSMUTATION OF METALS?

Schoolbooks pooh-pooh such attempts in the past to make gold and silver from base metals as foolish nonsense by people that did not know the properties of elements. To say some alchemists were rich does not prove anything, but what is very interesting is official reactions recorded to the practice of making precious metals from other metals. In 300 AD the Roman Emperor Diocletian issued an edict in Egypt demanding all books on "the art of making gold and silver" be burned. (This followed closely the event where the Praetorian guard Didius Marcus bought the entire Roman empire for the equivalent of $35 Million dollars!)

In 175 B.C. there was a law passed in China banning the making of gold by Alchemy.

In 1317 pope John XXII condemned alchemists to exile and heavy fines were issued to those found transmutating metals.

In 1404 King Henry IV of England issued an act that declared that the "multiplying of metals" was a crime against the crown.(book 11 pg 37-38)

Why were monarchs making laws against transmutating of metals if it couldn't be done? It appears that they *were* making gold and in enough quantities to be affecting economies of empires!

In 1688 William and Mary overturned King Henry's Law with the stipulation that they were to turn any gold or silver made over to the tower of London's Royal mint to be bought at full value no questions asked!

In the department of coins and medals of the British Museum in London there is a piece of gold that was once a bullet and is still in that shape. The caption reads "Gold made by an alchemist from a leaden bullet in the presence of Colonel McDonald and Doctor Colquhoun at Bupora in the month of October 1814" (book 11 pg. Pg. 39)

Obviously some atomic chemistry was known in the past that is not known now...or at least no one is admitting to this knowledge! One clue is that Mercuric Sulphide was very important in the process and mercury falls right between lead and gold on the element table...three consecutive elements very close in atomic weight. If the alchemists were a bunch of dreamers it's interesting that they used the elements that were so close on the element chart as they did not know the chart back then, and sulphur is a very volatile element. Even so it would seem that this would be just a chemical compound rather than actually 'gold', yet many governments made edicts to stop the making of gold and silver.

Democrates said there was in reality nothing but atoms and space.

Some Einsteinian knowledge appears evident in some old writings: Leucippus wrote in the 5th century BC Atoms "rush everlastingly through all space" and said they take on "Myriad changes under the disturbing impact of collisions" (book 11 pg. 52) , and Heraclilus (5th century BC) said "the way up and the way down are one and the same.

A table exist from 550 BC which shows the size of the atom which is "fairly comparable to the actual size of the hydrogen atom".(Book 11 pg. 55)

NUCLEAR WAR: WRITTEN EVIDENCE

An Ancient Babalonian text known as CT-XVI-44/46 reads "Ishum to mount most supreme set his course; the awesome seven [weapons] without parallel trailed behind him. At the mount most supreme the hero arrived, he raised his hand- the mount was smashed.... in its forests not a tree stem was left standing". (book 42, pg. 328-29) This shows some power or force was known to man, which was used to smash a mountain and level a forest! Other excerpts "...Even the crocodiles he made to wither, as with fire he scorched the animals, banned it's grains to become as dust, ...Who rained fire and stones upon the adversaries." "...he who scorches with fire and he of the evil wind together performed their evil, the two made the gods to flee, made them flee the scorching." These weapons were described as having a "terrible brilliance which overwhelmed them"

Indian texts (Ramayana) say the desserts were caused as the result of destruction from terrible weapons of the 'gods' (book 10 pg 142[again not in my copy of the said book.]) Is this the real explanation for desserts? It appears the ancients DID have nuclear weapons, so this explanation becomes plausible!

Pieced together from a few sources (quoting the Mahabharata) Remember this was translated in the 1880's... "Cukra flying in a vimana of great power, hurled at the triple city a (single) missile (projectile) weighted (charged) with all the force of the universe. An incandescent column of smoke and flame as bright as ten thousand suns rose up in all its splendor...it was as if the elements had been unleashed (unfurled) The sun spun around in circles in the heavens. The world reeled (shuddered) in fever, scorched by the terrible incandescent heat of this weapon. Elephants burst into flames by the heat and ran to and fro in a trumpeting frenzy to seek protection from the terrible violence. The rivers boiled, and those that had dived into them perished miserably. Animals crumpled to the ground and died. The armies of the enemy were mown down when the raging of the elements reached them. The raging of the blaze made forests collapse in rows (toppled like 9 pins) as if in a forest fire. The elephants made fearful trumpeting and sank dead to the ground over a vast area. Horses and chariots were burned up, and the scene looked like the aftermath of a conflagration. Thousands of chariots and horses were destroyed (incinerated), and then a deep silence settled over the land and sea. The winds began to blow and the earth grew bright. It was a terrible sight to see. The corpses of the fallen were so mutilated by the terrible heat that they looked other than human.

Never before have we seen such a terrible (ghastly weapon) never have we even heard of such a ghastly weapon. It was an unknown weapon, an Iron thunderbolt, a gigantic messenger of death that reduced to ashes the entire race of the Vrishnis and the Andhakas. The corpses were so burned as to be unrecognizable. Their hair and nails fell out, pottery broke without any apparent cause, and the birds turned white. After a few hours all foodstuffs were infected (or became unwholesome)...to escape this fire the soldiers threw themselves in streams to wash themselves and all their equipment. [that mighty weapon]...bore away crowds of warriors with steeds and elephants and cars and weapons as if they were dry leaves of trees... borne away by the wind..." Further description...a cloud rose after the explosion that formed into expanding round circles like the opening of a giant parasol. Another explanation of the explosion after the egg broke in half... "the upper half turned into a tree mushroom and rose high up into heaven" Again this was written down from old legends hundreds of years ago and translated in the 1880's! Other ancient texts repeat the same descriptions of elephants and warriors falling down like trees in a raging fire. This weapon called "Brahma's Rod" was described as "infinitely more powerful than Indra's Bolt [because it] can smite whole countries, and entire races from generation to generation" The Babylonians spoke against this weapon because "the lands would make desolate". Even descriptions of the aftermath are equally vivid... "drought would afflict the land for ten long years...and kill unborn children in their mother's womb" (Book 2 pg. 77,78, Book 6 pg. 215, Book 7 pg. 226, 227, Book 10 pg. 87, 143, 144, book 21 pg. 82,83, Book 29 pg 125-126, Book 35 pg. 176, Book 37 pg. 210, all quoting this source) A Myth handed down by the Pangwe of the Bantu people goes like this: The lightning lay packed in a special egg ...the egg broke and from its two halves came all visible things. The upper half turned into a tree mushroom. (book 10 pg. 87) If this "myth" wasn't a bazillion years old it could be used to describe a couple of cities in Japan at the end of WWII! It seems in the past many such weapons were being used! Back when these were translated this seemed like stuff of myths but now it is painfully clear what they are describing.

The Drona Parva speaks of Valadevas weapon which "fell down on the earth splitting her (with its might) and making the very mountains tremble". (Book 34 pg. 46 quoting this source)

NUCLEAR WAR: PHYSICAL EVIDENCE.

In 1947 in Iraq an archaeological dig which dug through strata which contained Babylonian and Chaldean artifacts and then below 14 feet of clay they came to a layer of fused glass, almost identical to the dessert floor at Alamogordo New Mexico which is the location of the first A-bomb test. (Book 6 pg. 215, 216, Book 30 pg. 66,)

In the Gobi desert was found vitrified soil (heated to liquid and fused into glass), which is the same as that caused by an atomic explosion. (book 37 pg. 207-208)

In Libya, Australia, France India, South Africa, Lebanon, and Chile there have been found areas covered with tektites (glasslike pebbles). These are not thought to be of volcanic or meteoric in origin because they contain radioactive isotopes Aluminum 26 and Beryllium 10. (book 34 pg 175, book 2 pg 128)

Vitrified forts have been found in Scotland, Ireland, Poland, Czech Republic, Germany France and Hungary. Though early attempts to reconstruct this form of rock showed that intense heat from fires places on the forts could accomplish in a small area, it's unlikely fort defenders would allow it to occur and easily have their way with the firestarters. And it would be virtually impossible to cause the entire forts to have this vitrification occur during a siege. And it's highly unlikely owners of the forts would do this to the forts as it weakens the walls. (see Atlantis Rising #118)

In Sacsayhuaman there is an area of 18,000 square yards, which is vitrified rock, which only happens, in extremely high heat. Usually it is suggested that this was caused my glaciers, except this "glacier" would have had to flow in six different directions in this very limited area. (Book 2 pg 38)

Ireland, California and Czechoslovakia have areas of calcined rock which is normal rock heated very high to become chalky but not quite enough to vitrify.(book 23 pg 208)

Death valley in Nevada has an ancient town that appears to have been destroyed in a catastrophe. The south sides of the buildings appear to have been in a furnace, and the rock on which they stands shows signs of melting. No grass grows in this area.(book 2 pg 128, book21 pg 60)

Forfarshire Scotland has several ancient forts that have been vitrified.

A skeleton was found in India which was 50 times more radioactive then the surrounding soil.(book 22 pg 160)

In Mohenjo-daro India and Harappa Pakistan, there were found a number of skeletons at street level which seemed, by their scattered positions, to be attempting to escape something and all the skeletons were highly radioactive. Nothing is known about these cities except they ended their existence abruptly. (Book 7 pg 228-230, book 6 pg 216)

MORE POWERFUL THEN NUKES?

The Mahabharata describes a weapon which "if you hurl it at a weak enemy it will destroy the whole world, there is nobody that cannot be killed by this weapon"(book 10 pg 152)

The Mansala Parva speaks of a weapon that was "capable of reducing the earth to ashes" and was destroyed upon royal command and ground to powder and cast into the sea. (Book 6 pg 215)

The Ramayana also speaks of a weapon so powerful it could destroy the earth. (Book 6 pg 215) I obviously have a very truncated version of this ancient text. Though mine was fun to read it obviously chopped out all the interesting stuff the Brahmins spoke of.

PLANET BLOWN TO BITS

My guess is that man before the flood blew up the planet between the Jupiter and Mars creating what is now the Asteroid belt. I thought this was a unique theory, but I am not alone!

In 1953 a chap named Orfio said a "space man" told him that a planet (named Lucifer) between Jupiter and Mars was "blasted'. This planet has also been named Marduk and yes, even... Krypton. The method of destruction is not stated. Some suggest a collision of two worlds, but if the solar system was created perfect with order prevailing this would not have been a possibility. Unless the offending 'planet' was a manmade world 'colliding' with the planet or causing the planet to be destroyed.

Actually in the 19th century Nikola Tesla believed that the power of resonated harmonic vibration tuned to the right frequency could in fact destroy the earth. The little device he stuck in his pocket and placed on the side of a 10-story building under construction illustrated this possibility. He made a link of the finest steel. The link was capable of bearing 100 tons. Crowbars and sledgehammers couldn't touch it, but with this device attached to it and then started up with a tuned timed rhythmic tapping on it ...tapping that wouldn't harm a baby, and within minutes the link started to contract and dilate like a 'beating heart" and finally broke. He had even come up with experiments that showed the earth to have a periodicity of 1 hour and 49 minutes and he believed this same power could destroy the earth. He figured this could be done with dynamite set off at this specific interval and within a few weeks the crust of the earth would be heaving hundreds of feet in the air. (book 52 p100-102) He once built what appears to have been a larger version of that pocket resonator and set it going on a pole in his apartment on Houston Street (NYC). Shortly the police station 14 blocks away on Mulberry Street began to shake with plaster falling off the ceiling and chairs moving around. The police knew where to go and when they got to Tesla's place they found him smashing the device, as turning it off would have not been quick enough! And to think it happened on Mulberry street. (Book 52 pg. 102-103)

Was the asteroid belt originally a planet? Pythagoras realized that in measuring the lengths of musical chords there was a mathematical correlation. He went further and theorized that the planets too moved in an orderly manner and that their orbits would also be arranged in mathematically natural intervals. We do know that gravity is related to mass and distance and these follow strict mathematical correlations that also work with magnetic fields.

BODE'S LAW

Similar to Pythagoras, in 1772 Johann Bode came up with a formula which predicted the distances of planets from the sun, and as it turns out his predictions are extremely close...so close that it's now called "Bode's law" except for one problem. There is no planet between Mars and Jupiter as his 'law' predicts. Bodes figures when compared to actual planets distances in astronomical units (AU) that is the distance of the earth to the sun is equal to 1 AU.

Bode's law predictions.

(1st planet) .4 au, (2nd). 7 au, (3rd) 1.0 au, (4th) 1.6 au, (5th) 2.8 au, (6th)5.2 au, (7th)10.0 au, (8th)19.6 au, (9th)38.8 au, (10th) 77.2

Actual distances of the planets from the sun

1) .39au(mercury), 2) .72(Venus), 3) 1.au (Earth), 4) 1.52au(Mars), 5) 2.77(asteroid belt), 6) 5.2au(Jupiter), 7) 9.54au(Saturn), 8) 19.2 au (Uranus), 9) 30.1au(Neptune), 10) 39.5(Pluto)

Because of these predictions astronomers decided to search the area between Mars and Jupiter for a planet...they found none. However this searching for this planet was how they discovered the asteroids. We did not find the asteroids accidentally, then come up with the prediction, the prediction found the asteroids, that is we found them based on the predictions of Bodes law, and many astronomers are convinced the asteroid belt was originally a planet but cannot figure out what could have happened to it. The asteroids do not have two axial revolutions indicating they are not from a collision of two planets but have a single axial rotation showing they all came from a single celestial body! In other words a single planet exactly as predicted by bodes law! (book 17 pg208-09, book11 pg69-70, book 6 pg207, telescope handbook and star atlas pg79, 91)

It would seem there was a time in the ancient past when man was extremely technologically advanced. Suggestions even indicate they could blow up an entire planet and indeed it would seem that a planet has been destroyed. Even physical evidence shows another moving body did not collide with it. My guess is man, for whatever reason, destroyed it. I explore some possible reasons later on. Not only do we see clear evidence that man really was advanced in the past but it would seem some of this advanced technology was in existence at a time when other men were mystified by this technology, suggesting some men were in a state of decline while others remained in a more advanced physiological and technological era concurrent with each other. This would also tend to confirm genetic decline of man and it appears to be a result of a by-products of the flood. But what would cause a difference to exist where some men were in a godlike state and some were in a state where they were grasping at straws to describe the technology evidenced all around them. Some of the people at the time even appear to be on a primitive standard similar to what we call cave men. We will explain what caused this state of affairs later on.

Now that we have laid the groundwork which shows mans technology was extremely advanced in the past we can now explain one of the biggest mysteries of the bible. Where did the water from the flood go?

Chapter 4

CAUSE AND MECHANISM OF THE FLOOD: WHERE THE WATER CAME FROM AND WHERE IT WENT

INVENTION OF WATER.(3RD ED. INSERT 2016)

Geologists say that there is not enough water on the earth now that would account for the Noah flood legend. This is true. Yet on the other hand they say that after the earth formed it rained and rained to form the seas. In fact that would be more water to create the seas than creationists says fell during the flood (when you consider lower average terrain that is known to exist on the earth at one time.) ...so where did *their* water come from? I explain where our water came from and where it went. No explanation for how their water formed or where it came from or why it even exists has been attributed for the existence of water. They just know water is here now so it had to have come from somewhere, but no workable hypothesis for the existence or origin of water is even out there. They would rather scratch their heads and hypothesize endlessly about where water came from, than, even for a second consider the biblical record which does, sort of, have an origin of water in Genesis chapter 1. "1:2 And the earth was without form, and void; and darkness was upon the face of the deep. And the Spirit of God moved upon the face of the waters."

Apparently water or waters have always been. It appears to be one of the attributes of God, and indeed the bible often equates the Spirit of God with water or it's attributes. Interesting. Well at least it's better than no clue. It might explain why we seem to be able to alter the properties of water with our thoughts. With us being created in God's image, we have an affinity for water too. Actually one of the physical attributes of space itself is similar to that of water. But we'll leave it at that...for now.

WE SAW IT THEREFORE WE RECORD IT.

(3rd ed. Insert 2016) Too often biblical flood proponents tend to assume the localized and continental floods are some of the evidences for the universal flood legend, and similarly people who don't want to believe the flood of legends and especially the biblical flood, point to the contradictory legends and evidences which seem to indicate a less than universal flood. Then with great authority in conjunction with physical evidence it's declare, "Thee flood" wasn't worldwide. This is one of those rare times when both camps are actually right, because both flood types are recorded in legends and in the geologic evidence seen on the planet.

Hawaiian, Chinese and Toltec Indians of Mexico all have the same flood legends as the bible and there are all told at least 270 flood legends. (Actually not many people realize the bible indicates a few different floods so you could push that number up a bit) When we've seen that there are two types of floods (Worldwide flood, and continental shifts causing water to overrun the continents), I think a collecting and careful analysis of them one by one would enable us to separate the universal flood legends from the slightly less catastrophic continental tsunami floods. By doing this, instead of confusing the picture, it would clear it up more, because when we realize that there are two types of floods and flood legends, we can look for the evidence and distinguish them, rather than trying to force all the evidence into one type of flood. I've often heard it said that the flood of Noah was only a local flood, for example the Urantia book states the flood of Noah was a local flood. No doubt this conclusion is either from looking at the evidence of a more localized flood, or deliberate attempts to undermine the ancient records and the faith they inspire...as indeed some have admitted.

It stands to reason that every people on earth would have a universal flood legend. Why? If only eight people survived that flood and they are the fathers of all the population on the earth, most certainly the flood story would have been passed down to their descendants...meaning all of us.

To the trained eye, clearly the physical evidence does support the occurrence of a worldwide flood. However there is indeed evidence indicating large local floods too. This was what was so confusing to the 19th century geologist as they couldn't understand why the evidence led to the conclusion that there appeared to be a few different floods on the North American continent as well as in other places. Realizing now that there are two kinds of floods to look for in legends and in geology, it will help clear up the big picture more and the legends, taken in categories, will help make a clearer picture still. However, one thing that can't be dismissed is the fact that these legends match up with the physical topographical evidence... meaning these events occurred in historical times and that the changes in the earth physical structures and changes in climate are specified in these recorded incidences. This is incredibly important in the overall scheme of things. Geologists insist the things that shaped the topography of the planet took millions of years to happen despite the fact that if this were true, erosion during those same millions of years would equally undo any physical changes. The fact that mountains and canyons exist is testimony to their abrupt creation, *and newness* due to lack of erosion.

For every geologic formation that they say takes eons to create, there are even better reasons to accept that these things happened far quicker and indeed during recorded history, and that is the very reason so many ancient texts, writings and legend speak of these very events. As will eventually become crystal clear, it's simply inescapable. Since recorded history only goes back little more than 5000 years (or about 7,000 if you include antediluvian material) we are forced into a corner that shows the earth and its geologic formations happened quickly and are far more recent compared to what are now accepted normal beliefs in an old earth, (as our evidence will further prove in chapter 5). Yet predetermined conclusions based on old earth hypothesis or evolutionary based logic means these proponents tie their minds behind their backs, because they dismiss the ancient legends, biblical record, or other superstitious "myths" as primitive tales made up to explain the world to children, rather than accept that they actually saw these things happen and thus told the tales and recorded the events.

WRITTEN AND PHYSICAL EVIDENCE

First, the flood evidence is there. They have found a universal layer of clay all over the earth and fossilized sea shells on mount Everest, so that alone would be enough to convince many that a flood did occur that covered the entire earth. Some clay might have been washed away or overturned in subsequent earth upheavals, but the flood has been found many times over. In fact in some opinions there are too many floods.

One of the main problems scientist have with the flood theory as mentioned in the bible is if the flood covered all the land to a minimum depth of 15 cubits, then A) where did the water come from, and b) where did the water go? I admit it took me a long time to figure out where the water went...but I did finally figure it out...and the answer will seem like it's out of science fiction. But let's start with where the water came from.

Although we covered some of this in chapter two a little review won't hurt. Ok there are clues in the bible. One... after the flood God gave the rainbow. So this means there was no rainbow before the flood! Clearly something is different! Two...The trees had no rings. This also shows a different global climate!

Paleontologists admit there was a time when the entire earth was a lush green house where trees grew at the same rate all year round with no fluctuations that would cause tree rings. They say this happened millions of years ago, whereas I say this is what it was like before the flood...we'll deal with tree rings and what they tell us next chapter. Three... man and animals lived fantastic lengths of time...900 plus years, so clearly the environment is different.

When people read ancient history and myths and legends they see that there was a universal flood spoken of in virtually every people and tribe on earth. Sometimes even the names of Noah are similar for example the Hawaiian call Noah Nu-U and the Chinese Nu-Wah. But some of the legends are confusing and they lead people to think the great flood was not the same as spoken of in the bible, because other histories speak of many survivors, or of no survivors (for example the Hopi say there were no survivors except those who went underground).

THE EASY PART; WHERE IT CAME FROM.

So what is the answer? Well it has to be something with a lot of water in it. The answer to where did the water come from is a water sphere or canopy which surrounded the earth! Actually people have figured this out before. I must admit to being curious as to the content of this water. Was it stagnant, pure, salty, mineral or caffeinated? You could take fish from the earth and put them up there. I doubt there would be anything for them to feed on, but what an aquarium! Though you'ld have to look at the fish through a telescope. Feeding time might pose a problem. And of course if they swam too low and fell through the bottom of the water sphere it would be raining fish.

Nineteenth century geologists couldn't understand why there seemed to be evidence of more than one massive flood. So the tendency is to downplay the biblical flood as more of a series local phenomena, especially because they don't understand how the entire earth could be covered by water to a minimum of 15 cubits (27 feet or 4 1/2 fathoms) nor can they figure out where the water went. It is the fact that no one can decipher where the water went that leads people to think the bible is more of myths and legends and poetic license rather than record of events.

However we will see that the bible is a series of historical, cultural, and geological factual recordings. The bible says that God would never destroy mankind again with a flood. So how could there be more than one universal flood? Though there have been many floods, and floods occur even today, obviously all of mankind does not perish in them.

The fact is there was more than one major ancient flood and most of them are spoken of or alluded to in the bible, but the second, third and subsequent major floods were not as complete as the first and greatest flood. The realization that there was more than one flood and that the nature of the floods were of different mechanics, but with similar outcomes, causes the confusion. The flood of the bible is of rain, drain, and geyser format, whereas later ancient floods were of wave or tsunami format. Actually people have realized there were incredible tsunamis in the past and so some have concluded that the biblical flood was one of these types of floods. But there is also evidence of deep clay deposits, and tsunamis will not cause this. Clay forms from massive sediments, such as would result by the type of flood described in the bible, with water standing for many months after massive disruptions of the earth's surface. This eventually settled becoming sediment. And this is how the biblical flood is described and it accounts for the universal clay layer. But how do you account for the other tsunami types of floods and just how massive were they? Those other floods will be spoken of and understood in chapter six "Peleg". This chapter will deal primarily with the universal flood.

WHAT BROUGHT THE WATER DOWN

Ok the first thing is to figure out where the water came from and what caused it to start raining. Well as we have seen the earth before the flood was actually inside of a water sphere. How thick the water sphere actually was could probably be mathematically deciphered, but one would have to do some tricky calculations because you would have to turn the clock backward to figure out the exact topography of the earth at the time of the flood to know how much water was actually on the earth. The mountains at the time of the flood were not the same as we have today so the actual amount of water on the earth at the time of the flood is not as much as people usually think, but we'll get to that.

If we can accept that the earth was inside a shell or sphere of water we can then at least clear up where the water came from. God separated the waters below the firmament from those above the firmament. He divided the waters and some went above and some stayed below. As for the mechanics of how he did this I can't answer that one, try as I might. If he pumped air into the oceans it would just bubble up. I'm guessing some sort of electro-magnetic interference with the molecules of the water, but that's just a guess.

The water was originally a few miles deep, like maybe two to three miles and no land was visible at the start. Genesis. 1:6 shows the waters were divided from the waters before the land appeared, with a firmament placed between the waters…that is an atmosphere. In other words before the land was visible it was originally already under all that water. In other words before man was made, the earth was exactly like it was at the end of the flood…all under water. Then he changed the molecules of a layer in the water into air, similar to electrolysis and then just kept doing this in progressive layers. Thus the water became atmosphere and less dense expanding this layer to what eventually became our atmosphere sandwiched in between two layers of water. Since all this atmosphere was in a single "bubble" inside the water spheres it didn't break up into smaller bubbles forcing their way through the water sphere, but the entire bubble simply pushed the water sphere upwards to a point where the pressure from the water equalized the pressure of the atmosphere. God in creation put it up there then made the remaining water to be all in one place (verse 9) and only then does he make the land appear from underneath. It's neat visualizing it.

GETTING THAT WATER BACK DOWN HERE

How did the water sphere collapse? To explain this I had to first establish that man in pre-flood times was far more advanced, otherwise to explain how the water sphere collapsed is going to sound like science fiction, and like I've been watching too many sci-fi movies. This is why I had to show first that man was so far superior to what we give our ancestors credit for as to be able to cause his own destruction. Sound familiar? But this destructiveness was done on such a grand scale that it becomes fantastic. Yet when looked at seriously this makes all too much sense and is completely logical….even if bordering on unbelievable. We simply have to stand and accept that man before the flood had technical skills beyond our comprehension. Some of these capabilities have been described in the previous chapter, and some more will be described in following chapters.

If we conclude that evolution is not correct and therefore replace it with devolution, we can reasonably presume all was created perfect and meant to last eternity. If this is the case we must presume there were no erratics, such as meteors, asteroids, comets, moons with wobbling orbits and so on. Some have theorized that God created these things to use for judgment of man. However if that were the case then man would have been created sinful to start with. I have to disagree with this assessment as it would seem eternity was part of the original plan for the earth when it was originally created. Subsequent actions meant consequences, which lead to the entropy of the earth and it's house. If this is the case, something after creation caused the erratics to come into existence. If we accept that man in the pre-flood era had and used technology to make a ship capable of roaming the solar system then we can presume he conquered space in ways that we can only dream of. Man was capable of making other planets inhabitable and causing destruction on the same scale. When one looks at sources of many disasters one often realizes mans own destructive nature brings about his environment's demise; we all too often fall in the very trap we create. But can such destructive ability come on such a grand scale, that man could incur the complete destruction of man by a flood because of his own actions? Hmmm… why does that sound all too familiar?

THE MOON GIVES SOME INDIRECT CLUES

The first time I read the bible one thing stuck out immediately, and that is that the biblical record says that the moon was a light meant for the night time. This seemed odd to me because the moon rotates around the earth and is only in the night times sky about half the time, and even then it is only visible about 1/2 the night because it is either in the early morning sky or the early evening sky. It is only visible at night all night when it is full. Now either their description of how the moon was meant to be is very poor, or something has changed causing the creation of what we call months.

A term known as tidal locking is used for describing the moon in it's present state, that is, it keeps the same face toward the earth. It would seem by the description of the moon's purpose in the bible that it was originally meant to be tidally locked with the sun, and it may have rotated at a different rate. The earth orbited the sun in between the moon and the sun rotating merrily along the way and tides being as stable as clockwork...and the moon did not leave the night sky...ever.

Now I will grant it's quite possible that I'm off on this theory. But I suspect that the moon originally rotated at a different rate. Yes it does rotate...but at the same rate it revolves around the earth so it keeps the same face toward the earth thus it does not appear to rotate from the vantage point of the earth, but possibly at one time we could see all sides of the moon from the earth. (Actually Tesla felt he proved the moon did not revolve, but, as near as I can figure, I think he believed it swung around the earth (like a ball on a tether?) as explained in one of his articles for the Electrical Experimenter. February 1917) The moon would have been used for timing events in a different way, with the stars moving behind it to allow an exact date to be discernible each night any time you looked at the moon. You could tell what day of the year it was at night by just looking at what star was near the moon, at the same time each night. (They were smart enough to be able to figure this out as easily as we look at our wrist watch to tell the time.) It's original orbit would have kept it in the night sky, always as a 'full moon', but it would have rotated in that position so that though the moon would have been in the same place it would have appeared different each night because it would show a slightly different face toward the earth each night.

Time would also have been discernible by the moons rotation on its own axis rather then it's orbit around earths. Impacts from asteroids changed this original standard to the current one. I don't think the moon would originally have had a wobble as it does now, and it certainly would not have had the craters in the beginning. They were a result of a catastrophe in the skies and they would have impacted the moons original orbital standards to new ones. That seems clearly aberrant to what should have been a stable orbit, not just for the moon but for all the planets and their moons. My premise is that asteroids and something else changed how the moon functions. Eskimo legends seem to suggest that the moon has done something that caused it to change its patterns though it's impossible to tell what happened from my sources and the legend's admittedly are obscure.

There are other moons and planets in the solar system that have screwy features that suggest extreme catastrophic occurrences since creation. If we presume they were not created this way then something happened after creation to cause erratic events to take place in the solar system causing these peculiarities. In the solar system we see moons blown up and reassembled, planets are tilted or now have debris around them in the form of rings. When I first understood what the rings of Saturn were I asked the question 'if the rings were made up of bits of…debris?, did those bits come from a crumbled moon?

MAN GAINS THE ABILITY TO DESTROY

Something did happen. The simple or "pat answer" is sin and the knowledge of good and evil entered mans make-up after Adam and Eve ate the forbidden fruit. But there's more to it than that. It is the very nature of the fruit that actually changed mans character. Oddly when one looks at the context we see that man gains something that God has. God says that man has become like "us" because man now has the knowledge of good and evil. Does this mean that God is evil? What one has to realize is that what we see as the meaning of evil is not the same thing as is meant in the bible (for the most part). Although we often interpret "evil" as meaning wickedness, "evil" in the biblical sense usually means the ability and capacity to cause destructive things to happen. I assume this also means "good" means the capability to create and invent. But with this ability infused into a being that was disobedient to God's word (don't eat from the tree) and thus sinful, we see a volatile mix, because now not only can we create great wonderful structures, we can also create instruments to cause destruction, something of an oxymoron. The bible says that man thought evil continually. This is different from wickedness as seen in Gen 6:5 where both words are used. Take this ability to create and destroy with the advanced ability of men before the flood and who knows what they could come up with!

Now things start to make sense. God has always had this ability but man did not. Like a potter he could make a pot and destroy the pot as he sees fit. Once man gained this ability he used it. But with man having an IQ that would make Einstein look like an idiotic child, he was able to cause creative and destructive things on an incredibly grand scale. Well beyond our skyscrapers and nuclear weapons. They would make our towers look like child's work with blocks, and our nukes look like firecrackers compared to what they could make in the pre-flood era. Obviously when you make a destructive force you want to try it out. Man before the flood made a bomb or force so destructive they couldn't try it out on earth. And in all likely hood it was not even shot from earth but more likely shot from a manmade satellite or even a small planetoid capable of orbiting earth or the fifth planet. They may even have made a huge permanent ship meant for traveling the solar system. Could man have built a craft such as this? Consider this. Jupiter for the longest time was believed to have 12 moons. But for a while a 13th moon was observed orbiting Jupiter. Then it vanished. There was seen a moon orbiting the planet Venus. But Venus has no moon! It too disappeared. Then there was seen a new planet orbiting the sun inside the orbit of Mercury! It was there long enough to get a name! It was called Vulcan. No I'm not stealing lines from space shows. I suspect that before the flood, mankind made a spherical space station or ship capable of supporting life to the same extent life was supportable on earth, with its own regenerating biosphere. It would have to have been pretty large so as not to have to keep coming to earth for supplies, and it would have had places for craft from earth to enter as it wasn't so much a craft itself but a manmade planet. If some evidence is to be believed this space ship or whatever it was, was big enough to be seen from earth in telescopes in a location as far away as Jupiter!! We will look in more detail at the evidence later on but for now let's presume man had such capabilities before the flood.

As to how they could do it, we can't be sure. One example of how a planet could be destroyed was explained by Nikola Tesla based on periodically timed explosions in one spot timed so that every time the reverberations from the previous explosions energy waves returned to the point of origin a new explosion would take place. In a month he figured the earth's crust would be heaving hundreds of feet in the air.

It's likely any destructive force that caused changes in our solar system would have come from this wandering manmade planetoid. And no, I did not get this idea from the movie Star Wars. I simply deduced this from the wandering planet seen in recent and ancient history and the premise that man was able to make such a thing before the flood. So if they built a weapon capable of destroying a planet obviously they are not going to use it on the earth. So they used it on the most logical spot. A planet immediately outside of Earth's orbit, far enough not to affect the earth yet not too far the event couldn't be witnessed from earth. As to why they would do such a thing one can only imagine but who knows, maybe it was just for fun! Sort of like fireworks on an incredibly grand scale. Or maybe there was an interplanetary war. Anyway it could have been a global event that all people on earth were aware was going to happen and they all watched it at the same time. Before the flood all the land masses on earth were in one continent, thus at a specific time all would have been able to see the blowing up of the planet at the same time. It would have been timed so all could 'see it live'. Another, more plausible, reason for the destruction of this planet will be presented later.

With space travel common before the flood, the great game of asteroids would have been a real life and death game and all space craft played to stop these asteroids from hitting earth. Man, proud and confident felt he could stop them all from hitting earth. They hit all the other planets in large doses. Uranus is orbiting the sun on its side with its pole facing the sun. Mimas one of Saturn's moons was almost blown apart. Miranda, one of Uranus' moons is felt likely WAS blown apart and the gravity of the pieces caused the moon to pull itself back together. Our moon was riddled with asteroids causing the scaring of the surface and the start of lunar changes. Such was the destructive force unleashed by the evil of man on what is no longer a planet but an asteroid belt. Some planets would have caught asteroids in their orbit turning them into "moons". Mars has two of the asteroids. Jupiter has moons that orbit in reverse or retrograde orbits as though they were captured. Who knows why they blew up the planet in the first place. I mean since we know they were intelligent this action seems the epitome of stupidity.

If comets are made up of mostly water and originate from this planet as do the asteroids, then it would seem that the doomed planet had water. If this is the case then that makes one think it was inhabitable, thus maybe we colonized the planet. Perhaps later on the people of that planet became belligerent to the people of this planet and so we destroyed them thinking we could cope with the resulting asteroid problem. We were wrong.

Was the asteroid belt a planet at one time? Many scientists have long felt that this could not be the case because there is simply not enough mass in the belt if all the asteroids were clumped together to make up a planet. They could all be piled up on Texas with a little spilling over the edge. I think this is somewhat short-sighted on the part of the theorists. Why do you think there isn't enough matter in the belt to make up a planet? Because the rest of the mass was blown out of the orbit of the original planet and strewn about the solar system, landing on the sun, all the other planets and their moons. Some may have even escaped the solar system, though I don't think this is actually the case. Asteroids from the destroyed and blown up planet threatened all of the solar system; the entire solar system was virtually under siege. No doubt a lot of that exploded planet landed on the sun, the largest source of gravity in the neighborhood, and this may be a reason for some sunspots, and no doubt this explains a lot of the missing mass from the asteroid belt. Even Jupiter has a big red spot that might be a result of a huge chunk of this planet landing there.

WHEN DID THIS HAPPEN?

There is a mathematical trick some mathematicians can do that to me is just extraordinary, but to some this is basic stuff. They can use math to predict orbits of items in space. Yes you know that, but that is worlds beyond me. They can also work backwards too! You can actually turn the clock backward by calculating the orbits of planets and asteroids backwards in time. I'm not certain if this mathematical science is perfect enough to calculate backwards 5700 years, but if you're keen to try here's what I want you to look for. Find as many orbits of asteroids as you can, Ceres and all the others and simply plot them backwards in time. (Though Ceres is a lost moon, so it might not work in the calculations)

Actually one source mentions this being done and they found around 4700 years ago there was the appearance of a bunch of asteroids in one vicinity at that time to confirm the theory of a blown up planet, but this may be a coincidence as I would think this was too recent, though I might be wrong in the timeline which I present later. However if we took Ushers age of the earth starting in 4004 BC this would put the destruction of the planet around 345 years before the flood. By my calculations I calculate this incident happening 353 years before the flood even though I add over 1000 years to the age of the earth. Possibly I'm wrong and these asteroids might be a key to getting the date right. But we'll get to that later too. I think the asteroid plotting work has to be continued back another 1000 years or so. But there has to be a time when all the asteroids and comets were in the same place.

The Russian Astronomer S.K. Vsehsviatsky observed "The rapid decrease in luminosity of periodical comets points to some unusual activity in the sky in the geologically recent past and felt this unusual activity took place in historical times, only a few thousand years ago" (Book 53 pg 139) Even historical observations of comets has diminished over the millennia.

Historical records show that there were many more comets in the sky in Roman times. Sometimes two or three comets were visible at a time to the naked eye. Some were even visible during the day. Often events were linked to the sightings of comets.

Diogenes (5th century BC) wrote that things in the sky *frequently* fall to earth.

The Jewish calendar is confusing, as by my reckoning it starts at 353 years before the flood. (see the earth age chapter) The Jewish calendar doesn't seem to start at the flood but only starts "when time started" to be counted as though some event occurred then...an event that starts time. My guess is since the Jewish calendar is tied to the moon, something about the moon started the calendar...but then I'm making that guess based on my theories so I might be biased.

The length of the year has changed. Yes there's reason to believe the year was 360 days long at one point. For example the Egyptian middle kingdom refers to the year as being less than 360 days long. It is quite simple to determine exactly how long the year is. By watching when the brightest star (Sirius) first appears then count the days until it disappears behind the sun and appears again. I mean you might not be able to get it to the minute as the earth would likely be facing a different direction the minute it comes into view but certainly to the nearest day. After a few years of observations you could start adding decimals. So to say the years were less than 360 days long and to be out by 5 days or more is beyond error and indicative of a different length of year, and not an error in the calculations. So at some point the Earth either rotated at a different rate, orbited around the sun faster or somewhat closer to the sun to account for a shorter year... or some combination of all three variables.

PERFECT TIMING.

(3rd ed. Insert 2016) Ancient Chinese records we know tell of times when the sun rose twice. Once the sun went back down and came back up. But another time (April 29 899 BC) it appeared to have risen twice because of an eclipse, right at sunrise. Because this eclipse happened right at sunrise they were able to pinpoint the length of the day at that time by charting backwards. By doing some calculations and correlating ancient Chinese records they were able to determine that the day back then was 0.043 second shorter. My glib comment about the earth slowing down enough to make the year shorter, (lost somewhere in this book) though valid, is not near as much as several days or a year before the flood, but a mere 6 hours. (World of the incredible but true Charles Berlitz page 193) Be that as it may, clearly a shift of about 5 days difference in modern years from ancient has been noted.

CALCULATE BACKWARDS TO FIND SOME ANSWERS.

My guess is at about 5700 to 5800 years ago all the asteroids and comets will be in one spot at the same time when they left the original planet in the explosion. There are of course some possible errors because some of the asteroids still in existence might have hit each other and changed their initial orbits. This may be impossible to calculate. One must also calculate the orbits of Mars and Earth backward prior to the flood. There are going to be some variables in this picture too. If Mars was hit by more asteroids, as I'm sure it was, as it would have been closer to the fifth planet, then it would have been hit more frequently. Mars' orbit would have changed dramatically because Mars is a smaller planet, so asteroids would have affected it more, and with more asteroids hitting it, the asteroids likely affected Mars' orbit tremendously. Not knowing what asteroids hit it and how big they were or what direction they came from and when they hit will likely make calculating all this an impossible task.

We also have to realize that some of the asteroids hitting planets were huge, so they conceivably could alter a planet's orbit. After all, Mars has an elliptical orbit now, indicating huge hits in the past. I have recently read that the orbit of Mars will be as close to earth as it has ever been, so obviously Mars' orbit has been worked backward but apparently without the variables of large asteroids hitting it. Without calculating asteroids in the mix we will simply come up with a calculated orbit reflective of the orbit of that planet based on present observations.

INEXPLICABLE KNOWLEDGE IN THE HANDS OF THE ANCIENTS

It appears the ancients knew that Mars had two moons and it appears that they were able to see them from the earth. Virgil and the Iliad by Homer talk about them, and even Jonathan Swift seems to have had access to old manuscripts which told of these two moons in order for him to describe them in Gulliver's Travels 150 years before they were officially discovered. (book 14 pg. 284) The two moons of Mars are tiny little things about as big as any comet or asteroid! How is anyone supposed to be able to see them from the earth? Well sure they had telescopes before the flood and after, but it would seem they were seen without them! But how is THAT possible? We usually can't even spot asteroids when they come inside the orbit of the moon! If this is the case Mars had to be incredibly close to the earth at some point.

ASTEROIDS CHANGE THINGS

If you're wondering what all this has to do with the flood and the missing water, it will come together soon. Already clues start to crop up. If we presume a planet was blown up and the pieces caused havoc in the solar system, effects from this havoc are going to take place. And ancient histories speak of these aberrations.

There are several catastrophes in earth's recorded history that might have altered earth's orbit slightly at the time they occurred. So even the earth may have wandered from its orbit in the past, but deciphering when and by how much might be pretty difficult to figure out. However the bible and other ancient records such as Egyptian and Sumerian and North American Indian and ancient India Chinese histories speak about many catastrophes so one might be able to decipher it all out. There were many catastrophes The Flood, Peleg, Exodus, and we have the earthquake spoken of around the time of Uzziah possibly around 1700 BC. There is the time when the sun went backward 10 degrees as spoken of in Isaiah. And of course there's the time when Joshua told the sun and moon to stand still and that was the longest day, (this event is confirmed in other histories). It also happens that several asteroids hit the Amalikites on that day and more were killed by them than by the Israelites, and this evidence has been found too. The Egyptians speak of the sun rising where it used to set on four different occasions, as do other records. All these events are indicative of huge earth catastrophes and any one of them could have knocked the earth out of its normal orbit.

If these things were happening on Earth, then they were happening on Mars and with more amplified results because Mars is a smaller planet and it was closer to the action. So no doubt these have to be equated into the mix. People generally say that the bible speaks of just one disaster, the flood, But as you can see it speaks of many, the biggest of them other then the flood itself was likely Peleg or the exodus. (see the Peleg chapter)

THE EARTH GETS HIT.

Back to that blown up planet and the ensuing asteroids. Well as you probably guessed some of these asteroids also landed here on earth. Theorist have often wondered why the earth appears to have escaped so much destruction when the moon, mercury and other planets seem to have gotten so much meteoric action. The answer is twofold. One, we were being guarded by the people in space and two, the water on earth erased many of the craters caused by the asteroids, and only the craters that hit after a later date remain. How much destruction from these asteroids was done? Enough to cause the flood. Maybe smaller asteroids might not have been a problem, and might not have disturbed the water shell enough to cause it to collapse and rain on earth. They likely passed right through the shell only bringing a little extra moisture to earth. But eventually man had to miss one big enough to cause harm.

God said He would bring the destruction of the earth and I have to think he did this by causing man to miss one. It says 'except God keep the city they who watch over it watch in vain'. Well they who watched over earth, watched in vain. One monstrously huge asteroid got through the gauntlet. Maybe it was dark and didn't reflect light and radar right, but one got through. How big was it and what did it do? I figure it was in the neighborhood 500 miles wide...or about the same size as Ceres. This size is strictly a guess but it was something on the order of this magnitude. It might have come from the daytime side in an orbit from the other side of the sun, or it might have come from above the orbital plane, and was missed until too late, or simply was missed altogether. As to how it was missed doesn't matter... it was missed... and it hit earth so hard as to not just create a crater, but to actually break through the crust of the earth and force the interior of the earth outward.

Some tektites which some people have deduced to have come from meteors are around the earth in varying amounts. The tektites from one particular incident or fall, have been estimated to weigh all told as much as 100 billion tons! (book 19 pg 163) All that from a single hit!? The asteroid that hit simply had to be huge!

You may be saying out loud 'O come on!' how could they miss one that big, and such a huge asteroid hitting the earth would leave an obvious scar visible even today? So where did such an asteroid hit? Surely something that big must still be visible even AFTER the flood. It is! It's as plain as day! It hit and created what is now known as Hudson's Bay in Canada, and also created what is known as the Canadian Shield. The Canadian shield is lava between 20,000-50,000 Feet thick and covers about 2 million square miles!! It just boggles the mind to just imagine where all that lava came from. People in the neighborhood would have been gone in an instant. But you say the earth wasn't destroyed by a meteor it says FLOOD! True. The meteor by itself might not have destroyed life on earth. Some would have survived, but it was the aftermath of the impact that killed all life on the surface. Some will insist such an asteroid would kill everyone. But the nature of the earth itself suggests it might absorb some of the impact shock. The meteor would have smashed through the water shell surrounding the earth and blown dust and debris into the atmosphere and even some of it would have blown out of the earth and come back down through the water sphere. All this action in the water sphere above earth would have destabilized it causing it to break apart and rain. The asteroid would actually have put a hole in the water shell that simply could not be fixed. It would have looked like a hole or a "window" in the sky. The asteroid smashed into the earth with such terrific force that it actually creates the fault lines in the earth's crust still in existence today.

EFFECTS OF THE BIG ONE

It says the windows of heaven were opened. This is a really interesting statement. It suggests that some smaller meteors may have gotten through, causing small holes in the water canopy creating "windows" in the water shell. Certainly the "big one" would have opened up the sky and caused the water at the edge of the hole in the sky to simply drain onto the earth. Possibly as the water shell broke up cavities in the shell became visible from earth. But this is also an interesting statement because a difference was observable in the sky indicating variations of colour in the sky. If the sky was previously green and then areas of the water shell opened up to allow space to be viewed, those areas would have been either dark at night or blue during the day.

Maybe even the sky dipped in those areas bringing the dark cold of space close to the surface of the earth making even holes of night visible in the daytime seen through the waters sphere. And it rained! Not rain as we know it now but literally either collapsing sky and or draining. The water shell would have been upset to the point where the gravity on earth pulled down on the shell itself. Pressurized air would have rushed "outside" the earth as these holes or windows opened up. With the rippling effect of the initial meteor the water in the shell would have been dipping into the atmosphere, breaking up then as the water broke up as it fell to earth it was simply torrentious rain by the time it got to the surface. Remember if the water on the surface of the planet reach to 4.1/2 fathoms above the highest mountain, that water was originally up there. The depth or thickness of the water sphere may have been as thick or as deep as 1-2000 feet! Some of the water shell would have come in with the meteor and then just kept coming.

What's amazing is that the people caught in the flood had no time to save themselves. If it rained forty days and nights one would think some other people on the surface of the earth could have saved themselves, but no one else on the earth survived. How could all that water get down here so fast? Maybe only 1% of the water coming down to earth came down as rain. And this water be it rain or drain had to come down fast, so fast that men didn't even have time to build more boats or even fly off the earth in smaller craft…unless they were already in the craft at the time of the hit

Perhaps the meteor had accompanying dust and debris with it frothing up the water shell and breaking it up so it could turn into rain. The rest of the water may actually have drained down rather then rained down; draining downward as it followed the meteor. It might have come down like water coming down a drain and all in one spot like a sink draining with a water spout or drain but watching from underneath you could watch the earth surface fill up. This may have happened in several spots wherever "windows of heaven" opened up. Perhaps if you were situated in the right spot you could see a huge water spout falling to earth like looking up from a lake floor at a whirlpool, but with the whirlpool being water, the water being air and the surface of the lake being the underside of the water sphere. It rained forty days and forty nights but the majority of the water may have been on the surface of the earth in a day or two…. maybe a week…enough time to get to higher ground but not enough to build anything substantial to escape the water…like a boat. Sure they could move huge stones but stones don't float. Maybe some people hung onto floating debris but with no food or shelter and the water being on the earth for a year they would all be doomed.

It's possible the majority of the water fell to the earth within a single day, thus no one could get out of the way. So why then did it rain for 40 days? My guess is once the water shell broke, this changed the air pressure. What was once air became humidity and vapor as the atmosphere expanded into the air we are now familiar with. The very atmosphere was changing it's characteristics.

Again I'm just guessing, and likely better explanations could be put forth. I just put that out there because it's fun to think "out loud". Sometimes one can make sense of the guesses because they steer you in a direction you might not have gone on otherwise, even if the guesses are not correct.

ECHOES FROM CHINA

(3rd ed. Insert 2016) Donnelly in Atlantis quoting a Sir William Jones (*Asiatic Researches 1788*) states "The Chinese believe the Earth to have been wholly covered with water, which, in works of undisputed authenticity, they describe as flowing abundantly, then subsiding and separating the higher from the lower ages of mankind". This shows not only that The Chinese also have the universal flood history, but also speaks of a higher and lower age of mankind, referring to ages of relative advancement and civilization, pre-flood being the more advanced. Admittedly the legend speaks of the water subsiding, as some creationists deduce it did, but we'll see the problem with that.

MORE THAN JUST THE FLOOD HAPPENED DURING THE FLOOD

Another effect of the asteroid hitting the earth is it pushed into the earth with such terrific force that the interior of the earth pushed outward, causing waters of the deep to come out of the ground like ten thousand geysers all at once. One specific mention in the bible is that of the fountains of the deep breaking forth. This puzzled me for some time. What could cause all the underground water to just suddenly shoot out of the ground? There had to be a cause. Nature does things on an action reaction basis. So what could cause fountains of water to just shoot out like this? Well if you were visualizing earlier you might have guessed. That meteor hitting the earth cracking through the surface of the earth pushed the interior of the earth outward. There's your "fountains of the deep breaking forth". Maybe the meteor didn't actually smash right through the crust and imbed itself into the interior of the earth but it certainly would have pushed inward enough to cause the interior of the earth to push outward in other areas of the globe. This indicates the huge size of the meteor hitting the earth. Water from the deep would have been forced outward, like an orange being smashed with a hammer and the juice finding its way out through the skin. If the asteroid was say 500 by 300 by 200 miles big that is about 30 million cubic miles entering the earth suddenly. This asteroid's mass has to displace other mass in the earth so 30 million cubic miles of underwater springs shot out of the earth's interior during this event, also bringing with it more debris to become silt and eventually clay.

MYTHS: FLOWERED UP HISTORY

Plato explains that some ancient stories which appears to be a "myth" are really just flowery language for bodies moving around earth and in the heavens apparently causing havoc here on earth. Sometime after I had come up with this theory I read this. The Aztecs believe the first world civilization (water sun) was destroyed by a flood caused as a result of a planet called Maldek situated between Mars and Jupiter being blown up and the subsequent asteroids hitting earth. It just doesn't get any plainer then that!

IT DOESN'T GET ANY CLEARER

(3rd ed. Insert 2016) Atlantis Rising #35 pg 32 "...Arab historians used the story of Surid, the ruler of an antediluvian kingdom, to explain that the great flood was caused when a "planet' collided with the earth." That's the same conclusion we came to here as the cause of the great flood, *without knowing about this reference*, though this references uses the word "planet" ...planet, asteroid...tomayto, tomahto...

Of note: this particular reference was used as an example to support the theory of what sunk Atlantis, which we will see didn't exist as an Island kingdom yet. This is also an example of minimizing the great flood and using it to explain a local event. (This chapter deals only with the global Flood. We'll get to the Tsunami type in chapter 6.)

SUBDUCTION DEDUCTION?

(3rd ed. Insert 2016) It occurred to me while looking at our globe's fault lines, that the mechanics for *all* the water from the flood subducting underground after the flood is both not consistent with earth mechanics or with the time frame for it to have it all recede. The water came from the water canopy and just fell on the earth when its stability was compromised. If the earth below it was stable before the flood, what sort of mechanics in the earth could possibly absorb all that water? None. Creationists assume the fountains breaking from the deep was a large source of water causing the crust to fall and then rebound again, subducting the water back into the earth. But that doesn't work. What about the extra water that fell down as rain!? Based on this theory, the Earth would be expanding to a larger dimension than previous to the floods original measurements. That can't be possible. Perhaps the amount of water that came from below would subside back underground, I'll give them that, but where is all the extra water from the canopy going to go? (remember, it was on the earth before it was set above. Read Genesis 1:6-7... 6: "And God said, Let there be a firmament in the midst of the waters, and let it divide the waters from the waters. 7: And God made the firmament, and divided the waters which were **under** the firmament from the waters which were **above** the firmament: and it was so." This 'firmament' is the air layer that was inserted between layers of water (the bottom 'layer' being the oceans, the top 'layer' being the water shell). It clearly indicates there was a lot of water above us. Before this happened the earth was as it was right after the flood occurred. The flood undid a key creation event. Remember, creationists, God moved the waters to one place so that dry land would appear. (Genesis 1:9) Before this the earth was just a water planet, like it was when the flood occurred.

Creationist either miss or don't get that a *wind* was the *key* piece of getting rid of the water, not subduction. Understandably wind isn't going to do it either if it's an ordinary wind. But *this* would be the first appearance of Typhon, the origin of the word typhoon. And such a wind was unwittingly demonstrated by Velikovsky to be from a planet close enough to the earth to wreak havoc here during the time of the exodus.

WHERE THE WATER WENT

Many scientists say the flood as written in the bible is just impossible because there is simply not enough water on the earth to do what is stated in the bible, legends, myths and folklore, that is the covering of all land up to 15 cubits deep. (A cubit is about 18-25 inches, which was supposed to be the length of your arm from the elbow to the tip of your fingers. Since my cubit is about 19 inches I might interpret this to mean that men in the past were of a overall larger stature. This would further suggest a reduced overall physiology of man...but I digress)

They say there is no way the water could have evaporated and sub-ducted into the earth to this extent. They have done accurate measurements on the moisture content of the sky and there is not enough water to even make a foot of water on the earth, let alone enough to cover all the mountains 15 cubits. So where did the water go, or is the biblical account a bunch of exaggerated hooey? Well we can see where the water came from, but as to where it went has plagued Creationists for a long time. Well now the mystery gets solved. Here's where the water went.

NOT AS MUCH WATER AS WE SEEM TO THINK

First there are two things we have to consider. Originally the earth had a more gentle terrain. There simply were not the mountains in the pre-flood era as we know them now. The average height of the continents used to be a mere 1000 feet and at some point this average rose to the current 2500 feet! (Book 9 page 126 using R. F. Flint Glacial Geology and Pleistocene Epoch as a source) So 15 cubits above the highest mountain wasn't what it would be today. As far as calculations would go this reduces also the amount of water that fell, that was originally above the earth. Maybe only 700 feet of water was above the earth in the water sphere. (don't forget if there is 700 feet of water fifty or a hundred miles up? that translates to maybe three or four times the depth when brought to the surface. But I'm just guestimating numbers out of the air. Maybe the variation in depth was negligible) Yes there were mountains before the flood but not on the scale we now see.

Mountains such as the Himalayans didn't exist on the earth before the flood. They were possibly created about 100 years after the flood! Now even if you're a creationist you might be saying NO! We know that mount Everest has sea shells all over it and as we've seen it was under water long enough to get sea life such as clams to live there, proving it was under water. It's well documented that the Himalayans were at one time underwater, true, but that actually proves something else. Yes it does show that Everest was under water at one point but consider this. If the water from the flood sub-ducted and receded from Mount Everest the clams and such simply would not have had time to get there. Why? Noah's ark was resting on land (Mount Ararat) by the seventh month and mountains were visible by the tenth month indicating Ararat was one of the tallest mountains as seen from the ark. But Ararat is much lower than Everest, so Everest would have had to be above water much sooner than this, thus not allowing the time for the sea creatures to reach that point and then multiply because if Everest was a mountain before the flood, it would have been the last mountain to get submerged and the first mountain to become free of water.

If we confine ourselves to believing mount Everest existed before the flood, then there simply was not enough time for Everest to have received the amount of sea life on it that is known to have been there, and certainly not clams and oysters on its surface. (Actually I'm just deducing this bit logically so there may be some flaws in this reasoning I'm unaware of.)

Some event after the flood brought Everest into existence. Suffice it to say there were no 29,000 foot monsters before the flood that we see now. The water was only on the earth visible from the vantage point of Mount Ararat for ten months. Everest did not exist before the flood, it was pushed up when India rammed into Asia after the flood. And to make explaining all this tougher the flood action did not create the mountains. Some of the Himalayans likely existed pre flood but they were probably not more than 1000-3000 footers, but they may not even have been molehills before the flood. And no this is not a cop out for making the water on earth disappear more easily. The water was here and the entire earth was underwater. It just wasn't 29,000 feet deep, it was about 3000 feet above current sea level. Mountains were just lower than that. Likely the highest mountains were in the 3000 foot range. So either way the question of where the water went is still a tough nut to solve…because even with 3000 foot mountains that's still 2500 feet of water we have to explain away. (some flood water still remains on the earth) So where did it go?

Ok, so if the earth was a flatter place before the flood, this does mean there was less water originally on the surface then one thinks when looking at the terrain of the earth today. Still there is too much water left behind to account for what remains on the earth today. Otherwise the earth today (presuming Everest DID exist before the flood) would only be maybe 10% land and 90% watery surface. Yes some water subducted back into the earth. The interior pressure likely forced land masses upward, but there's no way this alone can account for the water disappearing. Where did that extra water go? The only clue we have is that there was a wind after the flood that took the water away. People read that and assume this was the agent of evaporation. Nope. This was an agent of suction! That too would make the sound of wind. Something pulled the flood water off the surface of the earth! But what, and how could water leave the surface of the planet? There really is no other explanation because the water isn't here anymore.

HOW THE WATER LEFT EARTH

No we didn't invent a big vacuum to suck water off the earth just in case we flooded it.

This is a tricky one to be sure. But astronomy tells all. The first clues I had, I actually found when I was about 14 years old, in a set of cards that came out of tea. There was a space set and one of the cards gave a clue. Though I didn't realize it at the time I never forgot that card as it was so interesting. This card depicted a painting of a tightly orbiting binary sun.

There is a type of star known as binary stars. These are stars that orbit around each other. In some instances binary stars have very tight orbits around each other and in such instances they do something rather unusual. They exchange matter, similar to how molecules share electrons. Atoms sometimes lose electrons and often have to share electrons, so in actuality all the electrons of each atom orbits both atomic nucleus's. Similarly with binary suns they exchange matter back and forth because the gravity of each body pulls some matter to a common center. This matter would also become part of the other star, maybe for good, or maybe until the mixing up of the matter made that matter go back to the original star. Left long enough each star in a tight binary orbit would have virtually identical physical properties. Though the stars may be a million or more miles away from each other, the gravity of each star is enough to pull matter from the star into space and towards itself, so from a distance it appears that both stars are held together with a cord, like two people holding hands and spinning around each other. (**See drawing 5:** Based on Brook Bond Canadian card set "The Space Age" (set 12) card 44)

You now have all the clues.

Drawing 5

DID YOU PIECE THE CLUES TOGETHER?

This explains where the water went. Have you figured it out? At one time the Earth was close enough to another planet to exchange matter with it. But what planet? And how could we have gotten close enough to exchange matter with another planet. The nearest planet right now is 33 million miles away once every 16 years! We would not have been close enough to another planet long enough to exchange matter and certainly not enough matter to make a difference, and then certainly not in the amount of time allotted. The total length of time from the start of the flood to the earth finally being dry was one year and ten days or 370 days or less. (Shorter than a year)Though the water would have continued to subside for years. When the gods came down the records indicated there was still much flooding evident.

Consider this. What do you think is going to happen to the earth and other planets when they are hit by asteroids of this nature? The planets that get hit are going to stray from their normal orbit. Maybe permanently. Look at the orbit of Mars. It orbit is not circular, it is highly elliptical. Tiny little Pluto's orbit is so elliptical that it's actually brought inside the orbit of Neptune! Also when one looks into ancient history we find that Mars at one time came a lot closer to earth then it does now. Also Venus is shown as a crescent in ancient drawings suggesting it too came extremely close to earth. True if man was so advanced in the past they would have had telescopes and could have drawn Venus this way to differentiate it, but it would seem that by the time these drawings were made man had already become devolved and technology was lost. Either way, something is up.

Consider this. The moon orbits earth yet it only affects the tide, it doesn't actually take the water away and it is only 240,000 miles away. The water on the earth actually lifts toward the moon every time the moon passes over above. There is actually a hill of water when the moon passes over. But for the water to have actually escaped earth a planet must have come inside the orbit of the moon to do this! It appears Mars in recorded history was so close to the earth that it was rival in size in the heavens to that of the moon and bigger! And since Mars' size and thus gravity is considerably larger than that of the moon it's affect on the water of earth would have been a whole lot more than a high tide! (The Moon's diameter 2160 miles Mars' 4200 miles) This no doubt would have affected the moon's orbit as well, as if the asteroids hitting the moon weren't enough. Have you ever seen pictures of the far side of the moon? There is a crater dead center that is just gigantic!

But even if Venus wasn't close enough to earth, and it might have been, Mars definitely was MUCH closer to earth at intervals. (Velikovsky, citing many legends, determined that Venus [diameter 7700 miles] orbited the earth for a while and it's possible the atmosphere of Venus is made up of some of our water in vaporized form, as Venus' larger mass would make capturing some of our water an even easier task then that of Mars doing it.) Today Mars gets pretty close to earth roughly every two years and comes at it's closest to Earth about every 16 years. In ancient times this closeness far exceeded the proximity we get today. Mars got close enough to see it's disc with the naked eye! That's CLOSE indeed! But still not close enough to exchange matter. Post flood legends actually talk about Mars interacting with the earth, but we'll get to that later because by then the water was already gone, as these histories are all post flood, but at one time Mars WAS close enough to get some of our water. It's even possible Mars and Earth rotated around each other briefly, then the two planets catapulted themselves back into their respective orbits, likely with the "aid" of more asteroids. This would have even brought the moon into play, and this also might explain how the moon changed its orbit too.

This is the answer to where the extra water went...to Mars! It's also possible that after the flood during the time of Exodus that we were close enough to Venus that Venus later on took some more water increasing the water content of it's atmosphere. I know, this all sounds like complete baloney and originally I only thought this could be a possibility, as it did seem a bit farfetched. Then I saw something that said YES that's where it went.

Have you been keeping tabs on the news from NASA and the Jet Propulsion Laboratory? They now have pictures that are undeniable evidences of a LOT of water at one time being on the surface of Mars and they can't figure out where it came from. Some of these pictures show raging rivers at one time existed on Mars. Why would that water disappear if it was there to begin with? Here we have two mysteries that clear each other up. Where did the water on the earth go and where did the water on Mars come from? These questions answer each other.

Though they realize the water all sub-ducted under the Martian surface, they can't figure out where it came from. How could they? It wasn't there to begin with. They never banked on it coming from earth. Initially Mars would have been as barren a planet as say Mercury. No Atmosphere, no ice caps and no water. But obviously with the asteroids hitting our moon, the planets and earth, they were also hitting Mars, and they would have been pretty big to have caused Olympius Mons, the largest volcano in the solar system to come into existence. These asteroids and meteors threw the entire planet Mars into an elliptical orbit, originally much more elliptical then it is now.

One might ask why aren't there many really big huge craters on Mars if it was getting hit worse than the moon? Simple! Because the water from earth eroded the majority of the craters away.

Mars, originally a bare planet, immediately following the flood had to be close enough to the earth for a while to actually achieve matter transference. Mars could not give earth any of it's matter except for maybe the odd loose rock and some dust. On earth there is a layer of red dust! Martian? Mars didn't just steal our water it also took some of our atmosphere, in fact all the atmosphere now on Mars probably came from earth. That's why Mars even has an atmosphere in the first place! If Mars is going to be close enough to take our water it's definitely going to take some of our atmosphere, and if it was barren in the first place it wouldn't be giving any back, meaning there is less atmosphere on earth then there was before the flood. There are tales and legends of Martian meteorites landing on Earth. And actual Martian rocks have been found on earth. How did they get here!!!? One would normally think like I did when I heard these stories 'oh come on! How is Mars going to send a meteor off into space and have it land here? This theory clears that problem up! Had Mars continued to orbit with earth a whole lot longer Mars very likely would have been equally as inhabitable as Earth! In fact I'll make a deduction based on this theory.

LIFE ON MARS?

The thought of life being on other planets has been itching peoples scalps for some time. Though numerous Mars probes have been to Mars (where else would they go...except maybe Gilligan's Island) and so far they have turned up empty as far as life is concerned. I would bet that if they went to enough locations and dug down, not only would they find our water, they would find some of our water creatures in whatever form they may be. There would be plankton to be sure, probably Diatoms, possible some seaweed and maybe even the odd fish that got captured in the spout leaving earth. I don't know what the limitations might be as to the size of creature captured by Mars as it orbited Earth might be, but if we can get a rock from Mars, it can get a sizable fish from here. There could even be some pretty fair sized fossils on Mars. Especially if this thing about Martian asteroids hitting earth is correct. Boy won't that be a shock one day to have a Mars probe land and the camera bay open and the first thing it sees is a mummified porpoise right in front of the camera lense! No doubt the people of NASA and the JP. Laboratory would think they landed on earth somewhere by mistake!

Some might say the flaw in this theory is that the chemical composition of the atmosphere on Mars is different from that of earth. That doesn't bother me in the slightest. Actually the atmosphere on Mars is quite similar to earths in many ways. But we don't know the exact chemical composition of the earth's atmosphere as it was before the flood. Remember people were living 900 years! What could allow that? There may have been a whole bunch of one molecule high in our atmosphere that is almost completely vacant now as maybe Mars took most of that. Or what about the composition of Mars' surface? That may have reacted with the water causing an abundance of vapors and gasses not native to earth. I think with enough exploration of Mars we will find dead signs of "life" and it will be identical to what we have here, because it came from here! There may even be Earthen based airborne bacteria on Mars...maybe even the odd human skeletons that were floating on earth and got sucked up to Mars with their little rafts.

AM I LAZY, TOO CONSIDERATE, OR ASSUME YOU'VE READ MY SOURCES?

While rereading this for improvements for the 3rd edition, I realized this last bit didn't really present the evidence for Mars taking our water very well. You might be thinking this guy's dreaming! I didn't really site all the evidence, as I sometimes tend to think readers, familiar with this sort of material are familiar with the sources. And I tend to not want to put people through unnecessary repetition. But in submitting an article with this theory I felt I better do a cracking job and dig the evidence all out. I'm not sure what this says about the rest of the book, but here's the evidence, plus some cool new stuff I stumbled on in the last few years. I think this will be much more convincing.

A VENUSIAN FACELIFT.

(3rd ed. Insert 2016) It's nice finding more exact details. The Greek King Ogyges (thought to have ruled around 1767 BC) referred to in a later Roman historian's document (Varro 116-27BC) stated that the planet Venus changed her size, colour, figure(?) and course, something that hadn't happened up to and since that time. Now maybe Venus didn't come close enough to earth at that time to steal water or maybe it did, but clearly some big events happened in our solar system recently enough to be recorded when it did.

This event whether linked directly to events here on earth, or not we simply have to deduce that they happened; and that any such recorded solar system event would have been catastrophic here, either at the same time or in a closely linked one. The cause that altered Venus, was likely only possible in one way, that being an interaction between planets, which would be sufficient to create such a change.

Velikovsky deduced that Venus was a new planet coming out of Jupiter around 1500 BC and the cause of all the upheavals on the earth at the time of the Exodus also around 1500 BC. But there is evidence that proves he was wrong in this idea of Venus being a new planet, at least at that date. There is a diagram of the zodiac and the positions of the planets on a mummy case that is in the British museum indicating the time of the death of the occupant which was deciphered to be the autumnal equinox of 1722 B.C. They got a professor Mitchell and assistants to determine the position of the planets on that equinox of 1722 B.C. and the position of the planets the scientist came up with was exactly the same as those on the coffin, confirming their work of deduction. (Atlantis: Donnelly page 364-365) If Venus wasn't in the diagram it would have been noted, nor could it have been plotted correctly. This in fact could push back the date for the Exodus over 250 years if Velikovsky is right in linking Venus' close proximity to earth with the Exodus; though the effect in the camp of the Israelites I think he deduced incorrectly, as Velikovsky thought Venus' interaction might have been the pillar of fire and cloud in the camp.

So the supposed date of 1767 B.C. for king Ogyges reign (before the 1722 of the coffin) might be closer to the correct date of the change noted on Venus, as its most likely the Venus depicted on the coffin indicates its state after to this change.(I wrote this bit after submitting the article below.)

Consider this article I wrote for Atlantis Rising (which will appear sometime after #118) and some of my thoughts after submitting the article. This is as I sent it, though some editing might have occurred, and indeed good old Cornelius did some editing which I've decided to not incur to leave it as submitted. I tentatively call it…

MARS VISITING WITH THE NEIGHBORS

(3rd ed. Insert 2016) While researching ancient history to prove man was more advanced than we are today, I stumbled upon some very interesting material regarding the planets. Venus, Mars and a third planet had tremendous impact in Earth's early history. I realized that some people got Venus and this third planet mixed up and interchanged them. For example Immanuel Velikovsky deduced from ancient texts that Venus was a new planet which came from Jupiter and suggested it might be the origin of the Jupiter's red spot, and dated this incident to around 1500 BC. He claimed that Venus, a new planet, interacted with Earth and Mars causing upheavals on Earth. Based on this he came up with some deductions about Venus's temperature and atmosphere that proved remarkably accurate, making it difficult to discount his other deductions for Venus. (see Worlds In Collision)

But there is evidence that proves he was wrong about Venus being a new planet. There is a diagram of the zodiac and the positions of the planets on a mummy case that is in the British museum indicating the time of the death of the occupant. The planet positions of the diagram were worked backwards to determine these positions indicated the autumnal equinox of 1722 B.C. They got a professor Mitchell and assistants to determine the position of the planets on that equinox of 1722 B.C. and the position of the planets the scientist came up with was exactly the same as those on the coffin. (Atlantis: Donnelly page 364-365) If Venus wasn't in the diagram it would have been noted as its absence would have stuck out like a sore thumb, meaning Venus was obviously in existence in 1722 BC, thus disproving Velikovsky's new Venus theory. Furthermore, Bode's laws which show planetary orbits follow natural predictable distances from the sun would clinch it. This however doesn't disprove that Venus came close to the earth as Velikovsky maintained; it just suggests he mixed up Venus with another planet, but that's another story.

I say that to say this, even the best of the alternate archaeologists are fallible and a little work can ferret out some new insights: I found something else very key that Velikovsky missed.

In Velikovsky's work I discovered that Mars had a very important impact on Earth that no one else clued into, even though Velikovsky walked all around and missed the significance of his clues; partly because of the dates he attributed to the events he described thus he missed the connection to the correct period, and partly because he didn't deduce it.

The first thing that got me scratching my head and looking for Mars clues particularly was the discovery of fragments of the moon and Mars found in Antarctica in 1983. I could not believe this and doubted the deduction...I mean how the heck is a piece of Mars, let alone the moon, going to find its way to earth? This seemed to me like it had to be a misidentification of these rock samples. Zecharia Sitchen in the War of Gods and Men (Pg 110) noted this find and suggested a collision between Tiamat and one of Nibiru's Moons would explain it. I don't think so...neither of these is Mars and if an asteroid from one of these places smashed into Mars it's not going to eject bits of Mars out of its gravitational field, unless it was big enough to virtually destroy Mars, and no such impact seen on Mars could fit this theory. Another theory is that Mars' volcano Olympus Mons, the largest in the solar system, ejected stuff out of Mars which eventually made its way to earth. First, it's unlikely that a planet could eject anything out of its own gravity's influence, and even if it did it wouldn't escape Mars' orbit but would circle the sun until eventually Mars caught up with the debris and it came hurtling back down to Mars. Martian debris in space would be like earth's orbit where our atmosphere is slowly escaping into space leaving a vapor trail all along earth's orbit. It's not going to escape the Martian orbital plane.

So if that bit of rock found in Antarctica really was from Mars, something more significant had to have taken place to bring a Mars rock to earth. As it turns out history records actually show how that rock got there!

Velikovsky deduced through ancient myths that Mars' orbit was at one time so elliptical, it brought Mars close to Earth every 15 years, so close in fact that it interacted with the Earth. The reason it was every 15 years was because this is the duration it takes for Mars and Earth to be at the point in their orbits where they are closest to each other. (The origin as to how Mars got this highly elliptical orbit is another story)

Babylon called Mars the unpredictable planet, which makes the heavens dark and "moves the Earth off its hinges" (World's in Collision). The Babylonians even mentioned that Mars caused fissures in the ground, meaning Mars was close enough to cause serious earthquakes. But how close might this have been?

Greek Legends give a good clue. They refer to Ares (Mars) "flaming" and "blazing steeds", referring to Mar's two Moons Deimos and Phobos. (Ibid) But these two moons going around Mars when seen in space don't look fiery, do they? Unless they are close enough to the earth to interact with the Earth's and Mars' atmosphere, then they would indeed be fiery! But Phobos (22.2 Km/13.8 miles) and Deimos (12.6 Km/ 7.8 miles) are really small! And to be able to see them with the naked eye at all means Mars had to be real close, indeed well inside the orbit of the moon! Chinese legends take it a step further. "the five planets went out of their courses. In the night, stars fell like rain. The earth shook." (Ibid pg 260) This 'stars falling at night' is deduced as dust from Mars, and indeed Velikovsky deduced that Martian dust fell worldwide and was the cause of the Egyptian plague of the river of Blood. But I managed to show in my book this blood of the plague of Egypt, was in fact real blood, showing the cause, meaning placing this Martian dust blizzard during the Exodus was incorrect and allows me to move this event to a different time frame.

The Indo-Iranian Bundahis says "The planets ran against the sky and created confusion in the entire cosmos." (Ibid) The imagination reels thinking of Mars running against our sky and what that might mean. (The text also suggests Venus did so as well but our focus here is primarily on Mars)

Velikovsky comes closer still to this missed detail when he notes the Martian atmosphere changes shape, looking like a sword in the sky according to the Babylonians, and looking like a wolf or jackal to the Egyptians, Chinese, Romans and others. (Ibid pg 269)

Velikovsky now closes in and states that Maruts (Vedic name for Mars) was sung about: "be far from us, and far the stones which you hurl." Thus he deduced that Mar's proximity to the Earth enabled Martian rocks to be hurled at the earth, and it stands to reason because Earth's gravity is stronger than Mars' it can pull loose debris from Mars and pull it down to earth. So this explains how a Martian rock could get to Antarctica. Velikovsky notes some of these stones were subsequently grabbed by Earth's inhabitants and worshipped. And indeed some of these Mars rocks remain in some tribal hands today. A Chinese legend, Abel-Re'musat, quoted by Velikovsky, states "The planet Mars being in the neighborhood of Antares, a star fell at Toung-Kiun, and arriving to the ground, it changed to a stone." More Martian stones are said to have fallen in Greece, Mecca, or, like the dust of Mars, worldwide.

Velikovsky comes closer still quoting a prayer to Mars: I quote one key line "Who can run away from thy storming". Another place referring to Pliny's Natural History, says "a bolt from Mars fell on Bolsena", burning the entire town. Thus we have enough clues to figure out what Velikovsky completely missed! Have you figured it out?

If Mars and Earth were close enough not only to see the 'steeds of Mars' but close enough that when Mars interacted with earth's atmosphere making Phobos and Deimos appear like flaming steeds, and if Mars was close enough to the earth to throw stones at us, don't you think that maybe Mars took something from us?

Now I will add one more clue that gives away the game. In Genesis 8:1 after the flood of Noah, a wind blows which apparently takes away the water. A wind blows away the water? WHAT?! Well this seems completely useless as an excuse to get rid of enough of Earth's water to subside the flood waters, which are at the time 15 cubits above the highest mountain. If we interpret it as an evaporating wind it just doesn't work! There's not enough water vapour in the world's atmosphere to make a single foot of water, let alone evaporate 15 cubits just to see any ground. The theory that the water subsided underground is insufficient to get rid of enough water, so the biblical flood is thought to be impossible, at least as stated in record because of this. But saying a wind took the water is a vast understatement, and no one has realized this wind wasn't of an earthly origin; it had to be Mars. I maintain that at the time of the flood, Mars had already been thrown into a highly elliptical orbit which brought it close to the earth after the flood and it took the lion's share of the water from the earth. Though Velikovsky puts the proximity of Mars to the Earth during the Exodus, I place it closer to the time of the flood, though it could have been coming close to the earth for a long time, as indeed he notes Mars was a problem every 15 years. Needless to say, Mars also took some of our atmosphere, meaning Martian atmosphere, though thin, will be breathable.

Velikovsky had the key ingredient that would indicate Mars (and possibly Venus) were taking earth's water when he referred to Typhon being the 'pillar of fire' at night and the 'pillar of cloud' during the day in the camp of the Israelites. Typhon is in many legends and is said to be a giant that hissed and coiled whose head was of a hundred snakes which reached to the stars. Velikovsky translated this as an electrical discharge between the planets which was smack dab in the middle of the camp of the Israelites. But the description of Typhon is in reality a pillar of cyclonic water and air escaping the earth and going to Mars (and Venus?) with accompanying electrical discharges freaking out the inhabitants of the earth and indeed becoming the stuff of legends. Quite frankly if this is what was in the midst of the camp of the Israelites, it would have probably killed them all and sucked half of them up to Mars. The durability and widespread mythology of Typhon, and the periodic intrusion of Mars into Earth's close proximity suggests that Mars came to Earth, not only after the flood to take away our excess water, but continued to come periodically after that to do the same thing at different times and become an enduring legend. Typhon is of course the origin to the name of typhoon for earthly storms which we in the western world call hurricanes.

In my book I had already published that Mars would have had our water and air back in 2007, but I also stated that there might be fossils on Mars of earthly origin. Who knows what this typhoon pillar of water going to Mars and possibly Venus might be able to take with it! Every time I saw articles showing Mars had water it was just confirmation of my work. For example A.R #111 pg 20 stated that scientist now feel Mars had an ocean on it at one time the size of the Earth's Arctic Ocean.

What I thought really cool was something mentioned in #114 page 21, There is what appears to be a large crablike creature that has been spotted on Mars…most likely fossilized. And if Ancrew Basiagio's story of being teleported to Mars and breathing its atmosphere is true, (See Atlantis Rising #82) Mars may be far more inhabitable than anyone would have ever believed, and my deductions would all be proven true.

(I added this paragraph in an email the next day and it is probably included at the end of the article) After submitting this article, while riding my bicycle to my Girlfriends place, I started thinking. Though I'd proven Velikovsky wrong in his assessment of Venus being a new planet, he was so sure that Venus was new and he submitted all sorts of evidence to support his deduction (though I couldn't think of anything specific), that maybe there was something about Venus that had changed at this point in time. Maybe Venus wasn't new, but perhaps something about Venus *was* new. Consider. What if prior to 1500 B.C. Venus was just a hot dirtball in the sky closer in appearance to Mercury. It wouldn't shine very brightly, it would just have a low albido, like a dull star, something few people would take notice of, and just be another one of the 'wanderers'. Now assuming he is correct that Venus came close enough to earth to cause "Typhon" (take water from us like Mars did,) what would happen when the water went to Venus? With Venus being around 800 Degrees, the water would evaporate and turn to eternal steam creating the cloud cover we now see on Venus. That white steam would ramp up the albido of Venus 10 fold or more! Suddenly Venus would be like is now…the brightest object in the night sky next to the moon! This would fit with Velikovsky's deductions that Venus was 'new' and indeed it would have been a marvel to all on the earth…and indeed SEEM like a new planet. Furthermore it would likely continue coming close to the earth occasionally until the orbits of the planets eventually normalized. Thus with Venus' new look and it still coming close to the earth in this period, the phases of Venus would have been very obvious to those on earth. I know someone who can see the phases of Venus with his naked eye, but with our orbits temporarily closer we could have seen them easily. It would have been a little like a periodic second moon, and with it coming closer to earth for a while (or earth getting closer to Venus) it may even have rivaled the brightness of the moon itself! Maybe Velikovsky was right after all!

Also reading backwards through the issues I have (of Atlantis Rising Magazine) for material to use for this 3rd edition I read # 72 after submitting this. It's regarding Mars and it's bombardment from what can only be the Asteroid belt. I had concluded that the planet which exploded had smashed into Mars pushing it into a highly elliptical orbit making it possible to interact with and take water from Earth. At the time of writing this, my knowledge of Mars was basically based on what I recalled from school days with maybe a 1970's planet book keeping me 'up to speed'. I hadn't actually known of specific asteroid blasts, I just assumed or predicted they would be there. And as you just read I deduced it would unlikely be an eruption from Olympus Mons that would spew any lava far enough away from Mars to get to earth. I quote the article I read in A.R. 72. By Stephen Robbins, Ph. D. "There is no question that Mars was obliterated by a veritable shotgun blast of large, high velocity bodies. Over 3000 gouged 30 kilometer minimum craters; there were myriad smaller hits. Olympus Mons…rises on the planets side opposite three of the largest impacts (630 km, 1000 km 2000 km). A 4500-mile rift, the Valles Marineris, runs four times deeper, six times wider than the Grand Canyon" (quoting Hancock, The Mars Mystery) He further notes that "The crust of the entire northern hemisphere, 3-4 kilometers in thickness was ripped off." He then asks "But when, and where?"

Well after reading this I had to start thinking. First this confirms that such a series of asteroid hits from the exploded planet on what has to be the solar systems orbital plane confirms Mars was indeed knocked into a highly elliptical orbit making it possible for Mars to get close to the earth. However it also shows that I could be wrong in my estimate of Olympus Mons being unable to shoot something far enough to leave Mars' orbit and reach earth. Kinetic energy from asteroids hitting, in many cases probably simultaneously on one side of the planet forcing the other side to make that huge volcano meant a onetime incident could have occurred. However I think this article shows that even if that was the case, Mars' proximity to earth is more than enough to explain the presence of Martian material here on earth. And besides, what are the odds a *onetime* blast from Mars would actually have lined up right so that the ejection from Olympus Mons actually made it to the earth? Chances are it just followed the orbital plane of the solar system and crashed right into the sun. One interesting thing about this missing bit of Mars northern hemisphere. This would suggest which part of Mars was closest to the earth and just how much of Mars is actually here on the earth! (Though I deduced that quite likely some of that missing shelf just came crashing back down to Mars in various places…but who can say for sure? Is there really that much of Mars, down here on Earth? This would make Martian rocks practically common place around here.)

However, consider a couple interesting tidbits here. There's a little something about the moon's limitations. Our moon, if it were any closer to the earth than 11,500 miles, it would disintegrate! Earth's gravity would pull it apart and turn it into something like the rings of Saturn or just cause a massive mooneor shower. Susan B. Martinez noted in Atlantis Rising #104, that at one time in our past meteors, dust and stones "assailed the earth" and "fell in such quantities that it can be compared to snowstorms, piling up on earth in places to a depth of many feet, and in drifts up to hundreds of feet" (I'll repeat her quotes in relation to something else later) Is there really that much of Mars down here!?

I thought a bit about when these events would have occurred. I don't think Mars would have been hit too long before the flood itself as the same event that caused asteroids to smash into Mars also caused the flood. If Mars was coming close to the earth before the flood, Mars' proximity likely would have destroyed the water sphere on earth if the asteroid hitting it hadn't, and it wouldn't have been timed right to take the water less than two years after the flood. Meaning Mars was likely hit less than 15 years before the flood.

One thing I was surprised to see in my first edition, was that I had deduced that Olympus Mons was the result of an asteroid hitting the planet from the other side, I did not know it, I guessed!

Another thing I found subsequent to this article was a letter written to Atlantis Rising in #69 by William B. Stoecker. He notes some very interesting tidbits about Mars. The First Lander images showed a pink sky and Nasa said this was from suspended dust particles. Sounds reasonable but with Mars supposed to have an atmosphere 1% the density compared to Earth's means a 1% atmosphere suspending this much dust is not possible. Another picture leaked showed the US flag on the lander with a blue sky in the background! Blue would indicate a much denser atmosphere than had been reported. A 1% atmosphere could not possibly support the dust or obscure mountains in the background. Some other pictures actually showed melt water with icebergs and water coloured in graduating shades from light to dark blue, showing shallow and deep water, yet water cannot exist in a 1% atmosphere at sea level pressure as it would boil as fast as it melted. (Realizing this I had to think back on our earth's pre-flood water sphere talked about in chapter 2, and this creates a possible problem with the water sphere idea. Perhaps the outer surface of the water sphere would evaporate but create an outer atmosphere vapor shell? Not enough to obscure the sun moon and stars, but just veil them a little) This issue of A.R. came out just after I published my book (indeed it has the very first ad for my book.) So my book came out and immediately some of my predictions proved to be correct.

Afterward I read Atlantis Rising #68 (This is the first copy of Atlantis Rising I ever got but it seems I never read it. It was apparently sent to me after buying ad space in the following issue. Once I'd published my book it seemed pointless to do more research, I had other kettles of fish to fry and let the mags pile up) I found a very cool article in #68 and wrote the following.

TECH STUFF ON MARS?

(3rd ed. Insert 2016) Apparently there is some cover-up going on about stuff seen on Mars through lenses of Mars landers. It has been said that NASA is hiding things they've found on Mars (and apparently on the moon). Though NASA is thought to be "Civilian space research", they are in reality to be considered a defense agency, and not a civilian one. This means they can hide stuff in the name of national security, which apparently they have been doing in spades. Not only are they hiding some finds, "outright lying is permitted to protect the secrets" they know. NASA told former NASA contractor Ken Johnston in charge of Apollo photos during the Apollo program to destroy copies of official astronaut photographs taken on the moon. That's pretty odd, what could be in those photos they had to hide? Johnston was fired which boiled down to him saving some of the copies which were displayed at a press conference showing anomalies and artificial structures on the moon. Richard Hoagland (Who wrote "Dark Mission" with Mike Bara) and other investigators say that some of the NASA moon photos have been airbrushed and some paste in bits were done in some photos. This assertion has been confirmed by Russians who say some black strips have been overlaid in some shots to hide something in a 1960's shot, as well as the use of some airbrushing. Hoagland and Bara say some images of Mars have been altered similar to stretching, flattening, and turning to become unrecognizable. The pair state that remains of gigantic lunar domes and underground structures exist on the moon. Deep penetrating sonar has been used on the moon, but the results were never made public. Hoagland believes, not only 88 pounds of moon rock samples were brought back from the moon, but there were artifacts too.

But Mars is a whole 'nother kettle of fish! Ruins of cities bigger than Los Angeles are supposed to be on Mars. Landing sites where the …Mars landers…landed …on Mars…were so littered with artificial debris that NASA had to censor shots of things less than a yard from Pathfinder. Hoagland says an "…incredibly advanced civilization was swept away by a solar system cataclysm which destroyed Mars as a Habitable planet". However a Moonwalker from Apollo 12, Edgar Mitchell, says Hoagland is a "Flake". Either way there's some strange goings on. Others have said many Mars photos appear stretched, airbrushed or altered in some way to hide details. Why hide detail unless there's something to hide other than a barren landscape? Seeing Martian images on the internet you can clearly see large areas of Mars do indeed have these smudged areas, like a palette knife has spread the colour sideways.

My theory that Mars took our water could indicate some debris from Earth was swept up with the water Mars took from the earth, but more likely Mars was colonized before the flood and the exploding planet laid Mars waste, with subsequent nearness to earth and taking water further ruining the landscape.

I found something in a book called Alternative 3, which was originally aired as a science report program, then later called a hoax. But the author of Alternative 3, Leslie Watkins, insists the material in the book is true. In light of that, we can quote a little something from the book here. An unmanned lander lands on Mars and the techs exclaims "We're on Mars and we have air" However the secret but apparently genuine NASA video of this landing as aired in the TV program have technicians which say "Temperature 4c, Wind speed 21 K… Atmosphere 707.7 millibars, (on earth the pressure is 1013 millibars at sea level) then after landing "boy if they ever take the wraps of this thing, it'll be the biggest date in history… May 22 1962 … we're on the planet Mars and we have life!" and you see via the camera something crawling in the dirt.)

Alternative 3 suggests scientists and technologists that have been disappearing has a common thread (very bright technologically minded people) and a brain drain from earth's nations exists and the people missing have possibly been saved and sent off the planet in hopes of saving some of mankind from what was in the 1950's deduced to be the complete destruction of life on earth in the not too distant future. Both Mars and the moon appear to be possible final destinations for this 'brain drain'.

BATTLE OF THE BULGE

(3rd ed. Insert 2016) As we know Mars doesn't really have any moons, except a couple tiny things (Deimos and Phobos) whipping around it faster than the Martian day. These would not cause any crustal shift, displacement or bulge to the planet. But Richard Hoagland suggests that the Tharis and Arabia mantle uplifts of Mars are evidence of planetary bulges inflicted on Mars by an unknown planet designated "Planet V" (Atlantis Rising #35). I don't quite get his theory; it sounds like Mars was captured by some planet invading the solar system. (I suspect he is mixing up a Planet V with one called Elysia (See Chapter 9) However this evidence could also be used to confirm that Mars *was* close enough to the earth for a while to cause the same effect.

HOW BIG WAS THAT DISEASED CANCEROUS CRAB?

(3rd ed. Insert 2016) As mentioned I felt the water from the flood went from earth to Mars, which means it's entirely likely some of our creatures went with the water. I fully expect there to be some remnant of Earth creatures on Mars. Recently what appears to be a large crablike creature has been spotted on Mars… most likely fossilized. (Pic also seen in Atlantis Rising Mag # 114 Pg 21)

What makes this crab so interesting is a legend that started the crab as part of the Zodiac. A Giant strong crab named Crios guarded sea nymphs. A Monster named Typhon battled Crios who got a squid named Vamari to guard the nymphs (who instead ate them) while Crios battled Typhon. The crab won the battle and Poseiden placed him in the sky. (Atlantis Rising Mag #110 pg 49) Many legends are symbolic. Did Typhon take the crab into the sky…and land it on Mars? Could this crab spotted on Mars be this very crab now part of the constellations and be a completely unexpected confirmation of our deductions?

Some have warned that if there is life on Mars, going to Mars to find it could be incredibly stupid as they might bring home viruses we have no possible defense against here on earth. But I deduce that if there is some sort of life on Mars, that it came from Earth to begin with and won't be as dangerous as all that, though possibly, if it's like the H1N1 influenza virus that wiped out so many after WW1 it could be something of a problem if brought back to earth, but it won't be unbeatable.

MARS: MORE VINDICATION.

In an article attempting to justify panspermia with evidence of biological stuff in comets and stuff falling to earth like blood and frogs, the article notes some things found on Mars. It notes that the surface of Mars has lots of Iron Oxide. I had always wondered if this might be evidence of a large planet wide reaction to water. Well I might be close. It's noted there had to be a lot of free oxygen, possibly from photosynthesis, but I think water might do it too. Well as I've stated the oxygen came from earth to begin with, but the article also shows a picture of Mars surface finally released to the public in 2001 showing what appear to be plants…maybe swamp things. Another fossil appears to have been found too. Something resembling a Crinoids or sea Lillies has been spotted on Mars. (Atlantis Rising 117)

Back to Earth….

One apparent contradiction I find in some of this research is water volumes in relation to land masses visible above water. This contradiction may be a clue to forces in the earth structure and the dynamics of the earth physiology.

Ancient maps show more land above water and at the same time they show Greenland and Antarctica free of ice. The ice on these two land masses alone is said to be enough to raise the water level of the entire earth as much as 300 feet, thus enough to submerge many islands, and inundate many coastal cities, yet there appears to have been more land above water when Greenland and Antarctica were free of ice. Did the land sink and not the reverse? (sub-duction) **Has some event caused incredible erosion?** When one digs further one sees that it would appear at one time the entire continental shelves were at one time above water. There is evidence of beach sand and riverbeds continuing to the edges of continental shelves. The Hudson's canyon extends nearly 200 miles to the edge of the continental shelf a full one and a half miles below sea level. Saint Lawrence river also continues underwater for hundreds of miles to the shelf! Clearly there is evidence of a huge amount of water still on the earth that wasn't here at one time. This very fact alone proves there was a flood. Since the shelves are now 5-600 feet below sea level I have to think this is the single biggest bit of evidence that shows we had a flood as told in ancient legends. But there also seems to be evidence that the earth's crust heaves upward sub-ducting water beneath the continents, and / or the continents sink squishing water into the oceans, making the ice on Greenland and Antarctica merely factors and not key ingredients in the extent of the amount of water on the earth's sea level. *I suppose even the silt in the ocean bottoms could be factored in.* This silt amounts to thousands of feet on the ocean floor...which was all at one time above the sea on land. When we realize all this silt is flood period and later, that is a mere 5400 years of erosion creating all that silt, it makes one curious as to what it all means and how it contributes to the whole picture.

With the proximity of Mars to Earth for this short period of time a 'great wind' around the entire globe would have been occurring, sucking through gravity and this transference of our atmosphere and water in a vortex off to Mars. This has to be the great wind spoken of in Genesis after the flood. It must have been quite the sight every two years after the flood seeing Mars SO close to earth! And every 16 years being close enough to cause fear, as so many ancient documents assert.

So when did the flood happen? If it happened can we date it? Obviously it happened in historical times, but when? Civilized mankind appears to date back about 5500 years, yet mountains appear to date in the millions of years, and some say mankind dates back in primitive form for a few million years. But these guesses are based on evolution being true. But if evolution is not true, are the dates correct then? How old is the earth? Is it 4.5 billion years old or is it 10,000 years or less as the creationists seem to think it is. Some of the dates arrived at are because evidence is interpreted one way, but other interpretations of the evidence are equally or even more valid and these bring much younger dates.

Chapter 5 Part One

HOW OLD IS THE EARTH

There are three mainstream theories or schools of thought that have to be overturned in order for the theories presented in this book to gain credibility. The first two are the theory of evolution and the idea that man has been ascending from a primitive monkey and cave man. Basically those are really the same theory but in showing man today came from a superior specimen rather than a primitive one is virtually a new school of thought in itself. The third theory that needs to be overturned, is the established belief that the earth is far older than it really is. Believing this throws much of the physical evidence into confusion. Once we show that the earth is in fact very young, what was previously confusing will suddenly be looked upon in a new light and the confusion will disappear. In this chapter not only are we going to show and prove a very young earth, we are going to see *exactly* how old it is…no guesses, or estimates. Well there are some variables but these will be shown. Cosmology dates based on red shift interpretations have been dealt with in chapter one.

Actually after I finished this chapter and indeed the entire book I found something of a real stupid mistake in this section. Have you ever worked on something for ages…in this case about 25+ years and then found a real stupid mistake that sort of makes the whole work seem almost pointless. Well it isn't quite that bad but it does change things here. I wasn't quite sure how to correct this as it could mean some considerable reworking. So instead of reworking everything and possibly making another mistake in my haste to get it done, I thought I'd leave the mistake in here and show you what it is at the end because in the final analysis it doesn't change things all that much and really is only a variable. Indeed if one assumption is incorrect it doesn't change the final outcome at all! The most it changes it is 3 X 30 years. That's a clue. So if you are one prone to plotting these things and you find the mistake don't throw your arms up in disgust, but give yourself a brownie point for spotting it. That doesn't mean there aren't more mistakes in here and this is why I'm showing as many variables as I myself can spot.

This is the sort of chapter one writes when one takes the bible literally and then sets out to prove it. After each proof read I kept adding to this chapter and finding more stuff that was important to include. This chapter became something like a bucking bronco. Just when I thought I had it nailed I got bucked off and had to wrestle with this some more. And after all is said and done the very asteroid belt may end up bucking us all off again.

At least one person has said that I use the bible to prove the age of the earth. Not so. Principally in this chapter I'm trying to show or prove how old the bible says the earth is: big difference. We'll see eventually that other ancient legends, calendars and documents suggest similar ages for the earth, or at least civilization. The second half of this chapter will look at the dating methods to see if these ages are in any way verifiable.

MY CURIOSITY PIQUED

When I was a kid and realized Dad believed in God, soon after meeting him again, I borrowed a bible from him and started to read. The first thing I noticed as I opened the bible he lent me was that down the center of the page there was a strip of notes. I have since discovered this is an unusual type of bible. At the top of this center strip there was a date assigned to the 1st page of 4004 BC. This was the assigned age of the earth when creation took place. As I read I saw the date change at the top of the page. I thought this was fascinating to watch change.

Just like some kid trying to figure out where he came from I wanted to know how old the earth was. Naturally I wanted to somehow know if these dates were provable and if I could come up with the same date for the age of the earth myself. Not quite ready to accept that age shown in that column unless I could see for myself that it was correct. From that point onward I always wanted to know "exactly how old the earth is, and see if I could come up with an age, based on the biblical record. I felt this might be within my grasp to figure out. As we'll see, one of the variables actually came up with a date very close to this one.

As a kid I didn't do much research, but I kept my ears open to what science and other sources say is the age of the earth. The dates vary considerably...as you know. Regardless of what accepted sciences were saying about the age of the universe I wanted to see what exactly the bible stated was the age of the earth, so eventually I started plotting dates on a timeline. We may not be able to do much with the pre flood era as far as proving the dating is concerned but if we can find something that even fixes and proves the date of the flood we can then presume the dates for before the flood are in all likelihood correct because the pre-flood part of the timeline is complete. I felt that once the biblical age of the earth was established in my mind and on paper I could then go to science and see if the date I came up with could be confirmed using known dating methods. I know dating methods show a wide range of dates for the age of things so I wanted to see if any of them corroborated the date the bible might come up with and see if there was anything wrong with dating methods that didn't. Thank goodness other people have done some of this sort of research because that really would have been something of a hard task to do all by myself. It was mostly a matter of finding it assembling it, understanding it and hopefully explaining it.

LENGTH OF TIME FOR CREATION

The timeline is complete up to the flood so we "know" that the earth was only around a mere 1656 years before the flood. How long it took God to create the universe, has been debated for some time, and probably doesn't matter much, but for the sake of argument I state my opinion here. I have noticed over the years that some people tend to lean on long creation periods as a crutch to withstand the onslaught of popular opinion believing that the earth is really old. I myself at one point fell into this trap. It's easy to buffer this old earth belief if we allow thousands, or even millions of years for creation to have taken place.

Some have suggested creation took 6000 years to complete because they say with God 1000 years is as a day (or visa-verse). So they suggest the creation day was a period of 1000 years. In a way this makes some kind of sense because when Adam was told if he ate the fruit he would die in that day. Since Adam lived to 930 years some have taken this to mean he died the same day.

Remarkably some even use this period of creation or time frame to suggest when the fossils might have formed. Unfortunately even if this were the case we see that the animals were created the same day as Adam so there's no way dinosaur fossils could possibly be made in the creation process. We will see that it was actions that took place after the creation of man and even after the flood that caused fossils and mountains and other evidence to come into being. The fossils and the mountains (as we know them today) and the continents were *not* part of the original creation.

THE FIRST "DAY"

Some say this first day of creation was an actual day, but others point out the fact that a day as we know it did not exist until the 3rd or 4th 'day' thus the first "day" is simply an undefined period of time. So to my way of thinking the trick was to figure out what this period of time might be.

When one looks at the definition of "day" in light of what was created the first "day" (light), that 'day' could in fact be an infinitesimally small period of time! (People seem to think creation must have taken a long time simply because there's so much of it. But there is no reason to think God could not do it in an instant. If God can change us in a "twinkling of an eye" why not all of creation...remember he's God. Who really knows the limits of his power?) God on the first day created "Light" yet we see no actual source of light being created, but only that light is created. So what is light?

In physics light could even be "energy" or "matter" as $E=MC^2$. Thus mass, energy and light can all be singled out in one part of the equation to equal the other parts of that equation and shown to be aspects in relation to each other. So the equation of light can be written $C=\sqrt{E/M}$. In fact when one looks at matter or atoms, they are really just energy bits held together, by some binding force. When I was 11 someone once showed me Einstein's famous equation. Not knowing the significance, naturally I played with this equation and got $1=MC^2/_E$. The fellow asked me what '1' was. I thought a moment and said maybe it's that dark matter stuff. As simple as that might seem I still think it might be correct.

God's voice created light (Illumination) or by reading it in this "light", on the first day the atoms come into existence. God divided some dark or non-matter into electrons, protons and neutrons thus also creating mass and potential energy. So the universe's appearance on this first "day" must have been the definition of entropy at its maximum point of breakdown...just a universal greyish fuzz, maybe something like the sky on a uniformly dark grey overcast day.

I personally think the time referred to for a "day"...[a time period that existed before the sun and earth were created] was something indicative of what was created on the first 'day'. Atoms are termed the "building blocks of the universe", so it's not illogical to suppose that this is what was made on the first day. Or put another way, the item created on the first day [light] is the instrument by which the length of the day was calculated.

WHAT IS A "DAY"?

At this point there were no stars or planets or flashlights to make or reflect light. Therefore the definition of the time span called the first "day", must be something intrinsic to the characteristics of light, energy or atoms, if we conclude that it *was* atoms that were created the first day. So we look to the atom to find what might be a way of measuring time. Thus it would seem when looking at the atom as we know it, and the parts that make up the atom we find a natural time period that must then be defined as the "day" used as the creation 1st day. A 'day' would then become the time it takes for an atom's electron to circumnavigate the nucleus.

Before this 1st day "Darkness was upon the face of the deep" And God was upon the 'face of the waters' (In my mind this "darkness" appears to be this 'dark non-matter' that was all that existed, and this bit about waters seems to suggest a 'physical' property of dark matter, or collapsed matter, or more properly un-expanded matter). Interestingly we see that "darkness" still existed. On the second "day" God separates the light from the darkness (or matter from non-matter; something like Oil running from a grease fighter) This also fits the now known physical appearance of the universe. Not an expanding ball as the big bang theorizes but a series of clumped together "bubbles", like those of a bubble bath or like a loaf of bread, with large voids and then matter as we know it being the shells of the bubbles, and the contents or "air" of the bubbles being this unexpanded matter. Later the shells of the bubbles of matter conglomerates, solidifies or congeals into suns stars and what-not, but that's another story, for another day. Well that's how I see the time period for the day of creation period. Mind you with the nature of electrons still being not fully understood, this time period may be up for revision. And of course this is just my opinion based on my interpretation, but it would seem to me that the universe was then created in less than a millisecond.

THE DAY GETS SHORTER

Also consider another possibility. Since we know matter is in a state of collapsing, the time frame for this "day" changes over time. At creation atoms might have been as big as a solar system. But once entropy came into existence the electrons started to go into disintegrating orbits around the nucleuses. As the electrons move closer to the nucleus in their orbits their rate of orbiting the nucleus speeds up, similar to how Pluto goes slowly around the sun in 247.7 years but Mercury goes around the sun in 88 days. Perhaps when creation took place the electrons were the distance of Pluto from the nucleus and are now the distance of Mercury. But this is somewhat an interesting conjecture too.

PLOTTING

Back to the age of the earth. After the flood the timeline continues on up to Jacob and beyond that it would seem to break down and I stopped plotting, as there appeared no way to keep going. The time line appears to be incomplete until we get to Exodus 12:40,41 and then we see that it was 430 years from the coming into the land of Egypt to the time they left. So we use Jacobs's age to decipher exactly when they came into Egypt and again the timeline can be plotted a little further. Then it breaks down again as there appears to be no other points to plot beyond that. Then we get to 1st Kings 6:1 and we see that it is 480 years from the time the Israelites come out of Egypt to the time that Solomon starts building the temple so once again we have a point to plot. We can easily plot from that point and work back to Solomon and David's reign. But once again the timeline appears to break down sometime between Solomon's sons and the carrying away to Babylon or certainly between Babylon and Christ's Birth. So once again the timeline appears to be incomplete, because even using the kings of Israel we run out of points to plot. Though apparently the kings time line is complete up to the carrying away to Babylon, but in fact as we shall see, it may not be.

DEAD END?

With the realization that one apparently can't really seem to zero in on a specific date for the age of the earth, based on the biblical record I wondered how the date of 4004 BC was arrived at and I found it was some sort of guess with some sort of logic attached. As I understand it had something to do with astronomy but I have forgotten exactly how this date was arrived at, and since there are a few guestimations on the age of the earth based on the biblical record I may be confusing them with each other.

I have since found that there are four principle guesses as to the date of the earth based roughly on stuff in the bible and other scholars interpretations. Hales comes up with the time of creation at 5411 BC(A Dictionary of the Bible by Smith and Peloubet Published by John C. Winston 1884 ed. page 117), but for some inexplicable reason he uses the value of 627 years from the coming out of Egypt to the building of the temple. WHY? It states clearly in 1st Kings 6:1 that's this period of time is 480 years. Jackson says that creation took place 5426 BC and he too uses an incorrect time period, this time of 579 years for this coming out of the Israelites to Solomon's temple. Petavivs decides creation took place 3983 BC and he also uses the mysterious time period of 579 years from the Israelites leaving Egypt to the start of Solomon's temple. Though they all seem to rely somewhat on the bible to arrive at dates for the age of the earth in principal, Ussher appears to be the closest to the biblical narrative. The more accepted time of 4004 BC for the start of creation is that of Usshers and he uses 479 years for the period of between the exodus to the temple. Why does he use 479 years instead of the scriptural 480? Perhaps due to birthdays being out by a half year? However since the length of the year has changed over the millennia perhaps this is why the differing dates are used. True 479 is close to 480 but why not use 480? I haven't been able to find a copy of Ussher's book and I didn't even know he had one until recently, but it sounds that even though it was written 400 years ago it may actually be a pretty interesting read.

I've since found one more date for the flood which was worked out to 3446BC (Sept 7th) By a certain Dr. Seyffarth as referred to by Charles Berlitz in Atlantis: the Eighth Continent. In assuming his date is arrived at using the Bible I presume the same 1656 years for the pre-flood era and thus this date arrived at is quite close to the date I will arrive at as this would work out to 5102 BC for the date of Creation, thus his date will vary from mine by a mere 39 years. It would be interesting to see how this date, was arrived at. I know nothing about this doctor other than through this reference.

None of these dates arrived at seem to completely accept the bible at it's word, In fact a majority of Christians seem to NOT believe the bible to be the word of God. A survey around 1973 showed that about 64% of Christians back then did not completely believe the bible was the word of God. Small wonder there is less belief in the bible these days. If the Christians don't believe it, how are they going to convince others to believe it? It would seem "science" has eroded this belief. Actually I just heard that to an extent some of the early leaders of the church themselves started to doubt the biblical narrative causing the general population to become disenfranchised. So we may have ourselves to blame. Many people accept the existence of God but seem to pick and choose which biblical parts they accept. Bad trend.

I find it real weird and curious how people can come up with an exact time of a specific day for the time of Creation. I mean people pick exact dates and even the hour and minute. Heck, I'll be glad to get the year…that's plenty close enough for me. I mean how do you pick an exact minute anyway? Maybe I'm missing something.

We will eventually see the sciences when correctly interpreted can indeed verify the bible, so you might enjoy the ride, or the challenge.

Though all these figures for the age of the earth are relatively close to each other, within 1500 years, none match each other, and none appear to take the bible as 'gospel'. But obviously they all are very much at odds with the generally accepted age for the universe and the earth. Since I had no idea how to finagle and postulate some make believe age, it seemed to me for a long time that the date of the earth was indecipherable according to the scriptures.

Long have I realized about 8 or 9 of the old testament books are missing. Books like Jasher and Iddo, (not to be confused with the books in doubt included in other bible versions) I consequently assumed any missing pieces for the age of the earth might be in these missing books, and I gave up plotting.

EUREKA

I have also realized that some information in the New Testament alludes to things not found in the Old Testament and some information fills in gaps missing in the Old Testament. To my surprise I discovered with dating this is also the case.

One day I was reading in Matthew when something I read stopped me dead in my tracks! I had read over this part several times and missed it as I tend to keep reading even if I'm thinking about something I read previously, so sometimes it takes a while for my mind to catch up with my eyes. Actually with this part being something of a genealogy I sort of glazed over until I get to an interesting part, which is probably why it took me so long to finally see it. But one time there it WAS... the missing clue!

In Matthew 1:17 it says it was 14 generations from Abraham to David, and 14 generations from David to the carrying away of the Israelites to Babylon and another 14 generations from that point to the birth of Christ! Was this what I was looking for!? I assumed that 14 generations equals 14 generations equals the next 14 generations… (and believe me this is bucking the trend!). So I went to my now old and ragged plotted timeline and plotted from the point of Abraham's end to the beginning of David's rule. Interestingly we see that we do not know when David was born because there is no mention as to how old he was when he died. This is real strange! This is an exception to the rule indeed! So since we do not know when David was born do we automatically presume the timeline is incomplete? I had to presume that the point meant, must be the point when David started to rule, and this too makes sense because this is a very important point in history indeed! Important to the Israelites and indeed to all Christendom, as this is the official start of the lineage of the rule that would continue to the ruling of Christ, so I think it' safe to presume it is this point that is referred to when plotting the 14 generations, particularly in the light of the fact of the unusual exception that David's age is actually not recorded. So when plotting from Abraham to David, the time between these two points is 981 years. [By the way, you've just read that stupid mistake I was talking about earlier]

HOW LONG IS A GENERATION?

Since a conversation with my dad a long time ago I had always wondered how long a generation was supposed to be. So I naturally decided to divide 981 years by 14 to see just what a generation's time length was and got just over 70 years...70.07 to be exact, well to two decimal places anyway. But I thought this 981 years possibly a mistake as if you took off one year and made it 980 years (say due to birthdays being out by a half year), then a generation becomes exactly 70 years. But it turns out this may not be the right thing to do, as when it all works out I found I was further from an accurate date with 980 then when leaving it at 981. So to save time I will continue on with the time line of 981 years being 14 generations, odd as that number is.

Suddenly it dawned on me I had also discovered the biblical definition of a generation as I had heard many people debate this, questioning... 'exactly just how long WAS a generation?' as it is never actually specifically stated as to how long a generation is in the bible. I had heard 120, 70, and 40 years. My Dad said it was 70, but he said the length of a generation changed over time and at that time (in the 1970's) it was down to 40 years and the generation was getting shorter, to where he felt it would eventually drop to 30 and even down to 20 years. Well that aside, not only had I solved the length of a generation I was able to come up with a decipherable and provable (or disprovable) date for the age of the earth

Though because of some variables I suppose 980 might possibly be correct but I'm not going to go there as the time line to David is complete and using 980 means suggesting the entire timeline might be in error, so 981 years it is. Actually after finishing this book and on my 4th proof read I realized since David ruled 40 years and 6 months, if you added that ½ year in to the total it makes the line so incredibly accurate one wonders if it shouldn't be 981.5. You'll see why soon.

PLOTTING FINISHED

To that point on Abraham's time line from Creation is 2123 years. When we add 981 years we get to David, and 981 years again to get to Babylon and another 981 years to get to Christ's birth, we get the figure of Creation taking place at 5066 BC. We now have a complete and solid timeline right up to Christ. When we then add the current date 2007 we find that it's now is 7073 years for the age of the earth according to the bible, with the flood occurring at 3410 BC. If you know accepted biblical chronology you know David's supposedly ruled around 1000 BC, so if you're having a fit because of the lineage of the Kings from David to Babylon, I'll get to it. This is one of those variables.

WHEN WAS YEAR ZERO?

That was one of those questions I asked as a kid, and did they call it year zero and how did they know it was year zero...and what made them decide to call it zero.... I remember hearing about Leap year and asked what it was. I was told that every four years they added a day to February. So I asked when did February start and why did they make it and I couldn't wait until it was the longest month when it would have 32 days and I thought maybe when it reached 60 days long they would divide it again and there would be 13 months and maybe this was how February got started. I must have driven some people batty. (I still do, mainly because I'm some kinda nut.)

The date of Christ's birth is subject to debate and could vary by as much as 5 years. Some "scholars" seem to think the wise men were stupid enough to try and follow a star that was in fact Venus or Mars or Jupiter or some conjunction alignment of two or more of them. They assume these wise men were complete idiots and followed Mars and Jupiter and Venus in a rare triple conjunction to the birthplace of Christ. I mean think about it, how on earth are you supposed to follow planets to a point somewhere on earth? The theory of evolution seems to have made them think they are more advanced then these wise men of 2000 years ago. I have to admit that steams me. Maybe the date of Christ's birth is up for debate, but for whatever reason that that date might be wrong, it is NOT because some wise men were silly enough to think they could follow planets.

These 'scholars' thus suggest that Christ's birth is out because they trace back the circuits of these planets to a previous triple conjunction near but not at the supposed birth time of Christ. They thus assume the birth of Christ is wrong for this reason, because it would seem to these wise 'scholars' impossible for them to follow an actual star. Granted following a "star" as we know it, is obviously impossible. I mean the earth would burn up! "My! What is that incredibly hot furnace like object over our heads singeing our hair?" "I don't know, I think it's a star... lets follow it!" As to what star they followed we leave to the theorists. (I personally think it might have been a "chariot of fire" seen from afar, or an angel seen from a distance glowing as a star...as these theories have some scriptural basis..."Chariots of fire" are mentioned in the bible and there is a hint that angels and stars are somehow equated)

Since this date for Christ's birth was arrived at sometime early in the 4th century AD, it is entirely possible the date *is* incorrect. I just assumed by some stroke of luck the people who assigned the date for Christ's birth in the 4th century AD had something in their possession we don't have now and they got the date right first try and so I went with the current date as the right one. It turns out it is extremely close, possibly out by just two years! You'll see why shortly.

It's funny with me worrying about 479 years or 480, or Christ born 2, 5 or 0 years from year zero yet people saying the earth is anywhere from 4.5-30 billion years younger or even 1062 years older than Ussher's date: one might accuse me of straining at a gnat and swallowing a camel. It's merely a fun exercise in trying to find the exact date of the earth, to the year. If we try for the most accurate possible date, I would think we can only benefit from this practice. Nothing wrong with trying to get the most accurate date.

PROVING THE AGE OF THE EARTH

Actually though many fight the bible, scholars specializing in ancient history agree that the old and new testaments are the most accurate records in existence of events between 3000 BC and 100 AD. That in and of itself should indicate that the bible is not some subversive book bent on confining men to some interpretation of morality. Only when it comes to the miraculous and the apparently impossible do scholars waver in this appraisal of the 66 books and letters that make up the bible. If it's accurate in a historical way it stands to reason it is accurate in other ways. Many malign the bible and even say it is full of "contradictions" even though many who make this statement have in fact never even read it, and can't even point to a single so called contradiction. Having said that I will in all fairness shortly show some problems with the lineage of the kings. OK Since we now have a definitive exact date for the age of the earth, is that date of the earth being 7073 years old in anyway provable. Yes it is. You read me right YES it is!

ZEROING IN ON THE MOST ACCURATE DATING METHOD KNOWN

While reading some sources I had used for the rest of this book, occasionally I came across mention of a dating method that was always good for "nearly" 5400 years. It was called dendrochronology...or Tree Ring Dating. (This will show you how old some of my research sources and materials are).

In a nutshell, tree rings display environment changes in the growth patterns of the rings that are the same growth patterns for all trees in any area at a given time. The environment affects all trees in a given area the same way and this shows up in the rings and how they form. What's more, specific and exact dates can be assigned to each specific tree ring. The growth pattern of one tree will line up with the growth pattern of other trees in that area and they will overlap depending on when those trees lived. This overlapping can continue over thousands of years.

Actually even global factors can be determined by tree rings, whether the earth was warmer or colder at a specific year, decade or whatever so that this overlapping can be done for trees in one part of the earth and another and get general world climates during any give tree ring. This overlapping has been done all the way back, as these old sources kept saying, to "nearly 5400 years".

Since it was not yet 5400 years but only "nearly" I wondered when it would become exactly 5400 years. I wasn't quite sure what this might prove but it seemed important. One day I believe it was in 1993, I was reading some article in a 1988? publication and it mentioned tree ring dating was good for 5400 years. (I do not recall the article, and have not been able to find it again. It appears one of my roommates tossed out a bunch of my Time magazines, one of which contained this reference, and oddly I haven't been able to find another source that shows the date when dendrochronology starts at) In this reference to dendrochronology, it did not say "nearly" nor did it say "more than", it said just plain 5400 years. Had I stumbled onto the date I was looking for? Subsequent publications tell you in referring to dendrochronology that tree ring dating is now stated as good for MORE than 5400 years. So it appears I did stumble upon the exact date or a date very close to the exact date, as it's possible whoever wrote that article may have rounded up or down the odd year and just called it "5400 years" on the dot. So somewhere around or in 1988 tree ring dating was good for exactly 5400 years.

SOMETHING ELSE TO PLOT

I went back to my now very old and decrepit timeline drawing and placed 5400 years backward from the year 1988 and where do you think year zero was, that is, the first year that dendrochronology starts? Two years before THE FLOOD!!! **Bingo** we have something! If we presume that the 5400 years as mentioned in 1988 was a rounding off or if as is suspected the birth of Christ might be out by as much as 2-5 years we have an extraordinarily close to perfect date as to the age of the flood and we can conclude that it is the flood when tree ring dating goes back to and starts as the first year of dendrochronology. Thus it is the flood itself which institutes the beginning of tree rings! Using 5400 years plus the 19 to present date and the 1656 years before the flood we get an age for the earth of 7075 years. In fact if we presume dendrochronology starts immediately following the flood it would take one year for that first ring to show up! Meaning we get to within one year of the flood! This is an incredibly small margin of error! Since dendrochronology is in fact the most exact dating method known to man we have to presume some rounding off was present in the article or some miscalculation in the plotting of Christ's birth all those centuries ago took place or even that I've got the wrong year for that article. But all those things considered even the discrepancy of just 1 or 2 years is only minute, and it can no doubt easily be narrowed down to the exact year. And now consider this! If we add the ½ year we missed in David's reign we get to add 1 ½ years to the time period between the flood and Christ and we get the flood date exactly!!!! EXACTLY!

RINGS START AT THE FLOOD?

OK so you ask, why is dendrochronology only good back to the flood?... what about the trees before the flood?. The obvious guess is the trees from before the flood don't exist anymore or are all decayed and are unusable. But this is incorrect. Actually I find it astounding that trees could exist as long as this. I would have thought they all rotted away to nothing by now, but this isn't so. Long have scientists known of a time in "prehistoric" earth's climate where the earth was like a greenhouse and the trees grew at a constant rate all year round. What does that mean? It means that trees from that prehistoric period did not have the usual rings! You read that right...at one time trees did NOT have rings! OK since this chapter comes after the chapter about what was life like before the flood ...well I guess you knew that, but it's interesting to come to this conclusion two different ways.

It's all starting to fit! This is why dendrochronology is only good for 5419 years, because before a specific point (the flood) trees didn't even HAVE rings to use in the dendro-chronological timeline! These dendrochronologists have long known at some point trees didn't have rings, but because of the obvious climate change descipherable by wood with no rings those trees were just called prehistoric trees, supposedly millions of years old, but they were simply finding trees from before the flood!

But if you think about it, it does sound like deliberate deception. How? Well they tell us this prehistoric climate on earth existed millions of years ago, and one of the clues they use to prove this is of course trees with no rings. But if they can only find trees with rings dateable back to about 3410 BC why are they telling us the tree with no rings are from millions of years before that? Shouldn't they have tree rings dating to millions of years ago to substantiate that? Isn't it fair to assume that the trees without rings came just prior to the trees with rings, and not have this completely empty time span of millions of years before the last ringed tree and the trees they found without rings? There is no reason for this.

Obviously not understanding what could cause rings to suddenly cease will cause some sort of break that needs explaining, but simply saying millions of years happened in between is not logical in any way. I mean think about it, what they are in essence saying is every tree with rings before 3410 BC has completely decayed and they cannot be found...until miraculously trees without rings are found from ...what...2, 10? 60? Million years ago and are found in enough abundance to determine that the earth in that prehistoric time had an even climate in which trees did not grow rings. Could they tell that from a single tree? I don't think so because they would have suspected an extinct species of tree. They had to find enough of these trees to come to this conclusion that at one time trees didn't have rings. If this is so, then how can they explain the absence of millions of years worth of trees between that last tree with no rings and the first tree with rings. They can't. All that is in between the tree with rings and the trees without is a layer of flood. But with the land being jumbled sometime after the flood, this flood distinction is a bit indistinct. We'll see why next chapter.

So we see that not only can we decipher a specific date from the bible as to the age of the earth, we also discover a scientific dating system actually confirms age of the earth deciphered from the bible. And it's not just any old dating method either, it happens to be the most accurate dating system on earth, that is dendrochronology, that confirms the date in the bible...with an error somewhere in the works of just 1 or 2 years and possibly no error whatsoever!! In other words, science proves the bible is correct and thus the earth really IS just a mere 7073 -7075 years old! (As of 2007)

IS DENDROCHRONOLOGY PERFECT?

At least one author seemed to think there was some variable factor in the dendrochronology dates. He noted that some years two rings could be created in a single growing season. I have even found one source that suggested that tree rings date back as far as 8200 years. But this is the exception. Every other reference to dendrochronology is consistent in the 5400 year range. That 8200 year estimation may have been one that gave a single year to each ring, but was later corrected. I have to assume that the dendrochronologists have figured it out because it is considered the most accurate dating technique in existence. Which means no matter what, with dendrochronology we have a decipherable date for the age of the earth, at least from the point of the flood.

No matter when trees began to get rings that is when the flood occurred. It would seem that at present it is very close to 5419 years ago. When adding the 1656 years of time known to have existed before the flood, this makes the earth 7073 years old back to the creation.

OK Ok I hear you screaming about those other dating methods that show a far older earth and universe. I'll get to them.

CONFLICTING WITH ACCEPTED CHRONOLOGIES

The time before flood (1656 years) is pretty much universally accepted by Biblical scholars and why not, the ages and dates as laid out in Genesis are hardly deniable or debatable.

THE YEAR CHANGES LENGTH

The age people lived to before the flood was about 900 years. People tend to think no one could live as long as this. However the length of the year back then may actually have been shorter by 6 or more days and thus ages spoken of in the pre-flood era might actually be slightly less compared to today's calendars and ages...maybe as much as 2-3 percent. So someone living to 900 years before the flood might actually have only lived, based on today's calendars, about 878 years, so Methuselah may have only lived a mere 940 current years...*much* more reasonable.

This shorter year might actually be a factor in the pre-flood period of 1656 years, (and much post flood time too) if we are ever capable of finding an accurate dating method for items from the pre-flood era. This is assuming the actual day was the same length of time too! But for sake of argument and the lack of a way to accurately date the pre-flood era we will stick with the biblical 1656 years. With a completely different environment existing on earth before the flood, dating methods would need to be calibrated to account for this different environment. But as far as I know, no one has done this. With the earth in this period being an extremely stable environment it would be difficult at best to come up with a dating method that actually works on materials from this period of time. Carbon dating for example in this period is off the wall. We'll see why shortly.

THE DATING CONFLICT

Coming up with a date of 981 years before Christ as the time of the carrying away of the Israelites into Babylon, and another 981 years before that, getting you back to the time of David conflicts with <u>very accepted</u> chronology. This of course means we butt up against the scholars who say that the Israelites were carried away to Babylon about 587-586 or even 597 years before Christ, and furthermore they say that David ruled about 1000 years before Christ. In fact coming up with 1000 BC for David actually conflicts with the lineage of the kings of Israel too!

These dates were usually best guesses based on other archaeologists best guesses...and the best guesses of some biblical scholars. In fact the dates arrived at for other civilizations are often based on and lined up with the dates given in the bible. They tie other world events to events in the bible, and vise verse, but there have been found many errors or duplicate possibilities as to which events match up with which events mentioned in the bible. Because of the chronology of the kings in the bible this time period has been assumed to be a much shorter period of time, and admittedly due to some variables this may in fact be the case. Some scholars are a little liberal in their interpretations of some dates. With the apparent flexibility of some historical events on the timeline one might presume the dates for in between David and Babylon and Christ are similarly flexible or incorrect and up for debate, but actually these dates are so set in stone many will say these dates are NOT up for debate. Something is clearly amiss...but what?

THE EGYPTIAN SHUFFLE

Egyptologist scholars make a nice neat timeline for the Pharaohs of Egypt and say Pharaoh so and so was the son of so and so and he lived in such and such a dynasty for however long and approximately at such and such a time before Christ. As I understand it, not one single pharaoh has been positively matched up with pharaohs spoken of in the bible nor have they been positively placed in a correct chronological order.

The chronology of the kings of Egypt timeline is their best guess. They in private behind closed doors rearrange the timeline in all sorts of ways. They have NO IDEA which pharaoh followed which in almost

ALL CASES! To help date them they even try and use conventional carbon dating and other methods but that just throws their calculations into more chaos and makes the picture even less clear. In some occasions these dating methods might happen to confirm their assessment, but this appears to be more of chance then actual proof.

Many scholars have decided to agree upon dates assigned to certain points in history just to show a sort of solidarity between them to give the impression they know when these events took place. That's not to disparage their work,...good gosh not in the least! They have been very meticulous in their archaeology, their work and research. If not for their work we wouldn't know what existed in any way shape or form in history other then what is written in the bible and a few other works handed down through the ages. It's because of many an archaeologists work that we can ask intelligent questions! Many an author has done just that, and that is why I was able to read about this stuff in the first place and put my 2 farthings worth in. However, often some will suggest a more exact knowledge then is actually in existence, and then be offended if they are questioned or proven wrong.

NO INDEXES OR CROSS REFERENCES MAKES DATING IMPOSSIBLE

This is not to say my dates are absolutely correct either because there are some variables which will be gone into at length.

Though the dates for the old world are generally agreed upon, to show just how exact some knowledge really is, take a look at a new world date by way of comparison.

One construction at Teotihuacan has been dated as 6000BC, 1500BC and 600BC (Book 23 pg. 148) When archaeologist cannot match up artifacts with known events they simply are lost as to dating an item. However cut them some slack. This is understandable. It's almost impossible to date some stuff without cross referencing, and even that is only right part of the time. They like to think they are correct always in these cross reference match ups but Immanuel Velikovsky showed clearly there were many errors and points up for debate. Yet instead of thanking him for his work, he was ostracized and vilified to the day of his death.

INEXACT KNOWLEDGE NEEDS TO BE NOTED

Very seldom are actual dates ascribed to specific events. How easy world history would be if this was the case for every event. Strangely when an actual date is mentioned archaeologists often seem to ignore them, usually because they don't fit in with accepted chronologies. Gee you would think they would be glad for the help! But usually the case is events are not dated, but are placed in time by reference to kings reigning at the time. Thus the problem lies in placing Kings in the correct order and era. It's rarely an exact science and mistakes are made. Often errors can go undetected for years and decades. But as time goes on a best guess becomes really ingrained and then less and less up for debate.

Things that are in question should be clearly marked! This way people can focus on them to figure the dates out and match up cross references more accurately. But the fact is if this was done most of all accepted chronologies would be marked in bold with question marks. This would give people in school learning this stuff the impression that scientist don't know much. Can't have them realizing this. But why not? What's wrong with admitting a certain lack of exact knowledge. If something only has an 85% chance of being correct it has a 15% chance of being 100% wrong.

Knowing what we don't know would encourage people to want to find out for themselves what is the length and the breadth. But this knowledge of what knowledge is not known seems to be for the elite to know what is not known. The rest of us have to figure it out for ourselves or trust the experts. And believe me it is so hard to figure out, and should you make just one mistake, then they can laugh at you for your ignorance, and discount your entire arguments. Why hide what we don't know and pretend we know it? This doesn't encourage learning, it discourages it. It's possible Velikovsky made a few mistakes too, but they sure don't want to admit that even though many of Velikovsky's theories are reluctantly being accepted.

If we see clearly what is not certain, that only makes us more keen to figure out that area and nail it down. What kid will want to get into a field of research where all is known and thus feel he cannot contribute anything to the knowledge pool? It's not pretending to know everything that will make learning more fun, but admitting holes in the knowledge that will foster more interest.

ARE THE DATES SET IN STONE?

Immanuel Velikovsky found at least another 400-600 years in between the timeline of David and Christ, and conceded that there could be more. He found many instances where accepted chronology based on matching up of events and people's names were inaccurate. He found people misidentified and events wrongly matched up, thus sometimes throwing some things out by as much as 1500 years or more! Yet having said that, he seemed to understand how touchy tinkering with the timeline of the kings of Israel was and felt this period might be more set in stone then need be. He felt that tying biblical dates to inaccurately accepted dates for other events was a mistake, which thus threw out the biblical timeline, not because the bible was inaccurate, but because it was tied to inaccurate dates assigned to events which were far too accepted without question.

He was certain David's reign had to have occurred at least 500 years earlier than was shown by accepted archaeological chronology. (Book 25) When you work out the chronology one sees David in the lineage of the kings does appear to be much more recent. Whereas the chronology I present here puts David nearly 1000 years earlier than previous estimates. Although Velikovsky only managed to show maybe 500 years more was in this time frame, I have go out on a limb and say there may have been twice as much time as that! and to be honest I don't really know how. But maybe there is something I present in this work for the trained eye that I can't see.

BY-PRODUCT OF DIGGING THROUGH THE RUBBLE

As a side note Velikovsky also realized that the geology of the earth had a very cataclysmic un-uniformitarian history indeed. This bucked the trend of what was usually considered a slow uniform and gradual life of earth. Thus he suggested a shorter age for the earth, simply by showing that in our past there were so many catastrophic incidences in recorded history creating geological formations that were supposed to have taken millions of years. He deduced many of these incidences happened in a moment...a day or a week. In fact he so reduced the age of the earth evolutionists jumped all over him! He appears to have hit a sore spot and hit the proverbial nail on the head and consequently got ostracized by the evolution community at large who all stood in favour of the uniformitarian theory. Ironically Velikovsky was an evolutionist.

Since his death some of his findings have been reluctantly accepted and to some extent many of his theories have been adopted by evolution theorists today, even though they persist in forcing his theories and findings into an old earth picture. Controversy still goes on about this maverick. Evolutionists and scientists just keep trying to bury this guy. But reading this guys work shows he clearly was a lucid intelligent chap that was making honest appraisals of the information available to him. That's what researchers are supposed to do! But people get pet theories and are loathe to be proven wrong and go to obscene lengths to maintain credibility, even if it means vilifying honest appraisals of information. Had Velikovsky done his work in the 19th century he would be hailed as a genius to this day.

BORING LINEAGE PROBLEMS

I'll try and make the problems of the lineages as short and succinct and clear as possible. This bit is more for the biblical scholar's attention than anything, but you're welcome to read along, or go get a coffee while I talk to them. (Meaning some people have their eyes glaze over reading this part so skip to Chapter 5 part 2 if you like. Even I get lost if I start in the middle somewhere.) However if you are a bible scholar or even if you are prone to plotting my findings and the Kings of Israel on a timeline you may have had a conniption fit, as you will see or know of a huge problem.

The kings of Israel lineage is apparently complete right up to the carrying away of the Israelites to Babylon, but the time frame for this period is just 462 years! It's 519 years short of the 981 years! This means either there is something wrong with the 981 years, there's something is wrong with the lineage of the Kings of Israel, or the generation fluctuates in length. Needless to say there are some variables in the picture, this time frame being the biggest variable. I'm not a Bible scholar in the traditional sense and don't profess to know Hebrew and Greek sufficiently well to say empathically some mistake has been made, but I have found a few possible sources for confusion in this period.

DOUBLE TROUBLE

As anyone who has read the bible with some diligence will know there are the odd occasions where some people will have the same name. I remember reading one section and being very confused about the events. I spent about a half hour trying to figure out what I was missing on that page. I finally realized I was reading about two kings with the same name! Upon subsequent rereading of that part, the confusion returned but realizing I had figured it out once before I just kept on.

It's possible the lineage of the Kings has a similar confusing duplication, even though the lineage is written twice (in II Kings and in II Chronicles,) and they appear to support each other pretty well. But I would point out that it would seem both these lineages are written after the carrying away to Babylon and probably after they got back to Israel. If there is an error in the lineage these lineages may be repeating the same error.

UZZIAH UZZIAH UZZIAH

Problems started to crop up when realizing that King Uzziah is a key figure because of the major earthquake that occurs in his reign. I was working on the Peleg chapter and since this is a very major earthquake I decided to plot King Uzziah on the time line to get a rough estimate when this earthquake occurred and soon found a possible problem in the lineage of the kings!

In II Kings Uzziah is the son of Amaziah and Uzziah reigns 52 years. In II Chronicles 26:1 Azariah is the son of Amaziah and he reigns 52 years! In II Kings 15:1 this king is called Azzariah, but two paragraphs later, in 15:13, he is called Uzziah. In the lineage of the kings mentioned in Matthew, Ozias is equated with Uzziah but he is the son of Joram! All three names Uzziah, Azariah, and Ozias are supposed to be the same person...and that may be, because the names have similar sounds, and there are no vowels in Hebrew, But can Joram and Amaziah really be the same person?

TWO PAIRS : CROSS REFERENCES SLIP A DISC

I know that when you plot the kings of Israel they are usually tied to the kings of Judah by year of reign so one might think it would clear up there. One gets a bit of a headache trying to figure this stuff out, but a problem shows up there too.

When one plots the kings of Israel over the kings of Judah to my complete surprise the lineages don't line up! Usually they say such and such a king of Israel starts his rule in the 3rd year or whatever in the reign of such and such a king of Judah or visa verse, so you would think there can be no mistake. But the fact is, sometime the lineage works, like for instance with Pekah and Ahaz. Their reigns when plotted mesh perfectly. But when you get to the Jotham son of Uzziah a real problem occurs! Jotham is said to only have reigned 16 years in II Chronicles 27:1 and then he dies, but in II Kings 15:30 Hoshea starts his reign in the 20th year of Jotham son of Uzziah! Jotham is said to reign 16 years by one account and obviously at least 20 years by another. This simply has to be two different Jotham's and thus at least two different Uzziahs! This apparent duplication alone would add at least 68 years to the timeline.

In all the time I've been within earshot of biblical stuff I have only ever heard reference to some inconsistencies in the biblical timeline once, and that overheard when a bible college student was chatting. Are we afraid to admit these discrepancies exist? These don't mean the bible is wrong, it only means that the timeline is incomplete.

HENRY EDWARD THE EIGHTH OR IS THAT THE AYGHTH?

Often people kept a father's name going so many times in a lineage that the same name would be used over and over. This appears to have happened with the Kings as well and it has now caused some confusion. It may also have caused accidental elimination of some apparent duplications, when in fact they may have been missing kings. Since Hebrew does not actually have any vowels one person might have the same consonants as someone else in their names but have a different name. The vowels not being written are only indicated by little dots and such. So let's say we have two people with names like GHLB (I'm making this up just to illustrate and I picked four letters completely at random) GHLB might read Gohalab or Egahleeb. Actually there are "vowel" pronunciation marks and there may be some rules I'm not aware of but you get the idea, and as I say pronunciations for the missing vowels do exists.

TAUGHT KNOWLEDGE DETERIORATING TOO?

Actually if you can believe it, as I understand it by at least some accounts, the correct pronunciation for the name of God is apparently lost. Some say other than specific religious leaders the Jewish people were not allowed to know or say this name, so the proper pronunciation has been lost! Though the four letters YHWH are well known, the correct pronunciation of those four letters is, to some, up for debate. It could be Yahweh, Jehovah or possibly even Yahoo... who knows. At least so I have heard.

However when looking up this name in Strongs concordance (Copyright 1890) in fact it appears the exact pronunciation for YHWH *is* known. It has two pronunciations: Yeh-ho-vaw, and Yeh-ho-vee. I wonder where some people get their information from to say the Jews do not know the pronunciation of this name...is some misinformation creeping into bible colleges or am I missing something?

I remember one incident where a young man fresh out of Bible collage starts saying to our bible study that the lineage of the kings actually works its way down to Mary and not Joseph. This seems peculiar so I quickly flip to the appropriate verse and tell him he mistaken and point out the verse where it shows that Joseph is part of the lineage, and not Mary. (Matthew 1: 15,16 KJV) Oddly he was surprised to learn this.

Assuming the name for God might actually not be known though I repeat, Strongs concordance shows two specific exact pronunciations for his name, I stumbled upon a third possible pronunciation for YHWH. Actually I pick the pronunciation "Yahoo" because Velikovsky showed that people may have used this name in prayers to God and the people he refers to appear to have been in the vicinity of the Hebrews during the Exodus and got this name from them, so this too might be a possible pronunciation of the four letter name for God, assuming the pronunciation for YHWH really IS lost. But I digress.

EDITOR'S REMORSE

It would seem there must be at least two different Uzziahs, and both just happened to reign 52 years each! If that's not enough in II Kings 13:8 the son of Jehoahaz is called Joash, and then called Jehoash the next paragraph. Though the two are very similar and may indeed be the same, clearly there are some missing sections in the lineage of the kings. Again I repeat I am not a pro at this stuff and I may be missing something, as this was not the area I was concentrating in. My **guess** is things got mixed up at some point, likely after a war or the return from Babylon, and people tried to splice the lineages back together and possibly eliminated what appeared to be duplication at some later date and duplications of names caused confusion in the lineage. Perhaps where a new paragraphs begins may not be the same original chronicler, and may signify an incorrect splice. So what the case is, the words are correct but the scribes or librarians or whatever made a goof up somewhere... maybe in a few places.

THOSE UBIQUITOUS BOOK BURNERS

Not only is there a problem when we try and put the kings of Egypt together now it appears there was a similar problem occurring with the Kings of Israel too. The timeline though appearing to be complete up to the carrying away of the Israelites into Babylon, may actually break down at several spots and at one of the Uzziahs. (assuming there is more than one, and there may even be three)

With the plundering of Israel by several nations and the destruction of Jerusalem just prior to the carrying away to Babylon maybe some records got destroyed. We know many articles of Solomon's temple got used to pay conquerors or stolen and taken to, among other countries, Babylon, and even kings got taken. Did records get destroyed during this period? We know that people destroyed libraries and burned the books all through history. Many armies hated the Jewish nation and tried to destroy them and may have done the next best thing by destroying their histories as best they could. Older records would have had more copies made, so dates and chronologies up to Solomon would be complete but more recent lineages might only have had a few copies and they may have got destroyed.

All speculation of course, but it seems pretty clear there is something missing and likely some confusion about which King is which with the duplication of names. We do know that there were attempts to salvage and save records for posterity. For example the Dead Sea scrolls were very well hidden in some caves and not discovered for at least 2000 years. Why would they hide these scroll books or records unless there was a very real fear they would be destroyed. The very fact they were hidden has to mean some other records *were* destroyed. Maybe the missing 8 or 9 books were destroyed and the lineage of the kings also were partially destroyed. It's a miracle as much as we have has lasted this long.

THREE 14S EQUALS GENERATIONS OF 70, 33, AND 43 YEARS

As for the time period between the carrying away of Babylon to Christ's birth there seems to be no lineage whatsoever except for the Mathew lineage which has no dates, length of reign or ages assigned to the names. So plotting beyond that point becomes impossible and I have to rely on the assumption that 14 generations equals the time span of the previous 14 generations.

But does 14 generations equal the time between Abraham and David (981 years) or the time indicated for the lineage of the kings (462 years)? But then if we presume 14 generations is correct at 462 years that puts David at 924 BC and Solomon at 884BC and this would be considered a bit late by conventional chronology. So anyway you slice it, there is no way around it, something is askew with the chronologies of the kings as stated in the Bible. That, or the length of time for a generation varies because if the 462 years is correct, then those generations are a mere 33 years long. And if we add into the mix the presumed date of about 597 BC for the carrying away of the Israelites to Babylon to the time of Christ, (not in any way decipherable by the biblical chronology but this date is arrived at by other ancient history fields) that would make the generation during that period to be 42.6 years. This would mean we have a fluctuating generation!

OH NO...MORE NUMBERS!

If we are to accept these dates, that is 462 years from David to the carrying away to Babylon and 597 years from that point to the birth of Christ, we can further illustrate the problem. This would means the flood would have happened 2372 / or 2507 BC. (2123 years to Abraham +981[to David] +462[to Babylon] + 462 /or 597 [to Christ] [minus 1656]) This puts the flood at 2507 BC. This is clearly not correct...or is it?

Well it sure isn't when considering conventional chronology. Interestingly if we use the smallest dates we get creation happening at 4028 BC, just 24 years out from Usshers date. If this is correct how would we rectify this against dendrochronology, not to mention Velikovskys adding at least 500 more years in this time slot?

It is virtually universally accepted that this period from the flood to Christ had to be well over 3000 years, and curiously the time assigned to the known start of written records is curiously close to the time I assign for the date of the flood, that is 3410 BC. That coupled with the dendrochronolgy factor clearly indicates problems somewhere. So again there is missing about a thousand years or to be exact the timeline of the bible is apparently missing, by my reckoning, 903 years, that is if we presume an equal period of 981 years for 14 generations.

TIME VERSES NUMBERS

Admittedly the definition of a generation in Mathew appears to be an actual number of descendants and thus a fluctuating time period can be ascribed to a generation based on this. If this is the case, and I admit it could be, then this argument may be lost. And to further make my case seem hopeless, if 42 (3 X 14) generations are spoken of in Matthew, where do you shove another 903 years into the mix? (actually I count 41 generations including Abraham to Christ being the 41st. So Even Mathew appears to have at least one missing....possibly a duplicated name being thought to be the same person?)

Even if we try and make the Jewish Calendar work it means that their calendar started 400 or 1303 years after creation. [1256 or 353 years before the flood] That doesn't appear to make any sense either. Although if we take 903 missing years and take off the 400 we get curiously close to the 500 years Velikovsky places in between David and Christ...but this is just jerry rigging now, and no matter what, there has to be a way to justify adding years somewhere, and I don't know how to do it other than assuming the 14 generations equals 981 years. And of course this runs into problems.

MY WHAT TEENY GENERATIONS YOU HAVE!

(3rd ed. Insert 2016) I must admit since publishing this and subsequently reading Herodotus and Josephus in conjunction with the Bible I have come to realize that a slightly younger date for the earth is more probable; that is the length of generations seem to be determined by the ages between fathers and sons, thus generation lengths after David to the carrying away to Babylon had to be shorter, consequently reducing my date for the earth. Why? Because matching up Herodotus and Josephus, at least in a casual basis, shows fairly accurate dates for B.C. dates back to about 500 BC are well established, which gets back to the time of Babylon, a date I put to around 980 B.C. but which with these references place around 500 B.C. So I'm curious as to how Velikovsky got his dates such as in Ages in Chaos. When you think about it a shorter generation does make sense as people live shorter lives than antediluvian people, or people immediately after the flood. If a generation is meant to indicate ages between the death of fathers Father's and birth of sons, In theory this could mean a pre-flood generation could be about 700 years. The definition of generation seems to mean a group of people living at the same time. What would that make? A half life span? Biblically it seems to indicate just the number of people in the lineage. So if this is the case a generation would reduce after the flood.

IF WE PRESUME A DECLINING GENERATION THE SECOND AND THIRD 14 GENERATION SPANS SHOULD BE CLOSE TO THE SAME TIME LENGTH.

Logically one would assume, as the life spans of man declined and leveled off, the time span between David to Babylon (462 years) would equal or possibly be more than the time for between Babylon and the Birth of Christ. But it is shorter by 135 years. This just does not seem correct. If we assume the 597 years is correct and some kings are missing from the lineage, we have to double that 597 and that puts David at nearly 1200BC. Conventional thought says David was around 1000 BC. These two times spans of 462 and

597 years just can't be right. We can't artificially lengthen one span or reduce the other, we have to accept that something is missing or added where it oughtn't to be. But even if we presume logically that the latter two 14 generation periods are of equal length, and take the chronology of the kings to be complete, this puts the flood to 2372 BC! We can't have it both ways!

We can't say the timeline between David and the carrying away to Babylon is 462 years, the time from Babylon to Christ is 462 or 597 years and then say the civilization as we know it started somewhere in the neighbourhood of 3000-3500 BC and keep the biblical chronology from the flood to Christ. Something is going to break. Perhaps one could argue this dating is correct and actually does go back to creation. So if we added 1656 years we would get creation starting at 4028 BC, close to the date of 4004 BC reached by Ussher, which makes his date even more mystifying. But this would mean the dendrochronolgy tree rings start before the flood or that their tallying is incorrect, as well as other dates arrived at by archaeology. All these dates are confusing, but I'll get out of this part soon enough.

This definition of a generation and particularly a changing generation just may not be correct. One could argue a generation was never meant to be a definitive length of time. If a generation is determined from a son's birth to the father's death, a generation would change every generation. The fact is some prophecies are linked to the time period of a generation so it seems logical to presume the time length of a generation is not subject to change. As much as I tend to disagree with some of the dates that come about via mainstream archaeology it would seem pretty consistent that there are at least 3200 to 3500 years BC of civilization before we get back to a start from something or some event that seemed to spark civilization. (Obviously this has to be the flood or the gods. I will eventually explain who the gads were, so rest assured.)

There are calendars and other factors that would strongly support that civilization as we know it did start in this approximate time frame immediately after the flood. Since this date also matches up so well with Dendrochronogy (and as we shall see Atmospheric C14) one has to investigate seriously the possibility of a break in the lineage of the Kings of Israel as a possibility. The timeline seems firm and undeniable up to sometime into the kings after David, and that in itself is a remarkable wonder! But it would seem Israel's enemies in the latter times got to enough records before enough duplicates were made to disrupt the historically recorded timeline beyond Solomon's son Rehoboam somewhere. Heck even the kings of Judah and the Kings of Israel fought each other!

It's even possible the biblical record only speaks of historically significant events and the kings involved with them, though a pretty good argument against that idea I'm sure is more likely.

We know 8 or 9 other books referred to in the bible that are missing, so there is no reason to believe the entire record is all there, hard and sad as it is to realize that. Although this period between David and Christ seems to be the most certain in many scholars minds it may be the very source of the confusion. We have to assume a year is a year and a generation is a generation, so the chronology from creation to David and a little beyond is complete. But after that point no doubt there is much to be debated. If we can accept the 981 years = 14 generations equation things actually fall into place very well.

CHRONOLOGY PIECED TOGETHER AFTER THE RETURN FROM BABYLON?

Admittedly I do not know how to fix these clearly glaring problems. My only guess, and it's not a very good one I'll admit, is that the missing kings and apparently "duplicated" kings which then got chopped and spliced in the Kings and Chronicles account after the return from Babylon thus created a botched timeline which somehow got repeated in the Matthew account. But that can't be correct either because some of the names in the Matthew account simply do not match up with the Kings and Chronicles accounts. So it appears the Matthew account, is using a different source which is also missing names and finds more names not in the other two ledgers, and the real chronology might actually be a splicing of the Matthew account WITH the Kings and Chronicles account. Clearly there is much to be pondered and debated yet, to nail down an exact date for the age of the earth. It should however be clear if it isn't yet, that the earth is extremely young, anyway you slice it, at least as far as dendrochronology and the biblical record is concerned, not to mention other calendars. So for sake of argument I will continue on in the vein, that all three 14 generation periods equals 981 years, even if this is in vain. If this is actually incorrect, then it is an incredible fluke that the accepted dates for dendrocronology line up so perfectly with this assumption.

CALENDARS ALSO NEED TO BE PUT IN THE MIX

Many calendars still in use are at a date of around 5100 odd years from the start of something. But that start for some reason does not appear to be the flood! Calendars start at some event, but knowing the event isn't always easy.

The French after the revolution briefly started a new calendar making the revolution as year one. (well actually the calendar started when Louis said hello to lady guillotine in 1793) China's calendar current date starts at 3366 B.C. So by my reckoning it starts at 44 years past the flood. India has a couple, one starts at 3113 B.C. 297 years past the flood and another that starts at 3101 BC. The Mayan calendar starts at 3111 B.C. or 299 years after the flood. Even when people worked an Egyptian calendar based on some clues, they came up with the first dynasty starting around 3100 BC. All these are a longer time period then the Ussher period from the flood to Christ, that is 2348 BC, again indicating something is missing from the linage of the kings of Israel. Could all those calendars be wrong? The asteroids say… maybe.

HOW MANY YEARS?

(3rd ed. Insert 2016) Many researchers quote some of the long spans of time referred to by the Egyptians, Indians, or Sumerians as indications that the bible's dates are wrong in suggesting the earth is just a few thousand years old because dates referred to by these histories and their gods are often in the 10's of thousands of years. Or some say the ages of people before the flood can't be right as ancients often gave really old dates and ages to compete for who or what civilization was the oldest so some say the dates before the flood are multiplied by 10 or some other factor. Though we showed that man could, in theory at least, live to 900 + years (and if not that would mean some people in the bible had kids when they were 5 and 6 years old, if you divided the ages by 10 as some suggest is correct) I'm not entirely certain how to myth bust the real long ages given to indicate the gods life spans and times they ruled, however Sitchin seems to have unwittingly found a chink in the armor. He shows that some war and some retaliation happen soon after some event, but this 'soon after' time allotment he says is "300 years later we believe" (book 42 page 158) Ok. I don't care how you slice 300 years, it does not equal 'soon after'. This does seem to indicate that indeed some ancients did fudge a little bit when they wrote down time frames.

MY CIVILIZATION IS OLDER THAN YOURS.

(3rd ed. Insert 2016) Speaking of changing some dates around, I've not been able to figure out how to approach ancient Indian and Egyptian dates that skew chronology all over the map, as I simply am not qualified to dissect in detail some of these legends or "histories", and no doubt should I even attempt to do so, my ignorance in such matters would be abundantly obvious to some. But some Russian mathematicians have attacked virtually all the dates in history in a four volume work (Fomenko's history: Fact or Fiction), more than anyone would even think of doing. (See Atlantis Rising #96 cover story) They have suggested that all of the history of mankind doesn't go back any further than 900 AD and all major historical events date no earlier than 1300 AD. OK obviously this is a bit of impossible conjecturing as tree ring dating makes this deduction impossible, and virtually no historian takes their dates seriously. However their logic isn't entirely assailable. They maintain that history is available to the conquerors and the highest bidders. They note that nations wanted to have the oldest pedigree, whether real or invented so that like our arms races, they had oldest history races: they would spin the biggest yarns about their antiquity. In the Russian mathematicians crosshairs they had Egypt's 11,000 year history and Babylon's' 700,000 year history as complete fabrications, and Plato's Atlantis date of 9000 years before Plato's day was also not exempt and placed instead at 1500 BC, which as chance would have it lines up reasonably well with some other peoples dating for this event. This example is odd, as they seem to use BC dates as non historical events, even though they place the date of the sinking of Atlantis in the picture. If we have a verbal/ written recorded history of Atlantis doesn't that make Atlantis part of history?

I think it is safe to say the Indian dates of millions of years is not even close to reality. But there are some people that grab onto these fabricated dates such as those used by India to add veracity to dates assigned to fossils, out of place artifacts, or ancient civilizations dug out of the dirt. But like wishful thinking trying to make the earth appear older with 'pick and choose' dating methods, to get these impossible dates they use dates like those of India to add a slender thread of 'history' to validate them.

Though we'll see that some legends and verbal histories can be fairly intact after a few thousand years, I seriously doubt any civilization could maintain any real history for 700,000 or millions of years. If this were the case there would be a broad range of calendars dates around the world. But in fact the opposite is true, most world dates seem to cluster around 3100 BC as the beginning or a major key date in history… though the beginning or end of what seems at times is a bit obscure. I suspect, like Christians using Jesus as the starting for the calendar we use today, or Muslim using Mohamed for their Calendar, I suspect the date of 3100 BC is also linked to the arrival or departure of 'the gods'. We solve who those gods were in Chapter 9.

CALENDARS LINKED TO THE GODS? ASTEROIDS? CATACLYSMS?

It would seem the first Egyptian dynasty occurred after the reign of the 'gods'. Several of these calendars start within just a few years of each other and their start may be linked to a common occurrence or similar event. In fact some are so close that had the chroniclers forgot to incorporate a longer year at some point for just a century or so they would be, but that seems unlikely unless some dark ages way back somehow kept the same calendar. That or some series of events was making accurate calendars impossible. That may not be as farfetched as it might seem. There is a known period of about 25 years when calendars could not be calibrated. (See next chapter) The similarity of all these dates suggests something started or ended at that approximate time. But that date appears to be linked to when the gods left…? Has this got something to do with the devolution of man breaking down to some men in a devolved state and some in a pre-flood state? More on that later.

So one has to surmise that some major event occurred at 353 years before the flood (Jewish Calendar), and about 300 years after the flood. All these dates mean something and they can't be ignored when calculating the age of the earth, either by biblical or some other standard.

RECORDS OF INTERACTION OF CULTURES ARE FEW AND FAR BETWEEN.

Since archaeologists tie events and dates of one culture to another by cross referencing they have to take all the factors into play and since what happened, did happen at some point they will align correctly. Unfortunately except for wars and trade, many ancient civilization had little or nothing to do with other civilizations living on the earth that chroniclers would bother to record, so cross referencing and indexing may prove difficult to impossible in some situations. The trick is knowing how much time elapsed so you have a better idea when things happened and they will fit better. If you try and put 2300 years of events into 3500 years of time or visa verse, something is going to break. Either you have duplication or an inaccurate time slot to put the events into. Though as we have seen there are still some variables in this proposed timeline there are some lining up of events that also tend to support it too.

Curiously some of the biggest events in history which are of a cataclysmic nature are spoken of in many records, yet these are not being used to help date history because no one seems to believe these records very much.

NO CLUE

(3rd ed. Insert 2016) Speaking of things found dating before Christ, Rasmus Nyerp of Denmark in 1806 stated "We know that it is earlier than Christendom, but whether by a couple of years, or a couple of centuries, or more than a millennium, we can do no more than guess" (Book 13 pg 31) So why are we so accurate with our dates today? We aren't, we just pretend we are so we sound smart to the general populace. Oh sure some correlation between ancient texts in possible, but as mentioned they have no idea which Egyptian Dynasty was in what order for most of the pharos, but they create a time line and stick to it, to make it seem set in stone when it's really set in pudding. Few references in surviving texts can accurately match one Pharaoh with an event.

DATING METHODS AREN'T MUCH HELP

Since this is anything but an exact science, archaeologists tend to use dating methods to help. But the dating methods used have been known to have flaws. To the best of my knowledge none use dendrochronolgy. But then how can you tie dendrochronolgy specific dates to artefacts? I don't know that one can, unless you can match up an exact environment and date it to a specific artefact and a specific tree ring. I don't know that this is even remotely possible.

I suppose if strange weather is spoken of in ancient records one might be able to match similar accounts up in the dendrochronology. For example if in one area and chronicle, long winters came ten years apart, one could look to the tree rings from trees in that area and see where two long winters occurred ten years apart and get an exact date for those and surrounding events. This also might be possible for the time of the plagues of Egypt. Oddly the most bizarre weather event of all, the flood, is completely ignored when tying dates to events in the tree ring record and it is the most obvious. As it happens weird weather has been spotted in trees dated from 536-545 AD, See next chapter.

Interestingly the bible occasionally equates men with trees in a sort of metaphoric or allegorical way, for example equating godly men with trees that do not lose their leaves. I tend to want to stick with the dendrochronology match up, though that is hardly an argument to do so, simply because if the tree rings are interpreted correctly they can positively date the flood.

Perhaps like the earth and man, time slowly erodes the earth's ability to produce, mans abilities to invent and the records slowly get lost and changed. We know many civilizations have burned libraries and wiped out history and replaced it with their own version of it, or just left a void starting a dark age. Like the expression goes, those who win the wars write the history books.

There has been a war waged against the bible in our society. I remember hearing that the bible doesn't need defending, it defends itself. But I think it does need defending and even though I dare to show some of it's apparent breakdown due to whatever cause, we will see during the course of this work that it is still an incredible ledger that is still for the most part intact. We should cherish it and other ancient texts and ledgers carefully or they will fall into disuse and misuse and decline, and eventually be forgotten.

They should be part of school curriculum. We need to know our pasts so we can compare their stories to our times and make intelligent life decisions, and not base our actions and decision on some idiot on TV, but by how our fathers and forefathers lived, and the standards they held fast to.

Chapter 5 Part Two

DATING METHODS AND THEIR FLAWS

OK you ask, nay scream, what about the other dates given for the earth and the universe like 4.5 to 30 billion years given as the age of the universe by other dating techniques. What about the carbon 14 dating or other dating methods that shows bones to be in excess of 50,000 years old or light from stars that suggests the stars to be millions, nay billions of light years away thus 'proving' the universe is at least billions of years old? ((2ⁿᵈ & 3ʳᵈ ed. Insert 2008/ 2016) If you find a treasure chest full of coins you can tell how long the coins have been in the ground by looking at the dates on the coins. They could not have been buried before and probably not long after the most recent coin in the chest. Similarly there are clues in the earth that are limiting factors as to how old the earth and universe can be.

About every thirty years or so a star dies and explodes causing a nova or super nova. As these dissipate they leave telltale rings. If the universe is billions of years old why are there less than 300 super nova rings found? By comparison there are about 2 trillion stars in existence for every single human being on earth!

Red stars are said to take billions of years to turn into white stars. Yet the Egyptians (2000 BC) and Cicero (50 BC) describe Sirius as a red star. Seneca (4 BC to 65 AD) said it was redder than Mars. Ptolemy (150 AD) counts Sirius as one of six red stars. Yet Now Sirius is a white dwarf. (Kent Hovind lectures)) Cosmologists say it takes millions of years for this exact same transition from a red giant to a white dwarf to occur. This is another bit of evidence to show cosmologists don't know it all either and maybe the earth and galaxy are not as old as we have been told it is

As we can already decipher, the earth's environment before the flood and immediately after the flood is of two or three differing systems that will alter how things date when subjected to dating methods which calibrate ages by how the earth ages today.

For example with the water sphere surrounding the earth before the flood certain effects of solar energy on objects on the earth are not going to be the same as they are today. After all men lived to 900 + years, so clearly something was different in the environment. ((2ⁿᵈ ed. Insert 2008) For example, water blocks ultra violet light and X-rays.)

Since the components of solar energy that are not going to get to earth in such an environment are probably of a radiation nature, then dating methods that rely on radiation to date things are going to alter drastically and appear less radiated and thus seem considerably older. Also since man himself will alter his environment on a large scale as we will see next chapter, he will have introduced more dating variables.

Successful heart surgery has been seen on bones "100,000" years old... How do we know the heart operation was successful? The ribs showed regrowth for 3-5 years.(book 1 pg 48) If civilization is supposed to be about 5500 years old, what is successful heart surgery doing on bone 100,000 years old. Is there a problem with the dating methods or is civilization 100,000 years old?

THEM'S FOSILLZ, DEY MUST BE RILLY OLD THEN.

(3rd ed. Insert 2016) There's an automatic belief that fossils mean they are prehistoric bones, and thus must be zillion year old remains. This assumption however is somewhat diminished by the fact that Claude-Joseph Désiré Charnay found **fossilized** bones of swine, sheep, oxen and horses in the ruins of Tula in central America in 1870's, (Atlantis: Donnelly page 350) Thus strongly suggesting that maybe some evolutionists are drinking too much fossilized wine. They just don't want us to know this fact, that maybe, just maybe fossils don't mean prehistoric at all and are from much more recent critters than we are led to believe.

MORE ATMOSPHERE, LONGER LIFE SPANS.

Gravity keeps most of our atmosphere fixed close to earth, but at times when the sun gets nasty and our atmosphere expands, we lose a bit more atmosphere to space. It's well established that the earth has a vapor trail following it showing clearly that we are losing and missing some of our atmosphere. Even today we realize more radiation is coming to the surface of the earth than in previous times. This initial time immediately after the flood means we would have lost great portions of our atmosphere so ages of men would have declined in proportion, and this is born out in the genealogies shown in the bible after the flood. Ages declined rapidly from 600 to 400 to 200 and on down to 120 years. This is not to say solar radiation alone is responsible for the decline in the ages of man, but it has to be a major contributing factor. Eventually our life spans got down to our present "three score and ten.

As we've seen a lot of our atmosphere is on Mars. Mars may have periodically gotten close enough to earth to steal more atmosphere and even a bit more water as it would seem that post flood legends speak of seeing the moons of Mars. If they were close enough to be seen, Mars had to be close enough to cause more problems and steal more atmosphere. We will see that Mars indeed does come back into the picture. Immediately after the flood we had a whole lot more atmosphere and it protected mankind to the point it allowed them to live still fairly long lives. Also the atmosphere had less carbon 14 in it to work its destructive ways on life.

CARBON 14

One of the more fun carbon 14 (C14) dating errors was when a living mollusk was C14 dated at 5000 years old, and you read right it was still living! (Though with mollusks living underwater, they have been protected from carbon 14 influences and thus would seem to be this old. This simply adds weight to my arguments here that the pre-flood environment, protected by a water sphere makes things seem older when calibrated to today's environment.)

WATER SPHERE PROTECTS CARBON FROM BECOMING RADIOACTIVE.

As stated that there was a water sphere encircling the earth before the flood containing and holding ALL the atmosphere fixed to the earth. It protected our atmosphere from the destructive beta rays that change carbon in the air to C14. There was simply LESS radioactive C 14 in the atmosphere (if any) and in our bones at death to break down.

So we can presume after the water canopy was gone there was nothing remaining to keep all our protective atmosphere firmly fixed to the earth and our carbon dioxide lay open to the destructive mutating nature of beta rays. There was an unstable period of time after the flood when we had a larger portion of our atmosphere but it began to disseminate into space and other places and thus the earth's protective atmosphere simply allowed more radiation and other degenerative causes to reduce mans overall lifespan. The very loss of this protective water shell started carbon 14 to build up in the atmosphere in the first place, as we will soon see.

ALLOW ME TO QUOTE DR. FRANKESTEIN... "IT'S ALIVE!!!!"

(3rd ed. Insert 2016) A living snail has been carbon14 dated at 27,000 year old....who knew they lived this long! Living penguins dated 8000 years old with the C14 dating method.

DATING CAN BE FUN!

(3rd ed. Insert 2016) Freshly killed seals dated 1300 years old. (C14) Mammoths dated 27,000 and 44,000 years old. Both specimens were from the same mammoth.

Some bones were dated between 20,000 and 30,000 years old. After the dates for these samples was secured the bones were revealed to be from dinosaurs. Consider this little known fact. On occasion dinosaur fossils have have broken and they smell rotten inside. If they really were millions of years old, that rot would have long since disappeared and fossilized. Fossils are NOT millions of years old!

Some lunar rock samples were dated 10,000, 2.5 billion and 4.5 billion years. All these dates were arrived at by dating the same rock cut into 6 pieces. Guess which date they use. Eenie meenie mini Mo...

Carbon 14 assumes a constant amount of C14 in the bones and other organic matter like wood, shells, seeds and such at the time of death and a constant rate of decay afterward. The decay is constant, but to assume all organic matter had the same amount of C14 in them at the start is to assume the earth's environment was the same all along. It also assumes they absorbed the same amount and they lived the same length of time.

The ancient records clearly indicate the environment immediately *after* the flood that was different to the earth of today. Both pre flood and early post flood environments will affect the way bones and other things will carbon date. The earth before the flood and even for a short period afterward clearly shows a divergent environment. How else can you account for trees with no rings? I mean this is a clear and obvious oversight. If the trees had no rings at one time something in the environment has changed and thus radiation dating cannot be accepted without some calibrating that takes these changes into account.

C14 LEVELS HAVE CHANGED

Carbon 14 is inhaled and the amount of C14 in the creature matches that of the air, but there was simply less C14 in the atmosphere after the flood, and in fact there may have been no C14 in the air before the flood. Here's why. The pre-flood earth was a far more sheltered environment which was blocking out much of the suns damaging rays, allowing life to go on for a much longer time. But the point is the bones of people and animals before the flood simply were not absorbing the same amount of C14 as we do today. And before the flood they may not even have absorbed any!

Bones found from just after the flood date up to 50,000 years old. Bones found from before the flood date so extreme as to be completely undependable and date in the millions of years. This less C14 in the bones to start with at the death of any creature when found gives the indication that they are much older simply because we are presuming the bones were subject to the same environment and atmosphere we are subject to today. Thus when those people died their bones by our way of thinking already appear very old when compared to ours.

EQUILIBRIUM NOT YET ACHIEVED.

By one account it is said that Carbon 14 forms in the atmosphere at the rate of 18.4 atoms per gram per minute and the decay of C14 is at the rate of 13.3 atoms per gram per minute. This is a huge point! The C14 in the atmosphere is not at a point of equilibrium!

If the air was at a point of equilibrium the C14 formation rate would equal the rate of decay!!! The point of equilibrium has been worked out and determined that the atmosphere would need to be 30,000 years old for the point of equilibrium to be met! This means the atmosphere cannot possibly be thirty thousand years old! It's been worked out that at this stage the present atmosphere can be no older than 10,000 years old! It's felt that this is also the upper limit of the age of the earth, but this in fact is only the upper limit of the age of the atmosphere. There's more!

Robert Whitelow found an error in the calculations of the rate of formation of C14 in the atmosphere mentioned above and he came up with the figure of 27 atoms of C14 per gram formed every minute! That means over twice as much C14 is being formed than is being broken down! This too has been extrapolated and it means the present atmosphere is only around 5000 years old! Doctor Henry Morris appeared to feel that this gave a low figure because he felt that this C14 reading in the atmosphere was an indication of the age of the earth, on the apparent assumption that the atmosphere was the same before the flood as after. However we have seen that the atmosphere could NOT have been the same before the flood as it is now.

We have shown by dating the flood that the present atmosphere is about 5418 years old. This lines up with Robert Whitelow's figures for the formation of C14 exceptionally well as his figures thus indicate the present atmosphere to be only about 5000 years old, exactly as is shown by the biblical date for the flood. (Book 9 pg 164-165) A variation of just 400 odd years, an extremely close match up considering how much play has been seen in some of these dating methods.

So not only does dendrochronology prove the bible, so too does the atmosphere itself give the figure of about 5000 years for the time elapsed since the flood, thus confirming, approximately at least, the date for the flood. So the biblical record, the dendrochonological record and radioactive C14 all place the flood about 5400 years ago, an amazing match up.

As the formation rate of C14 in the atmosphere gets closer to the breakdown rate of C14 , that is equilibrium, the atmosphere will give an older age. Once equilibrium is established then the age of the atmosphere can no longer be determined except that it would then have to be at least 30,000 years old. (Of course were equilibrium the case how would one determine how long it took to get there?) But of course equilibrium has not occurred yet so we can still get a fairly close estimation as to the age of the atmosphere.

Realize of course that we cannot include the time before the flood in the calculations as that atmosphere no longer exists in its original form. We can only assume the age of the earth as shown in the bible (1656 years) is correct and then add that to the total after the calculations.

I mean this is huge! This means carbon 14 dates that give any date over 5400 years have to be wrong and calibrated. All carbon 14 dates are calibrated to today's atmosphere, but a sort of logarithmic scale has to be made to account for the smaller amount of C14 in the atmosphere in previous times.

FOSSILIZED BRAINS, ARE OLDER THAN WHEN THEY WERE ALIVE.

(3rd ed. Insert 2016) I've noticed a trend in dating artifacts and civilizations older because of accepted dating techniques. Take Gobekli Tepe in the Taurus Mountains in Turkey. Because there are noted to be ice age animals carved on some of the pillars, and carbon dating some wood found on the site, the assumption is now this site is about 12,000 years old. But it gets more extreme. If a carved figure is found in 70,000 year old deposits, instead of questioning the dating systems, it's now fashionable to accept that these artifacts were carved 70,000 years ago. If the shoe has a trilobite squished underneath then there must have been people living on earth 450 million years ago. It doesn't seem to matter or bother anyone that all the calendars and ancient texts, myths and legends around the globe seem to date civilization to no older than 7000 years. If the date given to the artifact is X number of years the people who made the artifact lived at that supposed time in history. No one wants to question the dating methods. Because of the wonderful magic of Carbon Dating we can now add to the list the Indus Valley civilization. Carbon dating has determined the Indus Civilization must have been in its heyday in exactly 7380 B.C. Isn't Carbon Dating Wonderful?! Throw that ridiculous ancient calendar away…it doesn't conform to carbon dating!!

Not only are these dating methods coming up with ridiculous ages for some relics found, but in order to add veracity to these dubious dates, even alternate archeologists are accepting the dates and thus assuming "modern" man and thus his tool making / ornate crafting techniques are 10's and even 100's of thousands, even millions of years old. No one wants to admit that just maybe the dating methods are flawed! Since the relics and artifacts are found in what is dated at millions of year old dirt rock, sediment or, heck under water, then mankind must have been living millions of years ago. Who cares that historical records over and over again speak of a young earth & show young dates for all the calendars around the globe. See how this affects logic. More on this later.

SPEAKING OF GOBEKLI TEPE

(I wrote this two part letter to Atlantis Rising. It was probably too long to publish in the letters column. But it shows the problems of dating the Sphinx older based on rain wear, (as we see in the next chapter) and it shows the problem of dating a site called Gobekli Tepe using Carbon 14 dating as we discuss in this chapter. I think it deserves to be noted by the archeological society so I include it here. {this also serves, with application, as something of a review of what we've just learned.}

First, a quick synopsis: Robert M. Schoch deduced the Sphinx was much older based on water wear and felt he had substantiation for this older dating because another archeologist dated Gobekli Tepe about 12,000 years old because of carbon dating some wood found on that site, meaning a couple sites dated older than conventional archeology would date ancient sites. What this does is open the door to other sites being dated really old. But there are fundamental flaws in the dating techniques that if left unchecked means this reasoning could cascade into dating many sites much older, all because people have unfounded faith in the dating techniques. My letter…

Robert M. Schoch dating of the Sphinx (and by association the Pyramids) and using Gobekli Tepe as a confirmation is a very flawed set of deduction for his redating of the Sphinx. There are a few things when looked at together show the error of this deduction. First the Sphinx and indeed the pyramids were under a lot of sand. You have to ask yourselves: how did that sand and silt get there? He appears to completely ignore the sand! He is basing his dating of the Sphinx on erosion from water. And the dating of Gobekli Tepe was done by Radio Carbon which is also very flawed.

First the Sphinx and Pyramids were eroded by water yes, but from it travelling horizontally carrying the sand and silt with it, it didn't all come from the sky. Many legends speak of water coming over the land. Abram came from the other side of the flood, not the Flood of Noah, but a different flood and the words used for 'flood' in each case are different. Similarly on another occasion the thirsty Israelites after digging many trenches got water when it came from across the land. Further afield the Hopi speak of water overrunning the continent, and we know Mexico was overrun by the Pacific at least twice. If we took the time we could see that at one time or other the entire globe was overrun by Tsunamis because the continents moved during historical times, as indeed I've previously stated that many legends speak of the land moving and stars fishing up islands and lands moving like fish, and of course continent flooding itself also shows they moved. The events that caused these worldwide tsunamis eroded the Sphinx and the pyramids alike bringing the sand that covered them with it, and indeed the sand itself would have eroded them faster. Though the proof of this is too long for a letter. [given in chapter 6]

Similarly dating Gobekli Tepe by radio carbon is easily shown to be flawed as well. We already know that Radio Carbon dating is only good for a short period as it is. But when you get to dates close to 4000 years and older things start to look older much faster. Why? Again it's a long proof to show the evidence, but in a nut shell, major world events changed the atmosphere. But to start we know for example that Radio Carbon build up and break down are not at equilibrium. Carbon 14 is being created faster than it's breaking down. It's been shown that it would take 30,000 years (from start to finish) for the radioactive carbon 14 to reach equilibrium…meaning the atmosphere in its current state cannot possibly be older than 30,000 years old!...meaning something BIG happened! Calculation show that based on the current level the atmosphere has gone towards equilibrium show that the oldest the atmosphere could be is 10,000 years. However an error in those calculations actually showed it was less and is actually closer to about 5000 years (Which by the way coincides with the age of accurate Tree Ring dating (5400+ years) and indeed the flood itself!) That alone should be factored into any dating using Radioactive Carbon 14.

Without going into great detail, we see by deduction meshed with written histories that before the Great flood a water shell stopped ANY radioactive Carbon 14 from being created making anything from before the flood appear outlandishly old, and not just with C14, but with *Any* dating methods. After the flood the atmosphere started leaving the earth when subsequent upheavals, which by the way caused these worldwide tsunamis to bring deposits everywhere covering up civilizations. These events forced upheavals in the atmosphere ejecting much of it into Space and of course as I mentioned in my potential article that Mars also took some of our water and Air as well, making solar radiation coming to earth much more dramatic and starting the carbon 14 build-up in the first place. Meaning dating the Gobekli Tepe site by Carbon 14 also flawed and a 12,000 years date for that site in fact impossible.

And of course if you account for the sand and silt deposits from tsunamis with the Sphinx this would reduce the age of it to the more standard dates for these sites. Obviously this means you have to accept catastrophism. So it's either a false reading of old civilizations screwing up chronology or an acceptance of those civilizations records that show catastrophism which prove younger dates. Archeologists can't have it both ways.

I hope this helps someone out there.

DATING SPHINX AND GOBEKLI TEPE PART 2

Realizing after I sent this that [first letter] I needed to clarify why I referred to tree ring dating / Dendrochronolgy as proof Gobekli Tepe could not date to 12,000 years old, with the 5400+ years reference. (or was it 12,000 BC, I don't have any of the pertinent mags with me right now)

You may realize that dendrochronology only goes back 5428 years (I think that's the exact date, but I might be out a year or two.)

Dendrochronolgy is the most exact dating method known to man...it gives exact years. Ever wondered why it only goes back only that far and no farther? To me it's obvious but no material I've ever read or come across seemed to make the connection. That is when the flood happened. That's right the trees tell us when the great flood happened, even if most people ignore it.

Well you might say "What about trees from before the flood?" They were in the greenhouse environment that every geologist knows at one time existed on earth. Before the flood trees grew at a constant rate all year round...meaning...they didn't have rings. Simple as that.

Now we can narrow down any wood used to date any relic or placement of any object if the wood has rings, it simply means it has to be from after that date, and in fact would one way or another be date-able to an exact year when you lined up the rings on the wood you want to date, with the rings on the dendrochronoligical record.

Oh yeah... on the Sphinx dating by water wear, as deduced by Robert Schoch. Obviously my deduction of water overrunning the sphinx with sand and silt means one side of the sphinx would be worn more than the other as that would be the direction the water and sand came from. This theory plainly predicts one side of the sphinx would be more worn than another. I'd always figured this, but since I can't afford to go to Egypt to check and didn't come across anyone mentioning it being more worn on one side than the other, I didn't think it would be of any importance. I don't think I even mentioned it in my book. I just figured it was a no brainer. People reading about all the water overrunning the land, when seeing the sphinx would just say oh yeah that's confirms it. However when I read... I think AR #76(?) (with the Sphinx on the cover) Robert Schoch *did* say that one side of the Sphinx was more worn that the other but he weakly stated it would have been from prevailing winds. Nah, it's just not enough. The sand wore one side down and did it quickly, not the rain. That's why one side is more weathered than the other.

thanks for your time. I hope this is of some interest. (We also deal with mega tsunamis next chapter too)

BADDISH DIGS, FADDISH JERRY-RIGGED DATES.

(3rd ed. Insert 2016) In an Atlantis Rising # 103 article entitled "Deep Time in Deep Trouble" by Susan B. Martinez she noted some dating methods are starting to show some visible cracks. First off, to my amazement she notes that "'the belt of meteors gave up its stones, and showers of them rained down on earth', would be a game changer." (for dating methods and results) And "In the early life of our planet, meteorites, stones and dust assailed the earth." These "...fell in such quantities that it can be compared to snowstorms, piling up on the earth in places to a depth of many feet, and in drifts up to hundreds of feet" The article partly quotes from a book entitled "Red Earth, White Lies" by Vine Deloria Jr. (I have not read that book.)

With the amount of 10,000 to 700,000 tons of cosmic dust falling a day on earth she asks the questions could any fossils even be dug out of the ground? [If the dates we've been fed for the age of the earth were true! see next section 'Dust on the moon']. Then the article starts on the dating so well ingrained in common usage, which show some boggling faults. Louis Leakey dug up a one million year old Olduway man but he turned out to be a "(modern type) buried less than 20,000 years in older deposits which had been scrambled by faulting". In fact other finds by L. Leakey were pulled out of similar sediments. But they were not dating the bones with carbon dating; because they assumed very old dates, so they just dated the ground around the bones with Potassium Argon dating. People are favoring Africa for digging up old folks because the formations they find them in date the bones so old, and as the article notes finding "older" bones get you headlines and funding. (Actually the continent of Africa seems to have nearly been pulled apart in historic times (See chapter 6) thus putting 'older' dirt near the surface where later inhabitants walked and died and are dug up now by our paleontologists. But the dates they were getting for these bones were in fact too old for the theories, dating as old as 23 million years! So they selected other samples and got dates more to their way of thinking at 4 million years. The article even notes that this process is called circular reasoning.

Furthermore many of the fossils are found near the surface and subject to torrential rain falls, mixing of old sediments and new. But this doesn't stop people from dating them as old as they can if those dates fit their theories.

Caves also are routinely flushed with deposits. Caves supposedly older than 150,000 years have just collapsed, so any cave in good condition is supposed to be younger than this...which by the way is where many fossils are found.

But just as good, is this realization: Martinez notes that the entire globe was once more tropical "in which case the decay of Carbon-14 may not have been so constant in the past" and not factoring this in would give older ages. She also notes something I had only deduced: "In addition, the amount of cosmic rays penetrating the atmosphere also affects levels of C-14, *research indicating tremendous surges of radiocarbon that once affected all parts of the globe.*" (My casual italics: This could also suggest my approximation of 5400 years for the start of the C14 entering our atmosphere is still *too old*.) Thus in one fell swoop she shows A) they rig the game by using the mixed dirt around fossils to date the fossils and not the fossils themselves. B) They don't carbon date the fossils on the assumption fossils are too old for C14 dating methods as they must be millions of years old and thus carbon dating wouldn't work, (It's believed C-14 dating only works for about 70,000 years: I say only about 4000 years) so they automatically eliminate C-14 dating anyway, and C) then shows that C-14 dating is giving dates that are too big in the first place because of less or more radiation affecting the planet. Thus we see here at least three degrees of artificially enlarging and compounding the dates of fossils found.

Furthermore she blows Potassium Argon (K/A) as a useful dating method dating out of the water. She notes that K/A dating gives volcanic rock (common in Africa) dates from 500,000 years to 17 Million years for the Tuff at Lake Turkana. But she goes further! She notes that K/A dating on samples dated from 160 million to 3 billion years was fixed for a sample that was known to have just formed 190 years ago! (I couldn't have found better evidence in a young earth / creationist article let alone an alternative science Magazine like this one than this!) Many of the fossils are found not even securely attached to the volcanic sediment they are found in indicating they came much later and were involved in mixing up of strata's or sediments, but they use the volcanic K/A dating anyway, even though the dates would be meaningless if attributed to the fossils found therein. Potassium Argon dating can't even date anything less than 500,000 years old to begin with, meaning using it at all is rigging the time game for fossils right from the start!

DUST ON THE MOON

How much dust would be on the moon? They figured that dust falls on the earth and moon at the same rate and they know how much dust falls on these two heavenly bodies each year. If all this dust falling on the moon was tabulated, the amount of dust accumulating on the moon after 4.5 billion years would be 137 feet deep!

One of the fears NASA had about the astronauts going to the moon was the possibility of them sinking into 137 feet of dust on the moon. But all the dust they found on the moon ended up being just 1/8th of an inch deep!

And this makes sense. Otherwise the craters on the moon would not appear the same but would have different edges around the rims. Asteroids or meteors when they hit solid dirt and powder make different kinds of craters. This probably should have been obvious to them by simply looking at the moon through telescopes. However even this miniscule amount of dust would suggest the moon was still over 4 million years old. But that dust probably accumulated in a very short period of time while asteroids and meteors fell continuously on the moon shortly after the planet was blown apart. And this is of course assuming there was no dust on the moon to begin with.

(3rd ed. Insert 2016)This lack of dust suggested to some that maybe the moon was new, or recently captured, (though I don't know how "recently captured" would mean any less dust). But the same holds true for Mars: no Mars Landers ever got lost in 137 feet of cosmic dust. Moon, Mars…all the planets are the same age.

OTHER DATING FLAWS

There are other dating errors too numerous to mention and disprove thoroughly here but when each one is closely examined they all show flaws, but some are easy and fun to show. Here are a few examples.

The Ngandong beds were dated to be 300,000 years old …ready for it?....with an accuracy rating of + or – 300,000 years!

THE GREAT BARRIER'S DATING BARRIER.

(3rd ed. Insert 2016) During WWII some of the great barrier reef of Australia was damaged. Studies were done to see how long it would take to repair itself. Then these studies were used to extrapolate how long it took to build the Great Barrier Reef itself and it was found to have taken 4200 years. (About the same length of time some creationist suggest when the end of the flood occurred. I'm hesitant to suggest that is the cause of the start of the reef, but suggest that some events on earth occurred sometime after the flood, before the reef started its growth. In particular when Australia moved to that point on the globe first; or somewhere in the neighborhood of 1150 or so years between the flood and when Australia settled in its present location and the reef began its growth.) Anyway the point is it didn't take a bazillion years. But one does have to ask the question…why did it start then? Pilgrims? Wagon train Settlers? Or some world event?

OLDER THINGS BURIED ON TOP OF YOUNGER THINGS

Dinosaurs will be dealt with later but they are presumed to be millions of years old. This is one of those clues that proves more than one aspect of this research. At Blue Lick Springs a mastodon was found 12 feet below the surface and 3 feet below the mastodon was found a cut stone pavement. This find is ignored or not accepted for proving dates via association. (Book7 pg. 219) Why? Simply because it doesn't fit with accepted chronologies. According to accepted chronologies the mastodon has been extinct for 12,000 years and man has been civilized for about 5500 years, so what is an extinct mastodon doing buried on top of something that's supposed to be younger than it. This can't be, so rather than admitting there is something wrong with the accepted chronologies, they throw it out with the baby.

MY WHAT BIG FANGS AND TUSKS YOU GUYS HAVE

(3rd ed. Insert 2016) Proving that the bones of extinct animals such as saber-toothed tigers found with bones of man and Vero pottery in the Florida area was flatly dismissed as impossible by anthropologists of the Hrdlicka School because claims of the late arrival of man on the American continent. Similarly J. Claude Jones showed that evidences of extinct horses, lions, mastodons, camels on the North American continent in deposits of La Brea tar pits and Lake Lahontin concluded these creatures lived into HISTORICAL times. This statement was opposed because it was "obviously erroneous, since [it] led him to the conclusion that the mastodon and the camel lived on North America into historical times" Velikovsy notes "But this is an argument of a preconceived nature, not based on findings of field geology. Either the ice age animals survived the ice age, or some of the vicissitudes (a change) of the ice age occurred in historical times." (Book 53 page 156) Meaning once again people are letting theories that are ingrained blind them to evidence that leads to contrary conclusions or divergent theories.

EROSION

If the earth was 4.5 Billion years old and if we are to presume that for the greater part of this 4.5 billion years rain and wind were as they are today, then the erosion due to these forces on the land and earth above sea level would erode at the same rate. A known amount of silt and dirt is washed into the sea each day, week, and year. If this was to happen for 4.5 billion years, then all land above sea level would have eroded away into the ocean 14 times over! We'd be hard pressed to make or find a sand dune, let alone an island or continent. Or said another way it would only take 321 million years to erode all the land we survey into silt onto the bottom of the oceans. Well there'd only be one ocean then wouldn't there? So any date you see above 321 million years you can automatically laugh and toss out as an impossible date! (And with the land as seen today would no doubt mean even a fraction of this 321 million year date would be outlandish if used)

PETRIFIED TREES, BOOTS AND PICKLES.

((2nd ed. Insert 2008) Admittedly I shied away from petrified trees as by the time the first edition of this book went to print, I hadn't found any proof that trees could petrify quickly, though I had guessed they could. I suppose I should have been a bit bolder as I knew petrified trees exist with rings in them indicating they are of post flood origin. Many geologic strata's have petrified trees standing through many of the layers, suggesting that the trees lived during the formation of the layers. This shows the layers formed quickly and likely the layers were the cause of the petrifaction of the trees. But trees can petrify quickly. Since Mount St. Helens eruption in 1980 (I heard the blast) trees which were uprooted and cast into the lake nearby have already started to petrify! A Cowboy boot with the leg still in it has been found and both the leg and the boot have petrified. A person found many jars of pickles in a house that had been abandoned since the 50's. But one had been opened and inside was a petrified pickle! The pickle could be no older than the thirties.)

ROCK HOUNDS SCIENTIFIC COMMUNITY

(3rd ed. Insert 2016) Scientific American 1998 Glenco Earth Science 199 Pg 649 notes that a Mars canyon was found which is much larger than our own Grand Canyon and which was deduced to have formed in just a few weeks.

Do you need me to make the connection…? Oh heck why not…I like two finger typing anyway. First this demonstrates that there might have been a lot of water on Mars to form such a canyon in the first place…a heck of a lot to make a canyon bigger than ours. Then it shows the abnormality of all that water disappearing, when the water that formed our canyon is still here. And then it shows that if the Canyon on Mars, bigger than our own, could be formed in a few weeks, then so too could ours… and indeed evidence when seen from space clearly indicates the Grand Canyon WAS formed in a very short flash flood scenario…and not by a river that would have had to climb uphill to form it!

That was the short version quickly typed before I realized I had already typed this next paragraph… But just for the record…

OK if a canyon on Mars…bigger than our local Grand Canyon can be accepted as taking a few weeks to create, then why not the Grand Canyon? Actually when the Grand Canyon is looked upon from above, it does become clear that it formed very quickly in a flash flood type / breach kind of event, and is not a slow erosion sort of river. But this fact is not told the general public because it quickly brings into doubt other long-term dates given for earth formations. Go ahead look on the net at the Grand Canyon from space… Google earth, and it is instantly clear that it t'wern't done by no tricklin' river!

Think about this. The Grand Canyon, if it took millions of years to form, why is there NO erosion evidence? Rain or avalanches or whatever would have, over such a long period, clearly marked much of the sides of the canyon walls, yet there is no trace of such erosion…. This is still more evidence to show the canyon is newly formed…and it happened FAST. Look at the delta for the Mississippi…Big Delta… Clear as mud…heck it IS mud, a whole 5000 years worth. But look at where the Grand Canyon flushed out. Look for a delta… taint nuthin thare! Why oh Why aint it there? Cuzz it moved so fast it flushed right out into the pacific! Snow Globe city! Consider this little known fact: the Grand Canyon whose top is at 6900-8500 feet above sea level had water from a river from the 1800-2800 foot level below run and climb upwards to create the Grand Canyon. This is complete nonsense! Thus scientist want us to believe it took millions of years to form and the water ran uphill to do it! I don't care how many million years you want to cut the grand canyon, water is never going to run uphill! It is clearly a breach, possibly from saturation from a lake behind, which eroded the softer upper layers of the Kaibab uplift (what is now the location of the canyon), rushed through in flashflood conditions similar to Mount Saint Helens doings. That's' what formed the Canyon…not this nonsense we are fed.

Speaking of Mount Saint Helens, when it erupted, a new canyon formed in a few minutes. It is 1000 feet wide and 140 feet deep. It was formed by water erosion in exactly the same way the Grand Canyon was formed. Looking at the canyon from inside one might suspect it was formed over a long period of time, but the mud flow through the Toutle river formed the canyon in as little as three hours. It all happened on March 19th 1982. Another interesting note is the eruption stampeded about one million trees into Spirit Lake. The trees stand upright and many are already deeply imbedded in silt deposits, which are already forming into peat. The peat is mostly composed of the barks and bits from these trees, which by the way is already forming into coal at the bottom of Spirit Lake just a few years after the eruption. (this was a long term effects of the May 18th 1980 eruption)

OK Back to Mars… Think of it…a huge amount of water had to have been on Mars to suddenly make a canyon bigger than our Grand Canyon. If there was so much water there, what on Mars made it disappear? If it was theoretically there for who knows how many billions of years, why did it disappear, or conversely why is our water still here? It is clear that it just suddenly appeared on Mars and then with the Martian surface not used to water, the dirt just absorbed it all. Meaning it had to suddenly appear…from where? The earth! The find of this canyon (and other Martian water created landscapes) is actually confirmation that Mars stole our excess water from the flood.

However, I've since realized this canyon might not be partially or entirely the result of water erosion in the first place! This canyon might be a large planetary fracture from the "shotgun blast" of the asteroid meteors crashing into the planet.

A MOON OR A RING OR SPIN SPIN SPIN.

(3rd ed. Insert 2016) The law of physics indicate that the moon should be slowly receding from the earth, and it is. The moon is slowly receding from the earth into space. The same physics laws determine a maximum and minimum distance from the earth the moon can be, before it would disintegrate or be loosed from the earth's gravitational pull. Too close and the earth gravity would tear up the moon and turn into something like the rings of Saturn. (I didn't know that!) The minimum the moon could be away from the earth is therefore known to be no less than 11,500 miles. At that point the tidal forces would destroy the moon. So for the moon to have slowly receded from the minimum of 11,500 miles to its present distance is **considerably less than a billion years** and definitely not 4.5 billion years, otherwise that would have set its initial position inside the limit and been destroyed and we wouldn't be having this discussion about the moon…what moon? And the less than a billion years is assuming that the moon was that close to begin with, which probably would have been disastrous to life on earth were the moon ever that close. This scientific limitation seems to be one of the reasons astronomers are suggesting the moon is a new moon added to the solar system, a lost soul captured by the love of earth to stay with us, not so very long ago. But folks creationist have no problem with the moon appearing to be young!…they don't have to come up with hypothesis for its apparent young age.

A similar problem exists for the earth. The earth is gradually slowing its rotational speed. To go backwards in time is to speed up the rotation of the earth, but if you go as far back in time as old earth scientists believe the earth is, the earth would have been spinning so fast that centrifugal force would have caused the equatorial region to be 40 kilometers higher, and the earth's oceans would have settled in exceedingly deep oceans in the polar regions. It's likely the dinosaurs would have been able to fly, as the centrifugal force would have sent them flying off the earth. Ok that's a joke (Thanks Kent!) Not to mention The winds from the corellas effect would be in excess of 5000 miles per hour (or about 8000 KPH

EARTH'S MAGNETIC FIELD'S HALF LIFE

The earth's magnetic field has a half life of 1400 years….meaning 1400 years ago it was twice as strong as it is today, and 2800 years ago it was 4 times as strong. If the earth was as old as they suggest then the earth's magnetic field at one time was the same as that of a pulsar, which is simply an impossibility! The physical limitations of the earth make it difficult to believe the earth could even be older than 10,000 years old with this present 1/2 life of the earth's magnetic field.

STAR DUST: READ THIS SLOW OR READ THIS TWICE.

Radioactive Technetium has a life span of only 200,000 years, so it is difficult for astronomers to understand how it can exist in stars supposedly thousands of millions of years old (Book 34 pg. 18) This is a huge limiting factor.

THAT'S A GREAT DISCOVERY! NOW GO STAND IN THE CORNER YOUNG MAN!

(3rd ed. Insert 2016) Robert V Gentry who wrote "Creations Tiny Mysteries" discovered radio polonium halos in granite. Everyone thought that was great and he was published in science journals around the globe. Then one day it dawned on the astronomical society that this discovery disproved the big bang theory. (I don't know how, I haven't read the book) but suddenly the door shut in Mr. Gentry's face. Suddenly he was persona non grata in the scientific community. So disproving *theories* is a bad thing, right?

IS THAT A COMET, METEOR OR A FORD GALAXY?

(3rd ed. Insert 2016) One problem soon understood in dating the universe with long long Looonng time frames, was the fact that comets still exist. This was a real problem to people who wanted to date the universe "Billions and Billions" of years old. What is understood about comets is that they have very short life spans. They are made from rock and ice and just get sucked into larger sources of gravity like planets and the sun. So why then does our ancient solar system still have so many of them flying around inside it? We already know that far more comets were visible from earth as recently as 2000 years ago than are seen today, so we can readily see that they do indeed diminish rapidly over time.

It's felt comets could not exist or survive any longer than 10,000 years, yet our solar system stubbornly shows many comets are still around. This is grating to old earth and old universe theorists. Biblical young earth scientists don't have a problem with the existence of comets today because many creationists are sure the earth is less than 10,000 years old. But old earth scientists had to come up with an explanation for the existence of so many comets. So the idea of a cloud of them outside the borders of the solar system far beyond the capabilities of any telescope to observe was put forth. This theoretical cloud of comets was named the "O0rt Cloud" after Jan Oort who theorized the idea. No evidence or proof for such a cloud of comets exists and in fact no logical explanation for such a cloud formation existence has ever even been put forth. Yet its existence has been accepted simply because it supports an old universe theory. But this then becomes a "belief system" to substantiate the belief in an old solar system. Old earth scientists then tell young earth creationists to prove it doesn't exist, which probably can't be done. But it's not the creationists that have the problem with comets still existing because they believe the earth and universe are younger than 10,000 years, so the onus is in fact on the old universe believers to prove the Oort Cloud *does* exists, which they have no interest in doing. Other than the "Oort cloud" no way is known for comets to come into existence at this late stage of the game. But what no one has bothered to note, is that the Voyagers 1 and 2 never showed any evidence of this so called "Oort cloud" once they traveled outside the outer edges of the solar system. I however maintain the comets came into existence when the fifth planet was destroyed. Water on that planet mixed with dirt and rock and froze when expelled from the explosion into the chill of space freezing instantly and forming the comets, which over the past 5000 years or so have slowly diminished in numbers as they fell into the planets, the moons and the sun. Comets were much feared in recorded history because they often meant certain destruction was soon to happen on earth. The very fact we don't fear the comets now is again more evidence they have diminished over recent recorded history.

Julie Loar refers to the Oort cloud in Atlantis Rising #73 when she says "…Jan Oort, who theorized its existence to explain the mysterious origin of long-period comets. The Oort cloud is a thousand times farther from the sun than the Kupier Belt. The Oort cloud is a hypothetical spherical cloud of rocky and icy debris, leftover material from the formation of the solar system, which suggests that the aura of our solar system is colossal. Scientists estimate that the distance to the Oort cloud is one light year, a quarter of the way to the nearest star." She also notes that the dwarf planet Sedan, one tenth the distance to the supposed Oort cloud is thought to confirm the clouds existence, and suggests the Oort cloud might be much closer than previously thought. (So then why didn't Voyager run into it?) She has no axe to grind and yet clearly notes the existence of the Oort cloud was "hypothetical" and dreamed up specifically to explain what must be very old asteroids, and comets, ("rocky and icy debris") because no one is willing to believe the solar system is younger than the theoretical life span of a comet. Apparently accepting ancient records that say the earth is a new creation are out of the question.

Ironically an exploded planet, were it to be generally accepted as true, would not contradict the old Solar system belief of astronomers if that planet exploded inside a 10,000 year time span backwards from today, the theoretical life span of comets, so acceptance of such an event could be construed one way or the other.

Another possible origin for some of the comets might be the result of Mars and Venus pulling some water from earth, but the water not landing on these planets, but it going astray into the solar system.

TURNING THE CLOCK BACK

(3rd ed. Insert 2016) A F. Whipple, after calculating the orbits of the asteroids in 1950, concluded that two collisions occurred between these celestial bodies, one 4700 and 1500 years ago. (Book 53 page 260) Might be interesting to see how well these dates tie into events down here. 4700 might indicate the flood period and 1500 might indicate something that started the Dark Ages (see chapter 6)

A DATED SMASHING

(3rd ed. Insert 2016) Australian astronomer George Dodwell studied solstice shadows recorded by the ancients such as Eudoxus, Amen-Ra, and Stonehenge and concluded that these places in fact record a tilt of the earth. Graphing this tilt he discovered the wavy line on the graph that was a match of the wavy line a spinning top makes when it is struck by an object. He deduced that the earth had been struck by a large object 4350 years ago. 4700-4350 = 350…Jewish start of time?

LAVA AND URANIUM

Uranium when present in substances is used to date other materials in the vicinity. But it's been shown even in new lava formations, when uranium is used to date the lava, the lava appears to be thousands, hundreds of thousands, even millions of years old. This is always the case for samples of known age. For example a known specimen of lava formed in 1801 subjected to uranium dating appeared 200 million years old! Oh yeah and a Dr. Austin took a piece of lava from mount St Helen and had it sent to a laboratory for dating without telling them where it came from. The lab dated the lava as 2.8 million years old. Dr. Henry Morris asked the question "Why should uranium ages be assumed correct when applied to rocks of unknown age when they are always tremendously in error when calculated on rocks of known age" (Book 9 pg. 144)

MORE LAVA…WHERE IS ALL THIS LAVA COMING FROM ANYWAY?

At Cuicuilco a pyramid is 1/2 buried in lava. The lava was dated at 8000 years old, but the buildings it is felt could not be older than 6000 years. When archaeologist cannot match up artifacts with known events they are lost as to dating an item. And dating lava is anything but an exact science.

700,000 DIVIDED BY 250K MULTIPLIED BY 122 SQUARED BY THE HYPOTENUSE: THUS 1959 = 8.5 MILLION YEARS

(3rd ed. Insert 2016) Mount Etna erupted in 122 BC. The lava was dated with potassium argon and dated 250,000 years old. A 1964 eruption of Mount Etna was also examined and the sampled dated at 700,000 years old. In 1959 a Hawaiian volcano erupted and they submitted samples from this eruption and they dated 8,500,000 years old. Why is it, if they can't date objects of known age correctly that it is assumed that rocks of unknown age are dated correctly?

YOUNG THINGS INSIDE SUPPOSEDLY OLDER THINGS

Living frogs have been found in coal veins supposedly millions of years old. But the metabolism to keep these creatures alive even in a dormant state simply would not last a million years.

Intricate manmade items have been found imbedded in coal…as have other creatures, including a living Pterodactyl! Coal is compressed vegetable matter which includes trees. Coal can even be found and seen with tree rings! Therefore much if not all coal cannot be older then the flood! Some actions *after* the flood had to create coal! (I'll get to that in chapter 6)

Often living creatures have been found inside rocks and coal, quarried, dynamited, or broken to reveal and free the creatures lying dormant within. The stones, rock or coal these creatures are found in are said to be 100's of thousands to 100's of millions of years old. We see that even coal is estimated at being 10's of thousands to millions of years old, so does anybody know how old coal is? And there is a problem... the creatures inside were still alive. Even creatures in dormant states still metabolize, even if at greatly reduced rates. The metabolism would eventually run its course and the creature would still die and fossilize if left inside long enough. Thus we must conclude that the rocks they are freed from are not as old as believed.

Before I go on I should address this as some of you might have caught this. If coal has tree rings this could account for those supposed millions of years of missing trees with rings we spoke of earlier. I'm willing to bet that those rings as seen in some coal will line up with tree rings we've found elsewhere. I maintain that tree rings could not be formed before the flood so the coal rings are found in must be of a post-flood origin.

Back to those creatures found in rock and coal. There is another real problem. Heat. Presumably when rock formed there was tremendous heat. If this was the case as seen in the area surrounding Pompeii the creatures inside the rocks would have been vaporized. All around Pompeii they found cavities in the lava that destroyed that city. When they poured plaster into these cavities they found that the cavities were of people that were vaporized by the heat of the lava. So why do rocks exists with living creatures inside them? Clearly heat is not always necessary for rock to be formed.

1818 Chalk drawn from a quarry 270 feet down yielded several *fossilized* sea urchins and newts. However three of the newts were well preserved. They were carefully extracted from the rock and put in the sun, and came to life! Two died shortly after but the third was fine and when put in water it escaped. Realize that some of the newts had already fossilized because they had died, but the living ones metabolisms was still in working order so they resisted fossilization. Here's the catch. They were still alive and metabolizing so the chalk couldn't be all that old, but the ones that died turned into fossils. But fossils once they exists are automatically assumed to be millions of years old, but here they were clearly the same age as the other newts which were still alive. This drastically reduced what is perceived to be the age of fossil formation to sometime within the period where metabolism ends.

1835 Near Coventry. A blasted piece of rock thrown on a wagon cracked open revealing a toad inside. The toad seemed to be hurt, and they resealed the rock with it back inside but it still died four days later.

1851 in Blois France a living toad was freed from a 14 pound nodule of flint.

1852 in Paswick Derby England a toad was freed from a large block of ore. It died soon after exposure to the air.

1853 A solid rock was broken and inside was a living horned lizard which lived 2 days after it was released. Clearly the lizard was encapsulated inside the rock when it was formed, but the rock could not have been hot when it formed or the lizard would have been cooked or vaporized.

1856 in a rail road tunnel during construction near the town of Gray, a fresh boulder of "Jurassic" limestone was split which freed a living creature that then fell and died. It may even have died because of the action that split the rock. Based on the description of the creature it could only be a Pterodactyl or Pteranodon, or similar creature!

1865 In Hartland Durham England a living toad was freed from a block of magnesium limestone. It was quite lively so it does not appear it was even in there long enough to run its metabolism down to reduce its strength.

1901 A lady in Rugby England stokes a coal fire and a lump breaks. She then notices something moving in the fire and pulls out a toad which survives for 5 weeks

Late 1500's a surgeon in Meudon France sees a huge lively toad emerge from a freshly split large stone

MANMADE STUFF FOUND IN PLACES IT'S NOT SUPPOSED TO BE.

It's assumed that the earth and its rocks were here long before man, and especially sophisticated man. Man is not supposed to have been doing much before 5000 years ago and it's naturally presumed that the rocks were completely formed long before man and certainly before he was making things other than pointed sticks.

(3rd ed. Insert 2016) In London Texas in 1934 a high quality hammer was found imbedded in "400 million year old" stone. The handle of the hammer had turned to coal. The hammer was made from 96.6% iron, 2.6% chlorine, and .74% sulpher. Debate on this one still goes on. No one seems to want to admit that ancient man had quality tools....and that things aren't as old as dating techniques suggest.

Circa 1787 40-50 feet below the original surface of a quarry was found petrified wood and a 1/2 worked quarried stone, with coins and petrified quarrying tools similar to the ones the Frenchmen were using when they came across them. Even coins don't back very far, as they are thought to start their appearance around 700B.C.

1845 at Kingoodie quarry Scotland that had been worked for 20 years yielded a rock with a nail in it. The protruding part was rusted.

1851 in Dorchester Massachusetts A Zinc and silver artifact that looks like a bell or candle holder, definitely manmade, was ejected out of blasted solid rock. Obviously the item was made before the rock formed. The rock it was found was supposedly '600 million years old'.

1852 an iron instrument thought to be a drill was found inside a lump of coal in Scotland.

1868 Near Hammondsville Ohio a coal mine was being worked when a slab of coal fell revealing a slate all covered with inscriptions. A school teacher in the area said the inscriptions were similar to Egyptian hieroglyphics. It was felt the inscriptions were inscribed when the coal was in its vegetable state. They oxidized before experts could examine them. Too bad they weren't acquainted with today's preservation methods, which would have been an interesting plaque to translate. This by the way is further proof that coal is a new formation, as it turned to coal after writing was invented.

In 1885 and 1877 in Austria a metal cube was found with two rounded corners and a grove down one side. Obviously manmade but it was found inside a lump of coal, supposedly 10,000 years old. Ridiculous arguments stated it was a natural object or a meteorite, and the cube vanished, but a cast of it still exists in the Ling Museum. (book 11 pg 29) Another identical cube was found in an Austrian Coal mine vein supposedly 300,000 years old. At first I thought I was reading about the same cube, but this one was found about 50 feet away from the other. This was in the museum of Salzburg, but it too has disappeared, along with the files. It was found to be made of a Iron Nickel alloy...yet nickel wasn't 'discovered' until 1751. (Book 5 pg 23) What is a machined nickel alloy metal cube doing inside ancient coal. After next chapter you won't have to ask that question anymore.

1891 June 9 Mrs. S. W. Culp found a gold chain imbedded in coal. When picked up coal clung to both ends of the chain. (Book 30 pg 46)

1912 Oklahoma Frank J. Kenwood found a pot encased in a large lump of coal. (Book 30 pg 46)

Though I referred to this to show man's advancement I present it here again. In 1961 a geode (hollow rock with crystalline interior) was found in California. When cut in half, it nearly destroyed the saw, because there was something inside completely unexpected! It was a manmade metal and ceramic object. When the halves were x-rayed it was unmistakably a manmade object, in a rock supposedly 500,000 years old?! Analysing the object came up with the result that it was likely a sparkplug! Either civilization is way older than we thought, or that geode is not 1/2 a million years old!

Human bones were found embedded in a silver vein. Over $100 worth of silver attached to the bones. (19th century silver values)

Shoe prints have been found in "Triassic" period limestone and a 22 inch foot print has been found imprinted in gypsum rock in White Sand New Mexico. What is a manmade shoe impression doing in ancient rock. (Triassic period dates 251 and 199 million years old)

((2nd ed. Insert 2008) A mortar and pestle (along with arrowheads and stuff) were found under a mountain by J.D. Whitney in 1880 in a Gold mine dug in California underneath a layer of lava supposedly 9-55 million years old.)

Obviously either the rocks and coal and such that these objects were found in are either not as old as is generally believed, or man has been around doing and making sophisticated items a lot longer than was previously assumed.

Some have taken the old dates assigned for the rocks these objects were found in as gospel and have thus assumed that man or some sort of spaceman came to earth here long before many of the rocks were formed to seed the earth and let evolution start? Really? The logic of this is silly, not to mention the chronology would be all screwed up. But we'll piece it together for you: Space man makes a print in 400 million year old *soft* rock…with an obviously highly advanced uh…wooden sandal… to better stomp on those nasty trilobites, 350 million years before primitive man shows up, so he can seed the primordial soup with something that will turn into a monkey. Then come back later and help the monkey turn into a man 2 million years later? Then they have that spacemen come back and give cave men these implements, thus being a reason man evolved from cave man to higher forms. Where is *any* logic in *this*? Boy you need a *lot* of faith for that one!

But this is only based on the belief of evolution and that these rocks are as old as current dating methods lead us to believe. ((2nd ed. Insert 2008) Though some fossils do get carbon dated and come up with completely unreliable dates, usually they are dated by which layer of dirt they are found in. The depth of the dirt is used to assign a date to the fossil. Similarly rock layers are dated by which fossils are found in them! This circular reasoning is silly and provides no concrete basis for dating either the rocks or the fossils. It is based on arbitrary dates assigned to them in 1830! A lawyer Charles Lyell invented something called the Geologic Column to aid dating stuff and he did so to deliberately discredit the biblical dates. (Curiously it was this book that steered Charles Darwin off course from being a preacher to what he is known for today.) This column doesn't exist anywhere on earth! There are only 26 places on earth where the fossils happen to correspond to the layers. Over 80% of the earth surface doesn't even have 3 geologic periods appearing in the correct order! (Kent Hovind lectures in reference to John Woodmorrappe).)

We have to conclude these rock formations are very young because not only have manmade objects been found inside formed rock, so too have creatures, some still alive when found! This forces the estimated age of these rocks to be greatly reduced. For some of these things to have become encapsulated and buried hundreds of feet below the surface suggests huge upheavals in a period when man was obviously around making sophisticated items.

In an interview with Captain Alexander he said "We also think that there are some problems in our carbon dating system. If we had cataclysms of a magnitude capable of destroying a continent, then with this catastrophe would have come radiational variations significant enough to actually change the radiocarbon dating system" (Book 30 pg 60-61)

Did he say… "destroy a continent"?

And he's just talking about the upheavals of the earth after the flood, and not the carbon 14 content of the atmosphere. And as we've seen the flood itself limits carbon dating to just 5400 years. Many objects have been found in sandstone and we know sandstone can be made in less than a week, and even in a matter of hours!! In fact the largest amount of fossils are found in sandstone and there is really no way to date sandstone. They date it using the "index" fossils found inside it! The only thing we can be sure about fossils found in sandstone is that they must be a few hours old. That's obviously a stretch but as we've seen fossils are not millions of years old in order for some creatures in rock formations to be still metabolizing.

ICE AND WATER

The Niagara Horseshoe falls are supposed to have come into existence at the end of the ice age. That may well be. The falls erode the underlying rock at the rate of 3.8- 5 feet a year (depending on source material) thus making the falls a maximum age of 7000 years old based on this rate of erosion. However with the volume of water from the melting ice it's deduced that there would have been considerably more water initially going over the falls. The more ice and glacial material there is to melt, the more melted ice there is going to be, so the volume of water in the beginning would have been considerably more. Thus the horseshoe falls would have eroded much quicker in the initial stages. With this factored in, it then reduces the age of the falls to as little as 2500-5000 years depending on source.

Several calculations when measuring glacier movement show glaciers to be between 2400 and 4000 years old but these calculations have been thrown out because they must be too young to fit in with theories. People insist the ice age glaciers were between 12,000 and 1 million years old! But actual measurements persistently prove these estimations to be WAY out!

Similarly the Mississippi silt deposits have been measured and it's been estimated that it took a maximum of 5000 years to accumulate the amount of silt found. However these estimations do not take into account the effect of melting glaciers, which would speed up erosion and the buildup of silt in the initial stages after the ice age.

Land locked lakes such as lake Summer, Albert, Owens, Lahontan, Pyramid, and Winnemucca which were formed from glaciers have all have been measured with various factors and all date in the same general age range of 2500-5000 years old. (Book 53 page 146-156)

RING AROUND THE GREENLAND

(3rd ed. Insert 2016) Another flaw in dating methods is found when considering the so-called annual snow layers on Greenland and other large ice masses. Greenland ice is thought to be 110,000 years old based on the number of annual layers of ice. However these are not annual layers as we have been told, but hot and cold layers where the snow melted then froze and more snow was added then melted and so on. There can be many hot and cold periods on a sheet of snow/ice over a single year. We can verify this. A group of historical buffs were intent on retrieving a plane that was abandoned in 1942 on Greenland during the Second World War. They knew it's exact location so they melted their way through about 250 feet of ice down to the plane, then took the plane apart and brought it up through the melt hole. Though the plane had only been in the ice for about 65 years at the time of its retrieval, they had melted their way through HUNDREDS of layers…these very layers that "scientists" call annual layers. This instantly brings the ages of the snow on green land to about at least a fifth or sixth or less of the previous ages attributed to the snow on Greenland. (and obviously this principal works for Antarctica as well) but even that date has been debated. With the top layers accumulating around 5 feet a year and the bottom layers compressed to about 8 inches means that by averaging the annual depth of the ice on Greenland the age of the ice is actually about 6000 years. AND I'll toss in, that accumulations during high volcanic action on earth would reduce even *this* age considerably. (see chapter 6)

Constantly geologists look for ways to 'prove' the earth is older than it really is and then allow themselves to be blinded to the facts, because…well it just can't be that young so they eliminate contrary evidence …it's unthinkable! This comes from blind acceptance of everyone else's dating assumptions and evolutionary based thinking. It just makes the truth that much more difficult to find or prove because they handicap themselves with an incorrect theory to base dating methods on. We have to be willing to dare and ask ourselves…'but could it be?' Or 'What if…' and never assume because everyone says it's so, that it is so. And what the heck even if it is so, you took the time to prove it to yourself, and if it isn't so, you've made a great discovery…that people will ridicule and ostracize you for. The rewards for research and discovery are endless.

PRECONCEIVED NOTIONS ELIMINATING POSSIBILITIES.

(3rd ed. Insert 2016) I suppose one could accuse me allowing the preconceived belief of a young earth / creation to bias me to young earth thinking. I'm not entirely certain I can honestly accept that as I stumbled on young earth dates long before researching this book, even before deciding to write it, but just to be fair I'll accept that. But it's not just happening with my young earth group. Evolutionist have for a long time assumed man in our current evolved state from lower forms of hominid only appeared on the earth as "modern humans", about 200,000 years ago. Any older and it conflicts with the evolution theory because it means **"modern man" fossil evidence becomes contemporary with our supposed ancestors.** (As indeed some paleontologists are beginning to realize)

Research by Michael A. Cremo has shown that for some time Evolutionist have been throwing out dates of fossils for homo sapiens bones that date older than the 200,000 years; that or they resubmit the sample until they get a date that conforms to their theories. Take for example a finger bone found in a formation 1.84 million years old. (See Atlantis Rising #115) It was examined and found to not be a finger bone of a gorilla, chimp, baboon, or monkey, and different from Australopithecus, or Homo habilis. They found it to be just like a finger bone of a modern Human. But the finger apparently cannot be of homo sapiens. Why? Because they did not exist 1.84 million years ago…or so the theory forces us to believe.

1470 man was dated at 2.9 million years old. But the KBS tuft it was pulled from was dated with the potassium argon method to be 212-230 million years, so they resubmitted the tuft bits and got dates they liked such as .52 million years, and 2.6 million years old. An error ratio of 500%.

Many examples of evolutionist throwing out old dates of human remains can be found from over the 150 years that evolution has crept into the worlds thinking. Another example of this occurring as noted in Atlantis Rising issue #116. Modern man, that is Homo sapiens bones, were found in Pliocene strata with the strata imbedded in the bones themselves indicating they were not recently introduced into the strata, but were imbedded in the strata when the layer was created. Cluing into this, a young Italian archeologists named Mauro Quagliati wanted to submit the bones to radiometric dating, but the person in charge of the bones. Dr. Guido Rossi, said there was no need to do that because they were obviously Homo sapiens. Meaning evolution states homo sapiens were recent thus precluded the need for proving it by seeing if the bones were older, which they apparently are.

So I'm not alone in this apparently setting the limits of dating, evolutionists are diehards at this dogma. But I will put a word in my defense. I have taken the time to see if there is anything wrong with the dating techniques, whereas it can be shown that others pick and chose the dating methods to get the results they want or expect. That's cheating. But the fact is if they took the dates as given, the theory would be so full of holes they would be calling it the Swiss cheese theory of human origins. They know this and this picking and choosing dates practice, is deliberate deception.

MODERN MAN AS OLD AS THE DIRT THEY ARE FOUND IN

(3rd ed. Insert 2016) Some have decided to accept the old dating results despite the problems shown to exist with those methods. I've also broken out of the mold, as many branches of Christendom are willing to accept older dates for the earth contrary to the biblical narrative's pointing to a younger earth. I've simply taken biblical and other legends at face value and decided to see if there's any validity to them. There's validity aplenty.

On the other hand I fully expect human remains to appear very old…well about as old as the earth. Ask yourself this, how old would the earth appear to date by any dating method you chose, 10 seconds after the earth was created? I remember as a kid wondering and asking how can you tell how old a rock is? It turns out they can't even date rocks. Well if you ask an evolutionist they will say by the fossils found in the vicinity. And if you ask them how old the Fossil is they will say by the strata in which it was found. Think about it. The dates assigned are entirely arbitrary and then they use jerry-rigged dating methods to prove these made up dates.

Mankind will appear as old as any rock, sediment, or deposit it is found in. Ancient archaeological sites are now being dated really old by the dirt found in the ruins which they are buried under. But this is just silly! If a volcano or a tsunami tosses dirt onto a city is the city suddenly as old as the dirt tossed onto it? Forget historical records…too limiting. In fact new technology is able to "see" underground sites called Ground Penetrating Radar, and doubtless these sites will break dating records … Superhenge will no doubt be an example. Artifacts are found in 400, 500 million year old dirt and coal. So instead of realizing hey something is wrong here, a whole new trend is occurring, the belief that man has been on the earth for this long…it's the natural progression of refusing to believe the ancient records. But as we will see these and other sites and artifacts were buried in catastrophic events that moved mass amounts of dirt, sediments and rocks and even mountains overtop of old civilizations. The dating possibilities under such circumstances are thus endless. But the events that caused these civilizations to be buried are all recorded in ancient legends, myths and records, meaning they all occurred in historic times…as you will see in chapter 6. The word "Prehistoric" is a red herring word which is meaningless, or at the very most, means pre-creation where no artifacts existed.

An apparently 100 million year old hair was found in Amber. Mysteriously they discovered it was the same as our hair today. They wonder why it hadn't evolved. (See Atlantis Rising #83) UH guys…maybe evolution is nonsense…ever considered that possibility? No matter how you find genuine human remains they will always be "modern", and no matter how old the gravel, dirt, amber, dust, volcanic ash, or rock you find these items in, they will always be modern, meaning man and the earth were made at the same time…well…OK give or take a week.

IS DEEPER DIRT, OLDER DIRT?

Archaeologists when digging deeper into the ground ascribe various dates according to depth because it is assumed that the further down you dig the further back in time those relics were put there. But they seem to overlook a very obvious point. How did all that dirt and whatnot get there to cover the items in the first place?

Does each layer just materialize out of thin air? Remember there is only 1/8 inch of dust on the moon. Does some pixie get out his bulldozer every 100 or 1000 years and add more dirt from somewhere else to cover up a civilization and allow a new one to start? The very fact that the objects are buried in the first place sometimes 10, 20, 50, 100 feet down is because something caused the dirt to pile up and cover up either what was there in the first place or whatever was brought with the dirt when it moved.

Many times items have been found buried apparently out of chronological order, that is to say an item was buried deeper then items above it but was deduced to be from a more recent period. Yet archaeologist never seem to suspect that perhaps a huge event might have mixed up items. In fact if a single event caused 50 or 100 feet of dirt to move over land and gather up relics from all over the place and pile them up on top of each other, it's conceivable that the entire archaeological dig, no matter how deep could all be from the exact same time period! Small wonder dating of events is so mixed up.

In fact something in the recent past did mix everything up and it caused a second huge flood. In fact it caused several floods and started the ices ages and it all happened after the flood of Noah. That's next chapter.

SUMERIAN DIESEL ENGINES?

(3rd ed. Insert 2016) Michael Cremo likes to find and flaunt discoveries of Human bones and relics found in what he believes to be extremely old Rocks and layers, which he uses to demonstrate that man is far older than evolution doctrines impose on the masses. I take the opposite tack, saying man and earth being created recently shows that any examples of Human bones or relics found in any strata simply means the strata such objects are found in was subjected to massive upheavals during the time of man and his civilization. But both our tacks completely discredit evolution as is it is known.

For example Cremo notes that human bones were found inside solid Pennsylvanian limestone with no possible way of introducing the bones into the rock at a later time, items which were found in Carboniferous period limestone dating from 299 to 318 million years ago, long before monkeys even appeared let alone modern man. This completely flies in the face of Evolution doctrines that stipulates modern man didn't appear until about 150,000 to 200,000 years ago. He goes on to speak of the little manmade pot found in

Carboniferous Coal (I mentioned this earlier) which supposedly dates to 305 to 312 million years old. Obviously if a young earth creationist brings these finds to the attention of an evolutionist the derision is epic. But even as an old earth archaeologist the derision Cremo finds attached to these discoveries is interesting. In a 1940 Scientific American (Volume 162 p.14) attention to finds like this is predictable: "What? You want man in the carboniferous? Entirely and absolutely – totally and completely — impossible." Admitting they don't know how to explain such a find, but they still liken them to "…asking the historian for Diesel engines in ancient Sumeria". The idea of suggesting man was in the carboniferous period was so impossible in their established theories, that they stated that if they were wrong, then the whole science of geology is so completely wrong that all geologists will resign their jobs and take up truck driving". (See Atlantis Rising #88) Diesel trucks? Unfortunately the Sumerians wouldn't hire them because they were already using Flying craft and diesel engines weren't being used.

Another example. Some Mortars and Pestles were found imbedded or 'cemented' in gold bearing ore (which had to be carefully picked off to not damage the items) in 1906 near a place called Waldo… maybe that's where he hides…find Waldo and you find Waldo…makes sense to me. Anyway it was 58 feet below the surface. Another was found about 300 feet away and about 10 feet underground. Naturally it was assumed these were a minimum of 2.8 million years old and throws evolution theories into chaos because the implements were obviously manmade, and that's much too early for evolution to work when our ancestors were supposedly only capable of this 200,000 years ago at most, and evolutionists balk at these finds. But even evolutions co founder Alfred Russell Wallace indicated in 1887 that for finds such as this, the proper thing to do is place it on the record. "to ignore it as unworthy of acceptance or subject it's discoverers to indiscriminate accusations of being imposters or the victims of imposters" was already becoming the case all too regularly. Naturtally Michael Cremo sees the artifacts as proving man was here this long ago and it disproves evolution once again.

And I say these objects were tumbled and jumbled in a far more recent cataclysm. I mean guys how do you think these items got buried that deep!?!? To just add 2.8 million years just doesn't work. (Atlantis Rising 117)

2 MILLION YEAR OLD SMILES.

(3rd ed. Insert 2016) This business of evolution really gets silly sometimes: case in point. In 1881 Henry Stopes was on the North Sea coast of England and pulled out of some dirt called The Red Crag formation, a clam shell that had a simple face scratched out on the surface. Big deal right? Apparently this gave the geological society a brain hemorrhage! The red crag is supposedly from the late Pliocene era. Gasp! NO!!! I can't be!!!!! tell me it isn't so! …WHAT the…? First it shows how highly we think of ourselves. This red crag supposedly dates 2 to 2 ½ million years ago meaning this couldn't be right, because man was a stupid rock thumper back then. Me No make face in Clam shell... what be clam shell? OOOH lemme see. God in Clam shell smile at me! Good Greif! Some kid with his Babylonian army knife scratches a face in a shell and tosses it away, the continents move, bury the shell in some red muddy muck and it hardens. A few thousand years later it's picked out and people go bananas about it. Because we think we are smarter than people who built the pyramids, even though we don't know how they did it, and these cataclysms that buried this clam shell happened after the pyramids were built. But by refusing to accept any form of historical cataclysmic in relatively recent history, they tie their brains behind their backs, and end up just looking silly. (See Atlantis Rising #81 Pg 19) Naturally Micheal Cremo who wrote this article assumes it shows no evolution but proves that modern man…lived 2-2.5 million years ago.

THE MISTAKE

You'll recall I said earlier I missed an obvious timeline entry. Did you figure out what it was? Then get an application for a trivia game show!

All along I kept thinking David was 70 years old when he died but the bible doesn't actually say this.

Then just recently I read II Samuel 5:4 and David was thirty years old when he began to reign and he reigned 40 years. There it was. I had figured this out before but just couldn't place it and thus couldn't be sure I was right.

So this means if the 14 generations between Abraham and David is from the death of Abraham to the birth of David instead of when he started to reign, this reduces this time span from 981 years to 951, and a generation would become 67.9 years. This also could reduce the age of the earth by 90 years if we assume a constant length of time for three 14 generation periods. But since the timeline matches up so well with the dendrochronological record by presuming the 14 generations ends when David takes the throne I sort of ran with it anyway. That's why I left it in there. Obviously this is another variable. This would mean (with the equal 14 generation time frame) the flood could have occurred at 3320 BC and the creation at 4976 BC and the earth is 6983 years old. Yada yada yada.

SUMMARIES: VARIABLES

Other dating problems occur that are a bit more intricate to explain that force the explanations of such things as closed and open system...which I have to read a few times just to grasp. I had a difficult time reading some of the proofs and they are hard to read and they quickly make your head ache trying to grasp them...and then I quickly get really tired while trying to figure it out or just plain forget. (for all I know I explained open and closed systems above!) When things are difficult to grasp they become even more difficult to explain and I'm trying to make this work readable and understandable.

Nevertheless when one takes the time, all dating methods that show extremely old ages for the earth and universe can be shown to have serious flaws. If there is still doubt I recommend a side study. Suffice it to say that it is a known fact that dendrochronology is the most exact dating science we have and it confirms the biblical date to the YEAR! Atmospheric carbon 14 content confirms dendrochronological ages as well. So the answer to the question "how old is the earth" is, the earth as of 2007 is 7073 years old, give or take a year or two.

HOWEVER. If in fact the tree ring dating method proves to be in error, for it has been seen that sometimes two tree rings can grow in a single year, then this would probably vindicate Ussher more then I previously thought.

The age of the earth would then become 1656 years (to the flood) 2123 years to end of Abraham's life, 3104 to beginning of David's reign. Then variables kick in. We get the Israelites carried away to Babylon at either 4085, 3701, or 3566 years after creation. Then we get Christ's birth happening at either 5066, 4298 or 4028 years after creation, and the earth being 7073, 6305 or 6035 years old, and the flood occurring at either 3410 BC, 2642BC or 2372 BC. This, compared to the Carbon 14 in the air estimated at about 5000 years for the current atmosphere, is reasonably close to these figuring's.

THE ASTEROID FACTOR.

The one thing that might force a recalibration of the tree rings is, of all things, the asteroids. With the calculation of all the asteroids being in the same place about 4730 or so years ago, some misalignment may still exists somewhere. If an asteroid caused the flood they had to be all in the same place before the flood occurred, meaning some of the variable dates for the age of the earth, the flood and all that other stuff have to be tossed out...maybe. Only some of the dates shown above show the flood happening after the time these asteroids were in the same place. My guess for the age of the earth of 7073 would be thrown out and that would mean the tree rings are lying somewhere. In other words though my guess for the age of the earth at 7073 years old, may still be too old!

Though I don't specifically show when the rings could be registering two winters in a single year, we will see next chapter the conditions that were occurring on the earth that might explain how this could have happened.

Then there is still the question as to when the Jewish calendar (5770) started and what event instigated it. 7073-5770 = 1303 or 353 years before the flood (a likely point for the explosion of the planet, or 6035-5770= 265 after creation or 1391 years before the flood... An unlikely point for the destruction of the planet...unless a different event in the heavens other then the planet exploding started the Jewish Calendar. The exploding planet pushing Mars out of its proper orbit may force the younger earth age, as it possibly strayed less than 16 years before the flood. It is possible that the flood did not occur because of an asteroid from the exploding planet, but from one of the moons of Saturn that was destroyed. But though this is possible, it still seems certain that the planet had to have exploded before the flood and not after it when technology was in decline, and indeed the legends place this event before the flood. So a double checking of the orbits of the asteroids in order to see if they were all in the same place 4700 years ago or if they were in the same place earlier then this is in order. If this is the only time that the asteroids were all in the same place we have to conclude the flood happened after this event and therefore sometime after 2700 BC, meaning the trees are lying, we have a variable generation, and something is wrong with many calendars. So figuring out the age of the earth is not finished yet!

I note that the Jewish calendar starts 3763 BC, Sitchen states it starts 3760 BC. And the reason for that date is not 'from the beginning of the world' as others have assumed but the number of years that have passed "since the counting [of years] began." (book 42 page 296)

SO MANY VARIABLES AND POINTS TO CONSIDER WHEN COMING UP WITH THE AGE OF THE EARTH

I try and show the points of potential error so that maybe what I might be missing is obvious to someone else. Those points are:

1   Point in time where all the asteroids are in the same place at the same time (planet explosion).
2. Problems with the Kings of Israel timeline, and the possible apparent floating generation time frame.
3. Fine tuning of the carbon 14 atmospheric dating methods. Any dates arrived at by carbon 14 must not be greater than the time it takes to reach equilibrium (30,000 years) and in fact must not be older then the degree to which we have proceeded towards that point, that degree being something of a variable in itself. (around 5000 years)
4. A second look at those tree rings. Although they are the most accurate dating method, they could be suspect in this. Although the amount of variation in these specifics is quite a bit in relation to each other they are minute in comparison to other errors used in dating methods compared to orthodox methods.
5. The tree rings starts 5419(+ or -) years ago (3412 BC date of flood)
6. Estimated date of flood by the biblical record 5417 (3410 BC constant length of a generation) 4379 (2372 BC variable generation) years ago. (possibly when adding the 1 ½ years due to David's ruling 40 ½ years the tree rings date the same as the date arrived at for the flood 3410BC)
7. Age of present atmosphere (carbon 14) aprox. 5000 years (3000 BC date of flood)
8. Estimated point of planet exploding 4700 years ago. (Aprox. 2700 BC probable cause of flood)
9. Jewish Calendar starts 5770 years ago (3763 BC)or 3760 B.C.
10. China's calendar current date is 5372 (3366 B.C.)
11. India is at 5119 (3113 B.C.)
12. Mayan calendar is at 5117 (3111 B.C.) (Another reference says it began August 12, 3113 BC [Atlantis Rising mag. #92 pg 25])
13. Egyptian 1st dynasty estimate starting time (5100+ or - years ago) 3100 BC
14. Other variables, the kings of Israel lineage and the time between the carrying away to Babylon and the Birth of Christ.
15. Shorter years. If we include a shorter year in the mix from 687 BC and back. Say if the years from before this time were 360 days long and not 365.249 and we use the age of the earth as 7073 or Usshers 6011 the difference can be as much as 48-64 years subtracted somewhere in the mix.

(3rd ed. Insert 2016) While it's still fresh, I thought I'd mention I found some more dates to compare with just mentioned ages above. Petrie dated Egyptian Menes as starting 4777 BC, Breasted at 3400 BC and others suggest 2850 BC. (book 34 Page 115) General consensus is he reigned around 3100 to 3000 B.C. Some of these dates line up surprisingly well with dates mentioned above.

3100 BC

(3rd ed. Insert 2016)This 3100 BC date, or near this date just keep cropping up as some big event or events happened here on earth. A Sumerian clay chart apparently says events were witnessed in the sky on June 29th 3123 BC. A world age named the Kali Yuga in the Mahabharata is dated to start 3137 BC. Mayan calendar starts August 12 3114 BC. An asteroid is thought to have hit Australia in 3100 BC. A comet is thought to hit in the Mediterranean Sea in 3150 BC. Worldwide erosion jumped from 20-30 tons to 140 tons per Kilometer around 2950 BC. The Nile delta experienced climate deterioration around 3090 BC. In Antarctica a peak in sedimentation occurred around 2900 BC, and an unusual spurt in growth of peat moss growth is noted to have occurred around 3100 BC in the south Shetlands. (Atlantis Rising 117)

Though none of these dates match each other exactly they are all very close, some of them extremely so. Though shown together they speak of errors in the chronology, the errors are small and making them clear this way may cause someone to be able to decipher exactly what the errors are and fix some things. For example we have by one account the asteroids being all in the same place at the same time 4700 years ago (this is probably a rounded off figure). If this is truly the case and working backward further does not put the asteroids together again, then this has to be the point when the planet exploded. If this happened at this point in time, and it is the cause of the flood, we can't then have the flood occurring before this now can we? We can't have the flood occurring before the cause. And the evidence of the date of the flood would be the tree ring record. Those three things alone can force errors out of the variables.

Maybe even the dendrocronology is subject to serious scrutiny.

But these all indicate a short time frame and definitely not millions of years. Though I favor the age of the earth as worked out to 7073 because of the closeness of the tree ring dating to my deciphered date for the flood, I am not married to this date. Particularly because the exploding planet seems to indicate a younger earth still, closer to Ussher's date. And ultimately I may simply have vindicated Ussher's conclusions.

If I could figure out for sure there was something wrong with the dendrochronological record I would bank on the earth being 6035 years old instead of 7073 merely because of the kings' lineage and the exploding planet. Perhaps the trees are fooling to us somehow. If we can figure out what the discrepancy is and why it is there we can maybe solve this to an even more perfect solution. It's possible in some years there were two winters...a normal winter followed by a short warm season followed by another "winter'. This could start and stop and start tree rings making a second ring for the year. We will see there may be cause for a time when two winters occurred in the year in the next chapter.

Next we will see that even though we have reduced the age of the earth here, this will actually clear up dating problems when associated with geology and not make them worse. Though calendars start at some point or event, knowing what those events might be is not always obvious, but later on I will try and deduce what started some of the calendars.

At the beginning I said I would show an exact date. I guess I showed many, and the correct one may be there staring at us. When I started this I thought I had it nailed but I kept finding more and more variables. Though the variables put off finding an exact date, they consistently show a younger earth. As we shall see next chapter a young earth actually solves geological mysteries that an old earth theory simply cannot explain, in other words a young earth will clear things up more than just saying these things took millions of year to happen. That, we will see, doesn't explain anything.

Chapter 6

PELEG: THE ORIGIN OF THE CONTINENTS

I suppose this chapter could be summed up in one question: If we speeded up continental drift would it account for what we see on the earth today, and would ancient legends and geological evidence support a theory based on this question?

This chapter could easily be a book in itself and in fact calculating the word count and comparing it to some of my research books it could in fact stand alone as a full book. (This whole book is over 1/3 of as million words, written mostly in the 1990's before I even got *near* a computer) I also had the most difficulty in organizing this chapter. Indeed I don't think that it is as organized as it could be. I tend to repeat some things, though in some cases I do that on purpose. It does eventually get where I want it to go, so I've left it as is. If it gets a bit tedious forgive me. I reread it many times reworking it each time and finally I'd had enough. The first time I reread it I was mad at myself and the obvious disorganization and repetitiveness. About the 3rd time I read it I was frustrated at how difficult it was to organize. About the 6th time it was just bothersome in some areas, but I didn't have the heart to dare restructure it anymore and risk some sort of continuity breakdown...so I just tweaked it a couple times and have left well enough alone. It does get where I want it to go so have patience with me on this one. (this 3rd ed. is starting to look a little better. You're lucky you waited)

The physical evidence of geology all around the world corroborates the ancient legends along with written and verbal histories and does not back up the theories most scientific disciplines present, yet the ancient histories are refused as evidence and even the geologic evidence is ignored simply because it does not mesh with current theories. But they are *theories* thus they are meant to be proved or disproved, not endlessly propagated. The very fact that all three types of evolution conclusively disprove the other two types clearly suggest we may be on our own to weigh the evidence, as it would seem "science" has shirked this responsibility and instead had decided to push their pet theories down our children's throats in buildings we originally made to teach the children truth about history.

But this has had grave consequences. Since they insist we are evolved creatures, they take God out of the teaching picture and thus make morality a state of mind or a cultural thing rather than an absolute and consequently our civilization has wandered so far from its moorings the ropes are starting to break.

After the flood mans advancements were so rapid, and technology advanced so fast when the gods showed up, that the earth itself, weakened and cracked from the flood, gave way to the pressures of this advanced technology and caused the dividing of the continents just 101 years after the flood using something still existing today.

PELEG

First off I guess we should explain "Peleg". After the flood the descendants of Noah are listed and one of the sons of Eber is named Peleg because in the days of Peleg the earth was divided. Now what could this division be referring to? Tribes or land separated or divvied up? No. This does not mean subdivided and surveyed. We can deduce it means that actual earth itself was broken up into continents at this time because the name Peleg actually means earthquake. So either an earthquake caused the dividing of the continents or the dividing of the continents caused an earthquake. Though a subtle difference, I go with the latter. We even know when this happened: 101 years after the flood, that is 3309 BC. (At this point I will continue on with the premises that the earth is 7073 years old. If we presume the earth is 6035 years old owing to the possible earlier planet explosion and the fluctuating generation length then you can subtract 1038 years and this date would be 2271 BC)

I Chronicles 1:19 also relates this incident. And unto Eber were born two sons: the name of one was Peleg (Earthquake) because in his days the Earth was divided: (the root word for split). But no normal earthquake is going to divide the earth, but the earth being divided would of course cause an earthquake. The bible specifically refers to the creation of the continents and the date given is when Peleg was born, and thus he was named so because of the incident. This means we have to clarify the fact that at one time all the continents were all part of a single massive continent.

PANGAEA SPOKEN OF IN THE BIBLE?

(3rd ed. Insert 2016) Believe it or not the bible makes more than a nebulous reference to Pangaea. In Genesis 1:9 we read "And God said, let the waters under the heaven be gathered together unto one place, and let the dry land appear: and it was so." If the water was separated to one area of the globe, doesn't that suggest that the land was separated to another part of the globe? That's exactly like the mass continent of the world which been stated to have originally existed before a break-up by geologists! Meaning history appears to have recorded it…as have other ancient stories as we will see.

NOT ALL AT ONCE

We can deduce that the meteor that caused the flood cracked the entire face of the earth creating fault lines throughout the earth, at the places which would one day delineate the edges of the continents.* Other fault lines could still break up the landmasses even more in future Peleg actions. We cannot however say this meteor actually caused the break up because we know the land was still in one piece after the flood. (* this isn't unique in the solar system. Mars has a major fracture caused by Krypton's explosion, as does one of the moons of Saturn: Mimas, and a moon of Uranus (Miranda) appears to have blow apart and reassembled.)

When this dividing happened the earth wasn't divided to the point the continents are at today. This was an ongoing series of geological occurrences that started and stopped according to events that happened after this time. For example, Charles Darwin was impressed by the clear evidence of recent uplifts of the mountains of Chile 1300 feet up finding undecayed shells on the surface. He also noted the mountains didn't rise gradually but in jumps as only a few intermediary surf lines were detected showing the land didn't rise little by little. (Book 53 page 79

CONTINENTS BROKE IN RECORDED HISTORY

So then what caused the actual movement of the continents to start? Believe it or not I am going to try and give evidence for the cause of the dividing of the continents to be something that was caused by man and his technology. For that to be the case there must be evidence of incredible technology in the past which, we have shown, and there MUST be evidence of upheavals in the earth on the order or magnitude that would be from such an event during *recorded history*. Furthermore I must find evidence in the past in written and verbal histories that say that this is in fact what happened, that is, the cause of all this havoc was caused by man himself! In other words this didn't happen over a period of millions of years it happened within the last 54 or 43 hundred years. A tall order! But you won't be disappointed!

We've already seen that man had vast capabilities and technology to enable him to destroy an entire planet and cause the flood itself so we can see this is a possibility. Already we have quoted one ancient text that speaks of this event occurring in recorded history [the bible about Peleg], so a few corroborating histories should seal at least half the work. Unfortunately we seem so stubborn sometimes we need to be hit with mountains of evidence so I'll give all I can find in hopes of convincing more than the usual smatterings. And besides, it's more fun.

AT ONE TIME THERE WAS JUST ONE LAND MASS.

Obviously it is already an accepted fact that at one time all the land was part of one huge continent, and we have concluded that the continents have come into existence since the beginning of time, that is since creation. So it does stand to reason that such information might possibly be found when we accept the young earth theory. So I think we already have a firm footing to believe it could have happened. Thankfully the theory of continental drift is now firmly established so I don't have to go through the trouble of proving it occurred. (It took about 100 years for that theory to be accepted. Surprisingly some creationist don't accept the continental drift theory.)

It is now conceded and established that there exists what is now termed continental drift, and the international geophysical year confirmed this theory, that is that the continents slowly creep across the oceans and were initially all part of a single land mass. Oddly this theory was very slow in receiving acceptance even though the bible and other legends clearly refer to a time when the land broke up and divided. ((2nd ed. Insert 2008) A curious and telling note deserves mention. Even kids in school, myself included, were able to figure out that Africa and South America were at one time joined, yet Geologists for over a hundred years refused to accept the evidence that even kids could figure out.) What's seems odd is no explanation seems to have been put forth as to why the continents just seemed all of a sudden to start drifting in the first place, or for that matter what could have caused the land to break.

Originally there was just one continent commonly called Pangaea but also referred to as Gondwanaland. Though it seems these names refer to the mass continent at two stages, that is a stage where there was no break up, and a stage where there was only a partial break up. It was this original continent that was divided into the continents as we know them today. Long has the cause for the break-up of this large continent gone unsolved, and thus the force which could separate the continents has likewise also gone undeciphered.

Before the flood this single continent would have been a sound and solid firm mass of land. With the meteor smashing into earth to cause the flood, we can at least deduce that the cause for the breakup of the original mass continent Pangaea into fracture zones known as fault lines was this same meteor. Though there were no actual continental masses, as are evident on the earth today, there now existed the crack lines which would soon turn into the edges of the continents. We might also conclude that with an additional 5 or 600 feet of water still remaining after the flood, some of the continental shelves…so to speak…may have already been underwater to allow water to flow as rivers there no more.

This meteor would have cracked this huge "floating" continent. This in itself is a huge piece of the previously unsolved puzzle of ancient geology. We also see that when the meteor hit the earth causing the fountains of the deep to break forth this action also pushed the land mass outward, or perhaps we should say 'upward', and though I don't fully comprehend the dynamics of such an action, it will no doubt be a clue to further understanding the physical makeup of the earth, and subsequent upheavals might be better understood in this light.

Now we will henceforth clear up the mystery of what caused the continents to "divide" and start their "drift".

MORE THAN ONE DISASTER

Although it is generally believed that the bible speaks of only one cataclysm; the flood, in actuality the bible speaks of several cataclysms and alludes to a few more. However the focus of the biblical text is seldom on the cataclysms, so the extent of the cataclysms is usually overlooked. I mean think of it! Here the earth changes it's physical characteristics from a single land mass to that of a series of continents...I mean this is big news, and all the bible says in reference to this is basically 'in the days of Peleg the earth was divided', then it continues on with the rest of the genealogy! This is simply because the bible often seems to have a different set of priorities. Geological history seems low on the totem pole indeed, but fortunately it is not entirely ignored and some clues do exists. Often cataclysmic events may have hardly affected the recorders of the event whereas in other parts of the globe that same event was simply massive devastations in their 'local' neighborhood.

One of the major problems with the flood legend is that there are several differing flood legends and they appear to contradict each other, so it is usually presumed the biblical flood was not one that covered the entire earth, as there are often more and varied survivors of these other floods which only superficially corresponds with the biblical account. And as we have seen 19th century geologists couldn't understand how there could appear to be more than one worldwide flood. We will now explain the other floods.

When we read of these other floods, confusing or supposing them to be other references of the biblical account of the flood of Noah, we see contradictory evidence and legends which tend to suggest the biblical account is inaccurate. There is sufficient evidence to show there was indeed a worldwide flood. And indeed everywhere there is evidence of often more than one, but certainly at least one flood. But as has been shown the flood DID encompass the entire earth just as stated. Once we explain what caused the other floods, the biblical food of Noah will be easier to distinguish from the evidences of the other floods. And everything will become clearer when we separate and explain what caused the other floods so that they can be seen as separate events, and not the same event.

The fact is there appear to have been many floods and three or four main floods, but this does not contradict the bible where it says God would never again destroy all mankind by a flood. He didn't, obviously. Though there were subsequent floods, vast in their consequences, they were not universal, but more local, even though the term "local" may in fact mean 1/2 of a continent or more (that is a continent by today's reckoning.) The cause of these subsequent floods is of an entirely different nature... not necessarily from rain but from incredible almost unbelievable tsunamis. They would not have been caused from tidal action so much as displaced water.

Many creationists in the 19th century couldn't understand how there could be evidences of what seemed like more than one worldwide flood, and so geological history got away from them, and geology found itself in the hands of evolutionists. But as we shall see when we understand that the ocean overran the continents in Peleg and subsequent continuations of this initial Peleg motion, it will explain the apparent confusion of flood legends, and the physical geological evidence will be much more easily understood.

A SECOND FLOOD SPOKEN OF

As it turns out and no doubt few people realize, the bible actually speaks of two fairly major floods! This second flood is referred to by Joshua just prior to his death.

Joshua 24:2) "... Your Fathers dwelt on the other side of the flood in old time, even Terah, the father of Abraham, and the father of Nachor [same as Nahor]: and they served other gods. 3) And I took your father Abraham from the other side of the flood,..."

Initially I thought this was probably referring to before the flood of Noah, but realizing Terah is Abraham's father, this has to be after this flood. So I thought it might simply mean *after* the flood. But then it occurred to me it might be a different flood.

If this was the case the word translated as flood might be different then the word translated 'flood' for the time of Noah. I checked and it is! The word used for the Noah flood is more descriptive of that flood.

But this word that Joshua uses is referring to something that comes out of the sea, and could possibly mean the flood of the Nile, or the word could be used in that context. However Joshua referring to this as "the flood" means this was more than a normal flooding of the Nile, and it doesn't seem at all to be in reference to this river at all, and indeed the location from which Abraham came was not from the direction of Egypt.

Furthermore the term "other side" doesn't mean before or after, it means literally the physical other side. So it speaks of a more localized flood that Abraham originated from that happened somewhere in between where the Israelites were at the time and where Abraham came from. And it's indicates the period when this second flood occurred. Terah was born 1878 (years after creation), or 222 years after the flood, and Terahs' father Nahor was born in 1819, or 163 years after the flood. It would seem to suggest that a second flood occurred sometime around this period. This then could suggest a different flood then that which might have occurred at Peleg pinpointed at 101 after the flood of Noah. So we see we have the flood of Noah, the flood of Peleg (101 years later), for indeed the continents moving would have displaced water and caused massive flooding, and if the flood of Terah and or Nahor is not the flood of Peleg then it is a third flood, shortly after Peleg perhaps somewhere between 150-200 years after the flood. And the more I look at the overall picture I start to be convinced that what caused Peleg, reoccurred a short time later, simply because the men of the earth didn't fully grasp what had happened the first time during Peleg.

A QUICK OVER VIEW

Ancient Indian legends speak of as many as 9 cataclysmic events in history. The Aztecs spoke of at least 4 world ages which can be interpreted in more ways than one, but each cataclysm or world age is given a name. They speak of a "Water sun" (What the sun might have looked like through the water shell and this seems to refer to the time before the first flood of Noah) Earth sun (earth pre Peleg?) Wind sun (Ice age?) and fire sun (a hotter sun?) In light of the evidence presented in this work, this series of four suns seems to indicate a progressively more inhospitable environment under the sun itself. As more atmosphere is pushed or pulled off or jettisoned from the planet during cataclysmic actions, the sun itself becomes more intense as seen from earth's inhabitants. This stands to reason as when there is less atmosphere the sun becomes progressively harsher to life on earth.

The Egyptians priests speak of four times when the sun rose where it set. In fact most cultural world histories speak of 4-7 world ages with this current age being the 4th or 7th. This is why the sky is sometimes called the 7th heaven. Literally they are referring to a sky that actually appears different from a previous sky. What could change the appearance of the sky?

Herodotus mentions that the Egyptians spoke of twice the sun setting where it used to rise and twice rising where it used to set, changing its position 4 times. Oddly they say Egypt was unaffected by this, either with harvests, the rivers or disease.

Legends speak of the lands swimming like fish and the stars changing their positions. Maps of stars exist in areas where some stars on the chart are not visible from that particular location.

Mayan, Chinese, Egyptian, Babylonian, Grecian, Mexican, African and Polynesian all have similar or even the same names for some of the constellations, even though the constellations so named have no similarity to the creatures they are named after. This suggests a closer link between these cultures then their present position in geography would suggest. If these people are so far away from each other, what could be the reason they appear so similar? Were they at one time closer together, before the continents divided? There are many hints in history that suggest this is the case. It stands to reason if all people are descended from one family (Noah's) and they named the constellations or the pre-flood people did, they would pass these names down through the generations and they would be the same even after the tower of Babel incident historically the cause of different languages. But if you don't buy this version of history, then many mysteries remain for you.

NO SINGLE LEDGER WILL REFER TO EVERY CATACLYSM

Since some cataclysms will be smaller and more localized than others where say a meteorite or a comet hit, they will be in some legends and not others. We can't assume cataclysmic events are all spoken of in a single ledger, and so consequently no doubt some that occurred may not have been mentioned in the bible, or Indian histories or Egyptian ect. But a look at all the histories should give a fairly adequate understanding of what happened in the past, particularly when these histories compliment and support each other. Obviously the bigger the cataclysm, the more ledgers will refer to it.

There appear to be about 9 cataclysms the bible speaks of which interestingly coincides with Indian histories, possibly because of the relatively close proximity of India to Israel. Many of the events spoken of in the biblical record could have been indications of huge worldwide or very major local cataclysmic events. These are: (1) The flood,(2 and 2a) Peleg and a second Peleg shortly after the first, (3?) Sodom and Gomorrah (4) the ten plagues of Egypt, (5?) The walking of the Israelites across the Red sea. (6)The Israelites crossing the Jordan River with Joshua (7+?) Joshua's longest day which followed rocks falling from the sky. (8) Isaiah speaks of the shadow going backward 10 degrees. (earth apparently spinning backwards) (9)The earthquake during King Uzziahs reign. One might even add the return of the two and a half tribes of the Israelites back across the River Jordan, though no mention of how this return trip was accomplished seems to be noted. Anyway these events occur so close to each other, within 5 years they may be looked upon as the same event. These waters of the Jordan river were even divided by Elijah and Elisha so these may indicate other earth events. Not to mention the times when fire called upon by Elijah rained down on the captains and their 50s.

DID THE EARTH HAVE A RING AT ONE TIME?

One can't help but wonder due to the frequency of some of these events that perhaps the earth for short periods of time captured some of the debris from the exploded planet, similar to how Mars has captured two asteroids. We may have had several asteroids temporarily orbiting the earth, which from the surface may have simply appeared to be comets. A shift in the suns intensity, possibly brought on by asteroids hitting it as well, caused excessive solar activity which in turn expanded the atmosphere of the earth out to the point where these asteroids orbited bringing them crashing down to earth. Some of this debris would have caught fire as it entered that atmosphere at 18,000 miles an hour, and appeared like fire coming down from heaven. This would also explain how some ancient historians spoke of stones often falling down from the sky. Though as we've seen, Mars tossed more than enough stones to account for the legends, but earth shifting would likely coincide with major impacts from above.

When one looks at old legends and ledgers there were apparently a whole lot more comets in the sky and these sightings were not welcomed. People were deathly afraid of them. And why not! If they came to earth anywhere near the people seeing them it almost certainly meant disaster. But it would seem clear that there were many more such incidences the further back in time you go, and this stands to reason. As meteors hit earth from a 'meteor stock", that stock dwindles and fewer and fewer meteors hit earth as time lapses and the time span between disasters becomes, on average, longer. Recorded sightings of comets are fewer and fewer as history marches on. The last major disaster spoken of in the bible appears to be the major quake during King Uzziahs reign, though some hints in other ledgers suggest there was another one about 700-500 BC. (Obviously one of the dating variables suggests this could in fact be the same time and event.)

The date 687 BC has been put forth in this regard as when the year reached 365.2423 days long. So the past had more major disasters and they had more comets. It would seem the two phenomena are linked.

Though this chapter deals mainly with Peleg some of these events mentioned here deserve a better look, and indeed some of these appear to be of a similar nature to Peleg as a continuation of the original division of the continents.

TEN PLAGUES OF EGYPT.

The ten plagues of Egypt were in all likelihood caused by some massive cataclysms in the nearby neighborhood, particularly when you consider the description of fire raining down from the sky. In cataclysmic events this is a very credible possibility. Rock with oil or some flammable substance stuck to them could ignite under heat of volcanic action when thrust into the air and would then come back to the earth as flaming bits or fire raining down from the sky. Even just flammable liquids could rain down in this fashion. We all know how much flammable oil is in the middle east!

Immanuel Velikovsky brings so many concurring corroborating stories of this period of time in earth geological history that it becomes abundantly clear this was no local phenomena, but rather more of a worldwide event being described by a local ledger. It just appears that Egypt was at the center of the storm or the consequences of it. Many of the ancient legends he brings into play corroborate with the biblical account perfectly. He talks about many ledgers and histories around the earth that refer to a low sky, and relates this to the origin of the idea that mountains hold the sky up. Something we usually attribute to little Henny Penny who believes the sky is falling. The African continent appears to have nearly split apart during this time frame.

At one time mountains fell and when they did, another event happened... the sky fell and / or it changed its appearance. So much debris and moisture was in the atmosphere that the sky appeared lower, and thus the legend that the mountains holding up the sky came into being because of the link between the two events.

In Deborah and Barak's song about the Israelites journey they speak of the earth trembling, the heavens dropping and the mountains melting, (Judges 5:4,5) and David's' Psalm concerning the same period says the earth shook, the heavens dropped and Sinai moved (Psalm 68:8) So not only do other legends speak of a lowering sky, the bible itself refers to such an event. I personally found this to be a surprise because though I had read the bible several times, I had missed this connection. In fact there are Finnish, Belgian, Samoan, Chinese, Eskimo, African, Japanese, Brazilian and no doubt other legends that speak of a lowering or collapsing sky. This is a huge weight in the argument of historical earth wide cataclysms. Some stories suggest the sky was so low you had to bend over to avoid having your head in the clouds so as to see and breath clear air! When one asked "how's the weather up there?" it was no joke! (book 14 pg 103-104, 132)

But a collapsing sky is only a symptom of what was going on at the time. The earth was trembling and mountains were dropping in some areas and rising in others, as mountains would also have risen in this same time frame, though not necessarily in the same place they were falling. As continents moved, some continuous action thrust and crumbled mountains simultaneously, often in the same place. In some cases it's difficult to tell if some of these legends speak of the original Peleg action or this time during the ten plagues and the Israelites exodus, but whatever event they speak of, they speak volumes all the same. No doubt a study of these histories in their context by more qualified ancient historians could decipher what time frame these legends refer to. And these ledgers are clearly contradictory evidence to what the earth scientists of today speak of when they refer to a calm uniform gentle geological history. Give the ancient records their due. Actually many have started to realize there must be something to these records. So many records speak of cataclysms and many comets that they are starting to reassess things in this light.

Many legends speak of differing heavens. This seems to say that the sky changed in appearance, thus the 4-7 heavens. It has been noted that if only a few more miles of atmosphere were added to the earth, the sky would be a different colour. I deduce that when the ancients said there was a different heaven the sky was a different colour, possibly a lighter blue or even a greener shade of blue. When one looks at the sky at the horizon and compares it to the sky above you, you will understand what I mean. The sky above must have been like the sky at the horizon at one time. At one time the sky might have been almost emerald, similar to looking through a little water or a lot of water, or a little window glass or a lot. If we lose some more atmosphere I would have to guess the daytime sky would turn a darker and darker blue then purple then were to it continue to it's logical end...black!

FALLING SKY... CHICKEN LITTLE

(3rd ed. Insert 2016) Initially I ignored references to falling sky and waves, as I still as yet didn't grasp the significance of these legends. But for the third edition I looked again at the books I used for research for stuff I initially passed over. I found another ancient record (and thus more confirmation) showing the sky fell in the distant past. "There is, for example, a passage in the Saxo's Gesta Danorum (VIII, 262), which could be describing either of the two cataclysms mentioned in the Oera Linda Book. It says: 'The sky seemed to fall suddenly on the earth, fields and woods and sink to the ground; all things were confounded, and the old Chaos come again; heaven and earth mingling in one tempestuous turmoil, and the world rushing to universal ruin". (Book 31 page 35) Again this falling of the sky is mentioned in a few ancient legends and is indicative of inordinate volcanic activity due to the continents moving. But here's more: a great cataclysm legend of China was recorded by Martinus, a Jesuit historian and quoted by Robert Scrutton...

"At the beginning of the second heaven, the earth was shaken to its foundation. The sky sank lower and lower towards the north. The Sun, Moon and stars changed their motion. [They appeared to do this because the inclination of the earth's axis was changing.] The earth fell to pieces, and the waters in its bosom uprushed with violence and overflowed it. ... The system of the universe was all disordered. The planets altered their courses, and the great harmony of the universe and nature was disrupted..." (quoting book 31 pg 41, including the [] brackets.)

It turns out even Easter Island has sky falling legends. (Atlantis Rising #82 Pg 69 Quoting from Mysteries of Easter Island 1968) "In the days of Rokoroko He Tau the sky fell. Fell from above on to the earth".

LAMENTATIONS OF THE AZTECS

(3rd ed. Insert 2016) Aztec legends, referring to earthquakes and fire from the sky, record long pleas to God to cease punishing mankind, and speak of the ongoing calamities going on around them. "...is it possible that this lash and chastisement is not given for our correction and amendment, but only for our total destruction and obliteration; that the sun shall never more shine upon us, but that we must remain in perpetual darkness and silence...?" and "...make and end of this smoke and fog of thy resentment; quench also the burning and destroying fire of thine anger; let the serenity come and clearness; let the small birds of thy people begin to sing again and approach the sun; give them quiet weather..." Book 37 page 195)

Berlitz, referring to the Popul Vuh, finds this tidbit: "During the Eleventh Ahau it occurred...when the Earth began to waken. And the fiery rain fell, and the ashes fell, and the rocks and trees fell down. And the Great Serpent was ravished from the heavens. (Typhon?) And then, in one watery blow, came the waters... *the sky fell down* and the dry land sank. And in a great moment the great annihilation was finished." (Book 37 page 196) my italics

My deductions for a falling sky: I think steam from Volcanoes going off in abundance (chiefly) in the Atlantic ridge, and in worldwide underwater volcanoes caused from continents moving evaporated, vast quantities of water, creating incredibly humid atmosphere worldwide causing clouds, mist, and fog cover to be so dense that what we call sky was filled with clouds from near the ground to the stratosphere, indeed so much cloud cover that little if any sunlight could penetrate to the ground level.

DIS BE MANNA AND DAT BE AMBROSIA...OR WAS IT DE UDDER WAY AROUND?

(3rd ed. Insert 2016) One thing that didn't quite sink in for a long time was that the Manna the children of Israel ate in the wilderness for 40 years was also being eaten by people around the world at the same time, but by different names. The Talmud said the clouds brought the heavenly bread. (Book 14 pg 146)

Icelandic legends speak of a world fire followed by a "fimbul" winter which only two northerners survived. During this period they fed on a morning dew. (Fimbul winter is the winter at the end of the world or a triple strength winter)

The Maoris of New Zealand tell of fiery winds and fierce clouds that lashed the water into tidal waves that reached the sky which were accompanied by intense hailstorms. The ocean fled. One result of all these goings-on was heavy and light dew. Boy it's all there in *that* one. (book 14 pg 147)

Rig Veda is quoted as saying that honey comes from the clouds, earth, fire, sea and wind (book 14 pg 148)

Aristotle is noted as saying honey falls from the atmosphere with the dew when the world was veiled in the carbon clouds which caused the honey-frost. (ibid)

Buddhist writings note that when a world cycle comes to an end, the world is destroyed, the oceans dry up, day and night can't be distinguished from each other and heavenly ambrosia serves as food. (book 14 pg 147)

In fact Asian, African, Hindu, and Finnish, all have legends describing honey-food being dropped by clouds during a shadow of death that enveloped the whole world after a worldwide catastrophe.

MODERN MANNA

In 1857 Napa California, particularly near Clear Lake the entire area was blanketed with what kids and dogs soon discovered looked and tasted like rock candy. Some naturalist attempting to explain it away said it was some 'exudations from some insect'. (book 62 page 142)

In 1939 in central Angola the Seles tribes along with their animals were facing starvation with no rainfall. Animals had fled or died, and the Christian missionaries were suffering the same fate as the tribe. The missionary's 5 year old daughter had wandered off into the bush with a wooden bowl and came back with it full of something she was eating. When asked what it was by her father she replied she was hungry and had prayed to have some manna to eat like Moses ate and then went out to look for it. The tribe followed the girl into the brush and every bush and bit of ground for hundreds of yards were covered with a honey like substance. Every night the stuff was renewed for an area of about half an acre, and it kept the tribe alive until the rains returned. Some of it was put in a jar for analyses later on and it was deduced to be some kind of honey. How it got on all those bushes for all that time no one could explain. (Book 62 page 174.

TERAFORMING EARTH?

It is theoretically possible to actually temporarily, that is for several centuries, reverse the sky and atmosphere to a previous colour and volume. One could conceivably do electrolysis on the oceans and reduce much of the water into its component elements. This would add oxygen and hydrogen to the atmosphere, and possibly other atoms and molecules found diluted into the ocean waters would find their way into the atmosphere. It would change the ratios of the contents of air somewhat, but probably not detrimentally so. And one could also turn some of the oxygen into ozone to replenish the missing ozone. Since there is about 300-600 feet of additional water still remaining on the earth from the flood, one could conceivably return that water to the atmosphere in the form of Hydrogen and oxygen.

Obviously before one does such a drastic terra-formation to the earth, studies would have to be done. This would probably result in an increase of the average heat of the earth and make the earth more temperate worldwide. The polar regions could be used to grow crops again. A whole continent could be opened up to new pioneers, as Antarctica could once again have a livable climate. But it could also have an effect on the amount of rain falling in some places on the earth. With more land becoming visible, less water surface would be subject to evaporation slowing the amount of moisture entering the atmosphere to later drop down as rain, but on the other hand the denser warmer atmosphere might also aid in that evaporation, speeding it up. Things would burn better, though this could be a benefit or a hazard depending on the situation.

With a denser atmosphere once again in place on the earth, more protection from ultraviolet rays would result in less skin cancer. Possibly even longer lives could result and even calmer dispositions could be a possibility, meaning less tendency to war. Though one cannot merely blame less atmosphere on the dispositions evident in many populations today. Clearly a receding from moral values has taken place which is being replaced with Evolution, devalueing human life, and less peaceful natures thus more violent dispositions.

Laboratory and computer simulations would prove to be interesting. Even gradations could be explored, for example say if just 50 or 100 feet of sea water was turned into atmosphere. People are afraid of global warming melting ice and raising seas. Such an action could eliminate this danger, by turning that extra water into breathable protective atmosphere. But again there are pros and cons to this. The salinity of the earth's oceans would be altered as salt (and other particles) to water ratio changed. How would this affect marine life? Obviously there are a multitude of scenarios that could be explored. This of course is pretty much hypothetical in nature as few would seriously consider doing this on such a grand scale and there would probably be little financial incentive to do such a thing.

Though the ocean has many elements dissolved in it, even the recovery of these would hardly pay for the process were it to be done. One might think this is somewhat an extreme theory or suggestion. But because man in the last hundred years or so has so altered his environment in such a detrimental way, extreme measures such as this might even become necessary at some point just to keep life on earth livable. There even seems to be some urgency. It has been noted that cosmic radiation is entering the earth at an accelerating rate. (Book 47 pg. 204)

If a sudden continuation of the Peleg motion were to transpire, more atmosphere would be lost to space, with the result being less atmosphere here to maintain life at the current status. As a result more radiation would enter to earth, more mutations would occur and less reproductive capabilities would also result. Obviously this is a catch 22 situation because the more atmosphere you make the more can be lost to space, so this would merely be a stop gap for however many centuries the air remained held to earth. And one has to ask how will the reduced weight of water affect land underneath? When the water is turned into atmosphere how will the land underneath react. Will it, with less weight, rebound and rise, speeding up the receding waterlines around the earth? More importantly how will the earth react? Would it set off volcanoes and cause destruction on a global basis? Thus effectively making the cure the cause of more trouble. All these things are items one would need to consider if one were to undertake such a drastic terra-forming measure. No matter how you crunch the numbers entropy will eventually take its toll, and indeed this very action could be considered slowing down entropy on earth or even speeding it up. But this would prove to be an interesting factor in the scheme of things were it ever to be considered seriously.

WINDOWS IN HEAVEN

When text speak of "windows of heaven" opening up, it seems this would mean either holes in the water canopy as seen during the time of the flood or vortexes in the atmosphere so enormous that parts of the sky would descend or recede from the incoming of the vacuum of space, making parts of the sky appear like there was a black hole in it, or a "window". This term "windows in heaven" is in other ancient histories besides the bible as well, and though I failed to make a note of exactly which histories used this term, I was pleasantly surprised to see this term used by other ledgers. Also I must note this term was used in the context of a post flood event.

Hurricanes could be said to have a window in them when looking at the "eye" of the storm. On a larger scale with more ferocious activity going on in the earth these vortexes could reach into space, not only making "windows:" in the heavens but actually bringing the chill of space to the earth's surface.

Curiously in the Israelites' journey, God comes to earth in a thick darkness. Perhaps that darkness rose to space appearing as a hole or "window" to observers from a more distant vantage point.

All these events speak of physical events going on in the earth and it would seem these actually describe a time when the land and continents were actually moving...in recorded history.

CROSSING THE RED SEA

One more direct reference to moving land might be when the Israelites crossed the Red Sea. It's been suggested that a land bridge south of the Sinai peninsula was raised and revealed for the Israelites to walk on. Possibly, as there is a land bridge in this area just under the surface of the water. But the text states clearly that the water was a wall on both sides of the estimated 2-6 million Israelites as they walked through to the other side.

What could cause this phenomena is difficult to say but some events in the Bermuda triangle are sometimes quite similar, with water becoming a trough that planes can fly through. This suggests something more than plain old gravity can affect how water sits. Gravity itself could even account for this phenomena if other sources of gravity were close enough to the earth to make water stand in this way. One somewhat extreme theoretical possibility is that both Mars and Venus were close enough to the earth to pull this water from both sides of the Israelites, though this seems highly unlikely. However it does not seem positively out of the question as often ancient pictograms show Venus and another heavenly body in the sky at the same time.

Remnants of old technology still appear to have existed at this time in order for the Egyptian priests to duplicate so many of the miracles Moses did with his staff. But this parting of the waters may simply be a faith miracle that affects the outer edges where the event took place as after all it was just a stick. To paraphrase a well known saying 'If you have faith as a grain of mustard seed you can move mountains'. However there is reason to believe this was also a result of a rather perfectly timed cataclysmic event. Consider Psalms 114

"When Israel went out of Egypt, the house of Jacob from a people of strange language; Judah was his sanctuary, *and* Israel his Dominion. The sea saw *it*, and fled: Jordan was driven back. The mountains skipped like rams, *and* little hills like lambs. What *ailed* thee, O thou sea, that thou fleddest? thou Jordan, *that* thou wast driven back? Ye mountains *that* ye skipped like rams ; and ye little hills, like lambs? Tremble, thou earth, at the presence of the Lord, at the presence of the God of Jacob; which turneth the rock into standing water, the flint into a fountain of waters." Apparently not only did the water part, but Sinai and the surrounding land moved, and no doubt these concurrent events are intimately linked in some cause and effect. Though by this time the continents had already come into existence they were likely moved further apart.

RED EARTH AND WATER

It's not understood why the Red sea is called by that name as it is such a deep blue. It's possible Mars may have entered the picture again during the time of the exodus. Interestingly red earth is not a predominant type on earth, but it is on Mars, though as I read more sources I see there are many places on earth where red soil is common. Curiously Adam means red earth, and it's been suggested Adam was made from such soil. One wonders if earth at one time didn't have similar dirt to that of Mars. Which raises the question 'did Mars steal our dirt or did we steal Mars' dirt? As we've seen Mars' orbit must have been more extreme at one time, in order for it to have come close enough to take the flood waters.

Further asteroid activity would account for the planets more circular orbit as seen today, though it would be impossible to figure any such asteroids hitting Mars into a gravity and orbit equation for that planet, because once the asteroid hit and the planet changed course, if one were not aware of this event, they would plot the new course as a stable one and plot backwards incorrectly because they wouldn't take the effect of the asteroid into the equations.

Many legends talk of red dust everywhere and water turning to blood... not just in Egypt. This actually appears to have been a worldwide phenomenon. Mayan records tell of a time when the water in rivers turned to blood. A river in Thrace flowing from a mountain was also blood thus accounting for the mountain's name "Haemus". A mountain in Egypt was also given this name for the same reason. (Book 14 page 65) Ocean waves became purple which would happen from red dust. Red tide as we know it today has been shown to be from pollution affecting marine biology so red tide is not an adequate explanation for this event in ancient times. If Mars got close enough to exchange matter with earth again this would account for all the red dust in so many legends, such as red clouds of dust, though it's possible this dust came from volcanic eruptions too, or both. Mars is blamed for many earthquakes in the past and is said to have destroyed buildings in Mesopotamia though the time frame isn't always clear. (book 14 pg. 279) We'll soon see another cause of this blood water.

MARS STILL IN THE PICTURE.

If Mars was close to the earth during the time of the Exodus, it could be a factor in this red coloring to so many water bodies around the earth and it's gravitational pull might have continued the continents drifting further apart and mountains falling and rising. This would suggest when two planets get close to each other that the gravity pull between them would cause quakes. This is actually confirmed. Statistically earthquakes have been shown to occur more frequently during new moons and full moons when the sun and the moon act in tandem with an increased gravity factor working on the earth's surface. In fact not only does the moon pull water towards it causing tides, it also actually pulls up on the land itself. With this data, one could see that with Mars close enough to the earth at several points in time it would have consequences on earth. This close proximity of Mars and earth explained where the water went after the flood and it stands to reason Mars didn't just go back where it belonged after the flood. It's orbit would have continued with its occasional close encounters with the earth for some time.

Sumerians and Babylonians speak of Mars as one of three planets which caused thunderbolts and cause the earth to "move off its hinges" and to shudder. (Book 19 pg. 172) This may be in reference to those planets moving close enough to earth to exchange matter with the earth and cause an electrical discharge and physical upheavals, as when any one of apparently three planets comes close enough to the earth the two planets interact in the atmosphere and would cause tremendous lightning displays as the atmosphere went berserk.

With the realization that the moon and the sun working in tandem can cause earthquakes we can see the ancients weren't just making this stuff up, but Mars really was close enough to earth at one time to do these things. But if that's the case what could be the other two planets? Mars yes, and possibly Venus as there appear to be legends of both these planets coming close to earth, but what could be a third? Mercury and Jupiter are just too far away as also would the destroyed planet that became the asteroid belt; and this planet would have been destroyed before the legend existed. So what could the third planet be?

It's been suggested that this third planet appears to be Jupiter, but this is simply impossible, unless the earth itself moved so far out of it's orbit to come close to Jupiter, but this is impossible too, or we would have the most bizarre orbit of any planet. But the legend appears to be linked with Jupiter, so maybe something from Jupiter came here. (book 14 pg 181)

One might suggest the third planet could be the moon as the moon has also been shown to have been considered a planet by the ancients. But this seems impossible because no mention of the moon actually getting close to the earth seems to exist in all of history in any of the reference material, no matter how whacko. And clearly with the moon the most well known, "planet" such references, were they to exist, would certainly be obvious. So although the moon's orbit appears to have altered it doesn't seem to have been a factor otherwise. I suppose it is possible one of the chunks of the exploded planet could have been large enough to appear like a planet and come close to earth and then later on ended up landing on the sun or Jupiter. This mysterious third planet to interact with earth will be suggested in a later chapter.

Polynesian records have very poetic language for a similar event. In reference to a cataclysmic event it says 'a star is used as bait in fishing up of the islands'. This is beautiful and also completely accurate. A planet will look like a star then become a large object in the sky, so this is an interesting legend indeed.

Legends also speak of worlds clashing with worlds. This could again refer to Venus and Mars in close enough proximity to the earth that a "clash" could be observed. Maybe even Mars and Venus got close enough to observe an exchange of matter between the two planets from earth. Obviously some interesting goings on were occurring in ancient history including the time of the exodus. Egypt was decimated as were other countries in the same area. Though the exodus seems to be indicative of huge upheavals going on, it is not the cause of the continents drifting, though it appears to be a time when they drifted further. And this of course is my deduction because these events happened well after Peleg, the initial cause.

With so much of the water on earth being turned to "blood", the question comes up, was the Egyptian river turned to blood or was it just colouring from Mars dust similar to the colour of blood? I have to admit at first I just believed it...it was blood. Then I read Velikovskys account and it made sense that it could be simply a river so red it LOOKED like blood. So to be fair I checked to see if the word used in the bible during this plague was either the word used for actual blood or if it was a word that meant the colour of blood. The word used is in fact blood. Could this be? I'll get back to this.

THE SUN RETURNS 10 DEGREES: POLE SHIFTS?

Isaiah speaks of the sun going backward 10 degrees. Interestingly he was given a choice of the sun going 10 degrees forward or backward...showing some divine interference is not out of the question. (Oh really?) If the sun were to go backward 10 degrees, this does not necessarily mean the earth stopped and went backwards and the lithosphere and everything on it hurtled away at up to 1000 miles an hour.

We have to assume the meteor that caused the flood is the reason the land breaks occurred and it might have affected the poles, though it might not have caused a pole reversal. As we will see it appears the earth's crust is floating (though not on water) and a sidereal motion could fling continents sideways from a central point through centrifugal force caused by the impact of some meteor or a pole reversal. The action might be similar to say paint on a spinning piece of paper but made to work on a sphere, like some complicated Rubik's toy. In some places on earth, the sun would appear to go backwards, in other places it would move sideways and some it would shoot forward and in other places possibly even stand still, depending on your viewpoint on the planet. The planet likely did not simply stop and reverse directions, but the earth and the continents simply slid to a different position as some force toppled the planet and the continents slid in direct reaction and relation to the earth's misstep due to some force acting upon the earth's surface... probably a meteor.

Evidence for a pole shift has been obvious for many years. In fact evidence for as many as four pole shifts has long been known. Back in the 19th century, scientists debated the causes of such a pole shift. At the time the thinking was that the earth was a solid sphere and calculations were made based on this theory. But with this view or theory, even a sudden drop on one side of the earth of 15,000 feet and a rise on the other side of the earth of the same amount was calculated to be insufficient to cause a pole shift of more than a few miles. Though the theory of a liquid or molten undercarriage to the continents was put forward it was rejected for many years and the continental drift theory drifted in obscurity.

It doesn't take much to cause the earth to wobble. Consider…

MAN MADE WOBBLE

(3rd ed. Insert 2016) Further proof that man can affect the earth in astounding ways. The Three Gorges dam built in China, is the world's largest dam by 50%. While the dam was filling up, the earth experienced a measurable wobble. And it's acknowledged that the dam and reservoir can induce seismicity (that's a fancy way of saying, it can cause earthquakes.)

POLE SHIFTS, ICE AGES AND MOUNTAIN BUILDING INTERRELATED EVENTS

Attempts have been made to explain what would cause a pole shift in the newer theory of the earth's physical makeup, that is with continents sliding on molten under lays. With pole shifts occurring four times, this coincided with, and would explain the ice ages as there also appear to be four ice ages. Interestingly ice ages are linked with mountain building and pole shifts...so things are starting to fit.

Cold alone cannot create an ice age and heat alone cannot create an ice age. Cold freezes oceans, heat causes massive evaporation and torrential rain. For an Ice age to occur torrential rain fall and staggering snow falls have been shown to have occurred at the same time and in close proximity to each other, showing that massive evaporation was occurring AND some cooling agent occurred at the *same time* to cause the ice ages.

Mountains rising at the same time poles are shifting at the same time ice ages are occurring at the same time as massive evaporation, precipitation and sudden blocking out of the sun causing crashing temperature, cooling the air and causing massive snowfalls. And this is normal?!? NO! This is indicative of incredible catastrophes going on all around the earth at some point or points in the past! Something is causing all these events to occur at the same time on a global scale! This event has to be the continents in motion, not at today's clip but clearly at a vastly accelerated rate. It is the ONLY event that will cause all these factors to occur simultaneously. Since the ice ages are supposed to be as recently as 11,000 years ago, that automatically has to reduce the ages of the continents too. But as we've seen glaciers and glacier lakes and Niagara Falls are far younger than this thus we can see these cataclysmic events happened even more recently than this! And indeed since these events are spoken of in historical ledgers this further illustrates this point.

A simple asteroid probably won't cause the continents to move from a standstill, though once the continents have started moving it could cause the continents to move more, and then these things could occur. But only the movements of the continents will account for all these events occurring simultaneously all around the earth.

The key ingredient in all these events is volcanic activity. Continents move causing volcanoes to form and go off. Since a large portion of these volcanoes will be underwater in the Atlantic, Pacific and other underwater ridges as the continents slide, the volcanoes evaporate the ocean, which turns into sooty steam. Realize that the Atlantic would have been a much narrower ocean at first with the initial Peleg motion. But the center line of that ocean would be where the majority of this action would have taken place as the continents sporadically moved further apart. There are many areas where land sub-ducted and many areas when it came out from underneath as seen in the Atlantic ridge. If one continent moved, they all moved and all the earth's ridges expel matter and all the subduction points continue to sub-duct.

KRACK A TOE MEANS 7 YEARS BAD WEATHER.

(3rd ed. Insert 2016) Somewhat related: A study was made by Dr. W.J. Humphrey (of the U.S. Weather Bureau, correlating weather patterns with foreign particles in the air over the preceding 300 years. He found that virtually without exception cool and rainy summers followed periods of major volcanic activity. For example the explosion of Tomboro of Sumbawa Island in the East Indies was followed by "The Year without a Summer- 1816." (book 62 page 221) This study, though only a short term sample (300 years) can easily be extrapolated for many volcanoes. A prolonged period of volcanic activity, as has been noted in ancient times, would have caused endless winters of back to back years at a stretch with so much snowfall as to create the glaciers we still have here today.

ANOTHER MODERN DAY EXAMPLE

Consider another more well known volcano. In 1883 Krakatoa went off. Yeah big bang, but one interesting thing about that volcano, was the dust from that one volcano reduced the sunlight coming to the entire earth by 10 percent for years! And there's another interesting tidbit about that volcano. After it erupted half the island disappeared under the waves the tsunami created which was a 120 feet high! The wave was reduced somewhat when it reached Sumatra an hour later. It was only 70 feet. This while the continents were standing still! Coral blocks weighing as much as 600 tons were thrown ashore! If a single volcano could do this, imagine what thousands of volcanoes could do going off at the same time...WHILE the continents moved! There's your erratics, there's your universal layer of sandstone created by waves overrunning the continents, there's your fossils, there's your mass extinctions around the world!

I'LL HAVE A NICE COLD GLASS OF AVALANCHE.

(3rd ed. Insert 2016) People might wonder how a continent or land could possibly move. Studies on avalanches show the material of the avalanche actually takes on a property similar to water or a liquid during the avalanche. Once the material in the avalanche overcomes friction, the body of the avalanches seems to move faster than one would expect, or put another way, the reaction is greater than the sum of the parts. This action can indeed move whole mountains and even whole land masses. Once land is moving it can continue moving over great distances.

When avalanches have been observed under laboratory conditions they have found that once land starts to move it takes on motion properties of water. The avalanche proceeds disproportionate to the parts or the friction we would think would stop it. So too would this occur when continents moved. We think the mass of land would stop any force applied against it, but once the land slips, that is overcomes friction, it moves easily in the direction of the force applied, with apparently little or no friction, not unlike wet ice on wet ice.

HOW IT PLAYS OUT

The soot, ash, lava, pumice, and steam from the volcanoes boiling the water, ejecting volcano stuff into the atmosphere, blocking out the sun causing drastic worldwide reduction in temperature, thus massive snow falls. Thus we have heat and cold going on at the same time, exactly what is needed for ice ages. Some areas not blocked out will have massive rainfalls. Ice ages, massive rain and as the continents moved, mountains rise. It all fits. Did this cause the pole reversal or did a pole reversal cause this? Anyway the poles probably changed during these events. However sometimes the magnetic poles flipped and sometimes they moved, suggesting different causes. Sometimes the sources seem to be equating pole shifts with pole reversals or 'flips', so it's not always clear which events caused which reaction, but my guess is that meteors moved the land and the poles, and something else caused the flips...which also occurred during the moving continents.

ALL RECENTLY YET STILL SOME PIECE IS MISSING

Geologists puzzle over the numerous violent earthquakes evident in earth's past and of those spoken of in so many historic accounts and legends yet oddly the picture still seems incomplete. Admittedly I may be missing some obvious stuff too. If these events happened in historical times why the need to say the earth spent millions or billions of years to reach the state the earth is in now, when the written and verbal histories speak of such events that would have caused the features evident on the earth?

WOULD A METEOR DESTROY THE EARTH?

Some have suggested that if a meteor of any consequential size hit the earth, all of life on the planet would instantly be destroyed. This might be the case for a solid sphere, but this is nonsense in light of the physical nature of the earth. In the area where the meteor hit, there of course would be vast devastation. But because the earth is somewhat like a breakable soft crumbly surface over a liquid, any such meteor would sink into the ground, break through the crust and enter earth's interior and the earth's physical nature would act like something throwing a rock at a wet sponge, which would absorb the impact...or similar to that bowling ball that gets tossed on that well known mattress not disturbing the next area. But obviously there would still be vast consequences on the earth and depending on the size of the meteor the continents would still shift suddenly and to varying degrees.

The water would react to these events too, overrunning lake borders and ocean water gets in the way of the moving land masses and huge tidal waves would result. The volcanic activity would immediately go crazy in many places all over the earth. And then there's the air. It would be subject to this motion too and huge swirling vortex's would result. The cold of space would plummet to some spots on the earth's surface and storms of unimaginable strength would occur in many places on the earth. Places that were temperate would suddenly be moved to areas that are cold and vice verse. Hurricanes of magnitude 10 or better, earthquakes of Magnitude 15 and tsunamis hundreds, possibly thousands of feet high would rush far inland, with these tidal waves even climbing hills and possibly mountains, and of course as the continents moved, mountains would rise as you watched. No picnic. This is to some degree confirmed by the tsunami that caused such devastation around the Indian ocean at the end of 2005. In some places the wave was over 100 feet high. If this is the case for a single localized earthquake off Indonesia, what would the consequences and effects on the water bodies of the world be if the continents themselves actually moved?!

FREEZE FRAME

(3rd ed. Insert 2016) One might have asked the question, why wasn't all life wiped out by these continental floods caused by continents moving, forcing water to rush on land. One explanation that might have limited the destruction of all life on the continents while the continents moved was the same thing that froze all the wooly mammoths. If the water in areas froze in motion from the chill of space descending upon the moving water, the water would have frozen solid instantly or fast enough to not drown everything. Indeed some still remaining ice seen in some arctic areas appears to have frozen in this manner. A woolly mammoth that was seen "moving" was thought to be still alive, but it's now thought it was seen in a solid block of super clear ice. And some completely frozen "waves" have been found, as though they were frozen in the very act of breaking, ready for a surfer.

ATLANTIS AND UZZIAH.

Then there's the earthquake written of during King Uzziahs reign. This appears to have been a huge one and it appears to be the same quake that destroyed Thera, and other Mediterranean sites, such as when Sicily turned into an island. It may coincide also with when the Bimini wall sunk and finished off Atlantis, and no doubt affected other sites around the globe.

LAND OR WATER DID THE CRUSHING?

Claude Schaeffer determined that the same earthquake that destroyed Troy, also destroyed Ugarit, Alaka Huyuk, Alisar, Tarsus, Tepe Hissar, Byblos, as well as cities in Palestine and terminated the old kingdom of Egypt...an area of over 600 miles wide. No earthquake today covers such a vast area. A little earthquake off the coast of Indonesia caused tsunamis all around the Indian ocean in 2010. What would an earthquake 600 miles long and wide do to places around the Mediterranean sea? A 50 foot wall was destroyed in Troy, Indus Valley crumbled, places such as Asia Minor, Mesopotamia, Caucasus, The Iranian Plateau, Syria, Palestine, Cyprus and Egypt were simultaneously laid waste, and the climate changed following this period. (Book 53 pgs 175-183)

Furthermore hundreds or thousands of cubic miles of earth heaved upward almost instantaneously in the Andes. The Sierras would have caused worldwide earthquakes. And we now know the Sierras attained their present height in the age of man. Not only that, but the ancient records prove it. Babylonian tablets speak of them and in even more recent times during the Punic wars (219 BC) in one year 57 earthquakes were reported in Rome alone. (Book 53 pages 137-138)

Some have suggested that Plato's referring to Atlantis may be a mistaken reference to some smaller lands inside the Mediterranean ocean. But just because a volcano or earthquake in this Mediterranean bathtub might affect a single island does not rule out this might have been an effect of a simultaneous event happening elsewhere. The Bimini and Bahamas area may have been part of Atlantis. Even the time frame is about right if we assume Atlantis sunk 900 years and not 9000 years before Plato's time.

Many plausible reasons have been put forth to explain this 9000 years was meant to be 900, not to mention the proof of a younger earth as discussed last chapter. Also there's no reason to think the Plato's retelling of the story is incorrect. For example he stated that the water beyond the pillars of Hercules (Strait of Gibraltar) were not navigateable by ship. Such a scenario is perfectly plausible. Volcanic eruptions in the island of Iceland and Sumbawa in 1783 and 1815 caused volcanic ash to land in water, but instead of this ash sinking it hardens on the surface and made travel by boat through these areas virtually impossible. This even illustrates in a small way that land can float on a liquid, such as the theory for continents.

When plotting King Uzziah's reign, assuming the earliest possible plotting point, based on the revised timeline, the earthquake in his time occurred sometime between 1707 and 1657 BC. This does fit well with other chronologies linked to major catastrophes in the period. However if we use the short 14 generation period (462 years) from David to the carrying away to Babylon and use that value again from then to Christ, the time of this earthquake works out to somewhere between 674 and 622 BC, very close to the deduced final catastrophe that altered the length of the year up to 365.249 days which is said to have occurred at 687 BC. Since no actual date can be deduced for the final 14 generation period one could suggest it was a little longer ...even just 15 years and this put it smack into Uzziah's reign and the two incidences; the earth quake and the cause of the revised year likely being the same event. (this could be a biblical indirect link to Atlantis.)

Worldwide ocean subsidence has been noted and dated around 1500 BC thus even this points to tremendous geologic activity going on during recorded history (Book 53 pg 165-66) This event closely matches the possible dates for the sinking of Atlantis and the older figure for Uzziah's earthquake as well. Wouldn't it be something if there were two Uzziah's (or three) and in both reigns similar events occurred? That would really make separating things difficult!

The Earthquake during Uzziah's reign is one of the few cataclysms actually mentioned more than once in the bible. Amos 1:1 speaks of an event that occurs in the reigns of Uzziah (Judah) and Jeroboam (Israel) two years before the earthquake. It would have to be a major earthquake to be singled out as "the earthquake". Zechariah 14: 4-5 also speaks of this quake in a prophesy about when Christ returns. Vs. 4: And in that day His feet will stand on the Mount of Olives which faces Jerusalem on the east and the Mount of Olives shall split in two, from east to west making a very large valley; half of the mountain shall move to the north and half toward the south. This Valley in verse 5 is said to reach all the way to Azal, which is strikingly similar to other names of Atlantis, though I can't be certain this is what is spoken of and it may just be a lost Israeli place name nearby. Verse 5 goes on to say "And ye shall flee *to* the Valley of the mountains; for the valley of the mountains shall reach unto Azal: yea, ye shall flee as ye fled from before the earthquake in the days of Uzziah King of Judah:... It seems as though the Israelites run toward and into the valley created but they flee it, and the "*to*" is inferred, so maybe the Italicized "*to*" might be "*from*"? It's difficult for me to be positive which way they run regardless of translation, though it does seem to appear they run toward the valley created by the quake...though I can't see how this makes any sense.

Research has shown there is a fault line that runs right through the mount of Olives in this exact location and in the direction spoken of! An east west crevasse from this point made long enough would indeed run right through the location of Atlantis spoken of by Plato...beyond the Strait of Gibraltar. What is particularly striking about this reference to this earthquake in Uzziah's time is that they fled from it. I mean think about it. We don't flee from earthquakes, we ride them out, or in extreme cases hide under doorways or get into open ground. I don't know of any earthquake where people fled from it. In the 19ᵗʰ century in the plains of America people could see the land move like wave action as the quakes rippled toward the observers, but no mention of fleeing them seems to be in the historic mention of these quakes. So the quake in Uzziah's time must have been incredible!

OK... PELEG. FIRST, SOME CLUES.

Archaeologists when digging deeper into the ground give dates to each foot of strata they dig down into because they assume the deeper down you go the older the relics they find must be. This seems like a logical presumption, but often items found at one stratum will be found in an entirely different stratum somewhere else. Not only does this put dating certain items into question, it also actually shows that cataclysmic events jumbled the strata in the first place. The very fact some things are buried to start with is evidence that there were cataclysmic events to bury the items. Think about it. I mean where is the dirt in these strata that covers all the artifacts supposed to have come from in the first place? Does it just materialize? I find this the most obvious problem about dating dirt levels. Where is all that extra dirt supposed to have come from? If the moon in what's supposed to be 4.5 billion years accumulated just 1/8 inch of dust, how on earth is 18 feet of dirt on earth supposed to equal 6000 years? We must conclude that the dirt did not fall from space or just spontaneously appear; it had to be moved from some other place on earth to cover something. How did it get there? I mean I find this the most obvious clue to massive upheavals in the past and I simply cannot understand why people haven't clued into this before. This single bit of evidence, that of deeply buried artifacts, all by itself should be causing geologists and scientists to rethink their theories.

FOSSIL CREATION

When digging through various strata, these layers of dirt are usually said to have formed rapidly as are subsequent strata below. ((2nd ed. Insert 2008) Again, paleontologists, archaeologists and other various dirt diggers date fossils or artifacts by the geologic column they are found in. Similarly they date various geologic columns by the index fossils they find in that layer or strata. This is in fact "circular reasoning". But the "geologic column" is in fact a myth. About 85% of the earth does not have the geological columns in the right order. Also some have as few as three stratas and some have far more. This is really not a way to date fossils or dirt levels for that matter, but it really is a clue to cataclysmic events.) Between the separate strata's no erosion from the previous strata exists. So entire formations are in all likelihood formed rapidly, and at the same time, and this mean by a cataclysmic event, or one heck of a bulldozer. No observable time break exists between the two most important ages: that of Paleozoic to Mesozoic and Mesozoic to Cenozoic. These "ages" merge subtly from one age to the next and the formations of all the "ages" were formed rapidly. Also many rock formation actually requires rapid formation, and in fact fossils in order to form at all also need rapid burial!

Animals that just die on the surface don't turn into fossils, but rather they simply decompose and get eaten and the bones just dry up and turn to dust. Rapid burial is a MUST for fossils to form and thus this means a cataclysmic event is the cause for all the fossils. This is not to say the SAME cataclysm formed all fossils or rock.

Though the majority of fossils are of marine invertebrates, it's not entirely understood why so many fossils of these creatures exist because even now they don't just fossilize when they settle in the soft sediments. When a fish dies it gets eaten by other water creatures, usually in a matter of hours. Some process of rapid lithification is necessary to turn them into fossils; that is a cataclysmic event. Fossils are simply not being formed in our present era, under the present conditions existing on the earth today. So what caused them?

Some evolutionary geologists insist that the past can be understood by what is occurring on the earth today. This simply is not the case, because fossils are not being formed, ice ages are not occurring, poles are not shifting, mountains are not being built and continents are not moving...certainly not at the clip necessary to cause these events. Something big happened in the past and something has changed for the world to be as it is today.

There is another problem. Even buried stuff doesn't just turn to fossils, it rots underground and is eaten by worms and crawly things. Another ingredient is needed. Salt is also needed for fossils to occur. This is a really big and important clue. Where might this salt come from? Obviously from salt water. And where do we find salty water? The oceans. Is it starting to make sense now? Could what I'm suggesting actually have happened?

Fossil bearing strata are virtually everywhere on earth meaning everywhere was subjected to at least one sort of catastrophic event that allowed fossils to form. So salt water had to be everywhere. A close look at what caused the flood of Noah and the mechanics of it seems to suggest to me this was not the type of flood that would bury creatures, just drown them. But if the flood of Noah didn't bury things and just drowned them, then that flood didn't make the fossils! A different flood with different mechanics had to cause the fossils. That's OK, because as we've seen there were many "worldwide floods" as the geologists point out, and as we've seen they deduced most if not all of them were of the tsunami type. Obviously not all of them because one of the floods (Noah's) made the clay…not the fossils. Show me clay with fossils formed in it. It doesn't exist…correct? (I don't know this for certain but I'm guessing this is right.)

Though usually the flood of Noah is 'blamed' for the bulk of the fossils, actually I suspect precious few fossils would likely exist from the flood period. The amount of water involved would just turn them into fish food and plankton munchies. The action needed to create fossils is not evident in the flood's actions, except possibly near the extremities of the Canadian shield, or in areas where the fountains of the deep burst forth possibly burying creatures in the immediate vicinity. Perhaps some giant wave of slurry went outward from this point and quickly buried many creatures which then got covered by the water of the flood. But this would mean many fossils would be found UNDER the Canadian shield or under a layer of clay formed by the silt from the flood. Though I don't think there would be fossils under the Canadian Shield because it would have been hot lava. And likely they would have vaporized and this meteor would have brought the water of the sphere in with it.

During the flood everything was just underwater and would decompose. Living creatures actually have to be buried to form into fossils, not just submerged. This does not appear to be the case for most if any fossils. The action of the flood does not suggest as many fossils would have formed as in other cataclysms as most of the organic matter would likely have been in silt or floating and sinking in the oceans then rotting or eaten. Remember in the flood the entire earth is under water so water bourn creatures would be eating dead matter or as the water subsided they would still only be on the surface of the land, rotting and not forming into fossils.

Wouldn't that be something if when Mars took some of our water it also took some of these floating dead creatures and deposited them on Mars? Some Mars probe lens could even see a mummified skeleton of who knows what or who! That is if they didn't decompose there too. But sometimes conditions exist where a mummification can occur in the open. For example some mummified seals or porpoises (I forget which as I saw this on TV) have been found on Antarctica, in open sterile arid air found in some places there. Curiously in the cold air of the Antarctic your breath cannot be seen because Antarctica's air is so pure and ones breath doesn't condense on anything. Perhaps similar conditions exists in some places on Mars where creatures can mummify on the surface there too.

The flood appears to be responsible for all the clay around the earth and not so much the fossils, whereas Peleg would have been responsible for the sandstone, and other rock formations where salty aquatic action is needed for them to be formed. The flood waters is basically standing water, whereas the Peleg motion as we shall see caused rapidly moving water. But if the flood of Noah didn't make the fossils, what did? what event caused the fossils?

After the flood the next cataclysms is "Peleg" which occurred a mere 101 years after the flood! It would appear this or similar and subsequent events caused the bulk of the fossils. So we may have found an event that moved dirt from somewhere to huge depths in order to bury things 18 feet deep and even deeper in many cases, and we may have found an event that moved massive amounts of sea water over the land to turn the buried things into fossils.

It would seem we could deduce that massive amounts of salt water overran the land to move the dirt and make the fossils. But this would mean the water had to virtually cover the continents, so the continents must have moved fast to force the water over the land. Could this be? There seems to be no escaping it... how else can the fossils get made?

SIZE NOT AGE DETERMINES FOSSILS ORDER IN THE STRATA

When fossils are found usually the smaller creatures and artifacts are found at lower levels. This is natural as when a lot of dirt debris and water are moved together the smallest stuff will settle first.

Size, shape and mobility determines the position of a creature in the strata through settling, not age or position in time. This then can mean that an entire stratum could all be the exact same age. This makes sense...how often is the water going to overrun the land...if this is indeed what happened. With water overrunning the land creating a slurry of dirt, water, debris and fossils, they are going to settle in a natural way.

Itty bitty sea creatures supposedly extinct longer then the creatures buried above have dates attributed to them merely based on their depths in the deposit. But they could have become extinct all at the same time, as indeed a massive tidal wave would not be discriminatory about what things get in its way. The smaller and less mobile creatures will often die first and settle at the bottom of a slurry. The larger more mobile creatures will have smaller items settle below them and they will likely be able to get away from cataclysmic events for a longer period of time, or struggle longer. Birds might not even be affected by cataclysms, or certainly far fewer and this explains why they rarely turn up in the fossil record...they just fly out of the way. If perchance a creature happened to become extinct in one cataclysm, they would not be found in a later cataclysm.

This tidbit is real interesting. Did you know that all currently living creatures are found in fossil form in all ages? Meaning at one time they were all alive on the earth at the same time. They could not possibly have evolved from each other if they all exist at the same time! However occasionally a previous cataclysm will wipe out a species so they are judged to be from previous eras like tertiary, Paleozoic, Mesozoic... etcetera. So true various ages or periods of time do exist where certain creatures no longer walked the earth, but the time between some "eras" or cataclysms is far shorter than is believed.

GEOLOGIC FEATURES THAT CONTAIN FOSSILS

The most common formation containing fossils is sandstone and it is virtually a worldwide formation. Evolution theorists suggest that sandstone would be formed now but it just doesn't form in sea beds and things that settle in sea beds just decompose and no current action in nature actually makes sandstone. Such fossils have to come from saltwater overrunning land, gathering cementing ingredients, picking up shore sand, creating a layer of sand deposits then quickly drying. And sandstone doesn't take millions of years to form when it does form...with the proper cementing agents are present, it can be sandstone in mere hours. This explains how human foot prints can be found in it. Water comes rushing in and subsides. Any people that might have gotten out of the way of the huge waves would then walk out onto the sandy areas looking for stuff washed in and making footprints. A few hours or days later those prints would be in rock hard sandstone, as the cementing agents did their thing.

Conglomerate rocks are also formed through hydroponic actions and they too contain a lion's share of the fossils. Such conglomerates cover an area of North America from Alberta to Tennessee and stretch right across the continent from California to Vermont! Could this entire area have been overrun by the sea at the same time?!? This is so vast an area I have to wonder if the North American continent wasn't two temporary land masses at one time as it even stretches this theory to conceive a wave that big could cross the continent, though I confess I am no specialist in hydroponics.

Maybe Mu and North America merged. James Churchward did seem to conclude that parts of Western North America contained clues and relics which he contributed as belonging to MU. When one looks at the Pacific ridge off the coast of North America one can see that this is actually the case. The Atlantic ridge pushed north America west and the Pacific ridge push something towards it and they met somewhere in the middle. Is that true? This suggests the land from the western part of North America came from somewhere else. Well it's another factor in the big picture.

(3ʳᵈ. ed. insert 2016) Jeffrey Goodman looking at the evidence asks "Were the Himalayas born in a few explosive moments? Were the Himalayas born when the Indian subcontinent slammed, not pushed, into the Asian mainland? Were colossal upheavals and uplifts triggered? Did it take millions of years or just a few centuries to create the Himalayas?

Later Jeffrey Goodman quotes Dr. Frank Hibben "We find literally thousands [of victims] together... young and old, foal with dam, calf with cow...The muck pits of Alaska are filled with evidence of universal death...a picture of quick extinction. And he also states this applies to North America, Siberia and Europe as well. (Book 19 pg 107)

Evidence exists that shows it was even faster than that, because fossilized clams in the closed position are found on Everest When clams die they automatically open so burial and uplift had to have happened quickly.

MOUNTAINS FORMED IN CIVILIZED TIMES

When digging down, sometimes civilizations appear to be built on top of older civilizations. It's sort of peculiar that so much debris can be in layers between these civilizations. In fact it seems very peculiar in the light of prevailing theories. The earth is supposed to be a very docile place where hills and mountains form over millions of years, and dust settles from space at the rate of 1/8 of an inch every 4 million years. I've never understood how three civilizations could appear to be buried and then rebuilt on top of the one below. I mean how is that possible? I could see possibly two, one from before the flood, and one after, but even then this suggests that in between the two civilizations should be mud and clay and this level of mud should be deeper then the highest building, but often it is just ordinary dirt. I mean what happened? Did the previous civilization just say, oh this city is stupid, let's bury it and start over with a new one? And the city below is in ruins, and then buried. I can see just ruined and then rebuilt, or abandoned... but buried? Where did the dirt come from?

However in some cases it's entirely possible when considering the lay of the land that sometimes a city could actually be on top of itself! For example in the Capitol Hill, Smyrna Asia Minor there is what has been deduced to be three civilizations on top of each other, but these may simply be the same civilization. Sand and debris could overrun a place from a major tsunami then upheavals bury one part and throw another part of the same civilization on top, then another as the land folded, while the land moved in a specific direction. Obviously this suggests enormous upheavals unlike anything seen on earth today...so this suggestion is ignored or laughed at. Also we are simply not talking about your normal tsunami here. The type we are talking about will become clear soon enough.

Though I don't know that this is the case for this particular location at Capitol Hill, looking at cross section drawings of this area definitely suggests this possibility has to be taken into consideration when identifying such things, especially in this city. It is important to note that it has been proven that this particular civilization existed before the mountains rose. (book 16 pg 130-131). In fact it's likely the folding of the city may be the same event that caused the nearby mountains to have formed. Thus we are faced with a dilemma...is this civilization older than the usual 5500 years or are the mountains younger then this? I think it's safe to say these mountains rose during recorded history. Odd that the text books seem to ignore this very important fact that mountains are thus proven to have risen during civilized times. (perhaps you think I'm glossing over stuff but eventually it will become undeniable here that the mountains rose during civilized times...and we watched them being built...if we survived)

Similarly a great civilization once resided in the Colorado desert in what was once a fertile land. This too has been proved to have been inhabited before the local mountains rose. The very same action that created the mountains also changed the area into a desert.

Other places show what appears to be the same civilization center broken into pieces and left to rest on an angle, like dominoes resting on each other as they fall, suggesting the land moved and broke the civilization center and then pushed it sideways creating a few folds in the land the civilization rested on. Such actions leave the place in a series of folds of land resting at an angle in relation to its original orientation. All over the earth what should be level striations in land appear at bizarre angles. And indeed in several locations these events happened to areas that were large population centers, simply making it plain that much terrain forming was going on during civilized time.

If this is the case, and it is, we also have to realize that mountains in uninhabited areas were also rising in these same time frames. There may be no civilization around for us to prove they rose during civilized times, but suddenly when one realizes mountains arose in one place with people watching or being crushed, we suddenly get an uneasy feeling looking at other mountains of a similar type.

Then subsequent actions actually buried some of these civilizations later on, as though more than one disturbance happened in the same place. What could cause such huge upheavals all over the world, and in recent times when advanced civilizations were on the earth? We continually see that such cataclysmic events had to have happened during recorded history, yet enigmatically evolutionary and uniformitarian geologist seem to just ignore these sites, like they don't exist and insist the mountains grew over a time frame of millions of years. I mean why? To what possible benefit could this be to advancing the spread of a more exact geologic branch of science? Are they afraid they'll start a panic? Or do they think these civilizations just stayed around while the ground underneath slowly over the millennia began to tilt? Do these archaeologists think these people were there merrily walking down streets resting at 10°, then 20°, and even 45°, angle streets eating on tables sitting at 45° and sleeping on beds at this strange angle too? Do archaeologists think that once they hit 46 degrees they decide they were tired of this angular living space and move to a different place and start again on a level piece of ground? Obviously a rhetorical and sarcastic question but NO!... these upheavals happened in a moment and suddenly.

This doesn't mean that a series of a few civilizations could not be built on top of each other. Often civilizations build up in areas that are perfect and logical places for them to do so. I mean rivers and fertile plains might mean a civilization might be built in exactly the same location. But what buried the original civilizations in the first place? It had to be water overrunning the land bringing debris from wherever to bury these previous civilizations, and the land had to be moving for this to happen. It just all fits the rapid continental motion theory, and all these events are interconnected and related. Though I can't say for certain which might be subsequent civilizations built on the same site as previous civilizations, and which ancient cities might be broken and on top of themselves, as I'm not the expert, but clearly this possibility has to be considered when one might re-examine the evidence in any given site. We'll get back to this aspect of geology.

CLUES THAT MAN CAUSED SOMETHING BIG TO OCCUR.

Above we have seen some clues as to what actions appear to have been occurring at some time on the surface of the earth, and we'll cover some more. We also see that these events were occurring during civilized times. This event or events in time we can call "Peleg" as it would seem that when the earth was "divided" the land moved and water overran the land. Though there may have been four separate "Pelegs" all continuing the action of the original "Peleg" spoken of in the bible. Keep in mind Peleg is really the initial creation of the continents. Since it would seem this Peleg caused a "second flood" (and 3rd and 4th flood) this then will explain why there is evidence of more than one flood. Since I have deduced that this initial Peleg was man's doing, then let's look at some clues to see how man might have caused this event referred to as Peleg. Which by the way is a natural follow up of the meteor that caused the flood, due to the extent of man's technologically advanced tools that were in existence prior to and after the flood.

Yes these *are* clues. Something caused the earth to divide that was in existence before the flood. This "something" was man made, but it did not cause the breakup of the land before the flood because the land was a solid mass. When the meteor hit, unbeknownst to man, the earth's physical structure changed creating a very unstable and volatile land mass. Once this something was put back into operation this hidden danger made itself known by suddenly changing the face of the earth.

Nikola Tesla detested the idea that people were paying outrageous amounts for electricity, when he apparently knew it was possible that after the construction of some sort of tower contraption we could get electricity for free by simply pounding a stake into the ground! By some accounts he planned or was actually doing something to the planet that would enable people to do this! Whether or not it would have worked is debatable as he felt he was sabotaged by the electrical companies. I feel certain he was onto something big in his understanding of the dynamics of the globe.

Consider these clues in Tesla's inventions. 1) he used energy within a space to operate lights in the room by just holding them in his hand. 2) He appears to have conquered gravity as he was seen lifting massive machinery as though it was lighter than a feather and silver appears to have played a part in this technology. 3) he knew the entire planet could be tapped into to be used as a power source, for electricity, and possibly other potential worldwide power systems. He felt that sound and molecular vibration was the key to achieving weightlessness.

Other references to antigravity inventions seem to be linked to silver and the tapping into the latent physiology of man.

A fortress or monastery is built in Ollantayparubo in Peru with blocks weighing from 150-200 tons that were 'carried' over the screwiest terrain imaginable, from quarries as far away as 1000 miles! The terrain is so rugged, and the task so unsettling to archeologist, that they are forced to suggest that it was built at a time when the terrain was more gentle. Here's an archaeologist's nightmare…being caught in a catch 22, either the land was more gentle before the buildings were built, or they were using antigravity to build the structures. So they are forced to suggest manmade structures were built before the changing of the landscape took place. Ironically in this instance this is not necessarily the case, because if the ancients had antigravity they wouldn't care what the terrain was like. Legends insist the stones of this fort as well as other sites around the world were flown through the air. (book 53 pg 78, book 37 pg 79) Even the pyramids appear to have legends attached to them about huge stones flown through the air by antigravity means.

Tesla said a proper harmonic frequency could destroy the earth. His experiments with harmonics caused local earthquakes and attracted violent lightning and thunderstorms in the vicinity of his workplaces.

Many things man now does causes earthquakes to occur: even a simple truck hitting an imbedded cement wall can shake houses for blocks around. Man's advancements during the 20th century may be a reason the number of earthquakes in that century escalated to such extreme numbers over previous centuries. Here's a few examples. September 10 1978 25,000 Iranians lost their lives in a quake considered to have been caused by an underground nuclear test 36 hours earlier 1500 miles away. U.S. Geological Survey felt that a quake on August 13 1978 in Santa Barbara was caused by activities at an exploratory oil well off shore four days earlier. After the US Army started dumping lethal waste down local deep wells in Denver Colorado, Denver suddenly started experiencing its first ever recorded earthquakes in the mid sixties. More than 710 earthquakes were experienced in this short period. Finally after much study and public pressure, dumping stopped and as quickly as the earthquakes started they stopped. (book 19) Personally I can't understand how dumping hazardous waste could cause earthquakes, but maybe the neighbors downstairs were knocking on the ceiling, telling us to stop. Above ground nuclear tests are known to affect the earth's magnetic field. Who knows how else we affect our earth. These may seem like small things but so too might have been the warning signs before Peleg.

Reports of a lithium bomb exploded by the soviets in 1953 on the neck of the Kamchatka peninsula caused a major earthquake, that "dented" the earth and a seismic shock wave traveled several times around the globe. (book 47 pg 183)

(Here's a few more I've found….

BIG BOMB

(3rd ed. Insert 2016) Looking on the net I found a larger Lithium Bomb (called Tsar Bomba) was exploded by the Soviets in 1961. It was 50-58 Mega tons (1350-1570 times the power of the one on Hiroshima or ten times all the conventional explosives used during the entire WWII) They had to use a parachute on it to allow the plane enough time to get away from it. Because of lead tampers rather than Uranium ones it was probably the cleanest Nuke ever, but they had to make it this way or the fallout would have landed all over the USSR. (USA did a lithium one that was the most contaminated nuke ever, destroying the inhabitability of Rongelap and Utirik Atolls and spreading radiation around the globe) TheTsar Bomba mushroom cloud reached 40 miles up, (Above the stratosphere and into the mesosphere) and the mushroom was visible from 600 miles away. All buildings in a village 34 miles from the epicenter were destroyed. People would receive third degree burns 100 kilometers away. Wooden buildings hundreds of Kilometers away were destroyed, and stone buildings lost their roofs and windows. Windows were broken 600 miles way. The seismic shock wave from the bomb was measurable even on the third trip around the globe.

IT'S ALL OUR FAULT

(3rd ed. Insert 2016) More evidence that man can cause the earth to hit back at man with disasters. Many atomic bombs were exploded at Frenchman's Flat in Nevada which polluted the air over the U.S. with radioactivity and with the subatomic particles of what had once been the bomb itself. That's bad enough, but then in 1953 the earth struck back. What was being noticed was a huge increase in tornadoes. By May 1953 130 had been counted; the worst year on record. Naturally the Atomic Energy Commission said "The A-bomb's effect on weather is only local in character." Then in April and then again on June 8 1953 they detonated a "very powerful A-bomb", and three days later a great wall of tornadoes formed in the skies of the Midwest, a formation like no other formation on record, killing more than four hundred person from Ohio, Pennsylvania, New York, and Massachusetts. Could that have been caused by the explosions? They studied the rainfall that fell during the tornadoes and it was unusually radioactive, in fact so radioactive "that the water could not be used for photographic purposes". The mud created by the rain was also highly radioactive. Those tornadoes were loaded with the radioactive material from those bombs a few days before, and it likely caused the tornadoes as well. (book 62 page 221-223)

THE ANTARCTIC "CHIMNEY"

(3rd ed. Insert 2016) The reason for blowing off nuclear weapons in the Antarctic was understood by the elite in the fifties. It was called "Alternative one", like throwing rocks at a green house to let hot air out. They deduced back then that the earth was heating up so they attempted to make "chimneys" for the heat to escape, by punching holes in the carbon dioxide high in the atmosphere above Antarctica. But unfortunately the cure may have been worse than the disease because they created a hole in the protective ozone layer. They abandoned the idea when they realized they couldn't patch the hole by replacing the Ozone. (Alternative 3 page 98) They later blamed the hole on 'Hair spray'.

By the way, Climate change advocates have been telling us that the ice caps are melting and we are all doomed unless we tow the line and buckle under...usually in ways that line climate change advocates pockets. But the fact is Antarctica's ice cap has been growing dramatically in record breaking proportions in the past 18 years (1997 to date). Some people such as Daily Mail's meteorologist John Coleman who wrote an open letter to the U.N. saying "There is no climate crisis. Man made global warming is a lie and not backed up by science." (Atlantis Rising Mag. #109 Pg 10) Yet you have people like David Suzuki saying if you deny climate change you should be put in prison. No room for debate, the science is settled...Off to prison with you! What is the agenda here?...but I digress...

MAN MADE DESTRUCTION OF PLANETS?

(3rd ed. Insert 2016) Some suspicion of the purpose or effect of the Large Hadron Collider has been put forth as seen in Atlantis Rising # 86. Checking the math of the project shows it could produce three microjoules per particle (I don't know what that means) but the writer C.C. vonWerklaag, suggested that such a result meant they could solve the world energy crisis in a week. But use of the collider has apparently created upheavals in the neighborhood of the collider. Buildings, bridges and roads alignment have been shifted out of true. Rivers and water-ways had also been skewed. Many cases of dementia and alzheimer's disease and depression have occurred in the neighborhood of the collider as well. The conclusion was that the collider had warped the physical reality of the area. Jokingly he suggested the entire planet could be warped by the actions of the collider and torn apart by the stresses resulting from opposing gravitational forces. This sounds very similar to what Tesla believes could happen to the earth with technology he appeared to understand. Ever thought about how sometimes we can hurt ourselves by accidents or miscalculations? Of note, two Physicists, Matthew Choptuik of U.B.C. and Frans Pretorius Of Princeton U. in New Jersey used Einstein's equations to show that the Hadron Collider could in theory open up a very small black holes... something everyone else missed. (See Atlantis Rising #82 pg 12) These little oversights just might one day cause us some big problems, for which we might have to pay dearly.

A lightning bolt that strikes a magnet will change the polarity of that magnet and reverse the poles.

Contrary to popular belief like magnetic poles attract not different ones. Cut or break a magnet in half to prove this. In theory the poles of the particles of a magnet should be north south n, s, n, s,... so when you break a magnet the opposite particles should be attracted to each other. But they are not attracted, they repel. Furthermore when you then turn the broken parts around and you then put the unbroken north and south ends of the magnet together they also repel. I'm not sure if this is a factor or clue that belongs in this column, but I mention it in case it is. Something sort of related to this is an observation I have noticed. People often say "Opposites attract" when referring to couples. Even as a kid I always thought this to be wrong as I noticed that often couples seemed to display similar compatible characteristics, not opposite and thus volatile ones...in fact the more similar couples are the more suited to each other they seem to be. As far as like poles attracting I'm sure this will come flying back at me, but I am so curious as to why broken magnets do not attract at the point of break that I'm willing to risk ridicule to find out the answer.

BACK TO THE BIG STONES

Although I covered to a large extent some of the huge blocks moved by ancient man in chapter 3 to show man's superior technology in the past, I mention some of this material again to show this capability is connected to a different aspect of the past as well... that is, it is connected to geology.

In Baalbek Lebanon there are several ancient structures that stupefy modern engineers. There is an ancient 'temple' that has 54 pillars that are 8 feet wide and 90 feet high...and that's the easy bit! (why are they always presumed to be ancient temples or monasteries? why not shopping malls? My guess is since these places were built by the "gods" these places have become "temples" and such simply because of the link of the buildings to the "gods". Initially they may well have been intended as malls.) If the method of lifting these pillars wasn't enough to raise people's hair while using their calculators trying to figure out how they did it, the roof is enough to give archaeologists heart failure. On top of the pillars are slabs so large they can't be accurately 'weighed'. They are estimated to be between 1200 and 1500 tons. As far as I know modern technology can't move these slabs yet they came from many miles away, and lifted them 90 feet! How did *they* do it?! In other parts of Baalbek where the original structures have been taken away and Greco-Roman structures take their place, there remain the original foundations. These foundations are comprised of stones weighing from 750 to 2000 tons! The sizes of these stones are so huge that bizarre theories suggest they were space ship platforms. How did they move them? But they did move them and they were still doing so when construction abruptly stopped.

In one quarry there is seen a stone that was about to be moved. It is 60-80 feet wide by 13 3/4 feet or by 15 3/4 feet estimated to weigh 2000 tons. (sources vary as to its exact size)

Easter Island statues stopped construction suddenly. During the construction of the Easter Island statues… "The ruins show traces of sudden interruption. Scores of the Easter Island statues were being worked on when something caused the carvers to drop their tools. Dressed stone blocks were stacked awaiting shipment and at Nan Madol some of the cyclopean walls under construction were never completed." (Book 37 page 126-127) So obviously the statues too were being made by the same advanced civilization that was making the megalithic stone structures around the earth.

In fact all around the earth construction stopped on many Herculean structures apparently all at the same time. What happened? Did the builders just all say at the same time. 'Ah forget this pushing 200 ton rocks on rollers' and just stop? Granted Solomon's Temple was made with actual hard physical labor, and archeologists seem to equate how that temple was made to how other monolithic structures were made, such as the pyramids. But by Solomon's time virtually all ancient technology was gone. And it would seem the other indecipherable structures around the globe all stopped being made about 1000 years or more before Solomon's time. What's interesting is that MANY structures were in the middle of a building process. Few if any were actually finished. Something stopped them all at the same time, almost as if the very act of building them was the cause for the sudden stop of construction. How could building something actually be the cause that ceases the building of the same things? Paradox? Nope it is a big clue. Though we've already deduced that the ancients had antigravity in the technology at their disposal, we will see the use of this technology at this time had consequences.

(3ʳᵈ ed. Insert 2016) My conclusion is the earth suddenly shifted due to the over use of antigravity wreaking havoc on earth, stopping all work being done with this force and the gods just left.

MORE THAN THAT STOPPED

(3ʳᵈ ed. Insert 2016) It's been noted that monolithic structures all around the world stopped in mid construction suddenly, as mentioned. But it was interesting to find that mining stopped around the world suddenly as well, some noted but not connected before: such as the lion coal mine in Wattis Utah. Diggers broke into a network of tunnels six feet high and wide with coal so old it was weathered beyond usability. This particular 'mine' might have been just tunnels, although no entrance was found on either side of the mountain, but mine rooms were found. The entrances could have been blocked off in an earth upheaval, so it's not conclusive in my mind whether these were tunnels or a mine based on my source. (book 35 page 50-51) However a copper mine was also found on the Keweenaw peninsula on Isle Royal in Michigan. They estimated 2 million pounds of copper were removed from the mine which was suddenly abandoned. Interestingly it is theorized that a cataclysm of such proportions to destroy the infrastructure and need of mining copper may have been the reason for the abrupt end of mining activities. The cataclysm thought to have ended the mining is suggested in an Amerindian "Dance of the Trident" where they turn the trident prongs downward to say "I remember the old Red Land of my forefathers, and how it sank beneath the sea" pointing to the east in the direction of the Sunrise sea referring to the Atlantic ocean. (book 35 page 52-53) If a cataclysm stopped mining and stopped megalithic structures from being built, it seems logical it was the same event.

Ancient legends and gifts from visitors in strange lands constantly speak of antigravity devices like gold discs and such being tuned to the original owners physiology.

Often when you read about legends of the pyramids you hear of stones flying through the air and gently being placed into position. And I don't mean little rocks you can throw. I mean those huge slabs man was moving around like they were as light as feathers. Antigravity is a natural phenomena. In recent history strange unexplained explosions have been heard followed by stones being observed to lift on their own, which then moved several feet horizontally then dropped, showing there IS something in earth's physiological makeup that can make stones hover and fly. Figuring out how and why is the trick…that and evidently making scientists believe these things actually occur. Clearly the ancients new about this phenomena and figured it out. Stones made to move in that time were possibly as large as 20- 50,000 tons or more. All this masonry just hovering about like hummingbirds. One stone appears to have been a mobile quarry, with stone cut out of it with two 90 degree corners indicating some lost invention capable of cutting stone like butter and pulling square blocks right out existed at one time.

Sites in central and South America have stone spheres up to 9 feet wide sitting on top of pedestals. Nothing is known about them. Some stone spheres around the earth in ancient cities at one point glowed at dusk and turned themselves off at dawn. Some sites when damaged and subsequently "repaired" stopped working. Some stone statues existed that hummed or sung in the sun, but were damaged by earthquakes and when they were repaired they also stopped working. It appears as though these sites initially tapped into some natural earth force phenomena.

Somewhere in the Brazilian Matto Grosso in the 1920's Col F.H Fawcett was trying to find a city the Indians there said existed, but were afraid of as 'haunted'. Such buildings therein were described as "a fat tower of stones which was capped with light that never goes out" Pyramids with lights on top? (Book 12 pg 27-28) Since Atlantis appears to have been right in line with the pyramid belt it's quite possible there were several pyramids on that small continent as well, and in fact at least three pyramids appear to be under water in the Florida-Cuba-Andros Island area. Hundreds of archeological sites actually exist under water in this area and would likely have been part of Atlantis. Quite possibly some of the pyramids originally in Atlantis could still be in working order, causing some of the phenomena seen in the "Bermuda Triangle". Some legends even appear to exist that say the Atlanteans used powers we don't use today like vibratory forces…again possibly linked to pyramids.

WHERE IS THIS GOING?

OK here's the gist of where I'm going.

What caused the creation of the continents and how long did it take for them to form? Scientists have told us this drift took 200 million years. They have dated lava under the Atlantic Ocean and it dates incredibly old, and so they come up with this time period partly based on this age derived from this lava. However sea water among other things does things to lava that make it seem incredibly old when subjected to dating methods. I repeat a certain pertinent fact here. A known lava example formed underwater in 1801 dated by these same methods appeared to be 160 million years old! That's four fifths of the 200 million years right there just since 1801!

With this Peleg theory we would see North and South America pulling away from Africa and Europe, and consequently water overrunning the west coast of Americas and simultaneously rushing up into the newly formed Atlantic ocean from around the Cape and the Horn. No doubt with 3-600 feet of water left over from the flood, perhaps a sort of Atlantic sea existed before the breakup of the continents. It's just not plausible that a meteor would cause such massive land movement without actually destroying the earth and all the inhabitants of the earth, even with the earth already cracked. It would have taken an asteroid almost the size of the one that caused the flood hitting the earth at the right angle to have done anything powerful enough to create the continents.

Originally my guess was that maybe some sort of massive asteroid on the other side of the earth might have caused the continents to break away and drift, but this just doesn't seem like enough force or even the right force as the asteroid would have to be so big as to destroy the earth and no legends seem to exist suggesting any of this, and no other landmark on the earth suggests this took place, though I suppose one could maybe make an argument to the contrary. As I can picture it, an asteroid would have to have actually drilled right through the planet again so as to in a sense start to turn the world inside out in order for the continents to drift, but the "drift" would have been so catastrophic legends of that would be as widespread as those of the flood, and this means the "fountains of the deep" would have had to have broken forth again, and this just does not seem to be the case, as only pre-flood legends seem to talk about this…I think…

Legends say that Mu had a hole in the middle of it and the land mass appears to have sunk into it. That would be on the opposite side of the Atlantic ridge. It would be interesting to explore this possibility. Some other force besides an asteroid drilling into the earth turning it inside out had to start the drift, in a far less destructive way…despite how destructive "Peleg" actually was. This hole in Mu and the subsequent sinking of land into it may be somehow linked to the forces at work here. I've seen an interesting ball shaped toy with holes through the center that as you push material of the toy into the hole it comes out the other side. I suppose it is possible the earth also works like this, though it seems like a absolutely fantastic idea, and doesn't really seem to mesh with the topography of the undersea beds, though again no doubt a sustainable argument could be put forth in favor of this theory.

THE MOON LIKE A BOAT BEGAN TO FLOAT UPON THE STARRY OCEAN

(3rd ed. Insert 2016) (I found this reference similar to something mentioned above) In Atlantis by Donnelly (page 431-432) he refers to Chaldean and American legends. The legends quoted appear to be speaking of a flood of the tsunami type and of the time when global catastrophes changed the earth. "The pillars of heaven were broken; the earth shook to its very foundations; the heavens sunk lower toward the north: the sun, the moon, and the stars changed their motions; the earth fell to pieces, and the waters enclosed within its bosom burst forth with violence and overflowed it. Man having rebelled against Heaven, the system of the universe was totally disordered. The sun was eclipsed, the planets altered their course, and the grand harmony of nature was disturbed." This flood does not appear to be of a down fall description but of something causing the oceans to overflow the land, and it's one of very few mentions I've found of the moon changing its motions. (Obviously the sun can't change its motion but the earth in relation to it changed, probably referring to a reversal or crust shift.)This bit suggests that water came shooting up out of the ground again like it did during the flood: another asteroid in the vicinity? It's difficult to see with this little information if it isn't another world flood legend, as some details are similar, but the Heavens sinking lower seems to place it post world flood and make it a local type, though apparently it was worldwide in effect, as both American and Chaldean felt it. To be honest, I can't quite tell if this is a tale of the universal flood or a continental one.

INVERTIBLE BALL?

(3rd ed. Insert 2016) I suggested that the earth could possibly be like one of those loop balls sort of shaped spherically round but like a squished 'O', where you push one side in and it comes out the other side. Whether this deduction holds water, who can say, but I found some stuff while skimming some of my old sources that reminded me of this. Physicist John S. Rine Hart felt "…the variations in Old Faithfull's timing was connected with Alaska's Good Friday quake in 1964. Rinehart feels the stresses building up in Alaska traveled through the earth at a rate of three to six miles per day, eventually reaching as far south as Yellowstone Park in Wyoming."

Similarly in the 'Continents in Motion' by Peter Vogt referred to by Goodman he writes"…is quoted as believing that the surge of molten material from one of earth's plumes (hot spots) "may travel through channels in the floor of the lithosphere[rigid crust]" and "that a horizontal plumbing system underlies the mid-ocean ridge." Vogt has found correlations between past molten surges off Iceland and eruptions from the plume under the far distant island of Hawaii."

So it seems that once things get going from some initial earth catastrophe, the entire globe could erupt similar to a community with a lot of dogs. Once one dog gets barking, all the dogs in the area join in.

Another note along this line is found in Atlantis Rising #118. On October 8th 2005 a 7.6 earthquake hit Kashmir Pakistan, and another one hit Central America. Three days earlier a Hurricane (Stan) hit Guatemala and the day before that Llamatepee volcano erupted in El Salvador. Connected?)

LEGENDS SUGGEST CATASTROPHIC GEOLOGICAL EVENTS OCCURRED IN HISTORICAL TIMES AND WERE CAUSED BY MAN.

Traditions and legends allude to science and technology handed down to or from the ancients that caused displacement of the poles, and changed the earth's protective belts causing climate changes with extraordinary disasters. This is interesting. This seems to infer that the gods gave us technology and we like kids with matches caused a 'fire'. Later science was condemned for fear of another reoccurrence of disasters caused by man's inventions, so consequently scientists were forced underground or they became priests. Many of the miracles Moses did for Pharaoh were duplicated by the priests, such as their rods turning into snakes, or turning water into blood. This even serves as a warning to us today. There are genuine miracles but there are also "miracles" possible through sorcery or science and technology. One has to be careful when observing miracles and not automatically assume the originator of the "miracles' are super Godly. Even Jesus said many who do miracles were considered workers of iniquity. One of the miracles done in the end times is fire coming down from heaven and turning a statue of the beast into a living creature.... very similar to what the Egyptian priests did with their rods. But I digress.

So what disasters did the ancients cause and how and with what did they cause them? We've already seen they had nuclear capabilities, but this capability is destructive in the wrong way compared to what happened. Yes nuclear bombs will cause earthquakes but not on this scale.

THE LAND DIVIDED SPEEDILY

Since this creation of the fault lines only occurred at the time of the flood this means the continental drift not only started *after* the flood but at a very fast rate to get to the point where the continents are at now in less than 4800 years, if we work back from the time of Columbus. In fact the continents moved extremely fast! Could continental drift be blamed on meteors? If the continents already started to drift, the drift could have been speeded up, but it's doubtful meteors started the drift. However if meteors didn't cause the continental drift they would have displaced the normal rotation of the earth enough to disturb water and moved the land, with huge tidal waves being the result, but not on the scale we are talking about, unless the continents had already started to move. They may even have shifted the poles somewhat, but would they have switched or flipped the poles? Very doubtful. It would seem to me that the event that caused the flipping of the poles is also the event that started the continents to drift. What could do both things?

So the meteors can't be blamed for the initial start of the continental drift though they would be blamed for disasters from subsequent motion continuing the drift. So something else had to start the drift. If we use ancient legends as a clue to decipher events in the past we see they speak of manmade technology causing a massive disaster. The only disaster I can think of on this scale to be caused by technology that accounts for the clues has to be the initiation of the continental drift.

RATE OF DRIFT

The rate of drift is now somewhere in the neighborhood, by some estimates, inches and maybe a foot or two a year...if that much. Five millimeters is the current estimate based on satellite findings. So clearly the rate has slowed down a lot, though it is interesting that it hasn't actually stopped yet. If the rate that it is spreading was added up for the 5400 odd years back to the flood at the rate of 1 foot a year the spread between Africa and America would be little more than 12 miles! By the same token if we go with the current rate of 5 millimeters a year, in 200 million years the distance achieved would be in the neighborhood of 519 miles or 837 kilometers, still too little, and with no known cause for the division to occur in the first place. Since we've ruled out an old earth we thus must conclude at one time the continents "drifted" VERY fast because of some as yet unnamed force.

If mountains formed at 1000th the part of the equatorial bulge (due to centrifugal force and tidal action) only a 2 or 3 mile pole shift would occur. Even if 1/10th of the entire land mass of the surface of the earth rose 1000 feet it would only deflect the poles 3 degrees 17 minutes. (though not much, it's considerably more than if the earth were solid) Some far greater force acted upon the earth to have cause all these events. Conclusions by scientists say the displacement of the earth's crustal shelf does not appear to originate from forces within the earth itself, but must have occurred from some external mechanism. They appear to be considering inter planetary causes or asteroids. This may be partly correct as ancient legends do clearly indicate the planets had a hand in these disasters. But it appears that some action by man, as extreme as that sounds was also responsible.

Studies done on the north pole in relation to large earthquakes (7.5 or better) around the globe found that in most cases such earthquakes actually shifted the north pole temporarily in some way. We could deduce from this that earthquakes do not flip the poles.

A SENSITIVE EARTH

Some geologic theories suggest that the weight of ice on northern regions can press down on the land mass to the extent that it disturbs the underlying crust. If subtle things such as ice build up on Greenland can cause earthquakes, maybe the Antarctic continent could be cause for concern. The center of gravity of the Antarctic ice cover is actually 345 miles from the geographic pole. It's felt that with the earth wobble and large earthquakes something could happen to this southern region that could cause the whole earth to tumble. If such mundane causes could be blamed for changes in the earth's form just think what a single decent sized asteroid could do. Such could be the straw that broke the camel's back.

(3rd ed. Insert 2016) Charles Hapgood and James H. Campbell (an engineer who helped developed the Sperry gyroscope) deduced that the whole earth wouldn't topple, but that the earth's crust moved around a liquid layer something like an orange peel sliding around the orange inside. (which by the way is fun to do with the mandarin oranges…) These and others like Hugh Auchincloss Brown, felt that periodic build-ups of ice on Greenland, Antarctica and the arctic sea could upset the balance of the crust which slips to compensate. (book 19 pg 147-148) Others argue crust moving from a thin layer of ice and snow compared to the thickness of the planet makes that seem an insignificant factor. The continents appear to be floating rather than rigidly housed so you can't take the thickness of the earth to debunk this idea, only the thickness of the lithosphere, so it could be a factor if not the cause of continental shifting.

Other theories tend to allude to a fairly sensitive earth. The shape of the earth is wider at the equator then in other regions, indicating that just the rotational movement and centrifugal force of the earth can make the land masses bulge at the equator. This single fact alone should give geologist reason to ponder.

An interesting theory that even Einstein supported was that possibly centrifugal force can move the continents and this force pushes the continents to a small degree toward the equator and up or outward. Indeed even the continents are subject to tidal tug by the Moon and the sun and pull toward these sources of gravity. In theory, perhaps this centrifugal force, if somehow something upset a balance such as a huge meteor, the continents could slide or rotate over or around what holds them in place and cause a relatively large shift in the continents. Even so it still would be inadequate to cause what is seen on the earth today, that is the separate continents. There would have been needed a substantial boost to break barriers and overcome friction to such a degree to cause mountains to climb as one continent overran another, otherwise they would simply stop moving at the next barrier. If the earth is as sensitive as this, maybe something less substantial than a massive asteroid moved the continents initially, and this again possibly puts such a force into the hands of man.

TIDBITS ABOUT THE PYRAMIDS

Ancient maps copied and redrawn show that some of the maps were oriented in a completely different way. It took a lot of detective work but they realized the maps were drawn with Cairo at the center.

Coincidentally when taking the entire mass of the continents, Cairo is in the center of the land masses, and before the continents came into being, Cairo seems to be at the center back then! (book 51) What do we find near Cairo? Three pyramids. These three pyramids are in the center of the world's land mass, and ancient maps were drawn in a way to show the least distortion of the land so they too were centered in Cairo. This alone speaks of some fantastic design. It would seem the three main pyramids were placed in the center of the earth's continental mass and this was probably done deliberately.

Though there is debate, it would seem the pyramids likely existed pre-flood as is evidenced by the deep based silt deposits surrounding them. There seems to be reference to a localized flood in Egypt, not connected with the flooding Nile, or the great flood. This could be a similar flood spoken of by Joshua. Since this flood covered the pyramids very early on after the flood of Noah I have to think these are in fact pre-flood structures. Though the origin of the pyramids is presumed to be unknown, there is at least one Tibetan tablet that shows the origin of the pyramids. It says that the people that built the pyramids lived in a land in the center of the great water. (book 12 page 111) That at first glance doesn't seem to say much. But they are talking about the lay of the land, but obviously the pyramids are not in the center of that continent, so this seems a strange thing to say. But when one realizes that the earth before Peleg was a single land mass and the rest of the earth was water it makes sense. Since Tibetan legend speaks of them being in the center of the land, this places their construction sometime before Peleg, that is 101 years after the flood at the very latest.

From space the earth might have looked like a big "eye" with one big landmass in the midst or center of a worldwide ocean. Granted Peleg happened 101 years after the flood, so this Tibetan tablet only narrows down the building of the pyramids to pre Peleg, because Peleg changed the face of the earth. Even if this doesn't seem like the correct analysis of this Tibetan tablet, we do know by other histories that the pyramids must have been built before the reign of the gods ended, somewhere before 3100 BC or about 300 years past the flood...so it fits.

WHEN AND WHY WERE THE PYRAMIDS BUILT?

Consider this. The problem with traditional geology, archaeology and anthropology is they discount the event of the flood and presume the face of the earth was as it is for a far longer period of time. Thus they can assume long periods of time for the population to build up to the point where they could have enough people to build the pyramids in ways they suggest they were built. But since the flood did happen, we have to take that event and the time that event occurred into account when considering theories on how and when the pyramids were built.

If we presume they built the pyramids right after the flood, why would they do this? They must have had prior knowledge that they would and could be built and for some purpose, otherwise building pyramids when you're trying to rebuild civilization doesn't make any sense. They could not possibly have been built for the purpose of burying kings, because people were still living to 400-600 years after the flood...so who died? ((2nd ed. Insert 2008) Remember after creation when life spans were so long no one on earth died for possibly as long as 800-930 years. The first recorded death (other than Abel) is that of Adam and he lived 930 years. Similarly after the flood with life spans still 400-600 years, no one would have died to supposedly cause the start of building the pyramids or this so called tomb. So it can't be the reason they were built as they were arguably around even before the Egyptians first dynasty, during the reign of the gods, around 3100 BC, or about 300 years after the flood)

Assuming they built them in the center of the land mass deliberately, they would have had to have surveyed the entire earth to decipher the exact center of the land mass. This might not have taken too long if they had space craft at their disposal, but if they did they would have had to have this flight capability immediately after the flood to start the pyramids right away. And they likely did not have this right after the flood, though I suppose there could have been room in the ark for a single flying saucer...but it doesn't seem like they had one, though I can't say this is by any means certain. But I get ahead of myself. Also if the pyramids were built in the center of the land mass deliberately this was clearly for a far grander purpose then just burying some king or god. In fact if they were built in the center of the land mass deliberately it speaks of a global purpose behind the construction of the pyramids.

If the pyramids were built in this period of time after the flood but before Peleg, this does not leave enough time or a large enough population base to build them, if we assume traditional theories on how they were built are correct. And in my estimations as we talked about earlier, were they built in conventionally ways, they may have taken 2223 years to build! We would have long since forgotten why we started the things, and there isn't just one! There are many! Then this seems to indicate the pyramids were actually pre-flood structures, and certainly not for burying people in.

Its known pyramids in China were opened up and used as burial places long after they were originally made. It would seem that if an important person died, perhaps one of the "gods", the person was interred in an already built structure. The pyramids were just used this way since it was not used any longer for any other purpose, and it was a way to show how special that person really was by giving them a final resting place in such a special place of honor. A stone "sarcophagus" was found in the main pyramid but it had no lid, and no treasure typical of stuff seen with the burial of kings has been found in the pyramid of Egypt, and that includes a body. The sarcophagus may have been placed in there after the pyramid was built but then some problem arose to not enable them to bring in the lid, or the lid may be somewhere else in the pyramid. But with all the secret passages and such maybe somebody is yet to be found…maybe even in the hands of someone who was going to bury the person there, as they may have got trapped, but all this is speculation obviously.

FRAUD FOR FAME. THUS THE PYRAMIDS ARE OLDER THAN THOUGHT.

(3rd ed. Insert 2016) It's often thought the pyramids were built by Khufu Cheops:the first pyramid (and later ones by Chefra, and Menkara), because their names were 'discovered' in a long sealed section by colonel Vyse. But this Mr. Vyse actually was an archeological fraud. He had blasted his way into the pyramids, and placed inside a coffin dating about 2000 years after Menkara lived with an even later skeleton in the coffin. Sitchin had gathered evidence that the Khufu inscription was a forgery and in 1983 the records of one of Vyse's assistant surfaced because of Sitchens work. It was in the hands of a great grandson of this assistant. The record noted he was an eyewitness to the forgeries, and because this assistant disagreed with Vyse' methods, Vyse had him expelled from the site and forced him to leave Egypt. On top of this, inscriptions exist showing the pyramids existed in Khufu's time, so he couldn't have built them.

Legends speak of sounds sung by priests which could open secret doors. If this is correct, the knowledge is lost as to how to enter some of the pyramids secret passages…if they are even there. Maybe something happened to someone that could open them. Radio and other technologies that might allow one to 'see through walls" proves ineffective in the pyramids as the readings never read the same way twice.

Back to deciphering when the pyramids were built. The population base comes into play. If the pyramids were built in the traditional way archeologists suggest, there simply was not the manpower available to build them if they were built after the flood. There were only 8 people in the ark and it would have taken longer than 100 years to build up the population to the point you could make 100,000 slaves with which to build the pyramids. We know the pyramids were considered old in the first Egyptian dynasty so they were definitely built before 3100 BC and probably well before this time. This leaves well under 300 years in which to build up the population and build structures with a hundred thousand men. But by some other people's calculations these pyramids may have taken as long as 600 years to build!

These eight in the ark originally lived pre flood and probably had much pre-flood technology with them and would have understood whatever still existed, and knew how to use it. Although they were still living long lives and would have been able to have kids for a much longer time, perhaps 3-4 hundred years past the flood, Shem, Ham, and Japeth were still having kids. Looking at some clues it would seem twins were a much more common occurrence at one time whereas nowadays the chance of having twins is one in 182 births. Reading one lineage of the "gods", several generations in succession were twins. This factored into any population figures would clearly play a part in a rapid growth of population, but even so, no way is the population going to reach numbers needed to build the pyramids before Peleg. Within just 80 years easily a thousand or many thousands more people were on the earth, rebuilding civilization, but not enough to build the pyramids in the way archeologists suggest. And time is a factor too, because the pyramids had to be built before Peleg, 101 years after the flood. Why must the pyramids be built before Peleg? Not just because of the Tibetan legend....

The pyramids were completed before Peleg, because Peleg caused the pyramids to be buried in silt in the first place! If they were built after the flood they would have had to take all the flood clay and silt away to get down to the bedrock they were built on. I've not read of anybody clearing away clay while getting to the base of the pyramids so it would seem they cleared the clay away at least before using the pyramids if not before building them. So they were built either before the flood, very fast or both. Though I suppose a post flood tsunami might have washed away any clay the pyramids might still have had clinging to them.

The pyramids were partially buried by silt and were at one time partially underwater in a completed state as an old saltwater line known to have been on the pyramids indicates. The silt was more than 30 feet deep. The silt was full of clams that dated 12,000 years old, but we already know of the problems of dating. Some action partially buried the pyramids and the rest of the ancient buildings in the neighborhood, so obviously the pyramids were built before this occurred. So they had to be built prior to 3309 BC. Again, it stands to reason they are pre-flood structures.

Also how long did they take to build? It's been estimated that the limestone casings (the bright white stone the pyramids were originally finished with) alone would have taken at least 27 years to quarry. Even though this is based on the lousy technology at our disposal today... it still involves a well established shipping infrastructure already in place. It would seem they could cut through rock like butter, and fly rocks using antigravity, so this would greatly reduce building times.

What constantly bothers people is that we still do not have the technology today to cut and place the limestone with the accuracy the pyramids were built with. They were all placed 0.02 inches apart and the cement in that gap is stronger than the limestone itself, and each of the limestone blocks weighed at least 2 tons. Not to mention they had the angle of the pyramid cut into each one as well. I mean imagine your average construction crew today trying to do this even with the tools we have at our disposal. They build bathrooms to fit a shower that goes in later and often we have to move the walls with sledge hammers just to get them to fit. If we have difficulty making a room exactly eight feet, what measure of success would we have making the pyramids with this level of accuracy being expected?

The likelihood that they used antigravity almost forces the pyramids to be built before the flood if my assessment as to the purpose of the pyramids is correct. Man appears to have had the capabilities to overcome gravity by using special devices tuned to their specific individuals physiology, such as Vril rods and golden disks. These antigravity devices were tuned to individuals similar to how divining tools are tuned to specific diviners...IE length of string, type of wood ect. So they could have built the pyramids with this technology first then gone onto building other things. But the pyramids would then have to have been built first and very fast and then the other mysterious structures around the earth would have been built after the pyramids were finished, and all this had to take place before Peleg. A very short period of time considering what was built. And this still doesn't mean they were built after the flood as there are just so many pyramids around the earth.

Maybe the pyramids did take a long time to build but then when did they find the time to build them? Where do you place them in the historical timeline? Considering many of the problems of time and construction one has to conclude the pyramids were built before the flood. Sorry to belabor this fact but it seems somehow necessary to show they had to be pre-flood structures as so many seem to completely forget about the flood altogether, when estimating when they were built.

A Coptic writer also suggests that at least two of the pyramids were built before the flood. (book 37 pg. 68)

There are also 7 other pyramids in a single plain in China, one being estimated at 1200 feet high and 2000 feet at the base. That is over and above the standard of a mountain! There are said to be at least a hundred pyramids in China alone. There is rumor of one in Mongolia or Tibet that is 1000-1200 feet high! It is called the Shensi Pyramid west of Sian-Fu two days caravan west and one day northerly from this ancient walled city that has the remains of colour on the four sides, East side green, South side is red, West side; black, and North side is white. The top is an uncapped flat area, with traces of yellow paint.(book 12 pg 20)

PYRAMIDS PURPOSE STARTS TO BECOME CLEAR

Pyramids have been studied by many and it has been noted that they appear to be placed around the earth in relation to each other, and it's been suggested that they were part of a worldwide interconnected system, in what is often referred to as a "Pyramid belt". This makes sense as they are an odd sort of "building" so it's certainly plausible they were built for the same reason, purpose and function.

This begs the question; are they separate entities, or are they interrelated and connected somehow? The clues seem to indicate or suggest they were to be used in a function all at the same time, like integral parts of an earth wide structure almost as if the earth itself was the housing unit. Even imagining this tends to suggest something fantastic. Pyramids built all over the earth for a single common use and all linked with each other by a 'belt' and some binding force, for the purpose or harnessing of some earth physiological phenomena. It boggles the mind. What ARE these things!?

Pyramids are known to be less sophisticated the newer they are and the oldest ones are the best made. So that would suggest that some were made after the flood, during the time man and the earth were in a state of decline. So man's capabilities had to be diminished not to able be to duplicate the master pyramids, and with the earth also in decline, more pyramids were needed to be built up the power of the grid as each pyramids maximum capacity was diminished by the earth's reduced capacity to be turned into some sort of power field. More devolution evidence.

But also the use of them changes. Later on they are smaller and used to bury people in or the older ones are opened up and used for burials. But it's clear they were not originally meant as burial places. However as to what the original purpose of the pyramids was, few can agree, and as far as I know, none have guessed at what I suspect they were used for, though admittedly my research sources are few in number. All I've found is that they are all over the earth and appear to be built for a common purpose as not only are they aligned to the cardinal point of the earth, they also appear to be built in relation to each other. So working with this deduction they appear to be some sort of inter connected grid with one common purpose. If they were built to be linked somehow to each other they must work in tandem to accomplish their task assuming they had a purpose other than burying kings. And this also makes it all the more impossible for them all to have been built after the flood and before Peleg.

It does seem obvious that some of the pyramids were built after the flood. In fact some were not even finished and they were built in inferior ways with inferior materials. For example in one plain in China there are 7 incomplete pyramids and they are made of dirt. The dirt pyramids in China were just compressed dirt with limestone being added after instead of them being built with stone throughout. But these were not finished allowing people later to dig into them to bury special people. If they were built with dirt, this suggest the theory they have secret passages in them may be incorrect. That is those built with dirt anyway. In fact if they were built with a variety of materials, this means what they were built out of wasn't important, but what was important was the shape of the building.

PYRAMIDS KEEP CROPPING UP.

Back to the condition of the earth immediately following the flood. Now all these fissures, cracks and fault lines would have been covered up with the flood and the silt and the earth would have appeared sound....maybe even from the air as settling would have hidden these physical signs. Maybe they would have been visible from the air or may even have been in plain sight but anyone living after the flood might not have understood or clued into the nature of the slightly altered topography all around them, and gone merrily on their way rebuilding civilization, with the advanced tools at their disposal.

They were not as advanced as the pre-flood generations, but light-years beyond us still. Assuming they were using pre-flood tools they would have been at least for a short while almost as advanced as pre-flood man, especially since it would appear they had some help from an as yet unnamed source, that is these "gods". They were still building pyramids, just not as good as the pre-flood ones. But that they were building pyramids at all shows they knew what they were for, and how to use them. Since the meteor that caused the flood also caused the earth's magnetic field to start a half life, diminishing its power capacity, more pyramids had to be built to beef up the power of the old ones, so this could explain why they would be building more pyramids after the flood.

With the sun now shining directly onto earth's surface with all its incumbent radiation and the earth's missing atmosphere and protective water shell no longer surrounding earth, man, though still smart, was rapidly declining in longevity and mental grasp. If you doubt the sun can affect people this way, people who have been lost in the desert stuck in the boiling sun for long periods of time have been observed to act incredibly stupid, and this is not from lack of water, but from the prolonged exposure to the direct sun and the heat. Some people of this early post-flood era realized this was happening and went elsewhere (see chapter 9) and some of course stayed and rebuilt, oblivious or resigned to the dangers. They would have had some of the knowledge of the pre-flood generation taken with them through the flood, and probably still had far more technology at their disposal then we have today. Much of the evidence shown in the Adam 900 chapter as to their technological achievements is of the post flood era, though some of it may also be a carryover of this technology salvaged from pre-flood times on the ark, and then there are these ubiquitous "gods". We are merely clutching at straws when we try to grasp the advances of the pre-flood generations...but if my guess is correct as to what the purpose of the pyramids was, we might just get a glimpse.

I must interject that I'm not talking about just the pyramids of Egypt, though I am speaking only of that type, that is the smooth faced limestone faced ones, not the stepped ones, usually called ziggurats as seen in Mexico and other places, though a small one of these also appears to be in Egypt. It would seem the pyramids and the ziggurats have two entirely different functions, though they apparently tap into similar forces. I'll suggest a possible function for the ziggurats in a later chapter.

PYRAMID CRYSTALS

There is said to be a white pyramid which was spotted by a pilot during WWII in early 1942 while flying a cargo plane. This pyramid is supposedly in the Himalayans, seemingly on route to, or in the neighborhood of Brahmapurta River in Assam India, or possibly over the border in China. This pyramid has been known about for centuries by many Asian communities. This or a similar pyramid was stumbled upon while a pilot, James Gaussman, was flying over the "hump", a 500 mile stretch of mountains between India and China, during the second world war.

During the allies flights to supply the Chinese with ammunition to help to fight the Japanese, WWII pilots saw all sorts of strange things in the secluded mountain regions as they flew over them; ancient lost cities, ruins, strange buildings in the middle of nowhere, and seemingly a few pyramids, apparently in various conditions. Gaussman's flight took him through "Dead man's alley" from India to China. His plane started to have trouble, probably from freezing fuel lines, so he dropped below the clouds and started zigzagging though the mountains in hopes of the wings warming up. He was on a route to Assam India and banked to avoid a mountain and came out over a level valley of undetermined size. There he saw directly below him a dazzling white pyramid capped with a crystal, like something out of a "fairy tale".

Though the pilot could not land he circled and described what he saw. The pyramid looked like it could be metal or some very white stone. The capstone was a huge piece of a jewel like stone that could have been crystal. (book 12 pg. 16-17)People tend to suggest this is a pyramid of legend and that it doesn't really exist. But consider this. The pyramids of Egypt were originally encased in polished white limestone that was so white; the light they reflected it is said could be seen from the mountains of Israel and possibly even from the moon. So the fact that someone saw a brilliant white pyramid without knowing this fact does tend to lend credibility to the story. I suppose it's possible someone altered the fabled white pyramid at some point after this sighting in the '40's, but that seems unlikely. There's more.

One thing that has been told of the pyramids is that originally they were capped with a crystal. I can't seem to figure out if this was a crystal sphere, cone or just a crystal, shaped to finish off the slope of the pyramids; all appear to be possibilities. This legend is fairly widespread, so there's no reason to doubt this...and in fact this was apparently confirmed by the pilot who saw the white pyramid which he said had crystal at its peak. The pilot who saw this appears to have had no foreknowledge of the existence of such crystals. There are pyramids around the earth but this one by its description was in virtually perfect condition and I think was only referred to by one other author in my sources, though I didn't go extensively into pyramid types of books. He had no evidence to prove this pyramid existed, though pictures of a similar very damaged Pyramid in this area does exist, with no crystal capping it. As far as I know, no other pyramid has been found with a crystal on top but there is always a flat spot on top of the pyramids where they would put one, indicating these legends have something to them and the areas where these crystals would go indicate that they were large crystals indeed!

These crystals seem to originally have been an integral part of the pyramids purpose and function, but they have all been destroyed. If they were not destroyed but merely taken away there would be stories of such huge crystals still existing so it seems they had to have been destroyed.

The largest existing crystal that I know about that seems linked to these types of crystals, appears to be that 11 1/2 pound crystal skull, found in the Mayan ruins near Lubaanun of the British Honduras. This rock crystal skull shows no tool marks and to me it suggest it was molded and the crystal may have been of an artificial manmade sort. Other stories exists that suggest these crystal pyramid capstones were manmade. But if they were destroyed we have to ask the question...why? When we answer this, things start to fall into place.

EVEN MORE PYRAMIDS?

Some pyramids may have been destroyed in the Peleg motion or their alignment disturbed in relation to each other and thus ending or drastically reducing their power, though remnants of the power remain. Other pyramids may have been completely sub-ducted in the mountain building process that appears to have occurred after the pyramids were built, and some are now underwater, again pointing to their very early existence. Possibly detailed studies of satellite photos in the areas in question would reveal whether this white still pyramid exists. Though a cursory search of the Himalayas in Google Earth, the internet virtual satellite earth image, came up empty. But there are a lot of mountains to look through. However I did come across some interesting ruins in the middle of the Himalayans, but then promptly lost the co-ordinates. This would tend to lend more credibility to this story of the fabled white pyramid, as Gaussman also spoke of these or similar ruins. Looking for the white pyramid on the internet shows it still hasn't been found, at least not as described, even with other people looking at satellite images.

The pyramids have been demolished to the point they are no longer functioning structures. Interestingly while Tesla was in the middle of an experiment which caused several city blocks to shake, he was found to be smashing a contraption attached to a pillar of the building he was in because there was not enough time to simply turn it off. Otherwise it would have kept running, slowly turning itself off for too long a period to multiply the destruction it was causing. Possibly if what the pyramids were really used for was ever to be tried again they could unleash their disastrous consequences again, or they may not even work anymore with the earth so reduced in power, and the crystal caps long destroyed. If this guess is right as to what the pyramids were used for, one does not want the pyramids to ever work again, simply because the earth is now just too weak to take the strain.

PELEG IN REVERSE

Originally with all the continents at the time of the pyramids construction actually still being a part of a single continent, the position of these pyramids would have changed somewhat in relation to each other when compared to the positions they are seen at today. However people have turned back time so to speak and returned the continents back to their original position by "reversing" the drift. It's really quite a neat film clip to see the continent drift in reverse. When one takes the time to match up features where the continents connect up it is said they match up perfectly, even to the rock formations and fauna. Closely matching up the continents can find mineral deposits on one side of an ocean that are known to be on the other side.

A PYRAMID BELT OR GRID?

What got me started on this idea was the noting of some authors about the pyramids being in a 'belt' on the earth. If we plot the known pyramids based on the topography of the pre-flood single continent Pangaea we see the pyramids could form an arched line around the center of the land mass. We could fill in a few spots if we deduce some pyramids in the Atlantis area and one conveniently plotted on the Antarctic land mass.

It's possible that when "India" came crashing into Asia a pyramid or two got destroyed. It's also possible the very nature of the power of the pyramids actually prevented some of them from being damaged, diverting moving land around them, as may be the case with the white pyramid. If there is even further bunching of Pangaea we get a straight line of Pyramids across the center of the land mass, though I may be missing knowledge of some of them. Where you plot unknown missing pyramids is somewhat speculative but I have to think they were evenly or mathematically spaced, though I'm no pyramid expert. It has merely been noted that they were built apparently linked to each other in their placement.

I do not think the step pyramids are necessarily part of the grid though they may also line up with the rest, and their similarity may even have aided in some sort of power harnessing, though I don't think they were part of the grid or even helped it any. So if we just go with the Pyramids of one kind and presume there are pyramids in Antarctica and Atlantis they seem to cut through the known center of the landmass before the flood. This would also quite possibly point out the original poles. So it seems like at one time there was a straight line of pyramids straight across the equator of the single mass continent from sea to sea. It makes me wonder if they didn't build them right around the globe regardless if there was water in that place or not. When the west coast of South America was pulled over the pacific bed or Mu, or folded over itself, it's possible a pyramid or two got crushed and sub-ducted into the earth. We know some manmade structures exist along the Pacific 6000 feet under water near Peru. Also at least one city has been seen in the Atlantic ocean from planes in strange occurrences that made the water sink in some areas revealing the structures. (3rd.ed insert 2016) The map of Scandinavia by Olaus Magnus from 1572 appears to show 3 or 4 pyramids on the southern coast of the northern part of Greenland, north east of Iceland. That might sound like an impossible placement for Greenland, but the map of Nicolo and Antonio Zeno from 1380 also depicts Greenland extending to this area too.

Assuming they were all created for the same purpose regardless of however many there were and whatever that purpose was, they seemed to have been linked with each other in some fashion, despite that fact this "link" would be over many hundreds even thousands of miles. Obviously they are all the same structure and they are all the way from China to the west coast of South America. Some might even still be undiscovered and thought to be mountains all covered in growth in the jungles. They are in widespread locations and clearly have a single unified purpose which is on a global scale. But to grasp this and see the magnitude of them in this light means they were far more important than just route markers or burial places. I mean it's just ludicrous to think they were created for tombstones but whatever they were built for must have been impressive indeed! And since it would seem they are a pre-flood structure, we start to glimpse something huge in scope.

CHANGE OF PLANS

(3rd ed insert 2016) That's what I wrote in earlier edition. My guess was originally the pyramids lined up horizontally, on what would have been the earth's original equator. One map I used appeared to bear this out. Though there may be a pyramid location link with the 12 sided aspect or anomaly magnetic hot spots of the earth. (one map I found almost seemed to form a circle of pyramids around the globe with the Giza pyramids in the center of the circle suggesting the Dodecahedron magnetic hot spot is more on target then the equator idea). Frankly plotting them on various maps of the earth from ranging from Pangea to current maps doesn't seem to bear this theory of the original equator out though. Admittedly some maps seem less exact compared to each other so it's hard to know which maps of Pangaea (and the stages in between) are accurate. Also mapping all of Pangea depending on projection messes you up somewhat too. (if you don't include Mu) the land mass appears to go vertically over the (current) pole. In fact you could almost argue the opposite: that using the pyramids pushed them towards the equator. Still regardless of plotting, it still seems the pyramids are linked with world antigravity and destruction, suggesting the two are linked. I started plotting pyramids on maps but then categorizing them and some possible pyramids, like for example Faroe Islands just gave me a headache. I just didn't know where to draw the line on what pyramids were really pyramids. So I'll leave that to someone else. Anyone doing so would need to plot them on the current map of today but also on the map of Pangaea and possibly stages in between like on Laurasia and Gondwanaland to include all the possibilities. I date Pangea at 3400 BC, Laurasia and Gondwanaland at 3100 BC. Further continental movements occurred at the exodus around 1500 BC, another at 687 BC and a possible final movement at 536-545 AD, when Antarctica's last 20 degree twist may have happened.

POWER SOURCE

The earth is a source of power if one knows how to tap into that source. It can be seen among other things as a giant magnet. Curiously when tracing magnetic lines of force this force is weakest over the central area of the magnet. If we consider the earth as a giant magnet, the weakest area of that magnet would be the equator, the very place where these pyramids seem to be when plotted on Pangaea, and it has been noted that the pyramid's shape is similar to that of crystal magnetite. There could very well be a connection.

Magnets when hammered lose some of their strength. Let's presume the pyramids were originally built to have something to do with tapping into the latent energies found in the earth itself...staggering as that seems. Maybe with the asteroid smashing into earth the pyramids didn't function up to speed with the earth generating a reduced amount of power. Maybe some of the smaller or dirt pyramids were added after the flood to beef up the system... built by the post flood generation as it's generally agreed that not all the pyramids seem to be equal in standard and precision, yet all are almost equally as impressive.

The foresight to builds these structures all over the earth (in ways we still don't understand) and the scope they encompass means they could only have had a worldwide global purpose and are not individual pyramids as we see them but are in fact all individual components with a single purpose, like parts of a machine... similar to how electric eyes have two parts on both sides of a door; They don't touch each other but are part of each other. If the pyramids are and were created as a single functioning item, what on earth WAS that function? Their function must have been linked to the very earth itself! It just boggles the mind!

EARTHS EARLY MAGNETIC FIELD

The earth's magnetic field is known to have a half life of 1400 years. This means in 600 AD it was twice as powerful. In 800 BC it was four times as powerful. In 2200 BC 8 times and in 3600 BC (around the time of the flood) it was 16 times as powerful. How powerful was it before the flood just before the asteroid smashed into the earth weakening this field and indeed likely 'creating' the earth's magnetic field's 'half-life" to begin with? Perhaps the magnetic field of the earth was a full 20 or maybe even 32 times more powerful originally! That in itself deserves study as to its characteristics and how it would affect life on earth. And since this was part of the original creation it must have been a factor in many things, possibly longevity, antigravity, flight, holding a water sphere above the earth...and who knows what else it affected. It might have interacted with our very minds and those of the animals. We know that the animals became frightened of man immediately following the flood. We know powerful electro magnets can affect men working near them, though this type of magnetic field appears to affect man in negative ways.

Certainly man tapped into this power. Even Nicola Tesla looked upon the entire earth as a giant generator. Speculation just goes wild when one reads about this fascinating man. He could see lightning was cyclic and tuned to the earth itself. He created voltages beyond what we've been able to duplicate today. As to how much the physiology of the earth itself came into play in his inventions I can't say, but he knew the earth was a factor and had a vital role in some of his discoveries and inventions. He even saw that harmonics, which if used in a destructive way, could destroy the earth. Sound familiar? If this man understood some of the latent powers in this earth with its diminished capacities, you can bet ancient and pre-flood man knew about and tapped into this power. Had Tesla insisted on his royalties from his inventions he might have made something far beyond his Niagara Falls generators, and Tesla coils. He spoke of "Vibratory electro-magnetic transmission forces" in his attempt to electrify the earth. This sound very much like the legends that talk of how the earth was destroyed and how antigravity was achieved. Maybe he would have made another pyramid, or realized what the pyramids might have been used for at one time and reinstated their use. Maybe it was a good thing he didn't!

There are the odd references to the 'destruction of the world" in history which legends say was caused by crystals. This likely refers to crystal blocks or spheres known to have been used to cap pyramids, thus this tends to suggest that the pyramids themselves are linked to the "destruction" of the earth, and this would explain the crystal's destruction and disappearance. Obviously the earth still exists so this "destruction" appears to be in reference to some aspect of the earth that is no longer the same. We've seen that the earth and sky have changed since the flood, and we'll see this continental drift action is described in the past. Whatever changes to the earth occurred, ended up reducing our life spans further and the only other major physical change apparent since the flood is the creation of the continents. Anger at the devastating results likely made people destroy all the pyramid crystals, so the same events could never happen again, and make things worse. Were the pyramids somehow responsible for this change? The pyramids didn't cause the great flood, so what did they do?

Possibly physiological aspects of the earth were harnessed through the pyramids to overcome gravity and move massive weights over great distances. This might employ a similar science to current technological advances which allow 'flux pinning'; that is hovering of objects in stationary spots through carefully tuned magnetic fields. ((2<u>nd</u> ed. Insert 2008) <u>Flux pinning is something like stabilizing a magnet being repelled by another magnet underneath so that the upper magnet stays hovering above the magnet below without sliding off the field. Normally such a magnet above would simply slide off the repulsion field and clank onto the bottom magnet.</u>) Interestingly silver is used in these experiments and silver which is the best known superconductor is constantly linked in clues to antigravity. The pyramids appear to have originally been built before the flood, and were likely repaired or merely 'dusted off" after the flood and put back into use. Since it's been noted that the shape of the pyramids is very similar to that of crystal magnetite, then some aspect of this crystal shape may build up some sort of force as is evident in the pyramids. Large stones around the world have been found to have silver set in holes in them when originally discovered. The pyramids also have stones inside with mysterious holes in them. Was silver set in them then taken out later? Crystals, silver, antigravity, and destruction of the earth; are all these things somehow linked with the pyramids?

EARTH FORCES KNOWN ABOUT

It's long been known that the ancients were fully aware of earth's magnetic field and its force line throughout the earth, and many researchers have come to the conclusion that they somehow tapped into this force. For example the Chinese have long practiced feng shui; the art of arranging towns, buildings, and even furniture to somehow interplay with what they call "dragon paths". Though it is generally conceded that the pyramids line up with cardinal points and stars, this may be a fluke. When examination of other aspects of this work are taken into consideration we find the orientation of the land itself as well as where the sun rose, changed several times during recorded history. It's possible the pyramids were originally lined up with each other more exactly and with the true original magnetic poles, and nothing to do with the current poles or the stars.

I suppose the pyramids themselves may actually be tied to some physiological aspect of the earth in a way that keeps them lined up with that particular aspect, regardless of the fluctuations of the earth's crust, similar to how a boat's stabilizing flywheel will stay aligned with the vertical regardless of what happens to the water the boat is in.

Also many stone circles around the earth seem somehow linked with earth forces. Though I have not taken the time to study the stone circles, such as Stonehenge and the medicine wheel, or ley lines, dolmens and menhirs, my guess is the purpose of these things may be twofold. One to identify areas of the earth where natural earth forces peak, and two, they may indicate some sort of earth grid similar to such seen on ancient portalano maps that use the 12 wind grid system. They tend to further suggest an even more extensive knowledge of earth forces.

PUTTING IT TOGETHER

Basically what we are saying here is that the continents before and right after the flood did not yet exist but just the single large continent existed at that time. Shortly after the flood due to man using the pyramids again they, inadvertently caused the earth to break apart and "divide the earth". So not only will I show the continents came into existence during recorded history, but I will also show that man caused it to happen.

Now consider the similarities. 1) legends exist of gravity being overcome and huge stones flying through the air.2) Holes have been found perfectly drilled in huge stones in Egypt and Central America, Baalbek and other places, suggesting closer ties and similar building techniques, likely involving antigravity. The central American stones were found by the Conquistadors to have the holes with silver rods still in the holes, which seemed to serve no purpose. (though when they were removed the buildings fell apart in a subsequent earthquake.) I've seen one of these holes as a result of a drill in a cornice brought to town in an Egyptian display.(Field work!) The hole was absolutely straight and perfectly smooth. It was most definitely drilled by some advanced machine beyond what we have today, the interior of the hole was absolutely smooth, like a polished surface. Typically in the display the hole was completely ignored in the write-up. I guess the motto is ignore what we don't understand and maybe it will go away. 3) Large crystals are known to have as yet still unsolved and unusual properties. They can tune radios and who knows what else. 4) Antigravity always seems to be linked to silver and energy fields of either of man's physiology or the earth's.

Conclusion? I think these pyramids were part and parcel of a single worldwide earth powers harnessing power grid which utilized earth's magnetic field and likely other aspects of the earth physiology. If my deduction is correct, then the pyramids, capped by large crystals, were part of a worldwide earth power harnessing antigravity system.

At the time of their building, the earth's magnetic field was at least 16 times as strong as the field is today. I presume most of them were built before the flood and the impact of the meteor that caused the flood. So the earth's magnetic field may have been as much as 20 times as strong or more when the pyramids were built.

Samples of rocks have been found with such strong magnetism(...as much as 100 times as strong as other natural formations) that people are at a loss to explain how the magnetic properties could have been so strong in natural rock. Whether this is connected I don't know.

Once the meteor that caused the flood hit the earth it would have immediately reduced the earth's magnetic fields strength and starting the decay of the same field that still continues today. Other aspects of the earth have also changed which may have aided in the original function and purpose of the pyramids. If, or rather when some near future catastrophe such as a meteor prophesied in the bible occurs, causing a drastically reduced magnetic field this could mean disasters on earth that could fit the other prophesies mentioned in Revelations, and a new sky. Actually Astrophysasistsasistphyisistsists...uh... star gazer people, say the same thing, that it's not a matter of *if* a meteor hits, but *when*. Right now most such asteroids seem to end up at the Polar Regions because somehow the earth's field seems to steer them there. But with the earth's protective belts becoming weaker and weaker, they may divert asteroids less and less.

I will admit, it's possible that if Mars and Venus did do what legends suggest this might be a plausible cause for the creation and movement of the continents. Though legends seem to indicate man was the cause, the planets may still have had a large part to play.

THE EARTHS POLES CHANGED...HOW AND WHY?

So what caused the earth's magnetic poles to flip? Two possibilities. 1)Possibly planets coming near enough to interact with the earth's poles. If this is the case then magnetic pole flips will be distinguishable on Mars but not on say Mercury. Admittedly I don't know enough about such events to know if this would actually do this to Mars' poles but it seems to me a possibility especially in the light of the fact that Mars actually did come close to the earth in the past. 2) The pyramids.

My guess is after the flood as more and more construction went on with more and more people tapping into the pyramid power grid, the system or rather the earth underneath the system became overtaxed. As populations increased the pyramid power grid work became over extended in relation to the now damaged earth's crust ability to withstand the forces used. Likely the stress of their use may have created imbalances in the magnetic field of the earth, kind of like a cloud collecting negative ions then discharging them all at once to create lightning. Magnetic fields coil around changing electric field and vise verse, and lightning strikes will reverse the polarity of a magnetic field.

By overusing of the pyramids, perhaps this coiled the atmosphere brought intense cold to the surface where the field was weakest, or vortexes occurred creating "windows in heaven". Then suddenly the poles shifted or flipped, and consequently the land moved, broke or "divided", and the water over ran the land and the vortexes caused large areas to suddenly freeze.

I repeat a paragraph here. One source says the Chaldean priests of On could conjure up storms to lift stones that a 1000 men could not lift. (Book 21 pg. 100.) Now this is actually quite revealing. The storm itself likely did not lift the stones but it is a result or byproduct of the power used to do so, similar to storms seen around Tesla laboratories. It is likely some byproduct of the technology used to overcome gravity, possibly similar to strange weather around missing boats and airplanes in the Bermuda Triangle and effects seen around UFO's. So it's interesting that the lifting of the stones also incurs severe weather. [weather of an electrical or magnetic nature]

As seen in a previous chapter the stones they were moving were massive, but we have saved the biggest stones for here. It would seem they were clearly trying to find the limits of what the pyramids could lift through this antigravity force.

A quarried mass of chalkstone has been found to be 3 **miles** long, 1000 feet wide and 1-200 feet thick and was moved an undetermined distance. If it weighs the same as other stone as calculated previously, this block of stone could weigh about **125 Million tons**!!!! Another huge one is found on the East coast of England, it is so large a village was built on it.(book 53 pg 11)

Possibly the weight of these two stones alone caused Peleg. They appear to have dropped where they were and there is no further indications of cutting on them. It seems to me that the ancients started not only moving huge cut and trimmed stones, via antigravity, they started moving the quarries! These may have been huge mobile quarries in the midst of transport when the earth just gave away under the strain of the forces and the continents wrenched apart.

With the earth's crust cracked from the flood, and with all the land and pyramids on one side of the earth and nothing going on, on the other side of the planet, where all that water was, except maybe a few plesiosaurs munching on a few trilobites, the earth's magnetic field became lopsided and eventually overstrained, and it had to right itself all in one go.

These earth power harnessing structures, strongly using earth's magnetic field, may have caused a huge earth wide disruption, or 'top heavy' overextension of the earth's magnetic field which caused an event similar to two magnets held tightly together in your hand with the dissimilar poles of a magnet held together then suddenly released. The magnets would suddenly flip over fast to allow the attracting poles of the same magnets to attract each other and clank shut to each other. Since this event was on a worldwide basis this caused the earth's fracture zones to pull apart causing the continents to come into existence.

If this deduction is correct then the entire planet went through a violent 'righting' or flipping of the magnetic field. Not just on the surface but also from underneath the surface. As it happens I found out that the earth's magnetic field had flipped in the past *after* coming up with this theory. In fact studying the Atlantic fault line and the magnetic fields of the rocks in the fault has shown the field has flipped many times in succession, and in RAPID succession...in the formation of the SAME rock as it oozed out in molten form. Naturally with 'accepted' dating methods they deduced much larger time periods for these events then I suggest here, but even in their exaggerated dating method they deduced a remarkably short period of time for each flip as though it was one long event and not a long protracted series of events.

ERRROR IN THE SYSTEM?

(3rd ed. Insert 2016) Since publishing this book I have heard that there are no areas in the world such as in the mid Atlantic ridge where reversed polarity or 'striped' excretions from this or other ridges (where one stripe would be positive and the next negative) exist, only areas of weaker and stronger polarity. That is to say no place where a compass will point south thinking it is pointing north if in fact it is pointing south. So maybe that discovery is moot and the point of whether the poles switched polarity doesn't even matter. The evidence that they switch positions *is* in history and earth formations anyway. Many ancient records say the sun rose where it used to set and the earth flipped four times. But does tumbling the earth necessarily mean the polarities of the poles would change? When you turn a magnet upside down does the polarity flip? No, so I don't think the earth's polarity would flip either. But that's just a Jonny on the spot deduction. I still say the geologic evidence shows huge global shifts and displacements, **and** I might add the 19th century and 18th century geologists thought these massive upheavals were **clear and obvious**…before they realized the deduction from this observation conflicted with unifomitarianist doctrines.

Perhaps the straw that broke the camel's back was these huge mobile quarries being moved around the earth simultaneously. Suddenly a huge electrical discharge occurred to flip the earth's magnetic field causing the earth's crust to "divide" and a time of storms and hurricanes (wind sun?) and even the chill of space descending to earth. I suggest that these flips occurred continuously until the actions stopped. Thus with this event all building of Herculean structures ended all around the earth at the same time.

Though possibly in some cases later flips happened after subsequent Peleg actions occurred, likely from Mars coming close to earth again during the exodus. Later incidences would have been more pronounced, not only dividing the continents further but hurtling or flinging the continents vastly outdistancing the original Peleg's consequences and freezing the woolly mammoths, and changing the climates of some regions in a heartbeat.

ANCIENT HISTORIES SUPPORT THIS THEORY

History may even have recorded the name of a person or persons directly connected with the breaking up of the continents. The "Club of Janus" and "the hammer of Vulcan" are said to have been the cause for breaking the earth in pieces. (book 41 pg 28) So here we see actual names of people or 'gods' associated with a break-up of the earth. This can only be the same event as that of Peleg, that is the creation of the continents.

Janus is also identified as Bel (Nimrod), or Chaos (possibly Cush: but obviously he can't be both because they are father and son). Janus is also identified as Vulcan with his hammer in this source. The act of "breaking the earth in pieces" is also attributed to the god of confusions (Chaos), but this seems more in line with the mixing up of the languages rather than the physical breakup of the earth. Hislop assumes this 'breaking of the earth in pieces' means confusion of languages as at the tower of Babel, but it likely is referring to the physical break-up of the earth.

I'm not sure if Hislop assumes Nimrod is Bel because of his deduction that what is meant by the breaking of the earth in pieces is the language thing, or if for other reasons. We do know that Nimrod apparently built some great cities, but these cities in particular do not seem to have the stonework on the proportions we need to prove Nimrod IS Bel or Janus so some misidentification may exist at this point. Though it would seem the Club of Janus or the Hammer of Vulcan speak of actually physically breaking of the earth, this has always been assumed to be allegorical. Many other people also constantly assume allegorical meanings to what appear to be literal events. But it seems that here all along we have had ancient histories that actually talk about the physical breakup of the earth into continents!

One could surmise then that after the break-up of the continents Cush and Nimrod went about trying to undo what they or Janus and or Vulcan did in "dividing the earth" and thus tried to tie the earth together with their tower of Babylon. This reasoning would then place the tower of Babel incident after Peleg. Were the tower incident a pre-Peleg occurrence, Nimrod would have had to reach his heights and done all this very fast, as he is the grandson of Ham. But I don't think they are responsible for the earth break up as they seem to have been more involved with the language breakup. The similarity of the legends of 'confusion of language' to 'breaking the earth in pieces' has thus been assumed to be flowery language to describe the same event, whereas it would seem these are two separate events.

Possibly connected to Peleg and the first ice age is a note about Set. It's said Set had power over his enemies on the day there were storms and rain upon the earth.(book 61 pg 205) And one deduces that massive rain storms accompanied the mountain creation which is in turn evidence of the land moving... and likely occurred simultaneously with the pyramids causing magnetic flips thus causing massive storms earth wide. Set may be Shem the son of Noah, as Seth and Shem are apparently synonymous, (book 41 pg. 65) and Set and Seth are also apparently the same person. Though one can't rule out the possibility of two people with the same or similar name, as the Egyptians also have a Seth (assuming this is not the same Seth). If however this is correct this may also help date all these events. And indeed as we deduced some of the consequences of this dividing of the earth were massive storms on the entire earth.

WEAPONS CAUSE?

Again alluding to another possible manmade cause of the divisions of the continents, the Drona Parva speaks of a weapon or "mace" of "Valadeva" that fell on the earth splitting it and making the mountains tremble. Hopi Legends also seem to corroborate this. Hopi legends seem to suggest it as the reason for the damage caused to the earth and the ensuing flood, though as said there were a few worldwide tsunami type floods and this may only have caused or be confused with one of them.

Though this may not have been the cause of the continental drift it sounds like it was an exceedingly strong weapon that may have at least cracked the earth causing a fault or split a fault already in existence. (Book 34 pg 46) But with the faults already in existence at the flood this weapon may have further cracked the earth, though it seems doubtful a weapon could divide the continents unless it actually interfered or wrestled with the very physically damaged areas of the earth itself especially if placed on in or around a fault line. But what kind of weapon could that be? It would likely have to be something that interferes with the earth magnetic poles, but then such a weapon seems too huge in scope to use on a single enemy. Perhaps if that lithium bomb referred to before were used right on top of a fault line this could have had far more serious repercussions.

Could a weapon also be partly responsible as the cause for the breakup of the continents? This would seem to indicate our nuclear weapons are more dangerous to us than we previously thought. Well I guess we have to consider it as a possibility, so it may have played a part, but it may have been part of the reason the continents drifted further, in a specific place on earth. We know explosions push outward so I suppose a strong enough explosion placed in a fault line could conceivably push the two fault lines apart. Sounds like something Lex Luthor would do in the Superman movie! I often wondered as I worked out these theories based on ancient histories if these movies didn't steal these ideas from ancient histories to make movies out of. I know Indian movies often use their ancient histories as plots for their movies. I mean in Star Wars a planet is seen to blow up and the context of the story is 'long ago in a galaxy far away', and no doubt other stories are similar. So it may be a different theory then I present here or it may be a factor in the same old theory I'm unaware of that so many books and movies are based on. It would be interesting now to find out where some of these authors got their ideas from.

THE CONSEQUENCES

Man using the pyramid energy grid over taxed the earth's magnetic field and whatever else is linked to this power grid and suddenly the earth gave way and the continents ripped away at many of the fault lines, virtually turning the earth forces inside out. As the continents ripped apart then drifted, the land was sub-ducted on one edge and was regurgitated at the other side of the newly formed continents. The regurgitating was in the form of the Atlantic ridge and volcanoes being formed hundreds at a time were all erupting at once under the new Atlantic ocean water as the Atlantic ocean became larger, pushing the Americas one way and Africa and Europe the other way. This caused steam and debris to enter the atmosphere in quantities like you just cannot imagine. Land moved in several directions at an incredible rate...in fact so fast it forced ocean water over the land. Then as the water went back more waves would have occurred. Tsunami after tsunami on worldwide proportions, but with the land displacing the water adding force and height to the water as it rushed away from the leading edges toward the other coast.

Western America would have forced water over the Far East coast and vice verse. Whales were deposited in Michigan and Alabama in huge numbers and the bones were in such good condition and in such quantities that farmers used the bones to build fences. Ships were thrust far inland on incredible tidal waves then crushed or entombed in raising lands which surrounded them. A ship was found inside a mountain in Naples in the 16th century and one was come across inside a mine in Peru. This is your second flood.

It's well documented that water overran Mexico...all of it... on at least two and maybe three occasions via cataclysmic tidal waves. The rocks in the area have been examined and shown to be of Pacific Ocean origins! (book 16 pg 247)

Hopi legends speak of mountains falling into the sea, lakes sloshing over the land and freezing solid, apparently from the cold of space. Only those that went or were already underground survived.

NO HOPINESSLESS

(3rd ed. Insert 2016) Finally able to obtain and read the book of the Hopi, I'm able to read and pass the tidbits here. I quote a couple paragraphs here.

"So again, as on the first world, Sotuknang called on the Ant People to open up their underground world for the chosen people. When they were safely underground, Sotuknang commanded the twins, Poqanghoya and Palongawhoya, to leave their posts at the north and south ends of the world's axis, where they were stationed to keep the earth properly rotating.

"The twins had hardly abandoned their stations when the world, with no one to control it, teetered off balance, spun around crazily, then rolled over twice. Mountains plunged into seas with a great splash, seas and lakes sloshed over the land; and as the world spun through cold and lifeless space it froze into solid ice. This was the end of Tokpa, the second world. "(book of the Hopi by Frank Waters. page 20)

"So he loosed the waters upon the earth. Waves higher than the mountains rolled upon the land. Continents broke asunder and sank beneath the seas. And still the rains fell, the waters rolled in. (ibid page 23)

And it seems these legends say that all at once the North American continent was depopulated. It seems that this may only have been an assumption on their part as presumably some animals and men would have survived this event. But the evidence clearly shows massive ocean waves may have come over the entire continent...maybe not all simultaneously or in the same cataclysm but the entire continent at one time or other was under fast moving water, and not just the waters of the flood but from some subsequent hydraulic action not compatible with what would have occurred during the great flood of Noah's time.

WHAT'S MISSING? OR MORE RIGHTLY... WHY IS IT MISSING?

(3rd ed. Insert 2016) Often strange ancient artifacts are found across North America, like ancient armor or buried soldiers in armor, buried walls, ancient coins, Ancient ledgers, ancient writing, toys, abandoned coal and copper mines, ancient tunnels and on and on. Archaeologists just dismiss them as hoaxes, or brought from somewhere else, or natural formations, because they say no ancient civilization existed on North America. They say this because no ancient buildings or town ruins are found here or no written history about North American ancient cities seems to exist. Sounds logical... but artifacts that defy this reasoning are constantly found here. The ancients apparently knew about this vast continents; people like Plato spoke of it. Ancient pyramids exists in central America, and ancient cities in the heart of South America. If they knew about it, could the ancients have deliberately avoided living in North America, when it is obviously such a rich and desirable land? Clearly something is wrong with this deduction. All the missing structures co-existing with little evidences of ancient goings on here is evidence of large civilizations and thus adds weight to a continent being overrun with water as the geologic evidence shows. This is why there are no ancient cities on North America; the water from the Pacific just destroyed it all. This is why it's missing.

Consider for example the Burrows Cave (somewhere in Southern Illinois). Hundreds of artifacts have been found and sold from a cave Russel Burrows discovered but he never told anyone its location. Many called the items hoaxes, yet the artistry of many of the items was above his ability to create. Many more items in locations near where Burrows cave is thought to be, have turned up over the past couple centuries in curious dips in the landscape by farmers over the years, but everyone who insists America could not have had ancient civilizations call all the items fakes, because it just doesn't fit into their neat little theories of ancient man.

Another bit of evidence that shows North America had to have had some major civilization here at one time is the obvious evidence of so much copper mining that went on here. Hundreds of copper mines emptied of copper and literally thousands of train loads worth extracted, much in the great lake areas, has been pulled from the ground, yet virtually nothing of that has been found in the way of artifacts here. Whether it all got buried in waves overrunning the continent, or it got traded to, or taken by the Phoenicians, is immaterial, it was here and now it's gone. Why?

What appears to be the case is that the pyramids with their crystals in place destroyed the continent Pangaea and turned it into several continents, and as the continents formed the water overran the land destroying millions of animals and people that got in the way of the waves and the debris they carried. Furthermore the land crumpled in this motion suddenly pushing land upward forming the new mountains seen around the earth. The land moved so fast it chased animals and they got caught and crushed in massive numbers all around the earth.

WHERE'D THEY GO?

(3rd ed. Insert 2016) Clues are piling up. It's acknowledged that elephants, lions, short faced bears, camels were once very numerous on North America, but no explanation for their sudden disappearance around the end of the last ice age has been convincingly hypothesized. That's because no one suspects that water could overflow the continents to such an extent as to wipe all these species out simultaneously. Why? Because no one is venturing into catastrophic theories much these days. Because the only conclusion you can draw from this theory, is that the continents moved so fast and suddenly as to cause the water to overflow the land, creating the Rocky Mountains and leaving the evidence we see; not 200 million years ago, but at the very most 11,000 years ago when the last ice age was supposed to be on our planet. And as we've seen that "ice-age" wasn't as far back as that, but may be just 4000 years ago…thus greatly compressing the time frames we are talking about. (see Atlantis Rising Mag #101 "Facing the extinction Threat") Ironically one of my ads, talking about the continents moving in recorded history, is directly across from the page this article is on.

PYRAMID STUFF: MAYBE I'M RIGHT?!

(3rd ed. Insert 2016) Looking through my material again I got to book 42 (*The War of Gods and Men* by Zachariah Sitchin) and suddenly the book starts to be more interesting the second time around. But his theory for the purpose of the pyramids being built was so that space people could figure out where to land seems silly. I mean build a couple fake mountains!? If spacemen are going to be able to get here they aren't going to need fake mountains to figure out where they are, and if they needed land marks why so big?... couldn't they use something like what's on the Nasca plains?...much less labour intensive. And if they landed safely the first time so they could build them, why would the need to build them to land safely again? (Sitchin also concluded that the step ziggurats, such as those in Mesopotamia, were built for the purpose of allowing airborne craft to land on them. {Book 42 page 266})

OK maybe I don't get his theory completely because he then starts explaining more stuff and I then start to doubt my theory. But then he refers to and shows what appear to be sketches of Cylinder seal impressions (I've not been able to find this particular cylinder seal, if that's where the image came from. I've drawn it as though it were a rolled with a partial repeating image). He points out that these images seem to show the pyramids being built? (They look complete to me). I passed over them the first time I looked at them long ago because the scale was so poor, I thought maybe they were just smaller pyramids of later origin. The pyramids are drawn small in scale compared to other stuff in the images, but hey if it's a cylinder seal, what do you expect… Davinci? So I look more closely this time and though they are two dimensional and poorly drawn, they seem to show pyramids as they were originally built and they appear to show or indicate their purpose! (Zitchin seems to think they show them being built, but they in fact appear to show they are for building!

One shows them with a spherical object on the top with stairs going up two of the sides. I've tried to draw it a little more 3 D though, with three sides visible (which of course is impossible from ground level... but this is what the image did too) **(See Drawing 6)**

My cover illustration guessed a spherical crystal on top, so that might be right, as a second drawing of the pyramids also shows a sphere on top, but I've not bothered to draw this one. The drawing seems like it's half path or maze and half pyramid (admittedly this one could be an indication of them being built, floor plan or paths inside the structures?...but it's a real simple drawing so it's difficult to glean or interpret too much from it). The more I look and think about the other pyramid drawings; realization dawns that I just might be right. One pyramid Sitchin says has wings (this one seems to just have a round apex rather than a sphere on top, but that might be poor cylinder seal art?) but his reason for the drawing of the wings on the pyramid is based on his theory of them being for flight and landing of flying vehicle land marks. (actually one of the 'wings' looked more like light shining from a beacon, but it could be a wing or maybe both? If a light, it recalls what I stated earlier that Colonel Fawcett was told by the Indians that a city in the Matto Grosso had a fat tower of stones which was capped with light that never goes out. But if the picture depicts wings, you might recall, I said something in the main text that made me think Pyramids flew, which of course I automatically ruled out (and still do) as silly and preposterous. (Said in chapter 9 actually) But these images if they don't mean the pyramids fly then maybe it means they make something fly....which we've already deduced was large stones. I had said they created a worldwide force that allows antigravity to lift huge stones.

Well that one seems to be plausible but not heavy on weighty evidence. **(See Drawing 7)** But as is my wont, I saved the best for last.

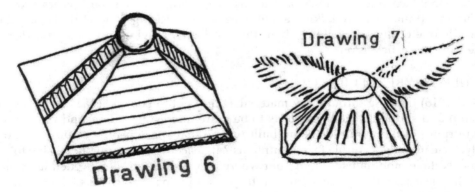

Drawing 7

Drawing 6

One drawing shows some people pointing at a pyramid, lifting their hands to one or pointing to or touching piled stones. WITH entwined snakes above the entire scene. This slowly sinks in. I think this one is BIG! If you recall in chapter 3...I quote myself "The Temple of Hathor in Egypt shows giants holding what appear to be huge glass bulbs similar to electrical tubes or clear light bulbs with snakes inside. The bulbs are connected to cables with what appear to be some sort of electrical transformers holding up the bulbs which might be "tet"'s, an Egyptian term used in relation to bringing Osiris back to life. The snakes in the bulbs could be indicative of a snakelike filament and how electrical power "bites" like a deadly snake might." (See chapter 3 drawing 2) My first mentioning of this was to just indicate the ancients had artificial lighting. But if my interpretation of the snake filaments as a power force in the bulb is correct, and then if the snakes in the cylinder seal mean a power force in the air and the snakes with their heads and tails starting and ending at the pyramid, mean that power and force has to have something to do with the pyramids, then the guys around the pyramid pointing to the pyramid and the stacked stones seems to mean the power or force of the pyramids is for the building of stones one upon another…antigravity. I mean I don't know if it can get any clearer? (Unless I can learn English) **(See Drawing 8)**

Drawing 8

I stumbled on another reference to Pyramids and Snakes found in the Carlos Crespi collection in Atlantis Rising # 86 referring to the Gold of the Gods by Erich Von Daniken so I started a little internet search. I found a couple plates showing Pyramids with snakes (and Cats?) hovering above them in among these South American artifacts. This particular pyramid drawing showed a sun like object on top of a pointed pyramid, which is likely a glowing circular cap sphere which is on top of the pointed finish, likely indicating what the pyramids initially looked like.

(See Drawing 9 maybe I'm putting too much into this drawing, but those nine dots with the cats: could cloning if done optimally only be good nine times on the same creature? The first sheep ever cloned only lived half as long as a normal sheep. And other successful clones are never as good as the parent)

DRAWING 9

If the picture showing snakes above the pyramids in Sitchen's work are genuine, it adds credibility to the Crespi collection which was called fake by the archeological society after Danikens work hit the stands. But then anything or anyone that doesn't conform to mainstream dogma must be a fake. Interestingly there was a huge crown in the Crespi collection that only a giant could have worn. The Crespi Mayan(?) artifacts and pictograms of South America are very similar in many ways to Egyptian, Persian and Babylonian ones. Actually eventually the Crespi collection did attract the attention of archeological world and suddenly their eyes seemed to have been set agog. What took them so long? Sadly it wasn't until after an arsonist had set fire to the original collection which destroyed many artifacts before this collection got any attention by the formerly cold society of mainstream ancient researchers. Sadly the local authorities appear to have sold, destroyed or melted down all the artifacts. (Atlantis rising #118 indicates the collection may still exist and purchased by the Central Bank of Ecuador)

One thing that caught my attention, was when Win Lambertson stated that he could feel radiant energy being emitted from the tip of quartz crystals. (Atlantis Rising #83 page 58) Considering the shape of Pyramids, and putting a circular crystal on top what is basically a crystal shape, strongly points to the likelihood they were using this 'radiant' energy at the tip of the pyramids as seen in the Crespi artifact. (My guess is that when these crystal pyramid caps were destroyed, the pieces were then carved into crystal skulls, indicating how deadly crystals can be.)

PYRAMID POWER PLANT?

(3rd ed. Insert 2016) I've been advertising my book in Atlantis Rising since #69, but with so much on my plate, after a while I just let the magazines pile up without reading them. Having finished all my research for a third edition, I decided to start reading the magazines to see if there was anything else that could enhance the book material, and started reading backwards starting with #115. I read an article in Atlantis Rising #90, by Christopher Dunn entitled "The Pyramid Electric".

From what I gather, Dunn's idea seems to be that the pyramids are something like a big battery or energizer that was disconnected sometime in the past. If restored it would be like a giant generator of some kind...but for what? He feels there were some wiring connectors that have been pulled out but evidences of electrical devices or connections and even corrosion are still to be found deep in the pyramid(s?) of Egypt. This idea never occurred to me. (I found in A.R. #85 a brief synopsis of his pyramid theory by William Stoecker: "He advanced the hypothesis that the precisely shaped structure was designed to resonate with our planet, absorbing and collecting the vibrational energies caused by earthquakes, tides etc., and then, via the piezoelectric effect of quartz crystals in the granite, convert that energy into electricity.") He sounds like he is on a similar track but completely reversed, like the effect is the cause and the cause is the effect. My deductions were that the shape itself, with the crystals in place and the knowledge of certain laws of physic to do with sound, harmonics, and magnetic fields would make the pyramids and the users capable of levitating large stone all around the earth as the pyramid belt was put into use. But it does make sense that the pyramids themselves would have to have the power 'turned on', or at least 'plugged in' to make them work, magnifying their latent power but then on the other hand just the finished structure itself might have meant they were 'on' all the time.

WE'RE CATCHING UP...

(3rd ed. Insert 2016) As noted some ancient legends speak of sound being used to levitate stuff. Science refuses to believe this was possible, but now they are using sound to levitate water in a drug so it can evaporate without forming crystals. Further looking on the internet shows that water is being levitated in little drops between a couple things. How soon before they start levitating little pebbles...and then bigger pebbles...(See Atlantis Rising #98)

Though I feel the pyramids started the continents drifting, inertia and centrifugal force kept them in motion at a slower rate but far faster than the rate of today, so when Mars came for a visit or when meteors hit, the drift motion was speeded up again for short bursts.

If this theory seems preposterous it's time to look at the physical evidence and see if it can explain what is seen around the earth.

THE PHYSICAL GEOLOGICAL EVIDENCE: THE WAVES

We've already talked about the massive amounts of earth moved around that buried things to 18 feet and often far deeper than this. In fact there seems to be some places on earth where not just 18 feet of dirt have been moved but literally hundreds of feet of earth have been displace and moved to some areas. For example, John Green spent 5 **years** digging a well in Texas county Oklahoma. He dug straight down and didn't hit damp rock for 233 Feet! But more importantly he didn't have to shore up the sides of the well at any time because the entire 233 feet was of pure top soil right down to the bedrock. (Readers digest Aug 1959 "Victory in the Dust Bowl")

I have to think this dirt was moved to this area from somewhere. I think the most important evidence to show and understand exactly what was going on in this period is the extent of the tidal waves and just how incredible these things were. One has to understand that the continents were actually moving great distance in short periods of time. This obviously is more than just some earthquake causing tidal waves such as we have seen in the 20th and 21st century. The waves were just beyond belief and imagination! This is why so much of the earth has vast layers of sandstone and fossils because the ocean actually overran the continents and few people survived. These layers of sandstone could not have been done in the Noah flood, they had to be done in a completely different hydraulic action...and after the Noah flood. This is why there is confusion in flood legends. Stories about these waves seem similar to the biblical flood, but they are of a different nature and cause. But there is other evidence of these massive waves that explains the inexplicable, and also give you a sense of just how incredible these waves were!

All around the planet there are things known as "erratics". These are rocks or boulders completely out of place in the surroundings in which they are found. These rocks can be examined and their places of origin can be positively identified. Boulders found on the highlands of the British Isles have been determined to have come from Norway! Erratics in Germany came from Scandinavia and the Harz Mountains in Germany have erratics that came from Norway. Finland erratic stones have been found to have overran Latvia and Poland and ended up in the Carpathian Mountains! Rocks originating in Labrador are found all the way from Maine to Ohio to Wisconsin. Some of these boulders are so huge as to defy imagination.

For example there is a block near Conway New Hampshire that is 10,000 tons and one in Warren County Ohio that's 13,500 tons. Can these really be moved by water? YES!, that is just how monstrous and violent these waves were! Unless they were moved by man... and the difference is easily distinguished, though the two may overlap and man quarried stones may have been moved by the waves as well, further confusing the picture. They were either moved by hydraulic action or were move by man's devices, or both... and either explanation is extraordinary.

Could the waves be this incredible to move these blocks this far or were these moved by man? One other possibility for motion of erratics is possible. The Ototoks erratic (quarried & partially cut?) near Calgary Canada came from 50 miles west and may have tumbled as the land moved underneath it! The land may have moved this fast! Likely the water and the moving land worked together to move some of the erratics. There are such erratics all over the world but these few examples give you an indication of what forces were in play at some time in the recorded past. This was no continental "drift", this was a continental race!

I even found another example of water overrunning the land. In II Kings 3, when the king of Moab reneged on paying the King of Israel 100,000 rams and 100,000 lambs, the kings of Israel, Judah and Edom went after the King of Moab. On the way they realized after seven days there was no water for them or their cattle. They come across Elisha and he says dig the valley that they are in full of ditches. Then he says "ye will see no wind, or rain yet this valley shall be filled with water." The next day water came from the direction of Edom and the valley and all the ditches were filled with water. (II Kings 3:20) This water had to come from somewhere, and it came over land. This sounds like the earth was hit and a lake overflowed its banks because of the jolt, and the water ran over the land toward the three armies, very similar to other legends that speak of lakes jumping out over their banks. After finishing the book and then deciding to finally get this third edition done I looked at my references again, specifically for references to the waters overrunning the land and here's some of what I found.

THE WATER FACTOR: ANCIENT WAVES SPOKEN OF AND RECORDED WERE STAGGERING

(3rd ed. Insert 2016) Velikovsky referring to the manuscript Troano the Mayans which describe a catastrophe where the ocean fell on the continent (Book 14 pg 82)

THAT'S A BI...BI...BIIGGG TURTLE!

(3rd ed. Insert 2016) Another legend exists, apparently derived from some native petroglyphs. The Great Spirit angered at the arrogance at some of mankind, pushed the lodge under the sunrise sea. Later animals and virtuous souls survived a flood by climbing on a turtles back which came from the ocean bottom. When all were safely on the turtles back it began swimming westward with the Great Spirit wading behind it through the water until they reached an unfamiliar shore to make a new home for themselves. Thus they named the place Turtle Island which is a tribal Indian name for North America. (Atlantis Rising #73 Pg 70) This could be interpreted to be a mega Tsunami overcoming the eastern coast (Volcanically caused), submerging Atlantis, land rising under the people and pushed westward, then the forces that did this pushed it, moving the island into the continent of North America moving westward during recorded history. Unfortunately I can't get an origin out of this reference to be able to go to the source and look at the legend closer.

Quoting the June 1880 edition of the Theosophist (Book 31 pg 109) a Yogi Brahmachari Baws writes '"Extensive works on astra-Vidya and other such sciences were at different times compiled in the language of the times from Sanscrit originals, [but] were lost at the time of the partial deluge of our country.' The discovery of these flooded lands – the carefully-planned cities of Harappa and Mojenjo Daru, in what is now Pakistan, overwhelmed by water around the time of Atland's [Atlantis'] destruction – would appear to bear out the Vishnu Purana Prophecy that 'the lords of the storm are approaching' and the land 'is doomed'. Needless to say this is recorded as happening to cities would mean of course, during history.

Zachariah Sitchen notes that after a series of world catastrophes the god Enki warned a man who then flees the earth to get away from the flood (presumably the great flood) but he also notes this god tells men to prepare for a flood with a boat and describes getting out of the way of a flood (describing something more like a tsunami). This boat was also headed to the Ararat Mountains. He apparently confuses both the great flood and a tsunami type of flood in the same legend, as they happened in the same region. This would appear to be the same flood that Abraham came from the other side of. This catastrophe indicates it had to be a post Noah flood so it makes the point that more than one flood type is described and that huge continental tsunamis were wreaking havoc on the planet at times. (book 17 page 389-403)

The early 19th century scholars got it right when they assumed so many of the erratic boulders found here and there were the result of huge waves sweeping over the continent. (book 14 page 89). Yet now geologists wonder, refusing to consider this hypothesis, because it means catastrophism. Can't have *that*!

Recent geological deductions show a toppling of the earth isn't farfetched in the least. Earth quakes affect the pole spin, and significant ones wobble the earth. German Meteorologist Alfred Wegener believed that changes in the earth's axis took place quickly, fast enough to cause flooding from oceans inundating equatorial lands.

Geologist Hugh Miller noted half of Scotland was inundated, in some places 15 stories deep of rolled pebbles, and fossils. The action that created the deposits was instant and sudden as seen by fish in contorted poses from the struggle. Signs of skin colour and soft parts are still seen, and being buried alive they fossilized before soft parts decayed. He wondered "...what could suddenly destroy... ten thousand square miles [half of Scotland] at once with instantaneous suddenness". (Book 53 page 18) Other Geologists have found the identical evidences in northern Italy, Harz Mountains Germany, Ohio, Michigan, Switzerland, and other places. (book 53 page 17-20)

3rd ed. Insert 2016) With trees uprooted by hurricane or flood…animals could have been dismembered by a 'stupendous wave' that lifted, smashed and tore millions of bodies with the trees. (Book 53 page 2) Most of the catastrophes were sudden…the last one had a twofold motion, inundation and afterwards laid dry the continents. (Book 53 page 12) France was sea, then land, then sea, land, sea and finally land again. (page 13) And with no mountains in areas of southern Sweden, Finland, or North-eastern Russia to powerfully abrade score and polish the flat terrain, it was concluded by Murchison (geologist) that what is seen must have been the result of the sea erupting onto land and leaving debris. (book 53 page 35) Similarly much of the low country of Russia, Poland and Germany covered by masses of stone, sand, clay and gravel was spread through aqueous action, that is powerful waves. (Ibid)

(3rd ed. Insert 2016) Quoting the codex chimalpopoca Drake writes "The sky drew near to the earth, and in the space of a day, all was drowned. The mountains themselves were covered by water. It is said that the rocks we can see today rolled about over all the land dragged by waves of boiling lava and that there suddenly arose mountains the colour of fire" (book 23 pg 157)

Drake notes Plato referred to ship anchors being found on mountain-tops, showing they were sailing on what is now dry land, which probably had risen quickly underneath the boats the anchors were attached to, that, or the boats were possibly tossed onto the mountains. (book 23 pg 209)

Legends in Peru, Egypt, Mayan, The Oklahoma Choctaw Indians, and the Epic of Gilgamesh are all said to speak of prolonged darkness in the span of what should be a day, and massive mountain high waves overrunning land.

(3rd ed. Insert 2016) Cuvier (1769-1832) the founder of vertebrate paleontology stated "Repeated irruptions and retreats of the sea have neither all been slow nor gradual; on the contrary, most of the catastrophes which have occasioned them have been sudden; and this is especially easy to be proved with regard to the last of these catastrophes, that which, by a twofold motion, has inundated, and afterwards laid dry, our present continents, or at least a part of the land which forms them at the present day. In the northern regions it has left the carcasses of large quadrupeds which became enveloped in the ice, and have thus been preserved even to our own times, with their skin, their hair, and their flesh. If they had not been frozen as soon as killed, they would have been decomposed by putrefaction. And on the other hand, this eternal frost could not previously have occupied the places in which they have been seized by it, for they could not have lived in such a temperature. It was, therefore, at one and the same moment that these animals were destroyed and the country which they inhabited became covered with ice. This event has been sudden, instantaneous, without any gradation, and what is so clearly demonstrated with respect to this last catastrophe, is not less so with reference to those which have preceded it." (Book 14 page 41-42 quoting Cuvier "Essay on the theory of the Earth" Pg 14-15)

(3rd ed. Insert 2016) Though I think perhaps some of the land was moving so fast animals couldn't get out of the way and were crushed, and here's something that confirms this deduction. H. Godwin deduced that somewhere between the first and second millennium B.C. the sea irrupted twice causing the fossils in England. However earlier, Geologist Joseph Prestwich deduced this irruption of the sea was far more widespread covering from central France, and the French Riviera to Gibraltar, Corsica and Sicily. (book 53 page 184) Whenever fossilized animal tracks are found (which means they had to be buried under fossilizing agents soon after they were made) they are of mixed species, predators and prey and the tracks indicate them running and together…not strolling about, but running at breakneck speed as if to escape some terror…no doubt the very agent that fossilized their tracks! (Book 53 page 204)

Geologists have shown with animation the continental drift from a massive continent to the break-up and to the current position of the continents. I'm pretty sure plotting erratics from point of origin to current position will not only confirm the direction the continents moved but also prove they moved fast.

What no doubt will also be very disconcerting is the motion that moved the continents also created the mountains. Disconcerting because "stone age" Human beings have been shown to occupy caves 8000 feet up, something unexplainable in current anthropological theories, because it suggests they rose during the time of man. Odd, it doesn't bother me.

Mountains uplifted many thousands of feet during the "Pleistocene" epoch (Ice age) when man is known to have been here which causes "great perplexity among geologist" who are forced to admit this conclusion. If that's not bad enough … "Not only in the age of man, but in the age of historical man, mountains were thrust up, valleys were torn out, lakes were dragged uphill and emptied." (Book 53 page 68)

WORLDWIDE EVENTS IN HISTORICAL TIMES

(3rd ed. Insert 2016) Here's a little quote from Atlantis rising #98 page 25 "Satellite images of our own world….show …eroded remains of ancient impact craters. In addition mainstream scientists have discovered ancient, evidence of mega volcanoes erupting in truly catastrophic form, as well as evidence for mega tsunamis and for sudden climate change."

Around 2050 BC worldwide erosion values of 20- 30 tons / kilometer jumped to 140. (Atlantis Rising #115 pg 60) This is contemporary with massive ash falls on the earth, documented by dendrochronology which is thought to be from comets? In the period from 2350-2000 BC at least 4 cosmic impacts hit earth. (2345, 2240, 2188 and 2000 BC) (Ibid) Around 3100 BC worldwide volcanic action peaked, particularly in the Atlantic Ocean. (Ibid) Worldwide volcanism has been noted to have occurred around 1600 and 100 BC that literally affected many locations around the globe, including several locations noted in the article (IBID) Some events around 1000, 1185 and 1141 BC flooded German forests, incinerated Bavarians Black forests, and rose the level of Turkey's Lake Van 250 feet in about two years.

Well we've seen that the Hydraulic evidence matches up with the legends. We'll see the rest of the world and legends match up too.

THE EVIDENCE OF RECENT SUDDEN SHIFTS

The very existence of volcanoes, mountains, sheer cliffs hundreds of meters high, and canyons testifies of some huge events in geological history and in recent history at that, because if they occurred at the rate they are said to have formed (over 200-500 million years) erosion would have countered the formations. If geologist's theories about mountains being formed were even close, mountains simply could not exist, because they would have eroded as fast as they were being formed. But they do exist... and not just a few, whole entire ranges exist, testifying to forces and movements simply not active in today's world. If mountain ranges the size of the Rockies and the Himalayans can exist formed by this action, so too can entire continents or at least large islands be swallowed and cease to exist.

Even if there were no historical records and legends about such sunken lands we could still surmise they once existed, but legends abound! Here's some I've found.

WE DON'T KNOW ABOUT THE ONES WE DON'T KNOW ABOUT...

(3rd ed. Insert 2016)
Though history records several cities that have sunk in ancient times some of which are visible from the surface, and they've been explored, such as the ancient Roman seaside resort of Baiae, Sybaris, parts of Carthage, Leptis Magna, Tyre, Caesarea, Alexandria and others, but when it comes to places such as Atlantis suddenly this is not possible? There is also a 400 foot regular shaped pyramid with a flattened top, east of the Florida Keys, 27 miles north of Cuba that rises from the sea floor. It's so regular it appears to be manmade amidst buildings, roads, stone walls, stairways, and shaped monoliths. Nope can't be…we don't know about it. (Not to mention it would confirm catastrophism…can't have that.)(World of the incredible but true Charles Berlitz Page 68)

Recently a remarkable series of pyramid like structures with an archeological site has been found underwater off the west coast of Cuba. **(See Drawing 10)**

DRAWING 10
Off west coast
of Cuba

Yet after all this evidences the evolutionists and geologists are afraid to suggest such speedy motions occurred and overturn their uniformist theories. It may be their very reluctance to put this idea forward that causes the ignorance which starts a similar event in the future. Yet even uniformist evolutionists note and admit that "violations of continuity" (meaning upwardly thrust features, angled broken and erratic features and rocks) in geological formations are more the rule then the exception. In fact many geologists are starting to favor or conclude that these features exist because of sudden upheavals, and not imperceptibly slow actions in the earth.

The uniformist theories, such as the slow continental drift, which are supported by the mainstream actually confirm nothing in what is seen in the earth, and a theory of fast sudden upheavals explains everything. Only the odd remaining flatter areas on the earth might be seen as conforming to the uniformist theories. But naturally some flat land would have to remain. This would be the remnants of the more older pre-flood terrain, though they may have been washed over with these tsunamis adding layers of dirt on them. Some might even have had dirt removed from that area and had more dirt washed onto the same area in subsequent disasters.

Evolutionists and uniformitairians disbelieve and ignore the obvious evidence. In fact some evolutionists actually ask for "faith" to believe the uniformist's theories despite the evidence to the contrary. Don't look at the mountains...they are not there just look at the low rolling hills and all will be well with the theory. Even so they are forced to admit tidal waves (a cataclysmic event) had to have caused some erratics. To a small extent they are forced to support cataclysms...when the evidence corners them.

They even supplement it with a theory which suggests icebergs dropped erratics on the ocean floor then the land emerged but then the land had to have emerged recently...in other words...fast. To further strain the credibility of these explanations one can find erratics at the equator... where it's hot and no icebergs venture. Even when their own explanations contradict their own theories, in order to explain a problem in an uniformist way, they still support the opposite theory. They just cannot get away from the cataclysmic theory altogether so they have now been, to some extent, forced to admit it into their theories. If only Velikovsky could see their faces. (Actually a significant sized errattic would actually sink the iceberg, or stop it from moving)

So in order to perpetuate the theory of a really, really old earth, they now suggest a short brief cataclysm occurs, followed by a long protracted time of uniformity then another short period of cataclysm then another long period of uniformity. So then what's the difference? The time span in the period of uniformity between cataclysms is thus either long or short. If a place has been uniform forever or a day there are ways to tell the difference as to how long that place has been uniform, through erosion. The area between strata's which are supposed to indicate millions of years show no erosion has taken place and it can easily be concluded to have all formed rapidly and at the same time!

MORE EVIDENCE AND CLUES

It's been concluded that at one time the Earth's Axis of rotation was significantly different in ancient times, and possibly as recently as the 8th century BC! (book 53 pg 132-133) Sounds like that earthquake during Uzziah's reign again.

Hippopotamus have been found in Northern Europe and it indicates sudden changes in climate because they just simply couldn't migrate that far.

Clear evidence of successful brain surgery was found in Chile and Egypt using identical instruments. Identical tools found across 2000 miles of ocean... what's up with that?

An Assyrian clay tablet describing a short term loan was found in the Pennsylvania river.

Bimini wall pottery (found underwater 1000 yards off the coast of Bimini) has been dated to 3-5000 BC, showing this wall sunk during recorded history. (Book 8 pg 73-74) This is obvious, as pottery itself is part of a more historical civilization, no matter how old the stuff is dated. Though I suppose someone might have dropped the pots over the side of the boat.

Cotton of ancient America is a crossbreed of a local type and the Mediterranean cotton and no one is really certain how it came about in ancient times. By great shipping routes or some other factor? In fact there are so many similar things in the Americas that are in common with things in the old world that often Atlantis is blamed for the things both have in common. And not just common artifacts and legends, but animals too. Granted no doubt Atlantis certainly did have a hand in some of that which is common to both coasts on each side of the Atlantic, but this Peleg action and second flood is in fact what created the Atlantic and Atlantis as a small continent (or large island) in the first place. When looking at where the land masses were originally, one can see that New England and Great Britain were not too far from each other possibly even in the same area at one time. This explains why there are so many dolmens standing stones and stone circles in both these areas. They were all built in the same area before the splitting of the continents, and not by a pan Atlantic culture exchange. This means the continents split after these things were made by man.

New Zealand and South America have identical fauna as though there was a very close physical relation to these places at one time.

Tiahuanaco, a port city, was pushed upward 2 miles in the westward movement of South America. TWO MILES! The very fact that this port city is 2 miles above sea level means that it was built before the mountains rose. This is so disturbing to archaeologists that some feel they have to date the city 11-12,000 BC, to match up with the presumed age of the ice age, even though everywhere else in the world civilizations are supposed to have started about 5000-5500 years ago. However this time carbon dating works against them because even carbon dating puts the city at only 4000 years old (2000 BC) and almost as if to corroborate this, on the other side of the mountains there is a surf line in Chile at 1300 feet above sea level with undecayed sea shells all through the line, indicating a very recent uplifting. (3rd. ed. insert 2016) Tiahuanaco as I mentioned was pushed up 2 miles and that others had noted that it was a Port city at one point. But what I didn't find out until reading Atlantis Rising #72 was that "Its massive stone docks are ringed with ocean fossils." (page 32)

Charles Darwin was impressed by the clear evidence of recent uplifts of the mountains of Chile 1300 feet up finding undecayed shells on the surface. He also noted the mountains didn't rise gradually, but in jumps, as only a few intermediary surf lines were detected showing the land didn't rise little by little. (Book 53 page 79)

THEY MOVED THE BEACH!?

(3rd ed. Insert 2016) "Either the land must have sunk two or three miles, or the sea once must have been two or three miles lower than now. Either conclusion is starling. If the sea was once two miles lower, where could all the extra water have gone" this was what Dr. Maurice Ewing Professor of Geology stated in November 1949 National Geographic when they discovered beach sand in the mid Atlantic Ridge 1200 miles from any land.

Found in a cave system of Yucatan were some statues very different from Mayan and more reminiscent of ancient Middle East. But even more striking was …"Evidence of water marks within the caves, now several hundred feet above sea level, had been under water after the strange stone figures were carved." Meaning these statues, obviously carved by man, submerged in a cataclysm, then in a subsequent cataclysm resurfaced. (Book 37 page 151-152)

MOUNTAIN BUILDING STILL A RIDDLE TO GEOLOGISTS

Oddly the current state of geology still hasn't actually solved what caused the creation of mountains. It's actually surprisingly simple. The flaw in their mountain building theories is they assume the mountains rose slowly over millions of years through tectonic actions as they are known in today's world. Granted the forcing of two land masses together would push land upward in the middle. But if it took millions of years the mountains would have eroded as they climbed, with the result of a more smooth profile and more humpy nature to the land itself. This simply doesn't account for the mountains we see.

This mystery is easily, though only partially, solved when you speed up the process. The very existence of mountains, not to mention fossils, and the massive amounts of moved earth burying so much stuff and no doubt a host of other physical evidences supports this theory. The mountains didn't form in millions of years, they formed virtually overnight. People actually watched mountains being formed! Incan and Mayan records speak of 25 years of gloom and new mountains rising. Other Mayan legends speak of gods moving mountains, but whether this was a deliberate action or an accidental consequence is not clear. (Or maybe both) If you survived it would have been a fascinating thing to watch.

No doubt someone will accuse me of taking more fictitious movies and turning them into this ridiculous book. I recall a very cool piece of movie footage that showed mountains being made in the distance. I've often wondered what that movie was. All I know is that movie must be at least thirty years old. I suppose to be honest, who can say just how much movies HAVE influenced these theories. And perhaps people with these theories have influenced these movies. Since I've only read maybe 75 books about related subjects who can say what movie writers were reading to add to their stories; just like we ask what was Jonathan Swift reading to put the two moons of Mars in his stories? Perhaps subconsciously these movies have been having an effect on me. After all something I saw on TV as a kid prompted me towards my theories on dinosaurs as seen next chapter.

The entire rocky mountain range would have all formed extremely fast as the continents moved westward. I see two types of formation possible through this action, though there are no doubt more. 1) Crumpling features as land pushes and suddenly halts from a smooth motion or from 'hitting' or overruns an obstruction, such as another land mass coming towards it or being overrun by it. 2) formations which form by thrusting from underneath as land overruns more firm underground formations.

There are actually arguments as to exactly what geologic forces made the mountains. Some suggest lateral movement of the land which caused pressure as two land masses met forcing the land in the middle upward, and some suggest vertical pressure from underneath pushed mountains upward.

When two land masses hit each other one has to climb over the other, and the other has to crawl under the other, that or meet in such destructive ways mountains just thrust skyward. Obviously some sort of substrata obstruction caused parts of the land moving over it, to stop a smooth motion and the extra inertia then pushed upward what the continent wouldn't allow to move outward, thus forming the mountains, somewhere in the middle of continental masses due to crumpling. Also when land overruns land it is pushed upward from underneath and when land hits other land masses the speed is slowed at one end but kept up at the other causing land in the middle to buckle and turn into mountains, or at least hills. This occurs either from the land underneath or from the slowed inertia, similar to carpet when it's being shoved across the floor. If one end is pushed faster than the other end moves away, the carpet will crumple in the middle.

Then as land overran other land, it sub-ducted underneath the moving land which then became an underground obstruction that forced mountains upward, or at least created very rough terrain. All this is pretty much as geologists have described it but it all happened at an exceedingly fast clip. Really all you have to do is take those movies of the continental drift and slow them down a little to find the actual speed the continents moved at. Eventually with computer simulations you should be able to decipher the real speed the continents moved at, by the amount of water that would be displaced and the ensuing damage and erosion. This is assuming you can correctly turn the clock back and unmake the mountains, undo the erosion, and replace the land sub-ducted underneath to full view. No small computing task. Actually ice ages, mountains, ice cap growth and mass widespread extinctions of creatures are all inexplicable in modern geological theories but this faster motion of continental masses clears it all up.

MORE PHYSICAL EVIDENCE

It's really amazing; once you speed up the rate of continental drift it gives a completely different picture and explains so much. One answered mystery just keeps answering others like dominoes. If this is true then such and such is true, and so on.

I used this before but I use it again here. At Blue Lick Springs 12 feet below the surface was found mastodon bones, below that, gravel, and below that a quarried stone pavement. If we consider that the cut stone pavement was built, then later a wave of sea water and debris caught the mastodon this easily accounts for the mastodon being killed and buried above the manmade cut stone...if you're willing to accept the mastodon lived during man's period of advanced civilization. I suppose a wave could have uprooted a dead mastodon's remains and planted it above the stone pavement, but even this tends to suggest maybe these extinct animals were alive during civilized times and before these cataclysms otherwise the dead mastodons bones would have long since turned to dust before they had a chance to get buried above a manmade object. We will see that in fact dinosaurs were contemporary with man, but we will work on the dinosaurs next chapter.

Aztec and Mayans had a calendar that was originally 360 days long and due to their ability to make accurate sightings this length of year is a mystery. Later the year was extended to 365+ after some event. (book 23 pg 158-159) It has been deciphered that the 365 day calendar starts 687 BC, and there is reason to believe this was the time of some final major earth upheaval before the relative calm that presides in the earth's continents of today. The Mayan year was calculated at 365.2420 days long, compared to the current 365.2423 days. This difference is so little that a single asteroid could slow the earth year down by that difference. Comets have been feared and linked to disasters for a long time. As recently as 1681 in Baden Switzerland a proclamation was made to attend mass, abstain from dancing and moderate drinking when a comet was sighted. Disasters have been linked to comets for a long time. Actually geologist wonder at what appears to be a lot of geological activity in historic times. Geologist are forced to come to the conclusion, or at least add in to the equation that in historic times there was much more 'readjustments' going on in the geologic strata. But this was supposed to be happening millions of years ago. They wonder how it could be happening a mere 3000 years ago. However it does explain how there could be climate changes and polar shifts in this time frame, though the question as to how, is still considered a mystery to orthodox geology.

HISTORIES AND RECORDS INDICATE CATASTROPHIC EVENTS DURING CIVILIZATION

Ancient chronologies handed down through time speak of places and events and indicate these things happened in recorded history. This was how Troy was found. Persistent legends coaxed a man to look for it and he found an apparently fictional city of fancy but with actual directions to its whereabouts. To top it off and help him find it, local legends constantly told of its actual location. All someone had to do was believe the legends and directions by the locals and dig, and there it was.

What were thought to be mythical tales of Minos turned out to be true when Knossos was excavated. Gold coins were found under Cochin China's coast bearing the likeness of Oc-Eo, a person who was previously thought to be mythical emperor. In fact most ancient legends handed down through time appear to have at least some basis in fact. As to how the owners of these legends ever obtained such knowledge is a mystery to many unless one assumes a time existed when man knew a lot more then we give them credit for.

Instead of believing these legends, historians, anthropologists, archaeologists, paleontologists, and geologists and the like come up with theories such as man crossing the Bering Strait / Alaska land bridge instead of believing the Native American/ Aztec legends. For example many legends say some of the peoples on America survived a cataclysm and came from a land that sunk under the Atlantic ocean: obviously referring to Atlantis. The Incas told the Conquistadors that their ancestors originated from a great empire in the east. But since this could mean a continental land mass sunk in historical times, this doesn't mesh with preconceived ages for the earth and the dividing of the continents and so these legends are simply dismissed and replaced with theories that mesh with other more comfortable theories that promote an old earth. Interestingly the Eskimo histories say they were flown to the northern country by the gods with bronze wings. Fit that in the history books!

I admit at first a lot of the ancient legends seemed like so much mumbo jumbo to me, but as various research authors kept presenting bits of these records in their work they became hard to ignore. Some of them still seem like so much mumbo jumbo, and I think some authors are reading too much into them, and possibly using or wresting them to support their pet theories, but clearly some are impossible to ignore. After a while when realizing there really was something to these legends, tribal and written histories I stopped glossing over them and actually took time to read them carefully.

To some it must be hard to accept ancient people's stories if you believe in evolution and view the people that tell them as savages or inferior beings. I think this mindset has really handcuffed us and put blinders on our eyes to prevent us from seeing what really happened in the past. We just like to think we are always and forever getting smarter and more advanced. If we keep thinking this we will never learn from our ancestors and their history as we will always think we are better than them. Conversely many ancient cultures, perhaps in an extreme way, revere their forefathers and strive to perpetuate their knowledge for us to learn from. I think if we did this in our society, perhaps we would be a much calmer saner and gentler society. It's too bad we massacred the Indians and didn't instead learn from them. One wonders what would be if Tecumseh had achieved his goals: what would and wouldn't exist today? What greed and "progress" hath wrought.

WHY SOME OF OUR ANCESTORS BECAME "PRIMITIVE SAVAGES".

Understand that after some of these catastrophes, cities, houses and dwelling places would have been destroyed, forcing mankind to dwell wherever there was shelter. Apathy likely set in the hearts of these men after these catastrophes making them less willing to build again, especially if this event happened more than once in a short period of time. Some of these events in some places would have happened over and over again, making rebuilding seem like a hopeless waste of time and the descent to junglizm or simplistic lifestyles seemed the only alternative. Indeed some of the legends seem to show exasperation and say "OH NO, not again!" They would devolve to what we now call "primitive tribes" or "Cave men". Eventually the advances of the past would have only been a glimmer in their stories, and knowledge and science apparently blamed for these catastrophes would have been an incentive to not bother with scientific discovery, and it may even have been considered bad to be inventive. In fact they would have realized the dangers of advanced science and carefully taught their children about these dangers by repeating in their histories what happened. This was the motivation for them to keep the stories in the first place. Their motivation lends credibility to the stories. They weren't trying to impress us, they were trying to warn their children...and us.

It seems that virtually every ancient civilization was at one time descended from a highly advanced culture in the past, and these legends are all that remains in some instances of those civilizations. There's really no reason to suggest they were any less sophisticated at one time than we are now. In fact all signs point to a civilization so far in advance to our own that in a sense the old 'legends' almost become more reliable than science in its current state with closed minds refusing ancient and even current evidence. All over, the earth itself corroborates the legends, all you have to do is believe what you see. Evolutionist want faith to not believe the evidence. Great is their faith indeed, not to mention their ability to ignore and even prevent others from viewing the evidence.

WHAT THE LEGENDS AND THE EVIDENCE INDICATE

We have already looked at many old histories and I won't repeat them though they could be used here, but here's a few more relating specifically to the subject at hand.

Hopi Indians say a second world ended when twins abandoned the north and south axis of the earth. Earth then careened in space changing the shape of the planet then a new axis and 3rd world was established. It's flowery language but it seems pretty obvious what they are talking about.

Other legends exist that show the "great bear setting". This is in reference to the Big Dipper, meaning that in recorded history the north pole of the earth shifted enough to make that large constellation set where it never set before. And of course legends exist of the land swimming like fish, for example the Japanese history of early earth events called Nihongi speaks of countries swimming about. (Book 10 pg 104) All this in recorded history just backs up the idea that the continents drifted very fast at one time and in recorded history. And of course the already mentioned biblical references to the days of Peleg when the earth was divided.

Tibetans speak of a time before the raising of the Himalayans. They lived in a flat fertile country surrounded by the sea. Tibet and indeed the world is anything but flat! Well not by post Columbus standards anyway.

Egyptians speak of four ages and four times the stars in the heavens changed their directions, and coincidentally there are considered to have been four ice ages. Not just mountains raising but continental motion and drift has also been linked to the cause of Ice ages.

The Eskimo legends speak of a time when the land they lived in had no ice suggesting their verbal legends go back to a time before the ice ages, climate changes, or a rearranging of the continents occurred. They also speak of a time when fire fell from the sky frequently. Sounds very similar to one of the plagues of Egypt. Instead of saying "Oh what nonsense, fire doesn't fall from the sky" we should ask ourselves what conditions on earth would account for fire falling from the sky? Meteors? Lava?

The natives of the area around the source of the Amazon River have legends in the chronicles of Akakor, which speaks of magic stones one could look in and see places around the earth, and wonderful subterranean homes. It also speaks of a great flood that was followed by extreme climate change and flying machines that could go over mountains and water, which were made of an unknown golden metal (orichalcum?) and were shaped like a clay roll. [rock boat? egg?] (book 10 pg 112-116)

Stories of Lake Triton's demise in Africa are found which occurred around the time of the birth of Athene. This huge lake disappeared after a large earthquake caused whatever was keeping the lake back from the sea to be destroyed, likely a mountain range, and the lake drained into the ocean. (book 14 pg 178) It's been deciphered that at one time the Sahara desert supported a great population, but the demise of this lake would explain the almost complete lack of populace in this area today. When one looks at the topography of Africa one can see it nearly broke into two pieces. Local legends often recount a time when things like the climate and landscape changed.

J.W. Gregory an explorer of the African rift concluded the rift wasn't a local fracture but included about one sixth of the earth's circumference… which must have been from a worldwide cause. He noted it first came into being at an early point but saw signs of movement at a recent date. Some features were so bare and sharp they had to have happened during the human period. Not only that, but he also found that "All along the [fracture] line the natives have traditions of great changes in the structure of the country" (Book 53 page 84)

The Sahara Desert has evidence of civilizations that once lived there, as well as a forest, and inland lakes which all indicate worldwide devolution. Incidentally finding the edges of the lake and previous riverbeds and you'll possibly find more ancient civilizations many missed.

A map of Antarctica (1737 Philippe Bauche) shows a waterway dividing the continent in two. This was not known to have existed until 1958!

A globe exists that is known to be older than its first mention in history (1531) by at least a couple centuries. Though it is very small it shows the complete American continents reasonably accurately considering the size of the globe. However one detail stands out. It shows the California Peninsula as an island. It is known that at one time this California Peninsula was not attached to North America, but in recorded history?

Maps exist showing Antarctica still attached to South America. Though it is conceded this was likely the case 11,000 years ago, how then could we have mapped it? The men of the time would have mapped the earth after each subsequent cataclysm. This is why some maps show Antarctica attached to South America and some show it as a separate continent or even two large islands, bare of almost all snow.

HEY THESE DON'T LINE UP RIGHT?

(3rd ed. Insert 2016) Geologists have deduced by the earth's wobble, Stonehenge, the Temple of Amen Ra, and other places, that the earth has moved extremely from a previous known position, and conclude that something huge struck the earth around 2350 BC. Meaning, that this happened during recorded history, because all these charts and ruins show they were built or made before this event happened. This, may in fact date when Antarctica moved as it twisted 20 degrees after it was originally mapped. In fact I'm confident using ancient maps of Antarctica in conjunction with current topographical maps and deducing where rivers were, will yield more ancient civilizations, of either early post flood or pre-flood origin. Infrared imagery of Antarctica might also reveal locations of former human activity.

Though scientists can't seem to understand how Antarctica could have had a temperate climate so recently they seem fine with the idea that North America was at one time almost covered in glaciers, even though these things happened in the same general time frame. What is interesting is that although there seems to have been a genuine "Ice age", the amount of ice on the earth during this period is only 6% more than the ice on the earth today. But the peculiar thing about the ice back then was not the amount of it, but the location! There has never been an ice age in Siberia for example, but there was an ice age at the equator in Africa, and the ice moved in the wrong direction...it flowed FROM the equator and not toward it!

Charles Hapgood showed that Antarctica was mapped accurately when it was still free of ice and at a time when it was rotated 20 degrees from the current orientation. Immanuel Velikovsky showed the earth during recorded history was full of catastrophes that changed the face of the earth. When Charles Hapgood presented his theories of catastrophism to Einstein he was "electrified" by Hapgoods presentations. Einstein originally opposed some of Velikovsky's theories but within an 18 month period his opposition to these theories diminished visibly. The very fact that he took these theories seriously is worthy of note. If Einstein took these theories seriously why don't modern branches of science?

THE EVENTS THAT CAUSED THE FOSSILS

As seen if we speed up the motion of the continents this explains the existence of the mountains. But we will see that this speeding up of the motion of the continents also explains the creation of the fossils. (Fossils are not explained in today's environment.)

As the American continent moved west the earth sub-ducted into the Peru-Chile trench along the west coast of South America and new earth was pushing through the Atlantic fault line, spreading America and Africa apart as the western part of the Americas sub-ducted or collided with Mu. You might ask just how fast could this have happened. Well there are some clues on the American continent, and indeed in many locations all around the world.

My first inkling of this faster movement came from the west coast of America in the California region. Because of the westward motion of the continent there are vast fossil deposits along the California coastline. Scientists have been unable to decipher why literally billions of fossil organisms all along the California coast line could have died so suddenly all at the same time and all along the coast? Simple. The continent moving sideways with all the seismic activity boiled the water and just scooped all the living creatures up, boiling and fossilizing them in the soup being created by the water and slurry all along the west coast as the land moved toward them. Maybe the water didn't actually boil but the continents were moving so fast they couldn't get away. There is a long stretch of fossils of every conceivable kind numbering literally in the billions. The movement was so fast, long and continuous, water spread deep inland wreaking havoc, and killing hundreds, thousands, millions maybe even billions of creatures in one swoop, and basically scooping them and whatever else got in the way. Some hydraulic action then settled them in this area along with the cementing agents needed to turn them into fossils. The water would have scooped up this lithifying agent and mixed it with the creatures and there they sat merrily fossilizing away for us to ponder over them a few millennia later.

MANY PLACES OF MASS CARNAGE AND FOSSILIZATION AROUND THE GLOBE.

There are several places on earth where the grounds movement was so fast that animals and even men were scooped up and crushed together with massive numbers of fossils or near fossils that are buried in appalling bunches.

Take Chalon-sup-Saone France. There is a concentration of bones of rhinoceroses, horses, bears, lions, deer, and others. These creatures appear to have swarmed and bunched together and then crushed together when Italy pushed Switzerland into France. Countries just swimming about until they hit something. Now this starts to give you an idea of just how fast continental "drift" occurred! Not even the animals could run fast enough to get out of the way!

(3rd ed. Insert 2016) I repeat this next bit for its relationship to fossils. I think some of the land was moving so fast animals couldn't get out of the way and were crushed, and evidence hints I could possibly be right in this analysis. H. Godwin deduced that somewhere between the first and second millennium B.C. the sea irrupted twice causing the fossils in England. And earlier, Geologist Joseph Prestwich deduced this irruption of the sea was far more widespread covering from central France, and the French Riviera to Gibraltar, Corsica and Sicily. (book 53 page 184) Whenever fossilized animal tracks are found (which means they had to be buried under fossilizing agents soon after they were made) they are of mixed species, predators and prey and the tracks indicate them running together…not strolling about, and running at breakneck speed as if to escape some terror…no doubt the very agent or event that fossilized their tracks! (Book 53 page 204) Geologist Hugh Miller noted half of Scotland was inundated, in some places 15 stories deep of rolled pebbles, fossils, and the action that created the deposits was instant and sudden as seen by fish in contorted poses from the struggle. Signs of skin colour and soft parts still seen and being buried alive they fossilized before soft parts decayed. He wondered "…what could suddenly destroy… ten thousand square miles [half of Scotland] at once with instantaneous suddenness". (Book 53 page 18) Other Geologists have found the identical evidences in northern Italy, Harz Mountains Germany, Ohio, Michigan, Switzerland,. (book 53 page 17-20)

(3rd ed. Insert 2016) Cuvier (1769-1832) the founder of vertebrate paleontology stated "Repeated irruptions and retreats of the sea have neither all been slow nor gradual; on the contrary, most of the catastrophes which have occasioned them have been sudden; and this is especially easy to be proved with regard to the last of these catastrophes, that which, by a twofold motion, has inundated, and afterwards laid dry, our present continents, or at least a part of the land which forms them at the present day. In the northern regions it has left the carcasses of large quadrupeds which became enveloped in the ice, and have thus been preserved even to our own times, with their skin, their hair, and their flesh. If they had not been frozen as soon as killed, they would have been decomposed by putrefaction. And on the other hand, this eternal frost could not previously have occupied the places in which they have been seized by it, for they could not have lived in such a temperature. It was, therefore, at one and the same moment that these animals were destroyed and the country which they inhabited became covered with ice. This event has been sudden, instantaneous, without any gradation, and what is so clearly demonstrated with respect to this last catastrophe, is not less so with reference to those which have preceded it." (Book 14 page 41-42 quoting Cuvier "Essay on the theory of the Earth" Pg 14-15)

Sites like this exist all over the world! In Patagonia South America, Bogata Columbia, and Peru Cordillera. Santa Barbara California is a site of about a billion fish fossils in a four square mile area in a place that was once under water. The list goes on… California, Mexico, Los Angeles, Fairbanks Alaska, Bering Strait, New Siberia, Llakov Island off Siberia is actually built of millions of skeletons, Harz Mountains in Germany, Switzerland, Italy(Monte Bolca near Verona,) Mediterranean islands, Gibraltar, France, England, Orkney Scotland, Nebraska, Ohio, Michigan, and Arizona, to name a few. Even whales have been found on the Himalayans. In Alaska animals are mingled with uprooted trees and at least four warped and distorted layers of volcanic ash, showing volcanic activity and earth upheaval was going on at the same time as the animals were literally being torn limb from limb.

(3rd. ed. insert 2016) William Buckland concluded climate change took place suddenly (Book 53 page 16)

A professor Frank Hibben (an eminent New Mexican archeologist) "…notes the layers of Volcanic ash interspersed through the piles of bones and tusks of the slaughtered animals, with implication of extreme heat and suffocation by volcanic gasses" (book 37 page 192) this links volcanoes with extinctions, which as has been noted are also linked with Ice ages, and continents moving.

Rutger Sernander concluded the entire climate and not just a single drop in temperature occurred suddenly in Scandinavia where it snowed for years on end during winter *and* summer. And a G. Kossinna concurred that not only did the drop in climate condition happen suddenly but occurred around the year 700 B.C. (book 53 page 158-159) If that's not enough, study of tree rings also show a dramatic alteration of tree rings in the years around 747 B.C., 702 B.C., and 687 B.C. (book 53 page 160) There appears to have been something dramatic in the years 536-545 AD as well as trees from this age were highly affected too which appears to be the cause of the Dark Ages. (Atlantis Rising #99)

In some of these sites animal were entombed so fast traces of skin colour remain. Insects are found with colours still visible, yet even complete insects are hard to find in some of these places. The geologic activity was herding all sorts of beasts as they fled to get away from the earthquakes: the land was folding in and around them and they were literally caught between a rock and a hard place and before they could get out the land smashed into them from both sides, tearing creatures into pieces.

In New Mexico there is a whole graveyard of dozens and dozens of dinosaur bones all intermingled with each other in one site. Even those that found them made the observation that they appeared to be overtaken in a catastrophe.

In Wyoming there are dinosaur bones and fragments in such huge quantities they look like a log jam.

Believe it or not these dinosaur sites are likely the same age as the other mass animal fossil sites of the more "modern" nature and content. In all these massive animal fossil graveyards sites when the evidence is first found, catastrophes are instantly and automatically suspected. Interestingly evolution theorizes that extinctions should be less frequent and slower than the emergence of new species, yet not a single case of a new species emerging from an old one exists, whereas extinctions are noted to have occurred suddenly all over the world!

Along the entire length of the west coast of North and South America similar events occurred all at the same time, as well as in other areas in the world, wherever land moved too fast and water overran the land too fast for man or beast to get away.

Darwin couldn't understand or explain all these mass extinctions. The obvious answer to him was a catastrophe but it meant one that shook the *entire framework of the globe*, and this seemed inconceivable. The evidence is there; it happened.

People want to think the earth is a nice safe place to live that will stay the same for millions of years. Well OK this is natural. Nothing of this sort is happening and hasn't happened for so long we tend to forget or even disbelieve they ever could happen. But take some walks or trips to interesting land formations and visualize what could make those formations. I have done this, and a look at some of the rock formations give me a very uneasy feeling about places where they are seen. One place gave me the willies and I just didn't want to be there. I suddenly felt like the land could move in an instant and the last place on earth I would want to be was is in the very spot I saw these crystal clear evidences of catastrophic geologic movement, as seen for example in some parts of the gulf islands off the coast of British Columbia.

CLUES TO THE ICE AGES.

This faster motion of the continents also gives clues as to the origin of the Ice age. With the continents taking a constitutional and the land mass coming up out of the newly formed Atlantic ocean, the volcanic activity would have been just incredible. There is a worldwide layer of whitish ash in all the seas and it has been deciphered as volcanic ash. (book 53 pg XX) I mean think about that. We are not talking about one piddly little volcano like Mount Saint Helens distributing a bit of ash in the neighborhood, we are talking about this happening all around the earth at the same time to make this universal layer of volcanic ash. What on earth was going on back then to make this happen?

With all this volcanic activity going on, the water in the ocean would have been constantly vaporized and turned into steam and entering the atmosphere. It's felt as much as 600 feet of ocean water would have turned into steam! There's your ice ages. The ice on Greenland and Antarctica is said to be enough to raise the oceans 300 feet. It would have all been in the atmosphere, then rapidly condensing, and coming down both as torrential rain and ice age blizzards. With the sun being blocked out with the volcanic ash, the temperature dropped in many places to explain these monumental blizzards. I mean consider that!

Currently it's felt that less than 1 foot of water is in atmospheric steam and clouds. The sun was not seen in some places for 25 years! That would have "precipitated" a lot of snow. A lot. One Ice Age blizzard comin' up! To spawn an ice age means a period of increased precipitation, but for increased precipitation it also means increased evaporation which would come from increased heat. Some legends speak of oceans drying up! …. Wow…. Oceans drying up…fantastic…scary and fantastic. It must have seemed like the moon's surface suddenly appeared off the coast. Just visualizing that is fantastic, like the surface of the moon suddenly existing in your back yard…that is if you lived near the ocean…man, what a haunting image. Visualizing some of these things helps to clarify and understand what exactly happened back then, but sometimes it is just plain scary. What a fragile planet we live on.

Thinking about this suddenly makes me realize this vaporizing of so much water may have helped spare much life on earth because less water was coming over the land in the form or tsunamis and more in the form of rain and snow, meant some people had more of a chance to survive these incredible disasters.

In some instance this was twenty five years of this eccentric weather going on and, as we will see, possibly longer.

It's also been deduced that the ocean level dropped all around the earth by 18 to 20 feet (book 53 pages 164-165) Three things could have done this. Subduction, but no cause for this seems logical. Mars or Venus coming by to take more water causing worldwide earthquakes, or a meteor from space large enough to start the continents moving again causing the volcanoes to go off around the globe evaporating the oceans this much to fall as snow and create glaciers and shift the poles. But this drop in the ocean level occurred around 1500 BC! This by the way is the date Velikovsky suggests Venus came to the earth (at the time of the Exodus), but King Ogyges thought to have ruled around 1767 BC when he states Venus changed, and likely linked to this drop in the water level, so some date checking is still needed to get this all lined up correctly.

People would have grown up thinking this was normal weather! It reminds me of a story I heard about it raining in some place for the first time in 30 years. People were in a panic because they didn't know what rain was!

IT'S A BUSY PLACE, OR DOMINOS ON A GLOBAL SCALE.

(3rd ed. Insert 2016) Referring to Dr. William Stokes work "Essentials of Earth's History" Goodman writes "Pole shift may also explain the overwhelming association between Ice ages, and mountain building. Stokes, in Essentials of Earth's History, says the "the one invariable accompaniment of glaciations appears to be mountain-building. Intensive mountain-building and continental elevation have coincided with all the great glaciations of the past…" Furthermore "…it was noted that certain geologists believe that the Himalayas were driven up suddenly during the last ice age.) Pole shifts may also account for the volcanic eruptions that are closely associated with ice ages." And "…oceanographers, Dr. James Kennet and Robert Thunell, believe that "this general synchronism is also certainly not coincidental."" And… "On the other hand, pole shift *could suddenly propel the continents forward.*(my italics) The slow continental drift observed today may be the residual momentum of a once great surge." Book 19 page 156-158) and here's some more… "S.A. Durant and H.A. Khan of the department of physics at the University of Birmingham, England, correlated various tektite deposits with both magnetic-field reversals and marine-organism extinctions. (? are there magnetic reversals or not?)Likewise in Nature in 1970, Dr. J.P. Kennet and N.D. Watkins of the University of Rhode Island Graduate school of Oceanography drew attention to the correlations between magnetic field reversals, widespread faunal extinctions, climate changes, and maxima of volcanic activity." Book 19 pg 163-64) (tektites could be of volcanic origin or meteoric origin and differ from each other in some ways) and you no doubt noticed both these people referred to above used the term "magnetic field reversals". So pardon me if I'm confused on *that* subject.

INCREDIBLE EROSION

Then there's the Grand canyon. This feature was always a focal point to me because it was continually stated that this was cut through by water for far longer than the age of the earth. But with the age of the earth being young or so I suspected, I wondered what might cause this canyon to erode faster. Either the earth is older or the grand canyon is younger; how do you account for the depth of the Grand Canyon in a young earth scenario?

Since creationists assumed there was but one flood some theorized the Grand canyon and Vancouver Island were the results of runoff from the flood of Noah. This is just not correct, and I feel this theory has made the creationist camp look worse for wear. Naturally some of you will think this theory will take the cake too, but I'm willing to bet it's better than the runoff from the flood theory.

First, suggesting that Vancouver island was built from silt deposits coming down the Frazer river is simply ludicrous because the island is not formed from silt, or even lumpy bits of debris. There are mountains and indeed the island does not differ in physical makeup from any other island or continent around the earth, showing that this is a normal island and not a sand bar on steroids. Though the Grand

Canyon is runoff from a flood, that is cut from this runoff, it is not runoff from thee flood. The flood of Noah is standing water which slowly subsided. The Grand canyon was made from different hydraulic forces.

OK you have North and South America moving westward running away from the Atlantic ridge. Though South America seems to have bunched up from this movement right at the fault line or water front, possibly preventing any water from surging over this bunched up land and newly formed Andes mountains, the bunching up land in North America occurred further inland creating the coastal and Rocky mountains. This meant that all the flatter land west of the Rockies was subject to inundation from the Pacific Ocean as the continent moved toward it. Possible early on some water got past the mountains before they were pushed up.

Actually a Chinese legend suggests the mountains (Himalayans) may have been overran by the water... but we'll get to that shortly.

There may even have been a split in the continental mass, making MU and North America became one solid continent rather than two partially divided land masses. There is a mystery attached to some of the mountain structures of North America. The Rockies were thrust upward and then eastward at least 8 miles over the plains and possibly many times this distance. No satisfactory explanation exists for this apparent sideways motion of the Rockies. This rapid motion of the continent westward probably explains this motion of the Rockies handily, as they would have been pushed up then broken off and then were pushed sideways by the other land being bunched up as western lands were forcing over and on top of the solid land as the continent moved west.

Back to the Grand Canyon. The western coast however far inland would have been temporarily submerged while the land mass kept moving, bunching up water against the Rockies and possibly beyond. When the land finally stopped moving fast, the water would recede all at once leaving tell tale signs of massive erosion and water runoff and all those erratics we talked about earlier. Thus the grand canyon would have been made in maybe a week, possibly less. However it seems there were a few "Pelegs" so the canyon likely would have taken a few hundred years, maybe a thousand years to complete becoming deeper and bigger with each succeeding continental drift. The canyon didn't take millions of years to create, maybe 50-100 years at the most, or during a few subsequent continental motions, further scouring away. Also with all the torrential rain pouring down after the oceans evaporated away, massive rainfalls on the new continent through the canyon would have vastly speeded up any further erosion. And as I say subsequent Peleg actions would have gouged this place further. So if you added up the total time it took to make the canyon it may have been a hundred years, spread over a period from 101 (3309 BC) years after the floor to about 687 BC, then it would have eroded at a much saner pace from that point onward. Canyon Lands National Park shows evidence of cataclysmic flash floods, and the Grand Canyon was likely created by waters overrunning the land as America went west. Not to be confused with the wagons crossing the prairies going west, as the land had to get there first before they could catch up with it.

((2nd ed. Insert 2008) Even if my conclusions about the Grand Canyon are wrong there is another way to show it is very young. Either the flood or Peleg could have made the Grand Canyon. The area where the Grand Canyon is cut into is 1800 feet above the level of the land up river. The entire area up river is below the level of the Grand Canyon. Were this land a lake at one time, and it appears it was, this would have filled up to the height of the plateau where the Grand Canyon now exists. Once that lake filled too much it would have overrun the plateau and started cutting through it. Once the cut starts, the cut grows extremely rapidly, like a swollen river overflowing its banks and cutting through an embankment. With a huge lake cutting through the plateau the canyon would have formed very rapidly as the water from the lake rushed through, and indeed the entire lake would have emptied into the Pacific. Oddly there is no delta at the end of the river which should be there if the river were millions of years old and it eroded the canyon in the supposed way. Certainly not a delta one would expect to find with that amount of erosion that would have occurred through the Grand Canyon. This suggests that the water rushed through the canyon to the ocean so quickly a delta wasn't formed as it was pulled out into the middle of the Pacific Ocean, and likely subsequent Pelegs destroyed any delta that may have existed at one time.) (Obviously my deductions prior to the more recently discovered material about the Grand Canyon in Chapter 5)

A MODERN DAY EXAMPLE

If you think this canyon could not possibly erode this fast, there is a modern day, though modest, equivalent to show what I mean. In July 1991 Mount Pinatubo erupted causing flash floods. A 16 foot wall had been built quite some time prior to the eruption to contain such floods. However the flash flood overtopped that wall and soon scoured its way underneath the wall. The onrushing flood quickly eroded underneath the wall and kept going until it got to a depth of 60 feet! SIXTY FEET! Leaving the retaining wall high up in the air as though it was not a wall at all, but an arch built to cross over a gorge. Just one Volcano! (National Geographic Dec 1992) Imagine the hundreds even thousands of volcanoes that must have gone off at the time of Peleg and mountains being created in a moment, while the land swum about diving for pearls. Some of the Rockies may be volcanoes but with the land moving and changing the terrain so fast, it might be difficult to tell which mountains were volcanoes at one time. It must have been neat to watch if you could get away from it! But there must have been thousands and thousands of volcanoes going off simultaneously as well. It must have been an incredibly frightening time to live...if you survived at all!

50 YEARS NOT 200 MILLION

Ancient histories are full of stories of endless noise from the volcanoes going off. Well that's another legend that confirms what was happening. Ancient references to a low sky are in all likelihood linked to this, as it is reminiscent of how a fire in a building acts where the only air you can breathe is the air at the lowest level in the room. Other ancient histories speak of ash being carried by the wind and covering the entire earth. (book 6 pg 201) Maybe the sky was so filled with soot and heat and vapor that only air in the lowest valleys was breathable. As time went on these have cooled off and fewer and fewer volcanoes go off, but this state of affairs lasted for years and years. If the Israelites exodus is an indication of the time frames involved, all this activity was probably happening over a period of about 50 years, probably in spurts. It would seem the majority of the continental drift took this amount of time, supplemented by the original Peleg 900 or so years earlier and the other events such as the sun moving back ten degrees, more meteors and other events as mentioned at the start.

THE RIVERS OF BLOOD

Back to the Egyptian river that Moses turned to blood. As we've seen the word used in the bible for this incident is in fact really the word for blood, and not just some rivers turning the colour of blood. Compare this to in II Kings 3: 22. When water came over a plain from Edom the Moabites saw this water from their vantage point as the appearance of blood. But it's clear this is in fact water. So there has been a distinction, this spot says the water looked like blood, but the Egyptian rivers actually turned to blood. How could the water just turn to blood?

One assumes it's a miracle and God can do anything, and no doubt God can interfere and intervene. Curiously the Pharos magicians could also make the water turn to blood, so there may have been two causes for this event, scientific and natural. Obviously we can't rule out simple miracles. After all Moses turned the dust into lice. This couldn't be done by the magicians. But we will also see there was a genuine natural cause for the 'river of blood'. I've noticed that while God is not adverse to doing miracles, he seems to use what is available to him and he seems to used natural phenomena quite often. He knows when the asteroids are going to hit and where. He knows the times and he knows how much time we have until a specific event will occur on earth and he can plan for it way in advance...but he is not adverse to a little manipulation of events for the sake of men. He has a timetable and it appears to be partly based on the event that caused the planet to explode. This does not mean miracles are out of the question, but this doesn't stop him from using what's already there too.

I asked myself, where did this blood come from? I then clued into something else in the bible. In the battle of Armageddon the blood of the warriors comes up to the horses bridle. An entire valley will be filled with death and blood. What a war. Then I asked myself did anything like this happen in the past that could be a source of this same amount of blood? Well we just read of many incidents all around the earth happening all at the same time! All those mountains moving and herding animal into confined areas only to crush them beyond recognition. This was happening all around the earth, and this was the same time all the water in the oceans and rivers were turning to blood. OF course! There is your river of blood in Egypt and Greece and everywhere else! I mean these animals were crushed, and the blood had to go somewhere...it ran into the rivers and even the ocean shores became red. Maybe Mars dust had a hand in this too and made the water redder but this answers this mystery. I figured then this must have meant the rivers were not pure blood but diluted blood. Then that mystery I had always thought odd was answered. I wondered if the rivers were turned to blood why wasn't the water they pulled out of wells dug by the river also blood. This answered that problem, because the water wasn't pure blood, but it was where the blood of all these animals in the neighborhood ran into. So consequently it wasn't in the water table and one could dig beside the river to get fresh water. This incident is similar to one prophesied to happen again as seen in Ezekiel 32:6.

CORRECTED TIMELINE CLEARS UP MYSTERIES

The reason this wasn't figured out before was because we assumed an old earth and these extinctions were supposedly tens of thousands or millions of years ago. So the two events were never matched up on the same time line before. The extinction sites are obviously there and those creatures all died and were crushed, and that means that blood had to run at some point in the past. We tend to forget that these extinctions were horrendous cataclysmic events that happened at some point in history. The blood is a cause and effect. We look at fossils and tend to forget they were at one time living breathing creatures, flesh and blood, and not just fossilized bone. We can now date the event, of so many extinctions, and the age of most of the mountains! The Israelites were led out of Egypt in 2668 after creation, or 1012 years after the flood. This period seems to have lasted about 45-50 years. Using the older 7073 date for the earth, that translates to sometime shortly before 2398 BC (or prior to 1360 BC using the younger date...which I think is far too recent), when the continents went rampant, mountains were made and the mass extinction happened and the rivers turned to blood.

A side note. With all this activity going on in the earth, one can see how more than one winter could be occurring in a single year and this in turn would affect the apparent age of the earth as seen in the dendrochronological record. If the tree rings can't be believed, then turning back the clock on the remaining asteroids by calculating their orbits backward through time may be the only way we can narrow down the point in time where the flood occurred, as this exploding planet is the source for almost all these cataclysms over the years. None would have occurred before this date...unless the crumbled moons that make up the rings around Saturn are part of the overall picture too. Great... nothing more fun than more variables...>Sigh<.

MORE LEGENDS, MORE CONFIRMATION THESE EVENTS HAPPENED DURING RECORDED HISTORY

The Aztec legends speak of a time for several years where the sun did not shine, doubtless due to volcanic dust in the atmosphere. They did not even know in which direction the sun would rise from! (Book 14 pg 130) I mean what was going on back then that they were even unsure of where the sun would rise from? With the dust in the air cooling the surface of the earth down, snow came down in monumental proportions for weeks and months and likely years. Forty feet can fall in one single storm if several volcanoes erupt at the same time creating a temporary shield over the earth of dust. This would have reduced the temperature over vast areas. Forty feet of snow in one storm! That's a small ice age right there, and it wouldn't have taken thousands of years...maybe thousands of hours! I mean even in today's world, New York got 5 feet of snow in 24 hours February 8-9 2007. At some points it was falling at the rate of 5 inches an hour! If this can happen in today's relatively calm world climatologically speaking, imagine what it was like during this insane time in the past!

THEN OF COURSE THERE'S ATLANTIS.

This land mass or area would have been created or isolated when the continents were made. A fracture with an isolated landmass that would become Atlantis as the land spread apart. It would have been a larger mass of land broken off from the mass continent as the new continents of Americas and Africa pulled away from each other while the Atlantic ocean was being created in this same action. Atlantis was probably more of a larger island then a continent in itself, though it might have spanned from somewhere in the middle of the Atlantic to somewhere under Florida. Land sub-ducted at the outer edges of Pangea and new land emerged in the mid Atlantic ridge as though the entire Americas were continents on conveyer belts, or actually part *of* the conveyer belt.

There's really no reason to disbelieve this small continent or large island called Atlantis ever existed. Atlantis probably existed from Peleg (101 years after flood) to about 1700-1500 BC (7073 year old earth) or 687 BC (6035 year old earth) when the earthquake of Uzziah's time finished it off. However the sharp minded will note that if Uzziah's earthquake finished off Atlantis in this later time frame this conflicts with the presumed 9oo year time frame as spoken of by Plato for Atlantis to have sunk prior to his time, so in any finalized date reckoning these conflicts would have to be considered and accounted for. Ok we'd better catch back up with that continent running away from the mid Atlantic ridge.

UNDERWATER EVIDENCE

In the mid Atlantic there was found beach sand at a depth of 2 1/2 to 3 miles and some sediments on the Atlantic floor are less than 100 feet thick instead of the usual thousands. (Man... one of those things you sort of come to grips with as you do all this research is all this sediment at the bottom of the ocean floors. I mean the 'usual thousands' of feet of sediment?!...all that lost land...all that entropy...all that erosion... such a weary old earth, disintegrating slowly into the ocean floors. It's gone and can't be retrieved, it's virtually in its maximum state of entropy. This planet is just slowly dying and eroding...sorry...where was I?) In some areas of the Atlantic ocean sediments are virtually absent altogether.

Ships logs recount occasions where they have come across temporary new islands that subsequently re-submerged in the middle of the Atlantic. They found ruins on these islands similar to those described in Plato's account, even down to the red and white stone pavements. These finds are ignored or refuted by orthodox geologists and archaeologists. Too impossible or controversial...but they are there. People have seen buildings under water in the western Atlantic from planes around about 45 miles northwest of Miami, and of course there's the submerged Bimini wall off the island of Bimini. Actually when you plot underwater finds you see many are in a small area north of Cuba, west of Andros Islands and east and south of the bottom tip of Florida. One could deduce that this whole area was at one point a large island, possibly part of or even the whole of Atlantis. Though people tend to put Atlantis in the middle of the Atlantic Ocean remember at one point the middle might only have been a few hundred miles away from the Americas and Africa. As the Atlantic ridge pushed more and more stuff out it would have pushed Atlantis further and further ...west I guess. There appears to be three or more pyramids in this area along with a couple walls and according to one source 14 buildings in one place somewhere off of Andros Island. The location of these underwater buildings was a divers secret and all that was said, concerning their location, was that they were not on the east side where the "tongue of the ocean" is. (book 8 pg 71)

In fact there are apparently over 50 underwater archaeological sites in this general Bahamas area. In addition there are things underwater like caves with stalagmites and stalactites; a formation made above water. Some of these sites are on an angle showing they weren't just slowly submerged by melting ice but sunk rapidly in some sort of geological calamity. Carved animals found in Yucatan caverns now well above sea level show signs of long submersion with oceanic fauna still present on the carvings, meaning originally the caverns were above water, sank in a Peleg action, then in a subsequent continuation of that action were once again returned to above sea level...unless someone carved the things under water! (book 6 pg 97) This indicates at least two upheavals with time elapsed between the intervals. But these last two upheavals happened after they were carved.

This is likely something of a confirmation to what paleontologists refer to as various ages in the earth. But the clues keep indicating these events happened during recorded or verbal history and the periods between these upheavals has been a far shorter time period then previously presumed. And indeed the very fact these animals were carved at all meant they were carved by civilized man, before these events occurred, again putting these catastrophic events during civilized time frames.

This also shows that the continents didn't just come to their present position all in one go but in a series of at least two Peleg actions and likely a few...maybe dozens. (For example like we mentioned about Chile's coastline)

This stands to reason, as we deduce from Egyptian records there were four times when the sun changed directions, four ice ages, etcetera.

ATLANTIS WEST, ATLANTIS EAST?

Many researchers seem to be unsure where to put Atlantis. I've stuck with Plato's story of it being off the coast of the pillars of Hercules AKA the Strait of Gibraltar. So why then do I show Atlantis as being off the coast of America and in the Bermuda triangle area? Simple. When Atlantis broke apart and sunk, it was the result of an asteroid smashing into the planet nearby. It then not only sunk Atlantis, it caused multiple volcanoes to emerge in the middle of what is now the Atlantic Ocean. The forces of the planet pushed outward from the middle of the Atlantic spreading the remains of Atlantis both east and west, moving the continents in the process. (Looking at maps of Pangea you can see Africa was very close to Mexico at one time, with what would be Atlantis in the middle.)

ATLANTIS TIDBITS

(3rd ed. Insert 2016) Though Raymond Drake adheres to the really old earth belief and also believing Atlantis to be dominating the world scene in ancient history (presumably ruled by space men who left the planet at some point for some reason. Seemingly everyone is a space man ...even God in his books (Book 23 and 34). Atlantis eventually, rent by upheavals for thousands of years, until about 11,000 years ago (obviously he's accepting Plato's '9000 years' date) it finally submerged. He thus concludes that the earth's upheavals and separating of the continents occurred during mans rule on the planet and was a not a prehistoric event. Thus one way or another we both conclude the dividing into continents occurred during recorded history.

Finally getting a copy of Ignatius Donnelly's *Atlnatis*, I use some info here. As early as the 1870's the Challenger confirmed Plato's Atlantis story by finding volcanic deposits where Plato said they would be, which he said at one time limited Atlantic ocean travel giving some creditability to Ignatius Donnelly's "Atlantis". (page 50)

One curious bit of evidence Donnelly came up with was the absence of several domesticated plants existing in the wild state anywhere on earth. His conclusion was that they were created either in vast antiquity or before the flood. (Which flood he assumes was of course Atlantis.) (page 61)

When the Canary islanders were rediscovered in 1395 they were surprised to see others had survived the disaster that overwhelmed their continent.

Have you got my statue? (Atlantis stuff.)(3rd ed. Insert 2016) I must have been sleeping when I read this bit the first time. In 1882 Cap David Armory Robson sailing the Jesmond from Sicily to New Orleans spotted at sea (200 miles SW from Madeira) muddy waters littered with dead fish (some species were unknown). Then he spotted an uncharted island, rocky and steaming as though newly emerged from the sea. He and some crew landed and among the usual basalt cliffs covered with marine growth, they found flint arrowheads, and small knives. The next day they found an apparently ancient tomb containing spearheads, axe heads, and a sword, along with figures of birds, and animals made of stone or pottery, two large urns with bone fragments in them and part of a human skull. Nearby was a 6 ft statue made from a solid block of stone which was taken aboard the ship. Pottery found had what appeared to be writing similar to Egyptian or Hebrew. The statue disappeared somewhere on route to the British museum and the island soon sank. The Atlantis statue is probably in someone's back yard, and its significance not known. (book 23 page 65)

ATLANTEAN SUBSTANCE.

(3rd ed. Insert 2016) Drawings in Lima Peru are said to have been drawn by a goddess "Orichana" who came to earth in a ship of the sky as brilliant as the sun. (Book 64 pg 108) Orichana sounds similar to "orichalcum" an unknown metal of Atlantis and there could be a connection. Maybe UFO's outer shell is made of this substance."

Whether or not she or her ship had anything to do with this metal, I can't be certain. But one thing that comes up while reading about Atlantis is that this metal was more valuable than gold and this substance was called orichalcum. Several authors referred to it and were mystified as to its contents. Charles Berlitz refers to it as a possible Gold alloy. (book 6 Pg 17) I'm not sure how he arrived at that, but he may have been very close. While reading Josephus as translated by William Whiston, I came across this in Antiquities' of the Jews Chapter V :2. "Now Esdras presented the sacred money to the treasurers, who were of the family of the priests, of silver six hundred and fifty talents, vessels of gold twenty talents, vessels of brass, that was more precious than gold, twelve talents by weight; for these presents had been made by the king and his counselors, and by the Israelites that stayed at Babylon." We might wonder why the vessels of brass were more valuable than gold. As it happens Whiston interjects here with an asterix by the statement "more precious than Gold*" with an interesting footnote. He says "* This kind of brass or copper, or rather mixture of gold and brass or copper, was called aurichalcum, and was of old esteemed the most precious of all metals"!!! He doesn't say why he knows this, he just states is as matter-of-factly. Clearly orichalcum and aurichalcum are read the same and have to be the same metal, and indeed are esteemed the same. Keep in mind his translation was done in 1737...about 150 years before Atlantis material became popular. So this clears up the mystery of what this metal is, and should thus be put to experimentation and see why it was so esteemed and what was so special about it.

UNDERWATER CARAVAN.

(3rd ed. Insert 2016) Frank Joseph found evidence of Atlantis's existence in a different way. We spoke of there being beach sand found in the mid Atlantic which showed this area had to be above water at one time, but since Plato spoke of specific animals in Atlantis, Joseph 'sifted the sand' so to speak. Plato spoke of there being so many elephants in Atlantis that tusks were an Atlantean building material. That seems like an awful lot of elephants, but when we realize some islands near the arctic circle are comprise almost entirely of mammoth carcasses, this doesn't sound quite so impossible. Anyway, in 1967 an issue of Science magazine reported a "...discovery of elephant teeth from the Atlantic Continental shelf between 200 and 300 miles off the Portuguese coast at more than 40 different dredge site locations from the depths of 360 feet. The teeth were recovered from submerged shorelines, peat deposits, sand banks caused by surface waves crashing against a beach, and depressions that formerly contained freshwater lagoons." By the way the article places the sinking of Atlantis coinciding with a series major natural catastrophes that happened at the same time, such as a huge eruption of the volcanic island Thera-Santorini in the Aegean sea and a "nuclear-like equivalent" simultaneously happening in New Zealand, which scholars have dated at 1628 B.C. (Atlantis Rising Magazine #71)

In 1964 Otto Muck (a German Rocket engineer) discovered two 'twin' deep sea holes in the ocean floor (exact location not mentioned) that were caused by an asteroid that had split in two before contact. They "...set off a chain reaction of geologic violence along the mid Atlantic ridge". (Atlantis Rising Magazine 35) This of course would have had the triple reactions activating the volcanoes, the sinking of Atlantis and spreading the continents further apart and consequently overrunning vast stretches of land around the globe with tsunamis, building mountains and causing more ice age snow to fall.

MORE ATLANTIS RUINS FOUND.

(3rd ed. Insert 2016) No One...and I mean NO one in orthodox archaeology or geology wants to admit Atlantis ruins have been found, because this would mean admitting underwater ruins in the middle of the Atlantic Ocean changes everything. Dating of artifacts and ruins and geologic processes are not what they are trying to force us to believe. Atlantis ruins under water mean this stuff had to have been built and above water in recorded history...which by and large means in the last 7000 years or so(or at the very least 12,000 years if you take Plato's dates at face value). A new underwater site of ruins has now been added to the pile of ancient underwater ruins, and they are clearly, based on location (about 30 miles south of the Bimini Islands) a remnant of Atlantis. Looking at the pictures as seen in Atlantis Rising Magazine # 98 there is no denying these are manmade quarried and finished stones. Some have tried to suggest that some of these manmade stones found at various places underwater are nothing more than ballast tossed overboard by ancient mariners, but it is clear these stones were "...obviously quarried for specific building purposes." Not to mention these stones are of immense proportions, simply illogical to be used for ballast if it needs to be easily thrown overboard. Columns and tool marks are clearly visible on some of these stones in the Bimini area. If the Bimini underwater wall wasn't convincing, these are. True they have ages of residue on them but even so there is no mistaking the evidence of civilization, but under just 3-7 feet of water depending on tide. The underwater site is 530 feet long (width not noted). The author of this article notes "Around this top area are massive blocks that appear to have been shaken down or impacted by some highly destructive force" Well considering where the ruins are located I would say that's reasonable assumption.

AN ATLANTIS PYRAMID FOUND!

(3rd ed. Insert 2016) I stumbled on a discovery of another pyramid near the Azores (...or is it in the Bermuda triangle area) which is apparently semi translucent, or made of glass and is larger than the Egyptian pyramid. (There seems to be some confusion as to its location.) Though the underwater scans and pictures show an absolutely geometric shape underwater, the Portuguese Regional Secretary of Education, Luiz Fagundes Duarte does not think it should be taken as a manmade object because of where it's found. What does it take to prove stuff to people? Personally I think this find is so dramatic it proves the 'legends' and a dramatic shift in ancient history is in order. I've drawn a **picture** of a photo seen on the net...yes the edges of the pyramid really are that defined! **(See Drawing 11.** As luck would have it a stwange cweature swam by while I was dwawing this. Fortunately I managed to qwickly sketch it. I'm not sure what it is or where it came fwum, but it may have escaped fwom chapter 7) The Azores are smack dab in the middle of where Atlantis would plot. Crazily someone has dated it 28 million years old. Sure, why not. More and more underwater archeology is being found like a step pyramid by Yonaguni-Jima Japan.

DRAWING 11

Old maps show a fairly substantial island called Friesland, south of Greenland, right smack dab where Atlantis, or part of Atlantis might have been…or maybe a little to the north. From the 1550's to the 1660's people from Greenland and Europe traded with this well populated island's people. But in the late 17th century this island just disappeared from maps and apparently from the face of the waters.

OTHER FACTORS IN ALL THIS CONTINENTAL MOVEMENT

Obviously we can't blame the pyramids for all four to seven huge historical catastrophic events, but only the initial one or possibly the first two. So probably Mars, maybe Venus and certainly we have to presume meteors had a large part to play in this continued motion of the continents, possibly at some point all these factors happened simultaneously.

This action of meteors on the earth's crust could be likened to throwing rocks at a small floating raft. Each time you hit the raft it will drift farther away from you. Any sizable meteors regardless of the angle they hit the earth at, would likely boil the continental undercarriage and just continue the Atlantic ridge spewing out liquid mantle from underneath renewing massive volcanic actions both underwater and above, and forcing the continents further apart. The angle of the meteors impacts hit the earth possibly giving some directional force to this movement. Some records speak of seven heavens or nine ages, so we can presume meteors played a big part in these ages and always with the same result…continuing the drift. We also see that man had mighty weapons and possibly some drift is due to them.

Again in the past a planet or planets (principally Mars) interplayed with earth on occasion so it also likely continued the drift…possibly every 16 years for many centuries, likely from the point of Peleg up to the point of the Exodus, maybe as late as the earthquake of Uzziah. Then one day Mars itself got blasted by a mighty meteor and it returned to a more normal, though still elliptical, orbit. If we consider that earth may also have had a more elliptical orbit for a while, then it stands to reason that every once in a while earth and Mars got exceedingly close, maybe even trading places with Mars coming inside the orbit of Earth, similar to how Pluto comes inside the orbit of Neptune now.

Again I must say this in some ways may never be provable because once a planet's orbit has changed due to an impact from an asteroid, that asteroid ceases to exist and the new orbit of the planet cannot be worked back properly unless you know the exact time place and size of the impact. Perhaps careful analysis of ancient history and legends might give some clues, but even they would be difficult to translate into changed orbital patterns.

Perhaps some meteors found on earth could give some clues, by their size and the angle they hit, and if we could ever perfect dating methods we might even know *when* they hit.

After the flood the earth likely had a more elliptical orbit, so only once in a long while Mars and the Earth got close enough to continue a Peleg action, maybe in more violent fashion than at other times. Maybe the earth even got close to Venus on occasion, though at some point meteors must have pushed Earth back into a more circular orbit. It would seem that anything that could go wrong did go wrong during the period of the Exodus where all these forces came into play in rapid succession or simultaneously.

Some of this deduction is based on ancient legends; Sitchin and Velikovsky concluded that planets came close to the earth, during this period. However Velikovsky suggested that the pillar of fire by night and pillar of cloud by day which led the Israelites in the wilderness might be this electrical charge that would occur between planets as they got close to each other. I can't really agree with this deduction even though it might sound logical. One has to presume if this were the case then it stands to reason that where such an electrical discharge were occurring would also be the point where the two planets were at their closest. But this would also mean this was likely the point where most of the upheavals were taking place. Though true, much was happening around the Israelites at this time, it seems they were more in the right place at the right time, always avoiding the physical geological activities, with the exception of the one family that was swallowed up by the earth. We have to presume that this pillar of fire or cloud was indeed an effect caused by the angel that led the Israelites around. So it was caused by some aspect of the angels abilities and not due to the events transpiring around the Israelites. Obviously angels in the mix will tend to alienate some people's opinions of this work, but it would seem angels indeed had a more apparent role to play in the more ancient past then they do now, though tales of angels still happen now. We see that this same angel castigated the Israelites after they got into Canaan, for not fulfilling their obligations properly. (see Judges 2:1-4) We'll get back to angels, in a subsequent chapter.

THE SUN AND THE MOON STAND STILL. STARS REVERSE DIRECTIONS

Just prior to Joshua telling the sun and moon to stand still, rocks fell from the sky killing more of the enemy than the Israelites had done. This again strongly indicates that meteors have something to do with the subsequent Peleg actions, as it was likely the effect of the meteoric impacts somewhere else on earth that caused the earth to alter its normal routine, causing the sun and the moon to appear to stand still in the sky. This does not mean huge meteors wiped out the army where Joshua was, but likely smaller cannon ball, or even marble sized rocks, otherwise *everyone* in the area would have been wiped out. But these smaller rocks falling from the sky in the immediate area were likely indications bigger ones were hitting somewhere else on the earth. If the sun and moon stood still for a whole day, the land Joshua was on was stationary in relation to the stellar bodies, thus one has to surmise elsewhere continents moved. As those land masses and indeed continents shifted away from or around this central location where Joshua was, water would have overran those areas. (And as we've noted many Martian rocks were thrown at earth when Mars got close to the earth: this could be a dateable / provable point if the rocks in this area (if we know the area) are shown to match radiometric readings such as the ones found in Antarctica that proved to be of Martian origin)

With all this happening the inner earth would have kept moving but the outer crust would have twisted and not actually stopped, but the twist would have centered near Joshua so it appeared that the sun and moon were standing still from that particular vantage point on earth. Perhaps the sun and moon were in close relation to each other in the sky and actually circled in the sky at a slow rate as to not attract comment, as I would guess the land they were on spun while other landmasses further from them flung away from this center. There may have been little else to distinguish this event in this particular locale, whereas in other parts of the earth complete havoc may have been taking place.

This is an incredible strain on the earth and something big would have happened world wide... possibly causing havoc in China, Africa, California and Siberia and doubtless continuing the original Peleg motion. This might be the event that twisted Antarctica 20 degrees, freeing it from South America. I suppose it is possible that a large enough meteor could have temporarily halted the motion of the crust of the earth then the underlying molten undercarriage still rotating as usual slowly started the crust moving again. But the sun and moon stood still rather than slowing down, but either scenario fits.

This biblical story of the sun standing still for about a day also corresponds with Mexican legends that tell of a night that did not end for a long time, thus confirming the biblical record and adding further weight to the continental drift occurring during recorded history. (Book 14 pg. 61) (Understand that if the Mexican and other legends confirm the biblical ones, this also means the biblical ones confirm the Mexican and other legends. When this happens this is like two witnesses testifying about an event to confirm this event happened. These testimonies should serve to overturn some scientific theories.)

Sahagun (1499?-1590) came to the Americas gathering aboriginal traditions and found a similar legend of the sun rising only a little and staying still as did the moon. (Book 14 pg 61-62)

Similarly in Peru, the sun did not shine for 5 days then suddenly the ocean overran the continent. Once again indications the continents moved and the effects of this movement were recorded, **though this is probably a different time frame and event.**

Egyptian records speak of stars changing direction and the south becomes north and the world turns over. Egyptian star charts show skies of two different eras, one with east and west reversed. (book 14 pg 119-120)

A sun clock was found in Faijum (somewhere in Egypt). The shadows cast on the clock do not correspond to any correct timing and does not work based on the location or anywhere else in Egypt like a sundial should. It's clearly accepted to be an Egyptian clock, but no theories exist to explain why it doesn't work. Things like moving the clock every hour have been theorized but these are ridiculous as you'ld need another clock to know when the hour was up, and then why the heck would you need the shadow clock in the first place!? Velikovsky feels it is a critical piece of evidence that would help us learn the length of the day, the inclination of the pole to the ecliptic, and the latitudes of Egypt in that historical period when this clock was made, which is understood to be before 687 BC and probably before 720 BC (Book 14 page 324-326) (I never realized sundials were location specific. I just thought they were all the same...just point it to the sun and voila...instant clock.)

Extremely accurate Hindu astronomical tablets show star positions changed and other Hindu records say earth shifted 100 Yojanas (5-900 miles) and a new star became the pole star. (book 14 pg 316-318)

Greek Authors before and after Plato speak of the reversal of the path of the sun. "Zeus...changed the course of the sun, causing it to rise in the east and not in the west" (Book 14 pg. 122) Hmmm sounds like a certain Egyptian legend don'tcha think?

A Nineveh tablet says the Vernal equinox was on the sixth day of Nisan and another one says it was on the 15th of Nisan. Their observations are considered accurate and precise and this discrepancy can't be explained under orthodox thinking whereas this work explains this as well. (book 14 pg 350) They also had three schedules for the movements of the moon and only one of them corresponds to today's observations. Thus adding weight to the theory that the moon changed its orbit and patterns in the past. The differences are so vast they cannot be explained by errant observations by such accurate methods, and can only mean vast changes in the earth's rotation and the moons orbit took place during recorded history. Even the length of the month changed. Daniel 2:21 speaks of God changing the times and the seasons.

Pictures from Mariner 7 of Martian landscape showed features surrounding the poles but were not centered as would be expected and it has been deduced this indicates a pole shift also occurred on Mars.

An asteroid missed the earth by 106,000 miles and another one sailed near a spot where the earth would be in a few days by far less than this. That may seem like quite a distance until you realize that is INSIDE the orbit of the moon! Or put another way, a distance of between six and twelve diameters of the earth away! If this happened in recent years with only a few asteroids in the heavens consider what was going on in the past when after the planet exploded and the sky was filled with asteroids, some possibly orbiting the earth for a while!

Underneath the north end of Ellesmere Island (beside Greenland's northern extremity) there is an item 15 miles below the surface and it extends to 80 miles below the surface. It is 65 X 64 miles long and said to be shaped like a "loaf of bread". It creates a huge erratic distortion of the magnetic field suggesting the temperature should be 2700 degrees, but counter to expectations the surface heat instead of being triple normal is in fact little more than *half* normal heat... a drop! (Book 29 pg 115-16) I can't explain these phenomena, but obviously this simply must be an asteroid underground, but it's not just the size of a house, it's 65 miles long! What would *that* do to the earth when it hit?

Geologists positively conclude by studying rock formations and paleomagnetism orientation of the earth, that the axis of the earth's rotation has changed. They want us to believe that these events occurred millions of years ago to make us feel safe, but as we see these events occurred during recorded history.

Even simple pottery can show a change in earth's magnetic field. While a pot is fired particles gravitate toward the nearest pole and the magnetic charge of those particles is known. At one time Italian and Greek pottery was fired when the south pole was closer. Either that or the magnetic polarity of the two poles changed. (book 53 pg. 133) Wow this seems pretty extreme for these places to actually be closer to the south pole. Especially when one considers an ancient group of rowers that, determined to find a route around Africa for trade purposes, noticed that the sun was in the northern part of the sky. When they finally got home they told people this peculiar detail about the sun and they were laughed at to scorn for this information. Though this proves they made the trip, it also may help date the incidents of the pole shifts which would have happened before this trip was made. And indeed we've already seen that the pole shift was likely during the time of the exodus. (I've forgotten and mislaid the information that speaks of this marathon rowing incident and the name of the captain of this ship that made this historical trip. Checking the internet it appears to have been Necho II who sent this Phoenician expedition out, seemingly headed by Heracles [interestingly here some misidentification seems to exists. Hereacles appears to have been black, but he could he Hercules, but was Hercules black?])

I am not aware of any records where the people in places spoke specifically of the sun changing from a southern placement in the sky to a northern one. So either I've missed that little detail or something is amiss with the pottery. What I really think is the pottery speaks of is a pole flip and not a displacement of the land in that particular location. If the pole flips the North Pole might appear as the south and a double flip would make the difference hard to find in some forms of evidence. If the pole flipped once then the pottery was made then the pole flipped again it would seem as though the land moved when in fact just the pole flipped, though we have to assume some movement of the land was also occurring. However some legends do speak of the earth actually tumbling, though as I say I have not found specific mention of the sun changing from a north to a southern location in the sky, though I may have missed it, and it may be there. But then I guess if the legends say the sun rises in the east then rises in the west that actually means the same thing. Pardon me while I go bang my head.

These pole changes were sudden. For example coral found in the polar regions speak of the suddenness of the change, otherwise coral would be found in a continuous reef or cordillera from the poles to a more climactic tropical region. For what would happen in a slow migration of the poles the colder zoned coral would die and the warmer area would spawn new growth as the poles slowly shifted.(assuming the depths of the coral didn't change) But this is not the case. Coral in the poles is confined to a small area and no continuous growth from one climatic region to another is evident in the record. There would also be a chain of deterioration as coral died, disintegrated or was eaten. But this gradual process is not observed anywhere. All evidences of pole shift are sudden, drastic and cataclysmic, and even just the fact that this change is reflected in pottery clearly shows this happened recently. Similarly coral can only grow in shallow areas, yet coral is found in places 1200 feet above sea level on pacific islands and no evidence of continuous growth of it from that point to a submerged area is evident anywhere, showing it was raised suddenly. Similar events have even happened in modern times, for example part of the Bonin Trench rose 6000 feet in May 1973. Yeah that said 6000 feet...that's over a MILE! Also when they were laying the Transatlantic cable in the 19th century it broke. Later on they found the reason it broke was because the ocean floor had risen 4000 feet suddenly. (Book 7 pg. 163) (Likely from an existing cliff rather than a sudden uplift occurring at the time)

Similarly palm trees are found in Greenland with no continuous growth in a line to a tropical area, and sequoias are found in Alaska, again with no evidence of gradual shifting of that growth to a warmer climate. All these events occurred suddenly and likely at the same time meaning worldwide earth shattering events occurred suddenly.

Not only are palm trees and coral reefs found to have once flourished in what are now arctic regions, coal deposits are found in Antarctica and on Spitsbergen (9 degrees from the pole) as well as places such as Egypt and Morocco. Coral growth is found in Spitsbergen, Greenland and Alaska, where it is far too cold to grow this stuff. Giant sequoias once grew north of what is now the arctic circle. Once Siberia, now the ice box of the world, was covered in massive forests. It's also known that at one time Greenland supported the growth of figs. The accumulation of sediments off Antarctica indicate it was a temperate zone for a long period of time.

Though Velikovsky concluded there were recent world catastrophes in the second and first millennium BC, he was surprised to find out after he published his book *Worlds in Collision*, that R. Sernander, a climate specialist ("and others") deduced that in 1500 B.C. and in 800 B.C. "there occurred climactic catastrophes of global dimensions" (book 53 page 257)...The same time frames Velikovsky deduced by both the physical and historical evidence, completely verifying his deductions.

With periodic catastrophes continuing the motion of the drifting continents, moving them further apart, Atlantis with it being in the center of all the action, got caught in the crossfire as more of the Atlantic ridge came up all around it.

Interestingly the ocean floor contains an incredible amount of red dust that contains nickel, a key clue to the presences of meteorites in the past. If you think all this blaming stuff on meteors and Mars is clutching at straws, there is so much of this red dust that 10,000 tons of meteorites must have fallen a day, 1000 times than what is expected by today's standards. By the way, we have a lot more meteoric activity on earth then is generally known. Recently it was admitted that on average every month a meteor the size of a house hits the earth! So what was it like back then with that happening a 1000 times a month, and obviously even bigger ones hitting the earth? Wishing upon a falling star meant you were wishing to see tomorrow!

OTHER CONTINENTAL MASSES

Other continents such as Atlantis, Lemuria and Mu likely existed as well. Atlantis with its more central location causing it to steal the spotlight, these other land masses often get overlooked. So many references talked about Atlantis whereas I only found one book on Mu, and none on Lemuria. There does seem to be some factual basis for the existence of Mu in bygone ages. I tend to think James Churchward tended to be over enthusiastic in his search for clues regarding it and consequently some of his conclusions seemed something of a stretch to me. He seemed to be seeing Mu under every stone in almost every part of the world.

Admittedly since he spent many years looking and learning to read ancient texts concerning this continent his enthusiasm may be more well founded then I was able to grasp. Even so he was convincing enough and his views were worth looking into. If Mu existed it was probably pushed under and fused with America as the Americas move westward and Asia moved eastward toward it. The Rocky Mountains may be the result of the two continents colliding, though Churchward placed Mu in the middle of the Pacific quite some distance from North America. Possibly some of Mu was part or is now part of the Americas, but if Hawaii was part of Mu as some legends suggest, that would make it a pretty large continent to just disappear. When geologists reverse the drift and piece together the continents to make the mass continent Pangea, they of course only piece together the known current land masses above water. For example they don't seem to show Atlantis, Lemuria or Mu. Mu may have been a substantial size continent indeed, possibly as much as 1/3 to 1/2 the size of the Pacific Ocean! But then if the islands that are deduced to have been part of Mu also moved along with the rest of the worlds land masses, Mu originally may have been considerably smaller then he deduced.

If these extra continents were as large as some people suggest then I do find some problems with all these continents that were supposed to have existed at one time. I have to think they were not as massive as their proponents suggest, but rather were likely well known well populated large islands which, because of their fame or at least the fame of their demise, their size has also become larger than life, similar to how people who have recently passed on suddenly become so important to us when we realize how much we miss them.

If these continents were as large as some suggest the area where water was before the flood had to be quite limited, though I don't completely rule this out as likely hundreds of feet of water came down in the flood. But these legends all seem to be post flood as far as I can tell, when so much of this land would have been permanently submerged, as our continental shelves testify. It appears all of the continental shelves were at one time part of the surface and they have been submerged ever since the flood to a depth of as much as 600 feet or more.

WATER TO LAND RATIOS HAVE CHANGED.

The problem I find with all these extra continents when one considers their supposed size becomes the water to land ratios. If Pangea was a vast single continent in a big ocean, and if these other lands were as big as some people suggest, then when added to the continent would seemingly almost eliminate oceans altogether.

At one time the earth may have been 50% land and 50% water rather then it's present 30%/70% ratio, but with such a low average height of land masses this was a delicate balance to say the least. Obviously as we've deduced there is about 300-600 feet of water on the planet that was not here before the flood covering the continental shelves which means to some extent this altered water to land ratio might have been the case.

On the other hand I suppose the time frames for some of these continents existence may not overlap each other. In other words Peleg actions would create one continent while at the same time destroying another. For example the destruction of Mu appears to have been first and the action that sunk it or merged it with North America also seems to be the same cataclysm that isolated a landmass between the Americas and the old world and created Atlantis. But the dimensions of the land masses we are dealing with seem extreme, and it would seem rather that the sizes of these continents is likely exaggerated, though I suppose deeper average ocean depths at one time might also be a factor or option to be computed into the mix. Indeed the very action of sinking a continent will speed up the sinking as water levels rise around the earth.

(Mind you I have seen at least one note that suggests at one time the Earth may have had a land to water ratio of 10 to 1)

THE SILT EXCHANGE

Certainly all those thousands of feet of silt in the ocean depths has to account for some of the change in water to land ratios. I mean if those thousands of feet of silt at the bottom of the oceans were in any way a solid mass, this could indeed be a huge factor when considering how land to water ratios have changed over time. I mean even if all that silt just came from land still in existence, that still pulls the surface of the oceans down well below the continental shelves. Re-displacements of water onto what was land by erosion of that land in the form of silt could among other factors account for the raising the water levels around the earth. This erosion would have been immense and a real factor during the time the continents moved. This silt would have come into existence since the creation, and indeed most, if not all of it came into existence since the flood. A more stable earth before the flood means very little silt runoff and erosion would have been made in that era, presuming man wasn't doing something then to speed it up. Having said all that there seems little doubt Mu existed, and its size may have been substantial.

EVIDENCE FOR MU'S EXISTENCE

Many ruins remain on Pacific islands that cannot be explained or built with the populations or resources existing on the islands, and legends exist that some of these islands were at one time part of a much larger land, similar to stories found in legends in and around the Atlantic.

Mangaia Island has stone ruins but no quarries. Tonga-Tabu has two 70 ton stone uprights and a 25 ton stone on top of them to make an arch, yet there is no stone on the island. Many islands have huge ruins that overlook the ocean. South Sea islands have such marvelous monuments that it is felt some great civilization was once there and is now lost. (book 16 pg. 92)

Included in Churchward's appraisal of islands once part of the continent Mu is Easter Island. If this is the case Mu was simply gigantic! Indeed his estimated drawing of the continent makes it the size of North America, but if North America actually collided and submerged Mu then Mu could be as much as twice Churchward's size estimations as some of that continent may actually now be part of the Americas.

Interestingly as I continued through my notes regarding this theme I found this bit of information. At the 1977 annual meeting of the American Geophysical Association they concluded there once existed an eighth continent they named Pacifica. Do I need to tell you where it was? They felt it collided with North America and created among other things, the Sierra and Rocky Mountains. It's safe to presume this continent they are talking about is Mu, which was populated with some sort of Civilization. So once again we see evidence to suggest the mountains rose in civilized times, as the civilizations were there before the continent sunk or was pushed under by being squeezed from both sides.

As a side note there is a remarkable testament to this isolated Easter Island being somehow connected with somewhere else. Over 20 alphabetic or phonetic language characters are identical to those of Indus script 1/2 a world away! This is beyond chance. There had to have been a connection at some point in the past between these two places. A friend of mine, John Newberry, who managed to decipher Indus script and is the now the foremost authority in the world of this lost language is aware of this similarity but seems to think this is just chance. Obviously in light of the theories I present here I disagree. I would assume, if there is a connection, some or all of these characters will mean the same thing and/or have similar sounds.

FLOOD EVIDENCE INCREDIBLY OBVIOUS

The bizarre Easter Island bighead statues have long been a puzzle as to how or why they were built. They were obviously built by someone with too much time on his hands. Perhaps somewhere under water is the answer. As you will recall the average height of all the continents was at one time a mere 1000 feet. We can deduce Mu escaped the process of mountain building evident on other continents because it sank first in the initial action that created the mountains, so it's average height above sea level may not have altered. When factoring in the water left behind from the flood one can surmise that as much as 300-600 feet of ocean water still extant on the earth today is a remnant of the flood. (Assuming this 3-600 feet isn't there because of the silt exchange) As stated some river beds continue underwater right to the edge of the continental shelves. I find this one of the most obvious evidences for the world flood yet people seem completely unaware of this tidbit of information or just ignore it. I mean a lot of the flood water is still here! If these riverbeds continue under water obviously they were not always under water as rivers don't flow underwater. There is simply more water here then there was on the earth at some point in the past. Looking at the continental shelves show that some of them are well under 600 feet of water, some are actually under more than a mile of water, but if the shelves were at one time the delineation of the land and seas edges there is simply a massive amount of water still here from the flood.

MORE WATER MEANS LOWER CONTINENTAL PROFILES ABOVE SEA LEVEL.

Back to Mu. This remnant flood water would substantially lower the average height of Mu above sea level after the flood. So when Mu existed before the flood it averaged 1000 feet above sea level, but with this extra 3-600 feet of water left behind from the flood…after Mars drank its fill, means Mu was then averaging 4-700 feet above sea level. With less land above sea level it would be easier to sink and since it was sunk first, it never even had any real mountains to resist sinking and it sank the fastest.

Interestingly this deduction tallies with legends that call Mu a land of "Vast Plains" and "Low rolling hill-lands" (Book 16 pg 46) This too was Churchward's deduction that the continent of Mu had no actual mountains. This also tallies with Peleg because it was during the Peleg action itself that mountains as we know them were created. Why would Mu have mountains when it was the Peleg action that formed them in the first place, and Peleg that submerged Mu.

Mu almost certainly must have been the first major land to be submerged by the Peleg action and because of its position on the earth and its low profile, so it would have submitted to the water much easier then subsequent lands, such as Atlantis which likely took 1700 years to finally submit to the waves. James Churchward also attributes vast age back to the time when the continent of Mu existed. He deduces it's destruction to a post flood era, so this likely places it's destruction at the time of Peleg. Mu may have had a lower profile still. With the fountains of the deep breaking forth in the flood, some continental land masses may have sunk a bit too, as water from below changed places with land from above. If continents sunk a bit during the flood and then slowly rebounded as underground pressures pushed the lands back up, Mu might not have been around long enough to enjoy this action. Mu may have been less than 200 feet above sea level on average! Though this is just a guess. It would thus have been very easy for this land to have submerged.

A HOLE IN THE EARTH?

There seems to be some suggestion that a hole in the middle of Mu opened up and the land sunk through it. Whether that is the case who can say, but it brings a strange picture to mind of the earth literally turning inside out! Picture it. Land sinking through a hole into the earth (Mu) and coming out the other side under the Atlantic creating the mid Atlantic ridge and Atlantis. This seems impossible but little is really known about the earth. The deepest we've ever dug or drilled down is only 8 miles. James Churchward seemed to think a series of cavities under Mu collapsed or exploded, but this seems unlikely or more would have occurred since, and it like suggesting the earth is made like a loaf of bread with more air bubbles then substance…though with the number of underground caverns this may be true.

MU'S POPULATION.

Churchward believed Mu was inhabited by 64, million people. With the distance of Mu from the place where Noah's ark landed I find it amazing it was inhabited much *at all*. With Peleg happening a mere 101 years after the flood, it's amazing that legends of Mu exist at all, but it's also a indication at the "fruitfulness" capabilities of the people that survived the flood. Though this is assuming the population and position of Mu as plotted by James Churchward is correct. This also assumes the first Peleg did Mu in. Possibly it lasted longer… up until the Exodus. This would give it a population base like legends suggest, though admittedly I've read precious few legends about Mu except mostly in Churchward's book.

CALENDAR RECALIBRATION

(3rd ed. Insert 2016) Churchward put the destruction of Mu very early, which I couldn't quite match up with the supposed population. He said 64 million, but if the destruction was the first post flood destruction, at the time of Peleg, a mere 101 years after the flood, this is obviously a set of incompatible deductions. However Frank Joseph (see Atlantis Rising #114) places the destruction of Lemuria (another name for Mu

I've found out) at 1628 BC. No details as to how he arrived at this date were mentioned and you have to see his book "The Lost Civilization of Lemuria"…which I don't have) but it does make a bit more sense as far as populations are concerned. Furthermore apparently many Thailand rituals still exist that are tied to Lemuria, something that also makes sense if we go with the more recent date for its demise. Could Atlantis and Mu have disappeared at the same time? (Atlantis submerged by volcanic action in the mid Atlantic ridge which spread the Atlantic ocean wider and pushed the Americas further west, forcing Mu under)

COULD A CONTINENT THE SIZE OF NORTH AMERICA JUST SINK?

Is it possible such a huge land mass could just disappear? And how could it? I suppose pressure from Asia moving eastward and the Americas moving west could force a lot of land in what is now the Pacific ocean downward, that is if there is a natural 'hole' for the land to have disappeared into. But it seems to me pressure from both sides of the Pacific would force some land upward causing mountain regions in the pacific and not just ocean. The lack of this sort of land in the Pacific area does suggest that the theory / legend of a hole in MU that sucked the land into it and pushed it out at other parts of the earth, as bizarre and extreme as that sounds, could have something to it. One would then conclude that for every ocean trench there would also be a ocean ridge. Or at least an equal amount of each feature.

Looking at the Pacific ocean floor for some sort of "hole" seems fruitless but the mechanics of the earth in this regard is anything but clear. Perhaps it just pushed it inward and downward as the oncoming lands encroached it, like the center part of a blender pulling down the top parts toward the blades. In fact the idea occurs to me that makes one wonder if such a continent not only got sucked under the ocean and forced land out the other areas of the earth via the Atlantic or other ridges, then this is like a sort equal and opposite action reaction, like cause and effect. This reasoning in a sense would mean that Mu was about the size of the Atlantic Ocean, if we assume the amount of ocean made in the Atlantic was the same amount of land sunk in the Pacific.

THE INTERLACED CONVEYER BELTS OF THE WORLD

Based on what we see in the Peru-Chile trench I have to think some sort of conveyer belt action is taking place with the continents, though I suppose one theory is as good as the next in light of current knowledge. Actually both theories could in fact be correct. The more I think about it the more this seems possible, so I guess I can't discount this bizarre "hole in the earth" theory completely, though I don't think there is really a hole in the earth that comes out the other side…now that would be a bottomless pit. But if we consider that the meteor that caused the flood could punch outward the fountains of the deep, then it also stands to reason that if the land masses were being sucked or pushed into the earth in one area, then 'land' was being pushed outward in some other area of the globe. This would in fact facilitate much easier continental movement.

Though I haven't really studied geology to any large extent, no doubt this science basically says the same thing. But it's interesting to think of this action happening at a far accelerated rate and what actions and forces would be acting on the areas where land was being pulled under via the trenches and pushed outward via the ridges. It's interesting looking at maps of the ridges and trenches of the earth.

Looking at the ocean floor maps we don't find any "hole" for land to be sucked into, other than trenches, though the floor is of quite a different nature under the western most part of the Pacific Ocean than in other parts around the globe. I have seen unusual mouths that are sort of crescent shaped. In this part of the Pacific Ocean there are some areas where trenches are circular or crescent shaped, so there may be something to this whole hole idea. I suppose if the land masses were moving at a speedy clip toward a subduction area it could well appear as a 'hole', for a while anyway.

Studying ocean floor maps we do see that land was pushed from the eastern part of the Pacific ocean into the oncoming continent of America so the idea that Mu Crashed into and became part of North America does seem to be a possibility. In fact maybe Mu was cut in half, half going toward North America merging with it and the other half getting sucked into the mouth of the earth. Interestingly Churchward would not have had these maps that show the Pacific ridges yet his surmising seems accurate when taking this ridge into consideration. This might also help in deciphering the actions of the water of the tsunamis. But If Mu was being pushed toward North America, then what continent is the American Geophysical Association referring to when they talk about "Pacifica"? Or put another way, just how big *was* Mu, and just how much water did fall on the earth in the flood?

This seems to confirm this earth is similar to an invertible ball hypothesis.

THE BEFORE AND AFTER PICTURES HELP DECIPHER THE EARTH MECHANICS BETTER.

It's difficult again to know what the continents originally looked like if you don't know what was there in the first place. One would have to study ancient maps and legends very carefully and compare them with today's to get a more accurate sense of the motion of the continents. Looking at the odd animated film clip of the continental drift they constantly show the land as it exists today and just move those land masses around. They don't seem to take into consideration the fact that some land disappeared.

For example we see off Peru some sort of manmade structures at 6000 feet below sea level. The west coast of South America got sucked underneath itself. I don't see any signs of people adding land to this area when they make these film clips. When these animation clips are run backwards showing where the land was originally, by putting the land back into the ridges where it was expulsed from, then the land you put back into the ridges has to come out somewhere else on the globe, likely out of the west Pacific mouths and at the leading edges of the various trenches around the world. Mind you no doubt this is a huge computing task.

To get a better idea of how the mechanics of the earth work one has to consider the before and after picture and see what has to be done to get from one to the other. With known ancient legendary land masses such as Mu, Atlantis and Lemuria (which I've since found out is another name for MU), any being replaced back onto a before picture and today's map of the world being the "after" picture experiments with the computing to see what motions are needed to get from one to the other will give a very accurate idea of just how the earth is made up. And this will also more accurately forecast future motions when more massive meteors hit in the future. Exacter evacuation plans could be put in place if a meteor of apocalyptic proportions was spotted. Assuming there was time and the governments actually decided to do this rather than "not cause a panic". "Please do Not Panic! You have three hours and fourteen minutes to get everybody off of Greenland"...or wherever. Well maybe some would escape...to what though?

As to how Hawaii got left so far from any continent remains a mystery to me, and it may merely be a volcanic reaction to pressure from both sides of the pacific, and indeed Hawaii is really a string of volcanoes...but then how do you account for the legends of these islands being parts of some larger landmass, if all they are is new volcanoes?

LUBED LAND LED TO A LARGER LURCH

One possibility, and this seems most likely given the clues we have, is the pyramids did something twice. So my guess is this. First the users of the pyramids broke the continents apart but they spread the newly formed continents perhaps only a mile or a few miles or so apart. Not realizing what caused the breakup of the continents or not thinking it was too serious they kept using the pyramids. Perhaps at first they were careful but when they got confident again they once again overextended the pyramid grid. However now that the drift had begun, with the motion started and the friction overcome, subsequent use of the pyramids exponentially increased this action because the continental undercarriage was all "lubed up". Once the continents had started moving it didn't take much to keep them moving, or speed them up drastically. In the second occurrence instead of a similar event happening the continents suddenly flung apart causing complete havoc worldwide.

THE SECOND FLOOD

As we referred to earlier we noted that the bible speaks of two floods. The second flood was the one that Abraham's forbears crossed over to get to where the Israelites ended up. We also suggested the mention of this flood seemed to indicate a possible time frame for this second flood to have occurred. So I repeat a bit here. Terah was born 222 years after the flood of Noah, and Terahs' father Nahor was born 163 years after the flood of Noah. With the original Peleg occurring at 101 years after the flood, this means Terah was born only 62 years after Peleg. It would seem to suggest that a second flood occurred around this period. This then fits with the deduction that maybe the initial Peleg didn't cause enough damage to cause concern and the pyramid grid continued to be used. With this continued use a further and far more violent dividing of the continents occurred and this second flood which is spoken of by Joshua then occurred. In areas around the earth the sea overran the land and this was when the pyramids ended up under all the silt and salt water that is evident on and around those structures.

ONE OF THE CONTINENTAL MOTIONS ACTUALLY MAPPED.

Ok if I've put you to sleep, wake up as you won't want to miss this one. Each meteor hit over time pushed the continents a little further apart each time, keeping the continents always in a state of motion. Residual movement would keep the continents always slowly moving and any additional serious meteoric impacts temporarily speeded up the drift in a renewed, though varying degrees of, cataclysmic fashion. All this was happening after the flood and thus during civilized times. This explains how the land bridge that connected South America to Antarctica could have been there long enough to be mapped. Ancient maps of Antarctica exist showing this continent turned 20 degrees from the present orientation. In the South Pacific (south 57, 120-140 west) is the Eltanin fracture zone and it is a twist of 20 degrees, this same 20 degrees… which means this twist occurred AFTER the continent was mapped. Again evidence that vastly advanced and civilized man was on earth at the time of the moving of the continents.

INDIRECT EVIDENCE: THE LACK OF CRATERS ON THE FACE OF THE EARTH.

One of the mysteries of the moon and the earth is that the moon has sustained bazillions of impact craters yet the earth seems to have somehow been missed by these impacts almost all together. The moon has thousands of impact craters, many of which overlap each other. Mercury too has this same surface feature. Yet oddly Mars and Earth show little or no such scarring. It was for this reason that initially, astronomers didn't believe that the surface features of the moon were even craters, but they thought they were some sort of feature done by volcanic action or some other inexplicable internal cause. But as we all now know these are in fact impact craters. So why do the moon and Mercury have so many and the earth and Mars so few?

One reasonable explanation has been theorized that earth and all the solar system did come under the same exact bombardment, but because of the nature of the earth and Mars these impact craters were healed because of action due to the primordial state of the planets as they formed. The moon and mercury being smaller bodies cooled faster so these craters remained. But this theory is based on an old universe and a mythical primordial earth that would foster some sort of evolutionary process. But as we have shown, that the earth and the universe are in fact much younger, and these primordial soup pixies evolving matter into life are nonexistent. So how DO you explain the difference. It's actually quite simple. Water.

As we have seen Mars took a lot of our water after the flood. At that time Mars would have been riddled with craters from the planet that exploded so near its orbit. But when the water from the earth splashed down on Mars it was like a chalk board eraser wiping out all the craters. Then the water subducted under the surface and some possibly migrated to the poles of Mars, leaving a mysteriously clean slate; an almost craterless face. Sounds like a cure for acne…just add water, scrub and dry: voila, no more craters.

((2nd ed. Insert 2008) My ad stated that recent information found on Mars confirmed part of this book. Before the add was placed I had always understood that both the polar caps were made of dry ice (carbon dioxide) and no water ice. A friend who had read this part of the book then told me of breaking news in June 2008 that the Martian lander had shown that the [North] polar cap was made of water ice. After the add was placed I found in a relatively recent book on the planets that it was understood that the north cap actually contained a lot of water ice and that only the south cap was all dry ice. I did not know this at the time I wrote that possibly some of the water migrated to the poles. Since this is still breaking news the results are not all in. But already it seems clear that water ice exists at the Martian North Pole, and as crystal ice in the dirt near the Martian North Pole. Furthermore it has recently been realized that the Martian South Pole also probably has a large water ice content as well. So I still give myself a three-quarter point for going out on a limb saying what I understood was supposed to be "dry ice", was in fact probably water ice.)

This subduction might have taken many years and Mars may have looked very similar to earth, possibly for even a hundred or more years. And Mars may even have returned periodically to get more water until another big asteroid knocked some sense back into Mars and told it to go back where it belonged. (3rd ed. insert I've since found out that Mars did have an water body the size of the Arctic Ocean at one time. See chapter 5)

We have shown also that man likely was trying to protect the earth from the asteroids before the flood, but they likely were not trying to protect the moon. But even if we completely discount the protection theory, then many meteors would have hit the earth after the flood as we can see that the number of heavenly objects falling to earth was considerably more numerous even in ancient recorded history. So why are there not more craters? Well I suppose those people that were protecting the earth before the flood could still be protecting it now, but again if this is nonsense to some, then there still should be hundreds of craters visible all around the earth. Where are they?

The answer again is water. But the water is where the water is and the land is where the land is. How is the water on earth going to erase all the craters that should be evident on land? This is more evidence and another clue that the continents moved at a rate fast enough to displace the water. When the land moved, the water in many places overran the land, and erased the vast majority of the craters like sea waves destroying sand castles.

Possibly the water that came rushing over the land in some areas froze instantly. How could this happen? Realize that not only is the land moving, so too is the air and even the entire shell of atmosphere is in disturbance as the continents move. Water would have leapt out of the lakes, and indeed legends speak of this very action. With the land moving and the air of the globe in upheaval causing incredible vortexes in the air, the chill of space in some areas around the globe descended to earth possible flash freezing the water, or land and creatures in some areas. If this happened with lakes this would account for some types of glaciations. Ocean water moving over the land would be one body moving fast, going over, then receding from the land, with no chance for it to freeze, though possibly some salt lakes would then form. Rapidly moving land and the consequences of that happening will explain and solve some of the mysteries found in geology and of course solve the riddle of the frozen mammoths.

German and Swiss lakes and fens were studied by H. Gams and R. Nordhagen and found that into recent times (Neolithic or recent stone age or the middle of the second millennium B.C. and the eighth century B.C.) the lakes were subjected to high water catastrophes, that were accompanied by very strong tectonic movements where the lakes suddenly lost their horizontal position, so that old strand lines could be seen to run obliquely to the horizon. Lake Constance rose 30 feet and the bed was tilted. These same effects were seen in the Bavarian Alps, in Norway and Sweden and it was concluded that all these places had these events happen in the same ages. (Book 53 page 161-162)

FROZEN MAMMOTHS EXPLAINED

Another interesting fact fits in here. People with their sled dogs have on occasion found their dogs eating something that turned out to be a frozen wooly mammoth. Since the meat from a woolly mammoth was no doubt extremely old they waited to see if the dogs would die, because in that length of time the meat surely would have become toxic.

However their dogs survived, so the dog owners also ate some and were fine. Though that story is easily found in many references I have not been able to find a reference for the following so this may be word of mouth, or I may have neglected to note it, but if my memory serves me, around 1896 there was a huge banquet and after the meal it was announced to everyone there, that they had just eaten the oldest meat in the world, that of a wooly mammoth. How could such old meat still be good?

Many mammoths have been found flash frozen, such as one found in perfectly crystal clear ice in 1799. In fact rumors existed that the Wooly Mammoth was still alive or certainly that it still existed as sightings by Peary's crew and hunters attest, but these may simply have been sightings of these mammoths encased in clear ice, possibly as the ice floated and moved. Autopsies done on mammoths have found tropical vegetation in their stomachs no longer growing in the areas where they were found.

But there comes a point when one wonders how wooly mammoths could freeze so fast? Experts have taken this story and wondered why the dogs and people didn't die because an entire wooly mammoth would take a very long time to freeze properly... in fact too long. The meat would be toxic before it froze, and those toxic agents would be in the meat and remain until it thawed or was eaten and would kill anybody eating the meat. The meat would have to have been frozen in an incredibly short period of time, far faster than the environment would allow. It's been a mystery as to how it could freeze that fast.

It is said that, for the meat of the woolly mammoth to have been in the preserved state it was in, the temperature would had to have suddenly drop to minus 150 degrees Fahrenheit, as much as 80 or more degrees colder than has ever been recorded on earth! But it would appear that it did just that, and that the animals died incredibly suddenly because in one case the mammoth was still in the process of eating buttercups! The very fact that the mammoth was frozen in mid chew means it had to have been frozen instantly! This is further evidence of massive global cataclysmic events occurring.

((2nd ed. Insert 2008) I had read the lowest temperatures on earth were something like -58. But reading "Icebound' by DR. Jerri Nielson after finishing this book, I found that the lowest temperatures ever recorded on the earth was -129.3 (Page 37) recorded in the Vostoc base Antarctica. When one considers Antarctica in the equation along with the rest of Peleg, we can get a pretty good idea of how the mammoths might have frozen instantly. At minus 58 a glass of water can be thrown into the air and come down as snow. Even at a mere minus 70 F a mere couple minutes of exposed skin causes frostbite. The altitude of Antarctica is between 9 1/2 and 10 thousand feet above sea level, with low pressure and little oxygen, thus facilitating extreme cold temperature.

If we consider the earth actually tumbling as we have to conclude occurred on occasion in the past, with temperatures like this -120 somewhere on earth this cold air is going to move and move fast. Any unprotected mammoths, not actually wearing deep freeze woollies are going to be subject to these temperatures coming at them at wind speeds of 100 to 3-400 miles an hour! The wind-chill temperatures I think would dip to minus 200 or more! That coupled with the thought of the chill of space actually plummeting to the earth's surface, makes instantly frozen woolly mammoths suddenly seem quite explainable.)

Autopsies have been done on at least one of these mammoths because they are in such a perfect state of preservation, and the findings are interesting. They found a fractured hip, and leg, clotted blood in the chest, unswallowed grass which all means a sudden and violent death. It's even likely the movement of the land caused the mammoth to stumble, cracking its hip! What could kill and freeze a mammoth that fast?

The answer is the sky went berserk as a result of the continents hurtling themselves away from each other. The chill of space came down and flash froze the mammoths while they were in a temperate zone.

This means a sudden temperature drop of at least 200 degrees occurred. The spot the mammoths happened to be was flung into or became a northern region. If the land moved slowly, the mammoth would have partially or completely thawed and rotted or killed the dogs. Though the place these mammoths have been found was never subject to an ice age, that is with glaciers, the temperature in this area has been so stable that these mammoths have not thawed out all this time, yet when the event occurred it was in a temperate zone. This means the land had to move very fast and or the earth had to suddenly alter its normal movements. Since some mammoths have been found encased in crystal clear ice, water over ran the then frozen the mammoths where they stood creating mammothsicles, not found at your local grocer. (I wonder how big the stick would need to be for these mammothsicles, or maybe they were meant to be Mammothkibobs)

The very fact that these frozen mammoths exist is clear solid evidence that these cataclysms occurred, and shows the extent of them.

Peleg gives the answer to these perplexing dilemmas that geologist gloss over to avoid the obvious conflicts with their pet theories. During the polar shifts and the rapidly moving continental drift, not just the physical makeup of the earth was being altered, but the very air and atmosphere was subject to this force. Vortexes of atmosphere were of such an extreme nature that there were areas on earth where the very chill of space itself came to fill these vortex voids, creating holes in the sky or "windows", by the rapidly moving land. Manned flight on the earth likely would simply have been impossible with the ferocious winds pulling any and all craft to the earth.

The actual vacuum of space and the temperature of that space touched down in spots briefly. Perhaps not the actual vacuum of space but maybe the stratosphere. The temperature of space is somewhere in the neighborhood of 4 degrees KELVIN! That is enough of a chill to even quick freeze an entire wooly mammoth. It has been noted that meteors tend to fall in the northern regions more frequently, suggesting the Earth protective Van Allen belts or some other physiological aspect of earth's protective atmosphere steer them that way, and it may also figure in the causes of the flash frozen mammoths.

MORE ON DATA CONCERNING FREEZING WOOLLY MAMMOTHS.

(3rd ed. Insert 2016) Meat freezes at the rate of about one foot of thickness every 24 hours. If the meat is too big, the middle of the meat would stay heated and rot out. Mammoths had to freeze within 5 hours or less because of the small crystals found in the blood. If it took longer the crystals would have been larger. To get a mammoth as found, you would have to stop the stomach from digesting the food. Even when the animal is dead the stomach continues to digest the food, and the food in the mammoths was not digested! The only way to freeze the mammoths this fast it to have the temperature drop to 300 below zero! But the coldest temperature ever recorded on earth is -127. Clearly the chill of space had to drop to the surface where the mammoths were and blow fiercely, and you have to ask yourself what could cause this. Something far more catastrophic had to have occurred on the earth than your modern scientists are willing to admit, otherwise the mystery of the frozen mammoths would have long ago been figured out.

NO RICOCHETS

(3rd ed. Insert 2016) As a confirmation for the deduction given for the cause of the sudden death and freezing so fast of the mammoths, another detail of their demise has been found. Both Bison and Mammoth remains in Alaska and Siberia have evidence of being hit by high speed blasts of debris from outer space. Holes examined in these remains were determined to be "…caused by high-speed collisions with tiny fragments coming from meteoric impact explosions of some kind". The fragments were analyzed and were magnetic and the combination of elements in them indicated they came from outer space. Some of the bison remains show continued growth around the wounds indicating that some of them survived the event. "-the case for a sudden catastrophic event becomes virtually inescapable." (Atlantis Rising # 68)

MAJOR EVENTS HAPPENED AFTER PELEG

If we presume that the continents started to drift at the birth of Peleg, and then in a subsequent Peleg shortly after this, we then find that there is a problem with the time frame.

Between 1880 and 1900 more than 10 million pairs of elephant tusks were found on mass extinction sites in Siberia. (not counting all the other mammoths found before and after that) This is where the bulk of carved ivory comes from. Peleg happened 101 years after the flood.

OK we know that Noah took two of each unclean animal and seven of each clean animal aboard the Ark. Assuming a woolly mammoth is a clean animal and one male and six females were taken and they multiplied at as fast a rate as they possibly could with twins in every womb, it is still highly unlikely that from those 7 mammoths they could produce over 10 million wooly mammoths in 101 years. This is a problem, but it also a clue.

If there is no way 10,000,000 Elephants and mammoths could be produced by the time of Peleg, then Peleg was not the main source of mass extinctions and the continents were only partially created in the initial Peleg action. This makes sense as we have already deduced, along with Mu's population.(assuming Churchward's population figures are correct)

MORE POSSIBLE EVENT MATCH-UPS AND CORRELATIONS

As we have seen the Egyptians speak of four ages when the stars changed their course in the heavens. Assuming the Egyptians were not counting what might have happened at the time of the flood when the killer asteroid belted the earth to who knows where, Peleg would likely have been the first recorded time the stars changed course, though possibly Peleg occurred before the Egyptians came into being, meaning Peleg could be a fifth such change in direction. (This is because the Egyptian 1st Dynasty started after the reign of the gods, about 300 years after the flood, and probably after the tower of Bable when they actually became "Egyptians". So Egyptians as we know them may not have become a factor in recording history until later, though as a people they would have remembered events prior to the end of the reign of the gods, so Peleg might be the first recorded alteration of the heavens anyway.)

A second Peleg around Abraham's grandfathers' time might be the second change in the stellar motions, and this too might also precede the Egyptians, as this second event likely happened before the reign of the gods ended. (We know Abraham's fathers served the gods) I think the second Peleg was the cause that ended the reign of the gods with them leaving and all the building sites around the globe then left unfinished. It appears that the time of the Exodus was the third time the stars changed direction, possibly Joshua telling the sun and moon to stand still was the fourth, and the sun turning backward 10 degrees during Isaiah's time the fifth age and the Earthquake during King Uzziah's reign (II Kings 20) (the likely time of the final destruction of Atlantis) the sixth age...an extra one. So the bible certainly has enough clues to corroborate ancient histories found in other cultures that speak of incredible disasters and changes in the motions of the stars and moon.

In Chinese history during a time of war between the Duke of Lu-Yang and Han the sun went down and the sun came back. (book 14 pg 242)

In the book of the dead Apep, the enemy of Ra makes Ra go back.(book 61 pg 168)

These histories and legends could allude to the same event as Isaiah.

Also clues that suggest the vastness of the population of Mu again would mean that Peleg 1 was not the cause of Mu's destruction either. So it appears Peleg only got the ball rolling...no pun intended. Subsequent asteroid impacts must have caused the continuation of the original Peleg motion caused by the pyramids. Based on the clues it would appear that the time of the Israelites exodus was the time of the worst and most complete Peleg actions. So the bulk of the mammoths likely were killed in this time frame as were likely the dinosaurs. This would be enough time for 10 million mammoths to have come into being. I suppose one could put the dinosaurs destruction at the time of second Peleg, but with the mixing up of the strata in the earth at the time of the exodus there's no reason to suggest the dinosaurs and mammoths were not contemporary. In fact some of the most well known dinosaurs may actually be still alive. (see next chapter)

THE TERRIBLE WATER

With the continents suddenly moving at a terrifying pace, the water around the globe was displaced, like someone shifting in a bathtub so fast that the water leaps over the edge. One can't stress enough the massive waves occurring around the globe. I read at some point about some ancient legends and the fear of the waves, but failing at the time to realize the significance I wasn't paying attention and didn't keep track of the references, but suffice it to say some ancient histories do speak of these waves. It wasn't the earthquakes and volcanoes that killed so many living creatures so much as the waves. Andrew Tomas does however ask, was "…an older civilization destroyed by tidal waves…?" indicating he too had come across this evidence. (Book 11, pg. 173)

Massive amounts of water overrunning the continents would also leave other strange monuments to the water taking land away. Though this would explain mysterious erratic boulders in the middle of nowhere, it would also explain other earth surface geological sites. Any firmer islands of rock or stone would be left high above the plains around them like pillars in a wasteland, like these chimney rocks seen in the deserts.

Huge rocks would be left lying willy-nilly around plains as the incredible amounts of water pushed rocks with movements that one would not normally attribute to water. This would also account for the vast and extreme movement of dirt to cover up cities and bury mastodons above them. This would also account for the lion's share of the silt on the ocean floors.

I saw this following bit of evidence long after I had come up with this theory. (Sorry I saw this on TV so I wasn't prepared for what I saw and didn't take notes so I recount this from memory)

In Washington state and to some extent in neighboring states there are details of topography that long stood as inexplicable. One "maverick" in the 19th century went to the sight and felt that large amounts of water must have created these features, but the amount of water he was talking about seemed to have no explanation, and he was ridiculed.

Upon further recent examination by other scientists and miniature scale models, it was determined that large amounts of water likely *did* create these features, but it was still not certain just where this water came from. So they devised a plausible theory, based on the ice age and a landlocked lake created by melting ice.

They felt a lake such as this would hold massive amounts of water that may have originally just been a melting glacier. The edge of this glacier which was still a frozen mass was actually holding back the billions of gallons of water. But as the glacier melted the ice dam holding back the water became saturated. Then at one point the dam just gave away and an entire lake came rushing west. Interesting how that now accepted theory so closely mirrors the theory of a westwardly mobile continent and the subsequent water overrunning the continent. The water went one way then as the water receded in the reverse direction. I suppose both actions could account for these features, and no doubt further study of the area would have to be done with this theory in mind. This could also explain the Grand Canyon.

A SATELLITE'S VIEW

I was looking on the computer at the Google earth program for some sites mentioned in this research. Google earth is such a fascinating site that one easily gets sidetracked when not sticking to an agenda. In one such sidetrack while looking for pyramids in the Himalayas and in China I stumbled across a vast and obvious landmark in the midst of the Himalayan mountains. Clearly this was a rippled plain and not a series of mountains. Even the terrain was fairly uniform in height above sea level and varied only by the ripples themselves. Although the vastness of this area is as large as the Caspian Sea, the details of the terrain instantly reminded me of ripples in sand caused by water, but these ripples had to be maybe hundreds of miles in length and several miles in width. I was convinced this was a hydraulic action that caused these features, though I couldn't recall any legends about this specific area. And these features seemed kind of extreme. The very next day while diving further into my notes I came across this...

Chinese history tells of a time when the sun didn't go down for ten days. (Was China a temporary pole?) During this period forests ignited and all sorts of "abominable vermin" came from somewhere. (Book 14 pg. 114) This account is very similar to the plagues of Egypt, and apparently this occurred at the same time, giving further evidence that the biblical record is an accurate one. Furthermore water over-topped the great heights threatening the heavens with their floods. This water swept over mountains and was trapped in valleys between the mountains. The land was flooded for decades. This occurred in the days of Yahou and this may be the time of the Israelites in the wilderness. (Yahou as mentioned before might be another possible pronunciation of the four letter Hebrew word YHWH, the name for God, so this fits very well indeed) Not to mention Velikovsky noted that people around the Israelites prayed to Yahou after learning that name from them.

Could water overrun the Himalayan mountains? Erratics on mountains such as the Isle of Man and Harz Mountains in Germany are there only because of waves putting them there. It would seem legends and evidence lead to the same conclusion. Now one might think there is just no way the waves could possibly reach 30,000 feet. I agree this does sound extreme. However there is one possibility here. We know India came crashing into southern Asia as the continents moved. We also are saying this motion was incredibly speeded up. This event may have happened very fast and the water got caught in between the two land masses as they collided together, creating China in the first place. Chinese history before this time is virtually nonexistent. There is more Chinese ancient history that speaks of the second or changed heaven. Consider this. In the beginning of the second heaven the earth was shaken to the foundations. The sky sank; the sun, moon, planets, and stars changed motion, the earth fell to pieces and water overflowed it. (book 31 pg 41)

I repeat myself here as one legends shows a couple points. Mind you once the water get's going who's to say it can't overrun the mountains. (Thus the reason for this part of my cover art, which has a likeness of that famous wave in it overrunning the mountains.)

A great cataclysm legend of China was recorded by Martinus, a Jesuit historian and quoted by Robert Scrutton...

"At the beginning of the second heaven, the earth was shaken to its foundation. The sky sank lower and lower towards the north. The Sun, Moon and stars changed their motion. [They appeared to do this because the inclination of the earth's axis was changing.] The earth fell to pieces, and the waters in its bosom uprushed with violence and overflowed it.... The system of the universe was all disordered. The planets altered their courses, and the great harmony of the universe and nature was disrupted..." (quoting book 31 pg 41, including the [] brackets.)

Is it legend, myth, or a remnant account of what happened? Looking at the geological evidence and the corroborating legends it must be concluded to be a witness account of an actual event.

IF WE LET OUR MINDS WANDER INTO THE LAND OF IMAGINATION.....

(3rd ed. Insert 2016) A few books in the mid to late 1970's based on seers like Edgar Cayce, warned of doomsday at the end of the millennium, looked into the possibility and wrote some fascinating books about what could happen. One such person was John White who wrote Pole Shift (I've not read this book, but it sounds similar to *We Are The Earthquake Generation* by Jeffrey Goodman from 1978 [Book 19 in my bibliography]) White asks us what would be the result of a pole shift, then he gives a list of events. "Enormous tidal waves would roll across the continents as the oceans became displaced from their basins. Electrical storms with hurricane winds of hundreds of miles per hour would sweep the planet. Tremendous earthquakes and lava flows would wrack the land. Poisonous gases and ash would fill the skies. Geography would be altered as seabeds rose and land masses submerged. Climates would change instantly." He goes on to mention poles would melt and new poles would form. "Last of all, huge numbers of organisms would be destroyed, including people, with signs of their existence hidden under thick layers of debris, sediment, and ice or at the bottom of newly established seas" (See Atlantis Rising # 81 Page 23) (I'll toss in signs of civilization would be found under and inside mountains as well) He felt this was a presentable case but not necessarily a provable one. Really?

I say look around you, and in the entire world we live in, and you will have your case adequately proven to the max. Legends of Atlantis and Mu, submerged buildings found around the globe, Boats found inside mountains, vast fields of fossils and masses of extinct species clustered together in fossil fields all around the globe, rock formations sitting at crazy angles, civilizations found deeply buried, evidence of water overrunning the continents, evidence of what we call ice ages, whole lava forming ridges underwater, evidences of sudden and dramatic climate change worldwide. He almost perfectly described the planet as it is seen today.

Clearly something like this has already happened, but more sobering, people wrote histories about these very things happening only a few thousand years ago. I would say that we've answered the question from the beginning of this chapter completely.

Time to wake up uniformitarian's and smell the fossils.

SOME 'RECENT' HISTORY.

(3rd ed. Insert 2016) Most of the events of world impact, like Peleg, Atlantis's demise, Mars coming close to the earth, continents shifting are all before Christ. So historians tend to completely discount any fantastic stories myths or histories linked to such events, even though the stories seem to be worldwide and are supported by each other when you can match up time lines, any legends or events. But a similar type of world event appears to have occurred after Christ as well, when supposedly records of history were more precisely written. ...and indeed though this next period is clouded in mystery, the dates of the events spoken of are more accurate.

To put a sort of exclamation point to this theme, Mark Andrew, while doing some research on the King Arthur story, which seemed a bit mysterious, consequently had some questions which caused him to come across some curious information. Was Arthur a legend? Myth? Or composite history? Before the Arthur period the Roman Empire, history of wars, treaties and such were precisely recorded, but the 6th century seemed to be filled with fantastic stories almost as if to fill in lost history...and not just for Britain, but seemingly the entire world. Indeed the 6th century history around the globe is behind some sort of strange obscuring veil. He stumbled on some curious facts about the dendrochronolgy from the period. From Europe, to Sweden, from Mongolia to California, and on down to into Chile...the whole world's tree records showed "dramatic effects from 536 to 545 AD". "A spring without mildness and a summer without heat", "Failures of Bread", which coincided with a plague in Britain that lasted about 20 years called the Yellow plague and might also be the same as the Justinian Plague which erupted in the early 540's. In China there's also a record of yellow dust raining like snow accompanied by drought, summer frosts, massive flooding and deaths from famine. Simultaneously South America was devastated by drought.

Of this time period it was commented that "It displayed all the hallmarks of nuclear winter." A loud noise that was heard in China in 535 is thought to have been Krakatoa, and ice cores from this period show evidence of mid 6th century volcanic activity. On top of this some scientists have concluded that a half kilometer sized comet appears to have exploded in the upper atmosphere and affected Australia around 535 AD. Around 530 AD shooting stars and meteor showers are recorded in China and the Mediterranean. One writer from the period wrote "something mysterious and unusual seems to coming on us from the stars". And in 538 a comet was sighted by a historian named Edward Gibbon which was seen for 40 days or more. He expected wars, and calamities because of it "and these expectations were abundantly fulfilled." This or another comet was written about by Zachariah of Mitylene in 538 through to 539 which was visible for 100 days. Another historian named Roger of Wendover wrote about a comet in Gaul in 541 that was so vast that the whole sky appeared to be on fire, and subsequently drops of blood rained from the clouds and people died afterwards. A monk named Gildas wrote around 540 that "the island of Britain was on fire from sea to sea". This bit of evidence is thought to have indicated to Wilson and Blackett that Britain was made partially uninhabitable because of a comet and was thus easily overrun by the Saxons because there were so few Britons left to stop them. Yet another record by a "John of Asia" (554 AD) described "the world shaking like a tree before a wind for 10 days." On and on. (For the whole story see Atlantis Rising #99.) If these histories are singled out, the way that some of the ancient myths are, these stories could seem fantastic. But because they are all dated reasonably closely we can only conclude these events were happening around the globe.

We see that the earth appeared to be in the middle of a perfect storm of comets, earthquakes, volcanic activity, and who knows what else that was a global phenomena and lasted between 10 and 20 years. But the effects were so dramatic it caused migrations of people all over the globe trying to find greener pastures…or in fact *any* pastures that could sustain them. No place on earth seemed to be unaffected. People stopped writing historic accounts in some places as just staying alive was more important. In fact it would seem that this series of events was in fact the very cause of the Dark Ages that lasted up to the renaissance. The point being, if this span of about 20 years of comparatively mild worldwide catastrophic activity from a relatively recent period between 535 and 545 AD could plunge the world into the dark ages, then we can see how the events spoken of before Christ could seem so incomprehensible, unintelligible, and mythical to historians and archaeologists.

FUTURE HITS TO COME

Nowadays people want you to believe that asteroids of any consequence rarely hit the earth, while at the same time governments are trying to set up asteroid smashing technology. What are they afraid of? Don't they believe the cosmologists, or do they know something they don't want to panic us with? As stated only recently was it admitted that on average an asteroid the size of a house hits the earth once a month! The bible tells of an asteroid that will hit earth and ruin much of the world's fresh water supply. Have observatories found this asteroid? Is this the reason asteroid smashing technology is being seriously looked into?

The bible speaks of many of these disasters in differing contexts, present tense, past tense and prophetic future tense. One of the earliest books is Job and in Job 28:9 it appears to be past tense. "He putteth forth his hand upon the rock; he overturneth the mountains by the roots." Habakkuk appears to be recounting Joshua's time with some interesting descriptions. Chapter 3 verse 6 …the everlasting mountains were scattered…" verse 11 The sun and moon stood still, and verse 15 they didst walk through the sea with thine horses through the heap of great waters. (this last description seems to be clearly about the Israelites passing over the red sea which suggests the whole text is concerning the time of Moses and NOT Joshua, thus hinting that the sun and moon stood still for Moses as well as Joshua.) I've tried to include as many of the more specific past or present tense references as I could find in context. Now here are some of the prophetic ones. When read in contemporary context of the geological history as seen above and then with others scriptures seen together in their prophetic context they paint a frightful picture that I don't think is wise to overlook.

TO SEE WHAT HAS BEEN, ALSO HELPS US SEE WHAT IS TO BE.

There are some interesting and frightening prophecies in the bible that resemble what it must have been like in the time of Peleg or the Exodus. Though these are prophesies they are also very logical in context of what we've just read. It would appear that we are due for a very similar event to Peleg sometime in the near future. Amos 8:8-9 Shall not the land tremble for this, and every one mourn that dwelleth therein? and it shall rise up wholly as a flood; and it shall be cast out and drowned, as by the flood of Egypt. (9) And it shall come to pass in that day, saith the Lord, that I will cause the sun to go down at noon, and

I will darken the earth in the clear day." (Interestingly it also speaks of the flood of Egypt, a third flood!, possibly the one that partially buried the pyramids.) Revelation 6:14 "And the heaven departed as a scroll when it is rolled together; and every mountain and island moved out of their places...." Shortly after this event the winds of the earth stop blowing (Rev. 7:1) Revelation 16:18- 20 mentions a similar event, possibly the same event or a follow up event. 18 "And there were voices, and thunders, and lightning's; and there was a great earthquake, such as was not since men were upon the earth, so mighty an earthquake, and so great" 20 "And every island fled away, and the mountains were not found." This could be a reversal of the motion of the continents, a sort of Peleg in reverse...or a sudden continuation of the original motion that caused the continents in the first place.

There may even be a warning sign in relation to this. First Thessalonians 5: 3 "For when they shall say, Peace and safety; then sudden destruction cometh upon them,..." Isaiah 13:10 For the stars of heaven and the constellations thereof shall not give their light : the sun shall be darkened in his going forth, and the moon shall not cause her light to shine.

Then as punishment for evil and wickedness, pride arrogance and haughtiness Isaiah 13:13 continues. Therefore I shall shake the heavens, and the earth shall remove from her place,...24:1 BEHOLD, the LORD maketh the earth empty, and maketh it waste, turneth it upside down, and scattereth abroad the inhabitants thereof.

Showing the intensity of what is to come it says that if you flee the noise you will get caught in the pit, if you escape the pit you will get caught in a snare... Isaiah 24:18-20 .... for the windows from on high are open and the foundations of the earth do shake(19) The earth is utterly broken down, the earth is clean dissolved, the earth is moved exceedingly.(20) The earth shall reel to and fro like a drunkard, and shall be removed like a cottage;.... (the earth being removed like a cottage could allude to the earth moving out of her normal orbit.)

Isaiah 40:4 Every valley shall be exalted, and every mountain shall be made low:... Ezekiel 38:20 (when Gog attacks Israel from the North) "...the mountains shall be thrown down, and the steep places shall fall, and every wall shall fall to the ground." To date no such earthquake has accomplished this feat so it speaks of an incredible earthquake indeed!

Ezekiel goes on in Verse 22:"...an overflowing rain, and great hailstones, fire, and brimstone." Gog is defeated and only 1/6 of the army returns home. The earthquakes and other events spoken of above may be a result of the weapon used on Gog when it attacks Israel, or it could speak of another time after Gog returns home and a bigger army...possibly the battle of Armageddon...attacks Israel.

The description of this weapon or "plague" is now very apparent as to what it speaks of. Zechariah 19:12 "And this shall be the plague wherewith the Lord will smite all the people that have fought against Jerusalem; their flesh shall consume away while they stand upon their feet, and their eyes shall consume away in their holes, and their tongue shall consume away in their mouth." This appears to be a very graphic description of nuclear war, and it appears it is so intense it causes the earth to go, among other things. a.w.o.l from its orbit.

Frightening stuff but ironically it may well mean the evolutionary geologists may eventually see how fossils are formed, first hand. I'm not looking forward to this.

FORESHADOW OF THINGS TO COME.

There's an American Onondaga Indian Prophesy that says the end of the world will be near when the trees start dying from the top down. In Toronto it's been noted that tops of trees are dying or have died in that area. This has been traced to contrails that use aluminum. (something that comes out of airplanes.) (A.R.m #113 pg 17) More evidence that we and the earth are slowly dying with us on board and we seem to be speeding up the process.

Chapter 7

DINOSAURS: WHEN? THEN, AND TODAY

I f as we have shown, the earth is really a very young place and creature fossils and ages shown in previous chapters are correct, then I should also be able to show that dinosaurs are not millions of years old as well. Since we've already gone over the basic dating methods used to arrive at these dates, we need more tangible evidence to show dinosaurs are a more recent creature then paleontologists would have us believe. Since we are showing a very young earth this means that these dinosaurs must have been contemporary with man. Paleontologists say this never happened, but rather they say that man came by long after the dinosaurs were extinct.

SWITCHING ERAS CHANGED SPECIES?

(3rd ed. Insert 2016) Darwin wondered how it could be that so many species could become extinct at the same time and that subsequently so many 'new' species could appear immediately following the extinction of those species. Simultaneously he kept trying to explain away the obvious evidence of worldwide catastrophes as the cause of the change. But there's no alternative to catastrophism to account for the evidence. As for 'new' species, the waves overran the continents as the continents moved, wiping out many species, and simultaneously this action lost much atmosphere to space and the effect, allowing more radiation to the earth stunting and reducing many species giving the appearance of new species. Louis Agassiz noted extinct fish species were better developed and further advanced than later 'modern' species. Similarly many 'ancient' versions of land animals were larger by far than contemporary versions; such as six foot beavers and wombats the size of Mini Coopers.

LE GASP...LE PANT.

(3rd ed. Insert 2016) One new theory on the extinction of dinosaurs is nostril size, which were the same size as that of a horse, which they think would have caused some dinosaurs to suffocate, though the fact they made it that big doesn't seem to have bothered them. But as we've seen the oxygen content was at least 35-50% higher, and the air pressure was higher too...probably double to triple.

MELLOWING FOR MILLIONS OF YEARS?

(3rd ed. Insert 2016) At least one oil company buys into the belief that oil took millions of years to create they and even show on their cans dinosaurs melting and mellowing underground for millions of years like beer or something. Maybe they don't know that radiocarbon analysis of the oil from the Gulf of Mexico measured the age of this oil, not in millions of years but in thousands...well within the range of Radio Carbon's dating accuracy range. (book 53 page 259) Furthermore oil comes from deep in the ground, yet no explanation of how dinosaurs got 1/4 mile or more underground has ever been presented. If that isn't enough, the number of dinosaurs needed to make all that oil are beyond the realms of reality as literally billions of dinosaurs would have had to roam around, die without decomposing on the ground or get eaten up by crows or whatever, then be planted deep underground. And if that isn't enough, the time limit for oil underground to maintain the pressure adequate to come gushing out of the ground when drilled into is maxed out at about 10,000 years before the pressure dissipates into the surrounding strata. Is any of this getting through? Don Gunter while drilling in the gulf of Mexico for oil drilled down through 14,000 feet of mud and silt then drilled through a tree for 60 feet. Think about that! And it was a tree, not coal. Hmmm… did I just contradict myself? If we think of North America moving west, meeting resistance that starts the Americas to sub duct under itself like a conveyer belt this could explain this tree found 14,000 feet down. >cough< and maybe even dinosaurs…but other things considered, still farfetched.

SUDDEN IMPACT

I recall watching TV when I was ten and I believe a segment of Galapagos Island came on, and large fin backed lizards were right there on TV. I sat transfixed waiting to see if they moved. (this was around 1968 when computer imaging was not a factor) It quickly became clear, it wasn't simply a very good painting or a photograph; these creatures moved! This was footage! This was real and I exclaimed "DINOSAURS!!!" Everyone in the room assured me they were not dinosaurs but just big lizards. I said 'No! I've seen these in dinosaur books!', and they insisted that they were not dinosaurs but just looked like the dinosaurs. At least that was a concession but I looked around the room and I couldn't believe they couldn't see how obvious it was that these were in fact dinosaurs. Yes, perhaps a relative species but dinosaurs just the same. This sudden realization that dinosaurs still existed but were called something else has stuck with me all my life. I wanted to see if in fact there was any validity to this theory. It turns out there is. But we'll get to that in a bit.

SOME DINOSAURS MIGHT NOT BE TOO FRIENDLY

Is there any evidence of them existing in ancient times contemporary with man? This might prove difficult because I'm sure dinosaurs might not be too friendly with man, so man would live in different areas…deliberately. Man would want to get away from them as far as possible, if not for the danger aspect to themselves certainly for their families sake. So finding evidence of them in the same place at the same time might prove difficult.

With this scenario likely the case, a site where dinosaurs would be found could then be interpreted as any age any paleontologist would want you to think, and how do you refute that, if there is no evidence of man in the vicinity? I mean do you want to go camping where there are known to be man eating dinosaurs lurking? I think not! "Just ignore it dear and pass the potato salad". So dinosaur evidence and man's evidence would almost be mutually exclusive…well unless you like living on the edge! So any evidence of man living with dinosaurs might be extremely scarce. However it does exist!

Important to remember also is that the people with these dinosaurs were not necessarily "cave men". They appear to be a cross section. Some were sophisticated people, some were "Cave men". We simply have to stop equating dinosaurs and saber toothed tigers with cave men. Remember too that some of the evidence found is on sophisticated pottery and figures, ancient buildings and written documents. These records and this evidence isn't from a cave man named Thag sticking his hand in the fire to discover pain here.

I will use the conventional dating methods just to show the apparent contradictions of the evidence, but most of these dinosaur fossils would likely have been made 3300-687 BC. (possibly even as late as 540 AD)

Usually I save the better items for last but some people are so against the idea that man and dinosaur lived together we need to start off with a solid item to promote more ready acceptance of that which follows.

The most famous and controversial site in the world that I know of is in the Paluxy River bed near Glen

Rose Texas. Dinosaur tracks are imbedded in the stone which at some point became exposed in a flood. With the dinosaur tracks were also found some human footprints in the same rock formation.

The prints of the men walking there were made at the SAME TIME as the dinosaur tracks. It's even been deduced by some, that the men who made some of the tracks were trailing or tracking the dinosaur that made the tracks. (actually it's entirely possible they were together.) Some of the human footprints even overlapped the dinosaur tracks, showing these were formed at the same time.

The fact that they are genuine dinosaur footprints has gone unchallenged for over 75 years and still there is no challenge to the dinosaur tracks. These dinosaur tracks are in fact dinosaur tracks. However when the human footprints were exposed, people started digging out the dinosaur tracks along with the human tracks to sell as souvenirs. Old timers also mention about the tracks seen at Paluxy. They said there were bare foot tracks as well as shod foot tracks, like moccasins or some other form of footwear.

But most of the tracks were chiseled out during the depression to raise what precious little funds they could sell them for. Eventually the number of close proximity of the two types of tracks was exhausted and people then started digging out just the dinosaur tracks and then started carving human footprints into the same piece of stone as the dinosaur print. So naturally wishing to discredit such a bit of evidence in order to continue the self deluding belief that dinosaurs existed 60 million years before man, the "experts" cried "hoax" "Fraud", and "Fake" and the site has been overlooked, and ignored, and the determination that they are fakes overrules any attempt to verify the findings simply because 'it can't be'. These known fakes, give them an excuse to bury their heads in the sand and ignore the genuine pairs. Well if you believe your theory blindly then it can't be.

However in 1976 the riverbed was re- examined and more parts of it were exposed using pumps and more dinosaur and human tracks were found, again in the SAME strata. The whole procedure was recorded on television cameras. (Book 57 page 36.) There is no doubt, the footprints are genuine and the same age as the dinosaur tracks. This is so explosive that paleontologist ignore, or vilify the site as a huge hoax, but there is no doubt about it, dinosaurs and man are contemporaneous, except in the literature still out there that deliberately ignores the evidence.

((2nd ed. Insert 2008) At first I was a bit hesitant to mention the dimensions of the human tracks seen at Paluxy, because it seems a bit off the wall. Some of the prints are over six feet apart! This would mean these men were giants! And indeed the prints are pretty big in themselves, some over 20 inches long. Though I won't go into length about there being giants at one time in the earth, this is some evidence for them. Indeed it seems many creatures were far bigger in the past than they are now...for example beavers reached six feet in length! Living things just lived longer and other factors such as higher oxygen content in the air (as much as triple) gave a better environment for things to live longer and reach larger dimensions. Similar to how a hyperbaric chamber can facilitate faster healing.)

Other footprints by humans have been left in rock with no dinosaur tracks about, but the prints date extraordinarily old. Thus by association we can presume they were made in the same eras when dinosaurs existed.

Human prints in rock at Mount Vernon are dated 140 million years old. (By the way compare these dates with the supposed ancestors of Man in the first chapter) Tracks in rock by the Mississippi near Arizona and New Mexico have been dated at 400 million years old. Evolutionists yell Fake! Hoax! and don't bother to examine the findings.

These ancient foot prints in rock have been examined as have those at Paluxy. If they were carved out, the density of the rock would all be consistent, but it's obvious that the rock was compressed. For example in sandstone the particles are denser, compressed and tighter under foot then in between the toes and the part where no print exists. People have even cut these prints in half to check for compression underneath the print, and it is compressed, and not all the same consistency as would be found if the prints were faked.

In some areas where prints are found, flood water has washed much of the softer material away, yet the prints remained as little pillars above the surrounding area, showing again that the land under the print was compressed and therefore resisted washing away.

((2ⁿᵈ ed. Insert 2008) Furthermore, human hands were found fossilized in "Cretaceous" rock along with an Ichthyosaurus in South America. (Kent Hovind lectures))

(3ʳᵈ ed. Insert 2016) W.F. Libby did radio carbon tests on plants associated with extinct Mastodons and found them just 3500 years old. (book 53 page 184) Dinosaur bones have been found with human bones in Russia, Lagoa Santa, Brazil, Matto Grosso, Ica Peru, Glen Rose Texas and Charleston California.

Obviously just as the dinosaurs are not old and their prints are not old, neither are the prints of the humans that made them but some agent is calcifying, and petrifying them at a rate far faster than science is believing. And this stands to reason. Otherwise such prints would be washed or blown away when new or even a year old and no trace of them would exist to harden. And once a rock is hard who can tell how old it is? Dating methods don't actually date rock, they date things found around the rock, and in many cases these ages are assumed. The simple fact is dinosaurs and man lived together at the same time, maybe not necessarily in the same tent, but certainly on the earth at the same time. Actually what some evolutionists say is that if this were true this would mean they were all created at the same time. Well that's refreshing. An evolutionist actually saying if their theory wasn't true, then creation is true. We are getting somewhere!

In a Russian museum there is an auroch skull with a wound made by a bullet. It was not made after the skull was found because the hole shows the animal lived sometime after the wound because it shows regrowth in the bone around the wound. Aurochs have supposedly been extinct hundreds of thousands of years....some time before guns were known to have been invented. Of course then there's those pesky monkeys and their gun factories they had in the Jurassic period that keeps gumming up the works and messing with the evidence. The Ramayana, a book which is about 2500 years old describes gunpowder and it's use perfectly. (Book 65 pg221. well at least my copy was good for something.) If we presume dating is incorrect we can see gun powder and aurochs are very likely contemporaries.

This is one of those things that proves three things. Dating methods are wrong and geological upheavals in the recent past…and now this. Although we already spoke of this incident (Twice!) in dating and Peleg, I bring it up again because it just keeps repeating on me…>urp…bleagh YUCK< I'll never eat one of THOSE again!

A mastodon (extinct for "12,000 years") was found at 12 feet below the surface near Blue Lick Springs. Three feet below the mastodon was found a manmade cut stone pavement…yeah civilization UNDER the creature not supposed to have existed until after civilized man came about. Unless it was the civilized monkeys and the sasquatches making the cut stone pavements. OK that's a wrap, put that smelly old Mastodon away now; we've milked that piece of evidence for all it's worth. Pee-yew! Get that thing outa here!

YE OLDE ART GALLERY

This next section shows 'prehistoric' beasts seen in art…so does art count as part of the hysterical …er… historical record? I think so.

The temple of Karnak has carvings of many types of birds which are easily recognized by zoologist, but there are many unknown birds depicted that stump the experts and are likely extinct types. It simply stands to reason that if man was drawing pictures of creatures that are now extinct they must have been alive when they were being drawn. Otherwise how could they draw them? You would be surprised at how many 'experts' cannot accept this. Some suggest these creatures were made up.

We have perfectly accurate drawings of Dodo birds. But these ridiculous birds just don't exist! Try and find one for me.! I mean the people who drew these creatures try and tell us they could not fly. I mean whoever heard of a bird that couldn't fly? Preposterous! So the people who drew these ridiculous birds obviously just made them up. They are corrupting our children to make them believe this bird actually existed during man's time on earth. Tsk Tsk. If you ask me this Dodo looked kind of dinosaur like, if a bird can look like a dinosaur. Ditto for the Moa... positively prehistoric!

People thought the platypus was faked and they had one right in front of them! If we haven't seen one before it just can't exist... now can it? Well OK, I am being cheeky, and obviously we can make up creatures that don't exist so one does have to careful. But the context clearly suggests these birds were alive at the same time as the other birds which are still alive. Did the Great Auk really exists?...naaah couldn't have. Ditto for the dodo.

MAPPED DANGER?

The map of Olaus Magnus from 1572 appears to be a collection of ocean events and depicts many sea monster. One ship is apparently sunk by one.

WARNING OF LOCAL DANGERS

(3rd ed. Insert 2016) During the 19th century expansion of settlements across the plains of America the natives Indians warned settlers to be careful of the thunderbird which they said had a wingspan of 20 feet and a bump on the back of its head. Clearly they were warning the settlers about a pterodactyl type flying lizard. And indeed some have still been sighted in America even in the 20th century. But every sighting receives disbelief and ridicule.

In the Grand Canyon a petroglyph exists showing a tyrannosaurus rex about to munch on an unsuspecting human looking the other way. Now this is important... they didn't have museums to go to, to see what a dinosaur looked like so they must have existed at the time in order for them to have drawn the beast **accurately**. Maybe the drawing was a joke or a record of what can happen in the area so people would be careful, like a sign today that might say "beware of fallen rock on the road". This one saying "caution! these beasts are in this neighborhood". Or maybe these were drawn by monkeys at the same time they were shooting Aurochs and playing with typewriters writing the bible.

Oddly paleontologists and the like are willing to believe the pictures of man hunting woolly mammoths that exist but when it comes to accepting pictures of dinosaurs they refuse to believe them simply because it doesn't mesh with their theory. This drawing is very old and it certainly predates the point before tyrannosaurus bones were assembled correctly, yet the T-Rex in this rock drawing is depicted correctly.

HERE THERE WAS A MONSTER

(3rd ed. Insert 2016) In 1675 the French explorer Jacques Marquette & Louis Joliet traveled down the Mississippi and stopped in Alton Illinois and saw a strange animal painted on a cliff. Here's what he wrote about this cliff painting.

"While skirting some rocks, which by their height and length inspired awe, we saw upon one of them two painted monsters which at first made us afraid, and upon which the boldest savages dare not long rest their eyes. They are as large as a calf; they have horns on their heads like those of a deer, a horrible look, red eyes, a beard like a tiger's, a face somewhat like a man's, a body covered with scales, and so long a tail that it winds all around the body, passing above the head and going back between the legs, ending in a fish's tail. Green, red, and black are the three colors composing the picture. Moreover, these 2 monsters are so well painted that we cannot believe that any savage is their author; for good painters in France would find it difficult to reach that place conveniently to paint them. Here is approximately the shape of these monsters, as we have faithfully copied it."

Asking the locals of the time what the painting was they said it was the Paisa bird or "Storm bird" and explained it was a giant bird that terrorized the village for a long time. It would swoop down and carry off Indians. Finally one day the chief figured out a way to kill it from a dream. After they were successful in ridding themselves of the terror they then painted the picture of the bird on the cliff. Since, after a long time of repainting the bird, locals finally made a metal plaque and hung it on the cliff. After a while fearing the plaque might fall they placed the plaque at the base of the cliff.

In the Hava Supai canyon there is a rock carving of a large man, possibly a giant battling a dinosaur and a mammoth. Though much has been made of this drawing I personally am not convinced. Being something of a fussy artist myself, I say the petroglyphs at this location don't look so good, but there is a resemblance, though it could also be wishful thinking to call the drawing this dinosaur. I'm such an art critique... but I'm just trying to be fair. The pictograph said to be a dinosaur could just as easily be a picto character rather than the drawing of a dinosaur.

A Diprotodon, the largest marsupial to ever live, about 9 feet tall, which walked and had the body shape something like that of a bear, was found carved in Alice Springs Australia. This was supposedly extinct about 40-50 thousand years ago. Obviously I'm assuming men made the carving...I know it's a stretch...and in all likelihood it was one of those monkeys again. *OK, enough with the monkey jokes!*

Near Lima Peru was found a carving of an Amphichelydia, which is supposedly the ancestor of the turtle. But they don't belong in South America, so where did the artist see them, especially when they were supposed to have been extinct for 180 million years? The rendering is apparently perfect even though even now it is only known by its fossil remains. How can they render an extinct creature perfectly? Only if you see one. Or could it be those monkeys again...my they *do* get around...There must have been a monkey art college that.... *What did I just tell you!!* Ow *NO* Ow *MORE* ok Ow *MONKEY* Ow *JOKES!!!* ...Ok Ok Okayy!

In Tiahuanaco there were found pottery shards painted with pictures of a creature identified as a toxodon, presumably extinct millions of years ago. Other pottery shows extinct llamas with 5 toes. (gone for about 12,000-50,000 years) At one time llamas did have 5 toes. It may have been an extinct species of llama or as some suggest an ancestor of today's llamas. Maybe it was a genetic manipulation to improve the llama...who knows. Also in Peru was found pottery depicting this same type of llama, and it is known that this type of llama did live in the area as 5 toed llama skeletons have been excavated in the same region. These drawings are on sophisticated pottery, which is obviously part of advanced civilization that is supposed to be less than 5500 years old. So what is a 5 toed llama and a toxodon doing drawn on civilized pottery if they were extinct so long? Obviously the dates are still wrong even here.

There are some carved stones called Ica stones in the vicinity of the village of Ocucaje and Ica, in Peru, which appear to have been carved soon after the rocks initial formation... however many millions of years you want to say these rocks were formed. Some of these clearly show man and a dinosaur together. On one there appears to be a man riding a pterodactyl. (wow! that would be KOOOL to have a trained pet Pterodactyl to ride around in the skies...but then what do you feed it... your hamster farm?) **(See Drawing 12)**

DRAWING 12

Another stone shows a triceratops and yet another shows something that could be a stegosaurus. Some of them show dinosaurs apparently domesticated. I don't find this in the least bit surprising. After all, do we not domesticate the elephant? Isn't it something of a dinosaur? Yet these elephants can love their owners and mourn for them when they die. Why not dinosaurs? Though I've lost the source I remember seeing a boy or girl leading a stegosaurus on a leash on some ancient pottery. By the way, there is no doubt that these Ica stones have been around for many centuries. Back in 1562 some were sent back to Spain! In other words these stones existed before we knew dinosaurs did, let alone what they looked like. However some of the natives in this region carve forgeries as a tourist thing "made in Peru", but they can be easily distinguished from the genuine older types through microscopic analysis. These dinosaurs are found on new ones and on genuine old ones. Naturally "experts", know about the forgeries and so claim they are all forgeries, then cry "hoax" and ignore them all. Why do we do that? Is it such a horrible thing to just say "OK OK, we are wrong the dinosaurs did exist during the time of civilized men and it's time to change the textbooks." I mean think of all the money they could make rewriting the text books and actually have something that justifies the cost of the new books for once! Rather than some little itty bitty update to force collage students to pay ridiculous amounts for only minutely updated versions every single year to prevent them from buying them from students who took the course before.

IMAGINATION OR EYEWITNESS?

(3rd ed. Insert 2016) Some of the dinosaurs depicted on Ica stones of Peru show dinosaurs with circles on their skin…no one knew why. Then around 1991 some dinosaur skin was found and it had circles on it!

HI YO POINTY!

(3rd ed. Insert 2016) One little trek into the internet found two examples of men riding a triceratops, an ancient sculpture that I couldn't find a complete picture of, and these Ica stones I've drawn here. **(See Drawing 13)** Other Ica stones show people riding dinosaurs which appear to be biting the riders. And other Ica stones show pretty hungry dinosaurs munching on men. Several of the Ica stones show dinosaurs with circles as part of their markings which we've shown such markings were proven to have existed.

In Big Sandy River Oregon an ancient artist left a picture of a stegosaurus.
Ancient ceramics found in Cocle Panama depict a flying lizard which is apparently a pterodactyl.
Similarly in Acambaro Mexico ceramic figures were unearthed in 1944 and on. Some resemble

Plesiosaurs, fish faced men (Oannes?), wooly rhinoceros, dragons, and some more apparently domesticated dinosaurs as they are made with women in the same figure in completely relaxed poses.

There is an exact replica of a brachiosaur, so perfect it's felt the person that made the figure must have actually seen one. Since they were discovered the owner of the land offered money for any more found so some fakes were made. So once again the "experts" cry hoax and ignore the entire find. But the originals have been carbon dated and found to be around 6000 years old! The fakes all carbon dated as new. (Here again carbon 14, as unreliable as it is, works against the evolutionists and paleontologists) It's easy to tell the fakes from the original ones, yet all the finds and the entire site is ignored by the "experts".

It's important to note that these figurines of extinct creatures were correctly configured. Originally many dinosaur bones when first put together were put together wrong and subsequent study of the bones made people realize these errors and the bones were later put together correctly. For example when I was about 11 I first saw a stegosaurus toy up close. (Though I was extremely familiar with the stegosaurus in King Kong, having a actual model in front of me started the wheels turning) I asked a fellow with me that it was strange the creature displayed two spines and I suggested it might be incorrect. Since this was a supposedly correctly depicted stegosaur, we thought and brainstormed and felt it might be like we have two shoulder blades, so it might be something like this all the way down the dinosaurs back. As it turns out my initial analysis was correct. The stegosaurus was found to have been put together wrong...it does only have one spine, and the plates are all attached to a single spine in a sort of overlapping way. Too bad, Ever since I was 5 I thought it would have been neat to ride on their backs in between the plates.

Also even when some dinosaurs were put together correctly the creatures method of standing and travel were deciphered incorrectly and later study showed the dinosaur in question to have walked or stood in a different position. The Tyrannosaur is an example of such. It was originally thought to have walked on all fours.

With these figures found in Mexico it is realized that the artists who made the dinosaurs molded them correctly, in many cases before paleontologists knew the correct stance of the animal.

Knowledge of dinosaurs and what they looked like is very new knowledge. 150 years ago few if anyone knew what these things looked like, yet these findings are absolutely accurate depictions of dinosaurs centuries before we knew they existed let alone knew what they looked like. The tyrannosaurus though known around the 1830's, was originally believed to have walked on all fours. This belief was held for about 50 years. Then around 1880 they realized that this creature walked on its hind legs, possibly with support from its tail. Yet the ancients drew these beasts correctly long before we knew about them or how they actually appeared! (As is likely the case with the Grand Canyon T-Rex petroglyph.)

ANCHOR WHAT? NO BONES EQUALS NO DINOSAURS?

(3rd ed. Insert 2016) A letter in Atlantis Rising mentioning a stegosaurus carving in Angkor Wat got me checking the internet and I found this amazing carving I drew here. (See drawing 14) As stunning as that is, it seems the artists of Angkor Wat vary in artistic skill as this stegosaurus sculpture pales in comparison to another dinosaur (?) or at the very least an unknown species sculpture found there. It looks like a web footed long necked dinosaur of some kind found on the Angkor Wat walls. (See drawing 15) Frankly the endless carvings / sculptures of Angkor Wat are stunning and deserve a look by anyone interested in ancient art. One comment I found about this stegosaurus on the wall of this stunning city goes something like this "if it's a stegosaurus, how come no bones of Stegosaurus have been found in Cambodia?" Kind of a silly question. What, people in one place can't draw pictures of species known in another? Some might say there was no travel from there to where any of these supposedly extinct dinosaurs might be. Also possible is they were hunted to extinction. Curiously there is a carving of an astronaut there as well! (See Drawing 4 chapter 3)If they had astronauts back then I think they could find a stegosaurus from *somewhere*.

Angkor Wat   Stegosaurus

DRAWING 14

Angkor Wat dinosaur **DRAWING 15**

HERE THERE BE DRAGONS

OK so much for culture and walking through this dull old art museum…now we've seen the people of old drew and sculpted these things, but now here are some very interesting historical records about "dragons".

"RARE" DOESN'T MEAN "EXTINCT".

Amos 9:3 "… and though they be hid from my sight in the bottom of the sea, thence will I command the serpent, and he shall bite them." Malachi 1:3 "And I hated Esau, and laid his mountains and his heritage waste for the dragons of the wilderness." (this is also evidence that mountains were destroyed after Esau's birth.) Jeremiah 51:37 And Babylon shall become heaps, a dwelling place for dragons. It would seem what we call dinosaurs, were at one time called dragons.

(3rd ed. Insert 2016) Note that the word dinosaur was only coined in 1841 by Sir Richard Owen. Previous to then they were always referred to as dragons, and this term was used synonymous with dinosaurs even into the 1940's. Today dragons are thought to be mythical animals yet as recently as 1946 dictionaries referred to dragons as something that still exist but were rare.

Early encyclopedias speak of dragons being very rare but still in existence. "Rare"? You mean in the late '40's dragons were still around? Hmmmm. We'll get back to that.

The bible indicates some dragons existed at the time the books of the bible were written. Micah 1:8 Therefore I will wail and howl, I will go stripped and naked: I will make a wailing like the dragons, and mourning as the owls. To make a "wailing like the dragons", one must have heard them to know what they sounded like.

The city of Nerluc in France was so named because there was a dragon killed in that city. It was described as bigger than an ox and had long sharp pointed horns on its head. Tricerotops?

A peasant killed a dragon May 13th 1572 in Northern Italy. This creature was mounted and a drawing was made of it. It looks something like a large boa constrictor with two legs that swallowed a pig.

A story is told of an Irishman that spotted a creature with claws that had iron on its tail that pointed backwards and had a head similar to a horse. Some believe he was describing a stegosaurus.

Flying dragons were recorded as existing in England as recently as 1649. The woods around Penllin Castle in Glamorgan was known to be frequented by winged serpents which were described as very beautiful owing to their skin as they looked like they were covered in all kinds of jewels. Some had crests (on their chests?) that sparkled like rainbows. However these creatures were something of a pest and they frightened young and old alike, because when they were angry they would fly over people's heads. It's felt they became extinct because they were so inclined to steal poultry that they were killed like foxes. Descriptions of these creatures match pterosaurs.

FAMOUS DUDES AND THEIR EXPLOITS

The story of a famed individual named "Wotan" was called a "queller" of dragons. That is, he killed them, or brought such beasts into submission. Though Wotan is considered one of the "gods' (also called Othinn, Wodan, and Odin) he was likely a human individual of vast abilities and capacities. Hittite and Greek texts tell of a chief deity that had to slay a dragon. (book 17 pg 67) Though that "deity" is not mentioned in that source it could be this same person. With the animals becoming dangerous after the flood, it eventually became open season on dinosaurs and anyone who managed to beat the more dangerous and ferocious ones were stuff of legends.

In 1271 Marco Polo reported that on special occasions a royal chariot was pulled by dragons. A post in China in 1611 was even designated as Royal Dragon Feeder. The Chinese zodiac comprised of 12 animals are all animals now alive, except the dragon. It doesn't make sense they would designate one of a nonexistent creature.

(3rd ed. Insert 2016) The book Beowulf written between the 8th and 11th century speaks of slaying dragons by pulling their arms off. Curiously a Babylonian cylinder seal shows a man pulling off the arm of a dragon...and Babylonian walls depicted dragons. Alexander the Great soldiers were scared off by dragons in some caves of India.

Job chapter 41 is the famous leviathan chapter. Some have suggested leviathan may be a whale, but the description just doesn't fit that of a whale...at all!

This is some pretty fierce creature by its account. Here are excerpts. Vs 7 Canst thou fill his skin with barbed irons? or his head with fish spears? (sounds amphibious) Vs 10, none is so fierce that dare stir him... Verse 14, who can open the doors of his face? his teeth are terrible round about (sounds similar to T rex mouth) Verse 15 and 16 No air can come between his scales, vs. 19 Out of his mouth go burning lamps, and sparks of fire leap out. Vs. 20 out of his nostrils goeth smoke... vs 21 his breath kindeleth coals, and flame goeth out of his mouth. (a fire breathing dragon?) vs 27 He esteemeth iron as straw, brass as rotten wood. Vs 29 darts are counted as stubble, vs 31 he maketh the deep to boil like a pot... vs 32 He maketh a path to shine after him. (possibly from a dragging tail sweeping clean the path behind him or a slimy trail similar to what a snail or slug might leave behind.) Vs 34 he beholdeth all things (a tall creature... still sounds similar to a T-Rex...or "Godzilla"?)

When comparing this creature he sounds something like Godzilla! Now we know where the "fire breathing dragon" legends come from. There's no reason to think this is a mythical creature. The book of Job speaks of many other known creatures like peacocks, ostriches and unicorns. (By the way a "unicorn" is a Rhinoceros. Long has it been known that unicorns were just rhinoceros's but they have become fabled horses with horns somewhere somehow since the 1500's.) Maybe someone actually rode one and they've been linked with horse ever since...but I digress.

As for fire breathing dragons legends... these things are in almost every culture in the world! And this stands to reason, it is such a incredible beast that if it existed, stories would be told about it forever!...and they are... so it stands to reason there is some basis in fact that they did exist...during recorded history! It truly would have been an awesome creature to behold! The saturation of this legendary beast throughout the world gives one pause to wonder, and the fact that it is even in the bible lends further credibility to the existence of this creature. And we appear to have bones of the thing!

Actually we know very little about creatures we find in fossil form only. I mean when you look at bones, you don't automatically say "Oh this was a fire breathing dinosaur" Whereas they were simply describing the creature as they SAW it...though interestingly, it is God describing the monster. Taken at face value this simply has to be some form of dinosaur. But to be fair and 'shoot myself in the foot' so to speak, Leviathan is mentioned later in revelations as something that would be destroyed and the inference is he is Satan, that, or there is an equating of the two as the same, just as Satan is equated with the snake and the serpent and similar to how we equate people who ignore unpleasant truths as ostriches who bury their heads in the sand...though ostriches don't actually do this, just evolutionist and paleontologists and... HAVE faith guys... this chapter will end soon!

Maybe no fire breathing dragons exist anymore but legends are quite full of them, and since they make such great imagery, naturally these work themselves into stories we make up to the point we mix up reality with fiction. But there is a interesting beetle that has similar features. The rocket beetle has two chambers for two types of a neutral fuel. When it gets scared it ejects fuel from both these chambers into a single chamber and they mix, explode and send the beetle off like a jet or rocket taking off, hence it's name. We even create hydrochloric acid in our stomachs, so why not fire breathing monsters?

Another dinosaur is referred to in the book of Job. If Leviathan isn't a dinosaur, behemoth is, and it is alive at the same time as Job. God said to Job in Chapter 40 verse 15 Behold (look at) behemoth. He's not going to ask Job to look at something that can't be seen. Some have suggested behemoth is either a hippopotamus or an elephant, but the description of this creatures just doesn't fit these animals. In Job 40:17 "He moveth his tail like a cedar..." Look at an elephants tail... is that a cedar? No! it's a twig, and a Hippopotamus' tail is little more than a sausage. Verse 19 says he is the chief of the ways of God. This indicates it is the largest animal. But today the elephant is the largest animal. Furthermore this is a land animal because in verse 21 it says he lays under the shady trees. Another indication of this creatures size is in verse 23 where it says he drinketh up a river...and trusts he can draw up the Jordan in his mouth... perhaps a bit of exaggeration but merely to indicate just how massive this creature really was. And this is no reptile because this creature in Job is said to have a naval...not something you find on reptiles. (verse 16) Behemoth may be similar to a diplodocus, or some other dinosaur with the trademark massive tails.

Lamentations 4:3 "Even the sea monsters draw out the breast, they give suck to their young ones..." This is the only time the word "monster" is in the bible. The term sea monster here could also be translated whale, but so too could whale be translated sea monster. When Jonah was swallowed by a whale the bible actually says "large fish" so some say this might not even have been a whale; and this too could also be translated sea monster. Jesus says that Jonah was in a whale but that could also be translated large fish. Something of a vicious circle.

Of course if we presume the ancients did not make the distinction between mammalian air breathing fish and gill breathing fish one can see the reason for the confusion. If it's swimming in the water to them it's a fish...no...that's aunt Dora...my mistake. I guess if the Hebrews lived under water they'd have more words for fish, like the Eskimos have so many words for snow, and it would be more obvious what exactly was meant by "large fish" or "sea monster". So although it would be neat to say "SEE! Sea monsters are even in the bible!"... but I can't say it unequivocally without qualifying it. Just trying to be fair. So many sources and authors speak of so much of this stuff obviously it has convinced many a person....though obviously not the paleontologists in their ivory...er...fossil towers.

AFTERMATH

Found in the homes of ancient peoples were utensils made of, and carved in, fresh mastodon ivory, not the petrified or fossilized sort. (books 16 pg 221) Similarly in Mexico was found a piece of mastodon bone. No big deal except on the bone were carved figures of a horse, reptile, and a type of mastodon thought to be extinct for 100,000 years. The bone was examined and found that the bone was carved when it was still fresh, and not carved on a piece of fossilized bone. The bone was carved shortly after the beast had died, and probably by the same hunter who felled the beast. It is also important to note that here we see an example of bone fossilizing AFTER being handled by sophisticated men, showing bone can fossilize in a relatively short time.

In the Brazilian state Minas Gerais, bones of man have been found buried UNDER bones of Toxodon, Megatherium (something of a huge ground sloth about twice the height of man or more), and a dinosaur.

It's also worth noting that dragons are mentioned in the bible 35 times. Ancient recipes call for dragon bone or dragon saliva; I don't think you can get that stuff if they aren't alive.

Campfire stories.

Zuni Indians have handed down stories through time that speak of reptilian monsters. Although people pooh-pooh the idea that people could possibly have seen dinosaurs and still speak of them, they have proven that American Indians killed elephants. More importantly is the fact that the native Indians themselves talked about killing the elephants in the past, yet the elephant has been extinct on this continent for at least 3000 years. This shows that spoken legends can stay intact and be completely true for incredibly long periods of time. There's no reason to discount other legends and written histories simply because they don't back theories. After all, these ancient histories were put together during the events in question. These histories should be used as reference sources, not as focal points of derision. If the Indians can tell stories for 3000 years about elephants, existing during their verbal histories then there's no reason do discount their ancient histories of a time when they lived with reptilian monsters, which in all likelihood lived at the same time frames as the elephants the Indians spoke of.

On the east coast of USA at Vero Florida, there were found many animal bones including extinct species (including the saber toothed tiger) in association with human bones and utensils. (Another site like this exists 33 miles to the north) This of course proved man was on the continent much longer then was supposed. Geologists concluded the humans and the extinct animals were from the SAME age. Well good for the geologists. Anthropologists concluded that this site was from first to second millennium BC. And good for the anthropologists too! Well there's hope yet! Here we see the saber-toothed tiger living as recently as about 1500 BC. But these creatures were supposed to be extinct 12,000 years ago. That in itself is a sore spot with archeologists and other anthropologists, and they still refuse to accept the findings of these sites, and all this physical evidence is all ignored in favor of the theory that man came from the Bering Strait. So many branches and disciplines of science are deliberately IGNORING the evidence to perpetuate their pet theories. I can't understand this weird phenomenon about all these scientists ignoring important scientific evidence? Is it so hard to admit we could be wrong or rethink a theory a little bit…or a lot? I mean a lot of this evidence is irrefutable, yet they continue to do so. It just boggles the mind. Very odd. I personally look forward to new evidence, even if it upsets my little apple cart… it makes learning all the more intriguing…sometimes a little scary, but interesting all the same.

This conclusion that extinct creatures lived into historical times has been reached in other ways at different sites in North America. Several lakes have been pinpointed to be of glacial age by analyzing things like sodium and chlorine, which helps determine the age of these lakes and it puts them to about 500-2000 BC. In the same areas there are extinct species such as Felix Atrox (a kind of cat), and different types of horses and camels. When comparing a glacier formed Lake Lahontan and the Labrea Tar pits, the conclusions arrived at was that pits and the lake were contemporaneous, and that the creatures found at these sites lived into historical times. Naturally these conclusions were disputed. Why? Because it was assumed to be erroneous to come to the conclusion that these sites were this recent because it led to the belief that these creatures lived into historical times. But this reasoning is flawed because this belief that they couldn't have lived to historical times is based on their unproved theories which are not based on the evidence found in geology.

As one looks at the nature of all the extinctions in the light of Peleg, it becomes clear that it is something of chance that certain species survived and others were all wiped out, in the action that caused the continents. Were things a little different we might be riding our pet stegosaurus to the museum to look at the fearsome Horseosaurus' and the vicious saber toothed poodles.

WHY DINOSAURS MAY STILL BE ALIVE.

Dinosaurs (depending on the type) are said to have been extinct for anywhere from a million to about 200 million years. More recent types like wooly mammoths and saber tooth tigers, horses and lamas with funny feet and such apparently died in the last ice age only a supposed 12,000 years ago. Obviously if you read this far you've seen that the first ice age likely started a maximum 5300 years ago and ended considerably more recently than that, with the last ice age ending as recently as 700-500 BC.

Yes, the vast majority of dinosaurs probably are extinct but as seen they died in datable cataclysms not all that long ago. There may have been "ages" which we call such flowery names as Triassic and Jurassic or what-have-you that ended, wherein dinosaurs roamed the earth then suddenly ceased to live because the land was in such upheaval they got in the way of the advancing tsunamis and land, and also likely got crushed by the tectonic action of Peleg. But there is another reason they appear to be extinct, because there is also another aspect of dinosaurs people tend to overlook.

The bulk of dinosaurs are of the reptile and lizards family. When you know a key fact about lizards and reptiles, things quickly start to make sense. Take crododiligators for instance. They can grow to huge proportions and they don't stop growing until they die. In principle you can tell how old a crocodile or alligator is, simply by its size, though growth rates vary with food availability and location of the critter. After a certain age their growth rate slows down considerably. Interestingly you can also tell how old a crocodile is by the growth rings in its bones. Though they grow slower in old age they continue to grow all the same. They might reach 7-8 feet in 7 years but they live as long as man, (from 70-100 years) and can reach about 20 feet long. How big would they get if they lived 300, 500, 900 years? Perhaps in post flood with the earth still a bit more hospitable, older lizards grew a bit faster than they do now, and more importantly they would have continued to grow all their lives. It's similar with other reptiles, and thus dinosaurs. The point being if they don't live as long as they might have at one time, they are not going to get as big as they used to.

WHAT SCALES?

Some carvings and drawings of reptile creatures are similar to dinosaurs as well as the small reptiles, so it is not always certain which creature they are depicting as the scale is not apparent. This illustrates my point: that is that some dinosaurs may still be alive. If we can't tell if they are illustrating a dinosaur or a small "cousin" what's to say they aren't the exact same creature? After all, the same creature, if it lives long enough will be a dinosaur eventually. Since reptiles continue to grow all their lives eventually your cute little lizard is going to be a dinosaur if it lives long enough. You see, the key point is reptiles and lizards never stop growing until the day they die. If you don't see how important that is, I'll spell it out for you.

THE LONGER THEY LIVE THE BIGGER THEY GROW

As seen there was something in the pre-flood era that enabled man to live well over 900 years old. Animals also must have had extremely long life spans, but most animals like man had definite growing periods, then they stopped growing. So if say cats' lived to be 300 years old it would be difficult to tell a 10 year old cat from a 200 year old cat based on size alone. Plant life grew to tremendous proportions because they continue to grow until they die. Reptiles also lived for extremely long periods of time, but owing to the somewhat unique aspect of reptiles they just kept growing...and growing; because like plants, reptiles also continue to grow until they die, and when you grow, you get bigger! I know that is a real lame and seemingly condescending and simple thing to say, but it really is that simple! Dinosaurs are almost invariably reptiles and the word dinosaur is almost synonymous with their huge size. All reptiles, no matter how cute or tiny they may appear at one time, are potential dinosaurs!

THE TIME FRAME WHEN THEY TURNED INTO DINOSAURS

The key period where reptiles would have become dinosaurs is the initial 1000 years or so after the flood when life spans of humans and creatures was still very long. The three sons of Noah lived to be around 600 years so if a dinosaur lived similar life spans to man they would have gotten large enough to be considered dinosaurs. If they lived as long by comparison as tortoises or parrots they could live three times as long as man. It's then more possible they became extinct around the time of the Exodus. This is all assuming the dinosaur fossils are post flood. Actually it's difficult to guess when they became extinct. Peleg happened 101 years after the flood and exodus happened around 1000 years after the flood. If they got as big as the dinosaurs fossils we have now in that short period between the flood and Exodus how big did they get BEFORE the flood? My only possible explanation which appears to be supported by historical evidence is that the dinosaurs must have survived Peleg, as there is no way they could become of dinosaur proportions in the 101 years after the flood to the time of Peleg. They must have become extinct in a subsequent Peleg action. Based on their growth rates, we see another clue that shows the exodus was the time of the most massive worldwide upheavals which includes the majority of the dinosaur extinctions, that or some possibly became extinct as late as 687 BC with the final major global destructions.

The standard belief is that dinosaurs all around the earth became extinct all at the same time and it is presumed some comet trouble caused their demise. Granted this is not a bad theory and actually corresponds to a large degree with my theory except for the dates and ages involved. Naturally the more well known theories which date the end of the age of the dinosaurs is somewhere in the neighborhood of millions and millions of years ago, whereas I say maybe they became extinct around 3100 (or) 2400-687 BC. As it turns out many of the "extinct species" are turning out to be not quite as extinct as we once thought.

MISSING THE OBVIOUS

(3rd ed. Insert 2016) We have shown that it's quite possible that man DID live far longer before the flood, but one piece of evidence staring us in the face all this time is found in the fact that we KNOW dinosaurs lived. How does that make it clear that humans lived longer? We've seen that the majority of dinosaurs are reptiles, and we've seen that reptiles never stop growing. One can actually guess how old a reptile is by how big it is. And it's entirely probable that some of the reptiles we have today, were they to live long enough would be the very same dinosaurs we've found in fossils. Thus this proves that something in the earth has to have changed to stop reptiles from getting bigger; and that is they don't live as long. So… ergo… if something stopped reptiles from living that long, don't you think the same thing is stopping humans from living proportionately as long? Thus we have another piece of evidence that supports the ancient texts, (Principally the bible) which tells of people living to 900+ years. But this also vindicates other ancient texts which speak of men living to fantastic numbers of years)

DINOSAURS TODAY

That aint no garter snake. (3rd ed. Insert 2016) Now this one isn't exactly a dinosaur, but it'll get your feet wet. The army in Ecuador had to hunt down a snake because it ate two of its soldiers. It was 100 feet long and the head was 5 feet long.

Plesiosaurs. On April 25 1977 a Japanese fishing boat *Zuiyo Maru* caught something near New Zealand 40 feet long, dead and rotting in their nets not usually served for dinner in Japan. Pictures were taken of the creature and then to avoid it spoiling the other fish it was dumped back into the sea. The people on the boat felt this might have been a Plesiosaur. Later the pictures were examined by many people and the creature was tentatively identified as a plesiosaur, supposedly extinct for 100 million years. Some have tried to dismiss the carcass as that of a shark but when the pictures and the structure of the catch is compared to that of a shark there simply is no comparison. (Book 57 pg. 149) Typing in "Zuiyo Maru pictures" On the internet and pics and articles about this creature can be seen.

MORE PLESIOSAURS

Lake Champlain has a creature that has been seen in it at least since Samuel De Champlain saw something in its waters and described it as "a 20-foot serpent, with a horse-shaped head and body as thick as a keg". This creature (or it descendants) has been spotted about 300 times over the centuries and even the odd photograph of the creature exists and it too most closely resembles a plesiosaur.

WASN'T THAT LIKE A SCENE IN KING KONG?

(3rd ed. Insert 2016) On March 24 1962 in Pensacola Florida, 5 older teenagers went scuba diving to explore the wrecked sunken ship "Massachusetts" off Pensacola harbor. Only one of the 5 (Brian McCleary) came back. They got caught in a storm and dragged out to sea. They were then stuck in a dense fog. In the fog they could make out what looked like a long pole with an inverted light bulb like structure at the top of it. It sounded like a porpoise and smelled like dead fish and they heard a loud hiss. Then it came near their raft and made a high-pitched whine and they panicked. They got on their gear and tried to swim back to the sunken boat whose mast protruded above the water. Brian heard his four friends one by one scream and disappear. He saw the creature when his last friend was taken. Its neck was about 12 feet long, brownish green and oval pupils and a head similar to a sea turtle but elongated and with teeth. When he told the story to the papers, not one of the papers would mention the sea serpent and said they just drowned. McCleary did a sketch of the creature and it is thought to be that of a plesiosaur. 20,000 people have reported seeing plesiosaurs in the 20th century. Note that in 1925 a sea serpent washed up on the coast of California which had a 20 foot neck and a bulb shaped head. It was described by the people of the time to be a plesiosaur washed up on Monterey Bay but the pictures I've seen are too indistinct to make this comparison. It would appear that knowing about these creatures has *put* them into movies.

The Potomac has had a plesiosaur sighting. Lake Eerie has "Bessie", a serpent like creature 35 feet long with a snake like head. In 1998 a taxidermist Pete Peterson found and stuffed a baby creature, found dead by Lake Erie, thought to be a baby plesiosaur. Pictures of it show it had a short tail.

In the White River of Arkansas a monster thought to be a bascillasaurus (or basilosaurus) was seen so many times that in 1973 there was a law passed prohibiting it from being killed or harmed.

Since 1816 over 215 sightings of sea serpents have been seen in Lake Memphremagog. Isaiah chapter 27 speaks of dragons in the sea.

NESSIE.

The Loch Ness monster has also been described as a plesiosaur and though seen occasionally swimming the lake it has also been seen shuffling on land surrounding the lake.

Several other lakes like Canada's Lake Okanagan in BC, Lake Champlain, Lake Manitoba, Chesapeake bay (sea serpent), Payette lake, Lake Memphremagog on the Vermont-Quebec border, Bynoe Harbour near Darwin, Australia are said to contain sea monsters constantly described as plesiosaurs, but they are given pet names like Ogo-Pogo, Caddy, Bessie and Nessie. They all seem to be 20-40 feet long and persistently classified as plesiosaurs. Actually a surprising number of carcasses have been found that keep being classed as plesiosaurs. They may be shy but they are persistently sighted.

AH SEEN HIM PLENTY -A- TIMES

(3rd ed. Insert 2016) Alexander Campbell was the game warden of Loch Ness for 47 years. He saw 'Nessie' 18 times, and one of those times was from just three feet away! He was in a boat doing his rounds when he turned around and saw the back of Nessie who also turned to see him: they both were scared of each other and skedaddled away from each other in a hurry. It seems Nessie isn't a violent to man type of Plesiosaur, whereas others have eaten four swimmers as mentioned (so a different species no doubt). Another guy on a motorcycle nearly ran into Nessie, and his headlight illuminated his entire form…on land. He has a blunt tail which wasn't known. Nessie scurried off to the lake. Two people on a camping trip saw Nessie leaving land with a sheep in its mouth. I guess you can't blame the wolves for everything. Seven other lakes in the same general area as Loch Ness have had Plesiosaurs seen in them as well.

OTHER SORTS

An extinct fossil that appears to have turned up alive is the Zeuglodon, some sort of "primitive" whale. What makes a creature "primitive" anyway? Because it's ugly and scary?... it hideous looking teeth? It's thought to be one of the possible explanations for the many sightings of sea and lake monsters, as are plesiosaurs. Actually in 1937 a 3 meter long sea serpent was pulled out of a whales belly, that was in all likelihood one of the sea serpents seen so often, and it had a head similar to an elongated camel head. If a whale can eat one sea serpent there must be other bigger ones around somewhere.

On December 19 1954 off the coast of Kentish, England a strange "boiling" in the water tore a valuable $1500 net. In the net was found a 14 foot unknown sea creature weighing one ton with smooth blue skin and eyes like those of a horse. It had rows of gills like a shark. A London zoo expert thought it to be an 'extinct species'....well that one is, but where there's one there are more.

Though not much of a "dinosaur", in 1952 10 neopilina's were pulled from a depth of 3590 meters below the sea. These are a sort of limpet shell mollusk. What's unusual is they were thought to be extinct for about 300 million years. Oh by the way these ones were still alive. I mean this sort of ties in with Peleg. If these things live at that depth normally, then one can see just how much water was thrown on land to have these creatures become fossils on land!

Of course then there is that Trilobite that was squashed by a shoe. That sort of says it all. A man squishing a bug supposedly 4-500 million years old. (book 30 photo section [many refer to this item]) Some suggest it was a space man. OK, sure...later on I'll tell you who that space man was. Maybe they lived or live with the neopilina's 2 miles down. How many of these are going to turn up? Not too many, but who knows maybe this creature will turn up too....though if someone went around squishing them with their shoe that sort of suggests they lived on land, and it becomes difficult to imagine what could cause such a small creature to become extinct.

LIKE WE'RE SPACE MEN, DUDE, LIKE TOTALLY AWESOME...AND DIG THE COOL SANDALS EH!?

(3rd ed. Insert 2016) Another thing about those trilobites squashed by a sandaled foot supposedly 500 Mill-yun yeeeerz ago... Some have suggested these were crushed by spacemen. C'mon...spacemen wearing sandals? Maybe ...just maybe the rocks formed /hardened far quicker and thus much more recently than we seem to want to believe. In 1817 at Herculaneum Missouri human tracks were found deep in a quarry imbedded in limestone...yeah limestone. (book 30 page 21) (Same general area where giant skulls of humans about 25-30 feet tall were found in mounds near Kansas) They were found back when very very few people thought the world was no older than 7000 years. No one thought anything of the tracks other than they were an interesting find. It wasn't until 1882, when people started to scoff at biblical dates and stuff, that they came up with ridiculous theories about these prints to explain them away in the light of 'Modern' thinking. They suggested they must be carvings though they were obviously foot prints. But seriously, were they carved then covered over by hundreds of feet of limestone waiting for some poor sucker to make the quarry, and dig down hundreds of feet to find them and be totally taken in by a hoax? Using what to perpetrate it may I ask? ...what is so hard about considering that catastrophes might have something to do with evidence of man underground buried by immense upheavals?

FRESH MEAT

Fresh dinosaur bones have been found. How fresh? So fresh they look like yesterdays dog bones and red blood cells have been found inside them. There is no way on earth red blood cells are going to stay viable for 65 million years let alone just 65 years! When people give blood the red blood cells start to break down in three months, and that with the blood preserved! A fresh dinosaur bone has to mean they are still alive! Showing her obvious bias, Mary Schweitzer (Of Montana State U) on July 9th 1994 said "It was exactly like looking at a slice of modern bone. But of course I couldn't believe it. I said to the lab technician: the bones after all are 65 million years old, How could blood cells survive that long?" She knows they CAN'T' last that long but willing to throw out the evidence to keep believing they are 65 million years old. I repeat something I mentioned before here...

Bones were dated between 20,000 and 30,000 years old. After the dates for these samples was secured the bones were revealed to be from dinosaurs. Consider this little known fact. On occasion dinosaur fossils have have broken and they smell rotten inside. If they really were millions of years old, that rot would have long since disappeared and fossilized. Fossils are NOT millions of years old!

THE HEART OF AFRICA: ONE WHO STOPS THE FLOW OF RIVERS

Some of the following information among other sources, is gleaned from the CEN Technical Journal of August 2001 as found on the internet.

There is a creature called Mokele-Mbembe by people that have seen it and the name is well known and established. This is pretty much the same creature we called "brontosaurus" [apatosaurus]. (Apparently brontosaurus was actually a mixed up creature that never existed. It was two creatures mistakenly thought to be part of the same creature, with the wrong head attached to the body, thus this name is not used anymore, though apatosaur is. I'm not sure why though as they are listed as the same creature.)

As a kid this was thee most famous dinosaur because it was the biggest. There is a full size model of one in Calgary somewhere. It's huge and I always wanted to climb that thing as a kid. The ones seen in Africa ranges in size from a hippo to an elephant and measure from 15 to 35 feet long, though much of this length is neck and tail. Their footprints are similar to an elephant but with claw marks. This creature is known to have been seen in the Congo for over 200 years in an area known as the Likouala swamp region in the Congo, long before the word "dinosaur" was coined. Tracks of a creature were spotted that were three feet in diameter!

Even its habitat, habits and diet are known by the locals. It is seen in swamps and its local name means "one who stops the flow of rivers". The creature has been seen at different locations and there are doubtless several of them.

Many local people have been interviewed and though the people interviewed had no communication with each other the descriptions of the creature are the same. It has a favorite tree it likes to eat and it has been seen driving hippopotamuses away from swamps where this tree is found. A creature named "one who stops the flow of rivers" that chases hippopotamuses away?... that's some creature! It eats tree leaves from about 20 feet Up...and no giraffes are in the neighborhood...so what else *could* be eating those leaves?

A certain Marcellin Agnagna a Congolese biologist, saw the creature in 1983 and was convinced he saw a living dinosaur. One of the arguments against this creature actually being a brontosaurus is that it would be impossible for such a large creature to hide. But as we have seen dinosaurs lived for hundreds of years to get to these massive proportions. This Congo version simply doesn't live as long so cannot attain the size of its ancestors. It's big but just not as big as the brontosaurus used to get, simply because they just don't live as long. I mean this is so cool! The brontosaurus was always one of my favorite dinosaurs, and it still lives!

Some have seen dinosaurs with spikes or horns on their heads similar to what Diplodocus are known to have had (Apparently females are missing this feature). (3rd ed. Insert 2016) Colonel Fawcett noted seeing a brontosaurus in South America.

KILLER OF ELEPHANTS

There may be more than one type of dinosaur lurking in the swamps of Cameroon and the Congo. Another creature spoken of by African pygmies is called Emela-ntouka, which means "killer of elephants"!

In Cameroon this creature is easily identified with pictures of the triceratops. Eye witness of this creature say it is dangerous and elephants give it a wide berth. The creature is rarely seen and hasn't been seen for quite some time and may now sadly really *be* extinct. Others have seen creatures with frills around their neck and with one to four horns on their head and nose that appear to be the Triceratops or creatures of this type!

People in these regions are shown black and white photographs of various animals from around the world along with other more well known African animals. They always pick out the same pictures of these dinosaurs as creatures that they've seen.

The sightings of these creatures in Africa are so persistent that many expeditions over the years (more than 20 since 1980) have been undertaken to document these elusive creatures: with varying success. It's almost funny that dinosaurs, some of the largest creatures in the world are the hardest to find...at least for us. Though we assume they would be walking on land and easy to spot, as so many dinosaur illustration show them, they just seem to be almost entirely aquatic, possibly due to their large size. They do venture onto land and live in amongst the trees as well but when men are around they scamper to the rivers. They are only tough when other creatures that conceivably could compete for their territory venture into their areas. But they are dangerous as they have killed some natives.

Casts of their footprints, droppings and recordings of the creature's sounds have been gathered. If you wonder how they could stay hidden so long, keep in mind by some accounts they live in the Northern Congo swamps regions which are as large as the state of Arkansas. Also these creatures don't exactly live in the most hospitable habitats. Often expeditions have to slog through mile after mile of swamp land and people tracking these monsters get foot rot, skin irritations, and insect bites while hacking through prickly vegetation, and "navigating" swamps where no normal boats can be taken and they are forced to use inflatable's or native canoes, often leaky at that.

Some of the rivers are simply impassable with these limited modes of travel. Not to mention disease and hostile natives also hinder such expeditions. To compound these difficulties the creatures themselves seem quite shy of men and usually dunk when they see us. They seem to have incredible lung capacity and once submerged just never seem to reappear when and where one might expect them to do so. When one plots the sightings of these dinosaurs they appear to be in a region from north Cameroon's to Northern Rhodesia to Gabon and possibly into Nigeria.

Other natives familiar with most of the native creatures in this vast area of Africa speak of a dinosaur they call Liu'kela-bembe. When shown pictures of dinosaurs they also pick out sauropod dinosaurs, and they don't think them unusual, though they are afraid of the things, partly because they have this tendency to scare away the hippos, elephants and even crocodiles. Remember hippos are the most ferocious African animals known, often besting crocodiles.

NO REASON TO DOUBT THE EYE WITNESSES.

Remember many of these eyewitness reports are not by people who know these things are supposed to be extinct. People merely ask them about the creatures they see around the area and are shown illustrated books or animal photographs. They don't know they are pointing to extinct creatures, they are merely pointing to creatures they have seen, and there is no reason to disbelieve them.

They don't think these creatures any stranger to them then gorillas and elephants. In most cases tribesmen identifying these creatures have never even been interviewed before. In reading these accounts it appears that often language was a problem and the pictures were the easiest form of communication. Given the fact that vast heavily forested and swampy regions of the interior of Africa are still virtually unexplored it's perfectly plausible that there are many creatures in these areas not yet known to science. There is no reason whatsoever these dinosaurs could not yet be still alive. Just because we say they are extinct doesn't mean they are.

Natives were not led or told the purpose of the interview, they were merely asked about the wildlife they knew. To us it would be like asking what old cars we've seen in the area. We may have seen a mint 1955 Buick, and people from the eastern provinces might have thought such a beast extinct! OK bad analogy but you get the idea.

Furthermore when the natives are shown say pictures of North American animals like the brown bear or even the African Hyena, they do not recognize them and they don't recognize pterodactyls or T-rexs, but when they see pictures of sauropod dinosaurs and triceratops they evoked excited responses.

MORE DINOSAURS AND EXTINCT CREATURES AROUND THE EARTH STILL BEING FOUND, ALIVE

There are several creatures that were thought to be extinct that still exist. The Tuatara thought to be extinct for however many years you want to say, was found in New Zealand in pretty good health and exhibited no change from the more "primitive" ancestor.

This creature has such a dinosaur look about it they have used it in movies, and magnified it to look like a Largemongous gigantosaurus.

Tuatara, mountain beavers, Queensland lung fish...actually the list goes on and on. Many plants, animals, fish and reptiles all thought to be extinct for millions of years are turning up alive and with no different features from their more "primitive" ancestors. Yeah in every case where a creature thought to be extinct for millions of years turns up it looks identical to the "extinct" versions found previously. Showing not only are some dinosaurs still alive but evolution to be a completely nonsensical theory because all these creatures, previously thought to be extinct, look exactly like their ancient primitive ancestors from "Millions of years" before. So what evolved?

It seems if paleontologists and evolutionists were genuinely interested in the evidence they would be all over the swamps of central Africa. I mean if they are disciples and followers of Darwin, you'ld think they would be just as ambitious in their search for these creatures as Darwin was in his search for unknown creatures. Actually I have heard that even non creationists are starting to take the rumors seriously and are leading expeditions into the heart of Africa. No doubt within the next few decades I would think some dinosaurs will leave the extinct lists with stunning footage of these monsters gracing our television screens, and it won't be a Hollywood special effect either, though I wonder if people will be able to prove they are not computer simulations to our computer literate population. Wouldn't it be sad that if real dinosaurs were found and videos taken of them, but because of computer technology people might refuse to believe the footages.

FLYING REPTILES!

People have seen large "birds" in the San Antonio region with a wingspan of "fifteen or twenty feet, if not more". When searching through books to identify the creature they identified it as a Pteranodon, supposedly extinct for 150 million years. Others have seen huge birds with bat like face standing as tall as them and later looked in books and identified the creature as the same Pteranodon. The little explored Mexico's Sierra Madre is a possible place where these creatures could dwell undetected. (World of Strange Phenomena page 205-7)

July 25 1977 a ten year old Marlon Lowe of Lawndale Illinois was picked up by a black "bird" in the early night with a wingspan of about 9 feet. It displayed a white ringed neck and a beak about 6 inches long. The boy was dropped after about 35 feet from about 8 feet up and was physically Ok. Consequently for a year he was unwilling to go outside after dark. Though the story got national attention and there were 6 witness's, few people believed the story and many dead birds were left at their front door.

A REAL THUNDERBIRD?

These stories receive curious confirmation from a story from 1890. Two cowboys discovered and shot down what they called a winged dragon which resembled something of a gigantic a pterodactyl. They measured the wingspan which was 160 feet! The body was four feet wide and 92 feet long. They reported it to a local paper (the Tombstone Epitaph which ran the story on April 26.) Another feature described about this flying monstrosity was that it had a piercing cry and thunderous beating wings. These measurement admittedly seem somewhat extreme, however the cowboys apparently cut off part of the wing to confirm the existence of the creature. As to how much the newspaper determined the validity of the story may be up for debate, but curiously, based on the newspapers description of the creature it's felt this was a Quetzelcoatlus, whose fossils are real and found in Texas. Could this be the legendary thunderbird spoken of by the Sioux Indians?

MORE XENO-ZOOLOGICAL DINOSAUR TIDBITS

LOCAL FAUNA

(3rd ed. Insert 2016) African explorer Frank Melland kept hearing vague rumors about a much feared animal called Kongomato, said to live in the Jinndu swamps. (located in Northwest Rhodesia near what at the time was the Belgian Congo) Asking the natives what it was, he was told that it was a bird, but not exactly a bird, but more like a lizard with wings and skin like a bat. So he showed them a picture of a pterodactyl and the natives pointed at the picture excitedly and said "Kongamato!"

WHATCHOO TALK'N 'BOUT, THOSE AREN'T EXTINCT!

(3rd ed. Insert 2016) An Olympic running team visiting the states was listening to Kent Hovind's lectures mentioning Pterodactyls and pteranodons and afterwards came to him and chatted with him asking him ' Why do your schools in America say they lived millions of years ago? We have those creatures in my village. They are rarely seen and they like decayed human flesh and they dig up buried people.

WE HAVE THEM TOO!

(3rd ed. Insert 2016) Adam **Hutchison a missionary to** Venezuela, heard the natives speak of a fearful giant flying bat that would capsize canoes and carry off Indians. So they sent their bravest men to the head of the (Muwada) River (around 1968) to kill one of them and buried it by the river. When Clint (another missionary) showed them a picture of a pterodactyl the natives eyes got "as big as saucers" and they said "That *is* the bat!". They positively identified the bat as what we refer to as an extinct dinosaur. Natives of the area still are afraid to fish near that river.

YEAH? WELL SO DO WE!... AND OURS GLOW IN THE DARK!

(3rd ed. Insert 2016) On the island of Seram (part of an Indonesian chain of islands) off the coast of New Guinea, Missionary Tyson Hughes says that the local people talk of a creature 4 ½ feet tall with leathery wings (similar to wings of a bat) which they call Orang-Bati (which means "man with wings") that lives in caves on the side of a volcano (You know, like in King Kong). They come at people when they are fishing to try and steal their fish. The people of the area say its favorite food is decaying flesh. It's said to glow in the dark and thus appears to have some sort of bioluminescence aspect in its skin. One missionary was fishing at night under water and his wife was holding a flashlight during which a glowing creature hovered above her dripping some of this glowing stuff around her. One lady from Indonesia while hearing about this story in a seminar came up and said that they have these creatures there and asked why do schools in America teach they lived millions of years ago?

OH THOSE!...BIG DEAL... WE HAVE THEM TOO.

(3rd ed. Insert 2016) Dr. Carl Baugh has gone to Papua New Guinea several times and interviewed many locals who have seen pterodactyl (which the locals call Ropen).

Jerry Williams missionary to the area for 28 years knows the creature is still alive because the natives talk about them so often. One of his missionary friends saw one and said it glowed in the dark, and indeed many have seen one and they too have stated that it glowed in the dark.

COELACANTH. MISSING LINK NOT CONNECTED TO ANY OTHER CHAINS

One embarrassment of the paleontologists is the Coelacanth. This fossil was figured to be 20 million years old. A true dinosaur, yet to their dismay they found some of them in fish markets in India and found more swimming merrily on their way in the Indian ocean and Madagascar areas.

These are a really cool fish to watch swim because of their unusual articulated fins. One might build a boat or submarine with similar working appendages. Though I can't seem to think why, they seem similar to humming birds in the way they are so exact in their motor coordination.

Even as a fossil this was an intriguing specimen and it was believed to be a missing link between the sea creatures and land creatures. It was called the fish with legs, and evolutionists claimed this creature evolved, and then went onto land to later grow limbs and evolve even further. But here "20 million years" later the fish is still identical to the fossils, except it has flesh, life, and still swims. No evolutionary change whatsoever. Nope, not so much as a freckle. But the evolutionists are right; it does go on land now...after it gets caught by fishermen and taken to fish markets.

DISTORTIONS WITH AGE?

It's entirely possible that when a creature such as a dinosaur continues to grow and grow for hundreds of years some physical changes may take place as it grows larger, similar to how men's faces can become quite distorted by growth as compared to babies, possibly making it quite unrecognizable in its later years compared to what it would look like in its early life. So what may have been a real cute little lizard in the forest might eventually turn into some ugly ferocious fire breathing killosaurus.

Basic shape and such would likely remain the same but things such as external bony structures might significantly be altered over a dinosaurs life span. It's quite possible the same creature in fossil form found in various stages of growth could be identified as two or three different dinosaur's which may in fact all be the same dinosaur. People have difficulty identifying sheep bones from goat bones and they are still alive! I have to imagine that maybe some similar problems are occurring with dinosaur bones too.

More accurate studies may indeed show that some of these dinosaurs started out like the very alive lizards we see here on earth today, and may indeed be the exact same creatures that we now call dinosaurs!

WHAT MAKES A DINOSAUR A DINOSAUR?

Many creatures in and on earth today could pass for dinosaurs if we hadn't known they still existed before we found their fossil remains. Take the leopard seal. This has got to be the most ferocious creature of the poles to rival the polar bear, even killing men. This is not a seal you want to feed fish to at the aquarium! It even looks dinosaur like.

Interestingly after I made this observation I read in a March 1959 Readers digest about the amazing adventure of Sir Ernest Shackleton and his polar expedition of 1915 that turned into an ordeal of survival.

At one point on a hunt for food, the hunters became the hunted. A large leopard seal jumped out of the water onto the ice floe and started to pursue one of the men. The description of this creature as told by the writer is interesting. "The beast looked like a dinosaur, with a long serpentine neck".

Take the paleontologist words with a grain of salt and allow yourself to imagine a time when we lived with dinosaurs, because we still do.

Chapter 8

SIGNS OF DEVOLUTION

This theory is meant to show that there is a perceptible decline in man and the animals of the earth, and indeed in the earth, the solar system and universe itself.

When we compare ourselves to the ancients we can see that we were truly an amazing creature that is still a remarkable creation, even though there is a marked decline evident in the human race...if you're brave enough to look for it. Evolution does not look for it, but ignores it, and suppresses the evidence. They want to make us think we are better than anyone before our time, and consequently we look down on our ancestors, their beliefs and living standards. For example to say the "wise men" were following the planets to some place on earth is really an insult. But I'll get to that in chapter 9)

Obviously if evolution is not true then we are not becoming more complex, superior, and climbing up some mythical ladder of advancement to perfection. Though the idea of evolving upward is actually quite old, with similar theories even being expressed by some of the ancients, it seems to be more a theory to compliment ourselves or make ourselves feel better, than to face the alternative.

One might argue that we are staying the same and we have been at this level all the time. Well possibly, as before I started this research this was what I thought was the case. I believed the creation theory but assumed we were created the way we are now. However the evidence does not suggest this is the case either. But if it is not the case, what is the alternative? It's not good. Not only are we *not* advancing to a state of perfection or at least staying the same but in fact the exact opposite appears to be true. Though creation appears even more plausible, the conclusions show we are declining from a state of perfection to the state we find ourselves in. This is very unsettling to many and completely unacceptable to the evolutionists who want us to believe the opposite. Not stuff people want to hear... doesn't sound too complimentary. But it may be frightfully nearer the truth than any branch of science is letting on. For any positive societal changes to be made, one thing we need to get a grasp on, is this declining state we find ourselves in. Once we come to grips with this inexorable fact, entropy can be tackled full force and slowed to its minimum.

More apologies.

This chapter seems to get away from me a few times and gets annoying, even to me. I seem to get sidetracked and don't know a good cut off spot so I left it. I get on some tangent and sometimes get off on some religious track so this chapter could use some editing as I don't seem to know when to shut up. But just as I think about slashing something, it stops and I make a new insight that make sense in the light of the chapter. So take heart, just when you think you wanna throw the book at the dog, or me, I change channels.

HOW FAR DOWN THE LADDER ARE WE?

One might argue that morals have nothing to do with a physical genetic decline. I would argue the contrary. Almost every major civilization that at one time reached a peak of civilization eventually also reached a peak of moral decline. Then almost as if to limit the spread of their obstinate aberrations they were conquered by some force and brought to naught. Pre-flood, Egyptians, Romans, Persians, Ancient Greeks, Babylonians, and on and on succumbed to these trends. But what often followed was a dark age either minimal or very pervasive. Now admittedly I don't know my ancient history all that well, so I can only give generalities, but many are aware of these facts so I state them to make a point.

These events triggered further decline in these areas. The ancient wars appear to have been of an elemental force, nuclear, or chemical variety and they appear to have been the cause for the greatest declines, with an impact to their environment and even on a genetic level. It seems the further advanced the societies were the bigger impact they had adversely on the earth and man when they fell. Though some might say their fall was welcome to get rid of their immoral ways from off the face of the earth. But with that eradication of the civilization also came the swing toward the eradication of their knowledge. Many many libraries were burned as a 'service' to mankind. But with genetic decline in the picture each time a new civilization started the upward trend meant it was more difficult to climb out of the previous dark age, with smaller incremental steps. Remaining knowledge, if it was any good, was often of an ancient form. People looked back at ancient maps and formulas to rebuild civilization because they no longer had the capability to come up with these concepts on their own. Once the ancient knowledge was lost, many steps and increments were needed to get back knowledge we once had which was second nature to the ancients and their forefathers. Only long arduous collections of what little ancient material was left has made us realize how advanced the ancients really were. But now with evolution we look down on those ancients as simple backward people. And so consequently evolutionists can't or won't explain the odd appearance of advanced building capabilities or advanced maps or knowledge of stellar information and on and on. Instead they hide and even destroy these evidences to perpetuate their theories. Thankfully they can't destroy some stuff. As dangerous as those pyramids became they still stand as a reminder to all of us of our entropic descent.

I tend to think moral values also have to be a part of the devolution picture. However in talking to some people I found it surprising to find some people think we are becoming more ethical and moral. Perhaps we are making more laws to enforce ethical behavior, but what has to be enforced now was at one time considered common sense or courtesy. So understanding the contrary view and opinions, I'll make my pitch then get off the subject and get back to the physical science.

If this decline is true, then what state ARE we in, and where are we headed?! Only holding fast to moral or Godly values has prevented us from slipping into the worst state of barbarism and licentiousness to come. But these principles are being thrown out faster than one can shed clothes to play in the mud. At one time bedroom talk was exactly that, but now it seems it's public debate and offhand conversation on busses. Since disciplining children has been all but outlawed, now the children are virtually devoid of patience and reasoning or respect for authority, parental or otherwise, and demand their way and tend toward bullying those weaker or smarter than them. Even the very teachers and authority figures themselves are being intimidated. In fact now extremist groups are demanding that not only moral values be tossed out with prayer in schools and out of teaching curriculums, but perverse lifestyles are being thrust on our children in school as if to speed up the process toward a completely depraved society, void of all value systems. One would think they want to outlaw morality and indeed outlaw laws themselves. This is not just my observation or conclusions. Michael E. Tymn states, we are "rapidly becoming a soulless nation…governed by "seven deadly sins." Lust on TV, Greed and envy by advertising industry. Pride or arrogance by revered athletes and entertainers, and "…gluttony and sloth are ever so obvious." "…clearly we live in an era of moral decadence, a time of egocentricity, intolerance, entitlement, hypocrisy, disorder, strife, chaos, celebrity worship, and fear." …"hedonism"…(not even a word I use). (Atlantis Rising #117) Intelligence is hardly valued anymore, but only power, wealth, fame, and things that do not indicate intelligence or strength of character are sought. If perchance some incredible scientist does come along and is admired often they are vilified by others out of jealousy until they die then they are set up on pedestals too late to spread their knowledge firsthand. Very few brilliant stars overcome these obstacles during their lifetimes. This rush to be a famous singer or sports hero is an empty ambition, as we will find we are not as satisfied with the result, unless we are truly happy with what we do, because we are not seeking to do these things for the glory or money they offer. It's said the American dream has changed from the seeking a home to call your own to the pursuit of fame. Fame is fleeting and certainly no guarantee of happiness.

To touch on an opposing argument. One area people felt we were becoming more ethical in, was in the area of treatment of women. Some felt that some laws such as ownership of women as property or women's lack of equality in voting were examples of how we have advanced ethically. Perhaps. But I have noticed a tendency for society to take wild swings from opinion to opinion over time, often traceable to very small incidents. I don't see a lot of evidence that such laws as these mentioned here existed in ancient times and the bible doesn't mention any such laws either.

Obviously some biblical rules for gender treatment do exist. But it seems some took these to extremes to insure the status quo that may have got upset in points in time by women showing men up. Perhaps as retribution, some ridiculous laws were then made by these same men. Say for example {though I don't know this for sure in this particular case} perhaps men introduced laws to stop any more Joan of Arcs from cropping up. Such new and unnecessary laws in turn got taken to further extremes. Only excessive abuse of certain privileges caused wild swings in the opposite direction.

Remember some Greek philosophers felt any change to society was ultimately a negative one. And of course any such laws would have been put in place long after the biblical laws were put forth. Jesus even spoke of the religious leaders also making traditions and then making them more important than the laws.

No doubt much could be made of all these opinions but this is not the place to discuss them simply because it could mean whole volumes of opinions contrary and endorsing these ideas. And these discussions probably belong in a book about sociology. But this does illustrate my point when I said "... we are making more laws to enforce ethical behavior, but what has to be enforced now was at one time considered common sense or courtesy." Meaning we are finding it increasingly necessary to come up with such laws because our willingness or capacity to uphold such "common courtesies" are, for whatever reason, diminishing over time. Similarly prior to the Leviticus laws being introduced, there were few such laws necessary because we either understood them naturally or declines in our physiology were becoming apparent. I'll get back to this.

HERD MENTALITY

This may seem like a diatribe but hear me out, there is a logical explanation at the end for what I'm about to go into...though I suppose good arguments could be made to the contrary.

Because of genetic decline it stands to reason that intelligent reasoning would be rarer and theoretically at a premium to the people. But all too often persons that exhibit brilliance, fair treatment, judgment or equal time for both sides of a point of controversy, are accused of being traitors to one side or the other and vilified. Even Tesla was fought against. Though Charlie Chaplin wasn't necessarily in this category, I use his example as he is a personal favorite of mine. His movie "The Great Dictator" was a brilliant hilarious spoof and stab at Hitler and his cohorts, yet he was vilified for his efforts and even an outcast because of them! I watched the movie and got it right away and marvel at his bravery, for no doubt the Nazis got it too. (3rd ed. insert 2016) Hah...is my face red! He wasn't exiled for this film as I had always thought; the McCarthy witch hunts pegged him as a Commie, and he wasn't allowed back into USA when he went for a holiday in 1952 to England. Oddly enough my next paragraph was about just that very period!)

Just look at the McCarthy era red hunts. We seemed to abandon reason and started pointing fingers at so many different people in an environment of fear. Few were able to reason logically and were easily whipped into a frenzy by advocates of these red hunts. Few realized opinions and standing up for the underdog or having a friend that might be a Communists did not mean that the person doing such apparently horrible things were Communists but were exercising free thought, loyalty and fairness, or just being friendly.

Even the courts were apparently challenging the rights to the freedom of thought! It seemed as though the McCarthies of the period were saying let government think for you. In the determination to avoid the extreme left, whatever that might be; liberalism, Nazism, Communism, they swung too far to the right. Edward R. Murrow found himself under personal attack by McCarthy when he questioned the sanity of the all pervasive red hunts. Fortunately Murrow was of stalwart enough character to withstand the onslaughts of the ridiculous accusations hurled at him for his efforts.

Consider how easily Nazi Germany overpowered the population of that country with their Aryan superiority complex. Even some people that had, and were loyal to, Jewish friends were killed. One wonders what a few Edward R. Murrow's might have done for that country had they been in place. He would have done his research and told the people exactly what Hitler's infamous book Mien Kampf was all about, maybe woke a few people before too many went to sleep. So easily do we get swayed by a few fanatical fear mongers, little giving ear to voices of opposing opinions if the fear monger has his way.

So often, radio or TV personalities condone a particular point of view and people who admire these people, that they have never met, just fall in line with that person views, and unless that person exhibits some restraint or ideas that involve a fair look at both sides of the fence, they will sway people to their point of view even if there is no logic to that position whatsoever. Some people are often unwilling to think for themselves but follow their idols. In fact this loyalty can be well beyond reason. It can get to the point they cannot be talked out of a ridiculous opinion no matter how logical the points of debate from of a contrary view might be to what they believe. Often people adopt another person's opinions just to be associated with that person, regardless of what that opinion is. I have been simply amazed at people that will do this. This may be why global warming nonsense has gotten so much steam, which had to be changed to "climate change" when global warming was found to be a farce. But don't get me started. There are books about that side if the argument if you dare to look at facts and not people like Suzuki that think people should be in jail if you disagree with him.

Just for example. From 1974 to 1980 or so global cooling was feared. Global warming was thought existed after that period but was later realized as just a fluctuation. For 19 or more years, well into the "Inconvenient truth" about "global warming" business, the world was cooling again. So global warming mantra has been dropped in favour of Climate change. They don't tell you they don't plug in the effect of the sun or the clouds into the computers models, even though the sun is the biggest factor in Global temperatures. (see Book 19 for some of this pg 131-132, and do some research for the rest of it instead of believing the famous people bought off by the people with pocket filling agendas)

We need to be willing to seek out and hear opinions of all sides of a point of view so we won't be swayed unnecessarily by an extreme opinion spoken from an otherwise charming person. Maybe some aspects of an extreme point of view might have merit, but that does not mean all points of that view will be correct. Be willing to sift the wheat from the chaff, the silver from the dross. Be willing to question something said no matter how much you like who said it. This will prevent extreme swings in popular movements. Stop being lazy, don't accept you're hero's word for it, prove or disprove it, and look at contrary opinions, and don't be afraid to have your conclusions challenged or overturned.

We need to be true to our principles but also willing to admit some of our knowledge or points of view might be wrong. There's no shame in being wrong. There is foolishness in being persuaded we are wrong then staying with the error for the sake of loyalty or pride. We need to be comfortable being ourselves with all of our opinions and points of view, and not be afraid to be seen as different sociologically & succumb to a herd mentality.

NO ONE WANTS TO BE ASSOCIATED WITH A "LOSER"

All too often people will root for the apparent winner. Look at the ways so many people root for sports teams. So often we cheer for the winner who isn't even the home team. We need to be of the mentality where we stand behind the home team, not abandoning them as soon as they go on a losing streak. (Obviously there are people who root for the underdogs too) I know this seemingly has nothing to do with standing on principles and knowing what they are, but I see a connection. If we are loyal to our friends and our home teams so to speak, we will less likely be swayed by extreme views and even be prepared to stand up for our own.

BUT WHAT HAS ALL THIS TO DO WITH DEVOLVING?

What I'm saying is diversity of thought and opinion is an aspect that maintains mental viability and inventive thought patterns in a society; similar to how diversity of genes maintains viability of a population, and diversity of the types of creatures in the earth and the types of plants in the earth maintains a more viable and complex ecosystem. Whereas making everyone think the same way limits diversity in society, and indeed can be extremely detrimental to that society.

Though we are apparently advanced in media, this mass media can also be used to narrow the focus of thought. For example when a single incorrect theory such as evolution takes hold of a society, it forms societies' thoughts and molds the character and moral standards of its individuals in direct response to that incorrect uniform thought. Thus the character of society takes on the error of the theory, and anyone that refuses or refutes the incorrect theory becomes a nonconformist and can even be perceived as a disruption to society.

With Germany having just Hitler and Goebbels dictating how Germanys people thought, virtually a whole population became tunnel visional with most thought dictated by their media and directed from the top down. Radio, school subjects, military training, newspapers, archaeological research, art, music, political perspectives, scientific "research", architecture, was all directed in this narrow focus to prove the supremacy of a race and the detrimental aspects of other races and religions. But this narrowing of societies focus isn't just something that happened in Nazi Germany. It has been done in the past in other societies too.

People have tried to use evolution to prove various races have smaller brains by filling skulls with ordinary flour and showing one race had bigger brains then others. In essence evolutionists are suggesting some races are more advanced than others, thus they are saying some are better than others, when in fact we are all the same species descended from the same mother and father. Thus "science" has been used by evolutionists to foster racism.

Evolution is also fostering some other negative aspects in our societies. The eroding of morals as based on evolution has justified behaviors that were not formerly considered of a moral sort. Consequently orders may be followed without thinking of the ramification of those orders. I heard of one nurse who when asked if euthanasia was legal and she was told to kill a 9 year child would she do it, and she seemed fine with this, no matter how the question was phrased. This is frighteningly close to what Hitler was trying to steer Germany into doing from 1924-1945. All it did was bring about the almost complete destruction of the German country.

Limitation and steering of thought in a society have extreme dangers to that society which can be linked to devolution of man as a whole, by limiting or destroying diversity of thought and opinion.

Though we claim we are a diverse open minded society, unfortunately by the nature of the two extremes they are mutually exclusive. People perpetrating obscenities bring down a society by virtue of their freedom and abuse this freedom at the cost of other people's peace of mind. And these same people that would abuse these freedoms strike out at the very people that would temper these freedoms with consideration for others.

Evolution has changed what we feel is morally OK, because the moral standard is no longer absolute, so instead of evolving it is eroding and devolving. By diminishing a societies' morals, and values based on evolutionary principles we also diminish a societies' understanding of what is right and wrong. As society shifts from a moral religious Godly focus to a relativistic, atheistic, materialistic man centered focus, the society will metamorph from the values of one focus to the values of the other focus. What we see in our society is the result of this shift. Back to Michael E. Tymn... He felt this period in history where the seven deadly sins have taken a hold of society could be traced back to the 19th century. This trend in man on earth today started in the "age of reason" and came from Darwinism's mistaken belief that "...biological evolution had completely nullified religious dogma". "By around 1870, materialism, scientism, and nihilism had become accepted philosophies among the educated." It got a good foothold in the roaring 20's, stalled in the depression, and took off with the advent of Television, and has reached an alarming stage with "... reality shows and uncensored lewdness and vulgarity." (Atlantis Rising #117)

UPWARD OR DOWNWARD TREND?

If the universe and all matter contained therein is not becoming more complex, then it is either on average staying the same or devolving to a less complex state. I think it's fair to assume that we agree it is not staying the same. Change is evident and obvious, but the question is, is that change in a upward more complex direction or in a downward less complex direction or an average balance where all things stay equal? Surprisingly this is less than obvious to us, otherwise theories like Evolution would never get off the ground, and originally I thought it was a balance that always stayed equal. Entropy was a real eye opener for me.

Considering the very fact that entropy is already proven true, I find it quite strange that evolution as a theory is even taught at all. In a sense this chapter is not really even necessary, as entropy has already been proven. But we seem to be unwilling to make the leap that says if the universe and the earth is in a state of decline then we must be too. We seem to want to believe that even as the earth and universe around us crumbles to dust we somehow are advancing and becoming more complex and perfect. This is just simply wishful thinking because it is just an impossibility.

WHAT IF SOCIETY NOW ABANDONED EVOLUTION?

What if society were suddenly to abandon evolutionary thinking and return to creationist centered belief patterns? There would likely be a rush of people clamoring for authority in the return to these principles as so many simply want power of some kind over people, be it educational or religious. Jesus said let the greatest among you be the servants of all and not rule over you like some do. (see Matthew chapter 23). Once again society would have a wild swing from one extreme to another.

Since few in our society are well versed anymore in this old form of religious godly moral standards, we would be even more prone to a society similar to the McCarthy or Hitler era. If a society has lost a firm grip on what is right and wrong and become lazy in the search to find out what is right and wrong, they will be more prone to accepting teachings of apparent authorities in these areas...probably based on the charisma of the teachers. But a look at the diverse religions in the world and their belief systems show that a mass return to "religion" would mean suddenly there would be massive competition for the minds of the people, probably on a global scale. Since we have allowed so many diverse religions to roost in our society, were a return to religion and God ever to become a trend, few would know where to go or which way to turn, and consequently we could easily be misled. We might become like India which is referred to by some as the land of a million gods. Though the true God does still have a place in India as ancient histories would still have these principals kicking around, the creator appears to be simply one of the many gods of India.

People with this 'root for the winner' mentality, would tend to go toward the most popular religion or leader, not really knowing if it was right or wrong, and could easily be misled by the teachers of that religion. Once a particular branch of religious thought became the dominant one it would become more powerful and soon force all others to join it or face very serious consequences. This would be the time when we would have to know and stand on what we believe or be pulled or forced into a dominant religion. It's entirely possible a huge outbreak of wars and civil wars could occur in this struggle of the various religions for superiority, until a single religion became universally accepted or forced upon the masses.

Freedom of thought would be subject to the dictates of that religion. Laws or overturning of laws would become subject to these dictates. And eventually that religion could be led by a small group of individuals. This of course is a worst case scenario, but based on some of the prophesies in the bible this could be a far more realistic scenario than it might at first seem.

To steer away from this scenario or eventuality, hero worship has to be discouraged, because all heroes will let us down, for they are human like us. Individual thought has to be encouraged and large councils of elders need to be relied upon for guidance. But obviously since our society has been in decline for a long time, many of our older folks have also given themselves over to perversities and only elders with a long track record of balanced moral values should be considered for these positions, though I think we should be willing to render respect and honor to all our elders, for even the foolish can learn from their mistakes.

Furthermore we once again need to return to a society that looks to learn from our forefathers. Why? Because with less societal entropy in the past, by learning and upholding our pasts standards we reverse societal entropy. This would likely mean less societal pressure to have the latest new thing. Sales of the frivolous items might plummet and a reduced profit margin for many would likely take place to take into account environmental and compassionate issues. Consider Quebec…

DELIBERATELY DESTROYING DIVERSITY FOR THE SAKE OF A BUCK

(3rd ed. Insert 2016) Reduced diversity is also a form of devolution. Quebec (A Province of Canada) has been a somewhat interesting social community that has resisted some of the changes of the outside world through culture, religion and language. They call it a "distinct society", and indeed it is. Were all localized populations like this, it would be very difficult to create a uniform world society, to force the will of a single world ideology on: So how is this "nut" being cracked? Through consumerism. The media hoped to expand their commercial operations in Quebec. "To maximize the impact of advertising they needed a homogeneous and unified market, rather than one that was broken down into different classes, mentalities, interests, and taste. It was important in this respect to integrate the rural population into the consumer society that had already taken over the cities and larger towns." This was part of a "…vast movement that was leveling mentalities, introducing a new form of social conformity, and, at the same time, unifying the audience for the advertising and the market for consumer goods." It goes on to state that educational reforms were geared to "…parallel that of [a] consumer society" The new objective had been "…the schooling of large masses of students to meet the requirements of industry and of the economy in general." The bottom line of this "Quiet Revolution" was to replace the influence the church traditionally had on this society, "inexorably imposing it's will, there began to emerge a new force capable of maintaining a form of social control very similar to that of the church in its method and its pervasive presence:…" (Quebec National Crisis Pg 34.) Consumerism's direct target was the church. So you see…you've been HAD!

DEVOLVING AND DISORGANIZATION NOT NECESSARILY THE SAME THING. A SERIES OF INTANGIBLES.

Since we've found that nothing actually substantiates the theory of evolution, it stands to reason we should be able to find something that substantiates the theory of devolution since these are two opposite theories.

The problem becomes what were man, life, and the earth like in the distant past? Had we not covered this in previous chapters, the apparent obvious answer to us likely would be we were primitive savages because knowledge has advanced amazingly in the last 200 years. The answer would appear to be that we are becoming more advanced and not devolving at all. But are we becoming more evolved or are we just becoming more organized?

With war and natural disasters often a civilization can be destroyed and become disorganized, where pockets or whole areas can regress to a more 'primitive' state in order just to survive. After wars, even of the 20th century, many countries were on the edge of economic collapse. Only the helping or iron hands of the sympathetic nations or the conquerors kept these countries from spiraling down to a completely disorganized state, similar to that of the dark ages. When there are periods of no war and geologic stability, a society can build or rebuild and become organized. Overall it would seem organization time has outdistanced destructive results of wars and nature, to allow us to reach this state. And we have introduced methods that speed up organization almost as fast as wars can inflict disorganization.

When one reads the written or hears the verbal histories of primitive tribes one finds still in this state around the globe, we see that they speak of a time when they were in fact more advanced, knew more knowledge and were anything but "primitive". Events have rendered them to this state, and they learned from those events.

Though they are still capable of climbing out of their current state to what most of us would consider "civilized and advanced", the very fact that to this point they have not done so shows a decline to a state where return to advancement is a longer and harder road to travel. (that or they maintain a high regard for their forefathers legends and are smart enough not to strive for what we call advances, because they know them to be destructive to their society as was the case in the past).

Be that as it may, my point here, assuming today's level of technology and organization are the desired end, is that each decline or Dark Age makes it harder to retain a previous status or state of organization. We can only conclude that there will eventually come a time when re-attaining such a status will in fact become impossible. And as we've seen to a large degree this is the case. We think we are more advanced than our ancestors, but we are light years below them. This will become even more clear as we show more of man's past physiology and advances next chapter.

So we see that it is not only the amount of disorganization that indicates a state of decline, but the time society needs to re-attain a previous level of organization, and the ability to grasp, manage and constructively use that amount of organization.

ORGANIZATION NOT THE SAME AS EVOLUTION

If we take devolution seriously, we become aware that not just society but our actual physical and genetic makeup is in a state of decline.

Is organization a sign of genetic evolving in an upward trend? No, because organizational skills are inherent in our genetic makeup. Whereas for example they are not inherent in say monkeys. Obviously no matter what animal I chose one could argue they are organized too. These are likely the people that believe monkeys had gun factories, drew pictograms and wrote the bible. But seriously, animals are not writing books, flying aircraft, making pyramids and philosophizing now are they. (certain space monkeys exempt from this argument)

We've seen that evolution may be a invalid theory. We shall see that with the showing of the opposite, that is devolution, being true this will further invalidate the evolution theory. Even evolution can sound plausible when presented right. But by the same token even creationistic ideas can sound right if presented right. This is why we need to be willing to think for ourselves. If we do not have our wits about us, it can be so easy for us to be misled. Some ascertain that if you say anything confidently enough and with enough authority you can fool anyone.

One might suggest that the very theory of evolution is proof that we are declining, because if we really were advancing we wouldn't be worried about such things as proving we are evolving, but I suppose one could argue the reverse is true too, depending on your outlook.

In fact to look at the technological advancements of our society one could immediately deduce we're advancing and not declining at all. I remember as a youth someone saying that we are declining to me and I wondered how that could be. It's not obvious. It has to be understood by careful observations of the evidence.

In essence this chapter shows how resilient the human species is, that even in our devolved state we can accomplish so much, and we get a greater appreciation for what once was, and the creation as a whole. It should also demonstrate how dangerous we can be to ourselves, and our environment, as if THAT hasn't been stated enough by the environmentalist's movement of today.

Though certain somewhat radical elements in our society tend to look upon all technological advances as declines for reasons other than those presented here; one could argue to the contrary with completely different reasons than I present here. But radical views aside, though no doubt some will think me radical, to show devolution is likely the case, something fairly concrete should be evident to substantiate the devolution theory.

ENVIRONMENTAL DISORDER

As we have started to see with the breakup of the continents, the reduced life span of man, the destruction of the 5th planet, the rings around various planets and the collapse of the water shell that caused the flood, clearly things on earth, and in the solar system have been disintegrating from a high state of organization to more randomness, disorder and less viability.

Things are not evolving to a state of nirvana and perfect order, they are disintegrating *from* that state toward complete matter chaos and heat death, and life on earth is disintegrating to a point of non-viability and eventual nonexistence. If creation is the correct theory we must also assume there is a creator with whom we have to do.

I present a few interesting tidbits, maybe the odd insight, and of course more weight to support this as well as other aspects of this work.

Entropy is true for the cosmos, and for life on earth. Planets slowly have their orbits disintegrate and fall into the suns they circumnavigate, (or do they get free of the gravity of the suns? My research seems to suggest both possibilities exist.) suns blow up, and here on earth, erosion slowly wears away the rock so that all the earth would eventually turn to silt.

Indeed the ocean floors have already accumulated thousands of feet of silt that was originally at one time part of the surface of the land. Eventually all land above the surface of the ocean will be below the surface in the form of silt.

Before the flood there was no rain so this form of erosion and entropy was virtually nonexistent. Thus when rain became the way of distributing moisture on the earth, erosion, if it existed at all before the flood, was now sped up ten thousand fold. We do know they had rivers before the flood but as to what fed these rivers is somewhat speculation. If the riverbeds were pure bedrock, erosion would be almost nonexistent.

Possibly the mists were of such volume they fed these rivers, thus erosion might have existed before the flood, but if the world was created to last forever these rivers must have been like underwater springs of an extremely unchanging nature. Likely what kept the springs even running was the pressure of tidal actions from the moon and sun and the rotation of the earth. Almost as if these geological and planetary forces acted like a pump on the underground water sources.

Since even rock will erode over time we must then conclude then, that before sin entered the picture this law of entropy and thus erosion, was not in effect. When man changed his physiology due to sin, this very physiology began affecting the very environment he lived in. Admittedly this is somewhat speculation, but interestingly Evolutionists consider there must have been a time when the laws of entropy did not exist and something changed to start entropy on the course it is now taking us too. Well this may be the cause and effect they are looking for, if they are willing to accept it.

This is also the case for atoms where the orbits of electrons are known to slowly lose energy and left to their own all matter would eventually collapse.

It's been admitted and noted, that many creatures of today's world, when compared to ancient fossils of the same creature, descend from creatures more advanced or perfectly structured than the same creatures of today; completely the opposite of expectations. And I might add, is a surprisingly short time.

This makes perfect sense for if all was created we must assume a perfect God created a perfect creature. If there is any change evident from that point onward it, for whatever reason, can only be disintegrating in details to whatever form they posses today. So whatever the detail of those changes might be, they can only be negative downward changes.

I find it interesting that they found this bit of information at all. I would have assumed the creatures stayed physically the same, possibly only not growing as large. It would be interesting to see what creatures they observed these downward trends in, and what those downward trends were. All I have found is the fossils seem to suggest the creatures before were often bigger. But here's a few I found...

Everything was bigger back then.(3ʳᵈ ed. Insert 2016) Fossil deer antlers have been found with a 12 foot span. Kangaroo fossils 10 feet tall. Wombat the size of a Morris Mini, and a "Prehistoric" goose found as tall as an elephant...which would have weighed a half ton! Christmas goose for dinner...invite the town and those from the next town too! Salamander's found 6 feet long. Shark teeth can give a rough estimate as to the size of the shark and a shark tooth was found that indicated the shark was approximately 80 feet long. Oyster shells were found 11.5 feet wide. Dinorus Maximus, a bird, was only 13 feet tall, and donkeys found 9 feet at the shoulder. Yet evolutionists knowing about these fossils, are "willingly ignorant" and refuse to even allow even the slightest possibility for giants in the past. I don't get it.

The tracks at Paluxy showing dinosaurs and men prints together in the same strata had strides of the man tracks 6 feet apart. Try that. My deduction (as I've not heard it said) is that the feet were impressed in such a way as to show the guy was walking (not running). But I'm no expert.

And what about us? I know evolutionists absolutely will not allow giants into the past of man in the evolution chart. Oddly many giant skeletons have been found and they are ignored or called fakes or hoaxes by evolutionists and the like. Why? I don't understand this mentality at all. Am I missing something? Is this a clue to something that unravels evolution before their eyes completely?

As a kid, I asked, "How do we keep our atmosphere, why doesn't it get sucked away from the earth because of the vacuum of space?" Obviously this sort of material has always interested and fascinated me, and I've constantly tried to understand what makes things tick. I was told gravity holds our atmosphere to the earth. After a question or two I accepted this. But I've since found that we *do* in fact lose atmosphere to space, and there is a vapor trail behind the earth.

This eroded or lost atmosphere is solid evidence of more entropy and seems to me a cause for concern. It is also key to understanding hitherto unexplained biblical statements such as how man could live to such long ages and why animals became more violent and afraid of man. At one point earth had all its atmosphere it was created with, and it affected life in ways no longer happening. Obviously more atmosphere meant less destructive solar rays getting all the way to the surface of the earth. And more radiation means a faster disintegration of all life.

If we accept the biblical text and the line that states we were created a "little lower than the angels", then one wonders what our original created state was. If we look at the biblical record on one hand and then look at most evidence and understanding of angels on the other, one might tend to think we were created a lot lower than the angels. But we were at one time so wonderful we tempted angels and some came to earth and took our women for wives.

The angels themselves felt the difference in stature between man and angels was not enough to prevent this action. This says a lot. Later on the women are told to cover their heads for the angels sake, though I'm not sure if this is to prevent their wrath or for some other reason. However, often after the flood people look to angels in awe and even tended to worship them until the angel themselves told them not to, because they were fellow servants. This alone is evidence enough for the people that believe in angels to show an incredible decline has occurred in the human race.

ENTROPY OR "DEVOLUTION" DEFINED

As we have seen we have descended from lofty heights indeed. In fact when one considers the whole picture, we are in actuality near the bottom of the viability ladder.

As more and more radiation enters the environment we become less and less viable as a species and indeed life itself is at risk. If we were to descend much further we would all exhibit varying degrees of down-syndrome or become primitive savages where the strongest destroy the weakest. That is if we were even able to continue reproducing. Clearly reproductive males and females would be at a premium.

If this is all true then there must be signs of devolving man, but not man only but also animals, earth, and universe, and clearly there is.

COSMIC CAT CALCULATIONS

Interestingly entropy is described as the gradual breakdown of organized to disorganized, complex to simple except where life is involved in which case life itself reverses entropy. I don't know if I can entirely agree with that definition. A chair just sitting there will eventually turn to dust by itself after maybe 1 or 2000 years but my cats are alive and they seem to be able to turn my chairs and couches into devolutionary material a whole lot faster. There might even be some sort of devolutionary equation with cats and chairs... If 2 cats will completely erode 2.6 chairs every 6.4 years, then how long would it take 50 cats to completely demolish an apartment block. Though that is said in jest, it does make an interesting point. One could also impute similar 'equations' to the human race as we seem to be able to turn a mountain into rubble pretty quickly, when we set our minds to it.

ENTROPY

Another definition of entropy is the degradation of energy and matter to the ultimate state of inert uniformity. In other words devolution, that is entropy, is like a man working on a rock with a hammer. The rock breaks apart and the hammer wears away. Eventually there will be no more big rock but little bits and the hammer itself will be worn away. Bigger rocks might be of use for building things but the smaller bits are almost useless, except maybe in the bottom of a fish bowl.

Another way of looking at it is like all the ingredients of a cake mix. Separate they are easily distinguishable and readily useable, but when you mix them together the individual ingredients are far harder to sort. Well the whole universe is becoming more and more like the ingredients of the cake mix; when mixed, more work is needed to sort the particles.

Eventually all matter will be a uniform mass of evenly mixed elements, similar to the silt at the bottom of the ocean. This is the ultimate end to devolution. But with mans tendency toward organization one could quickly come to the conclusion we are obviously advancing because we are organizing. We appear to be sorting the cake mix into its individual elements, but curiously at the same time we are turning the mountains into rubble. So is this a balancing act, and are things staying the same but with change evident? I don't think so...you can't put that mountain back together.

Two of the laws of thermodynamics and entropy are when there is no energy for work you have heat death and when matter is broken down completely you have matter chaos. The second law (Law of energy decay) has been proven experimentally thousands of times. You need energy to sort the cake mix.

Astronomers began counting the number of radio sources in space back through time. They found more radio signals existed in the distant past than now. (I don't know how they do this so I can't explain it, but this is established regardless.) The obvious and inescapable conclusion is the universe is inexorably moving toward heat death. Astronomers are always finding stars that blow up. They do not find them being made. They theorize them being made, but they can't find them. The matter contained in the stars turns to dust that no longer sheds heat and light and diffuses to a state of inert uniformity.

But forget blowing up, it seems just the very act of giving light causes entropy. Stars emit radiation and light and these have energy therefore light itself is the diffusion of mass to this eventual state of inert uniformity. (book 44 pg 197)

DUST TO DUST

If we momentarily accept creation, Genesis chapter one shows a universe in this state of complete entropy at the time when God said "let there be light". Before this point all that existed was darkness upon the face of the deep. During that point there was a state of complete heat death as the theory of entropy might deduce it, and matter as we know it didn't even exists. After this point all that existed was light and darkness uniformly mixed together until God separates the light from the darkness, or the particles of the cake mix if you will.

The universe was in a state of inert uniformity, and then creation took place because life (God) existed to undo that state, and indeed create that state in the first place. So even the creation story might be perceived to suggest we went in an upward motion, evolved from inert uniformity. But life was involved in the process of organizing the atoms so this upward reversal of entropy is explained by the definition. So here we see the time when the laws of the universe were indeed reversed! But the agent of reverse entropy is therefore God himself.

One aspect of entropy is it becomes necessary to do more and more work to get less and less results. For example it used to be real easy to get oil and gas from the environment. It was easily found on the surface. But now more work is necessary to get it from below the earth, and thus fuel costs go up, so more work has to be done for us to be able to afford the fuel. Then increasingly difficult forms of energy are sought for. First we used wood, then coal, then oil and even nuclear fuel, and now more and more complex means of energy are needed and the rate of disintegration of the earth also speeds up and vastly more work is needed each time a new source of energy is sought. (Jeremy Rifkin went into more detail in his work. Book 49) This is a simple illustration to show what is happening all around the earth as we exploit the raw materials of the earth. These material become scarcer and scarcer and more expensive and more work is done by any individual to be able to afford those forms of energy.

If we could somehow tap into the energy the earth itself gives off, we might suddenly reduce entropy occurring on earth to the same rate at which the earth itself disintegrates at…in other words exceedingly slowly.

MORE WORK AND WASTE FOR LESS RESULTS.

Since there is life where man is it stands to reason we would appear to be evolving from disorganized to organized, the opposite of devolution. Even after disasters in the past man still organized what little there was left to organize just to cope. But it is the extent to which we are able to organize, that is in question.

If as we assert man's intelligence was somewhere in the range of 900-1000 IQ before the flood and we only average 100 now, and people with 50-80 IQ are barely able to cope, it would seem we as a race are in the last stages of devolution, before complete implosion of the species could conceivably wipe us out.

ONE STEP OR 100 STEP INVENTIONS

If as we deduce we are becoming more mentally, physically and physiologically deficient, then more work is needed to produce the same results.

Take the inventing of technology. Much work and wasted material is used toward advanced organization which is essentially wasted energy with excessive intermediate steps between advances that would normally not be necessary. Did that make ANY sense?

In other words in the past if we wanted to invent an airplane we didn't start with a barely workable model such as the plane the Wright brothers came up with, we would have started with space flight and supersonic travel...without all the intermediate steps of advancing a previously imperfect invention to a more superior state. Yeah! It would seem people back then were just this intelligent. All those intermediate advances would not have been necessary and all the materials used to make those intermediate steps would not have been wasted.

So for example all 100 years of improved automobile manufacturing would have been completely unnecessary. Instead of barely workable and unreliable automobiles at the start improved from year to year we would have started right with fuel efficient safe methods of travel.

In fact I'll take this a step further. They wouldn't have bothered making specialized vehicles, for land travel, water travel, and space travel, they would have made vehicles that were capable of all four methods of motion, that is on land on the sea under the sea in the air and into space. Such vehicles might even have made surface travel obsolete before it ever got invented in the first place! No doubt in this light Noah's ark must have seemed to his peers extremely primitive. What?... a boat? for animals? does it fly? no? why are you building such a silly thing?

This presumes we were intelligent enough in the past that intermediate series of advancement and innovations were not necessary as they are now. They simply would have foresaw the problems before they built them into machines.

We've seen this was likely the case, as the evidence of mans inventive ability in the past show highly advanced technological skills were employed in simply making the buildings they erected.

VICIOUS DOWNWARD SPIRAL

As our physical integrity becomes diminished we live shorter lives and have shorter times where we can be productive and reproduce. Eventually all ability to reproduce comes to an end and all productivity ceases and all life becomes unable to cope or simply ends.

Is this happening in our environment today or are we merrily becoming more advanced despite anything we do to affect our environment? Has our environment becoming more complex? Animals are becoming extinct at the rate of 17 per hour (Discover April 1990) This in itself is evidence of devolution. The earth is becoming less and less diverse and less complex, and less able to support the complex and diverse life forms we find here. And no surprises here, man is the agent whereby the earth's environment is becoming increasingly hostile to life on earth.

By devolution on earth I do not just mean the earth and its inhabitants are declining at a slow long continuous gradual rate, but the rate of decline also appears to be linked with the rate at which the earth itself becomes less accommodating to the inhabitants. However the habitation is being devolved by the inhabitants so they are mutually destructive and supporting, something like sawing the branch on which you rest. The faster we destroy our environment the faster our environment destroys us. A vicious and ever increasingly speeded up downward spiral.

Decline can and did come in bursts as activities on or in the earth mitigated.

When the water sphere collapsed this started the reduction in age and mental grasp of man. Then as the atmosphere escaped earth, man's lifespan and mental grasps were further reduced. Then when continents moved around more radiation entered earth's biosphere, further declining our genetics, life spans and mental grasp. And all these things were caused by man, almost like a fight, every time we hit the earth the earth hits us back.

CROSS PURPOSES

With the earth in upheaval under our feet, above our heads, and indeed the very air we breathe is disintegrating, all these events are in themselves evidence of devolution as the land itself becomes broken up and thus further speeding up erosion.

Instead of one big continent we have several and erosion is speeded up. The ocean floors are often filled with hundreds or thousands of feet of silt, and our air becomes more laced with radioactive Carbon 14. With the last major earth upheavals apparently around 1700 and 700 BC the earth reached a more steady state and devolution also reached a minimal pace, and so mankind himself was in a more stable state, so men of this period onward would be just as devolved as us. Though with the decreased strength of the earth's magnetic field one could argue they were more physically sound even if less organized than us. From that time on only wars and ignorance would limit the progress usually accomplished with peace.

Some indications suggest civilizations in the past, possibly in the 12 or 13th century, progressed as far as we were maybe around 1910 or so with inventions similar to ours in existence in various places around the globe, then wars or fear of these inventions being used for evil happened, and the advances were destroyed, subdued or the knowledge of them once again became lost and a new dark age began.

It seems many dark ages occurred as knowledge was lost. We would make two steps forward and one back, two forward three back and so on. Glimpses through what escaped the wars and fires, such as the advanced maps, books and tidbits of information about ancient flying machines boggle the researchers. We think we are the first to be organized in millennia yet even in the 13th century Roger Bacon wrote "Flying machines as these were of old, and are made even in our days". This statement still boggles historians!

Also, possibly contemporary with Bacon, is a book called the Voynich Manuscript were apparent drawings of nebula and cell structure in plants give indications that microscopes and telescopes existed at that time. This is in the 12 hundreds!! (Though I see some date this manuscript to the 1400's as well.) However this manuscript is still un-deciphered and the drawings thought to be astronomical could also be "crop circles" for all we know.

Furthermore even in the 1700's a Chinese emperor destroyed flight blueprints in case they got into the wrong hands. When certain civilizations became strong and able to defend against marauding hoards, organized progress could be made and less regression occurred until we came to the point where we are at today.

Are we more organized now than we ever were before, or has each successive natural catastrophe and war diminished our capacity to organize just a little bit more? The problem with figuring this out is, that which was before, has been wiped out and is almost off the face of the earth, so how do you tell? It appears we are more organized and intelligent than ever before. So we accept this evolutionary idea wholeheartedly, because it seems so obvious that we are doing better than what was before. How does one tell? To what do we compare? And by what ruler or standard do we measure? Marauding hoards burned library after library with a net loss to knowledge and organization that is still felt for its loss.

We tend to think automobiles are an advanced form of transportation and some of us measure previous civilizations by this ruler. Since we haven't found any cars except wagons and chariots in the past, we tend to think we are more advanced than our forefathers.

Yet only now are we beginning to realizing how deadly the fuel we burn in these cars is, and how many people are being killed in accidents. Look at the unrest in the world simply because we all wrestle for the same fuel resources. Yet these automobiles are really little more than a luxury. As China becomes more and more technological, they too will start to vie for this limited resource. But that will almost double the pressure and demand for these limited resources as the population of China is a real source for concern when added to the mix.

Obviously new energy sources are needed and fast! But the truth is our hunger for the fuel is increasing faster than the technology that would be necessary to replace the need for these fuels.

Perhaps our forefathers never bothered to go through the stage of development of the automobile powered by carbon based fuel because he knew all along the dangers of such simplistic forms of transportation. He knew that not only would it harm the environment, but also was aware of the countless heartaches traffic accidents would cause. He skipped this form of transportation altogether and went right to the vimanas spoken of in the ancient Indian texts. These vimanas may have been incredibly safe with some form of magnetic repulsion guaranteeing no collisions ever occurred, and this form of transportation may have even had the ability to phase matter through matter so no collisions would be felt and cause any damage. Cars as we have today were in all probability beneath their dignity to invent.

Maybe we won't find any ancient cars as we know them back then because they were not dumb enough to make the things! (I pick on cars because I like them so much and I think the vintage ones are so cool, so I speak to my own devolved state here as well) Knowing how to conquer gravity and avoid accidents made the invention of automobiles as we know them a simplistic, polluting, dangerous and barbaric invention.

Steam by some accounts is actually more advanced, yet just when we perfected the steam driven car in the 20's we abandon it for the cheaper easier gas powered monsters that pollute our air today. Why? Because we are just so brilliant. Instead of doing the smart thing and supporting steam technologies we do the cheap easy thing. Sounds like me when I shop. We may still have had all the accidents but we would have had a lot less pollution, and competition for oil reserves...an incredible source of friction in our world today.

WHAT WOULD HAPPEN TO US IF OUR ADVANCED CIVILIZATION WAS DESTROYED?

Many people can drive cars but few can build them and even fewer can engineer them from scratch. And extracting oil from their sources is becoming an increasingly difficult task. Few if any would bother to go through the trouble. So cars would likely become flotsam on the roads and would be piled up on the sides of the road to make way for transportation that actually worked...like horses. By the same token many can operate a gun but few can build them, or engineer them from scratch, so back to bows and arrows, slingshots and nerf guns we go. Computers, TV, radios, telephones, all would cease to work anymore, and we'd be back to localized communities with little outside contact or communication, and our desire to communicate with them would wane as well. Families would be closer families once again. You would be surprised at what happens in families in a short while when they decide to turn off the TV for a few weeks. They rediscover books and inter personal communication. Suddenly they care more about what goes on with other members of the family.

We would be a happy bunch that the occasional wandering marauding hoard would sack every few years. But if this state of affairs were to happen again likely due to extremely destructive weapons, quite possibly our earth would border on being a hostile environment toward life.

Our society would feel the ravishes of a catastrophe even more now, because of how computers do so much of the work, and how reliant we have become on these things. Very few of our youth retain or know even simple crafts and skills. Cheating is rampant in school, college and university. This is diminishing the viability of diplomas being earned in our learning institutions. This so called advanced computer technology may be a huge factor in reducing civilization to rubble.

Few actually are well versed in the learning fields they are engaged in, and rely heavily on the computer and the internet for knowledge. Who can say how accurate the knowledge is. Some is terrific, and some is of doubtful value. Civilization would almost completely collapse if a new Peleg were to occur, particularly a Peleg on the scale prophesied in Revelations.

As for the computer this, is Jeremy Rifkin's conclusion too. He felt the reliance on the computer was a recipe for disaster. "It seems the more information that is made available to us, the less well informed we become." (Book 49 pg. 170) He notes that decisions become harder to make and our world becomes more confusing. He also sees the trend in mental health as a symptom of entropy, noting that mental health is reaching epidemic proportions and an ever increasing burden on the medical dollars available. (One in five are now said to be dealing with mental health issues. Even I've been diagnosed at one time as Manic schizophrenic, which might explain this book in some areas to some) Confucius scorned science in favor of relationships among people. TV and the computer seem to be the exact opposite. This trend suggests we could be easily led by people with less than our best interest at heart.

As has been shown man was far more advanced in the past then he is today, with space travel, antigravity, even the ability to destroy a planet, if you count that as "advanced", though it is more properly described as an advanced ability to create entropy on a faster scale. But consider the time taken to reach these 'marvels'. In 1656 years before the flood man managed to destroy a moon of Saturn, one planet and almost destroy this one in the bargain, and who knows what other damage to the other planets. We have taken 4300-5400 years to come to the ability to do none of them, though we have managed to come up with the ability to wipe out all life on earth. That's pretty advanced... I guess.

Though these are essentially destructive abilities they are on an incredible scale. I mean they did have nuclear war in the post flood era so I guess we are catching up... if one considers the ability to destroy massive amounts of people something of an advancement. Not just indiscretionary use of these weapons will cause destruction to societies, but any use of these weapons at all will cause destructive elements in our very living environment. Who knows how much all the nuclear tests have done to the living space.

Though some of the original native Indians of North America seemed to have learned from ancient history and were careful to maintain a balance in nature, we do not seem to have learned from history and indeed we have burned it and forgotten it and not passed on the knowledge faithfully down through the ages. One could then conclude that some of the Native Indians were more advanced than us simply because they managed to keep nature around them in balance. We however cause entropy on a vast scale in our endless determination to advance. There is nothing so dangerous as a child with a match. The further advanced we become the more dangerous we become to ourselves and our environment.

CLONING IN PAST DEGENERATES INTO THE BELIEF OF REINCARNATION

Another indication of how we have devolved is gauging our response to the practices of advanced science.

Man as we have seen demonstrated incredibly advanced creative abilities in the past. Adam cloned himself and this does not appear to have had much impact on his pre-flood peers. They understood exactly what occurred and it was no big deal, whereas this does not seem to be the case after the flood.

This ability to clone may have been taken though the flood on the ark. As deduced, it appears some genetic tinkering was going on just after the flood and some documents tend to strongly suggest that a clone may have been made of Nimrod (or Ninus). There is often confusion of the husband of Semiramis and her son as is also the case with Isis and Osiris with him being the son and the husband. (book 41 pg 22) For example Ninus (Nimrod) is the son of Bel But Bel and Nimrod are said to have started Babylon and Nineveh. Set (Seth?, Noah's son,) destroyed him, cut him in pieces and the pieces were scattered and later retrieved. Then it appears Nimrod was cloned, possibly from a cell in his eye. So the husband in a sense becomes the son.

There is an earth wide Mother and son worship (queen of heaven) that has confused missionaries because of the similarity to the Virgin and child. When missionaries reached Tibet and China they found the mother and child idolized before any trace of Jesus and Mary were known there. (book 41 pg. 77)

When Nimrod/ Osirus / Ra was killed Semiramis/Isis cloned him and he became her son. A Tet that looks like an electrical tower was set up every year in memory of the resurrection of Osiris. (book 61 pg. 116) This cloning may even have been done or assisted by one of the "gods" to further mitigate the problem. (see later chapter UFO's) This seems the likely origin of the worldwide belief in reincarnation that persists to this day.

People then began thinking these gods would return and revive to life all that were revivable if their flesh remained intact after death. They may simply have stated a simple fact that the flesh had to be perfectly preserved in order for a clone to be successful. This information was likely taken to mean they would come back and raise them all. But clones are just as human as the parent and they die too. This manmade "resurrection" appears to have inadvertently misled the observers of this technological feat, into believing something that was never supposed to be seen in an eternal perspective.

My point being here is not just the ability to do things has diminished, but our ability to understand and comprehend what has been done has also diminished. Was this clone of Nimrod taken in stride? NO. Now many religions in the earth appear to have concluded from this act of cloning that we will be reincarnated, or some variation of this theme. Many ancient cultures were obsessed with preserving the flesh so it wouldn't rot and see corruption, so it could rise as the same person once again.

Mummifying was not just done by the Egyptians. Incans and Mayans also mummified their dead. Even the early Christians were very cognizant with the fact that Jesus rose again without his flesh seeing corruption. Even in ROME in 1485 was found a perfectly preserved body of a woman in an ointment type fluid. The tomb was at least 1500 years old, though probably much older. When the tomb was opened a lamp was burning, lighting up the tomb. The ancients were certain that flesh would become alive again if it was preserved... that can only speak of cloning, yet it appears to has devolved to the belief in reincarnation.

SIMILAR THINGS OFTEN THOUGHT TO BE THE SAME THINGS

It is amazing how many similarities and correlations there are in history to biblical truths, and they can easily become confused. The bible clearly says it is given unto man once to die, and it says we are like a vapor that comes and then vanishes, and states flesh and blood will not see the kingdom of God.

A clone of any one of us would be an entirely different person with an identical physical make-up and identical abilities. But the nurturing environment in which a clone would grow up would make them an entirely different person.

People want to do things like cloning Lincoln and Einstein, but how would these people act if cloned and raised up in our society? They might be very clever brats, depending on how they were parented, as parenting has everything to do with the state of the child's mental and spiritual well-being and behavior standards.

It appears by looking at ancient history that cloning is the origin of the belief in re-incarnation. Though two people were cloned (Adam & Nimrod) the reaction of the contemporaries to this act were worlds apart. Obviously the belief in God existed prior to and after the flood and the knowledge that there would be a raising from the dead to meet our maker was most certainly understood. But cloning after the flood somehow has confused this to inadvertently or deliberately mislead man to think this raising from the dead is going to be accomplished in a physical body, and only careful preservations of tissue would insure they could be raised again. This led to so many cultures becoming fanatical about preserving the body after death.

Though cloning is not something man has as yet re-attained the ability to do, we are close to this ability, and now as we have become organized enough once again, we would understand perfectly what happened and not confuse it with "reincarnation".

Since it appears Adam cloned himself and it would seem this was something he would have been able to do right at the very beginning of creation. So cloning was an automatically understood knowledge in Adam and his peers, yet after the flood cloning starts religious beliefs because it seems impossible that such could be done by man, and it was the 'gods' that did this. This is ironic because many ancient histories show that the 'gods' were in fact humans…and thus subject to death just as we are. And as we have seen whatever abilities some gifted individuals have been able to do in the present era, Adam and his immediate descendants were able to do. All man had these abilities until the flood.

This then is the point. These are signs of devolution in mankind so that although we might be able to do similar things that our ancestors did, the time taken to achieve these things takes vastly longer to accomplish. Not only that, it also takes a longer time to grasp what has been done, so this grasping ability is also diminishing.

SOME FACTORS OR EVIDENCES OF DECLINE IN OTHER AREAS.

Some histories speak of some of the 'gods' eating ordinary people food in the past which consequently weakened them. What we might think of as normal food might be of reduced or detrimental value to someone from before the flood, and may also be a mitigating factor involved in our own devolution.

Radiation in our atmosphere which is at "normal levels" finds its way into the food chain, whereas food from before the flood may not have had any exposure to radiation, or certainly not the amount we consume. And obviously some other factors would be changing the quality of the food and our physiologies over time.

Many foods have apparently become poisonous to us over the millennia. Genesis 1:29 says we can eat every herb, but it appears this is qualified later after the flood where it says we can eat every green herb (Gen 9:3) and I dare say even now we probably can't even eat all of them, though I'm guessing.

Even the people before or immediately after the flood lived three to ten times longer than we do now showing a decline in our cells ability to replicate itself beyond a certain number of times. Mutational radiation no doubt is responsible for this breakdown as well. Maybe even the drinking water itself played a part in their longevity. Water modified by "electro-vibration" and given to guinea pigs in some cases doubled their life spans.

Recently life spans increased in America right up to about 1950 when it leveled off. Virtually all the advances in the increase of the average life span were due to a hand full of diseases that were conquered up to that point. The rest was attributable to improved sanitation. Since this time, life spans have leveled off and have even begun to decline. It's even been acknowledged that a relationship exists between a rise in disease and waste generated by our "petrochemical economy". A direct correlation exists to the number of deaths attributable to environmental causes. In 1900 12% of deaths were traced to environmental causes, in 1940 it increased to 38 % and in 1976 it stood at 59%. (book 49 pg. 178-79) Cancers have been positively linked to environmental factors, and not *just* from radiation sources.

BUT BACK TO "DEVOLUTION".

(3rd ed. Insert 2016) Looking through 'Entropy' by Jeremy Rifkin again, some more items merit mentioning. In noting as we use up old sources of energy each new one is harder to procure and speeds up entropy of the planet. Shifting to nuclear energy, radiation from nuclear plants is a real problem. Every nuclear plant on the planet leaks SOME radiation into the environment. The industry says these are acceptable limits. Rifkin clues us into a key statement "Every dose of radiation is an overdose". As if that isn't enough, each reactor's bi-product is Plutonium (4-500 pounds per year) which is used to make 40 more nukes…well what else are you going to do with it? As of 1980 700 pounds of plutonium were 'missing'. He further notes you don't even need nukes to destroy life…just the plutonium "…dispersed in the open air over a city, an area of 40 square miles would be contaminated for a period of 100,000 years." (And I'll add the population of that city might not even be aware the deed was done!) Nuclear waste is still a problem to dispose of …no one has figured out what to do with the radioactive waste. Many sites have been contaminated, including hundreds of acres of aquifers that have been contaminated above drinking standards. Constant reports of leaks and accidents involve dumping sites. People are worried about oil pipelines, but this is the real danger, and no one is squawking. In 1978 the state of Kentucky closed down its nuclear site at Maxey Flats, because an EPA study showed that "radioactive particles were migrating off site." And more such leaks were also going on in at least three other U.S. sites at the time. (Book 47 page 108-110)

How bad is radiation and our environment to us? Well further on Rifkin states some shocking stats. Most taxi drivers in New York have such high levels of Carbon Monoxide in their blood they are not allowed to give blood transfusions. Human breast milk cannot be found without pesticides, and carcinogens, and infant formulas contain lead deposits. A government report concluded that 60-90% of all types of cancer are caused by human-made environmental factors ranging from food preservatives to toxic chemicals. Between 20 and 40% of all cancers are work related as a result of contact with many metals and chemicals considered essential for industry. Because of environmental contamination and other factors Rifkin felt cancer could become a runaway epidemic. In fact most diseases are environmentally induced, caused by an accumulation of waste (Book 49 pages 177-181) Do you remember the fruit fly experiments in science class in school? Life on the earth is starting to mirror the graph of fruit fly experiments we did in school showing the rapid increase of population then the sudden downturn due to the waste of the flies in the environment. We are them now reaching for the top of the curve, if we haven't already reached it.

PSYCHOSOMATIC INABILITIES?

One thing that baffles scientists is that the frogs and reptiles can grow new limbs, and though we humans have the same features as these creatures in this regard, we do not regenerate limbs. However Jesus when he healed a withered hand it regenerated to its normal size. This tends to suggest that faith or even simply how we think has something to do with regenerating limbs. We don't generate new limbs simply because we don't believe we can. It's entirely possible that man before the flood automatically regenerated limbs when necessary.

ANIMALS SUCCUMB

Even animals appear to be subject to this downward trend or syndrome. Interestingly many fossils are regularly found that seem to go against the theory of evolution. When they find fossils of creatures that are still extant, often is found a more perfect specimen in fossil form than found in the living creatures of today, and it's deduced they were simply better specimens all round at the time when the fossils were still alive.

Animals, it's deduced, were tame and not afraid of man before the flood yet after the flood they became afraid of man. Some animals also appear to have gotten more belligerent toward man. No kidding!

To sort of corroborate this, it has been noted that animals in the dead sea area are tamer and more docile. And why not? They are under an additional 1300 feet of far denser atmosphere with more protection from the solar influences and maybe even a better oxygen content causing a calming effect.

Nikola Tesla hated the direct sun and said it caused pressure on his brain. Similarly people that have been known to levitate have been found to have less trouble accomplishing this feat in early morning or late evening. The middle of the day somehow interferes with this ability. This again suggests that solar energy and power interferes with mans physiology in a negative way, just like it affect people's stranded in the desert.

After the flood God gave us through Noah permission to use all animals for food. As to why one can only speculate. They became dangerous to man so if we killed them in defense we could eat them. But the question occurs to me, why do the tamer more docile domestic animals become food? Perhaps if they became too populous they would become a threat to the available plant life meant for our food? I'm probably asking myself real stupid questions here. No doubt the answer is herding sheep and cows is considerably easier and slightly less dangerous than herding wild cats and bears. Wow... branding would be one dangerous job!

Though the animals had been sorted into clean and unclean when they submitted themselves to the ark, there seemed to be no distinction as to which were meant for food. Even this statement that all animals are for food is surprising because later on certain animals are not only deemed unclean, they are no longer considered to be meant for human consumption, suggesting in the 1000 years after the flood they too became potentially dangerous to eat or possibly even toxic to man, and God needed to further narrow down the areas for us in which it was safe to operate. Furthermore he even needed to explain which were clean and which were not to us, because we became considerably less able to decipher this stuff on our own.

One of those interesting trivia bits that I tell people is there were two of every animal aboard the ark, except seven of the clean ones. Not only are people surprised to hear this, they wonder what I mean by "clean ones". I can't really tell them much myself except it has something to do with their feet and whether or not they chew their cud, and it has nothing to do with hosing the animals down before they got on the ark. "Oops, two filthy pigs got on…don't let any more of those on… Now hose down those two cats will you…"

PERCEPTIONS OF SOME MEN AS GODS

Man in the past when meeting men of renown and genetically less devolved individuals, seem to have given them the status of gods. This is not to be confused with today where every Jane and Dick can declare themselves gods and goddesses for no apparent reason other than they think themselves better than their neighbor. More often people tend to declare others as such, simply because they look good to them. But when looking into the ancient gods, back then it seems these people were actually worshipped or certainly served cheerfully and believed to be gods. (We'll see who those gods were in chapter 9 and 10)

Our comprehension of these men and their abilities took on mythical proportions and their ancestors were looked upon as gods. And this stands to reason. If they were living 7-900 years with all these abilities like lifting million ton blocks and they came in contact with someone living a mere 120 years that could barely lift his own weight, the tendency to awe is enormous. Even if these 'gods' tried all the explanations they could to the simple observer so that they understand, man is going to remember these persons as something far above himself, thus ergo some sort of 'god'.

Even now some writers look back on these people and their abilities, which seem so incredible to the writers that they can't seem to conceive of them as just men, but some sort of supermen or gods and if they are not gods, then they call them space men. Even as our society once again achieves a more advanced state of understanding and organization we still credit some of the abilities of the ancients to aliens from some advanced corner of the universe. We just can't seem to grasp that it was within man's ability to do the things that we see were done so long ago. That or we attribute illogical practices to achieve the things the ancients did.

Even the pre WWII Japanese emperors were thought to be the descendant of a god. Maybe there was a direct lineage to a specific individual declared a 'god' in the past, but no doubt this person was a human as us, and definitely not another species.

TWO STRATA'S OF MANKIND CONTEMPORANEOUS

If immediately after the flood we were all devolving at the same rate, as one would assume should have been the case, then all men contemporary with each other should be able to look at each other as men and sons of men, and not fall into some trap where other men appear to be as gods. So something in the past was making man appear to be in two leagues; men like us and men like gods. We have to ask ourselves: what situation existed in the past where men were not devolving at the same rate, to make this difference between the two states of man so apparent?

THE GODS NOT TO BE CONFUSED WITH THOSE WHO EQUATE THEMSELVES AS A GOD.

Some men such as Nebuchadnezzar have lifted themselves up as gods and initiated idol worship, and became so wrapped up in themselves that they gave death penalties for those who refused to worship them or their images. Interestingly, in chapter 2 of Daniel, though Nebuchadnezzar falls down to worship Daniel for declaring and explaining his dream, in the very next chapter he commits Daniel's three friends Shadrach, Meshach, and Abednego to the furnace for not falling down to worship his statue. So here we see, if we allow this conclusion, that not only were people devolved to a lower state after the flood where we worshipped the gods, we continued this downward trend and began to fall into the trap of worshipping each other, that is men with the same amount of devolutionary decline as ourselves. Furthermore some have fallen into the trap of thinking themselves so above others they demand or expect service and adoration meant only for God himself.

And again we see this problem of men making and worshipping images. One of the ten commandments was specifically not to make any image of God, or gods, or even animals or bugs. What is it about us that seems willing to adore images? Perhaps since these images can do no wrong and they can't interact with us they seem as images of perfection, somehow remote from us yet there for us to adore.

So easily do we like to adore a beautiful person, particularly members of the opposite sex, though just as easily it seems that so many of us have this need to be led by those of our own gender with better capabilities or charisma. Yet seldom do the objects of our adoration, if they be flesh and blood, allow us to gaze on them for long periods. Chances are when they do allow this prolonged gazing they take on an attitude of superiority, and lose the beauty we saw in them. How many people have fallen in love with some movie stars, which are really just images on screen? But it's all acting. Often we come to our senses when we meet them in person and realize they are human just like us.

I myself have been somewhat amazed how some beautiful adorable starlet can seem so angelic in one role and so despicable in another one, no doubt a pretty good actress to pull off two such roles so convincingly. Occasionally some movie star lets this public adoration goes to their head, and they seem to think they are above the law or so much above those of the masses. I personally think no person should star in any more than one movie, to prevent this very problem, as it affects them and those who watch them.

It seems man has this built in longing to gaze and adore. Just as a man can love his wife and a wife loves her husband and enjoys gazing at each other so too does mankind have this weakness to gaze on things and adore them. God wants not image or idol worship but worship of him in spirit only. Worship really means to "kiss toward", something of a gesture of affection and adoration. Though the more well known relationship of God and man is as his creation and thus his sons and daughters, it is no coincidence that God also refers to the people that do his will, as his "bride". We are the objects of his affections, just as he should be ours.

THE GODS MADE IT CLEAR THEY WERE MEN.

There are many incidents where men expected adoration or worship from other men. But this doesn't seem to be the case with the ancient 'gods'. It seems this status is endowed on them from other men, and not so much expected by the 'gods' themselves.

Actually some religions are against the Christian religion because most Christians think Jesus is God, (though some sectors of this religion believe he is Michael the archangel or just a teacher). It stands to reason that someone at some point in the past was God that appeared to look like a man. And most certainly this is not an unreasonable conclusion, nor should we think this couldn't be done. Could not the creator also appear as a man to communicate with men? After all he says we were created in his image, and God walked with Adam.

One philosopher said something to the effect that "God made us in his image and ever since man has been trying to return the favor". Before the flood it appears that the only person referred to as God is in fact God, but the situation changes after the flood. Suddenly there are a myriad of gods. Where did they come from, and why can't man seem to discern who is who? This too seems an aspect that has declined in us since the flood. Also with so many gods in the past how does one discern which one is God and which ones are just men looked up to as gods for their charisma and abilities?

ANCIENT SCIENCE DEVOLVED TO MIMICKING

The point here is in how we perceived the ancestors' science and the people in control of that science. We seem to have made religious practices out of what were originally advanced sciences. For example take astrology.

In the past astrology was used to guide our lives but this following was done somewhat blindly. We have started to realize that some aspects of astrology may have been originally based on scientific observation. Yet during the time of Elizabeth I an observation (attributed to her physician Dr. John Dee) notes that astrology and astronomy in the past were "married sciences", [and not the bunk astrology had become]. During world war II the US deliberately used astrology to boost morale and promote support for the war. The result no doubt was more belief and exposure to an apparently non viable directive.

Now newspaper astrologist look at what house so and so planet is in, if they go that deep, and come up with these generic horoscopes as though there were only 12 different sorts of people on the earth and the position of the planets would affect people of birth in various months in specific ways. More generic horoscopes suggest there are only 12 kinds of people, one for each month, as though all people born in one month are all similar and should follow identical "advice". This is the height of an insult to our intelligence. Though true, we are all human so some aspects will be common for all, but to read astrology and take it seriously is to put a straight jacket on your abilities to think as an individual.

We are vastly more individualistic then astrology would have us think. Admittedly serious astrologers take the exact date and time of birth into consideration when making up an individual's astrological chart, but even this can lead people to depend on something that really has little bearing on what a person will be like.

To follow the advice based on these charts is to give up responsibility and control for our lives and become fatalistic. It can't be wise to place our lives in the hands of people that likely do not have our best interest at heart. Charts are made up and some people take them so seriously they stop living normal lives and allow the charts to petrify their action or promote illogical actions based solely on someone's interpretation of how such and such a planet can affect an individual. God never wanted us to give up control of how we respond to life as it happens. He didn't want us to "observe times'. (Leviticus 19:26.) He only wanted us to guide our lives by his principles and be in control of our destinies. Having said all that...

SOME MUMBO JUMBO ORIGINALLY BASED ON EXACT SCIENTIFIC OBSERVATIONS.

Actually it has been seen that in certain months more conception are achieved and people born in certain months tend, on average, to be smarter individuals as though the three months where there is no gestation period is more harmful to fetus's. It has become evident that the position of Saturn and Jupiter and to a lesser degree the other planets can affect the sun and solar activity. We know that every 11 years solar activity is at a peak and it vastly increases locust populations and activity. These planets also can extenuate solar activity by way of sunspots which are known to wreak havoc in our atmosphere, and even interfere with electrical systems and indeed our very own biology.

So astronomy is showing that some aspects of astrology might have had some basis in truth if only on a more broad scope, that is for all life in general as opposed to individualistic prognostications.

There is now an aspect of astrological science that appears to be reducing accidents in Japan. When astrology, per se, is boiled down to pure science there seems to be some genuine aspects of it that can actually be of benefit. They have considered planet positions and solar emissions in relation to four factors of biorhythms in professional drivers and apparently can pinpoint when a particular driver is at risk for accidents and can either tell them to be careful or pull them from the road for that day. Apparently this has met with some marked success and driver insurance premiums in Japan are coming down as a result. (If nothing else, showing this aspect of astrology shows I'm trying to be fair in my assessments here. I can't stand astrology, yet I've taken the time even in this regard to attempt to glean fact from fiction.)

Solar flares have been linked to higher accident rates, riots and increased incidences of suicide. It's been found that the position of Uranus (if Mars is at a peak wobble and more at odds with its orbit then usual) can have some correlation to earthquakes here on earth. This might seem peculiar that a planet so far away could affect us, but Uranus is a unique planet in that it's poles are tilted 80 degrees and nearly parallel and not perpendicular to the solar systems orbital plane. It's felt its magnetic field could influence other planets showing the distance and extent to which these planets can affect things.

So we can see in astrology another example of ancient technological knowledge being devolved, and then mimicked and eventually being perceived as something that it was not initially meant for.

ADVANCED KNOWLEDGE USED TO CONTROL MEN AS THEY DECLINED IN UNDERSTANDING

Statues of Isis were seen to flash their eyes fostering continued worship of Isis. Though initially these lights may have been just for effect, they may have been perceived as some sort of sign to the more simple minded. Priests catching onto this, used the "sign" to manipulate the masses, to extend and perpetuate their power.

Some science went underground, partly for fear of retribution as science was deemed to have destroyed the world, and partly because it was a secret power to manipulate the masses. Possibly part of the reason God gave the third commandment "Thou shalt not make unto thee any graven image…etc. relates to this tendency of man in his devolved state to confuse technology used in statues as some sort of sign from a god or some higher power.

Possibly statues were even robotic representations of people as it appears some "came to life" causing people to adore ANY image of a person that was deemed to be something of a god. People not realizing technology or science was tricking them, were very easily mislead. Robots even appear to persist into more modern times.

Stories exist of robots in China as recently as 976-922 BC. Someone named Yan Shi made a robot to entertain a King while he did a tour. It could dance and sing and had artificial organs like a real person. Clearly such technology could be abused and used to mislead people.

A Shiva statue had an iron rod attached to it which was 18 meters high, to attract the blessings of heaven which of course came down as lightning and shattered the statue which was then rebuilt ready for the next "blessing".

COPYING THE GODS

Even today examples of this sort of misunderstanding of technology is seen in less advanced civilizations. Melanesians long believed that gods would be brought to this stone age tribe by big canoes and big birds.

In 1943 these natives felt their beliefs were fulfilled when supplies were dropped for the Australian forces and afterwards they started building flat areas for big birds to land (air strips) and created bamboo masts (aerials) and radio sets made out of bamboo and such to contact the gods. This is understandable. The Australian forces were using such equipment to contact other planes, and the natives looked at their instruments as something they could duplicate, not understanding the technology involved. They wanted supplies from the gods too so why not try and do what they were seeing work for the Australians?

I remember looking at this very cool footage of a bird coming over the horizon and I wondered what kind of awesome bird this was, when it became clear I was looking at a Concord jet approaching the camera head on.

The point here is that these natives may have unwittingly started a false religious belief system simply by copying advanced technology.

REPRODUCTIVE PROBLEMS

After the flood barrenness starts to be a factor in reproductive abilities. Sarah is the first known case of a barren woman. As events like nuclear blasts, nuclear waste, solar activity, distortion of the magnetic field and other protective features of the earth, like the Van Allen belts, the earth living space is affected and more radiation gets to the earth. This ends up further debilitating our D.N.A. One probable result is chlamydia which is inducing or causing sterility, which would become more rampant after such incidences and indeed sterility and barrenness is becoming more and more of a problem on the earth today. This makes perfect sense as it is our reproductive organs that are the most susceptible to the effects of radiation.

WHO DID CAIN MARRY IN THE LAND OF NOD?

Another factor that shows a decline in our genetic makeup is who we can marry and reproduce with. Although the age old question about who did Cain marry in the land of Nod is supposedly some sort of enigma, it is actually obvious who he and his brothers took as a brides. They took their sisters.

It stands to reason too. There was only Adam and Eve having kids so who else could they marry? When you grow up with your sister all your life in a loving environment who would you love more than your sister? Our genes were so perfect before the flood that marrying ones sister was not a problem. After the flood it is still not too much of a problem where even Abraham's brother Nahor took a niece Milcah, the daughter of his and Abraham's brother Haran, as a wife, and there is no indication this was considered wrong. Though this is not a sister, it is a niece-uncle relationship.

It's mistakenly believed that Abraham married his half sister Sarah, but it seems this relationship as a "sister" is only by marriage. Sarah was Haran's daughter in law through her marriage to Abraham. Sarah's fathers name is not mentioned. But by association any sister of a brother in law is therefore a sister in law, even if that "sister in law" is your wife.

But this association make perfect sense because at one time we were able to marry our sisters, thus this title of our spouses as sister in laws by association still stands after all this time.

Correction: (3rd ed. insert 2016) Abraham _did_ marry his half sister. I had thought he did but when I checked the lineage and genealogy I couldn't find it, as Sarah isn't mentioned in the genealogy, so I decided to play it safe. But the proof is in Genesis 20-12. And yet indeed _she is_ my sister; she _is_ the daughter of my father, but not the daughter of my mother; and she became my wife. This actually further substantiates the point.

Later on marring relatives this close becomes a problem and God disallows even this and says we are not to not even look on our sisters and half sisters or marry them, though marrying a cousin was not ruled out.

If there's any doubt as to how the decline of man's genetics is taken into account in the laws of the old testament, compare how bad it was considered to take one sister in the Mosaic laws to the undeniable fact that the sons of Adam and Eve had to have their own siblings as wives and husbands. There is simply is no other way to decipher this.

Now many societies make it unlawful to marry even our cousins because it has become obvious that such marriages often have physically troubled children, such as Down syndrome which is often one of the problems with children of these marriages.

There have been found in the genes of mankind over 60,000 mutations. Any given individual will have as many as 300 mutations. The environment we live in is constantly increasing the number of mutations we carry in our genes. This is why the law was put in place that we should not marry close relatives. When two individuals with the same genetic faults combine, often the offspring will display a physical manifestation of these faulty genes.

When one also takes into the equation how God wanted unblemished sacrifices and a pure people, this indicates that he was trying to prevent things to devolve the race further. Perhaps that is somewhat speculative, but it appears he was also trying to limit our downward devolutionary trend with some self preservationist laws, and prolong life on earth as long as possible in a more preserved state.

Though the Jewish people tended to think the laws were just for them it is very evident that God was always considering the Gentiles as they observed the Jews, and he wanted the Jews to be an example for the Gentiles, that they might do likewise.

Accumulating genetic mutations of our DNA gradually lowers the viability of a population. The net effect of mutations is harmful to a population be it flies, elephants or people. This is likened to carrying a load down through the generations. The load gradually gets heavier and heavier until a collapse of the gene and the organism which then becomes sterile or incapable of producing a viable offspring, or the individuals are unable to cope in their environment. This mutation rate has increased in our environment mainly through ionizing radiation and mutagenic chemicals. (book 9 pg. 56) A foetus exposed to gamma rays can devolve into a "monster" in a few days. (book 22 pg 177)

POSSIBLE WAYS OF SLOWING DOWN GENETIC ENTROPY

One way to slow the aspects of man's genetic deterioration is the mixing of genes; that is interracial marriages. Now one might think this contradicts this theme as I have presented it, in relation to the bible. Not so. We see that Moses actually had a Negro wife. In fact this was even a point of contention with Moses' sister Miriam, and in essence God spit on Miriam's face, by turning her leprous for a week. (Numbers 12:1-14) We also see that Ruth, a Moabite, married Boaz and this line carries on down to King David. I find it so curious that so many religious people try and justify segregation and even racism on biblical grounds, when obviously mixing races was not a problem. What God was trying to prevent was mixing beliefs, not races, so that one of the faith is not led astray by the spouse. How many people in the church have been snagged by less scrupulous spouses and are seldom seen in church after their marriage?

MORE THAN ONE WIFE

I mean consider it, even Solomon the wisest of all men, fell to this exact problem.

Most use Solomon as an example to prove people shouldn't have more than one wife, but it wasn't bigamy or even polygamy that was his problem. He multiplied wives, which in fact was ruled out because of this very potential problem. (Deuteronomy 17:17) Polygamous marriages were never ruled out: David had 7 wives and Abraham had several after Sarah died. In fact there were laws given saying men ought to treat each wife equally, buying goods in equal measure for each wife. (Exodus 21:10. see also Deuteronomy 21:15)

If God was handing down laws about treating each wife equally he sure as shootin' wasn't saying bigamy was wrong. Even in the new testament bigamy was not ruled out. It only states that those who are preachers should be husbands to one wife, not everyone. (I Tim. 3:2,12)

Even after the return of Christ seven women shall cleave to one man, (Isaiah 4:1) as likely there will be so few men after Armageddon, women will throw coyness out the window, and aggressively go after a man and be completely willing to share a man with other wives, to avoid the "reproach" of being single and without children.

Though most women will say they would never share a man, and indeed some wouldn't, but I've come across a surprising number of women that would. Some may even say they won't ever, but when push comes to shove and they feel their territory is slipping from them if the suggestion comes up, many will share rather then lose their man altogether.

There are some very fundamental differences in men and women that can allow this sort of scenario to occur and still maintain a happy marriage. True some conflicts could arise but the right man can keep all his women quite content. Now where was I before I wandered out into left field? Oh yeah slowing down genetic entropy.

AS THE WORLD TURNS AND THE GENES DEVOLVE.

I never understood why people seem to act cruel toward children of mixed marriages, that is "half-breeds". My observations were that they always seemed better looking. I couldn't understand the prejudice against them. I always thought the half-breed girls look prettier and the boys were better looking. They even seemed smarter and more charming. So my conclusion as a youth of 11 and 12 was that this attitude towards them by others must be because of jealousy.

My guess is there is a sound reasoning for this apparent better look to the mixed races. Mixing of a wider variety of genes appears to be a way of compensation in the genes. It used to be sisters could marry brothers before the flood, but now the closer related the genes are the better the chance of children with problems. So by the same token it stands to reason the further the genes are unrelated the better the offspring should be.

Obviously I'm not advocating forced mixed marriages as you have to pick someone you're attracted to, though many arranged marriage have indeed worked out quite well. More often than not you will likely meet someone of your own race you are quite content with. But there should be less resistance to interracial marriages.

I guess the one thing that slows this down is the racism factor. This too is a mystery to me. True sometimes a war can really escalate these feeling towards that other race. But people get over these feelings when the war ends. Thanks to Edward VII liking French stuff and being of good cheer, England and France are on good terms. The Japanese were slandered left and right during WWII, but we seem to have forgotten these feelings now. Obviously if predominantly people of a type are working subversively against your country, naturally there will be some concerns and suspicions, but if we just treat them and care about them like human beings anyway, maybe love will soften their stance. If they had said over and over 'love your enemies' during the 50's McCarthy would have withered away.

True, various races have tendencies toward different outlooks on life; for instance religious, or local upbringing. People brought up in the jungle will just have a different set of living standards than those of someone brought up in the city. People of hotter climates might tend to take siestas to get away from the heat of the day. To some this may appear as though that were a lazy race, and a marriage between such differing people would be endless conflicts. An African bushman and city slicker and or an Eskimo might find it somewhat hard to find a happy life together that they are both content with.

What I find quite distressing is racism simply because someone is of a different colour or country of origin. There are real extremes in this view too. So when I meet a person of this persuasion I try to show them the logical end to this negative way of thinking.

WHAT IF DIEHARD RACISTS HAD THEIR WAY?

This may seem like some more wandering, and I suppose it is, but once you see the theoretical logical road racism could conceivably travel down, you will see it sort of fits here.

Let's say you do not like or even hate a particular group or race of people. You can add whatever group you want here, it works for all. Can you honestly say that your race is perfect? Are there no criminals or murderers or lazy people in your race? Of course not. You are as an individual what you strive to be, regardless of your race. In each race there are honest and upright people and there are complete jerks and scum. We cannot judge all of a group based on a single person from that group. Granted there will be tendencies found in a group but these are usually due to necessities and upbringing rather then race itself.

Now let's say you are an extremist and would actually kill the race you hate, like the Nazis tried to do from the 1930's to 1945. Let's say you actually meet your objective and the end of the race you hate has come about. That race no longer exists on the earth. Will you finally be a happy person now that that race is extinct? Maybe for a day, but not for long. You will then find a new group of people to hate. Yes! The Nazis were going after other groups when they were finished with the Jews...and they even had some of their own people targeted!

You will then blame the ails of the world or whatever on another race or sector of the population. So let's jump ahead.

OK let's say you now achieve you're objective and no other race on the world exists, just your race, whatever that race may happen to be. Will you be happy now? Nope. You will find that you now hate members of another country, or religion, or sector of the population for whatever contrived reason, they will be next on your hit list. You will find another and another group to vent your frustrations and jealousies on. When you act on hate and justify the actions taken because of that hate, you will continue to hate others and on and on. If you actually were to destroy all other peoples except those of your own country and religion or lack thereof, you will find yet another sector of humanity to hate. If you are a city person you will hate country folks, If you're a farmer you'll hate city folk. If an islander you'll hate mainlanders. There is no end to ways people can be segregated or grouped. It's almost as if such hatred is directed at the very diversity that enriches the earth.

In a movie about Sgt. York there was even a note that some "bottom land" owners looked down on people that lived in the mountains with their rocky hard land to work and vice verse. The very lay of the land that people lived on created prejudices! The haves and the have-nots. This seems to have been at the bottom of the problem not too long ago in Africa.

The slaughter of people even of their own race in Rwanda should make it clear that even an almost imperceptible variation in a group of people will find these murderous ways expressed when civility is tossed out the window. This was virtually a war of the have-nots verses the haves, not too dissimilar to the causes of the French revolution and the subsequent reign of terror. If you judge that all of one race are not worthy of life, then by the same token you are not worthy of life, because the standard can work both ways, for the exact same reasons. God judges us by the standards we judge others by. (Matthew 7:1-2) Love your enemies.

Some fears or jealousies have caused people to behave irrationally and even hatefully. Sure one has to defend oneself against others that would destroy them, but some of these slaughters have been completely unprovoked. Prejudice is not solved by destroying a race because it is not race that caused the perception of a problem. It is something inside, some personal inadequacies, or jealousy or fear that stirs people to these extremes, and the religious, physical or economic differences between peoples seems to merely draw some sort of more distinguishable line in our minds.

The inadequacies you see in others are in fact reflective of your own insecurities. Sometimes individuals also seem to want to appear better then someone else so we feel more acceptable to our peers, so we put down someone to build ourselves up. This is really again a sense of insecurity as we don't feel we could be acceptable on our own merits to that same group. Since we want to be accepted by our peers, we pick on a group not associated with our peer group to look down on. But sadly this can lead to real abuses of other people's lives. "Love your neighbor" and do unto others as you'd have them do to you.

The most important accomplishment of all is not the building of a better mousetrap but the bridging of interpersonal relationships. This can never be done successfully when one group feel superior to another. We are all equals in potential and in the eyes of the creator.

If we find ourselves feeling such toward a different group of people we need to ask ourselves what it is about ourselves that is feeling threatened by this group of people. Are they going to take jobs from your sector of people? Maybe they are better qualified. And certainly jobs should go to the better qualified.

On the other hand jobs should not be reserved for people of a particular race to fill some sort of quota, otherwise the viability of the product made by the job becomes of an inferior sort because companies are forced to fill quotas regardless of qualifications. Just what you want at the nuclear plant, right?

If one black or white or Irish or Canadian or what-have-you person steals or causes you grief you cannot automatically assume every person of that group will act the same. It's like saying because one man or woman hurt you that all men or women are the same. This is ludicrous. I have had my investments stolen from me so that I couldn't buy a house, but to seek revenge or stew in anger and plot will only make my life more miserable, not theirs.

The ills we have done to us can never be righted by doing like ills to others. This only escalates hatred and steals peace from our hearts. And one can see that even if one does declare war on all other races and countries, in the end there is still no peace from this.

We are all individuals with different outlooks, personalities, moral standards and priorities. I like M.L.K's. line about being 'judged by the content of our character rather than the color of our skin' and might I add gender, our religion, our …well you get the picture…

As a side note, curiously were a more readily mixing of races be accepted, eventually individual races would virtually disappear, thus ending races and racism.

So the point here is with a decline in society to where hate can be motivating factors for laws and actions, such as eliminating races, you thus further reduce diversity on the earth and creating an environment where even more mutations can become physical manifestations, speeding up entropy.

Ok I suppose it's a weak reasoning for including an expose on the illogic of racism here, but I guess I just wanted to inject some logic in the picture for a possible racist to reflect upon. I once met a person degrading willy nilly another race, so I walked him though this logic and he got it. So if this can help one person maybe it will help another. Sorry for the straying from the main theme of this chapter. Ok let's get back at it…

THEY ARE JUST AMOEBA'S

(3rd ed. Insert 2016) When a theory like evolution takes hold of a society and changes how that society or at least its leaders think, it causes actions, laws, and sweeping changes that reflect the theory that society clings to. When one previously predominant world view such as a God/ creation centered world view that values each individual, is exchanged for a world view that evolution offers where individuals and even life itself has little or no meaning and people are looked upon as parasites of the earth and in varying degrees of evolutionary progression, extreme changes in societal actions can take place. Lenin, formerly a believer in God and creation, turned from this belief system to evolution through the influences of Darwin's book and killed mass numbers of his people. Cambodian leader Pol Pot killed 3 million of his own people: 1/3 of his country's population. Mao Tse Tung also followed Darwin and killed over 60 million of his people. Hitler believing Jews were "pure ape" and being unable to give them to other countries in luxury yachts, attempted to exterminate them from his population and killed 6 million of them. Mussolini also believed in Evolution and felt Italians were the superior race and thus had no problem starting wars in Africa. Theodore Roosevelt was also influenced by evolution theory and thus thought Indians were inferior and shouldn't be allowed to breed. Karl Marx dedicated his book "Das Kapital" to Charles Darwin. This book changed Stalin's philosophical outlook and consequently he had killed between 60 and 100 million of his own people. Now in our so called modern world society, some have felt it unacceptable to vote for people that have a creationist point of view and that they should vote for leaders that have a belief in Evolution. Why? So the voters can die at that leader's hands?

Consider some of the attitudes that permeate. A document signed by the USA on June 4th 1993 that came out at the convention on biological diversity which states "that we must either reduce the Earth's human population to one billion or reduce the standard of living to an agrarian peasant status". This clearly is materialistic in nature, and simply another way of saying 'Those who have need to get rid of those who haven't, to maintain the status of those who have.

Richard Weikart in his "Dehumanizing" article in Atlantis Rising (#93) clues into this too. He notes for example that bioethicist Peter Singer and Darwinian biologist Richard Dawkins "…argue that based on the Darwinian understanding of human origins, we need to desanctify human life, divesting ourselves of any notion that humans are created in the image of God and thus uniquely valuable." He further notes an evolutionary ecologist of the University of Texas, Eric Pianka, wishes that 90% of the human population would be extinguished, perhaps in a pandemic. Does he hope to be part of the casualties?

Weikart also realized that evolution based thought, led to the belief by some people in power who considered themselves as part of a master race, that they could then dictate who were inferior beings and consequently reproduction rates should be restricted, and only superior people would be encouraged to procreate. Furthermore the death camps were an outgrowth of this philosophy, and Nazi Germany used them simply as a way of getting rid of bad heredity found in 'inferior races'. But who decides who's superior? Again it appears to have boiled down to the haves and the have-nots. Thus prevailing 19th century opinions of Europeans felt that Africans… specifically Black Africans and American Indians were 'less evolved' due to biological inferiority, and some people were thus considered less human and partially animal. (Though I could argue they were simply less materialistic…because they hadn't learned it from these "superior" societies.) Because of Hitler's embracing of biological determinism, not only did he kill 6 million Jewish people, he killed 200,000 disabled Germans and hundreds of thousands of Gypsies. Weikhart also concluded that "…false conceptions of humanity can lead to destructive behavior and harmful policies, both by societies and individuals. It can and does affect the way we treat other human beings. Human rights are meaningless in a world of determinism…" Ultimately he concludes that those who see man as created in the image of God have different values than those who think of man as the sum total of environment and biology and thus that they can believe "…that humans can create whatever truths they desire."

Ultimately by destroying people you destroy diversity. Many fabulous people have come out of poverty. Many great ideas and inventions have come from these people that others would have wiped out. True some people take the easy way out and become dependent or parasitical of people they can get a hand out from. But this behavior is learned from parents and rich societies too.

CAVE MEN?

People explain the appearance of cave men and primitive tribes and scientists in the same era living contemporaneously, as though they were like some sort of primitive species and advanced species evolving on earth at the same time. They are said to be some pockets of a less advanced evolution still coexisting alongside each other. This is actually somewhat insulting to people of these less technologically advanced cultures.

People try and compare our civilization to that of rocket scientists and Australian bushmen as though they were less capable human beings or more primitive, but take a pigmy or bushman out of the bush, feed him a good diet and teach him in school and he can reach our body proportions, match the attainments of the rocket scientist, because he has the same ability. Therefore this is a bad, not to mention insulting analogy.

The correct analogy would be the atomic scientist and the person with Down syndrome. They do NOT have the same ability and never will. As hard as this is to swallow, our civilization is the Down syndrome compared to the civilization that existed before and immediately following the flood. All the clues lead to this conclusion.

Cro-Magnon man was not less capable than us but was equal or superior to us. (book 7 pg. 216) In fact he even appeared to be a more perfect specimen of humanity then many if not all of us. Neanderthal man was just as advanced as us except he had rickets. (3rd ed. insert. Though as we've since realized this may have been a misdiagnosis, and indeed their bone structure was, among other things, 50% thicker)

People keep equating cave men with inferior types of humans. But after wars or disasters people often dwelt in caves, simply because there was no other shelters built yet. After the destruction of Sodom and Gomorra, Lot and his daughters lived in caves. After the Benjamites were almost wiped out, the Benjamites lived in caves. King David and King Saul often spent time in caves. After Atlantis sunk, some of the survivors that made it to the west coast of Europe lived in caves and drew those cave drawings.

Though they weren't permanent dwellers in the caves, it was a shelter from the elements away from home. Job 30:2-6 speaks of people fleeing to the wilderness and living in caves. Hebrews 11:38 speaks of the persecuted wandering the earth and living in caves. For all we know some of these "cave men" were normal Joes, on a camping trip! I guess when we go camping and make a campfire and eat meat cooked over the campfire we suddenly turn into Neanderthals. Weird how that works.

COMMANDMENTS NEEDED

One of the biblical evidences for devolution is the fact that God gave commandments during Moses time. Now you ask what has that to do with devolution?

Even the bible itself is a series of increased revelations about God, as though the more devolved we became the more revelation was necessary for us to find our way to God and understand him. God didn't give these commandments before the flood or even to 1000 years after the flood, because what was a "new law" as given to Moses was something we originally knew and understood. We knew the law. It was obvious to us at one time. For example no one had to explain to Noah what a clean or unclean creature was...he knew. Also as we've seen, as we devolved we could no longer take our brothers and sisters, aunts, uncles, nieces and nephews as spouses.

Some of His laws were about simple things like sanitation and civilized rules of order, like do not steal and do not lie and kill. I mean we needed to be told that? YES! Before the flood little revelation was necessary to man because man knew these things and understood them. God has taken our devolution into the equation and once we became dull enough he found ways to reveal himself to us so we could be drawn to him and understand him more.

Biblical scholars recognize this trend in the bible to continual increased revelation until the time when Christ returns to rule the earth.

WAR IS NEW?

There are indications that exist to show war was a new thing that occurred AFTER the flood, originating with Ninus (Nimrod) being the first to learn the ways of war. (Book 41 pg 23). This new idea of war amongst us at this point in time shortly after the flood corroborates with a more perfect environment before the flood where animals were more docile and even man was more docile and soft hearted.

Even Jesus indicates that though divorce was allowed by Moses, originally it was not so, indicating that before the flood marriages lasted a lifetime...all the time. Divorce was a fairly new concept in Moses' time. In fact it was Moses' choice to allow it. It wasn't part of the law. I guess he figured it was better than having spouses at each other's throats.

We were simply more docile before the flood and divorce didn't happen because our hearts didn't harden towards our spouses like they often do now. In fact we even had to be told not to harden our hearts toward our spouses in the new testament, indicating an even further decline.

After the flood with the sun burning directly onto the earth, animals became afraid of man or belligerent toward them and men became more belligerent toward each other. We tend to think of pre-flood people being really atrociously sinful and wicked and yes there are indications of that, but it seems the pre-flood people's downfall was their "continual evil" which as we have shown was advanced ability to cause destruction, which ended up causing the flood. Once they were flooded, end of story. Very little is known to us about life before the flood. Why? The amount of information known about this period could fill a single small book. Why is so little known about a period that I insist was the most advanced time in the history of man? The answer is surprisingly simple, they didn't need to record anything.

UP IS DOWN: WRITING IS A SIGN OF DECLINE

The most touted sign of man becoming more advanced and civilized is the advent of language and the written word...communication as we know it. But is this a sign of advancement or is it something entirely different?

We as a civilization believing the theory of evolution conclude that man was an ape and then a cave man and onward up the ladder to the point when suddenly the light went on and language and writing was born. What if the theory of evolution really is bunk? Then to what do we attribute this thing called language and writing? It then becomes evidence for the exact opposite! Yes! Writing is a sign and evidence of entropy!

Originally our memory grasp was so perfect we didn't need to read or write as it was a superfluous thing; we knew or we could pass on innovations to others without the need for writing the ideas down or drawing pictures. Not only did we have the ability to visualize things in such detail we could see them in three dimensions, we could apparently have others visualize the same things with us, by projecting imagery onto film, a screen or in a sort of holographic three dimensional image.

This is why scholars are baffled as to why the Sumerians just pop up out of nowhere to start an advanced civilization apparently with no build up from a primitive society to an advanced one. It starts out advanced. Why is this? Because before this time we didn't need records and writing. Before this any knowledge to be had, we all had and didn't need to write it down to teach our kids, they automatically had or were able to glean this information without the need of books. Even if children were taught in schools they didn't need to take notes, they listened and learned. They just built and did things based on their advanced abilities before and shortly after the flood.

Our mental grasp was just phenomenal. Now few of us have photographic memories or automatic memorization. Even now our older people tend to have to make more notes to themselves as they grow older so they don't forget stuff that a few years prior would have been deemed unnecessary. I have been so bad at times I've gone to the store for two things, bought a bunch of stuff and not bought either of the two things I originally went to the store for! If I don't have a note or list with me I have the worst time remembering. Remember the gods and various "space men" are constantly referred to as "the people who knew everything". So they just didn't need to write anything down.

Well the whole of mankind became in need of actual reminders such as books. Thoth is said to have given writing to the Egyptians. Ancient Egyptians wrote that it was something of an insult to the children to make them learn language and writing as taught by Thoth. (book 8 pg 98) Writing was deemed a threat to society because children had previously been forced to apply themselves, and to learn and retain whatever was taught them. Sounds like what happened when calculators and computers were introduced into classrooms. In this light, writing still could be thought of as an advancement but, one can also see writing as a decline in man's ability to grasp without study. Originally we were intelligent enough to memorize what was said and taught. But the advent of the written word means we had declined to the point where we needed to write it down! As hard as that is to believe, it makes absolute perfect sense.

This trend to dumbing down trend is still going on. For example kids used to be expected to remember lines for songs or church plays. Now we seem to think it's too much for them and they just do actions to the songs played on sound systems. Adults aren't using their creativity either, but relying on canned or scripted plays and often as not puppets or 'actors' just mimic and no speaking by puppeteers, relying on someone reading or sound systems to present the story. Challenging the kids won't break them and challenging yourself won't crumble you.

One thing that has always surprised me is how long it took to come up with the printing press. I was making carved letters up when I was a kid, until I was told there were rubber stamp letters to be had. It seems such a natural thing to create. Making a printing press would have been my next step, and I was just 5 or 6 years old. However I've begun to grasp why the printing press took so long to invent. Back when the printing press was invented few grown-ups, let alone 5 year olds, could read or had much use for doing so... because society had deteriorated so much through so many dark ages, that writing and reading was for the rich and the privileged. Few had much use for reading, they just did what their fathers did in the same business or on the same piece of land. Even reading had declined. With the destruction of so much reading material in the burned down libraries over the centuries, reading became less and less widespread or useful. We only learned from our parents the trades we grew up in. Who needed printing presses?

WRITING HELPS ORGANIZATION

Though the written word is a sign of devolution by the same token it is also a method of organization. Writing was once known to have existed in ancient Peru but the ruler abolished writing under penalty of death because it was a plague then besetting the ruler's kingdom. (book 37 pg. 64) Though writing existed in many cultures at one time, often the ability to read that writing was lost.

Printing speeded up the process of organization in intellectual, spiritual and scientific progress. Originally it seems books were quite simple, written on tablets because we needed less to remind us of more. But if one continues this theme down through the ages one could almost say the computer is a sign of even further decline. True the computer is an incredible tool and is no doubt a marvel of advanced ability to organize and invent, but by the same token it is also a sign that we have become lazier or less able to cope with the more arduous task of research. It saves time, but it also saves energy that might be more constructively used in mental exercise. Now if we want a subject matter we can type in the key words and that subject matter is instantly available. Mass organization but at what cost?

Are we becoming mentally lazy? The old saying is 'if you don't use it you lose it'. Are computers causing us to lose the ability to think for ourselves at a faster rate than ever before?

NEW LAWS A GOOD THING?

We tend to think change is usually for the better, but there is reason to believe this is not necessarily so. The Greeks Plato and Aristotle felt society should change as little as possible because change did not create more order but less. They felt it their duty to have society be as close to the same when they left it as when they entered it. They felt the greater the change the greater the decay. (book 49) There are 380,000 regulations in Ontario on how business is run. Europe has 450 regulations for towels and 200 for spoons. They have a 65,000 word document just for selling cabbage! I don't think this is making society better.

This is evident in our society today. We make all these laws to improve our society. This decay is sped up by liberal judges that interpret the laws to their own liking, and hand down controversial rulings, not only declining organized society but also causing less respect for people in these positions. Consequently pushing some sectors of society toward preferring anarchism or a ruling force similar to France after the revolution.

ABSENT MINDED PROFESSORS

In his book Entropy, Jeremy Rifkin states "As entropy builds, our bodies internalize the disorders in the form of cancer, birth defects, diminished I.Q. in infants and so on". (pg 240) He notes that behavioral problems in school children have been linked to lead levels in the children. This no doubt was the reason lead was taken out of gasoline, but it shows how we don't seem to think sometimes about the obvious.

This is even a tendency in inventors, who are supposedly genius's. Not to say they aren't but the term "absent minded professor" is apt in describing a lot of inventors, if not all of us.

Take Mr. Cugnot. In 1769 he built the first (known) automobile. It was a steam powered tractor made for pulling artillery pieces. It was a huge boiler mounted on a wooden vehicle that could have been a wheelbarrow for a giant, as the vehicle is huge, standing taller than the average man. He started it up and it worked and went forward. However he neglected to put brakes on the vehicle, and steering was virtually nonexistent. Since the steam was good for 15 minutes it continued moving until the steam was all used up and the vehicle just went virtually straight...into a building. I believe he was arrested for public nuisance. The first vehicle was involved in the very first accident in 1771 with no other vehicles around! We should have stopped while we were ahead. Actually one of the original Cugnot vehicles still exists and it really is a cool piece of machinery. (I saw it on the internet while checking up on some of these details)

I heard a story that early in the days of automobiles there was a city with only two cars in it, and they managed to get into an accident with each other!

Henry Ford in 1896 built his quad cycle in the garage but neglected to put reverse on the car. Unfortunately he built the car facing the wrong way and had to smash a hole in the back of the garage to get the car out. Actually many of our inventions and advances in technology have been put into use not realizing the full extent of the negative side effects and dangerous byproducts of the advances. No doubt the reader can think of other advances that we may have been better off without. And similarly no doubt you can think of other products introduced to the public that proved more harmful than good to the users, from toys that harmed children to drugs that harmed the elderly. Even in our inventions we sometimes turn out to be our own worst enemies.

MORE INDICATIONS OF DECLINE THROUGH THE AGES

(I repeat a lil bit here) When the Canary islanders were rediscovered in 1395 they were surprised to see others had survived the disaster that overwhelmed their continent. They were no longer able to read their old writing and their buildings were all in ruins and no attempt to rebuild them was ever undertaken.

Quipus were a form of writing done with knots in Central America but the ability to read them was lost. I suppose one might be able to translate them if one re-invents the same thing in a different "language" and see what is common.

Some ancient tapestries were found to be phenomenally advanced with as many as 500 two ply woolen strands to the inch. We could barely attain 100 before the advent of the loom, and 300 is considered very fine and dense.

One ancient city of the Peruvians reached a dimension of 11 square miles, a size not attained until the 19th century...if you count size as a sign of advancement.

Seldom before 1900 did buildings have more than 5 stories as this was felt to be the safe limit to the height of buildings yet the Romans built 7 and 12 story lighthouses. (book 33 pg 222) They also built at least one water aqueduct that was about 16 stories high...which still stands 2000 years later! I mean how dare the savages show us up!

Schools of Thales and Pythagoras (c550 B.C.) taught the true nature of the solar system concerning the motion of the earth and the solar orbit, yet in 317 AD Lactantius was teaching that the earth was a plane surrounded by sky composed of water and fire, and he warned against the heretical teaching of the earth's spherical nature.

Though 14 stone buildings have been found in a five mile underwater area near Andros Island, the natives of Andros Island never built any stone buildings. Book 8 pg 71-72)

Incas cultivated cotton but did not use the loom, and Mayans built roads but did not use the wheel... though I'm not sure what these things prove.

Pockets of isolated population can tend to degenerate into a more primitive state. The Tasaday of the interior of Mindanao in the Philippines somehow became isolated 500-1000 years ago. At that time they were practicing agriculture, and producing a variety of tools and weapons. When rediscovered they had no knowledge of agriculture or weapons and only crude stone or bamboo tools. (book 54 pg 144)

The ancient Andes civilization came up with cotton that could be spun and they grew different colours of cotton still unattained today. Again this ability is so advanced writers credit this ability to the "gods" or spacemen. We just don't seem to be willing to grant that our ancestors could do these things because we insist that we are evolving upwards. Who were these gods?

Easter Island has been shown to have had three successive cultural levels, the oldest being the most advanced (book 37 pg 128)

Intricate and convoluted cave paintings have been found all along the western coast of Europe in dark caves which had to have been painted with artificial light because there is no sign of smoke on the ceiling or walls. These paintings are an apparent attempt to retain a sense of civilization and past cultures in a circumstance where survival had become more a necessity, giving further evidence of decline. Even sewing needles with small eyes found in these caves indicate more articulate dress than is usually associated with "Cave men" (book 37 pg 160) The Altamira cave paintings were ridiculed as hoaxes and it was felt they were done to discredit the then (1879) new science of prehistory. Once these paintings were accepted as genuine they have now somehow squeezed their existence into their prehistory theories, when previously they were deemed to discredit the very same theories. It goes to shows you that it's all in perspective how we interpret evidence, and what we want to believe.

Europeans never used forks or spoons until the latter part of the 15 hundreds yet in Central America they were used 1000 years prior to this and the Egyptians used them in 3000 BC.

The Sahara desert at one time was a vast fertile land with large lakes. The very fact that this dessert is expanding speaks of a time when it didn't exist. Desserts are not signs of anything but the earth's devolved ability to reproduce.

THE HORIZON IS MOVING AWAY.

(3rd ed. Insert 2016) Evidence that the earth is indeed waxing old like a garment: also the Sahara Desert shows it was inhabited with ancient civilizations and fossils of dinosaurs having been found in its midst. But now it is a vast desert that is spreading a few miles every year; it's been tracked as spreading 90-100 KM from 1958-1975

We tend to use the most easily available energy or source of material for our work and when that source is exhausted we go to the next easiest source and more work is needed to get that energy or material.

Originally man used something that was called Vidya Astra which means scientific (Vidya) manipulation of the electrical field of the earth (Astra). (book 31 pg. 109) As seen the ancients used the earth's magnetic…or electric field to do work. It was readily available to them and they understood how to tap into it. When civilization collapsed sometime after the flood (or our comprehension dissolved) other more polluting and difficult to access forms of energy were used.

Europe is a typical example of how we go from a simple form of available energy to a more difficult form. In Europe originally everything was made of wood, and it was their source of heat. As the forests became depleted and wood became scarce, they went to coal which started the industrial revolution. Then as coal supplies began to dwindle the next form of energy used was oil, and then nuclear power. Each energy form also had the waste factor to consider as it entered the environment. Even now we still do not know how to dispose of nuclear waste, and each energy form takes more work to extract.

In 1960 2,250,000 BTU of energy were extracted for each dollar (1973 dollars). In 1970 that went down to 2,168,000 BTU's for each 1973 dollar spent and by 1973 it dropped to 1,895,000 BTU's for each dollar spent. Though the data is old the trend is clear. (Book 49) This trend toward more work for less result is evident in clothing too. First we used animal skins and as animals began to vanish, we went to wool then cotton and then synthetic fibers. Each more difficult to procure than the previous. (Though I have to think tanning hides wasn't easy work)

RADIATION AFFECTS LIFE ON EARTH IN A DOWNWARD TREND

So many items indicate a decline of man, as a result of the devolving state of the earth. It's well known that earth magnetic field is declining in strength and could come to a complete end as soon as 4000 AD.

Though some scientists want us to believe it will then reverse and gain strength, I don't know that this is founded on solid scientific evidence.

Though it is true that the magnetic poles have reversed several times in the past and at the point of reversal or "event horizon" there is a time when a larger amount of radiation reached earth speeding up the devolution of life on the planet. Every indication suggests these pole reversals were sudden so the appearance of a nonexistent magnetic field was simply the short period of time at the event horizon the instant the poles switched. These pole reversals have been linked to times in the past of mass extinctions but this theory assumes a long interval between the switching of the poles and that the radiation coming to earth during this period accomplished this. But they overlook the obvious devastation the very act of pole reversals would do. It wasn't the radiation that caused extinctions, it was the physical havoc on earth that accomplished this, all occurring simultaneously with the pole switch. So they have the correct incident, but because of the belief in evolution and the old earth theory, they come up with the wrong cause to reach this incorrect conclusion.

Nevertheless as the field weakens, more damaging rays enter the biosphere. Though some seem to think that radiation will advance the species of earth, all evidence point to the conclusion that radiation is completely destructive to living organisms. Previous polar switches are blamed (or credited) for new species and the advancement of evolution in other species, but no evolutionist would volunteer himself to mutate into a higher form of life, because he knows full well radiation is destructive. Show me one evolutionist that would want to be present in such an event so he or she could be "evolved" into a higher life form. Were the earth's magnetic field much weaker, things here would decline at an accelerated rate and earth would be a dead planet like others in the solar system. (book 22 pg. 178)

Experiments on midges exposed to 4000 roentgens of X-rays does not cause them any organic damage and they can still reproduce, but the offspring are reduced in number and size, and the reduced capabilities are passed on to the *all* generations afterwards. (book 4 pg 82) (though I suppose in theory if a unexposed midge were brought into the mix he would help to some extent bring about an upward trend in the gene pool and he would be looked up to as SUPER MIDGE! Which, by the way, is what the gods might have been; Super Midge…er…man, when they intermingled with men.

Ultra violet rays from the sun weaken the immune system and disrupts DNA. (Time Jan 2 1989, pg 41)

Interestingly Eskimo legends say that the first people were much stronger than people now. (book 56 pg. 230, 240.)

Biologist Martha Adam's experiments with embryo chick hearts showed something in the environment was affecting biological processes because the results periodically swung from a positive stimulation to a depression. After much detective work it was realized these downturns in biological variability were found to originate during increased solar activity, which also precluded or seemed linked to large magnetic earthquakes, showing not only was solar activity affecting living creatures biologically in a negative way, with increased sickness for at least short terms; it may also be linked to increased geologic activity. Symptoms such as fatigue, vertigo, chills, headaches, nausea, ringing in the ears, and excessive bleeding were found to be linked to the increased solar activity.

A medical center was not in the least surprised by her findings, and corroborated her findings by saying their patients had these symptoms just prior to earthquakes. To prove the point they then predicted the next earthquake. (Science Digest October 1982 page 73-74)

If increased solar activity is affecting us negatively, obviously one can only conclude that **any** solar activity is affecting us this way, and thus our lives are shorter since the advent of the protective water shell's collapse during the flood. Thus it seems as our environment diminishes its capacity to protect biological beings on earth then as a result, those biological beings suffer with shorter and less healthy life spans. ((2nd ed. Insert 2008) To further substantiate this notion that the sun is as bad for us as it is good, in Antarctica they found a curious observation. Wounds at the South Pole during the months of perpetual sunlight do not heal as fast as when the pole is in perpetual darkness. (Icebound Page 58))

THERE WERE GIANT HUMANOIDS.

(3rd ed. Insert 2016) The evidence for the existence of giants in the past seemed pretty obvious to me, so for some reason I didn't bother to tabulate the evidence because it didn't seem relevant, thus the first two editions of this book leave this subject virtually untouched. Many authors mentioned the evidence of giant remains and I just agreed it was so. Curiously, showing the evidence doesn't prove devolution, or creation, or disprove evolution so it seemed out of the scope of the book... and this book has a pretty wide scope!

Though giants were spoken of in Native American Indian legends, in the bible and many other ancient legends, they don't fit the creation story either. What I mean by that, is it seems they were not part of the original creation but appear sometime afterwards, and it seems they were not entirely human, thus devolution apparently doesn't apply.

John Battle states "You might think these big boys were nothing more than an overgrown human. That was not so, the original race of giants differed from humans in several ways. They were treacherous people, with enormous jaws and a double row of teeth. We have species of reptiles with a dual row of teeth today, so this is certainly not beyond the scope of nature" (book 12 pg 134). Perhaps someone spliced human genes with reptiles? Thus the double rows of teeth and the excessive growth could be explained without using evolution or creation.

So proving they existed thus doesn't really disprove evolution, nor does it prove devolution, at least in my mind because though giants did exist in the past, there seems to be no definitive link to them being completely human, but rather a crossbreed between man and... what?! But they at the very least prove another species of Hominid exists or existed. Wouldn't that be something evolutionist should be crawling all over then? Is it because they know instinctively they are somehow related to man and that's just a can of worms they'ld rather not open? It never states in the bible that the giants that existed before the flood were of the line of Adam, nor does it state categorically that they are the result of angles marrying man, though that seems to be inferred, and though likely, there's always the possibility they were results of genetic experiments...but I think the angel interbreeding is the most likely as we shall see.

So proving giants existed doesn't really seem to help illuminate the concept of devolution in reference to man and the earth. However, John Battle also states "the older the skeletons we dig up, the taller and more powerful our ancestors appear to have been." (book 12 pg 137) (People always refer to the middle ages armour as evidence we were short in the past, but this is mostly due to nutrition deficits...and middle ages is nowhere near old enough to get back to the age of the giants.) Similarly "It is a remarkable fact that all terrestrial animals are continuing to diminish in size. ...this has only been investigated for a short time, but it already seems clear that the largest members of the animal kingdom are either becoming extinct or shrinking as if touched by a magic wand". (Book 21 pg 26)

He then goes on to demonstrate this trend also appears to be happening with mankind as well... as reference further on will show. So at least some giants...or big old men, do appear to substantiate devolution, and thus creation as well. That's a good thing...right?

Evidence for giants does vindicate many ancient legends, histories and does, heaven forbid, substantiate the Bible too, but again not my main thrust...though admittedly, I do like finding things that prove the bible. On the surface giants may appear to substantiate devolution and in some cases they actually might, as working on this has shown me that man was somewhat larger in the past than we are now. I had always assumed larger men back then were just giants. But then such "normal" men that are on average bigger does further substantiate devolution....which might account for some peoples aversion to their existence.

Evolutionists really hate the concept of giants existing in the past. Consider this quote. "To date, scholars will not admit that any human has ever stood taller than the height of today's average person" (Book 12 pg 133) and "To date no scientist in the established disciplines has bothered to view the evidence on giants" (Ibid) I believe it is because it would seemingly counter the evolution theory immensely. How can man have been a giant in the past and be just 4-8 feet tall now...that seems like devolution, not evolution, so on the surface it seems disastrous to the evolution theory and it just can't fit with evolution doctrine. Thus many giant finds have gone mysteriously missing or are vociferously discredited because of this mindset.

However it's dawned on me that it might help for me to explain their existence and thus dissolve the notion that 'gods' came to earth way back and created mankind through evolutionary means as though earth was lifeless or filled with monkeys before they came, like so many authors have put forth and so many people now seem to think is the way it was. Giants and gods in the ancient past do fit in the big picture and many an author has taken their evidence to go down strange garden paths and lead many astray. Lucky you, I've decided to add what is virtually a whole chapter worth of evidence of giants here, be they half breeds of men and Angels, offshoot branches of evolution, humanoids or what have you, here they are. (I've put Yeti, and sasquatch in the next chapter for reasons that will become apparent, though in theory they could be put here too, as indeed some fossil finds could possibly be some of these 'creatures'.)

WHO WANTS THEM?

However the very existence of Giants in the past on earth may even be more explosive to normal patterns of thought because if we weren't created as giants, then how could they exist at all? Thus Evolutionist and some Creationists seem to be at odds with their existence. Biblically they appear to be crossbreeds of man and the sons of God...so it *does* fit with the big picture. But the fact that it bothers both sides opens the door to 'mavericks' and 'radicals, because giants simply DID exists and to say they didn't exist or ignore them, only fuels the flames of those who are certain they did exist and then they try to explain them without evolution or creation parameters, thus coming up with even stranger theories.

Secular writers like Von Daniken, make those that came to earth (the same that occasionally interbred with mankind) out to be God, or gods that either seeded earth, advancing human evolution, or mingled with mankind similar to the ancient and biblical stories. Any one of these theories really knocks evolution for a loop. By showing angles and thus God exists, or gods from off the earth came here and either created man, or helped advance man's evolution, just doesn't sit well with established 'disciplines". It appears injurious to evolution because if they did this...where does that put the gods in their evolutionary time slot in eternity? It just seems to be a can of worms evolutionists don't want to look into or even acknowledge exists. It's just too much for evolutionists and they wave their hand and call Giants, fakes, or the finders Liars. It's just easier to bury their heads in the sand on this one.

Actually, as stated, it is a bit of a bother to some creationists as well. Later editions of the bible tend to change or obliterate the existence of giants in the past because evolution has filtered its doctrines into church beliefs, and so, few religions have faith in the bible as the word of God. Warren Smith stated as much saying: "Incidentally, if you wish to check the biblical references to giants, you should consult a King James or similar edition. The scholars who have revised the modern editions are nonbelievers when they hear of giants. They have eliminated, or changed, many references to these creatures."

I think another reason Giants bother some creationists, is because they are mentioned AFTER the flood. The bible explains how they came to be before the flood, but if they all died in the flood, then how could they exist after the flood if they weren't of Noah's family? This must really boggle some creationist's minds. Clearly the bible cannot be a complete record of the events...where did the sons of Anak (Giants) come from, or Og or Goliath. Though Goliath for some reason doesn't bother creationists too much...maybe because he's such an intrinsic part of key Jewish kingship lineage, they can't escape him. But these son of Anak are a real problem because the word for giants here is the same as that before the flood...Nephalim. As you can quickly see it's a conundrum for just about everyone concerned. Thus writers like Von Daniken get off the ground digging into these quirky mysteries that few creationists or any evolutionist seem to have the answers to, or the intestinal fortitude to even wade into the mystery.

What is quirky about Von Daniken is though he shows just how impossible evolution is as a theory, (book 10 chapter 5) he humanizes the God of the bible and puts him into the category of 'the gods'. (forgetting that we are created in his image so we have the same psychological attribute in many ways)

He minimizes the idea of God making Man, but seems ok with the gods advancing mankind. So he on one hand says the gods gave evolution a push, but disproves evolution, so he never says where the gods come from, so he thinks he proves… what? Furthermore God said there are no other Gods, yet curiously he says not to revile the gods. And Jesus himself said that the scriptures say we are gods, when they went to stone him for equaling himself as God and a son of him. So this is something of a can of worms *"Chariots of the gods"* never really digs into or solves.

The most frightening conclusion to the creationists mind is suggesting that some giants survived the flood, but then that appears to contradict the very bible that stated all man on dry land died in the flood (except Noah's family). They say the bible is infallible, and true, but this very bit seems to blow it out of the water and undermine their faith…so pretend it doesn't exist? But it does, so is the bible wrong?... or is there a rational explanation to this serious problem? Quite frankly when I started this book I wasn't even aware of this problem and stumbled on it during the research. To make it worse, the word for giant is Nephilim, the same for the preflood giants. I did however find the answer from a completely different tack, so by the time I had realized this apparent trouble existed, it was already solved and furthermore, it was just a confirmation of my conclusion, as you will see next chapter. For now let's just look at what evidence of giants exists.

For the record we have to use Robert Wadlow as the bar, or the control so to speak. Any single skeleton found shorter than Robert Wadlow doesn't count as a "giant" as his height was reached earlier in the 20th century. (Though a *group* of skeletons found this tall should be considered confirmation of the existence of a giant race) His height was 8 feet 11 inches. This will be our measuring stick…unless the giant spoken of has the peculiar attribute of a double row of teeth. Though they often have 6 fingers and toes I won't even bother to mention them as occasionally humans have this too, though it could easily be considered proof as well as a person being a descendant of giants. But then some evolutionists could just as easily say it's a mutation or a sign of evolution. Actually when pictures of Robert Wadlow are seen I'd say he looks like a giant all by himself compared to people all around him, but apparently he had some disease that made him grow too much. So apparently we can excuse him for his inexcusable appearance.

Actually, believe it or not, giants may still exist. They were reported as late as the 19th century, and may still be in the back woods of some jungles. (book 12 pg 134) We'll get to them…

THE LEGENDS

(3rd ed. Insert 2016) The book of Enoch as quoted in Book 12 page 135 says "…the Grigori broke through their vows on the shoulder of the hill, Ermon, and saw the daughters of men how good they are, and took to themselves wives, and befouled the earth with their deeds, who in all times of their age made lawlessness and mixing, and the giants were born and marvelous big men of great hostility."

This quite mirrors the biblical reference to them and seems more clearly to state they were the result of the intermarriage, and also confirms Battles description of them. By the way I looked up "Grigori" and it means 'watcher' and or 'fallen angel' watcher angel or angel watcher. (ok we get the picture).

The Olmecs say Teotihuacan was built by white giants. Hindu 'mythology', speaks of Daityas which were a race of giants. Aztecs tell of the Quinametzin's, a race of giants that populated the world during a previous era. Guam legends state that a race of giants built the latte stones found there.

Quoting books of Ischtlil-Tschotschitl (an Aztec king) we glean Giants were horrible monsters with "habits of ugly vices" and they were there before the Aztecs. They were slain by the "angry gods" by the seas rising up and mountains turning into volcanoes. Similarly he quotes the "Saxo Grammaticus" which states there were three types of men which included giants of immense height, and the other two types of men (Prophets and ordinary men) conquered the older race and exterminated the giants. (book 29 pg 155-156). Let me repeat… "Immense height".

The Greeks were pretty sensible folks and even they have legends of Giants. They tell of a time when the gods, including the giant sized 'Titans', walked among us.

The Roman commander Quintus Sertorius was shown a mound by the people of Tingis (Tangier Morocco) in 81 B.C. and was told it contained the remains of a Libyan giant named Antaeus who was said to have fought Hercules. Well this was too rich for the commander and he ordered his soldiers to dig it up and they discovered a giant skeleton that was apparently 60 cubits long! (85 feet) (Atlantis Rising #69) Immense height.

Though shorter than Robert Wadlow, but apparently not diseased, the roman emperor Maximus was 8'6" tall, which was why they called him Maximus.

Some biblical references to giants "Numbers 13:33 "And there we saw the Giants, the sons of Anak, which come of the Giants : and we were in our own sight as grasshoppers, and so we were in their sight". Other versions actually use the term Nephilim. These weren't just tall, people. They don't refer to Saul as a giant though he was head and shoulders above the rest of the people...he was just tall.

But how tall was a giant. King Og's bedstead was measured at 9 cubits which works out to about 13 ½ feet.

The Mayans and Incans refer to the first race of men created by the gods before the flood as a race of giants and refer to two in particular: (Atlan (Atlas) and Theitani (Titan).(book 4 page 34)

The Olaus Magnus map of 1572 appears to depict a Giant Attacking a smaller man on the southern tip of Greenland.

SOME MERGING OF THE ROADS

(3rd ed. Insert 2016) Before reading Atlantis Rising magazines I'd never heard of Michael Cremo, so to my surprise he was recognized by a friend while I was looking at a copy of the magazine in which Cremo has a regular column. I was asked what I thought of Cremo. I mentioned that he seems to hang his hat on Indian ancient legends of world Vedic ages for the earth and so if finding a supposedly million year old artifacts hits the grapevine, in his mind it seems to confirm his beliefs. I also mentioned that in one letter and an article I wrote I directly took aim at this ancient earth acceptance, though I didn't mention his name.

But at the core he is still a reasonable archaeologist despite this difference of opinion as to the age of the earth. If you have complete faith in dating techniques who's to blame him? In Atlantis Rising #89 as an example of his fair handedness, he says he's looking forward to finding genuine Giant bones to give that branch of archaeology some credibility, even if he *is* referred to as "The Forbidden Archaeologist". After all, ancient myths and legends speak of giants, including ancient biblical and Indian legends, so their existence is entirely feasible. He cites some historic mentions of giants such as the Boston Journal of Chemistry (Volume 24 Number 8 P113) speaking of remains of a giant that had to be between 10 and 11 feet. (Why would a *chemistry* magazine be reporting giants, were paleontology publications already ignoring these finds back then?)

Then he states something so blatantly obvious in the light of the devolution theory that I had to include him here. He states:

"That living things were larger than they are today over 5000 years ago is also part of standard science. Paleontologists tell us that in the Pleistocene period, which ended 10,000 years ago, many mammals were bigger than they are today." Then he gives some examples like the Irish elk Megaloceros was bigger than any modern example of the deer family and it had antlers that grew to 13 feet wide, and the wolf Canis dirus was bigger than modern wolves. He notes that plants were bigger too, like the giant redwood tree of the Sierra Nevada Mountains were 350 feet tall. (Today the average height is 164 to 279 feet [Wikipedia]) And he concludes that if plants and animals were bigger than they are now it's reasonable to presume some humans were too. So he's quite open to examining giant remains, but so far none have been available to him or if they were, they were hidden from him when he showed up. Though it may be the people who had them to show might have been pulling his leg, it's equally possible they became afraid that they would be confiscated from them like the Smithsonian, or "government" has done so many times to other giant finds, which after their visits these apparently nonexistent remains just vanished. So kudos to him for even being willing to look, where many in his field have literally turned their back on such evidence.

Now I ask you to seriously consider the elephants in the room. If many species, if not all, are conceded to be much bigger a mere 5000 years ago, (or if we accept some dating methods, as much as a measly 10,000 years ago), where the heck is the evolution in that? If it isn't utterly obvious to you it seems plain as day to me that this is not just devolution, it's pretty dammed FAST devolution, especially when you consider some of the dates attributed to many species. Others Atlantis Rising writers have also keyed into this obvious fact. (Though I neglected to take notes as I just nodded my head as I read their columns) Even today devolution continues at a rapid rate, with genetic defects in genes running rampant, infertility becoming a huge problem and on and on. This rapid rate of decline in…apparently all species seems to me to have an upper limit in the time or devolution scale…both past…and present. Why is this not obvious to so many? A certain individual once said words to the effect that not only were certain people not accepting the truth, they were deliberately stopping others from seeing it too. Things don't change much in 2000 years.

A SMATTERING OF GIANTS: NORTH AMERICA.

(3rd ed. Insert 2016) In Wausaukee Wisconsin, on October 4th 1904 there was found a skull that was three times normal size and the other bones found with it were correspondingly large.

In February and June of 1931, large skeletons were found in the Humboldt lake bed near Lovelock, Nevada. The first two skeletons found measured 8 1/2 feet tall and were wrapped similar to the Egyptians in a gum-covered fabric. The second skeleton was almost 10 feet long..er high…well it was lying down. (Review - Miner, June 19, 1931)

Tucson Arizona in 1891 yielded a skeleton 12 feet tall, which reported in several newspapers in the area at the time. It had 6 toes, long hair and a bird shaped headdress.

Twenty 9-foot skeletons were found in a layer of shell about 30 miles from Los Angeles.

Near the outlet of lake Noquebay in Wisconsin was a mound which when dug into revealed hundreds of skeletons. One skull was triple normal size of average humans, with other bones that were correspondingly large. (so presumably an 18 footer)

In 1879, a nine-foot, eight-inch skeleton was excavated from a mound near Brewersville, Indiana.

In 1642 Maryland started a war on many native groups including the Susquahanock group which had some very tall members in their tribe, whose chief was just 7' 6" and he had 2 rows of teeth. He was apparently a half breed son of the Cat people, who were a neighboring tribe. These neighbors were referred to as the "Cat people' because of the way they talked, roared and screamed: they averaged 10 feet. Their bowls, discovered by Archeologists were between 48 and 90 inches wide. I've not been able to find what happened to the Cat people.

Twenty 9 foot skeletons were found imbedded in clam-shells under Shreveport Louisiana. This was reported in "The Daily Town Talk" December 9, 1902

The bones of a twelve foot man were dug up in 1833 by some soldiers at Lompock Rancho, California. The skeleton was surrounded by giant weapons, like a massive stone axe, and the skull featured a double row of teeth in both uppers and lower jaw. There were also tablets engraved with unknown symbols, which no one could decipher. They went to a settlement of (Delaware) Indians nearby to see if they knew anything about the giant buried there. The Shaman stated that he was an Alhegewi, part of a group of men of great stature their people had defeated, that used to inhabit the United States. Both the Delaware and Iroquois Indians needing new lands went west until they came to the Mississippi region when they came across a settlement inhabited by these giants. Asking them to go further east through their land, they were refused. The two tribes desperate had no choice but to combine forces and after several years they finally wiped them out. The surviving giants went west. This legend matches up with the evidence as many giant skeletal remains have been found west of the Mississippi in Minnesota. (Book 12 pg 141-44)

In 1877 four prospectors found, imbedded in rock, the better part of a leg from 4 inches above the knee down to the foot which was found near Eureka Nevada. The rock dated to the time of the dinosaurs and was chipped away. It revealed a lower leg that measured from heel to knee 39 inches and extrapolation showed the bones came from a man over 12 feet high.

Charles Hankley of Temecula, California went to a small private museum in Virginia Nevada and saw two 9 foot skeletons in a glass covered pit. The owner of the museum had found them in a cave nearby. Ten years later Mister Hankley went back to that museum to see the skeletons, but they were gone. The owner said to him that someone from the government had taken them away and wouldn't return them.

Thirteen human tracks 22 inches long (and 8-10 inches wide) were found in 1932, imprinted in gypsum rock near white sands New Mexico. (Book 30 pg. 31) Giant tracks in rock before it turned into rock...this must really give some people conniptions.

In Toledo Ohio in 1858 twenty giant mummified bodies facing east were found which had teeth and jaws double those of normal sized men. A mound in chesterfield Ohio was opened for building material in 1829 and it contained a skull so large that an ordinary skull could easily fit inside, and it had many more teeth than a normal skull. (see Atlantis Rising #69 for a story about giants several of which are included here)

In around Kansas city Missouri in 1877 a mound was dug into and there was found a giant skull and tracks belonging to a 25-30 foot giant.

Even Laurel and Hardy could find giants. In 1925 some newcomers to archaeology unearthed 8 giants 8-9 feet tall 20 miles southwest of South Bend and Walkerton Indiana wearing heavy copper armor. Archaeological museums weren't interested in the bones, and consequently through apparently amateur mistakes the bones and armor have been lost.

Also in Indiana a mere 9 foot 8 inch skeleton was found and then displayed in a glass covered pit in a private museum. When the government got wind of it they came and took it away and never returned it. Can't have evolution being discredited you know; it's un-American. The Smithsonian institute is actively hiding and discrediting finds proving giants existed. After all we can't believe the ancient records and heaven forbid...the bible. Internet sources say the Smithsonian was forced by the supreme court to release some classified papers. In those papers was found that they had gathered tens of thousands of giant bones found in America and destroyed them as ordered by high level officials to protect main stream belief of the Human Evolution. One 1.3 meter long femur bone had been secreted away from the Smithsonian by one high official and it was shown during a court case. This destruction of the bones was apparently done deliberately to discredit the biblical, ancient texts and other legends of Giants in the Earth. I'm surprised the Smithsonian didn't swipe Robert Wadlow's remains. Trying to find the website again I found some of this information again and we find the Smithsonian called this revelation not true. But sites can be found showing old news clippings of giants being found in various American neighborhoods. In fact so many stories of giants being found in America exists as well as news stories, one wonders if there are so many people finding giant remains, why *are* none in any museums? Were all the Soldiers, farmers, archeologists, witnesses and whoever saw or found these giant remains just lying, or *is* there a cover-up going on? Let's go somewhere else where the Smithsonian can't touch.

GIANTS O'ER YONDER

In Egypt bones were found which indicate a man was approximately 13 feet tall and some have been found indicating giants of 16 feet tall. Von Daniken describing flint tools found, extrapolated that the people using them would have to be about 12 feet tall. (Book 4 page 32)

A wee giant was found in an Italian Coal mine. In 1856 a miner fell through a shaft hole in an Italian mine and found a giant that was just a measly 11 and a half feet long. (Atlantis Rising #69)

Dr. Louis Burkhalter a onetime delegate to the Prehistoric Society, wrote in the 1950 Revue du Muse's Beyrouth: "I want to make it clear that the existence of gigantic men in the Acheulian age must be considered a scientifically proven fact"

A human skeleton 17 feet tall was found at Gargayan in the Philippines. Bones of humans 'creatures' over ten feet tall have been found in south-eastern China which were dated at 300,000 years old. (Book 21 pg 26)

In Agadir In Morocco, French Captain Lafanechere discovered a whole arsenal of ancient hunting weapon including 500 double edged axes weighing 17 ½ pounds each, "twenty times as heavy as would be convenient for modern man and he figures the people that used them would have been about 13 feet tall. (Ibid)

(3rd ed. Insert 2016) In Tura, Southwest Assam state of India in 1960 a construction crew hit a mound of rocks around 4 feet down. Below the rocks they found a skeleton 11 feet tall. Evolutionists claimed it belonged to a giant ape but never even went to India to examine the remains. The "ape" had a cup and flint buried with it. A cup? Yeah *must* be an ape…before they got hired by organ grinders.

A 15 footer was found in south east Turkey in the late 1950's, and a 19' 6" skeleton was found under an overturned Oak tree in the canton of Lucerne Switzerland in 1577. A 23 footer was found in 1456 beside a river in Valence France, and a 25 foot 6 inch skeleton was found in 1613 near the castle of Chaumont in France.

Ancient records show that between 640 and 650 BC Carthaginians uncovered two 36 footers and a third of this size was uncovered during an earthquake. That's 6 times the average height of man today…truly you would feel like a grasshopper compared to them. Even I was stunned to find giants 36 feet tall existed. They make Goliath (about 13 feet) seem like a kid.

In South Africa a footprint was found that was 4 feet long, indicating the woman that left it was 30 feet tall!

Pictures found on the net show skeletons or partial skeletons that would verify the existence of this thirty foot girl.

I repeat this bit from chapter 5: Shoe prints have been found in "Triassic" period limestone and a 22 inch foot print has been found imprinted in gypsum rock in White Sand New Mexico. What is a manmade shoe impression doing in ancient rock. (Triassic period dates 251 and 199 million years old) Note the size of the print.

With the internet and some pictures you find there now, it's difficult to eliminate the hoaxes from what people want you to believe are hoaxes. Technology has gotten so good, that many a hack can fake some pictures. ..as indeed some appear to be obvious fakes, some so large as to defy reason, or incorrect shadows, so it's sometimes hard to know what's a fake and what's just plain freaky) I do know that the giant footprints found in Paluxy riverbed were cut through horizontally and this proved the impressions were done with massive weight and not carved.

There is a well known picture taken in 1895 of a fossilized giant in an open casket standing up beside a ladder somewhere in Ireland. The ladder is slightly tilted away so some reduction of real size is necessary for a fair estimate. If ladder rungs are 1 foot apart, let's allow 9 inches per rung, then the giant in this picture would conservatively measure 13 feet 9 inches.

In 1941 on Java, some giant bones were dug up, by an unnamed anthropologist (?)He was figured to be from 10-12 feet tall. And considered to be "a giant off shoot of the main line of evolution" which is still accepted in the scientific paradigm…yeah he's still on the books! (Atlantis Rising # 69) ("…a giant offshoot of Human evolution"?)

South America More Giants(3rd ed. Insert 2016) An Incan named Garcilaso de la Vega who fought against the Spaniards with raids, was captured and escaped and then captured again and given the choice of death or, due to his looks and wit, was given the option of going to see the king of Spain. Being a realist he chose Spain and over time wrote some of the legends of the Incans in five volumes. The books also castigated the Spanish conquerors, so the books were burned, but a few copies were saved and reprinted years later by a Brazilian publisher. One part tells of beardless white giant men nearly 20 feet tall with strange large eyes and long hair, who arrived there from the sea. Some wore skins, some nothing as they had arrived without any ladies present. They dug huge wells lined with rocks which lasted for centuries. Unable to kill enough game to feed themselves, they raided native villages taking men and children for food. Women raped by them all died from the experience. Apparently an angel came and wiped them out, with only a few bones remaining to tell of their existence.

The natives actually brought the Spaniards a massive thick bone which convinced them there were giants there at one time, and furthermore they said... "the height of an ordinary man would reach only from the hip to the knee." (I'm not sure how to read that... I think it means ordinary man would only reach from between the knee to the hip of a giant. but the grammar and order seems odd...like I know grammar..) (book 29 page 159-160)

Pizarro was told that a giant race had existed as late as the 10th century and a Historian Fray Diego Duran was told the Aztecs systematically drove them over cliffs to get rid of them. Captain Hernando Cortez was shown a giant leg-bone and it was as tall as he was. He shipped a giant thigh bone to the monarch, accompanied by a story that there were giants in older times but the natives killed them off because of their bad habits.

Similarly Don Antonio de Mendosa, the viceroy of Peru in 1560 had been hearing rumors of a "sacred tomb" in the mountains guarded by the natives which contained giants bones used for curing diseases. They finally found the tomb which contained several skeletons of huge men along with "objects and curiosities". These too were sent to the king of Spain which were then forwarded to the pope. (Book 29 pg 160)Diego de Ordez (1480-1532) while looking with soldiers for the seven cities of gold (Cibola) stumbled onto more evidence of giants. He found a sanctuary near a volcanic mountain in which a somewhat worn giant thigh bone (hip to knee) was found. It measured 5 cubits or about 8 1/2 feet. Its width was proportional to its length. That would be four to five times the height of a normal man, by my reckoning (24 – 30 feet). (Book 29 page 161)

Keep in mind they weren't out to prove or disprove anything with these giant bones: finding them really only confirmed what the vast majority of the world accepted at the time...that at one time giant roamed the earth. They had better things to do then perpetrate hoaxes, like steal more gold.

In Mexico, Charles Clapp in 1908 found a cave filled with around 200 giant skeletons and all were *at least* 8 feet tall. One he pieced together was 8' 11".

More giant skeletons were found in 1928 in Ecuador, by men building a railroad and blasting rock to reveal a cave. Inside were several coffins of 8 foot giants. The bones sent to the University disappeared. (book 29 Page 161)And still more giant skeletons were found in 1936 near Tepic Mexico by Senor de Valda. In an ancient grave mound he found seven 9 foot skeletons of men and women under thin tablets of blue-grey slate, along with unglazed pottery, painted bowls and other stuff. (Ibid)

Who **did you say?**(3rd ed. Insert 2016) But this to me tops them all, not so much the giants, but who found them. None other than Ferdinand Magellan when he came near the horn of South America in 1520 anchored his fleet at Port San Julian to get water. The crew was stunned to see a giant walking along the beach...yes a living one. A historian (Pigafetta) on the fleet wrote "... Our heads barely came to his waist." and "...his voice was like a bull." This was confirmed when 58 years later Sir Francis Drake stopped at the same port for the same reason. When the crew landed, a howling horde of 7 1/2 foot to 8 foot giants roared out of the jungle and managed to kill two of his men before they got away. A little further south near the bottom of South America in Patagonia treacherous ten foot giants were known about and recorded by explorer Sebald de Weert. Anthony Knyvet (1507-1554?)said he didn't see any living giants but did find some skeletons of giants that measured ten feet. Later in 1764 Commodore Byran anchored the Dolphin in Magellan strait and saw peaceful natives. An officer of his staff wrote that "...some of them are certainly nine feet tall if they do not exceed it. ...the women run from seven and one half feet to eight feet in stature..." (Book 29 Page 162-163)

Our Pet Explorer. These Patagonian giants appear to have vanished after this and a Sir John Marborough (I couldn't seem to find the right one on the internet but someone presumably between 1768 and 1849) thought they did not exist. But in 1849 the giants surfaced again. While getting supplies for the John Allyne from New Bedford, Massachusetts, John Bourne and others were approached by "huge barbarians" pretending to be friendly, talking to them in poor Spanish when they suddenly grabbed the landing party, and demanded ransom. Tobacco, rum, bread, flour and stuff were brought which were exchanged for all the party except for John Bourne who was held for extra ransom. The boats returned to the ship and were scheduled to return the next day, but during the night a storm came and drove the John Allyne from its anchorage. Bourne, assumed to be abandoned, was now in real danger and many of the giants wanted to just kill him and be done with it, and some wanted him to be their slave. John who was five feet 10 inches noted that they were all taller than him by at least a head and many were over 7 feet with large heads, high cheekbones and the only attractive thing about them was their teeth. They had very guttural speech like someone with pudding in their mouth, and were all "great liars" and that "falsehood is universal and inveterate with men, women and children." He further noted that not only were they thoroughly treacherous but were also "excessively filthy". Bourne was dragged around with them for several months as with wandering nomads (which explains why they seemed to disappear for almost a century in a place hardly ever visited) and they eventually ended up at the mouth of the Santa Cruz river, where they spotted a settlement of English men on sea-lion island and traded John Bourne for more goods. (Book 29 page 163-165) Based on these account, giants could still be roaming around the backwoods of South America somewhere.

EASTER BUNNY GIANTS

(3rd ed. Insert 2016) When Jacob Roggeveen, the first explorer to reach the Island of Te Pito o Te Henua (Navel of the world) on Easter day 1722 (it was subsequently renamed Easter Island.) he documented two races of people on the island, referred to as long ears and short ears. The short ears were described as normal people but the long ears were apparently descendants of magical builder gods and they made the stone heads walk through the air. These long ears were an average of 12 feet high! The tallest members of the expedition could walk under their legs without bending their heads. (Atlantis Rising #90 Pg 71)

THINGS TO COME

Isaiah 51:6 ...the earth shall wax old like a garment, and they that dwell therein shall die in like manner...

MY LITTLE RANT

Though one cannot halt entropy, one can slow it down to a crawl, by managing how large areas are used or pillaged for their resources. But we need to watch out for over reaction to the realization of a problem. I have my doubts about everyone suddenly jumping on the bandwagon to stop global warming, throwing money and politicians at the problem and potentially coming up with ridiculous laws and extreme measures to cure the ills we perceive. We need to just correct schooling and teach correct preservation methods and we won't have people arrested because they find eagle feathers on the ground and make things out of them for gifts, or accidentally run over an endangered rodent or have ridiculous laws that say you shouldn't walk in the forest. I mean it's there to enjoy.

If we are taught proper respect for our environment we won't ...well whatever it is they are afraid we'll do to despoil the nature of the area. Take forests for example. I've seen places where they want you to stay on paths and not venture into the forest. I mean what are they afraid of anyway? That we'll kick a rock over and despoil the way it looked naturally? Individuals are not going to destroy the forest, by walking through it, and this sort of protective measure is more straining at a gnat and swallowing a camel, as it is the big corporations and poor government policies that destroy forests.

Don't get me wrong. I hate litter too and we should all be conscious of how we affect our environment. If we care about the little can or piece of paper carelessly tossed into the forest we will also care about how the corporations we work for or own, alters our environment. Look at Brazils "management" of that huge rainforest, burning millions of acres of forest. Or some of the horrendous clear cutting practices. Take care of the governments and corporations destroying forests and you won't have to worry about individuals bending reeds or kicking over a rock in what little forest is left. The forest will be able to take care of itself.

Teach children not to chuck garbage into ponds and when they grow up they will take care of the cities that callously pour sewage into waterways; and you won't have to have ridiculous laws about being on the beach or telling us not to swim in the water. This idea of making laws so that individuals can't enjoy what little forest or beach is left in the world is hypocritical when the same powers that be, clear-cut or burn forests and pollute waters with impunity. It isn't the little individual that ruin the beach or the forests or the lakes or the mountains, it's the laws that allow big corporations to do these things. As long as this destruction is allowed to go on unchecked, and as long as big business lines the pockets of politicians, in the name of progress and industry, no amount of enforced environmentalism on the little guy is going to do one iota of good and the earth environment will continue to devolve at an accelerated rate. I can just see someone being arrested for walking on the beach or swimming in a lake or climbing a mountain or walking in the forest; yet how many big corporation owners and politicians end up in jail for polluting great lakes and huge water Straits?

((2nd ed. Insert 2008) People seem to think things are as they always have been. I have lived in this area all my life and I remember in 1964 the water in a local bay was so clear that I thought I could climb off a log and touch bottom. It then dawned on me that the water was very deep and I had to be rescued from that log! The water appeared shallow because it was so clear yet the water was about 15-25 feet deep. I've gone back to that bay to compare and the water is so dirty one can't see down more than a couple feet. Whether or not sewage has anything to do with the murkiness of the water I don't know, as studies show additional treatment is unnecessary. But in just over 40 years the ocean water has turned from crystal clear to blackish.

Chapter 9

UFO ORIGINS: WHO THEY ARE, WHAT THEY ARE, AND WHERE THEY COME FROM.

Some of the source material used to substantiate the theories presented in this chapter and indeed this entire work may be considered to be of limited value and even of a skeptical nature. For example Geologists and Paleontologists aren't taking the North American native histories into account when they come up with their respective theories. People tend to dismiss a point of view if they know the source material that substantiates that point of view to be a controversial one. But ask yourself, if the same fact is mentioned by Erik Von Daniken, or by Albert Einstein, does the person quoting the fact change the nature of the fact? Perhaps the context in which they used it may be of debatable nature, but the fact itself still remains a fact.

A fact can be manipulated to prove a variety of points if you have an agenda and a preconceived theory you want to prove. I didn't have either of these when I started studying UFO's. I just wanted to know what these things were and let the facts accumulate to see what sort of picture came out of the pile. In fact that could be said for most of this work. Granted I'm coming from a Creationists point of view, but what are the alternatives if Evolution is false? So if these other scientists are taking evolution as the basis for their theories, doesn't that mean their material is also of a skeptical nature and of limited value?

Obviously one can see that I do not necessarily agree with Erik Von Daniken's conclusions, which you might find curious since it was basically his work that started me on this information hunt. Nevertheless he did use facts and archeological material to arrive at his conclusions; and some of his points may be valid. I have taken his theories under advisement, usually with a grain of salt. I have merely accumulated the facts, and then tried to make sense of them when gathered altogether. I've even tried to verify them whenever possible, regardless of who stated them, at least as much as is possible for an armchair researcher. I can't afford to go to Egypt or Peru, but I can afford to go to a book store or a library and look up things on the internet. Yeah some even feel the internet is a suspect source for research. But the questionable internet can sometimes collaborate or conflict with a piece of information helping one come up with a more balanced view or at least a second opinion. I've seen some pretty lame theories there, some of which will be noted here, if for nothing more than pure amusement, but the internet can indeed be quick access to a whole lot of valuable information…Yeah, yeah OK I'll get on with it.

This chapter is difficult to create a logical order for the material to place in. So I have to repeat some stuff, as so much material has double and triple value. For example the Hopis have a legend I used I think four times as it just speaks to so many aspects of this chapters material. Occasionally I refer to stuff I haven't yet explained. Sometimes it's frustrating to order it, and it might prove confusing at times. But as you go along all will eventually be explained. For example I mention Blue Moon I think out of order, but that gets explained later. It partially rests on Chapter 3's mentioning mans ability to destroy a planet with such a planet. Anyway it will get there and hopefully this third edition will have it even more sorted out as I have been printing out each chapter alone and dealing with just one chapter at a time, rather than dealing with the entire book at once. So hopefully it will be a bit easier to grasp. I've realized this chapter is actually longer than chapter 6 by over 18,000 words. My apologies for any reading and comprehension difficulties; it will all make sense… eventually.

ESTABLISHING THE ANCIENT HISTORIES AS CREDIBLE.

As a rule I tend to ignore material if it seems somewhat in doubt or inconclusive, and indeed I tried very much to eliminate dubious material from the more lucid and credible. But due to the fact that I deduced some of the things presented in this chapter, then later found some of this dubious material actually lent support to these theories, it tended to make me think there may be something substantial to what would otherwise be considered dubious. And indeed the very existence of UFO's are considered by many to be in doubt.

I have heard of people actually attacking a person's character simply because they believed UFO's existed! So in essence one might even suggest I used dubious material to prove something whose very existence is in doubt. Can you prove UFO's exist by saying you saw one to someone who doesn't believe they exist? Some might even equate this with proving the bible by what is written in the bible. In fact people have completely negated any point I have made in conversations when I or others have proved the bible using the bible. Fair enough, I can see this point has some merit. (Why would I try doing that? Keep reading.)

In addition to just seeking interesting material to see what's what, I have also tried to lend credibility to the sources such as the bible and ancient histories by using each to verify the other. Since there was obviously no collusion between the various authors of these sources, any similar events spoken of in more than one source automatically lends credibility to both sources. Did you catch that? That is important! I'll say it again in another way. I have not used just the bible here to prove these points thus far. I have also found other ancient histories which collaborated the events spoken of in the bible. By doing this we see that ancient records prove each other because there could not possibly be any collaboration between the authors of these histories. So now we see geology and other histories confirm much of what is written in the Bible, but vis-a-vis we see the bible also proves the other ancient materials too…to some extent. Thus we all become forced to accept what otherwise we might have thought in doubt. Many of you will have to accept the biblical record even though it is popular not to, and I in turn had to accept many of the ancient histories other than the bible.

Still we have to be careful too in just accepting them carte blanche. For example many books were attempted to be included in the bible, but the scholars found reasons to seriously question the nature and origin of these books so they were not included. Similarly what few ancient records or histories I have managed to read often have either indecipherable gibberish or clearly fictitious accounts formulated to come to some moral.

Once many ancient histories are substantiated in my mind and now hopefully yours as well, we can start to depend on them for more than corroborating each other. When we see that the bible substantiates ancient Egyptian, Mayan, Indian and other histories with no collusion between the chroniclers, and we see that each of these ledgers lends veracity to each other by speaking of the same events. We can start to see that each of the ledgers then becomes more credible.

Actually few people seem to realize that the bible itself isn't a single book but a collection of books that were written over a couple thousand years which support each other. For example the four books Matthew, Mark, Luke, and John were written by four people about the life of Christ. So much is common to three or all four books that they do lend credibility to each other, similar to how two witnesses in court will help establish and event.

By this same logic we have seen that many ancient texts and histories lend credibility to each other. This is important, not only for all the other aspect in this book we have already covered, but for UFO research.

For example modern theorist insist North Americans migrated across the Bering Strait. But the histories of the natives completely contradict this theory. Now since we've seen these ancient ledgers corroborate each other often, we can become more reliant on these histories, so the modern theory has to be discarded in favor of the corroborating ancient histories about this same area of study.

Originally I wasn't willing to believe other ancient histories. This mutual corroboration between the various ancient texts convinced me to not be so narrow in my focus. This was how I was able to show mans advancement in the past being so much superior to our own civilization. But this wasn't my original purpose in searching for evidence for mans advanced nature in the past, I was just curious, and then realized I was finding things that did corroborate things written in the bible. Things that other people might want to read about. But in doing this research, these pesky UFO's kept cropping up. No matter how much I swatted at them they kept buzzing in the research material.

Eventually being curious I wanted to figure what UFO's were too. Since it would seem we have substantiated the bible and several ancient histories, we can further rely on their accuracy to prove other things. Once realizing they occasionally speak of UFO's I have tried to prove the existence of UFO's and their origins partly by using the bible and ancient history. Similarly ancient histories corroborate and thus lend credibility to UFO's. Yes...even the bible does this!

You may be wondering what explaining UFO's might have to do with a book of this nature. Wait for it.

UFO'S ENTER MY VOCABULARY.

When I was 5 or 6 years old I overheard people talking about UFO's and didn't know what they were talking about. After asking them what a UFO was I was told it meant unidentified flying object. So I say 'Like a bird you don't know?'... to which they replied, no that's known to be a bird... something not an animal. Ok now I knew.

Maybe a week or even just a few days later I was outside and a plane flew over. This is in the days when they made sonic booms. I loved those booms. OK this plane didn't go boom but I just wanted to reminisce... I saw a bumper sticker that said "I love airplane noises"... I guess that's me...well I can't stand those high pitched whining noise some of those jets make... Anyway back to UFOs. This plane goes by and I ask my big brother ...what's that? Of course I know it's a plane but I wonder if he'll be able to identify it. But he says it's an airplane. I say "what kind" he says he doesn't know. So I say 'so that's a UFO?' He say no because someone knows what type of plane that is even if he doesn't. Then he says UFO's are things that NO one knows what they are. Ohhh! The light goes on.

Fast forward. I'm about 10 and come home from some outing in the evening. As we drive up the long driveway. I mean long...about 1/2 a kilometer... OK I'm reminiscing again...anyway we get about halfway up and a couple kids come running up to the car exclaiming "We saw a UFO!!!"

Oddly I didn't doubt them, I was just sad I missed it. They were clearly as excited as anyone seeing one would be. They said that it came over Mount Doug and flew toward them and passed over and continued on in the direction of the cottage and on over toward the west. OK not their exact words but that was the gist. I'd missed my one chance to see a UFO. Years later while doing this research I found this exact series of sighting in one of the books I read. This was a series of sightings in late September 1968 that occurred in and around the Esquimalt dockyards area near Victoria BC. That was neat. It took me back and confirmed that these kids did see that UFO and I really did...just miss one. That's as close as I ever came to seeing one.

In a way I'm almost glad I didn't see it because then my clearing up the mystery of the UFO's might have seemed like a lifelong obsession. But don't get me wrong I think it would be cool to see one. But by the time I started work on this project I didn't really care about them, because I guess I felt I knew what they were.

MEMORIES KICK IN

(3rd ed. Insert 2016) I recalled more regarding the UFO sighting that I mentioned those girls ran up to me in the car to tell us about so, first the continuation of that story. I remembered seeing the event after the girls had seen the UFO, but at the time thought nothing of it. This makes perfect sense too, since I would have been on the road coming home and, based on their description and notation of direction travelled, it would have crossed the road we were driving on shortly before we arrived. Oddly enough I didn't even connect what I'd seen with their story at the time!

I saw the craft maybe five minutes before we drove up and they came running up to the car. We were driving home (north) along Blenkinsop Road. Being the passenger and thus not needing to mind the road, I saw in the distance an odd glowing flying craft meandering from right to left and a little up and down in along the edge of a treed area at around tree height. This was at the far end of Blenkinsop just before the road veers right toward the intersection. It would have come from the Mount Doug direction on the right, as the girls described and gone in the direction toward Royal Oak, weaving slowly along. It inclined slightly upward to get over the 'hump' of the trees and then downward and was gone. I wasn't even excited. I said to the person driving the car. "That was an odd plane" The driver just said. "Uh huh". Though probably half a mile away, it was right in the line of sight as we drove down the road. I just thought… 'I'm just a kid, but, he's probably seen plenty of those.' (Thinking about the girls sighting, the craft had to be just 30-50 feet above them as it flew over them, and I would guesstimate, based on the height of the trees, the craft was probably about 15-30 feet wide…quite the exciting sighting for them indeed, especially since the craft was a glowing white craft.)

As a kid, I didn't automatically think "UFO!". My thought was, 'Well that's an unusual "plane", but I'm just a kid so I haven't seen them all, nor do I know all about what we've come up with yet, so to me, this was just one I hadn't seen before'. So I thought nothing more of it. Thus I never connected what the girls saw with what I saw…in fact it completely slipped my mind.

During the next school week I was with a group of about five boys and they were going on about UFO's and stuff. None of them had seen one, but I guess the recent sightings brought the subject up readily as research has revealed that at the time there was something of a local "UFO flap". Since I'd never seen a UFO, or so I thought, and didn't know much about them, I basically just listened as the other four or five boys talked about them, as I didn't think I could add anything knowledgeable to the conversation. Realizing none of these had seen a UFO I recalled the odd craft I'd seen and said I'd seen an odd plane recently, thinking maybe they could tell me what I'd seen as they seemed quite familiar with flying craft. Suddenly all eyes were on me and they were asking me to describe it. Well I did of course and since it had no wings clearly they were convinced I'd seen a UFO. I kept trying to convince them it was just a sort of craft I'd not seen before that and I tried to convince them that they were just kids too and that they probably hadn't seen everything either. But they insisted all planes had wings. I'd mentioned helicopters didn't have them and they asked if what I saw was a helicopter and of course it wasn't. They were convinced based on my descriptions that I had in fact seen a UFO. Eventually they did convince me I had seen a very unusual craft indeed, possibly even a "UFO", as they called it, though I still was certain it was just man made craft we weren't too familiar with. I wasn't buying their "aliens" silliness. But recalling it now…well, It's kinda neat that I saw one.

MY FIRST WORKING HYPOTHESIS

I had asked a Christian what he thought they were and he said they were probably demonic manifestations. This seemed as good an explanation as any though I thought it unusual that they could appear this way. Since they are primarily known to have surfaced around 1947 it seemed to gel with the prophecy "In the last days there would be signs in the heavens'. This explanation seemed reasonable and I accepted it. I hadn't actually done any research on them but I used this answer to anyone else's inquiry as to what UFO's might be. I must have sounded rather closed minded to anyone who felt they knew better.

I have now done some research on UFO's. Needless to say I've changed my mind. Perhaps some UFO's could fall into the class of "demonic manifestations", but clearly there is something here that goes beyond this pat answer.

In doing the research for the rest of the book I stumbled upon these UFO's continually in some of the material and I couldn't understand the fixation so many people had about these things, or even why the authors were even bothering to mention them. I figured 'Big deal, fuzzy lights in the sky, whoopee ding." I'd roll my eyes, gloss over the references and carry on. But they kept cropping up in the research. Many authors referring to them were bright and lucid in their material when suddenly they'd refer to UFO's seemingly out of left field… 'Where'd that come from?'

One thing I found a bit irksome was how people who disclaimed and debunked the sightings of UFO's as mass hallucinations or Venus, a known airplane, or 'swamp gas' seemed in essence to be saying only they and apparently Astronaughts and pilots have a corner and monopoly on sound minds, and anyone else seeing strange lights or moon men were only simple peasants tetched in the head.

So as a sort of break I decided to side track and read a few books specifically devoted to them. Not sure why but, hey it sounded interesting and maybe a good read or two and it would give me an interesting break from my other research. They didn't seem important, I was just curious. But with the tentative explanation of them being "demonic manifestations", this diving into research about UFO's took on a kind of ominous meaning. I mean if they are not human what are they?

STARTING TO DIG.

Well as potentially disturbing as finding out what these things might be and what they might mean, I delved into the reading about UFO's. Since I didn't know one UFO book from another, I basically took any one and then followed the bibliographies to what might be more credible sources...if UFO books could indeed even have "credible sources". Who knew this sidetrack would fit right in with my research!

As I said, I kept seeing them crop up in my research material, in places I wouldn't expect to find them, like in ancient history. Though I wasn't "seeing" them as such but only some author's strange interpretation of ancient data that kept making this connection, so I just humored the authors and glossed over the references.

As it turns out some UFO data was already staring me in the face in my research but I had completely missed it thinking it to be something else or just ancient tetched peasants making up stories about natural phenomena...or tetched authors. Some ancient UFO sightings that were normally interpreted as allegories became so obvious when it was looked at in this light, that it is amazing how we missed it at all!

THEM THAR FLYING SAUCERS IS MIGHTY PECULIAR!

As I read about UFO's I became aware that people were not just seeing "fuzzy lights", but were seeing actual craft. That wasn't what I expected...at all! OK so at first I discounted these sightings as wishful thinking on the parts of one or two eyewitnesses. Maybe they wanted to see space craft and space men so they saw them.

Then the witnesses started becoming pilots and astronaughts who are supposed to know a puff of smoke from an actual flying craft. Suddenly this UFO business started taking on the nature of a genuine mystery! I suppose even I was one of those that felt only pilots and officials had sound minds, but I soon changed my tune and started taking the more lucid "tetched peasants" stories at face value too.

I started gathering clues. I wanted to figure this thing out! This is real cool stuff! But understand, this was also somewhat scary ground for me to walk on. Since I look at them from a creationist point of view the potential for upset exists. If these are not us in the UFO's and they are actual craft, who is piloting them? How do these fit in with the big picture, and with my preconceived ideas? Already they do not appear to be just demonic manifestations, though some might be, clearly these are piloted craft. So to be fair I will admit my perspective on the "big picture" and you can see if I'm forcing the UFO's to fit.

UFO'S ARE A POTENTIAL PROBLEM TO CREATIONISTS' POINTS OF VIEW

Since I believe in creation it seems to me that nothing can exist that was not created. Since evolution appears to be a bunch of malarkey and is easily disproved, then only what is created is what exists. So who are these UFO's then if they are not us? Angels? Demons? Foreigners from some distant galaxy? But if they were from another world this didn't make sense. (I'll tell you why in a sec') I mean you can see why the theory that they are "demonic manifestations could be so easy to accept under the circumstances. Even my 'old school' way of thought seems to force them into this box.

OK I know angels / "sons of God" exist and I know some of them descended to earth in the pre-flood era. Could this somehow be connected? (Since some people do not believe in angels you can see once again the biblical perspective really forms a lot of my understanding of the earth and universe. And as you've seen so far I have yet to come across any reason not to believe in the bible.) So then, what are these U.F.O.'s????

All the research here so far actually confirms the bible, and the bible itself actually speaks about the things mentioned in this work. So far the only problem we have seen with the bible is the chronological record does not appear to be complete and some of the timeline appears to be missing thus the confusion of the various dates accorded to the age of the earth because of this. This research into UFO's constitutes the biggest challenge by my way of thinking to the biblical point of view, and as I research them, I honestly did not know what the conclusion concerning UFO's would be. But these UFO's are not simply men or angles, they are craft...flying machines, something mechanical built by hands. Angles don't need craft... and neither do demons, though I suppose this does not mean they couldn't have used them or made them, though that seems like a completely bizarre thought.

WHY UFO'S, AS WE UNDERSTAND THEM, ARE A PROBLEM.

If evolution is not true for the earth it is not true for anywhere else in the universe. This would mean these UFO pilots must be created beings. But then where would they come from? If God created them and us they are as important to him as we are. Could God have created two earths and then come to both of them and lived and died for people on two planets? It says he died once for all mankind...not twice. Is there a planet out there with sinless beings on it? I mean what am I to think?! What are these things...Who are these pilots flying them?! Now you can see why so many either say they can't exist or they must be secret craft the governments of the world are not admitting they built. But as we will see, neither conclusion works!!!* As you can see the bible is very much influencing my ideas as to what these UFO's could be. This is why I'm telling you this to be fair so you can determine for yourself if I'm forcing them into my belief patterns or I'm correctly analyzing the evidence. (* 3rd ed. insert. further research shows some may be contemporarily manmade. We'll get to them)

TUNNEL VISION

At one point in my life I refused to read anything but the bible. Once when I was about 15, I read a book that was in a cupboard to get some culture or something, a book which turned out to be just smut disguised as literature. It was my one wander into other books and after reading most of the book I stopped reading it. That ended my ventures into "literature". After that all I would read was the bible or text books and the like. So even reading any other book at all for this research was to my way of thinking being bold. But read them I did and sometimes I felt to be on very strange ground indeed! And now UFO research?! Trepidatious ground for me to say the least!

The idea of them being from another planet seems very mysterious indeed. So you can appreciate the potential for a serious upset in deciphering just who and what these creatures and UFO's might be. But I was willing to figure out what these UFO's are and then see how they fit in with the big picture, even if I had to alter some things as I saw them. As it turns out these UFO actually do fit in with the "big creationist picture"... if I made one major concession. I had already deduced that pre-flood men had space travel. The 'major concession', if you haven't already figured it out, I will make clear soon enough. I feel honestly that this is an accurate deduction as to what UFO's are. They not only fit but they confirm my conclusions thus far. Now you decide if I have shoved these into this preconceived notion or if they fit it without me forcing it.

THE WITNESS'S

As it turns out the average UFO witness is anything but a simple minded peasant tetched in the head. A poll was taken of UFO witness's in the '60's and it revealed a decided lack of peasants and irresponsible uneducated or unbalanced people. Most witnesses had a high school education and 16% of those polled had higher education, with 4% scientists and teachers, 5% engineers and Technicians and 8% being police officers.

Are flying saucer real? On October 2 1954 the French air ministry ordered an investigation of them after 267 people in widely separated areas in France all reported seeing saucers. In the spring of 1954 over Birmingham Alabama, 4000 people saw a cigar shaped saucer hover above the city. It was seen to fade in out of view for an hour. (book 47 pg 82)

On November 8th 1954 150 Italians were gathering around the perimeter of a sports field in Monza. Through the boarding they could see a UFO and its occupants doing some field work. Some threw bricks at the saucer and hit it without making any sort of noise, like the UFO was soft. The crowd eventually broke down the gates and rushed the saucer and the pilots which wore helmets, white pants and grey shirts. They got back into their ship in time and the saucer took off vertically.(book 47 pg. 250-251) Here we see just a few instances where many witnesses saw these craft. Tell *them* these things are not real.

UFO'S: ARE THEY REAL? PUFFS OF SMOKE? VENUS? WEATHER BALLOONS? SWAMP GAS?...

On January 25th 1954 British air ministry warns all personnel not to talk to flying saucers. (book 47 pg. 119)

One UFO seen near Nha Trang in Viet Nam very much scared the 40,000 service men watching it descend from an estimated 25,000 feet to about 300-500 feet and light up the area like daylight. (book 28 pg. 99)

In April 1966 during a huge wave of UFO sightings, hearings in congress admitted that the civilian scientists and investigators have come to the conclusion that verify the existence of UFO's and that no doubt the US Air force had come to that conclusion long ago. (book 28 pg. XV) They felt that some public declaration should come forth from them. But the existence of UFO's are persistently denied.

Former CIA director Admiral Rosco Hillenkoetten acknowledges that no earthly power such as Russia or the U.S.A. could attain speeds and manoeuvrability seen with the UFO's. He states the governments of the world are "soberly concerned" about UFO's, but in public they ridicule UFO's as nonsense. Speeds of up to 11.8 miles per second have been observed by these craft.(book 28 pg. 244) This is absolutely remarkable for a couple reasons. For one, our satellites only orbit the earth at 5 miles per second and for another reason anything we made to go that fast in our atmosphere would just burn up by the friction. They have somehow eliminated friction or are phasing through the matter in the air to avoid the heat.

Sometime previous to 1974, U. Thant considered UFO's the most important problem facing the United Nations next to the Vietnam War. (Book 28 pg. 242)

YES UFO's ARE REAL. So what and who are they? And where do they come from. As I gather and put the clues together the answer becomes clearer.

WHY IS THERE DOUBT ABOUT THE EXISTENCE OF UFO'S?

If UFO's are real and are seen by so many witness's why is there so little formal study of the things, and no admitting of their existence by authorities? Doctor Paul Santorini a student and personal friend of Einstein said it's been concluded that there is a worldwide blanket of security regarding UFO's because authorities are unwilling to admit the existence of a force to which the earth has "no possibility of defense". (Book 28 pg. 102) No doubt the 'race' is on to master their technology and any knowledge gained from the UFO's would be a closely guarded secret, so denial of their existence would also deny they have any of their technology.

SOME UFO SIGHTINGS THAT GIVE SUBTLE CLUES TO WHO AND WHAT THEY ARE AND HOW THEY FLY.

Now that we have established they are real we can start to look at some sightings in more detail.

The vast majority of UFO sightings are at night or early morning, either for the purpose of eluding detection or possibly avoiding some negative aspects of solar influences on them. Power disruptions are often associated with their sightings. Our technology pales in comparison to the UFO's.

Though some UFO's have been noted as noisy this is not the case for all. Many sightings involve completely silent methods of flight, even though observers are close enough to them, sometimes even directly underneath them. If they were powered by conventional methods witness's would certainly hear such engines or be burned to a cinder if they stood underneath them. This strongly suggests some sort of antigravity rather than conventional propulsion system is in use. For example a completely silent UFO with not even the sound of the stirring of air was seen by several people in April 1966 at Beverly Massachusetts, though earlier it had been observed to make a soft 'whizzing' sound. (book 28 pg. 128-130) Not even the stirring of the air? This is indeed a most curious observation.

They have been seen hanging around power lines as though they acquire some sort of charge from the lines, and are often observed flying in a sort of pendulum motion as though under some sort of magnetic influence.

From January to July 1954 gold coloured discs were seen very high above, flying in a "V" formation over Victoria Australia.(book 47 pg. 63) Interestingly some birds, in particular Canada geese, also fly in a "V" formation. Birds are known to be able to view magnetic wavelengths of light not visible to man and it is thought this helps guide them in migration flights.(Though evidence garnered in the 40's and fifties tends to suggest birds can direct themselves by the stars.) This "V" formation follows the air currents behind the lead bird similar to the wake behind a boat and it's fairly certain that the V formation is flown by the birds to reduce drag, with each bird taking it's turn at the head of the "V". However it is interesting that birds can see magnetic wave lengths and fly in this formation and since it's felt that UFO's also utilize some aspect of magnetism in their flight, is there a connection? Or were UFO's merely flying in a "V" formation like the Snowbirds of Canada and using the air currents to reduce drag? This seems unlikely as the air seems to have little effect on the UFO's. Though admittedly I am not aware of any sightings occurring during storms. Thus suggesting storms might somehow affect UFO's flight ability, either because of the turbulent air or the violent erratic nature of electrical storms. Or perhaps I just haven't read enough about UFO sightings to have come across them being spotted in storms, after all storms are not the sort of weather one goes out into to look for UFO's. (One researcher notes that only 4% of UFO sightings occur during rainy weather)

At 3 A.M. October 3 1958 four star like objects were spotted from a train going from Monon to Indianapolis. They too were moving in a V formation. They came in close to the train and they were seen to be four disc shaped vehicles about 40 feet across and the edges were fuzzy, a common phenomena with flying UFO's. (though landed craft are more often clear and sharply defined.) These craft were not especially bright in the close up views so glare does not appear to be the cause of the soft indistinct "fuzzy" edges. So presumably a strong magnetic or electrical field could to be a part of their method of flight as this might account for the lack of hard edges which might be caused by distorting of light around the craft. The four UFO's buzzed the train a few times and even flew in a straight line. This sighting seemed almost like the UFO pilots were playing rather than a purely methodical mission. When the train reached Kirkland they flew away. (book 50 Pg. 31-34)

ANALYZING THEIR METHOD OF PROPULSION

When the lights went out all over the Eastern seaboard in 1965 there were a flood of UFO sightings related to this event. It reminds me of how Tesla blew out a complete cities generator doing his experiments in the Rockies. When the power that drives these UFO's is talked about, occasionally Einstein's Unified Field theory is brought up. The way Einstein and Leopold Infeld explain it sounds a bit convoluted but basically they say that when a strong magnetic field is cut crosswise with a strong electric current and some sort of third dimensional unknown factor comes into play, some sort of unified field is the result, though exactly what that result would be seemed unclear. (I tend to use the term 'Unified Field' a bit loosely, but refer to the general science.)

This apparently was done in some fashion in 1943 in the now famous Philadelphia experiment. Strong magnetic field generators were set to running on a couple of military ships, one in a harbor and one in the open water. The ship in the harbor was seen to become invisible down to the water line and the ship in open water was not seen at all unless you got close enough, then you could see the cavity of the water in which the ship sat showing its displacement. Oddly at this distance you could also see the sailors walking on the invisible decks as though walking on air. This is a most curious observation too, because it means a unified field will act differently on living beings when compared to inanimate objects like ships. Also this "walking on air" observation is interesting and does tie in with some ancient legends.

Interestingly the areas where these experiments were carried out also showed strange greenish hazes similar to those seen in the Bermuda triangle where so many disappearance have occurred. The ship in the harbour apparently started in Philadelphia then dematerialized and appeared briefly in Norfolk / Portsmouth Ohio area 425 miles away then back in Philadelphia in a matter of minutes. Apparent instant transportation or teleportation was a byproduct of this field.

A BRIEF LIFE' CALLING

While looking through a chemistry book I opened to a page that made my jaw drop. There was a light spectrum which had continued on to show radio waves and magnetic waves as a continuation of the same spectrum. I had no idea that magnetism was related to light, but I immediately understood how something could become invisible. I thought I had not heard of this Philadelphia experiment at this point but I then recalled having this same realization occur to me in school while I was in grade nine. (actually I had heard of the Philadelphia experiment in grade 9 but had forgotten about it and this look in the chemistry book brought back this memory.)

I remembered in grade 9 I was looking in the text book and saw what I thought was some sort of error and raised my hand to tell the teacher. After he asked me what the error was I said that they put magnetism in the light spectrum. The teacher said that magnetism WAS part of the light spectrum. [electromagnetic waves move at the speed of light thus a similar relationship exists. "...there must exist some connection between optical and electrical properties of matter..." and the same mathematical equations describes electrical induction and optical refraction. Book 44 pg 150] I then instantly deduced and said "well if that's true then a strong enough magnetic field could make something turn invisible" (I kid you not! I said this in grade nine science class!) Thereupon the entire class laughed at my deduction, and I determined right then and there that I would make something turn invisible when I grew up. I had my life's calling... for about 45 seconds!

Then the teacher said that this was true and it had been done in 1943 in the Philadelphia experiment explaining generally what happened back then. I then realized if it was already done there was no point in my reinventing the wheel, and the process must have been perfected by now. So in 2 minutes I had a life calling and then had the decision of that life's calling overturned. One wonders what would have happened had he said nothing about the Philadelphia experiment to me then, but rather told me about Einstein's Unified field theory instead! (By the way this was the same science teacher I asked about the DNA information in chapter one)

UNREQUITED EXPECTATIONS

I must confess I was wondering when this invisibility invention would become something we could buy and play with, and I looked for signs of it in ads and stores for many years with no success. Yeah! I'm serious! I even asked people in stores for it!" "Hey, you got anything that turns invisible? I realize it might be something quite expensive but if I can get an idea of how much it costs I can save up my allowance for it." I know I asked one store owner pretty much this exact thing with pretty much these exact words when I was about 14. He must have thought I was out of my mind!…or very misinformed.

As time went on around the early eighties, I was even beginning to wonder if it wasn't some sort of secret invention…(gee… you think?) But I asked myself, then why would the teacher know about this experiment? And surely after nearly 40 years it must be more well known and in the public domain! I kept wondering if maybe I shouldn't start experimenting and making this thing anyway as no one else seemed to be promoting a new invisibility invention. But I kept putting it off thinking yeah as soon as I spend tons of money figuring it out someone will put it on the market. This is how obvious the invisibility theory seemed to me, so I couldn't figure out why it wasn't coming on the market…it had to be obvious to someone else too. Apparently not. I mean especially since they had done this very thing in '43. Why wasn't it coming up for sale. I kept thinking if you scaled down the invisible stuff it might fit in say a box similar to a chemistry set. But then it never occurred to me it just might be too expensive to sell. After all you can't go to the corner store and buy a rocket to go to the moon with now can you. These things would be a pretty expensive item to place in aisle 11, even for Shoppers Drug mart.

COULD I HAVE BEEN WRONG?

This is not to say I am some sort of genius. I could be missing something real obvious here. For example I once thought I had the key to perpetual motion (didn't we all?) and altered an electric clock second hand to move with magnets. But I had completely missed a real obvious aspect of magnets. The clock did one tick and then stopped. So these observations I'm making here about invisibility could be way out of line. But they are fun to make all the same. Maybe this flop with perpetual motion is why I shied away from trying to make something turn invisible. I mean if I missed something that obvious with magnets, maybe I'm missing something really obvious with invisibility, and mistakes can be pretty expensive.

By this time (early '80's) I seemed to have completely forgotten about the Philadelphia experiment or I might have tried anyway. Hmmm maybe if this book sells really well I can work on it… or that man powered flight I've always been contemplating… or those cool bikes… Being poor can be really restrictive. I mean what sort of invention can I do with just wood I find at construction sites anyway? A particle accelerator? A nuclear wessel? Maybe with all that wood I could invent a storing device for holding numerous articles such as books, but it seems to me I've seen something like that before.

ALTERED DEDUCTIONS

Anyway, as to why I felt that a strong magnetic field would make something turn invisible I can only deduce my original reasoning was flawed but that I was on the right track. I originally felt a strong magnetic field could warp the light of an object so that you see around it or through it. The object might look like water in front of water or like a heat wave.

Though I still feel certain a strong magnetic or electrical field can turn something invisible, I have since revised this deduction as to why such a strong magnetic field would work and how something would appear under the influence of a unified field. Magnetic fields also generate electrical currents and vice versa. It's known that atoms are basically composed of electric fields and magnetic fields, that is atoms are simply little more than charged particles. My guess is that a strong magnetic field will interrupt the integrity of the normal workings of an atom causing the electrical components to alter their normal vibrational frequency.

HOW TO MAKE SOMETHING INVISIBLE

To understand how something can turn invisible one has to understand the mass of an atom. Extremely little mass is involved in matter that we see. By way of illustration, if a nucleus of an atom were the size of a baseball and in the place of the sun, the outer shell of the atom, that is the electrical / magnetic component or forces of that atom (electrons) would be as far away from the center of the nucleus (the baseball) as the planet Saturn. And one must understand that in this analogy that mass of an electron is a microscopic speck or maybe the size of a pea in comparison to that nucleus we mentioned that was as big as a baseball.

Now consider this. If you were on say planet Pluto and you looked into the solar system would you see that baseball and those electrons? No! they are so infinitesimally small they would not be observed in the panorama of the solar system, and they would barely even be detectable. This is to point out how much or rather how little matter there really is in matter. Matter just so happens to have energy that pulses, vibrates or whatever it does in such a way that we can see it. In fact scientists wonder why we can see anything at all, because there is simply so little matter in matter to be seen. It is the frequency of matter that allows us to see it, similar to how the frequency of sound allows us to hear it.

We can hear sound in a narrow range of frequencies then the sounds become ultra sonic or subsonic, that is to say, we can't hear it. A strong magnetic field will disrupt or interfere with the normal pulses of atoms and matter, so that matter will pass into the ultra visual or sub visual field and thus become un-seeable, or invisible. It appears UFO's use this science and it's possible that UFOs when in this state may also be able to alter their solidness, traveling in a solid state or stationary in a solid state yet invisible. On May 2 1953 a plane took off from Calcutta and 5 minutes later it disintegrated. Witnesses said nothing was seen near the plane, yet close examination of the wreckage indicated that it did not explode by some sort of bomb on board as one might expect, but that it had struck a "fairly heavy body". (book 18 pg. 216)

One UFO visible to people from the highway was seen hovering over a pond with the interior visible and normal looking occupants which appeared to be working on some repairs. When they realized they were being observed, one of the mechanics pulled two levers and the craft just disappeared. (book 35 pg 189)

Though Einstein and Leopold felt a third factor had to be introduced into the formula to create a unified field, they did not appear to be sure what that factor was and assumed it was some sort of dimensional ingredient. My guess is sound is the third factor. Sound also vibrates, and based on ancient legends where sound was a factor in lifting huge stones, levitation, and apparently invisibility, then this may be the missing ingredient. If you tune magnetic fields in some way with electrical fields and then introduce sound this might have an extraordinary affect once the sound is in unity or tuned with the other two fields. UFO's are sometimes said to travel with a nice almost musical sound. This tuning of sound might perhaps be similar to how when an airplane or a vacuum is droning you can hum until you match the frequency of those objects and you get a resonance. Ok it's weird but it makes vacuuming more fun...if vacuuming can be called "fun". Some UFO's have been heard to make interesting noises indeed, though it unlikely these sounds have anything to do with this capability as in all likelihood any sound needed would be ultra or subsonic.

WHAT IS WEIGHT?

(3rd ed. Insert 2016) What makes things heavier? You might say...more weight...but what is weight? What makes elements heavier? Heavy elements have more nuclear protons and neutrons, with the appropriate number of electrons whizzing around. But where do nuclear particles reside? They hang out in the center of atoms…they don't fall down to the bottom of the atom. Thus extra weight in essence floats so it's not heavy at all. Thus we are not lifting weight, we are countering energy that is simply electrical and magnetic in nature, and really has nothing to do with weight at all. Consider the spinning bicycle wheel. A Bike wheel by itself is easily turned in your hands. But if the bike is upside down and you peddle the bike so the wheel turns really fast and then try to turn the whole bike, the bike with the spinning wheel resists being turned. I think the power here is similar to the power in an atom that makes elements "heavier". Stopping the wheel stops the resistance, stop the atoms motion (or unify it) you control it.

Could sound lift weight? Keely started motors by hitting the right note on his violin. A harmonious sound in tune to matter might make atoms move in sync and then might be moved easily.

CLUES TO MOVING AT THE SPEED OF LIGHT

Since realizing magnetism is a form of light and that magnetism always has an electrical field and electrical energy moves at the speed of light, and electrical fields all have magnetic fields, one can make deductions from this. One could conceivably conclude that in amplifying this magnet field in matter one amplifies the electrical and light properties of it and probably diminishes or diffuses the visible nature by upping or lowering the frequency of that light/magnetic field. This would not only render the matter invisible but potentially actually turning the matter into a form of light and thus infusing the ability of matter to move as light *at the same speed*. This may account for the ship in the Philadelphia experiment transporting 425 miles apparently instantly. It got there at the speed of light. This may also explain some disappearances of people and planes and lost time in some cases. Thought this may not be related I can't help but think of when Moses was with God on the mount, how when he came down to the Israelites his face shone so brightly they had to put a veil on his face. As we do possess an undistorted magnetic field in our brains, there may be some link to this shining skin to coming into contact which that which can create the universe, that being God.

Apparently there is a heavy concentration of UFO sightings on magnetic faults. They may be studying it, using it, or it may even be a point of entry and exit into, onto, or even out of the earth. This might even cause one to speculate that not ALL UFO's are space worthy, though there is no real basis for that conclusion. It has been observed by a Dr. Wilbur B. Smith that whenever a UFO came within reach of the sensitivity of his equipment it registered a sharp disturbance of the earth's magnetic field, deciphered as a "gravitational distortion". (book 62 pg 131) So gravity is also part of this whole equation. And why not, as these UFO's clearly have mastered gravity, as so many are observed to "hover" with no apparent method of propulsion being used to stay stationary. Indeed some are completely silent in such sightings. This association with magnetic faults might have a connection with what was seen in the Peleg chapter and the "pyramid belt".

There is an aspect of the atom that was recently figured out which is quite interesting in light of this theory of instant transportation. Originally the electrons were thought to circumnavigate the nucleus of the atoms. But it was later realized that the electrons seem to randomly appear at various parts of the "orbits" with no apparent continuous motion. The electron might appear here then disappear and appear on the opposite side of the atom with no apparent motion used to reach one side from the other. When I first heard this, this seemed like science fiction, but if this is indeed the case, then this fits very well with the apparent teleportation of people and ships from one place to another. As a natural part of the workings of the atoms transferred in a unified field to the complete mass of an item so that when all molecular parts work in unison then all parts of the matter can do the same thing at the same time. Once all the atoms are working in a unified field then all the atoms can shift simultaneously from point a to point z with no traveling through points b-y. Well it's a theory anyway.

TECH CLUES

(3rd ed. Insert 2016) The story above about a UFO seen as a kid, wasn't particularly pertinent to the book's content, but because this sighting was mentioned in the first edition I figured my sighting of the craft would add to that story…for whatever it's worth.

However when I mentioned that story to a friend he told me about a UFO sighting of his own that speaks volumes.

A FRIEND'S SIGHTING GIVES CLUES.

(3rd ed. Insert 2016) This, in his own words, is of a sighting of a UFO over Victoria. The reason I include this one is because of the unusual nature of the "gantry".

"My sighting of an unexplained flying object happened one evening at dusk about eight years ago. [c 2007] It was a summer's night and nearly dark. I was standing with another bus driver on the sidewalk of Fort Street in Victoria, B.C. I happened to look towards the west and noticed a dimly lit circular object heading in an easterly direction at what appeared to be between 1,500-2,000 feet. This object was actually heading our direction and I pointed it out to my friend. As we both looked, a group of young people in their early 20's noticed us looking skywards and they too observed this strange object. I remember their expressions of 'cool' and 'wow' without me speaking to them. My observation was of a strange kind of gantry or triangular structure projecting from the curved surface. This gantry would instantly disappear and reappear on the opposite side of the circle, and then instantly show up 90 degrees or so further. The dimly glowing circle suddenly changed course and headed north at a constant slow speed at which time the dimness faded to complete darkness and disappeared, but then, almost immediately, some strange wavering streamers descended, on fire, numbering about eight, they could be seen on fire for about fifteen seconds before the fire went out. The passing group expressed amazement at this and they continued on their way along Fort Street. This happened on a clear summer night. I reported the matter to Victoria Police the same night but they said it is not in their range of interest. I also contacted Air Traffic Control for Victoria who told me there was no flying activity over Victoria at the time I mentioned the sighting. John Roberts."

These "streamers' are consistent with other UFO sightings, but this gantry's motion is of particular interest. As a youth growing up the standard model of the atom we learned about was of electrons zipping in very tight circles around a nucleus. I have found out during the process of working on this book that the electrons of atoms do not move this way, but instead the electrons will be in one spot, then another and another in no particular sequence. They are just here, then there with no apparent motion of going from one place to another, just like this "gantry" as seen on this particular UFO and I am certain this is a very good clue as to the way it works. I think this is an example of a unified field acting upon all the atoms of the UFO which are thus in synchronicity so the motions of the multitude of atoms in sync is transferred to the whole of the craft so in a sense the craft acts like a large atom. The interior occupants, like the people in the Philadelphia experiment would not be subject to this erratic behaviour of say the 'gantry", and were unaffected by the experiment visible on the exterior, whereas the people on the deck of the ship in the experiment were subjected to the full force of the field and their bodies began to act erratically like electrons or this 'gantry', thus they would disappear, act nutty and walk through walls. This effect was achieved with a very strong magnetic field (apparently a Tesla Coil?) and indeed this also allowed the ship to teleport, like an electron from one side of the sphere to another part…be that sphere the earth or the spherical craft.

Thus we can see that the working of the atom has been used to work on the UFO. Unifying the motion of all the atoms in the craft with a power source has transferred this ability of the subatomic to the craft structure itself. Likely the interior of the craft is in appearance as normal as any other interior, that is not acting like the superstructure.

UNIFIED FIELD AND ITS EFFECTS CROPS UP IN STRANGE PLACES.

The results and uses of such a unified field might have some predictable effects other than simply invisibility. Matter could conceivable pass through matter, maybe even in a visible state. Since there seem to be properties involved in a unified field (electrical, magnetic and sound) tinkering with the variables may create these results. If you could control your own field and alter it you could do some bizarre things. Some "primitive" cultures on earth have been known to push sticks through their mouths by way of their cheeks and then pull them out but no wound was visible because they phased the molecules of the sticks with the molecules of their own cheeks and then unphased them when pulling them out. One could perform incredible magic tricks were one to have control of this phasing ability. One could even walk through a mirror or make a statue "disappear", possibly overcome gravity and fly or maybe even appear to teleport oneself. (If you are familiar with any famous magicians you can guess to whom I allude to)

Jesus appears to have done something like this. He was back in Nazareth at the time where he grew up and the townsfolk were displeased with his sayings and they took him out of the town to the "brow of the hill" and they were going to throw him off the cliff and then, in Luke 4:30 "...but he passing through the midst of them went on his way" He did so because it wasn't his time, thus adding weight to the statement we did not take his life, he laid his life down. Though they had a firm hold on him he was able to just pass through the midst of them. Very interesting.

Other uses of a unified field could be utilized, possibly where an item has broken one could subject both adjacent broken pieces to a unified field and mend it seamlessly by re-fusing it at a molecular or atomic level. Paper cut in half could be restored to wholeness if the two halves were carefully lined up and "unified". Apparently "aliens" have demonstrated something similar to this very ability. Possibly one might be able to match the frequency of specific matter with other matter by say raising or lowering the average frequency of the atoms of a rock to match that of the atoms in the air, rendering a rock to be the same weight as air. Well it sounds good but obviously very precise and tuned experiments would be necessary to calibrate such forces to a more manageable state.

One might be able to change the very atomic structure of matter through a unified field. Atoms of a rock could disassociate and combine like soap bubbles and become something completely different like gold or lead or air. This could be the secret to "cold fusion". Alchemists were said to have done this very thing. Though it's thought incredibly expensive and technology is needed to bombard atoms to change matter to different elements it seems this was accomplished in the past, by more mundane methods. Laws were even being passed to stop alchemy and gold made from this art. Or gold made from this method was sold to the governments with no questions asked to stop economic chaos or collapse.

WE ARE CATCHING UP.

(3rd ed. Insert 2016) When they came out with Cold Fusion, everyone laughed. Why...it was impossible right? Wrong. Because it scared the hell out of those who profit by selling you power. It's been noted that the cold fusion experiment results have indeed been duplicated in other people's laboratories. Mark Dansie has come up with a "Over Unity Disc" which has an inexhaustible source of energy because it recharges itself by pulling charge out of "thin air" or ether (Earth's magnetic field?). But it's not a battery because the colder it gets the more powerful it becomes. Perfected it could easily replace batteries...but who would want that? Everyone! Because once you have one, you NEVER need to buy another one! This means no more extra $ for those who sell batteries. (See Atlantis Rising #98)

Does this remind you of certain cave lights "burning" for thousands of years? I say we are starting to get close to what the ancient's thought was normal technology. The problem with these new inventions is once you apply for patent on them, the details automatically get sent to the government to determine if they should be considered secret inventions. Over 6000 patents from 1942 to 1993 were and still are listed and buried under secrecy policies. Some people have dared to bypass this by sending copies of the technology to several colleagues, and simultaneously publishing the technological details on line...basically giving their discoveries away to be sure the public finds out about them. "Most ufologists that I know believe the the Cabal-which is also known as the 'shadow government'- in the U.S. is in possession of the technology we are looking for, but keeps it secret for reasons of their own power and profit" (Ibid)

DANGERS OF UNINTENTIONAL UNIFIED FIELDS.

But there could be dangers as well. If the atom's electromagnetic forces were stopped completely or slowed sufficiently, matter could change its atomic structure, or possibly even collapse. Though it is usually thought absolute zero would cause matter to cease to have energy, perhaps a magnetic force acting upon matter could stop the electrons buzzing, and then with no inertia the particles could crash into the nucleus collapsing the atom. One has to wonder if this is not what happens in instances of spontaneous human combustion. Perhaps the magnetic, electrical and audio components of the victim happened to unify and matter crashed inside the body. Often such victims leave almost no physical remains and it is a wonder where the rest of the person disappeared to. People have been seen to turn invisible and legends speak of human sound as a component in ancient mysteries connected with antigravity. Since it's known we have perfect undistorted magnetic fields in our skulls perhaps sound can interact with this field present in every human body. Perhaps the victims of spontaneous combustion hummed themselves to death. Wouldn't it be something if after reading this, investigators of causes of spontaneous combustion found out the people were all persistent hummers? Then the warning in schools would be "STOP humming you might blow up!" Well who knows...but the unified field theory might shed light on the poor victims of spontaneous combustion, and vise verse.

TURN...NOW!

(3rd ed. Insert 2016) In the main text I explained how UFO's either turned invisible, or teleported, and were not disappearing into some 4th dimension as so many theorize. But I completely forgot about the instant turns and acceleration which needs to be explained. People have said the UFO's cannot possibly be inhabited or controlled by real flesh and blood people, of any kind, because of these technologies which instantly bolt to 300 miles a minute, or turn 90 degrees while doing this speed because it would kill the occupants. (Some *have* concluded this might indicate they are piloted by spirits or ARE spirits.) Now while this could be an opportunity to play the demon card, I think this is actually technologically explainable.

What I deduce is occurring, is that while these maneuvers are taking place, the UFO's are in what I called phase mode; that is they are halfway between solid state and invisible state, or instant teleportation state. Thus they can be seen moving, but they are moving half way between normal travel methods and instantaneous (or teleporting mode). Remember the Philadelphia experiment where the ship instantly traveled 425 miles to Norfolk / Portsmouth instantly and then back again? No one was killed by this instant travel, because their molecules where in teleporting mode as well. But the travel was instant so no one saw the ship move, it just disappeared. Similarly while these craft are traveling they want to get somewhere quickly, but it may be quicker to just travel in phase mode rather than plugging in co-ordinates for an instant travel at that time to some place a mere 100 miles away. It's probably just easier to just jump to phase mode and bolt there in 5 minutes...or seconds.

NO HAMMER AND SICKLES ON ANY UFO'S.

(3rd ed. Insert 2016) One of the common fears was that the UFO's were of enemy construction, and during the cold war this meant they might be Russian. But recently Vasily Yeremenko, former head of the KGB stated significant resources were devoted to the study of UFO's. They were constantly collecting, evaluating and analyzing data on them. They even came up with a good way to get them to just show up! They would simulate a military alert by increasing aircraft and hardware traffic in a particular area. They did make sure however not to appear aggressive as that might instigate a hostile reaction. He stated that most of the UFO's that turned up in Russia were luminous spheres. He also stated that for security reasons UFO's should be taken seriously. (See Atlantis Rising mag # 100)

MAN MADE TECHNOLOGY?

(3rd ed. Insert 2016) Some hints in man's research suggest that just maybe man is making *some* of these UFO's. In 1934 Westinghouse Research Laboratories found that magnets made of cobalt shaped like a RING, with an enclosed frame holding one fast the other one will float above it, like it's resting on water and bob like a cork...reminiscent of how UFO's move. If one visualizes on a larger scale the earth being one of those magnets and the other ring shaped magnet being a UFO...?(Book 47 page 20) Around 1921 Hendershot invented a motor that derived power from the earth's magnetic field. This invention very much impressed a U.S. army Major named Thomas Lanphier. They built a model airplane that flew based on this engine. Oddly on March 10 1928 he ends up in hospital from his machine zapping him and the machine disappears after this date.

Some years before 1936, an experiment was done, possibly at Wright Field in Dayton Ohio, where several men with all metal removed from their persons held a railroad track suspended on cross sticks between them in the center of the airfield. Then a plane took off from another part of the field, circled and then flew over the group of men. When this was done the rail disintegrated and disappeared. The men were given no details, but the story was told some years later in 1936.

In 1906 a German scientist named Levetzof (or Lewetzov) discovered a ubiquitous ray originating in space that, if interfered with correctly, could weaken gravity, induce weightlessness, and be a huge source of power if man could find a way to manipulate the ray. Apparently (according to a magazine called Frankfurter Illustrierte) in 1929 Germans were sent to USSR in an exchange program to witness or work on technology based on the Levetzov ray theory. By 1942 a Russian Physicist Andrei Goryev was at work in the Urals hoping to make an 'aerofoil' using the Levetzov rays. Though apparently no 'aerofoil' of this kind was made they did appear to create some sort of crystal apparatus that interfered with the rays at least partially by polarizing or neutralizing them.

It's said that in 1944 a motor car was being driven by this ray, and this ray was even propelling aircraft in the USSR. By 1948 the Russian Air-marshal K. Vershinin had 5 planes flying by then that could reach "almost unimaginable speeds and service radius, in theory equal to that of half the known space". (book 47 page 24-26) In 1952 Russia had in their possession "...a type of aircraft already past the experimental stage, which was propelled by a newly discovered energy of extra-terrestrial origin.". (Book 47 page 27...Quoting a report by the Zyalkovsky Institute from Feb 20 1952) Description of the craft stated the crew is suspended within the hub and is basically stationary and the crew doesn't feel any acceleration or deceleration as they are shielded from the rays. Whether or not the Soviets say they have a UFO or not, it's interesting to note that in 1954 a Scandinavian skipper of a small trading schooner found a strange disc with Soviet markings that had crashed and burned near a Kamchatka coastal village. (Book 47 page 238)

Also in 1954 a café owner saw someone come out of a disc shaped saucer with a domed top and approach him and say to him in French "I am not a Martian. I'm French", and then asked him where he was, then got back in his saucer and take off, vertically at high speed.

But USA is in the mix too. Professor Hermann Oberth a former Nazi scientist working for USA at the time stated "We know of a material that will, in practice insulate from the pull of gravity [of] any object covered by it" Date not given for this quote but before 1955). (Book 47 page 28)

Herman Klein, another former Nazi Scientist in Zurich Switzerland at the time of these statements said that he was in Prague, Czechoslovakia when the Germans started work on a terrestrial saucer. In 1942 they sent a very maneuverable pilotless disc made in Peenemunde that flew from Stettin (on the Baltic) to Spitsbergen. Klein says the American Air force was instructed not to shoot foreign saucers but to force them down. (book 47 page 252)

GERMAN CRAFT?

(3rd ed. Insert 2016) While looking for any indication that at least some of the UFO's might be of earthly origin, and specifically WWII German origin I found this. Shortly after WWI (for protection's sake in the text a pseudo-name was used) German Dr. "Rhinelander" was contacted in Germany by "non terrains" from an underwater habitation, and was given plans for building a "marvelous aerial craft". He was told to move to some location in the States by some played out coal mines. (A byproduct of coal was needed for the craft). The non terrains with seemingly unlimited funds assisted and apparently 4 or 5(?) ships were built with earth escaping capabilities. However the first three were confiscated (with the pilots on board) by other non terrains not wanting [surface] man to have the technology. The fourth craft finally countered the capturing capabilities of the non terrains. The book goes on a side track about some fuel for the craft and lots of cloak and dagger stuff about the fuel and the non terrains stopping all attempts of the scientists to profit by the formula. But what happened to the craft themselves was never explained. (book 30 Pg 175-180) As I recall from other sources suggesting a German connection with some UFO's, was that some of these craft found their way into Germany's hands for them to study, and replicate. Could they be the same ones, and / or origins of the apparently German UFO's spotted over time?

SOMEWHAT EARTHY VENUSIANS

In March 1953 in Los Angeles 2 bluish "Venusians" men 6 feet six inches showed up in a newspaper to seek publicity. To prove their origins they scored a hardwood desk with their fingernails to a depth of 1/4 inch deep, apparently in one pass. Later they also scored a piece of steel the same way. They were said to be very smart and tracked a missing person in less than three hours when normally it would take a pro two to three weeks. When the steel furrow made with their finger was analyzed 14 elements were found there that were not present in the rest of the steel. (book 47 pg. 30-33)

A 'spaceman' named "Bill" with whitish blue skin appeared at a bus stop in Santa Monica out of the blue. He cut his name into cold steel with his bare fingers. (book 47 pg 34)

LATENT PHYSIOLOGY WITHIN, AND INSTANT TRAVEL

It would seem that apparently instantaneous travel is linked with these saucers and this ability may also be something latent in our own physiology, possibly making us capable of teleporting items or even ourselves. Saucers have been seen to phase in and out of what people consider a dimension. But this may simply be control of the forces necessary to become invisible.

A Fay Clark was "seen" to become invisible for 2 minutes while speaking to a crowd of people. She felt strange as though she were having a heart attack so she sat down and it was then she became visible again. Though she never left the room and could see all around her, they could not see her. No one has suggested she teleported from a different dimension, she was simply invisible. Yeah...simply invisible...real simple. (book 30 pg. 215)

Possibly this latent ability may be linked to teleporting people through doors or other places. One person on an ocean vessel was cleaning his knife. It slipped from his hands into the ocean. At that same instant that same knife fell through a roof window at his house and stuck into the table. His wife saw it and kept the knife and showed it to her husband when he got home and he realized it was the same knife, and further comparisons made it clear that it happened at the same time he dropped it. (book 47 pg. 99)

If we have the ability to become invisible through whatever force it is that is doing this, it seems that we become linked to the part of magnetism that is considered to be part of the light spectrum. But if this is the case, do we become light, and if so do we move at the speed of light or even that of thought? If so then this could explain apparent teleporting incidences. One thing that is interesting is that so many UFO-nauts have asked people what time it is, suggesting their phasing abilities and apparent teleportation abilities interfere with their chronometers. As Einstein's theories shows time slows down for those moving when compared to people not moving. So presumably less time passes for UFO's in motion then those on, or in the earth.

People tend to think the UFO's are going into some other dimension but I think they just turn on the super magnetotron or whatever and then their atoms slow or change the visible light wave length and are able then to move as light and invisibly. When they turn this machine off suddenly they just appear wherever they happen to be at the time they turned it off. To you and me not being versed in the mechanics of the machine then assumes they are ghosts, or coming from another dimension. I suspect that moving at the speed of light is not a matter of speeding up a vehicle, but has to do with altering the pattern of the atoms contained within the UFO or what-have-you as shown above with strong magnetic generators as experienced in the Philadelphia experiment. Apparently these UFO's have mastered the technology that can do this, possibly from observing it in nature or the physiology of humans which seem to be able to do this.

For example in 1593 on October 25th a man that was in the Philippines suddenly found himself in Mexico... clear across the Pacific! He told the people in Mexico a person was killed the night before in the Philippines and they had no idea if this was true as there was no way he could have gotten there in one day. He was jailed for desertion. Later it was confirmed that the person he said was dead, really was killed on that date and it was also proven that he was in the Philippines on the 24th of October 1593...the day before he appeared in Mexico.

A doctor and his wife were driving in Chascomus Argentina when their car was enveloped in a dense fog. When things started to make sense again they found themselves 4000 miles away in Mexico. Their watches had stopped and their car had strange burn marks like a blow torch had been taken to the car. They also found it to be 48 hours later. That much time lost?? Was it teleportation or as some suspect UFO's, or is there something in nature doing this too?

Another example of instant travel is in the bible. In John 6:21 after Jesus walks on the water during a tempest he then gets into the boat "...and immediately the ship was at the land wither they went".

A VERY GOOD CLUE MISINTERPRETED

There was a peculiar event recorded at the Mississippi Power Company that happened in 1931. A cloud formed over a turbine. At first it was thought the turbine was overheating but a careful check showed everything was in order. Then in the cloud appeared a woman lying on a couch. The image was quite clear and they could even see her jewelry. The woman however apparently did not notice the people at the power station...they would have been invisible to her. The image lasted about twenty seconds then things went a little haywire at the power station. (book 30 pg. 136-137) Interestingly, the engineer present noted a similar event occurred in Great Britain, though details were not given.

The important thing here is the scene of the woman in a cloud over a turbine which obviously is electrical, and thus a magnetic field is in play here. Very much like what is needed for the unified field. There was obviously that unknown third ingredient, whatever it was, present to create the unified field.

The immediate assumption was that they had briefly opened up a time portal to be able to see the woman. This seems like a logical assumption because obviously there was no woman present at the time so they felt the woman was in that exact same place at a different time. I don't agree with this appraisal. I think the woman was on the earth at the exact same time as the people at the power company, but on a different part of the earth. Consider our friend in Mexico who came suddenly from the Philippines. I expect that had the people at the power company walked toward the woman in the cloud they would have immediately been with the woman wherever she was. To the woman the power company personnel would have just appeared out of nowhere...or out of another dimension. Sound familiar?

It would seem this occurrence was an accidentally byproduct, closely associated with what occurs at power stations, well at least the type in Mississippi, in 1931. Interestingly UFO's often cause power outages or disruptions and the unified field is also closely related to both these phenomena. Many inventions are come across by accident. But this fulfillment of this invention has not come about simply because we tend to think what we are seeing is some sort of spirit, vision, or past event. It would appear that we have come within inches of discovering instant teleportation technology on a few occasions, and misinterpreted the evidence of the events.

MORE DISAPPEARING PEOPLE.

Though not much is mentioned about this one incident it seems relevant. A man disappeared in 1879 after going out for a walk and was never heard from again. In 1950 a man dressed in period clothing blundered into traffic in Times Square and was killed. This man turned out to be the missing man from 1879! (book 30 pg. 220)

On September 23 1890 in Gallatin Tennessee, a David Lang walks into a field in full view of his wife and a friend just arriving on a horse drawn buggy. He is suddenly seen to just disappear. They looked over the spot where he was last seen and there was no sign of him even though the whole town checked meticulously for any sign of a sink hole or unknown crevasse and dug in many places turning up nothing. Oddly the exact spot where he disappeared was then avoided by bugs and no animals grazed there. Only his children would go there from time to time and ask out loud "Father are you anywhere around?". Then suddenly in Early August 1891, nearly a year later, the children got a reply to their question! It was definitely David Langs voice which was also heard by his wife and two kids. It was speaking as though from a long way away asking for help. His voice was heard for five days gradually becoming fainter until it ceased. (book 50 pg. 41-46)

What happened? And how is it he was still alive though apparently stuck in the same spot for nearly a year? Did he eat? or was he in a state where food would make no difference. Will he just one day reappear like the man from 1879 that turned up in a busy street in Times Square 71 years later? Maybe at one point he did just suddenly get loose from the force holding him and he turned up in Uzbekistan or some such place 20, 40, 75 years later and was arrested as a spy and shot and no one knows who he is.

Several examples of people just disappearing in plain sight exist...A man vanished in Greece while walking in town on July 13 1889 in plain sight of witnesses. He was noticed because he was saying to no one in particular "let me go". Though witnesses went to the exact spot he was last seen he just wasn't there.

Another man who was descending a hill, while being watched by two people at the same time, was seen to just disappear on April 23 1885. Though they went to the spot he was last seen, no sign of him was found. These people were never seen again.(book 50 pg. 46-48) They too likely appeared somewhere else on earth. They might have materialized in the middle of the ocean for all we know, though my guess is they would likely materialize on land somewhere near a receptive place with some form of energy in harmony with the energy in the place of the disappearance. Of course there is also the theory that UFOs in invisible form are swiping people, but I tend to suspect there is a natural phenomena that occurs near an energy source or possibly these people are actually creating this energy source themselves. I would guess that occasionally some of us trigger these little known abilities.

SOME POLTERGEISTS EXPLAINED?

Similarly occasionally rocks are seen to fly out of nowhere. I seem to remember once when I was about 6 many of us kids were throwing rocks at some items for target practice. Then one of the rocks that was thrown made no noise when it should have hit something. There were a few of us around and we all wondered what had happened to that rock. Occasionally rocks are seen to just fly out of empty air. Though poltergeists are often blamed for such activities it's possible some kids are throwing them from 500 miles away for all we know. This however might explain some "poltergeists". They may be people that have control of invisibility with nothing better to do then terrorize someone, or maybe they are in places where someone is stuck in the process of teleporting from one place to another and they are trying to get free, with the result being things flying around. With time not meaning much to them in that state the events could go on for years. That is likely not the answer to what poltergeists though it could be something like some anomalous activity occurring in conjunction with people disappearing.

THE OUTER LIMITS OF THE ANOMALY

It is fairly certain that UFO's use electromagnetic fields to travel and apparently to teleport. It would therefore seem logical that the limit to the distance to which they can teleport from one place to another would be limited to somewhere within the magnetic field that encompasses them... that is the magnetic field of the earth. Put another way, it may only be possible to warp, phase, or teleport from one spot in that field to another spot within that field or magnetic sphere. The distance you can teleport is limited to the size of space influenced by the electrical magnetic sphere, because the ability to do these things is partly because of the magnetic sphere itself. If this is the case then UFO's can't be warping from star system to star system, and coming from planet Zorgon in some far away distant galaxy, because there is no natural link between the two. This also suggests that UFO's are limited to the space contained within the magnetic field of earth as far as instantaneous travel is concerned. To get outside of the influence of the electromagnetic field of earth they would have to utilize a different more conventional type of propulsion.

Occasionally one or more small disc UFO's are seen entering a cigar shaped UFO as though they are catching a bus. If the UFO's use some sort of unified field as a propulsion method one can only guess how this field would produce thrust, unless as some have guessed the UFO's ride currents of the earth's magnetic field somehow. Possibly the field is used only for cloaking and travel on and in earth and more normal mercury engines are used for flying out of earth's gravity. They may use similar engines as described in the ancient Indian text Ramayana where it speaks of Vimanas acquiring great power when the mercury held in four strong containers is heated and the craft then looks like a pearl in the sky. (Book 10 pg. 147 [well obviously I have to find a better and more complete copy of this book!]) Though no doubt as we improve our cars from year to year the UFO-nauts might be improving their UFO's over the centuries and mercury engines might be obsolete to them. But some UFO's which look like eggs may be a long term effective design that has no need for improvements or changes. If they were made before the flood then they would have been made right the first time, and any post flood types might have been of inferior design which needed occasional improvements. But I'm getting ahead of myself.

MYSTERIOUS BERMUDA TRIANGLE DISAPPEARANCES EXPLAINED

In March 1952 a US aircraft carrier reported seeing a UFO off of the coast of Korea. That same day in the same area a WWII ace British Wing Commander J. Baldwin, flying with a group, flies into a cloud and is never seen again.(book 18 pg. 217)

Similarly on November 23 1953 a plane and 2 occupants disappears over the Soo Locks of Sault Saint Marie. (book 18 pg. 219)

On September 10 1971 an aircraft watched via radar after takeoff for 85 miles southeast of Miami suddenly disappeared off the radar over an area where the water is just 30 feet deep, yet a search over 25,000 square miles of water turns up nothing. (book 27 pg. 152)

In June 1953 an F-94C Jet fighter interceptor was dispatched to intercept an object seen on radar failing to respond and identify itself. Suddenly all the electrical equipment of the plane failed and it took a nosedive on a collision course with the ground. At 600 feet, after the pilot told the radar officer to bail out, he bailed out just in time. His chute reached maximum efficiency just before he touched ground. After landing he looked for the plane and his radar officer but to no avail. The plane should have exploded and rubble should have been strewn everywhere but there was no sign of it. It was never found, nor was the radar officer. (book 28 pg. 279)

Here is my guess as to what happened to the plane. The plane and occupants became encompassed in a unified field presumably from being in the vicinity of a UFO utilizing this power, and all the molecules and atoms of the plane and occupants began phasing through matter. When the airplane "impacted" with the ground, instead of a collision, the plane continued phasing through matter, until it got out of reach of the force that was causing the planes atoms to phase. Then suddenly inside the earth the atoms returned to normal and fused with the dirt which surrounded it. My guess is if you dig around where the plane likely would have impacted you will find an area where the composition of the dirt changes radically as the plane passed through the earth. (remember the furrowed steel with 14 elements not found in the rest of the steel) The plane in its "altered state" would also alter the matter in the dirt it "flew" through; a sort of alchemy at high speeds. Follow this trail of altered soils and you will eventually find the plane. However this plane could be several to even hundreds of feet down and following the trajectory of the fall. The molecules of the plane itself would have fused with other molecules of dirt and some third substance would result as the atoms of each (dirt and plane) fused to likely make heavier atoms. This also would have happened to the molecules of the radar officer. He would appear to be a perfectly sculpted figure in all his gear, but he would be a human with his molecules fused with the molecules of the dirt he flew into in the state of phasing. This might even explain myths and legends of people turning into stone. If this is the case, this might also explain many lost ships and planes in the Bermuda triangle as some of the stories about losses in that area are very similar to this lost F-94C jet fighter.

On February 27 1935 at about 10 PM a plane was seen by hundreds of people as it fell into the water less than one hundred yards from the beach in front of the Hotel Daytona in Florida. No wreckage or even so much as an oil slick was found. No missing planes were even reported so the event, even now, enjoys the status of a "rumor". (book 24 pg. 138)

If this plane was caught in a unified field vortex it might have been in it for years, though it would have seemed like normal time to that pilot. So a search for this, and maybe other missing planes might have had to go back further in time to find one as "missing" to match up. If it was in phase mode, the plane would have phased through the water and the ground under the water and come to rest once it escaped the force. I believe I read about this plane in another source and it was seen to make no splash as it entered the water and the plane was silent. "Sounds" like some UFO's.

Between February 1 and 14 the 572 foot tanker V.A. Fogg disappeared and was later found: sunk. It apparently sunk so fast no distress signal was sent and the captain was still in his chair holding his coffee cup. Oddly the 38 crewmen were never found.(book 26 pg 133-134) If this ship passed into an area where phasing was taking place, the atoms of the ship would have passed through the atoms of the water and fell at the speed gravity would let it fall. When it got out of range of the source of phasing (presumably a UFO as the 38 crewmen appear to have been taken. Maybe they left the captain to "go down with his ship") it would have resumed normal molecular structure and continued sinking until it hit bottom. The captain might never even have realized he was sinking as he and the ship phased through the water, then when the phasing stopped suddenly water was in every spot in the ship where previously there was air or other molecules. They would all have instantly combined with the atoms of the ship or the captain.

UFO'S PHASE THROUGH THE EARTH?

Curiously a husband and wife were boating and came across a trench in the ocean. It was about 4 X 20 feet and it looked as though a bulldozer had carved out the trench, only this rectangular 'trench' was in the water, similar to what was seen during the Philadelphia experiment where the boat was invisible but the water displacement was still discernible. This trench appears to have been right in their path, and as they came to it the boat they were in lurched under them and they were propelled forward so violently that the wife broke a couple ribs. It would appear they hit something invisible that was displacing the water. The displaced shape is very similar or identical to an Unidentified Object seen in Alberta.

If we presume our theory of being able to phase through matter inside a unified field is correct the strange Unidentified Object sighting of June 7 1971 in Rosedale Alberta takes on new meaning.

A woman realized something unusual was taking place outside and took a look. She saw a lit box like capsule with two inhabitants, one apparently deliberately hiding a control panel with his body and arm. A third person was a few feet from the capsule. They all had sort of claw like hands covered by gloves. But their adeptness with the claws was pitiful as though the claw like hands were a disguise to hide normal hands. The inhabitants appeared like normal humans otherwise. The one away from the box was clumsily picking up rocks or soil samples. Leaving for a brief moment, the woman returned only to find they had disappeared. They were not seen to fly away, they were just gone. The box like shape doesn't even suggest the UFO was of a sort that flies. The next morning there was found a dark sort of rectangular burnt patch 20 feet by 5 feet where the UFO had stood. Note how similar or identical this burn patch is to the shape of the displaced water of the above incident. (book 46 pg. 65-67) My guess is, as weird as it sounds, this particular UFO did not fly but was more of an elevator for traveling through the ground...or water.

AN ESKIMO VISITS THE UNDERWORLD

Eskimo legends about underworld kingdoms exist. A strange scene was witnessed by Peter Freuchen while with a group of Eskimos. One Eskimo in sealskins was drumming and chanting, in such a way his voice got stronger and stronger. So strong in fact he checked to see if others in the room were helping, which they weren't. Then the chanting got fainter and appeared to be coming from the outside, then the chanting was gone altogether. It was then that he saw the chanting Eskimo was actually gone, even after a thorough search there was no sign of him.

After some quiet and disorder, someone restored order and got people to sit and sing because the Eskimo was coming back. The unusual chanting again was heard. Peter saw a skin flying through the air and in his attempt to investigate almost got his arm broken, when trying to grasp the flying sealskin which presumably housed the chanting and apparently invisible Eskimo returning suddenly 'from the underworld'. Though a younger Eskimos present thought it was all lies and tricks, the author wasn't so sure.

The Eskimo told of traveling through dirt to talk to underworld spirits or people or whatever. Was this a case of deliberate invisibility and phasing through matter theoretically possible with the unified field theory? It's known the human skull does not distort a magnetic field something thought to be important in experiments concerning antigravity and related sciences. And what of his so called visit to the underworld? Whether or not it was trickery, the belief in underworld civilization is known in the Eskimo legends as well as many others. (book 56 pg 226-229)

MORE BERMUDA TRIANGLE STUFF

Some force in the Bermuda Triangle (possibly UFO's or an underwater power source) disrupts the normal workings of the atoms of matter in the lost boats and planes via the unified field, causing them to phase through the air and the water. This might explain the complete lack of debris in areas where the planes and ships are known to have disappeared. Suddenly a plane or ship phases through the air and water and is imbedded deep in the earth under the sea until they get out of range of the object or objects causing the phasing. Perhaps the molecules only phase with the water itself but the end result would be the ship or plane and all the contents would be heavier than water (the weight of the water molecules plus the weight of say a piece of paper still adds up to heavier than water molecules) and all the debris sinks, with nothing floating. If this is the case, then the planes would enter the water without breaking up because it would hit the water in phase mode and only under the water or under the ocean floor would the plane end it's phasing. Then the plane or boat returns to its normal atomic state somewhere deep underwater or underground. This would mean debris wouldn't even be a factor. Since so many UFO's are spotted in this Bermuda Triangle area this may actually be a way they get to an underwater dwelling place. There may not even be any openings to such a place, they simply fly through matter until they reach their destination. Similar to our Eskimo friend who visited the underworld.

Actually there are some peculiar phenomena admitted to exist in the Bermuda triangle area. There is a known radio dead spot in this region. But more interesting was something noted in satellites. Some force in the Bermuda triangle area was affecting magnetically taped pictures in satellites during the time they flew directly above this area as high as 800 miles up. Oddly only this function was affected, yet it was noted that a power that could do this from 800 miles below should also have sent the satellite swerving out of orbit which it did not. (book 24 pg. 15)

SLOW LIGHT

Other strange things though not officially documented also occur in the Triangle. Slow lightning strikes that lasted 5 to 6 seconds have been observed. Similarly radio signals have been stalled as though caught in a vortex.

One pilot while in trouble sent out a radio mayday message. Afterwards he was able to get out of trouble and then landed safely. When he landed he was told a plane had just sent a distress signal and he was asked to help search for the plane. It soon became apparent that he was being asked to search for himself as his radio message had been delayed by 15 minutes. (Book 24 Pg. 135)

This anomaly might be some aspect of unified fields. Light and radio waves might be caused to slow down in their travel and held in spherical paths and then be suddenly released. If time is slowing down for those in a field, lightning could be observed to last for unusually long periods of time, possibly because the people in the field have been "speeded up", slowed down or out of sync. (take your pick)

UNCONTROLLED POWER CREATES BIZARRE SIDE AFFECTS

People subjected to such strong fields might show side effects. It's also been deduced that prolonged exposure to strong electrical or magnetic fields can have an adverse affect on people working near such power sources.

People from the Philadelphia experiment were seen to be phasing in and out of sight for weeks after the experiment. Some of the sailors went "mad as hatters", and some dematerialized forever. One sailor walked through the wall in his quarters in sight of his wife and child and was never seen again. Some sailors apparently raided a tavern while invisible scaring the waitress beyond comprehensibility. (book 30 pg. 159)

CONFIRMATION OF DIAGNOSIS.

(3rd ed. Insert 2016) In subsequent material read after the publication of this book I stumbled upon a bit of information regarding the disappearances in the Bermuda Triangle that confirms my deductions as to exactly what the fate of the missing was… and is. I found this information in "The Bermuda Triangle" by Adi-Kent Thomas Jeffrey.

Normally in the Bermuda Triangle disappearances (if you can call that *normal*) ships, planes and people completely disappear, never to be seen again. But occasionally there is the odd different occurrence. As we know occasionally the odd ship is found eerily with no one aboard and all the people missing which are never seen again. But one particular boat, the Carroll A Deering, had the missing clue as to the fate of the people that disappear in its story.

The Deering was found in early February 1921 with her prow dug into the beach of Diamond Shoals with all five masts in full sail and no one aboard. The night before was "all clear and calm" in the area as noted by the previous watch, and there had been no distress signals the night before. There was no damage to the recently constructed ship. The lifeboats were missing and a ladder was hung over the side. She had apparently been abandoned (except for one very hungry pussy cat), but in very peculiar fashion because the tables were set with plates of food only partly consumed as though the men just pushed back their chairs and left the table in mid meal. There was no cargo to steal and no signs of any struggle. Her journey was traced as far as possible.

After delivering her load of coal to Rio, the very experienced captain William B. Wormell left there on December 3rd 1920 sailing "light", that is with no cargo, for the return trip. Making her way back to Barbados, the captain complained of not feeling well but not bad enough to need replacing, so on January 9th 1921 she left Barbados's, but still with no cargo. She was later seen by the North Carolina lightship (a "Lightship" is an anchored boat that acts like a lighthouse in deep water) off Cape Fear on January 23rd. She was last sighted with her crew 6 days later by the Cape Lookout lightship off of Diamond Shoals. The distance between the last two sightings was just 80 miles yet it had taken 6 days to travel. When last seen, though still apparently sailing with a crew, something very weird was going on aboard that ship.

On that last 'normal' sighting, the captain of the Cape Lookout lightship was hailed by the Deering regarding her lost anchors from a storm in the last week and to warn others as she approached Norfolk. That was the last anyone on that ship was heard from. During the subsequence inquiry it was found that the Captain of the Cape Lookout lightship thought the people on the deck of the Deering were acting peculiar, that is not functioning like a proper crew. They were scattered about the ship in a way that suggested lack of conformity and discipline. Furthermore the person who hailed him appeared to be the captain, but upon subsequent examination of the captain's description, they realized it did not tally with the description of the Deering's Captain Wormell. What was going on aboard that ship? What's particularly odd was there had been no storms in the vicinity the ship had passed through, so why was it delayed? Yet the person who hailed about the anchors said there had *been* a storm, which caused him to lose his anchors. Did it also cause the loss of the lifeboats? Between the 23rd and the 29th the logbook had a different man's handwriting other than captain Wormell's. (This source however does not mention if the logbook mentioned any storm during that 6-day period)

Captain Wormell was known for his popularity with his crews, so mutiny appears out of the question. Did the crew leave in a real hurry: as the food still untouched on the tables and chairs pushed back would suggest? It seems she was in some sort of trouble, yet there were no signs of struggle or disturbance and the people left, possibly to be picked up by another boat, the Hewitt, which was also in the area. But it's gets even weirder.

The clues to what happened start to heat up. In early February coastal residents of New Jersey saw a brilliant flash then a pillar of smoke, suggesting the Hewitt exploded from its cargo of sulphur, but no wreckage or bodies from such an explosion ever turned up. No one was sure as to whatever happened to the crew of the Deering. What's curious is another ship disappeared in the same general area: this same Hewitt! It's thought possible that the people from the Deering abandoned ship and were taken aboard the Hewitt. This Hewitt disappeared sometime between January 20th 1921 and "early February", the same time frame as the Deering, and in the same area. In fact shortly after the Deering went by the Cape lookout lightship so too did a second vessel that did not respond to an international flagging signal, which is a piercing hailing whistle which can be heard for 5 miles, indicating the lightship "have important message" to pass onto the boat. The signal was sounded to hail that ship to warn her of the missing anchors of the ship ahead of it: (the Deering) This second ship was never identified though it could have been the Hewitt. It too was acting peculiar in that it did not respond to the hailing whistle. That would be January 29th. Sometime between then and "early February", the Hewitt; boat, crew and cargo and the crew of the Deering just disappeared.

But one clue tells all. After being discovered the Deering was still near the beach, Diamond Shoals, where she was found and the residents of that area declared that she was haunted. People could plainly hear the anguished cries of 'spirits' clearly on her apparently deserted decks and in her cabins, many months later, so the boat was going to be taken out to be sunk. However the weather beat the demolition crew, apparently smashing it to bits the night before as it completely disappeared. (Bermuda Triangle page 115-125) (As far as I know, no wreckage was ever found, so it's quite possibly that the influence that made the people on deck invisible but audible, finally pulled the entire ship into the same realm.)

Have the clues above in tandem with the rest of this work given you the solution of the Bermuda Triangle?

Now admittedly though this does give the definitive clue, there is, as you will see, a problem. But let's ignore the problem for the time being. I've mentioned some curious anomalies about the physiology of the earth. As most people that research these mysteries know, there are other places around the globe that also have these curious 'Bermuda Triangle" like areas and happenings, the most famous being the Devils Sea near Japan. But the earth apparently has exactly twelve of these zones and they are spaced equidistantly around the globe at 72 degree intervals…5 in the northern hemisphere, five in the southern hemisphere and one at each of the poles. If you know the many types of dice there is one called a dodecahedron or 12 sided dice…the earth apparently is something like that with regards to magnetic 'Bermuda triangle' zones. These twelve zones have heightened and unusual magnetic anomalies, and it is in these areas that these mysterious happenings occur. But they don't occur all the time, or no one would travel in these areas, but rather it is apparent that something triggers these areas to flare up.

The mystery is not tied to just the water's surface as the occurrences happen under water (as submarines have also fallen prey to this phenomena) in the air affecting airplanes, and even up into the area where satellites travel, as satellites have also been affected above these areas. So we can clearly see it has to be partly tied to the physiology of the earth as other aspects of the earth also reach into space such as the van Allen belts and such. So what is triggering the occurrences then? It has to be something that works in conjunction with the nature of these to heighten their effect so drastically that allows these things to happen, but apparently *we* aren't doing it, (that is known people and technology of the earth). Then who or what is? If we go back to the Philadelphia experiment we will see that there are some interesting parallels here, that, when compared to these Bermuda triangle disappearances clearly gives the solution as to what exactly causes these disappearances. The Philadelphia experiment story and subsequent events has key clues.

During the Philadelphia experiment, incredibly intense magnetic fields were produced on the ship that caused the ship to both disappear, that is become invisible, and to teleport from one location to another over 400 miles away then go back to its original location. The key linking bit of information here is what happened to the crewmembers that were not inside the ship. Though they too moved with the ship and were either invisible or appeared to walk on air. However with them being on the outside of the ship that factor did something to them that did not happen to those inside the ship. Some of them phased with the matter of the ship becoming part of the hull. Some of them continued to turn invisible occasionally even after the experiment was over, going to places in that state and freaking out the locals. Some of them walked through walls, and some who did so just disappeared for good. Some of them acted extremely erratically or as one put it as "mad as hatters". If we now take the results of the Philadelphia experiment and compare them to the Deering, I think we can see what happened to the victims of these bizarre disappearances in the 'triangles' of the earth.

During the Philadelphia experiment the crew on deck of the ship were the only ones affected by the forces generated during the experiment. Thus people outside the forces used are the ones that had the effects happen to them…not those inside. Were they all to be inside the ship while the forces generated were in use, they might have traveled this way not realizing how these forces might affect those on outside the ship. Thus I hypothesize it's quite possible then had they done this experiment in the "Triangle" or any of the other 11 zones around the earth where these areas have heightened magnetic anomalies, and where these disappearances occur, they would have triggered anyone in those areas close enough to the ship to also have had a 'Bermuda Triangle' experience…be it in a strange confusing fog, or people disappearing or the entire vessels vanishing. The forces used on the ship appear to be the very same forces that cause the 'triangle' zones to trigger these occurrences. But these Philadelphia experiments were (as far as we know) stopped because of the effect it had on the crew. So some other ships or craft in these areas using the same forces appear to be causing the disappearances.

It's well known that UFO's are often seen in the triangle more than other areas of the earth. With the Philadelphia ship moving across the globe 400+ miles in a non triangle area, what would have happened in a triangle area? It seems to me the answer is it might have teleported vertically as these areas appear to be power sources compatible with and heightened by the forces generated. My guess is these twelve earth zones are the "corners" of the earth mentioned in history and are useable gateways to the earth's interior and the UFO's use these twelve gateways to phase in and out of the earth to where they live. But with the Bermuda Triangle and the Devils triangle being more used by surface man, it's these areas that the phenomena are most associated with. So anytime they use the gateway they cause a disturbance in the area that excites there very air and water to also become like the men on board the ship (used in the Philadelphia experiment). People have noticed the air doesn't look right, and they can't tell which way is which…they appear to have been caught in the very air or water these craft travel through. The whole area becomes unstable for a short while in a way that allows teleportation through the water, and the ocean floor into the earth's interior. It doesn't affect the people INSIDE these craft, it only affects those outside the craft in its immediate vicinity which explains why so many people that have been heard from or survive these occurrences often speak of seeing UFO's. So why don't UFO's then have this effect in other areas where they are spotted. It appears, generally speaking, they only turn on these phase mechanisms in the 12 areas of the globe that facilitates and beefs up the power to be able to phase through the solid mass of the earth, even though they have been spotted in areas with known "magnetic fault lines). So people don't disappear in normal UFO sightings because they (usually) (UFO's) aren't using the forces that cause the dissapearances. They only use them when they go back inside or come out of the interior of the earth usually …in these twelve 'triangle' type zones. So let's go back to the Deering.

They spoke of a 'storm' that lost their anchors, though no storm had taken place. On the Deering they were seen acting peculiar and not functioning like a proper crew, scattered all over the deck. So it would appear that the crew was subjected to a similar disorienting magnetic force. They spoke of a storm that never occurred so again suggesting some form of power encompassed the ship similar to a storm from the inside but not from the outside looking in. And the people disappeared, again similar to the forces of the Philadelphia experiment. In Bermuda triangle disappearances "normally' the entire ship or airplane and crew completely disappears. But occasionally just the people do, but I think the same thing is causing both manifestations and side effects. Humans have magnetic fields in their bodies, so they would be more susceptible to the effects. The ships or planes they are on would follow soon after the effects take hold of the humans aboard. So it appears there's an area where the effects though fully affecting the humans don't quite get a hold of the craft they are in to the extent they disappear. What we've shown is likely the vessels start to phase with matter thus sinking into the depths by passing through the matter of the water and continuing on through the matter of the ocean floor until the forces causing the phasing dissipate, after which they become solid and combine with the matter in which they find themselves. But in the cases where only the people disappear, it is partly due to the force acting in tandem with the forces we already latently posses. So we would "disappear" first, but if the force acting on us dissipates early enough not to affect the craft we are on then the craft stays in "this world" while we go on somewhere between the two. We might stay visible for a while but function strangely and eventually the force causes any to disappear all together. (We noted places and times in the past where people have disappeared on land or teleported on land. This might be partly because of a mostly inert capability in man that we as yet have not entirely harnessed or grasped, though the odd magician may have done so.)

But what happens to us…that is the people subject to this force? Well as other clues clearly show we are still alive but are unable to solidly grasp this solid mass aspect of nature but are "translated" in a sense into a magnetic force with our conscience stuck. Only a similar force could bring us back out if we knew how to calibrate it properly. Thus all people lost, no longer being part of the physical bodies entirely are still alive. Also what might be causing strange behavior during these occurrences, is when phasing, man's body, 'absorbs' material through phasing which gets caught in the physiology and messes up normal functioning, or just messing with our magnetism physiology.

We saw a person disappear in one spot and be heard a year later by his two kids. He had been in that area for over a year not eating or drinking and apparently not even aware of the passage of time. The people were still on the Deering but only partially connected with the solid world and they too could be heard "haunting" the ship months later. They had phased entirely with the molecules of the matter of the ship so as to be vibrating at a different frequency than our eyes perceive. Scientists wonder why we see anything at all. So those people were still and always will be on that ship or in those planes drifting on and on or stuck in the solid matter of the interior of the earth, alive and stuck in timelessness as the voices haunting the Deering testify. So why the missing lifeboats and the ladder tossed over the side?

My guess as to the proceedings is something like this. During the meal, the affecting force came on the ship and the men of the crew eating suddenly realized they could not grab the food properly or eat...or might have been only partly able to do so to the point that they realized something very weird was happening to them. Looking at each other they say "hey! What's going on here?" And rush outside, as obviously nothing in the room would appear to be a source of the weird happenings. Once outside what occurred then is anybody's guess. They may have seen a UFO, or the surrounding sea might have appeared strange and ominous, or the boat might have appeared to be in trouble and they may have known of the boat behind them and hailed it. With both boats in the same vicinity and subject to the same forces, communications between the boats may have been possible and appeared perfectly normal. Acting somewhat erratically maybe each man just grabbed a boat and let her fly, possibly with only themselves in the boat. The lifeboats also subject to the forces might have succumbed to the forces quicker and quickly phased with the sea quickly submerging with occupants. Some others in the life boats might have seen the others and climbed back aboard the boat via the ladder. Others might have made it to the other ship the Hewitt, something like going from the frying pan to the fire.

The question and problem is this. Normally places or ships in these Bermuda triangle like vortexes, sooner or later either disappear or escape entirely the forces and survive. Why did these two ships travel on, apparently for at least three days still gripped by this force? Speculation at this point and one can only guess as clues are lacking. One could suggest that a UFO was shadowing the boats causing them to be exposed to the forces for a more prolonged period: Maybe even just for a short while to the point where more of the forces acting upon them and the boats built up inside the molecules of the boats and the people so that the boat itself became a lingering source of this force. How do you escape that? One ship caused its inhabitants to turn invisible. The other (the Hewitt) had the force first act upon it's cargo of that boat (Sulphur) and explode it as was seen by people from the coast, but then continue acting on all the molecules of that boat to make all the molecules phase and sink, disappearing completely. Just like the people from the Philadelphia experiment some of them were around for several days before the forces acting on them finally finished their work causing them to disappear days later. Remember some of the people on deck were subject to the forces of the experiment for the entire time, while UFO's tend to just "pass through" and usually don't hang around long enough to make the affects permanent. As is occasionally the case, UFO's sometimes stay with people or trains of cars long enough to affect them, even on land. If such an occurrence happened in a Bermuda triangle area the effects on a ship could linger and eventually pull it 'out' of this visible world.

TEN MINUTES

Other strange effects possibly linked to this unified field theory have apparently manifested themselves. Around 1969 a National Airline 727 in its approach to Miami suddenly disappeared from the radar screens tracking it for ten minutes. Almost needless to say they were coming from over the Bermuda triangle area. After ten minutes the plane suddenly reappeared on the radar screen. When the airline landed and the personnel were informed about their disappearance they said nothing unusual had occurred in the flight. However when they checked their watches and the airplanes time pieces, all time pieces on the flight were uniformly behind ten minutes. (book 7 pg. 125)

CURIOUS CONTRADICTIONS. UFO'S LIVING CLOSER TO US THEN IS COMMONLY BELIEVED.

Conversations with UFO pilots, if they are to be believed, raise and reveal interesting points. They are very intelligent, but apparently lie about their place of origin and specify they live on Mars or Venus, though it's felt they actually live in the earth somewhere. Who can say what planet they are from, but if they are living underground somewhere this would explain their seeming preoccupation with us.

They know every language on earth suggesting they are obviously very nearby to bother learning them in the first place. Apparently they showed up to try and stop further atomic explosions again betraying a personal interest, as why would such experiments affect them on Mars or Venus? Such action on earth would however very much influence them if they lived in the earth somewhere.

People who say they have visited a 'mother ship' say they are normal looking people like us. Again no surprise here. UFO occupants are always seen as humanoid suggesting a common origin. When two types of UFO occupants are seen together, the ones most closely resembling us are always in charge. They say their crafts are powered by free energy and do not use any type of fuel. Some have deduced this to be electro-magnetic energy, which is linked to unified fields.

MOON MEN

However there is some evidence to suggest some UFO activity is occurring on the moon. Occasionally perplexing lights are seen on the moon. On December 19th 1954 astronomer Fox Holden saw a dark speck on the moon move in a straight line, make a 90 degree turn then vanish. On October 29 and November 27 1963 astronomers at Lowell observatory saw a ruby red point of light on the moon near the crater Aristarchus, then later on its rim. Lights have also been seen in that crater in 1821, 1825, 1835, 1866 and 1867 from observatories around the world. In 1880 on January 23 a thin line of light like a cable of light was seen across this same crater. On March 3 1903 brilliant lights were seen in this crater flickering intermittently. In 1958 and 1961 gas was detected escaping from the moon near this same crater. Spectrograms showed this gas to be composed of carbon and hydrogen. (book 62 pg. 223-224)

On July 29 1953, The science editor of the New York Herald Tribune and a foremost astronomy writer observed in a 90 power telescope in an area known as Mare Crisium a shadow of a bridge like structure 12 miles long. After raising the power to 250 the feature became unmistakable and was not there 5 weeks prior to this sighting. To avoid ridicule he notified other astronomers who also saw the object.

This area of the moon has had curious sights seen in it before. In 1869 observers noticed a series of strange lights set in geometric patterns. Then these vanished. (Mechanics Illustrated June 1964 pg. 82)

MOON MEN AND THEIR FLASHLIGHTS

(3rd ed. Insert 2016) On April 19th & 20th 1787 Sir William Herschel saw three bright lights on the moon, and in 1790 he observed over 150 red luminous points of light on the moon as well. In the same time frame (1788) Johan Hieronymus saw a point of light as bright as a 5th magnitude star on the moon east of the lunar alps. Later on in exactly the same spot during the day he saw a grey shadow.

LOOK OUT BELOW!

It would seem that with this recent surge of UFO sightings around the world since 1947 has fostered some bizarre psychobabble theories about what is happening in the world, such as a fourth dimension merging with the third or the earth evolving into a new form raising it's vibrational frequency to that of the inter-dimensional beings we now see more often. I think this is all a bunch of hooey and new age nonsense.

My guess is the UFO's have appeared more recently because we are affecting the earth more...our earth and theirs. Since they can utilize the unified field to become invisible and phase through matter, we with our limited knowledge assume some other dimension exists. It would seem that other inhabitants of the earth are very much concerned about how we are abusing the planet simply because some of them live here too. We have by our own destructive technology stirred up the other people that reside here. But since that sounds like as much hooey as the other theories, my job here is to show there is a lot of evidence to point to this in fact being the case. Yeah! I'm going to actually try and do this!

A Doctor Salsbury who studied UFO's came to the conclusion that they had been around for at least several centuries. He felt they were here seemingly to manipulate us for their own purpose, be that purpose for good or for evil and he seemed to suggest they have a similarity to devils and angels, but did not feel they were actually these entities because they also seemed to be at cross purposes with them. (book 20 pg 21-22)

This would seem to make sense if we conclude they are as human as us, simply more advanced technologically and mentally than us, or rather less devolved, and of course there would be some good and wicked or anti surface dweller UFO-nauts. So some UFO's and their pilots might come to earth's surface to do studies and tests, to gauge our effect on earth and how we might influence their living space, and some might come just to mess with our minds and perceptions of them. Still others might simply come to inflict misery on the hapless civilian they stumble upon. ("Let's go play with some surfacers")

Some conversely would try and steer us in a less self destructive life path, for a real benefit to us and them. They have an investment in how we treat the earth because they live here too. They appear to have some laws in place that restricts or forbid their interference with surface dwellers, but nevertheless they try and influence us possibly in more subtle ways in hopes that we might 'get it'. But we, not understanding who they are, and when hearing contradictory stories we simply get mixed messages and confused understandings of who and what these UFO's and their pilots really are.

CROP CIRCLES

They are in all likelihood responsible for some of the crop circles, with programmed designs in devices that create the specific design in a particular field. Maybe they are responsible for only some of the crop circles. Small balls of light have been seen in the vicinity of fresh crop circles. Maybe a programmed design in each ball is meant as a progressive series of revelations in hopes of diverting disaster, but we are just too dull witted to understand...well just more speculation. Footage shows very small globes of light appear to be making the circles. Naturally some crop circles are indeed hoaxes made by some noodle brains wrecking some farmer's fields, but others seem far too complex even for sophisticated jokers to create. The circles are getting quite elaborate and the fear is what if surface world technology has secretly advanced to the state where we can do these circles to steer the populace toward some end, similar to how the U.S. used astrology to steer the civilians in favor of entering the second World war. One "crop circle" drawing is a picture of an Alien as seen in Star Trek holding a [antigravity?] disc. But this one is starting to look like the jig is up. It just screams hooey....or...?

UFO'S DIVULGES SOME SECRETS.

One indication that these UFO pilots are probably of human origin is that it has been noted that often people viewing UFO's at close range are rendered immobile and this appears to be directed at the individuals rather than as an unintentional accident. These effects on humans are usually temporary and no harm comes to the individual. (book 28 pg. 144) This indicates that knowledge of our physical limitations is well known to the UFO-nauts. How better to know our physiology unless you have the same physiology?

UFO's pilots have been seen to breath our air in many instances. For example one person after hypnosis revealed that he recalled seeing their breath in the cold weather. Interestingly he also mentioned that they said their UFO's were driven by "reversible electro-magnetic energy". (This description fits with the unified field theory) He also stated that during these conversations they said they lived in underground and underwater facilities. Some specific locations were mentioned. They said there was a place under water in between Florida and Bermuda... yup in the "triangle", and they also had a place off the coast of Argentina and in the polar region (this might explain why some believed the pole was a hole to the "Hollow earth".) They also stated that there were a couple places under the United States that they resided in as well as numerous other places around the earth. (book 29, pg. 184)

Our airplanes have markings on them to distinguish country of origin. The trained airplane buff can also determine the country of origin of the planes simply by the design. It would seem that there are a variety of UFO's and that they, like our plane markings, determine the 'country' and or race of origin of the UFO's inhabitants. It would seem that certain types of UFO pilots are seen reasonably consistently with specific types of craft, though I haven't bothered to go into depth regarding this. Supposedly at one time 5 various kinds of saucers landed voluntarily at Edwards Air force base displaying the ability to dematerialize or turn invisible in front of witnesses (book 47 pg. 41-42)

PRE 1947

So where do UFO's originate? People think they are either mass hysteria or a new craft by some governments unwilling to share the secrets, and not old at all since they seem to have started appearing in 1947. Some have suggested the war produced them and they have been government secrets ever since. 'I… know…nothing… about… them…we've never seen or heard about them before. We are all victims of being hypnotized spontaneously and in unison to believe we see them….' Yeah great secret.

Or perhaps the reverse is true. Perhaps "UFO's. originate in ancient history, where people just knew what they were…the same way we know what an airplane is because they were invented in 1903…or so we are led to believe. If we go to a place where no one has seen an airplane…though such places are disappearing fast if they even exists anymore, when such a population sees our airplanes, to them they may as well be UFO's. But they aren't to us, because they are known by us. They are just planes. Maybe someone in our past knows what the mysterious things we call UFO's are!

Maybe these machines as described are also seen in ancient history. But if they were why have they not kept flying about all through time, or did they? Are there records of UFO's previous to 1947? I had no idea if such a request for this sort of evidence could even be fulfilled. Written records rarely go back that far and if there were UFO sightings back then how would people describe them without the words "airplane" or "weather balloon" in their vocabulary? Thankfully the people that write the UFO book have done a lot of research and a lot of this information can be readily found. It is just a matter of assembling it and studying it to find some logical conclusions.

I was finding a lot of evidence that suggests "UFO's were in history and even ancient history. I was finding what might possibly be UFO's all through legends, and tantalizing references. But also we have to realize that these "UFO's" in ancient history would have been described differently. For example sometimes we describe them as flying saucers. But maybe ancient peoples did not put their cups on saucers for afternoon tea. Maybe they didn't eat buttered scones. Maybe they were completely barbaric cave men and prehistoric savages that put their cups on magazines or comic books! Saucer?… what's a saucer? Maybe they called them something else, like sky boats, houses or eggs that fly? But evidence for them in the past does exists and indeed it seems that they do originate in ancient history. Though there was precious little evidence it soon became clear that these or similar objects have been seen before, for a long long time. So let's work backward through history.

Keep in mind that people do not record normal events in the sky as something unusual…like saying the sun rose and the sun set. Even a simple eclipse though unusual was still understood to be an eclipse. To keep track of and bother to take the time to record these events means something extraordinary took place.

In 1946 over 2000 reports of unknown wingless objects are reported in Scandinavian countries. (book 28 pg. 227)

Hundreds of sightings of strange globes in the air were seen over Europe during WW II by pilots of both sides. Both sides thought these were observation or radar jamming devices of the opposing side. Both sides after the war were surprised to find out they didn't belong to either side.

They cropped up in the 19th century, but because of the more simplified nature of the earth, their need for disguise doesn't seem to be present and they simply appeared as eccentric inventors to whoever spotted them...yeah real people. So if they are real people what were those UFO's we hear about today with them "greys" and spooky bug eyed creatures?... I'll get to that...though you already have the clues.

One series of sightings concerns a mysterious airship that kept cropping up in newspapers across America. On April 26 1897 this airship was seen to dangle a long rope under it attached to a heavy object. A man climbed down the rope cut it and took off. The airship had several lights, the chief one being in the front which was deemed to be similar to a train light. (book 29 pg. 132) This might not really be a UFO though and could be an inventor's airship and an attempt to keep it secret while testing, with some accident causing it to disappear from history. (Atlantis Rising #80 story by J. Allan Danelek for example has this hypothesis) The story reminds me of Jules Vern's 1886 book, Robur the conqueror and his airship. This airship may even have been inspired by the same book!

September 28 1890 a red fireball that moved slowly across the sky toward the east was observed over Nankin China (Internet source)

As I dug deeper it became evident they may have been seen talking to Napoleon and other men of history. But only clues and suspect conversations with odd tall red, long lived, individuals remain. It appears to be well known that Napoleon talked with a strange RED man on three occasions while in Egypt. (book 35 pg. 134) Though what personal reason they would have for trying to steer the course of Napoleonic history is unclear.

It seems he was trying to influence Napoleons actions in some way. I've even heard a school teacher mention this red man that talked to Napoleon. She couldn't understand how it might be an American Indian as some had suggested. [because they weren't wont to travel across wide oceans to advise military strategies and such.] If I remember correctly she felt no historians seemed to be exactly sure what race this individual was. Also she seemed to understand this was a very red man...and she made the comment that even though we tend to call Indians "red" they were in fact brown.

I then looked at my pencil crayons and pulled out the one that was called "Indian Red" and used it to see what colour she was talking about. I hadn't met any "Indians" at that point in my life yet so I was curious what colour an Indian was. I mentioned to the teacher that the colour was still a pretty red colour, but she said the pencil crayons weren't necessarily accurate, and besides it was an even redder red.

I had a somewhat humorous addition here about naming pencil crayons after skin tones but thought I better not play with fire, even though it was all pretty innocent.

MORE UFO'S THROUGH TIME

August 18th 1783. From the Windsor castle an oblong cloud was seen to move basically parallel to the horizon. Under the cloud an object slowly became clearer until it was clearly a sphere that seemed pale blue. Slowly the light from this object became brighter until it lit up everything on the ground. An engraving was done of this event by Thomas and Paul Sandby. The event was recorded in the Philosophical Transactions of the Royal Society of which Thomas Sandby was a founder. Internet source; describing and showing UFO in medieval art.

In 1710 a painting is made by Flemish artist Aert De Gelder called the Baptism of Christ. It shows, what for all intents and purposes, appears to be a UFO disc radiating four threadlike beams of light in the sky shining down on the proceedings.

November 4 1697 two "glowing wheels" were sighted above Hamburg Germany. A drawing of the event at the time shows the wheels to look like spheres with bands wrapping around the globes horizontally and vertically and intersecting...very reminiscent of similar spheres I've seen in more orthodox churches which have crosses attached to their tops.

A 1680 French medal is absolutely extraordinary. It shows a huge flying disc like mechanism in the sky.

It's also on other coins from the period in 1656. A 1648 coin or medallion appears to be depicting the same craft **(See drawing 16)**

DRAWING 16

Several UFO's were seen over the skies of Nuremberg Germany on April 14 1561, apparently battling for control of the skies. They were described as globes, tubes and crosses near the sun. These items were drawn in a book at the time and the images can be found on the internet. The images in the drawing however are somewhat over simplified and possibly figurative. (Book 29 pg. 133) (Internet sources: UFO's in art)

These sightings go right back to the discovery of America. On September 15 1492 a bolt of fire was observed by the ships of Columbus in the area that shot across the sky and disappeared into the Sargasso sea. So UFO are long known in the area.(book 7 pg 81)

In 1491 seven dark RED skinned individuals met with Facius Cardan (father of mathematician Jerome Cardan) and said they live up to 300 years and were prohibited from sharing their technology with men. They said they were made of air, and that the earth was created ongoing every instant. (Book 5 pg. 86-87)

This in some strange way makes sense. Scientists have wondered what keeps atoms together as the nucleus is composed of both protons and neutrons. Neutrons have a neutral charge but protons have positive charges, and they wonder why the nucleuses do not just fly apart. Even playing with them in a unified field does not seem to disrupt their stability, unless those spontaneous combustion victims have had this happen to them.

I personally wonder if this accepted fact of like charges repel make any sense at all. When a magnet is broken, in theory one breaks a negative pole from a positive pole so a broken magnet should pull and hold itself back together when the pieces are put back together at the break: but this is not the case. When a broken magnet is held together at the break line the magnet parts REPELL each other, the reverse of the expectations.

I asked my grade 9 science teacher why this happened if opposite poles attract. He was stunned to hear this detail about magnets, so I've always wondered if I wasn't onto something. Who knows maybe this very basic observation with magnets reveals an amazing hitherto unknown phenomena. Maybe LIKE poles attract, at least in some instances, or maybe our entire understanding of magnetism is all wrong... yeah... sure... that little magnet is going to overturn science...ok on with the book.

Jerome apparently met these people too as he says of them that just as man is more intelligent than a dog, they were more intelligent than man. These people said they know the guardians of the sky but they were not them. (book 5 pg 92)

What's this? Our skies are guarded? What are they talking about? Is this related to WWII pilots that spotted "Foo fighters" and early earth orbiter that spoke of UFO's? Interestingly Shumer (Sumer) meant "land of the guardians" (Book 42 pg. 76)

Several Gemini and Apollo orbits and flights to the moon were accompanied by UFO's, several of which were photographed. Sounds like they've been guarding the sky...for what? and why? The Rig Veda speaks about people journeying out of this world and that they must first come to the moon to answer questions and if they can answer them they are allowed through. Through to what? (Book 10 pg 154-55)

Sounds like a humorous part of a show I saw once. "To pass you must answer me these questions three…" One of the questions is about the airspeed of a swallow. Asked to clarify what kind of swallow he is referring to, the guardian becomes stumped and is suddenly hurled off into the abyss, leaving the path unguarded.

Some of the lamps that do not burn oil or any other known substance which stay lit seemingly forever or at least centuries (as talked about in Adam 900 chapter) are said to come from the watchers of the sky. It's said by some that to touch these lamps is prohibited because an explosion could occur that could destroy a whole town. Seems a bit of a stretch but then one must remember that we are not supposed to touch halogen light bulbs when installing them or the oil in your hands would destroy the light. There could be a connection. OK not a whole town but there could be something to it. Small scale tactical nukes?

The book of the dead speaks of gods who dwell in the divine clouds and are exalted by reason of their scepters (Vril rods?) (Book 61 pg 146-148) In the book of the dead there also appears to be a reference to people with red skin. "the red ones have their faces directed toward me" (book 61 pg 178)

BEFORE COLUMBUS

These meetings with inexplicable strangers in recent centuries only made me wonder if there might be evidence of them even in ancient times. I was still willing to consider the possibility that maybe just a few strange individuals existed and some were just eccentric scientists and some were just demonic manifestations. I was still not quite sure what to make of these craft or creatures.

It bothered me that people were trying to suggest that man on earth was a product of spacemen from another galaxy. However this also suggests that "UFO's have been sighted in ancient history...or were the authors just clutching at straws? Some writers were suggesting that the origin of man, as a product of spacemen really seemed to me like passing the buck. They weren't willing to believe that God created the earth and man but that space men might have...so the logical question to me was, well, then who created the spacemen?

No this didn't make sense, yet I wouldn't force the UFO question into the creation doctrine. I was willing to read any interesting account of the UFO's that might give insight as to who they were or try to find something in ancient history that might prove to be a UFO when examined carefully. Then see where that got me in the light of the context they were spoken of.

It was somewhere around here I found something on the order of great magnitude. This started to allow me to suggest something unthinkable to the normal way of thinking, based on what I assumed the bible said. That being the idea that maybe some of these UFO's come from a pre-flood time. For a while I ignored that possibility, as that would mean someone or something survived the flood other than Noah.

In some ancient records these "UFO's are described in such detail that they are not thought of as "Unidentified" at all. Take the Asian Indian Vimanas. These are very specifically described craft. Even stating how many different types of metal they were made from. In fact so detailed are the descriptions, that Scientists in India are reading the manuscripts carefully to see if they can decipher exactly how these engines worked, so that they too can conquer space travel. They were written versions of the verbal legends that had been circulating by word of mouth for centuries...even millennia, possibly for as long as 5000 years!

The manuscripts talk about these craft as driven by mercury engines. This is interesting because one of the options for power sources when trying to accomplish travel to the moon in the fifties and sixties was mercury engines.

But one thing I found very interesting indeed, was the description of the outside of the ship. You could take those descriptions and put them into a present day UFO book and it could be a description of the UFO's seen today! For example late April 18 1966 at Sharon Massachusetts a UFO seen then was described as "Oval". An egg is oval and the ancients often speak of mysterious eggs.

It said these mercury engines were so powerful they could make the craft look like a pearl in the sky. A modern description of a UFO after take-off (which was estimated to be 30 feet high and 300 feet long) was described as a pearl or opal that turned into vapor. (book 47 pg. 37)

Another egg shaped craft was seen at Henzies France at 6 AM on October 7 1954. Two men dressed in black came out of a red egg shaped object. (book 47 pg. 242)

When ancient legends are looked at in this way to see if UFO's existed back then, they appear to be all over the place!! Lets continue our walk backward through time. I do this to show these UFOs have been here all along. Not just in ancient history and now but in all the intervening centuries. I suppose if I were to do an exhaustive timeline there might be written records of sightings of them almost every year. Looking into the past it seems that UFOs and sky people visiting people on earth were fairly common occurrences, and the people to whom these visitations were made often took the visits in stride as though this was nothing to write home about. They appear to make their way into art, even religious art, as can be seen on many internet sites devoted to ancient and renaissance art depicting UFO's.

In Ireland in 1490 a silvery disc flew over a church dislodging a church bell and some cattle received burns on their backs (book 30 pg. 124)

In a document at Ampleforth with a date ascribed to it of 1290 AD, is described a very interesting event. Just before dinner an excited monk named Joannes enters the room and tells those at the dinner table something amazing outside deserved their attention. All rushed outside and saw a silvery discus flying slowing above them all. (book 47 pg 71)

In Bristol England 1207 AD something hit a church during a service. When they went outside to see what it was, they saw an aerial ship hovering over the church with a rope dangling with an anchor caught in the steeple. A little man crawled down the rope, apparently to try and dislodge the anchor, and he fell to the ground. The crowd was on the man beating him and calling it all sorts of names. Another little man came out and cut the rope leaving his fellow pilot at the mercy of the crowd. Shortly afterwards the little man died.

The suspected reason for the cause of his death was he was suffocating in our atmosphere. This would sound like an extraterrestrial, but my guess is the fall and the beating made it difficult for him to breathe, as he may have had a collapsed lung or broken bones making breathing virtually impossible to maintain for long. The subsequent beating by the people around him finished his chances of surviving. (book 29 pg. 130-131)

In 1150 King Richard sees a flying cross in the sky. This could be a group of UFO's flying in formation. Flying crosses were seen in France in 1118 AD. During this century they were also seen in Holland, Poland and Italy. A similar sighting was seen in England in the '1960's? (date not given) (book 29 pg. 133)

900 AD a burning wheel is seen over Japan

European tradesmen in 840 AD were forbidden to barter with the "sky people" that drove "ships from the clouds". Formerly they would trade them fruits and vegetables. Four sky people (3 men and a woman) were caught and held and after a trial were executed by stoning. These appear to be normal looking people (book 35 pg 177.) It seems that after this point in time they become a little more leery of surface men.

Sometime around 840 AD 3 men and a woman claimed they were taken to a country called Matagonie in an airship in which time went slower than outside the ship. These people were stoned for their story. (Book 5 pg. 134) Remember Einstein's theory of relativity proves time moves slower for those in motion than those stationary. This is a pretty odd time and place to find this story!

A monk named Laurence in 776 AD saw flaming shields from heaven spitting fire during Saxons besieging the Franks at Sisburg. The shields came out of the sky and whipped the Saxons with fire and smoke. (book 43 pg 235)(book 29 pg. 128)

312 AD Constantine sees a flying cross in the sky. (book 29 Pg 133)

In 193 AD three stars were seen around the sun. (Raymond Barnard quoting various ancient manuscripts and historical books notes this and 5 other points placed in reverse chronological order throughout this section) (Book 43 Pg237-241)

In 70 AD many sky chariots were seen to go through the sky and surrounding cities, presumably of Israel (Book 43 Pg237-241)

SOME BIBLICAL REFERENCES TO UFO'S & THAT ENIGMATIC STAR

Pardon this section...I get a bit lost in biblical debate. Reading it again, it could get a bit tiresome. What about this "star of Bethlehem"? Dare I go here? Actually I've seen a few other people come up with this theory, but before I go there; let me show a completely opposite theory. I saw on TV some joker suggesting that the star the three wise men (actually there was a multitude of them not just three) followed may have been the rare triple conjunction of Mars, Jupiter and Venus known to have occurred around this time. However this is a completely lame and insulting theory unless you presume these "wise men" were complete idiots. Some sources suggest that these wise men were in fact astronomers, so they would know the difference between a star and a planet and they would know you can't follow a planet to anywhere. And even if this were the case, a triple conjunction of three planets breaks up very fast. In one day the changed position of each planet in relation to the others is very clear and obvious. These wise men came from the east and would have been traveling for weeks if not months. No triple conjunction is ever going to last that long. At best the triple conjunction might have served as a sign of something big about to happen, but nothing more than that. Even a person with absolutely no knowledge of astronomy would know you cannot follow a star or a planet in the sky to some place on earth. Besides, the earth turns away from it too fast.

Even people who know nothing about astronomy will notice a conjunction of two bright planets and comment on them. When Jupiter, Venus and Mars were coming together to in a recent triple conjunction, friends of mine who never gave stars a second thought were commenting on this apparition in the skies. And even they know you can't follow them.

Look at II Kings 23: "...That burned incense unto Baal, to the sun, and to the moon, and to the stars, and to the planets, and all the host of heaven." This shows the ancients clearly knew the difference between the stars and the planets. There is simply no way they followed planets. However this burning incense to the host of heaven is an interesting bit in that it refers to them. Host here means large number.

Similarly in the Book of the Dead Chapter 124 :16 the writer says "I shall speak with the Disc and I shall speak with the denizens of heaven"(book 61 pg. 355) Denizen means inhabitants and this bit is coupled with the disc.

By realizing the wise men could not be following a star as we understand stars, it then has to be something closer to earth that would enable men to follow it. In fact it would seem they were following it because they could, suggesting the "star" was allowing them to follow and even leading them. It would seem the Wise men had some sort of prophesy because they knew it to be "HIS" star.

This leaves three possibilities, I think, as to what this "star" could be. It could be an angel appearing as a star, or it could be a chariot of fire appearing as a star as so many of these "UFO's have appeared to look like stars to observers. Or possibly some sort of miniature glowing orb or star tuned to the child...whatever that could be. Small glowing orbs have been spotted over the years.

As we are starting to see, these UFO pilots are clearly starting to look very human and if there is a connection with them and us in the past they may actually BE humans. If they are, then my guess is people not only of our surface world were aware of prophesies concerning the messiah, but I believe so too were those others not of this surface world aware of this prophesy.

We see even in pre-flood times that it was prophesied that the seed of the woman would bruise the serpents head. So at one time all of mankind knew this would happen sometime. Is there any reason to think God wouldn't call a human UFO pilot to this event? It would seem this "star" was exceedingly patient to allow these wise men to follow it for so long. But actually the scripture does not actually say they followed this star all the way from the east. (Mathew 2:9 "When they had heard the King, [Herod] They departed; and, lo, the star, which they saw in the east, went before them, till it came and stood over where the young child was." This indicates that a star appeared in the east and the Wise men knew it to be the star of the king of the Jews. Since it was obvious to them where he would be born they then started on their journey to Israel, so they didn't actually have to follow the star. They knew what it meant and where to go. It then reappeared after their visit to Herod.

But some say this still means that it could be an actual star, as some have suggested it was a super nova. What nonsense, why would a super nova make an encore appearance directly above the stable, or wherever he was at the time, as this happened about 18 months after the birth, another indication this was a long journey by the wise men. Thinking this birth was known to the general population of the Israelites they stop in on King Herod to ask where this child was. This was news to King Herod and they check the scriptures and find out he is to be born in Bethlehem. The king then said 'find him by looking diligently then come back and tell me where he is'. This is when the star appears a second time and they follow the star to the child.

This shows the star was not a normal star shining in the heavens. Also if it was a star millions of miles up then who could say where the star was directly over so the 'star' had to very close to earth for it to be obvious who it indicated. Admittedly this does not necessarily indicate a "chariot of fire' or UFO, but at least some kind of directed shining energy globe that looks like a star.

If as we presume this star or UFO was indeed of human origin and of the sons of Adam then God wants all his creation to know of this very important event which we celebrate every year.

UFO art...like totally spiritual, Eh.(3rd ed. Insert 2016) If my suggesting that a chariot of fire might have been the star of Bethlehem seems a bit way out there, it seems medieval artists thought nothing of including them in their paintings when showing Mary and the child or various religious scenes, indeed a few such paintings have what appear to be obvious UFO's in the scenes. **(see drawing 17)** A: the Baptism of Christ by Aert de Gelder 1710. B. The Madonna with saint Giovanino (close up) by Domenico Ghirtandalo (1449 – 1494) shows man with dog looking up at UFO behind Mary. C: 776 Saxon painting from a book about historical and religious events. D and E: Tapestries (D: Unknown and E: The Magnificent) in the French Basilica Notre Dame in Beaune, both showing the "sombrero" type UFO's well known in current sightings.

Consider an event in II Kings. The Syrians, upon realizing that God was telling Elisha what their plans were regarding their planned attacks on Israel, decided to go and get Elisha. They surround him, and Elisha's servant (presumably Gehazi) sees that the city they were in (Dothan) was surrounded by the Syrians and he appears to have been in a panic. Elisha says to him in Chapter 6:16 "...Fear not: for they that be with us are more then they that be with them. (verse17) And Elisha prayed, and said LORD, I pray thee, open his eyes, that he may see, and the LORD opened the eyes of the young man; and he saw: and behold, the mountain was full of horses and chariots of fire round about Elisha."

DRAWING 17

We see that clearly the bible appears to be speaking of UFO's. I must admit I don't know what the horses were doing there, but they too were invisible. And they were horses, and not some misinterpretation, as the same word for horses is used elsewhere when there's no reason to suspect any other creature. I have to guess that it was to have the army hear the horses without seeing them causing them considerable discomfort. Also what would Gahazi think if he saw a bunch of shining "eggs"? I'm not sure that would comfort him, though obviously he knew they were chariots of some kind, so we have to presume the chariots were manmade, as never has an angel needed a chariot...have they? [that question will make sense later] We see they were invisible to him and apparently everyone else except Elisha. We also see that there were no angels present. In fact there is no mention of even any invisible people otherwise it might have said a great multitude.

Though we have to presume there were some people inside the 'chariots' suggesting it was a closed chariot where people inside would not be apparent. This is very much like UFO's of today, whereas if you describe our chariots driving on the road, the people can be seen inside if you look in the windshield. No description like "a great army" is here. Simply chariots and horses, so the people may well have been not seeable simply because they were inside the chariots.

They may have brought the horses in case it was decided to use the sound of invisible horses" to spook the Syrians, as has been done similarly in other places in the bible. For example in II Kings 6:24-7:7 an almost identical thing happens. Ben-hadad king of the Syrians besieged Samaria and there was a famine in the city. The story of two women eating a son is there to show the famine was very dire. Elisha is in the city and prophesies that the next day food would be sold for very little implying that food would be abundant. Yet the city is still surrounded by the Syrians.

That night some starving lepers go out into the camp of the Syrians figuring it is better than just starving so they take a chance and find all the Syrians gone and everything else just left behind...horses, tents, valuables and food! lots of food!

The reason for the disappearance of the Syrians is given in Chapter 7 verse 6. "For the Lord had made the host of the Syrians to hear a noise of chariots and a noise of horses, even the noise of a great host:..." Although these horses and chariots were not seen they were heard and they may have been invisible but really there, as when Elisha and Gehazi were surrounded. These were invisible yet potentially seeable, and under God's direction.

This ability of them to be invisible indicates they are not your average chariots at all but of some other origin. It would seem that God by whatever means called those in the chariots of fire, from wherever they may have originally resided in to come to Elisha's aid. If then they are participating in a surface world rescue there then is no reason to think they wouldn't participate in the Christmas event as well.

This would dictate that we have to stop thinking of UFO's as "aliens" but as real people who just are constantly seen in these chariots we call UFO's. It is their safe method of travel from wherever they are. It seems clear that when they are away from their chariots they are as vulnerable as we are, because they are merely another series of races of humans, not aliens.

I know this sounds off the wall, but if we consider that these people in UFO's are as human as us, and as much the descendants of Adam as us, this makes perfect sense. Just because we don't know what the UFO's are doesn't automatically mean they are some freaky aliens from some dimension X from planet Zorgon coming to steal our resources and eat our cattle and play mind games with us.

Admittedly there could be another perfectly plausible answer for the star of Bethlehem, but this too seems possible and it fits. Often UFO's start out to appear as stars but when they get close they become obviously chariots or craft.

However there is some flaw in this logic. If the wise men saw "His star" and knew it to be "His star" and UFO's are seen throughout history, then what sort of UFO was this that made it different from other UFO's so they knew it to be his star?

On the other hand UFO's are seen to shine in all sorts of colours. Maybe a specific colour or series of colours was what they were looking for, but I'm just guessing here. A craft could maintain this star like appearance even at close range. Just as the angels went to the lowest of the Israelites (the shepherds) to tell of the good news, he may have similarly gone to the lowest of the UFO-nauts to inform them of the events on earth.

If this is the case then no doubt whoever was in that "star of Bethlehem" went to his peers and told them of the events. This does not suggest all UFO's are under Gods direction or more properly following God's will. We see many examples of UFO's apparently just doing nothing in particular or even doing what can only be mischief to whoever they happen upon. Or should we call them "Chariots of fire" (COF) so we don't keep equating "UFO's with aliens?

Having said all that we see some strange verses indeed in the scriptures. In Psalms 68;17 "the chariots of God are twenty thousand, even thousands of angels: the Lord is among them, as in Sinai, in the holy place".

Chariots of God!? I have to presume we are not talking 1957 Mercury's here. I mean this is mind boggling. God has chariots. This texts also possibly suggests these chariots were also helping in the time of the exodus at Sinai. Also take Isaiah 66:15. "for, behold, the Lord will come with fire, and with his chariots like a whirlwind,..." and Jeremiah 4:13 "...his chariots shall be a whirlwind:..." This all seems to suggest that some form of chariot is in the hand of God and quite likely in the hands of actual angels! This description of whirlwinds with chariots has also been used to describe more recent UFO flights. Could this be the explanation for how the water of the red sea parted…invisible UFO's blowing the water apart then some invisible force field to make the water appear as a wall on both sides of the Israelites? I have to admit being dumbfounded to come across these verses. This tends to suggests many thousands of UFO/COF's are in the hands of God and angels. Perhaps it WAS angels in those chariots that surrounded Dothan. And as we have seen some are also in the hands of men and some possibly in the hands of devils.

So clearly some discerning which is which and who is who is important. This might be part of the reason the bible says to test the spirits. But if the deduction is correct, why would angels have Chariots? I can't answer this. But life is supposed to be fun and unlike the stereotype we envision of us and angels playing harps on clouds, it sounds like there just might be a bit more fun than some have led us to believe in the afterlife! Chariot races? With chariots that can be invisible…hide and seek with the whole universe to play in?

But we see sons of God have had some visual, physical, and social interaction with the sons of Adam in the pre-flood period, so the answer may stem from this period. Maybe angels have some of the chariots men had from before the flood. I mean there are all kinds of possibilities as to why God has so many chariots. I mean think of it… superfluous completely unnecessary chariots in heaven. It's just hilarious.

As strange as all this sounds, we can still be certain that angels do not actually need chariots to get around, say when traveling from the place of God to where we are, as seen when one angel came to talk to the parents of the yet unborn Sampson. They make an offering to God and the angel ascends to the sky on the smoke of the offering, [Judges 13:19,20] and in no case am I aware of angels being spotted in the vicinity of a chariot, but this doesn't mean they are not and just making the chariot invisible.

Still this really does put a crimp in the neat explanation of UFO's simply belonging to sons of Adam. But we must be careful and not assume from this verse that they belong ONLY to the angels. We shall see that some definitely belong to men. We have to be very careful here because if we presume they only belong to angels we might tend to think these charioteers can do no wrong, and possibly be led astray. With the numerous UFO sightings seen around the earth today, such a scenario is not out of the question. Even the very fact that some UFO 'churches' exist show that men can follow and serve such show such a scenario is all the more possible. It only takes one devilish UFO pilot of this sort to seriously lead all of mankind astray.

If say a human UFO pilot were to begin to take control no doubt his peers would nip that in the bud. We can be certain that no angels would allow such a scenario to occur because they know we have the prophets to follow. Though I can't say then that the "star" the wise men followed is a chariot, it seems a possibility. It could also be an angel. Stars are equated with angels in revelation 1:20 and stars fall to earth in Revelation 6:13. Though usually these seem to be allegorical relations between stars and angels we see a third of the stars (fallen angels?) do not shine and a third of the stars are cast to the earth and the heavens are rolled up like a scroll. Is it allegorical or is there some very peculiar properties to the universe completely outside our ability to comprehend? Are stars a sort of symbiotic part of angels? Again I don't say with conviction any of these scenarios is correct, I merely like to think out loud and chat about such things.

Let's get back to the biblical "Hosts of heaven". Immanuel Velikovsky tries to equate the Hosts in the bible with planets but we saw that the planets were mentioned as different from the hosts in the same verse mentioned above. Deuteronomy 4:19 goes further. It says when you see the sun, the moon the stars and the hosts of heaven you are not to worship them, and later in verses 17:2-3 it specifically states not to worship the hosts of heaven.

We've seen that the hosts of heaven are something that can be seen, but they are not the sun, moon, stars, or the planets! What's left!? Now, one could argue that the host are angels such as the heavenly hosts seen when telling the shepherds of the baby born in the manger, but this viewing angels in this manner seems to be an exception. This incident also shows angles don't need chariots to get around. I strongly suspect the 'host' of heaven' may be UFO's or those cigar shaped craft that disc UFO's have been seen entering on occasion. Guardians of the sky?

In a prophetic scripture concerning the end times, which also further indicates the hosts of heaven are not the angels, we read in Isaiah 34:4 "All the host of heaven shall be dissolved, and the heavens shall be rolled together as the scroll: and all their host shall fall down, as the leaf falleth off the vine, and as the falling from the fig tree." This seems strongly to suggest that all flying machines shall suddenly be unable to fly, but it also refers to the "host of heaven", and would angels be dissolved?

Often flying saucers are seen to fly in undulating motions not unlike tree leaves fluttering. In fact some descriptions of UFO in flight actually use this comparison. On the other hand this could be the same event referred to in revelation where the stars fall and the heavens are rolled up like a scroll. Suggesting hosts of heaven could be fallen angels, or "demonic manifestations". Demons changing themselves to look like men, just like Satan can make himself look like a angel of light. Revelation 12:9 speaks of the devil and his angels being cast down to earth, so this interpretation of hosts of heaven could be a very valid one. This might also suggest that at a point in time any UFO's in the air would suddenly be unable to fly but possibly survive their fall to earth by their undulating leaf like falling, possibly due to their electromagnetic drive tied to the earth's magnetic field.

We obviously can't rule out the possibility that demons are piloting the craft which suddenly can no longer fly and they fall to earth after this war in heaven. But this rolling away of the sky like a scroll also suggests some huge distortion of that same field, thus making flight impossible. Other flying machines simply plummet to earth like the falling of fruit. These may be a different type of UFO or COF, but they could simply be our airplanes as this was seen in a prophesy and often the prophets didn't understand what they were seeing, but were told merely to record what they saw.

The unsettling comparison here is that the Hosts' of heaven fall to earth in an event where the heavens are rolled away like a scroll, and the third part of the stars are cast to the earth just prior to an event where the heavens depart like a scroll, and this comparison to stars as angels. This forces the distinct possibility that at least some of these UFO's, these fallen stars, may mean as many as a third are demonically piloted.

UFO'S BEFORE CHRIST

On February 10, 9 BC according to Japanese history 9 sun disc appeared in the sky. (book 34 pg 98)

In 42 BC at night a light shone so bright that people got up to go to work as though a new day had begun and three suns were seen in the sky which then merged into a single orb.(Book 43 Pg237-241)

In 100 BC at sunset a circular object was seen to cross the skies from west to east, just north of Rome (book 29 pg. 128)

In 113-110 BC in a Roman war with the Cimbri in France, the Roman army was terrorized when a bright light shone down from the skies. (Book 29 pg. 128)

In Gaul in 122 BC 3 suns and moons were seen. (Book 43 Pg237-241)

In 163 BC something like a sun shone at night and later on in the day two suns were seen. (Book 43 Pg237-241)

In 218 BC two moons were seen at night. (Book 43 Pg237-241)

A Chinese poem speaks of a flight in a jade chariot *not affected by the wind* in the 3rd century BC (book 11 pg. 109)

3 moons were visible at night in 223 BC. (Book 43 Pg237-241)

Shiny 'shields', repeatedly dived at Alexander the Great and his army in India stampeding elephants and horses and then going back to the sky. (Book 43 Pg237-241)

667 BC the chronicles of Japan record about one who flew down on a heavenly "rock boat". A flying boat that looks like a rock? Sound suspiciously similar to the egg craft spoken of in other legends. (book 34 pg. 97) Remember the Schist disc (chapter 3) was apparently made of molded rock and possibly part of a flying machine. Could this "rock boat" really be made of rock as the Japan legend says?

In the times of Pharaoh Thutmose III (estimated at about 1504-1450BC) "circles of fire" were seen to soar across the skies. (book 29 pg. 55-56)

Chinese records state that in 2346 BC 10 suns were seen in the sky. (book 34 pg. 79)

ORIGINS

Interestingly the further back in time you go the sighting begin to change to stories of origins. Back to about here the stories are of sightings, but the further back in time you go, when you get to legends and ancient histories, the stories appear to know when and where the UFO's come from as though there was a more intimate knowledge of them, their inhabitants, and their machines.

Hopi Indians say their ancestors came from "endless space" and visited other worlds before coming to earth. (book 3 pg. 71) No doubt one of the reasons people including Daniken, suggests we are descendants of aliens. But this conclusion is likely incorrect. Things start to make sense if we consider the pre-flood space technology existing in space and visiting other planets in the solar system before and during the flood, and then coming back to earth after the flood.

Indians of the Northwest believed an 'all father' lived in a house in the sky, and the Iroquois, Huron's, and Wyandotte Indians believed the first people lived in the sky. (book 23 pg. 106)

A Tiahuanaco tradition says a person named Orejona came from Venus in a craft brighter then the sun. (book 22 pg 42) Could there be some of us on these two planets... Venus and Mars? An inhabited Venus seems highly unlikely.

Peruvian and Chilean Indians say their ancestors traveled on (in?) great golden discs kept airborne by sound vibrating at a certain pitch made by continuous hammer beatings. (book 21 pg 206) And Peruvian histories claim Peru was originally inhabited by people born from Gold, Silver and Bronze eggs.

Drawings in Lima Peru are said to have been drawn by a goddess "Orichana" who came to earth in a ship of the sky as brilliant as the sun" (Book 64 pg 108) Orichana sounds similar to "orichalcum" an unknown metal of Atlantis and there could be a connection. Maybe UFO's outer shell is made of this substance.

IT'S MADE OF WHAT?

(3rd ed. Insert 2016) Further in the same source, Patrolman Schirmer noted that the UFO pilots had said that their craft was made from pure magnesium. (Book 29 page 180) I thought at first this was something of a red herring as planes in World War II were made of magnesium in some cases and when they got hit or crashed the magnesium burned, often killing the occupants. Why build something from an element that will burn up? But I found something shortly after in my previous research book that I had passed over the first time: "Ultra pure magnesium fragments were retrieved from an exploding UFO at Ubatuba beach Brazil in 1957." This magnesium was manufactured in a way called "Directional casting" a method of magnesium manufacturing that was not known in 1957! Thus one has to ask, what are the properties of this metal in its pure form in electrical fields…does it glow in rainbow patterns, and how does magnetism affect it, to duplicate effects reported to be seen with UFO's.

The Machiguenga Indians tell of a time their forbears communicated with celestials from the sky. (Book 23 pg. 179)

Many Ancient legends speak of men coming from the sky on a rope, chain, thread, ladder or cobweb, similar to more recent sightings. African tribes such as Madi, Morui (ladder) Ashanti, Lobi (chain) Yu Kun (thread) Jagga (thread of cobweb) Ndorobo (rope) speak of these happenings. Ganda traditions say two women came down from heaven. In India legends, heavenly beings came down from heaven with gifts.

Osiris or Ra (these two are equated as the same person) is in an egg and who shineth from his disc and gives a blast of fire from his mouth (book 61 pg 104) The book of the dead gives the dimensions of the well known "Eye of Horus". The eye of Ra (Horus) Measured 7 cubits (about 12-13 feet) and the pupil (door?… dome?!) is 3 cubits or about 5 feet. (Book 61 pg. 305, 306)

This exact measurement of the eye of Horus shows clearly it is not the sun that they are measuring and obviously it's no "eye". So many scholars insist "Ra" is the sun but this clearly eliminates Ra, Horus and the "EYE" as the sun, but as some smaller measurable item…and since it flies through the air it has to be a UFO, COF or whatever you want to label it. It is measurable and about the size of a room. Compare this to modern sightings.

A UFO that looked like a "lighted egg" appeared in Exeter in March 1966. Similar oval domed craft were seen in Michigan and in Maine the previous month described as metallic, oval and with a dome. If one turns an oval domed UFO on its side it might look like an "eye".

In Socorro New Mexico on April 24 1964 an Officer Lonnie Zamora investigating what he thought to be a wreck was amazed to see an "egg" shaped object about 15 feet long, though no dome is mentioned. Another "football" shaped UFO was seen with a dome, the whole of which was estimated to be about 20-30 feet across, was seen March 29th 1966 in East Elliot Maine. (book 28 pg. 113) The majority of UFO's are about 25 feet across with a dome. (book 62 pg. 15) Eyes of Horus? Maybe Horus had this propensity to fly on his side while coming in for a landing and it looked like an eye to those watching him circle.

A line out of the book of the dead again seems to indicate UFO's in the past. "The goddess Hathor, who dwelleth in the spacious disc as it advanceth to Annu (Heliopolis) Book 61 pg 232) There is a lot of evidence to show that these UFO's of today are the Vimanas and the disc of Horus' and such of yesteryear. For example UFO's have been seen to be lit in one colour and then change to other colours. Horus flew back to the boat of Ra in the winged disc that shone in many colours (Book 42 pg. 27) Again, the sun doesn't do this.

Ancient texts speak of Etana who was given a ride during the day in an eagle that reached the 'plane of the fixed stars'. (in daytime when you get above enough atmosphere, the stars will become visible) Eventually he can't distinguish the seas from the land very well. Similarly astronaut Scott Carpenter noted that when you get farther away from the earth the general appearance of the earth is blue, likely due to the atmosphere colouring all that is seen.

Tibetan legends. Out of a light came an egg. The outside was very bright. It had no wings, but it could fly, no mouth or eyes but a voice came from it. After a time it opened and a man came out of it. (Book 10 pg. 123) November 9th 1954 a UFO is sighted in Belgium which is described as a six foot flying egg that landed in a cow pasture and screams were heard to come from within. Maybe the husband and wife were on a holiday and they couldn't decide on a suitable hotel. (book 47 pg. 251) When people have seen UFO's at first they look like lights in the sky but when they get closer the shape of the craft becomes evident.

These Tibetan legends go on and speak of flying machines that look like a "pearl in the sky" (book 2 pg 77) They say the first 7 kings came from the stars and could walk on the sky.(book 11 pg 117) This sounds very similar to stories I heard about a bridge of light which might possibly be the fusing of air molecules through the Unified field somehow, or simply walking on an invisible ship, as was seen during the Philadelphia experiment. If you were at the right distance, the people on the ship of the Philadelphia could be seen even though the ship itself could not be seen so they appeared to be walking in the air. Legends of India also refer to the Vimanas as "Pearls in the sky" (book 37 pg. 40) and they flew with a melodious sound.

Ancient Chinese Historical traditions speak of a flight to the moon and mention a certain How Yih in 2309 BC accomplishing this feat. He had chronometers telling the exact rising and setting of the sun. This craft mounted into space on a current of luminous air and went to a place where the movements of the sun were not seen. (book 11 pg. 114-115) In space the sun appears to stand still.

Easter Islanders Rapunui legends tell of the gods who came to them in an egg. (book 4 pg 121) Other south sea islander say they are descendants of a god "Tangalao" who came down from heaven in a gleaming egg. (book 4 pg. 162)

Zachariah Sitchen deduces a 'god' named Tuashtri provides flying machines and weapons sounding similar to nukes in their destructive capabilities. These flying machines could fly in air and the water, change colours and were very bright. He also deduces that wars were fought in the air, on land and in the sea by these gods with a city underwater existing. (book 42 pg. 62-65) A description of these fierce weapons is in the Indian text Mahabharata as described in the Adam 900 chapter. (Book 29 pg 125-126)

The Ramayana, an ancient Indian text is referred to as saying a fiery chariot shines like flame in the sky, it was as fast as a comet, and it looked like two suns were shining in the sky. When it rose the heaven was brightened. In a city named Ayodhya, the sky was full of flying machines. (book 21 pg 81 [once again my copy misses these juicy bits.])

One petro glyph or rock painting or fresco found in the Fergana Uzbekistan is interesting for its depicting astronauts and a fairly modern drawing of a UFO. I felt the petro glyph was also interesting for it showing 4 suns in the sky. The disk shaped UFO is shown with a pillar of fire and smoke or exhaust beneath it like it is taking off or landing. Though it's not sure what the artist was depicting whether a dream or some sort of surrealistic depiction it seems to be blending of things known about UFO's. But one aspect seems ancient; the astronaut in the foreground is holding some sort of disk that is very similar to disk designs of ancient times, possibly one of those antigravity discs tuned to the individual who owned it.

The checkerboard landscape seems similar to interesting tiled floors seen in UFO's and is possibly similar to checkered floors Plato talks about as seen in Atlantis. Although the checker board pattern seems black and white some reds might turn black with age. It is a peculiar rock drawing to be sure, and some suggest it a hoax because it is simply so fantastic. It is somewhat unique because it seems to be the only surrealistic rock drawing known. I couldn't find the date this rock drawing was found, though it dates back at least to 1967. Others have studied it and dated it to be very ancient. It might be a copy of an illustration used in 1967 so this one is in some doubt.

Indian Texts: Flying craft could go around the earth, hover, and *look like a star*, and could radiate so much light it could look like there were two suns in the sky. (book 10 pg 151) Though the Indian texts seem to be describing UFO's they seem to be more intimately acquainted with them, their capabilities and weapons.

The Mahabharata speaks of what might be about a ship in space. It speaks of the abode by saying infinite is the space populated by the perfect ones. (book 11 pg 117)

The Indian books of Dyzan said that fathers descended to earth on a moon. (book 34 pg. 27)

Ancient India texts speak of a person named Phaeton that drove a chariot of the sun and was about to set the world on fire when he was smitten by the "Supreme God" and was cast down to earth. (Book 41 pg. 233) This might have tower of Babel implications. I'll repeat this later.

Winged circles or spheres are found in many ancient pictograms such as those seen in Mexican, Naacal, Hindu, Guatemalan, Syrian, Persian, and Egyptian pictograms, suggesting if these are indicating flying spheres or circles they were seen virtually worldwide. But the ancients seem more familiar with them suggesting they were either intimately acquainted with them or they were far more prevalent back then than now. They even appear to know the pilots by name. Interestingly Horus was said to fly in a winged disk. (book 42 pg. 27) A.K.A. eye of Horus.

(I repeat this bit from an earlier chapter) The natives of the area around the source of the Amazon river have legends in the chronicles of Akakor, which speaks of magic stones one could look in and see places around the earth, and wonderful subterranean homes. It also speaks of a great flood that was followed by extreme climate change and flying machines that could go over mountains and water, which were made of an unknown golden metal (orichalcum?) and were shaped like a clay roll. [rock boat? egg?] (book 10 pg. 112-116)

Incans have legends of giants coming from the clouds taking Indian women, and Greek Mythology speaks of gods and goddesses' coming from the sky to live with mortals. (book 29 pg 167) Incans also believe a couple was sent to them from the sun to instruct the people around the lake Titicaca. They came in a great shining light. When they left from the island of the sun on lake Titicaca, they rose up in an object as bright as the sun.

A Sumerian text in the first person attributed to a certain fellow named Enki says "when I approached earth, there was much flooding" (book 17 pg. 291) Because this is Sumerian and thus extremely early, this strongly indicates he came to the earth shortly after the flood.

A Babylonian story is incredibly descriptive. A large egg came from heaven and landed in the Euphrates River. It then came to the land by the help of fishes that pushed it toward land. (this could be a propulsion from under the water line causing a bubbling wake making the observers believe fish were pushing the 'egg') The egg hatched and out came a woman named Venus. In this story she was said to have come from the antediluvian (pre-flood) world. (book 41 pg. 109) This is pretty plain language. Yet often this and similar stories are "interpreted" rather than taken at face value. Now see how this connects to this next bit found in the same source...

A woman named Astraea is also identified as Themis (goddess of justice) or she is possibly Themis' daughter. She is said to have lived on earth before the flood. She forsook the earth just before the catastrophe (flood) occurred. This Astraea is the same as the Syrian Astarte, who is also identified as Venus! (book 41 pg 309) Interestingly though Hislop deduces that these females are all the same girl, he disassociates these two events in his book and separates them by 200 pages!

We see Astraea leaving earth just before the flood. How she does this is not stated. But we then see her coming back to earth after the flood in an egg and landing in the Euphrates river in another legend. This places the egg shaped craft to the pre flood era! Since this mid 19th century author cannot accept that anyone leaves the earth before the flood or returned to earth after the flood, his primary goal in speaking about these legends turns into showing the symbolism of the egg and the women, not realizing he had evidence to show some people other than Noah survived from pre-flood times.

Since space travel was something of fairytales in the 19th century this was simply an impossibility to him. Because such a statement had to seem allegorical, his only alternative was to presume since they couldn't really have survived the flood, then some analogies were meant by these stories. Thus he identifies the egg as the ark of Noah and equates Themis with the spirit, apparently failing to recognize the obvious connection and similarities in these events and neglecting to ascribe any significance to them.

With the deduction that Adam had space travel the idea of a craft in space at the time of the flood becomes perfectly plausible. The egg is often spoken of as the ark of Noah or woman and fruitfulness or whatever. Why not exactly as it is described here in these references, that of people who survived the flood because they were not caught in it? They were able to "forsake" the earth and later on "come down from heaven".

True Noah and his family were the only survivors of people caught in the flood. But ancient sources indicate others were not in the flood to begin with such as this Themis, Astraea or Venus. Granted it would appear that since there is some equation of Venus with that of Semerimas a girl assumed to have been born after the flood, indicates some confusing and mixing up of these ancient texts is still occurring in ancient histories. We have to presume that the stories about these women coming down from heaven in an egg are specific events not to be confused with later events or people or meant to be interpreted as allegorical.

Indeed when one reads these stories and the equating one person in one legend with that of another person in another legend it seems some of these equations are a bit of a stretch, though admittedly deciphering where if any confusion actually takes place is way beyond me.

UFO'S MUST BE CLOSE BY.

The very fact that these UFO's have been around for centuries does NOT suggest they came here from some different galaxy or solar system but strongly suggests they actually live here and have lived here or at least close by [our solar system] since ancient times. But if not in some other dimension, as seems to be the popular view, then they have to be living somewhere solid and findable in our own dimension.

However this does not mean they do not make themselves invisible as it seems they do not really want to be found by us unless on their own initiative.

As we see UFO's originate not in 1947 but they stretch way back into pre-flood times! 1947 is a renewed surge for some reason, apparently due to our advances in the form of destructive capabilities. The way they just pop up reminds me of a beehive that is docile until disturbed. Since we've shot off a few nukes and dumped toxic waste into their living space we have disturbed the hive and they are buzzing us.

The very first a-bomb test site in New Mexico was the scene of a UFO sighting and landing, though no occupants were seen...small wonder! Canada's first nuclear power station near Port Elgin Ontario was also the scene of a series of UFO sightings lasting about a week. People felt it may be monitoring water qualities as it was seen to drop something into the water and returned on subsequent nights apparently looking to retrieve it. (book 46 pg. 117-119)

On the last night of 1975 a UFO was seen hovering above a Pickering Ontario reactor by lake Ontario that had been shut down for 5 months because of leaking heavy water. The UFO's returned a month later and monitored the plant for a 1/2 hour before shooting off.

It's been noted that UFO's have visited every important communications and industrial center, and military installation on earth. Even Jesus said in the last days there would be signs in the heavens (plural). We saw a rare triple conjunction of Mars, Jupiter and Venus on June 7 1991 (one heaven) and these UFO's have since 1947 been pretty prevalent in the local atmosphere to be sure. (another heaven) He may have understood they would come looking when we got dangerous to our environment. Paul speaks of several heavens and even creation speaks of a couple heavens as well, so it stands to reason these UFO's may very well be some of the signs in heaven Jesus talked about. Once we see that UFO's originate in history we can easily conclude that these are manmade structures whose origins predate the flood, though no doubt some are of post flood origin, maybe even like our cars with new makes and models. Some shaped like eggs, some like saucers, etc.

THAT ONE CONCESSION I HAD TO MAKE.

I had thought that maybe if there was nothing new under the sun that maybe Adam and his pre-flood peers had space flight. Though this was merely a deduction based on minimal evidence given to that point, other Christian authors have come to this conclusion as well. (book 38) The logic that man was created perfect using all his brain capacity and the apparent cloning of Adam speak of stunning technology potentially in existence before the flood. I mean if we as devolved as we are have come up with space travel why not Adam? He was created perfect and had the brain capacity of a million Einstein's...plus a few Mozart's and such. I felt confident that they had space travel back then.

I started to think about some of the people in space today. I imagined being up there looking on and realized if people were in space at the time of a meteor hitting earth they would not be affected. Then it struck me!! If pre-flood people had space flight, and many biblical scholars are willing to accept this as a possibility, it seemed with this as a logical conclusion, maybe someone survived the flood other than Noah and his family, because when the meteor that caused the flood smashed into the earth, they were in space at the time.

This means that people in space before the flood were never actually *in* the flood, because they were in space at the time of the disaster. This was the major concession I had to make, to fit UFO's into the "big picture". This actually makes perfect sense in the light of technology as we have it today. Understand this is not to say anyone *on* earth at the time Noah survived the flood. But people not actually in the flood because they were not on the earth at the time thus they continued on.

Though few if any other authors actually suggested this, the evidence they were citing seemed to point to this as a real possibility. In fact it seems to be the only conclusion possible, because these UFO craft, don't just belong to angels and God and devils, we also see that man was making them and had them.

However according to the conventional line of reasoning this idea of someone else surviving the flood just seemed impossible. So I quickly went to the verses in Genesis, and other flood references in the bible about the flood to slap my wrist with and show me that no, all mankind died in the flood, and how dare I think such a thing, and I just went to the bible to plant my feet back on good old terra firma so to speak as I needed confirmation. Such a wild speculation just couldn't be true could it...could it?

But oddly the flood accounts did not slam the door in my face! I didn't expect this. It said that all those on earth perished. All those on dry land died. Why the qualifiers? Why doesn't it say all man died? It's seems oddly specific, saying only those on earth and those on dry land died. What about those off the earth? Was I clutching at straws? Though it seemed incredible I wanted to give it a fair shake. It seems the scriptures leave the door open to this possibility. I wanted to find out why... is there something to be found out?

I mean even in our day and age at almost any given day there is someone up there orbiting the earth. Maybe at the time of the flood they reached a state where there was ALWAYS someone up there. Right now we are in the process of making a space station and there would likely always be someone in space, this in our own era. Remember as in the days of Noah, so in the last days, and there is nothing new under the sun. Even this verse allows for it. It doesn't say there is nothing new on earth, it says there is nothing new under the sun! Another curious qualifier. It sounds possible. One begins to see that if this verse is still valid, and I believe it is, then the time before the flood, man was no slouch in the inventions department, as we have seen.

If the deduction that men were in space at the time of the flood and therefore were not in the flood and thus survived is correct, it actually answers quite a few questions and solves several mysteries indeed. However because of the potentially explosive nature of this theory I figured I would just let that theory lay low but would keep my eye open and see what I might find out. I would simply discount the theory unless I found something that just could not be ignored. This was just too much to accept cart blanche. But just in case...just in the teeny weenie chance there actually did survive a ship out in space any evidence to suggest this could then be filed correctly on the off chance this was indeed true. You've seen some of the ancient evidence. Obviously some of it got out of the bag in chapter 8 with giants...but...there's more.

If the deduction that Adams race destroyed the fifth planet is true, I suppose it does not necessarily mean he did it from space on some moonlike manmade planetoid. Granted based on the evidence it makes more sense, includes more evidence and fits better, but with his inventive ability, pre-flood man may have been able to accomplish this with an earth based super gun or energy focuser, or whatever for all we know.

REHASH...DID I MISS SOMETHING?

We've seen that the pyramids are in all probability a surviving relic of pre-flood technology. Just stunning to think that a structure built before the flood could survive this long and still be this massive, this impressive, this visible and still be un-deciphered. People have come up with theories that suggest them as being built over a period of 600 years, with 100,000 slaves, or built by alien astronauts. Both theories are just on extreme ends of the reality scale. Why would aliens come to earth from who knows how many light years away to later build things, many unfinished, and just leave. And how could so many slaves be forced to build a structure for an unknown reason for so long without organizing and rebelling and ceasing the construction of the pyramids or whatever. Maybe one might suggest this is a reason so many cyclopean projects were halted all at once, but there is no evidence for this whatsoever.

Many archaeologists will concede that some of these structures are way beyond even modern mans ability to reproduce, but stop short of making maverick guesses as to how they were built, possibly for fear of ridicule from their peers. Tibetans say a three story pyramid means; the bottom: when the ancients rose up to the stars, the middle: when they came down from the stars, and the top: the new land the world of distant stars. (book 21 pg. 69)

BACK TO UFO'S.

There is a tendency today to make more of these UFO's than they merit, and explaining them here may help people to get a more balanced view of them. Rumor has it that even UFO churches exists, suggesting we are beginning to fall into the same trap the ancients fell into, worshipping, among other things, the people of the sky, or put another way "worshipping the host of heaven".

These deductions of the UFO's are disappointing, marvelous and sad. Disappointing because to some who believe in UFO's as superior aliens from space with whom they were hoping to do mental osmosis with, are going to be disappointed. Marvelous because it give us a glimpse of what we were originally created as, and sad because it shows us how far we have declined.

Keep in mind I still think some of these "UFO's may indeed BE demonic manifestations as some of the stories about them are horrific indeed, and even these stories stretch back into ancient times. Some of them may also possibly be fallen angels bent on destroying man in any way allowed. If they are weird looking creepy aliens they are NOT friendly toward man as a potential redemptive creature in God hands. They want us to have the final end that they have. But this is a glimpse of that dogmatic slant I have on UFO's still showing itself. Biblical indications are that God turned some fallen angels into unclean creatures, thus often in demonology they have two apparent looks, manlike and beastlike. At least that is most biblical scholars deductions regarding fallen angels. I put it here for the record. Remember the bible says even Satan can turn himself into an angel of light, suggesting he is in fact something else. We are to test the spirits. But I'm not dealing with those sorts of UFO's, what few there are of this sort, if indeed any do confirm my original suspicions of them as "demonic manifestations". I'm dealing with the ones that did not fit into my preconceived notions. I'll look into that in more detail soon.

IF THIS IS THE CASE THEN...

It seems inescapable, in all likelihood pre-flood man had space flight, and the post flood generation might have had space travel too. Though the post-flood were likely inferior to the pre-flood mother ship planetoid inhabitants, they were still no slouches in the invention department and could out-think us out of any paper bag you put them in.

Just doing a study on agriculture and the crossbreeding and genetic manipulations of plants in this period shows they were astonishingly advanced. No further substantial advances were made subsequently until modern times. And we still haven't perfect what we've done. In fact we may be making it worse. Genetically modified foods may in fact be one of the causes of the bee population declines.

If post flooders life spans were 600-400 years and their IQ's were about the same they would easily have advanced at an incredible rate too, and all signs indicate this is the case. Buildings as we have seen were built of monstrously huge stones and they appear to have been moved and built after the flood as most of them are still standing clear of any mud or debris that might partially burry them, and they are unfinished. This however does not necessarily mean just post flooders built these things as it seems pre-flood people may have come and helped as well. So though these buildings may be post flood buildings they could in essence be pre-flood technology as built or assisted by pre-flood standard humans. This might have gone on for a several decades, maybe a hundred years or more until it became clear man was being affected by the new post flood environment. The pre-flood survivors would have gone back to their home, presumably a vast moon sized ship, and some of the post-flood descendants may have started to grasp the problem and went somewhere safe too.

It appears the pilots of these vehicles were thought of as "gods". So somewhere a division starts to take place. Which would mean we have to check out ancient sources other than just the bible as it would not have, say, Hopi or Ancient India histories.

OTHER RECORDS, HISTORIES AND BOOKS ARE VALID TOO

One thing came out that was an interesting insight. One person while trying to track down a bible in India some time ago found this to be a virtually impossible task. It dawned on him that what the Christian segments of the world takes as an important book is or was not known by many people's around the world. They have their own important historical books.

Remember at the time of Babel when language changed, the word, name or meaning for God also changed depending on the language. What might be a word for God as we know it in English or Spanish or French might be perceived to be a different deity all together in another language and culture. India is known as the land of a million gods. There is one god in India that is rarely worshipped anymore and the descriptions of Him are incredibly similar to that of God as we know him from the bible. Maybe the creator was worshipped in India originally until the confusion of languages of the tower of Babel and the multitude of gods showing up made the true creator become pale and insignificant to them, and became just one of many 'gods' to chose from.

JAPAN'S SHOCK

(3rd ed. Insert 2016) Right after the flood, all people knew the history of the flood, and how the true god saved Noah, and this history was handed down to the children. Then at the tower of Babel, the people with their new language went their separate ways, but the history didn't change, just because their language did, so all of earth's peoples would have this history in common. So such alternative names for God come of course from the tower of Babel as noted, but it would be the same God but simply a different name depending on language, but all meaning the same. Thus all peoples if they search their history will find the true God in their past was sought and followed.

Japan is considered closed to any introduction of other cultures gods, particularly Christian teachings. However research shows they too once sought and served the same God. Researchers trying to find evidence of the most high God in Japanese history and culture found high towers in Shinto, and the Isamo shrine shows a trinity of gods of one is named "the god in the glorious center of heaven" or "Amenominnakanushi" as his name is spelled out. The Books of Kojiki and Kami speak of creation by these three, strikingly similar to the story of Creation by the trinity (or Eloheim) and mirrors the story of creation in Genesis 1:2. Needless to say it's something of a shock to Japanese people to find out that they have all along believed in the same God of the foreigners.

Even in our society today, the God of the bible is becoming less and less acknowledged as more religions come into favor and practice. People now ask what makes the God of the bible the right one?... because they say there are so many gods and religions. Such a question would have been inconceivable in our society 40 years ago. Ironically the origin of many of these gods and religions stems to a time when people were using high science and is even traceable back to these UFO's! Some were apparently merely people of pre-flood origin! Even the bible acknowledges a time period when the gods ruled, though sadly it does not explain them. Even Abraham's fathers served them.

Though other societies may not have our bible scriptures they appear to have histories handed down that also instill moral standards that God recognizes, and why not? This is not in any way to diminish the bible. We, all being created in his image, will know right from wrong if we are taught properly. Even the most primitive tribes have distinctively evil doers and righteous men, and they have no written language at all. Just their local histories which they teach their children. It may be on a more simplistic level though, but who is to say what is simplistic.

Jesus acknowledged the whole of the law could be said in two lines. Love God with all your heart and love your neighbor as yourself and in doing so, all the law fulfilled. This isn't difficult for ANY race or people to comprehend. It's even good and understandable for children and people with Down syndrome. If you know this and follow it you will not hurt your neighbor, you will not steal from him or take his wife, or kill him, bear false witness etcetera. So any organized society with these values also can understand telling the truth and handing it down for generations.

The truth handed down in ancient records often give glimpses of ancient history that other records don't speak of. Mind you in some ancient stories the true meanings are so confused in allegorical gobbledygook they become indecipherable and almost have to be discarded as they appear to make so little sense.

Also consider the fact that things that happened in India or China are likely not going to be recorded in lands like Africa or Mexico. But if the stories they tell ARE the same as in these other cultures they indicate vast antiquity of the legends which would then go back to the time when all mankind lived in a small area after the flood and the people of earth spoke one language.

Many legends persist and insist that a time existed when the whole of the earth's inhabitants spoke one language...not just the bible. Now some legends will be more localized because the events would have happened after the division of languages and the continents. Events like a comet or a mountain or the name of a local hero would likely be localized. The North American Indians have legends about "Thunderbirds". Boy that sounds an awful lot like airplanes to me! Other similar legends exist of men coming out of giant birds.

If these are ancient stories about flight in somewhat conventional aircraft, these are likely post flood craft. Aircraft are simply inferior to the UFO's and these do not look at all physically like the Vimanas of India. There's no reason not to conclude that at different times in ancient history, as we declined, so too did our inventive ability disintegrate. However it's likely short bursts of organization reinvented flight. Remember model planes have been found in ancient Egypt and other cultures. Men might have had normal looking planes as we know them, whereas the earliest and most advanced flying machines seem to be wingless, resembling the sun, stars, eggs or the moon. This might be why there is such a abundance of winged discs in so many ancient pictograms. They understood winged flight so added wings to discs to differentiate them from heavenly bodies. (that or they just added bird wings). Remember during the 13th century Roger Bacon talks about flying machines being common in his day, and Greeks and Chinese legends speak of manned flight. It would seem possible that at various times through history flight was re-achieved then lost again for a period of time. We've seen maps that had to date to after Peleg that people felt were aided by the use of flying craft.

MAN MADE MEN

OK what about the strange shaped aliens, the "greys' and the short midgets so often mentioned? Adam was so advanced he cloned himself. It seems that even before the flood, green, red, and blue skinned peoples are said to have existed. And though I thought giants were a result of the breeding of angels and men, it also seems possible that they existed before the sons of God came to earth. Genesis 6:4 "There were giants in the earth in those days; and also after that, when the sons of God came in unto the daughters of men, and they bore children unto them, the same became mighty men which were of old, men of renown." So we could deduce that before the flood using genetics they were making clones, giants and different coloured races. (Giants may be caused by breeding or genetics, or both)

If we presume these UFO'nauts might be sons of Adam they too could work with genetics. If these UFO people are so advanced and worked with genetics, their making new humanoid creatures is by no means out of the question. Why expose themselves to the risks of dangerous radiation on the earth's surface when you can get subhuman genetically engineered workers to do that for you?

Legends even exist that some apes were manmade to do mans bidding. Although the current theory exists that man came from monkeys, originally this was not the case but was in fact reversed. Old legends speak of a time when we or the gods created a species of monkey like creatures that were moderately intelligent to do the work. These were apparently cross genetic creations half man half ape like creature and by all accounts these were fairly intelligent creatures. This may even be the origin of Sasquatch. More on that shortly.

It may be that these apes also degenerated into the apes we now have on earth; creatures that have left the service to fend on their own, but have gotten a bit more wild due to over exposure to the elements on earth as we know them. Astoundingly a new theory has developed; that monkeys came from man! Where did they get that idea?

With the combinations of creature being simply endless who knows what genetic combinations they made up in the past. Even the red people who have talked about things to leaders and such in the past have admitted that they have made worker class of creatures, which clearly suggest these are not red people of the surface.

Though most UFO's sightings include what appear to be very normal men, they also include these apelike creature, midgets and "greys" and it appears they are just genetically altered or cross breeds of some sort.

Looking through ancient history we find all kinds of legends of monsters and half man half creature. And they are almost invariable from the same very early period, as though someone was making experiments willy-nilly then suddenly stopped. These are usually just thought to be legends, myths and make-believe creatures. But if, as we surmise, genetic manipulations were going on in the past we could conclude they are not legends at all.

Quite possibly creatures like Medusa, women that are half snake, half girl. Pan...half man half goat, half man half bull (Minotaur) Cyclops, Griffins, Lilith or Inanna (winged lady with bird feet) are genuine if only unique creatures. In fact the legends are so widespread it would appear that they were just making creatures at a whim. Some of these appear to have attained 'god' status, and demons could easily blend right in. Even the bible speaks of some of these creatures. There were men that had the features of lions. (II Samuel 23:20)

MADE TO ORDER

It would seem genetic operations were going on almost as a fad. You could have kids with leopard like lines in their hair. Indeed it was an age of confusion. This is even a plausible origin of varying races. Maybe the geneticists would say to the potential parents "what colour would you like your kid to be?".

ORIGIN OF SASQUATCH

In the Wyatt journal of 1888 (referred to in book 30 pg. 117-119) the writer through much contact with the Native Indians spoke many fluent Indian languages and dialects. He records the story of an unusual creature the Indians referred to as "Crazy bears" which by the description in the journal could very well be what we now call Sasquatch. They looked manlike and they were tall but their head seem to have no neck and they were very hairy all over except their palms and feet.

The Indians saw these creatures arrive and fed them, as they felt they were sent to bring them powerful medicine. The writer became inquisitive when he noticed the Indians taking meat to some unknown destination. Curious as to where they were taking this food he managed to persuade one to take him to where they were taking the meat and came to a cave where this 'crazy bear' dwelt. Though their origin was still a mystery he persisted and offered many gifts to hear the story.

Finally one native took him to a place and was told this 'crazy bear' had been brought to these woods from the stars. A "small moon" had come down and landed on a plateau a few miles away. Three crazy bears had been flung out of the moon, then it took off again to the stars. He told of other crazy bears being left by these people over the years. This Indian and several others had seen this moon on occasion and the men within it. These occupants appeared more like ordinary men but with shiny cloths and shorter hair. When seen, they would wave to the Indian witness's and go back to the stars.

The "Crazy Bears" were befriended by the Indians, which offered no resistance. Presumably they believed them to be some sort of gift from the heavens and no harm came to the Indians from the crazy bears.

It would seem we can now get a look at the entire picture of UFO's and their occupants. It appears Sasquatch and maybe other UFO occupants are some sort of genetic manipulation. Possibly Sasquatch are occasional errors of theirs or just getting old, so they just leave them here to fend for themselves. As for other UFO pilots, it seems plausible that completely human UFO occupants do not want their living places known and so make these genetic manipulations to throw us off the scent. When these "greys" are seen they are presumed to be aliens, when in fact they may be a manmade genetically altered semi intelligent creature, made as some sort of information gatherers sent to the surface of the earth to gather environmental data. Some forms of strange creature associated with UFOs such as Sasquatch seem to be short term temporary sightings. When the creatures die local sightings stop. If they chose to leave these creatures in the same place over time then renewed sightings occur of sasquatch or whatever.

IF YOU DON'T SEE THEM, DO THEY EXIST?

(3rd ed. Insert 2016) After reading *Sasquatch* by Don Hunter and Rene' Dahinden to get more info on the critters, I found some interesting tidbits. First…There seem to be many sightings of these things and the sightings go WAYYY back! Now I'm not discounting my conclusion that they are a man made creature as mentioned. I still think this is plausible, but these sightings go way back and in very diverse areas, meaning if they are dropped off by UFO's occasionally, they are dropping them off in quite a few areas, and that seems a bit inexplicable.

They are seen in British Columbia and have been known about for hundreds of years in my home province. But they've been seen in the whole area south of BC like the entire range of the Rockies in Washington as far as California, and even farther afield. But as many are aware, they are also seen in Tibet and called Yeti and in Russia and called Alma's, or Almasti. Those who take them seriously and study sightings feel there appears to be at least two species or more.

I've been aware of them since the famous Bluff Creek film hit the general B.C. public, so accepting their existence doesn't seem like too much of a stretch to me. This film has been studied, and not just by anthropologists, but by biomechanical experts. They concluded the gait, walk, and distribution of weight, flow of muscles etcetera indicates this could not possibly be a man in a monkey suit. They even deduced the shape of the foot by characteristics it would need to support such a heavy creature, which, as it happens matches so many tracks seen around. It seems the only people that don't believe it exists are people that either haven't seen one and won't believe it until they do, or people who seem to favour Evolution because this creature somehow throws a monkey wrench in the theory. Why? It's possible this creature could be a type of Australopithecus man, and if that's the case, it really hurts evolution. (That's not to say if they are this creatures it eliminates them as genetic manipulations, it only shows this has gone on for a while.)

But if you're a scoffer of their existence, take a look at who has seen them, or their evidence.

Jose Mariano Mozino in 1782 wrote of the natives unbelievable fear of the creatures. (So maybe two types exist here, fearsome and just nuisances) David Thompson in 1811 wrote about the Rocky Mountain Indian's belief in the creature on Jan 5th and two days later wrote about seeing its tracks, noting specifically they were *not* bear tracks. Theodore Roosevelt though not a witness to them, was convinced his friend Baumann saw such a creature that killed his hunting partner in a frightening manner. He was an experienced trapper and clearly saw the attacker was something very heavy that walked on two feet.

In 1884 the local newspaper 'Colonist' printed a telegraph regarding one that was captured (descriptions lead me to conclude it was a young one not reaching its full size at the time of its capture) It would seem the creature still managed to escape when on a train because it was never exhibited as it's captors intended.

Albert Ostman insists he was captured by one in 1924 and taken to a family of four of them, apparently for both mating games and a food source, but his wits kept the creatures interest distracted long enough to escape.

If that seems unlikely, apparently one was domesticated near the town of Ochamchire on the Black sea. The female named Zana was captured when quite young by some hunters in the late 1800's. At first she was chained, but becoming accustomed to her keepers and the free meal ticket, she became a house servant, who could understand instructions though she could not speak. She became a mother by several human fathers, and her descendants were traced, all of which had unusual body strength, and it's thought she may have been a half breed herself. To have descendants clearly indicates some human genetics, otherwise they wouldn't be able to have grandkids.

But she was not the only captive. During WW II one was known of and captured in the Caucasus (somewhere between the Black and Caspian Sea). It was captured to be sure it wasn't some sort of enemy in a monkey suit. When national security is on the line there was no hesitation to hunt the creature and capture it. It was examined and determined to be completely real, wild, and animal in nature, and not a saboteur in disguise. It was 180 centimeters tall, and made inarticulate sounds. Once it was determined to be a creature of some sort and not a man, it was just let go. All evidences closely examined come to the conclusion that it is "absolutely non-typical of man".

PRACTICAL JOKES?

Some types of creatures persist through time and appear to be normal inhabitants of the earth though no biologist has successfully found and classified them, simply because they are very few in number and die and temporarily become extinct on the surface until the UFO's drop off more or similar examples.

There may also be one time mistakes or laboratory freaks they leave here, possibly just for fun to confuse us, like some practical joke. "Oh look at that cube shaped spiny thing we made...we can't use this. Let's have some fun and take it to the surface, and watch them scream at this one." I copy this next sentence from Adam 900 to show what I refer to.

"In 1878 an incredibly frightening creature was obtained and led through London. It was about 2 feet long, two feet high, described as a "living cube". It had hair like wire, It had a head and a tail like a boar, but it's eyes were said to be "satanic". It had no abdomen, and its hind feet were unusually close to it's front feet. It was so disturbing it caused a panic and many accidents and the owner was told to get rid of it in no uncertain terms! It had been originally found in the Pyrenees in southern France."

No other creature like this appears to be noted anywhere else. If this was a UFO practical joke, the UFO pilots may simply have been in the crowd watching the fun. This of course is just speculation but I know of no other creature like this that has been seen before or since, and we certainly did not have the genetic know-how back then to make such a creature.

In Ramsgate Kent two unknown creatures have surfaced over the years. In July 1951 there was seen a creature with the head of a cat, hedgehog like spikes and a tail like a rat. Also in April 16 1954 in this same area was seen a creature with a long snout, short tail and claws. This creature, which was as big as an

Alsatian, was spotted by a Police constable S. Bishop and was described as a "walking fir-cone". (Book 47 pg. 95 96.) Has someone been yanking our chain?

TOWER OF BABEL

Allow me to think out loud here. If we presume the pre-flood people made a giant moonlike space traveling craft it likely still exists. We will shortly see that it does. After the flood, they came down to earth to live back on earth and helped the Sumerians with their science and rebuilding civilization. Maybe the Sumerians didn't know how to use the pyramids or they were temporarily inoperable, and the pre-flood people from the manmade planetoid fixed them and showed them how to use the things. Being oblivious of the dangers they caused the continents to come into existence.

The thought occurred to me that maybe it was the people from this manmade planet that came down to see what this tower of Babel could be. But it seems the bible is very specific in this matter and says GOD came down and saw the structure and confused their language... there is simply no other possibility here. God stopped this project, because if they completed it then they would be able to do anything.

With man's knowledge of good and evil, it seems some sort of incredible power was possible with this tower. They said this tower would make a name for them and stop people from scattering all over the earth. So it is a huge mystery what the Sumerians were building that could make a name (shem) for the Sumerians.

Earlier I wondered if the term "renown" used as a description of the giants before the flood was similar to this term "name" that the Sumerians wanted for themselves. So I decided to look up the two words. They are the same word in Hebrew! The giants were men of renown meaning they were famous, so this tower would have had the same impact on the people of the earth.

...BAKED BRICKS???

Curiously all they were building was a tower out of baked bricks and mortar, whose top could reach unto heaven. The building of the tower would somehow cause them to be able to do anything, be famous and stop mankind from drifting further apart. How? What's the big deal? All they were building was a tower made of baked bricks! Yet this tower of baked bricks and mortar caused God to intervene. Why?! Are we missing something or what! Is there some mysterious nature in baked bricks and mortar when arranged in a ...what? ziggurat or pyramidic shape that just causes man to have great power and causes other men to just stick around? No. Well not that I know of. People aren't flocking to Mexico or Egypt because of these pyramids or Ziggurats. Well OK maybe a bazillion tourists are going to these places, but they aren't staying. What's going on here? The answer probably has to lie in the top that can reach unto heaven that would allow them to do anything. But what could that be?

CLUES IN OTHER PLACES

Something referred to as the "pyramid texts" interprets the pyramids as a ramp to the sky, so that man can go to the sky. (book 11 pg. 110) Anthropologists just assume this meant they could get closer to the sky, but if that was all they wanted to do, they could just as easily have climbed a mountain, and a taller one at that. These ziggurats had a purpose we haven't grasped that is so incredible that they could do anything and it was to make a name for themselves, whatever that means. We all have names, even God has a name, but how could a name for themselves be so important and keep all mankind centrally localized. The term "a name to be reckoned with" comes to mind here.

A pyramid shape is similar to magnetite crystals. Is there something in that shape that assists in antigravity? But they were using the pyramids for this, so that can't be the complete answer.

Mount Shasta appears to have some unusual effects on the air above it causing strange formations of clouds. It even creates its own weather patterns. Interestingly though I only thought of Mount Shasta in regards to this interesting phenomena about its weather, oddly there turns out to be a group of people that live on this mountain that claim to be descendants of survivors from a lost continent, and they say they are visited by silver space ships. Furthermore they say the mountain has tunnels that link to the underworld. (book 23 pg. 57-58)

Does some similar effect happen when a geometric ziggurat is built, or is Mount Shasta just a peculiar magnetic anomalous area on the earth? Does this have something to do with Ziggurats and Pyramids?

We deduce the ancients saw natural phenomena and honed and mastered them. The pyramids are known to do strange things with cosmic rays, and antigravity is linked with them. Maybe anything of huge proportions that has to do with antigravity has to be built on top of the "tower" like some sort of antigravity focuser that infuses this power into what is built on top. OK that sounds lame but it might only focus this energy, so that whatever is built on top or lands on top can tap into and harness this power...such as another moon shaped planetoid, or possibly your average UFO.

The pyramids were known to have crystals on the apex...man made crystals at that! Were crystals going to be used here as well for a different function than the pyramids? My guess is this Tower of Babel was the beginnings of another space planetoid that could reach into heaven, and the ziggurat shape somehow aids in this function, a place where one could land and take off, and maybe God wanted to stop a repeat of the planet exploding thing, especially with a more belligerent human at the helm.

There is evidence that strongly points to man having nuclear war on earth after the flood, as shown in a previous chapter. There are a few points on earth where the only explanation for what is found there could have occurred from a nuclear bomb, and they appear to all be POST flood, after man learned war. With man apparently even more belligerent after the flood and already a bit more dull witted, this could have spelled disaster for the earth were we to once again make another 'blue moon'. (We'll get into what this "blue moon" is shortly)

This deduction is somewhat speculative and I don't know if making another site for an off earth roaming planetoid to land would in itself be enough to keep people rooted to the neighborhood. But if it was a place where you could take off from earth to visit the 'gods' of the Sumerians... these moon 'gods', maybe they would want to go up to see them in just the same way as they were coming down to see us... and it might have been a powerful reason for people to stay in the neighborhood. I repeat a previous bit here. This might be why God stopped the tower. ...

TERRA OR TERROR FORMING THE PLANETS

My guess is the Sumerians were trying to equal the Sumerian gods with a blue moon of their own with the same capabilities, and somehow a ziggurat is linked to this capacity. This would mean such huge spherical ships needed these towers to safely land on earth and ascend to heaven. If this is even close to correct with mans devolved and more belligerent nature after the flood, this power in their hands means they could have used the power to destroy a planet... onto the earth itself. They could have done anything. Ancient India texts speak of a person named Phaeton that drove a chariot of the sun and was about to set the world on fire when he was smitten by the "Supreme God" and was cast down to earth. (Book 41 pg. 233)

Boy with this power, were they to do such a thing, they could force people to do their bidding or they would destroy the earth, or at least the place where the disobedient resided. They would have made for themselves a name to be reckoned with. One then might ask the question why wouldn't the other blue moon people do the same thing and why were they not stopped. Simple... because with their pre-flood nature still intact they were calmer and saner people, and since this original large manmade moon was built before the 5th planet was destroyed this scenario might not have been assumed to have occurred. But then one might ask if they were so sane and calm, why did they destroy the fifth planet? My guess is that the 5th planet was inhabitable...and thus inhabited by a colony from earth. Boy is this getting whacko or what!?

But one bizarre conclusion just seems to lead to the next. We have often thought of terraforming Mars and Venus to make them inhabitable.

NINE PLANETS TO LIVE ON?

People have suggested that massive amounts of blue algae dumped into the Venusian atmosphere could consume the carbon in the carbon dioxide in the atmosphere and increase the oxygen content, thus reducing the temperature and cause rain to fall in massive proportions similar to the flood, but on Venus and make the planet, with a bit more work, inhabitable. This might be entirely feasible!

Maybe all these planets we have are potentially inhabitable with the correct terraforming procedures. Maybe this was all originally part of the original creation plan! For man to subdue the earth and eventually the others. I mean consider it. If we were meant to live forever, then eventually this earth would be over populated the entire solar system would have been there for us to inhabit! We would terraform each planet as the populations grew. This fifth planet may have been the easiest to do and it was done and colonized first.

As we have deduced the earth was originally completely enveloped in a water shell. Maybe the earth looked like Neptune and Uranus at one time. (Oh no!!! ...Neptune and Uranus are possibly terrformed planets and are possibly inhabited?...don't go there!...this is already strange enough!)

People have talked about colonies on Mars tapping into the poles and underground for water sources and also breaking the water up by electrolysis to get oxygen. No doubt the pre-flood people thought this too, but with one difference. They did it, or that fifth planet was already inhabitable in the first place. If this is the case then they inhabited it… but with who? Who would want to live on a planet not earth. Ok maybe lots of people would, I don't know. With their capabilities it might have been considered a fun thing to do like we might rough it camping in the woods or like the pioneers going west, they might rough it on a new planet. Today some corporations are working to get to Mars with a one way trip. With no possible way back to earth, people are still lining up to go!

ALTERNATE REALITIES

Some bizarre ideas come to mind. For example how long did Adam and Eve live before they ate of the tree? Did they have kids before that event? This is PURELY speculation. But remember God brought all the animals to Adam to see what he would name them. How long did this take? Remember he's likely naming as many as 30 million species. This is no afternoon project. Though this might be considered to have occurred before woman was made and likely was, there is some apparent overlapping in the creation timeline. Perhaps Adam and Eve had a kid before the fall. OK I'm not really suggesting this, but this is more of a "what if"? I have found a surprising number of people that actually think this or other scenarios are a possibility!

We seem to think that because Adam and Eve had the fruit that this was the only eventual outcome that would have happened. But since we were made with a free will, any number of things could have happened. What if only one of them had eaten the fruit? or if neither did but some of their kids did? Some have even suggested since man was originally made alone, that is without women, maybe originally we were meant to multiply in a different way. Maybe like some creatures we were initially created to reproduce asexually. Maybe this happened before Eve was made or maybe they had a couple kids before they ate of the tree and there were two types of man living on earth. Fallen man and unfallen man.

There is no reason to believe this in the least, so again I'm sort of just coming up with a "what if" scenario for fun. I think these are in essence all possible outcomes that had to be considered before anything actually was created. I would guess that God knew the possibilities, but with the "mystery of iniquity", as to when it happened it might have not been a sure thing that the first humans would eat the forbidden fruit.

People are sometimes fatalistic and tend to think what happened was all that could have happened that is it was "fated", but conversely we must remember that "time and chance happen to all men" and "all things work together for good..." no matter what had happened God would have worked with that scenario. He created the angels first and who knows how long heaven existed before Satan went off the deep end. He was originally an angel part of creation. Conceivably generations could have gone by without anyone eating the fruit. I mean if the serpent hadn't tempted Eve, maybe no one ever would have eaten of that fruit. Some suggest the tree was put there to tempt man, but remember God walked with Adam and was Adams friend. He planned on being here a lot and made a tree for himself to eat. After all God put the tree of life here and it was meant for man to eat in his original state. Clearly eternity was an option and possibility!

All interesting points and scenarios. Perhaps most would agree there really was no other possibility. But the reason I think other possibilities could have occurred is maybe with free will Adam and Eve never would have eaten the fruit. Or what if Adam had eaten from the tree of life first!? Living forever in a state of falleness. Terrible. Maybe this occurred with Satan, and so he is in his state forever. So stopping a sort of repeat, God guards the tree of life to prevent man living forever in this state. After all eternal life for humans might originally have been in the plans. But since the Fall it no longer became an option and flesh and blood shall no longer live forever.

Often people wonder what would have happened in any such scenario. We often speculate what the earth would be like if Adam never ate of the fruit but some of his children did. A whole new parallel history would have occurred, with a completely separate set of events. There would have been two types of men on earth, fallen and unfallen. Maybe as time went on the fallen man and the unfallen man decided to live on their own planets and fallen man got jealous and just wasted them. There is of course no reason to suspect anything like these scenarios ever occurred and it actually seems too farfetched to me, and unfallen men would not have died and been able to compensate whereas man in a fallen state would be easy prey and subject to death. What a situation that would have been. But speculation on all these scenarios does bring to mind one scenario that makes more sense. A clue to a more plausible scenario for the reason of them blowing up the fifth planet is in the bible.

WHY WAS THE FIFTH PLANET DESTROYED?

As we know, "sons of God" (presumably angels) came to earth before the flood to take women as wives because they were beautiful. As a result there were giants in the earth from the angels coming to earth and marrying the women. (As mentioned before it's entirely possible that giants were genetic manipulations and not offspring of the angels and women. But it's just as possible they were, so we will continue on as though they were.)

It would seem that as they populated the earth these giants {Nephil} offspring became "men of renown", and started to cause friction amongst normal men here. The Nephil appear to be linked with the extensive evil and wickedness occurring on earth before the flood, and that may have been a focal point of friction and tension. Remember the angels knew God face to face, and the men originally knew God, and this original knowledge of God would have been a pacifying element in their nature. But these Nephil possibly never met God, and were the result of mixing of genes which possibly meant a more volatile disposition. It appears their very "giant" stature made them think of themselves as better than normal men and the term Nephil also indicates they were bullies or tyrants. Also they were "...mighty men which were of old..."(Gen. 6:4) which appears to indicate they lived a long time, longer than men...and that stands to reason as they were the offspring of angels which were eternal, and indeed the word "old" used here can be used to mean eternal.

With the likening of a thousand years to a day for God, and man dying inside 1000 years, this could mean man was dying inside one day when compared to God. And God did say in that day they would surely die if they ate of the fruit. So all these Nephil 'men of old' had to do was live for more than 1000 years and they would be men of "old" or eternal compared to men. If this deduction is correct this means the angels came to earth well over 1000 years before the flood, or within a few hundred years after creation. So they likely dwelt with us for a long time.

Realizing this boggled my mind. I had always assumed that these sons of God came to the earth just prior to the flood and things went downhill in a hurry. But if they lived here for well over a thousand years this was virtually the norm on the earth. Men, Angels and Nephil all living together here for most of the pre-flood era!

The Nephil were also "men of renown" suggesting they were leaders and may have led mankind to ruin. Friction between the races may have started divisions and they separated themselves, with them and their wives going to the new planet and man staying here. Something of a friction escalated, and interplanetary war, if it could be called a war in the traditional sense, ensued and man somehow won, but at the expense of the fifth planet and the subsequent flood. There were countless legends of wars in heaven. I've clued into a reason for some of these wars during this third edition.

Often these angels that came to earth to take the daughters of men are referred to as fallen angels, but this may not necessarily be the case. There's nothing says that angels taking wives from the sons of men was even forbidden. We know that is no longer an option for them as it clearly says angels wont marry. Since men originally married their sisters but later on this was disallowed for the sake of the children, due to genetic disintegration. God may have told the angels "no more", or the angels may have decided amongst themselves this was the wisest course after witnessing the fiasco before the flood. Angels marrying the daughter of men may have originally even been part of the big picture. After all, birthrates of women tend to be slightly more numerous than men. If man was meant to not only inhabit the earth but eventually colonize the rest of the solar system, such marriages may have never been meant to be out of the picture, but indeed part of the plan, or one of the options. It was this mistake of doing something God said not to do, eating from God's fruit tree, that put the fly in the ointment. What a fly too. What a fascinating world it might have been.

As soon as the angels took wives of the sons of men the Lord said "My spirit shall not always strive with man, for that he also is flesh: yet his days shall be an hundred and twenty years." (Genesis 6:5) This life span didn't come into play until well after the flood, so he completely grasped the situation well over 1000 years before it all came tumbling down…no doubt long before Noah's birth.

ANGELS WE HAVE KNOWN.

Man was created a little lower than the angels, not a lot lower like we are now. Pre-flood men likely might have actually have been able to hold a candle to angels at one time. After all they thought our women good enough for them. I mean think of it. Here is a society so superior to ours, angels thought nothing of coming to earth to live with mankind and marrying our women folk. In order for angels to feel comfortable in such a society man himself must have been an exceedingly wondrous specimen.

By way of comparison how many of us would feel comfortable simply choosing to marry with the severely mentally handicapped. We would tire of the lack of intelligent conversation and feel like a fish out of water. The angels were obviously comfortable in the presence of men, and they stayed with us as we deduce for well over 1000 years! So we have to conclude man was indeed fantastic in his original state.

The angels themselves that came down in all likelihood would not even have been a problem in pre-flood society, and they may even have been something of a benefit. With their experiences living with God and seeing him face to face would only have made God seem all the more desirable to men who had not seen God face to face. The angels could have told stories about creation and heaven that would have had men starry eyed for God. But if the angels were not a problem, their kids certainly were.

A VERY WIDE GENERATION GAP

Due to mixing of the angels perfect genes with the fallen death ridden genes of man, and their superior physiology compared to men, things went a little off kilter. With escalating friction on earth between children of men and children of angels and women, a separation may have eventually been deemed necessary. This might have made living on two planets a logical option.

With their advanced ability this was no doubt an easy thing to accomplish. Then continued friction kept occurring, even though the two races were even on different planets. Man may have felt the only way they could end the friction of the children of angels and the children of men was to destroy them, and their planet before they did it to them. It seems entirely plausible the entire reason for the eventual complete breakdown of the human race before the flood was due to these disruptive children of angels. This war might have been inevitable and seemed the only recourse. Maybe this is close, but who knows why they blew up a planet, but this does make some sort sense if we can accept all the other things leading up to that conclusion.

HISTORIES SPEAK OF SOMETHING VERY MUCH LIKE THIS HAPPENING

Some of the authors based on their interpretations of ancient texts have concluded or suggested there was a clash of people on two worlds, so this scenario we've just speculated on may actually be closer to reality than one might think.

However with Mars wandering around interacting with earth who can really decipher all that ancient gobbledygook correctly. Those two warring worlds may not have been earth and Mars, but the blue moon and the fifth planet. Or both scenarios may be correct. Thus written in very similar ancient histories and consequently confused to be the same.

Battles of the planets, and battles of the gods. Jupiter, Mars and Venus seem to run through so much of the ancient stories. Who can decipher it all correctly? I mean with Mars, Venus, the fifth planet and the blue moon, it must be easy to confuse one with the other in ancient texts. One has to compare what was, to what is, to get any logical sense, and even then some confusion will likely continue and some will say it's all speculation.

When I first read others accounts of these planetary wars sometimes I couldn't help but roll my eyes and feel they are stretching their interpretations of the clues to the limit, so I don't really take some of my guess's too seriously either, as after all some of my theories are to some extent based on other researchers clues, and some of these researchers conclusions are controversial to say the least! But it's fun to speculate all the same. However I have to think there just may be something to this. I mean that fifth planet isn't there anymore. It did blow up and it appears to have been done by man, and ancient texts do speak of these wars in heaven, so they have to be based on something that happened and so there had to be a reason. No doubt the people on the blue moon know and probably even the UFO's-nauts know the story as well, so I think it will be known eventually. But the bottom line is, that planet is gone and it was there before. The solar system was created perfect and planets just don't blow up for no reason. We did it, I don't know why, but who else could have? That scenario is simply my best guess.

CONFIRMATION FROM THE MOST UNEXPECTED SOURCES.

Maybe a piece of the fifth planet caused the rings of Saturn. Apparently people who have talked to space "intelligences" say the rings of Saturn are debris of a moon shattered by a comet. (Book 23 pg. 17) So if they know this they likely know why the fifth planet was destroyed and it may be part of their history lesson in school.

An interesting statement does exist that throws some light on this. A man named Orfeo apparently had some conversations with spacemen. Naturally our eyes roll, maybe because spacemen never talked to us, but if this statement is to be believed my deductive guess may be closer then we think. This spaceman said that an Elysian world blasted a planet named "Lucifer" which was situated between Mars and Jupiter. No reason was given for the destruction. (book 47 pg. 34)

WHO MADE IT AND WHO IS LIVING IN IT?

When searching "Elysian" on the internet apparently this Elysian planet is inhabited by angels. Others describe this planet as paradise, similar to Valhalla. This term makes its way into several sources and appears to mean a place of perfection or heaven. If it is a duplicate environment to that of pre-flood earth it is as close to perfection as we know it.

The describing of this Elysian planet as responsible for the destruction of the 5th planet when all things are considered, is indeed a telling story if it to be believed and based on the research and evidence this seems entirely correct.

It would also seem our "blue moon" has a name: Elysia. But it would seem again some confusion exists. We know that angels came to earth before the flood, but people on Elysia are also equated with angels. I suppose, with angels living on earth for more than a thousand years, it is entirely possible this artificial planet was a joint project between men, some Nephil and angels. But as we've seen men from this artificial planet are likely men of pre-flood origin. If these "Elysians" come to earth after the flood similar to how angels came to earth before the flood this would be a source of confusing the two incidences as the same event, or even a continuation of the same event. We've seen in ancient histories that the 'gods' were men and they came down to earth so they weren't angles, they were men.

We have to presume the people on Elysia are in fact men, Or men and possibly some Nephil, because it seems incredibly unlikely that angels would go about destroying planets, and it seems certain that this planet Elysia is the cause of the destruction of that planet.

Also one can presume angels don't need chariots, but even this is up for debate because as we have seen God has thousands of chariots. But they wouldn't need a artificial planetoid to live on, as they would go to where God is. One could argue if God has chariots why can't devils? As we've seen possibly they do, and indeed some of these UFO pilots have been considered hideous unclean creatures so it's entirely possible they stole some of them or owned them all along.

We have to assume angels are with God and presumably God certainly wouldn't need an artificial planetoid to live on either; but then who can say where God chooses to dwell. But clearly the scriptures indicate that God does NOT live with men now because in Revelations 21: 3 notes "behold!" God will dwell with man in the new Jerusalem, strongly suggesting he hasn't before, for example on some manmade moon. Earth is merely his "footstool". I guess all sorts of possibilities exists. After all God hung around Solomon's temple for a long time. Of course with the omnipresent characteristic of God he can be in many places at once. But there seems no reason to believe this planet is where angels and certainly not God actually dwells.

It doesn't seem logical that this Elysian planet, which destroyed the fifth planet would be inhabited by angels at all. Possibly there are nicer Nephil and more wicked Nephil, in partnership with men sympathetic to their causes and leadings. With this artificial planet, the fifth planet and Earth, there could even have been three factions accounting for three moons seen coming to earth like the Drona Parva indicates. So it's really difficult to come up with any logical reasoning that would conclude in the destruction of a planet. But then destroying a planet is anything but logical.

In fact in the light of pre-flood men's, Nephil and angels capabilities this has to be something similar to today's world where the further we get away from God the more easily we are influenced by negative and destructive aspects in society. Anger, hatred, love of money, selfishness and all the other negative traits all lead to mutually destructive actions. So I have to think the pre-flood inhabitants were at this state where logic and reason were overcome by these other negative characteristics we so often display.

We can resist these influences or be led by them. If we resist Satan he will flee from us, but eventually when one gives oneself over to evil continually, resistance no longer becomes an option. "And God saw that the wickedness of man was great in the earth, and that every imagination of the thoughts of his heart was only evil_continually_" (Genesis 6:5)

I have to wonder what happened to the angels living on the earth at the time of the flood. I have to think they were eternal beings, not subject to death as we know it, so they wouldn't die in the flood even if they were caught in it. So where did they go? We can't equate them with devils because devils were here at the time of creation tempting Eve. The angels came later, and they did the right thing by marrying the women. So I have to think they were sad, but went back home with their hat in hand.

I suppose the theory could be put forth that the "Elysian" planet is the place for the angels that came to earth to take the daughters of men. One could argue that they had no place to go. But this doesn't seem to fit, and there's no indication the angels did anything wrong, so why wouldn't they go back to where God was, once the earth was demolished. They may be on a more familiar personal relationship status with the men of Elysia than with us on earth. I'm guessing they changed from the status of "sons of God" to angels (messengers). Since they lived with men and had wives, they may have a more personal interest in how we turn out and chose to be part of things as they occur. This may add some understanding to that scripture where it says we will judge angels. (I Cor. 6:3)

One might even suggest this Elysian planet is the place where fallen angels dwell, that is the unclean spirits that follow Satan, as it is presumed these unclean spirits were at one time angels which were subsequently changed into unclean spirits at some point in time. Maybe they were also living on the earth before the flood. I don't think this fits this Elysian planet either.

INFLUENCES

I guess any document that is going to talk about God and angels is at some point going to talk about devils or demons. These appear to be disembodied spirits that seem to occasionally dwell inside men and animals as influence is followed and control is given to them. As the world before the flood wandered further from Godly influences it was influenced more by the other side. Since angels could come to live here, it's even possible that the devils came in human form, though there's no indication this was the case. On the other hand the serpent is often referred to as the Devil. So maybe they came as animals that talked, after all it doesn't seem like Eve was particularly impressed by a talking serpent.

As the society before the flood became more and more influenced by destructive desires eventually this fifth planet was destroyed, but I have to think it was destroyed by men, or men and Nephil. I don't think angels would do it. God gives Satan permission to temp and try our spiritual fortitude or cause ruination, but his permission when given appears to be in influences over men, such as when God talked to Satan about Job, and God gave Satan power over Jobs stuff. This power or seizure was accomplished by hoards of invaders subject to Satan's influences. (Job 1) Curiously some of this destruction was caused by fire coming down from heaven. How this was accomplished is up for speculation. Curiously we see that this same feat is accomplished by God's servant Elijah (II Kings 1:10-12) and Satan's servant the "second beast". (Rev 13:13). Still these Nephil were people, subject to like desires and whims, and just as important in the whole scheme of things.

Devils in space? When Jesus cast devils out of people they were loath to be cast into the deep...wherever that is. (Luke 8:31) The "deep" could be the abyss, the depths in the sea, the bottomless pit, or possibly someplace off the earth out in space somewhere. One could read this to say they don't want to be sent off the planet, but contrariwise, we see in Revelations a time comes when the devils and his angels are in fact cast down to earth permanently suggesting space or at least "heaven" is temporarily a welcome place to them. (Rev. 12:8)

This also makes one curious. Is the event in Isaiah 34:4 where the hosts of heaven fall to the earth like the leaf and the fruit, the same event spoken of in Revelations 12:8-10 where the devil and his angels are cast down to the earth?

We've seen that the host of heaven likely refers to UFO's. My guess is these are similar events, one a phenomena that causes flight to be impossible for a while, and a spiritual battle in heaven that cast the devils to earth. But if it is a single event talked about twice in two different ways this is a sobering incident to come.

We've often seen the same or similar thing happens over and over like in how we saw the Indian texts speak of a person named Phaeton who drove a chariot of the sun, when he was about to set the world on fire, him being smitten by the "Supreme God" and cast down to earth. This is similar to these scriptures and repeated wars spoken of in heaven in the past. So many things are occurring over and over, one has to be careful in drawing set in stone conclusions in saying they are all the same event.

Also what we need to be aware of, is that some things could be indications of good and or evil. In fact some of the same identical actions could be done to accomplish good or evil depending on the motivation of the individual accomplishing the task. How you ask? Well for example a person could help someone to get in good with them to later take advantage of them, like so many scam artists do, or the same help could be given for the sole purpose of helping the person because they need it and they care about them.

It seems likely to me, if anything in this theory could be considered "likely", that this Elysian planet is built by and for pre-flood men. If they were just men and no Nephil they could escape the negative influences of the Nephil. The men of Elysia are of such a state as to appear like angels to those who have met them. And after all they (we) were created just a little lower than the angels so we now, in our devolved state, might confuse them with angels. It's even possible some of these Nephil still reside among men in the Elysian planet as we see the term "Nephil" is used once more after the flood in regards to the giants in Canaan. They may have been a result of blue moon "Elysian" Nephil mingled with men after the flood again, making a sort of 1/4 angel status type of man. Indeed they would be highly prized individuals as their genes being of an extremely longevity sort would be welcomed into the mix.

Is there more than one artificial planetoid?... there are smaller spherical ones that have been seen. Interesting questions.

If one wants to force it and say only eight souls survived the flood, it does offer a convenient cop out to say the blue moon is inhabited by angels, if this Blue moon still exists and is inhabited. But the evidence keeps pointing to the people on this manmade planet. (or should I say artificial, as possibly Nephil and sons of God helped put it together) Legends of these gods continually, when broken down, indicate they were in fact merely nothing more than physically, genetically and physiologically superior men, thus it would seem again this indicates the people on the "Elysian" planet are nothing more than men. This really is an interesting subject. One could even suggest that if there were two such artificial planets out there one with men and one with Nephil, that maybe there will be another "War in heaven". One could even speculate this is what is spoken of in Revelations chapter 12. I seriously doubt that, as it's pretty clear that the angels cast Satan down to earth.

CASTLES IN THE SKY... THREE OF THEM?

(3rd ed. Insert 2016) Raymond Drake quoting the Drona Parva says "formerly the Valiant Asuras had in heaven three cities. Each of these cities was excellent and large. ...When the three cities came together in the firmament [they] were pierced[(with a] terrible shaft ...consisting of three knots. [the people] were unable to gaze at that shaft inspired with the yuga fire..." (book 34 pg 46)I don't know if the three cities in the sky were destroyed or if they still exist. It sounds like when these inter planetary craft came to earth's atmosphere together huge bright bolts of lightning were shot out at each other, probably electrical discharges. My point being, if these cities didn't exist, what would make the recorders of the Drona Parva come up with descriptions of electrical discharges? (...assuming I'm reading that bit correctly)...as I think that is exactly what could happen. If these three "cities' were of a spherical type, like artificial moons this could indicate there's more than one. I've stumbled on Richard Hoagland and some of his theories a few times in Atlantis Rising magazine and consequently listened to some of his theories on line. He seems to think there was more than one artificial moon and one of Saturns moon Iapetus is one of them. He also thinks the people with this technology actually may even have moved some moons around the solar system.

BACK TO THE TOWER OF BABEL

With the Sumerian tongue no longer spoken, the people on the Blue Moon might have come back to earth after the tower of Babel incident only to find they could no longer converse with men, and they may have stopped coming to earth altogether, only to be spoken of in legends. Men might also have become exceedingly barbaric by this time in comparison to the "Elysians" and further direct contact was out of the question.

With men becoming simpler and tending to adore them, they felt out of their element and returned to the stars awaiting the day when the earth would be restored. With the confused languages at the Tower of Babel, creating the second 'blue moon' became an impossibility. The Elysians may have taken the time to learn the languages, but with their vast intelligence this might have been an overnight stay. In fact since all languages stem from Sumerian and these "Elysians" likely still speak the original tongue, they might automatically understand all the languages. Anyway at some point they left and likely haven't been seen in person by men on earth since.

THEIRS IS BLUE TOO.

(3rd ed. Insert 2016) The Hopis speaking of the last Great War say a Blue star (now invisible, [too far from earth to see]) will appear. Could they also be talking about Elysia? (Book 35 page 214)

Back to the age old question "what's in a name?" or "Shem". Zachariah Sitchen describes a shem as a rounded conical item and shows a coin of Byblos (Gebal) in Lebanon, with a "shem" at the top of many stairs. (book 17 pg 140, 164) I have not been able to find a photograph of the actual coin but have found a few different drawings of the coin, drawings which don't match each other exactly. **(See Drawing 18** I've focused on part of the coin for this illustration. The coin appears to show the roof at an angle as though it could rise, lower or rotate similar to an observatory. But this might be a poor perspective meant to show the top and the side in one projection. I might be wrong, but it could have looked like the drawing to the right)

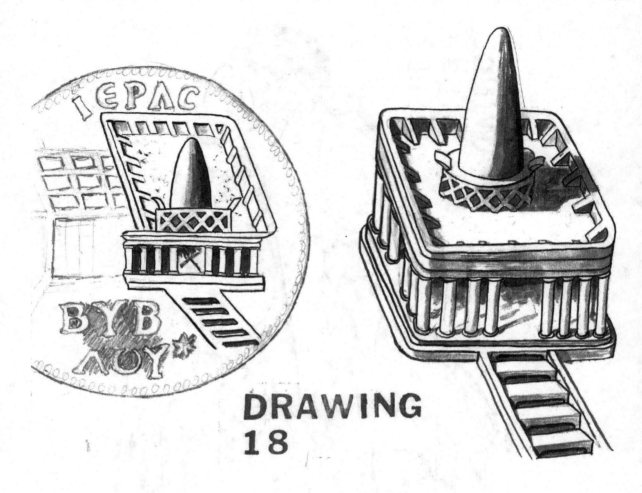

DRAWING 18

Whether or not this coin even has anything to do with what a "shem" is, is up for debate. Shem means "name" or "renown" that is 'famous', so what that has to do with a cone at the top of stairs is anybody's guess. However the fact that these conical structures are at the top of many stairs does suggest they are at the top of Ziggurats, exactly what the Sumerians appear to have been building to get to heaven. Furthermore it was the top which was to reach up to heaven, right where these conical items were placed, so there may be a connection.

Interestingly another ancient conical item is seen apparently at the top of many stairs. In a rock carving called the "Stelle of Naram Sin" are seen two suns, one in the sky and one on the tip of a conical tower similar to what Sitchen calls a "shem". People appear to be climbing many stairs to get to the base of this cone. Seeing two suns on the stelle, is reminiscent of ancient UFOs which appear like two suns in the sky, and this stelle shows one sitting on this conical item at the top of what also might be another ziggurat. Admittedly the stele doesn't really look like they are on a Ziggurat, but it does very much give the impression they are climbing toward a man made conical object, extremely similar to the conical object of the coin mentioned earlier. **(See drawing 19)** This item has many interesting features, but I focus mainly on the conical item.

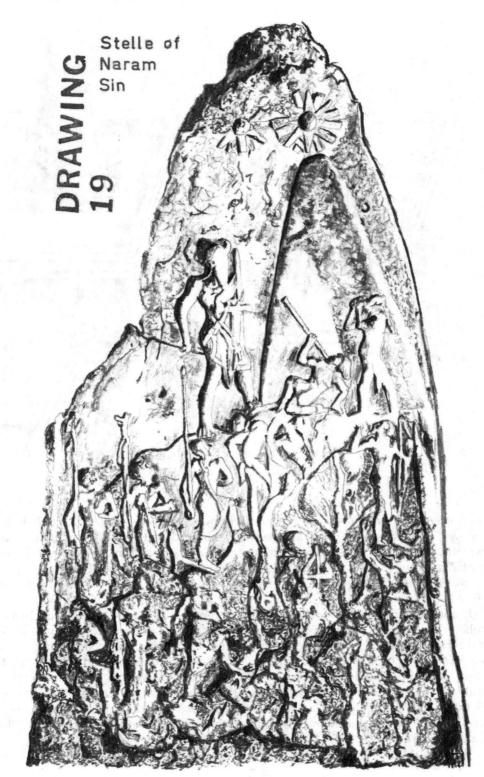

DRAWING
19

Stelle of
Naram
Sin

Oddly this one appears to depict two cones one (smaller) in front of the other. Curiously these ziggurats were called "stairways to heaven" (book 17 pg. 16) The cone in the coin appears to have a removable roof. Though the stelle appears to be incomplete there doesn't seem to be any such superstructure around the cone depicted on it, and in fact there are a couple trees depicted on the stelle, so it probably isn't on a Ziggurat. Still this rounded cone seen on both these ancient artifacts is very curious and may be a good clue. (Richard Hoagland, has suggested some movies like Star Wars show true ancient history disguised as fiction. One Doctor Who movie shows a flying craft with a doughnut shaped landing area coming off one of these shems as seen in these last two drawings. I wonder....

TALKING IN CIRCLES

We will seemingly talk in circles for a while (as if I haven't been doing that so far) simply to slowly show some of the problems we find in what is thought to be understood. But a picture and some clues will come out of all this so bear with me....hopefully I can find my way out of the loop.

These people after the flood were presumably what are now called the Sumerians. They all spoke the same language. Looking at ancient Sumerians just mystifies historians. They knew so much and they just popped out of nowhere and built stuff that stymies modern men and engineers. Well naturally this would happen and why not?! Think about it. After the flood, what remained on the earth? NOT MUCH! Something has to "pop" out of nowhere because they have to start all over. It's this assumption of evolution that is the reason for this mystification that stumps so many archeologists and the like. They ask how can something pop out of nowhere if man was on the earth for millions of years evolving to this point. So to them it is a mystery, but when you accept the ancient text it makes perfect sense.

They started at the top of the scale and cave men came after the destruction which occurred afterwards, such as the flood, Peleg, loss of atmosphere and such. To the evolutionary archaeologist cave men had to occur long before Sumerians, but that was before the flood when they were even more advanced. So cave men had to occur long after Sumeria and the flood, meaning they didn't happen very long ago and their dating techniques are shown again to be flawed. This once again makes perfect sense.

After the Peleg disasters, (man couldn't build with the pyramids like they used to) the gods left and so men submerged, succumbed and declined into simple folk or even savages living off the land. The dinosaurs likely all perished in the last major Peleg type disaster, likely around the Exodus, so few if any "cave men" were able to bag the dinosaurs for breakfast, thus no dinosaur relics are seen with cave men, though we've seen Saber-toothed tigers were with "cave men". But I digress

The degree of this advancement immediately after the flood also speak of the advanced nature of men at this point in time. No doubt if the pyramids were built before the flood, Noah and sons would have known what they were for and probably understood how to use them. The ancient Egyptians knew of the Sumerians and that they were highly advanced, and it would appear that to the ancient Egyptians the pyramids were old even to them. They are certainly hardy enough to have survived the flood even the flood as previously described. Since it is known that the pyramids originally had crystals capping them, clearly they were intact after the flood if they were not built then. The fact that these crystals are known about shows they likely existed after the flood because so precious little is known about pre-flood structures. It's doubtful if they had crystal caps before the flood, and they came off, that we would know this small detail about them, so the crystals had to be there after the flood, and this means the pyramids were in working order after the flood. Consequently they caused the continents to come into being which as we've seen had to have occurred after the flood.

One has to wonder just how much pre-flood architecture still exists. There are enigmatic structures all over the world that are just a mystery as to how they were even built. Knowing that the earth only had 101 years after the flood before the first "Peleg" certainly strains credibility to think the Sumerians could have spread out across the earth as much as these structures around the globe suggests. Though this is not by any means impossible with the technology at their disposal, population is a problem. It's just how many people were there in the earth 101 years after the flood and how far would they have dispersed? We've seen there were a million wooly mammoths to be destroyed to make the bone yards that exist today, showing again this first Peleg didn't destroy everything. We have seen that the first Peleg didn't complete the spread of the continents, so at what point does the tower of Babel come into play?

The reason I say this is because it is known that many structures and civilizations were in an incredible state of advancement all around the earth, but construction stops on many of them abruptly and presumable simultaneously. Plotting a few ancient megalithic spots on any map shows these were spread out across the earth, meaning there existed a global organization and building capability so the cause of its sudden collapse had to be huge, virtually on a global scale.

The question I've not been able to ascertain is whether the tower of Babel was built before Peleg or after. This may be a big question which could affect the theories presented here because of this at present indecipherable problem.

Some evidence does suggest that confusion of language occurred away from the site of Babel as well as at the site dividing further what was already divided. For example, if I remember correctly, a central American legend speaks of this confusing of languages regarding a local tower. Could the event have occurred on the earth at two places at once? That seems unlikely, but it might have happened in Sumer at the same time someone else was building another tower somewhere else and confusion of tongues in America was thought to be because of the tower they were building not realizing it happened because of another tower.

Some creationists tend to see the Peleg and tower of Babel as the same event. However the tower of Babel incident had to of occurred after Peleg but the number of advanced city's around the earth throws this guess into question, unless some of them are pre-flood structures as well. But then why weren't they finished and not covered in clay? Did the flood stop construction? Well no doubt it did stop some construction somewhere, but many if not all of these ancient cities do not shows signs of the Noah flood on top of them (clay) and only show the Peleg type of flood overtop, or they are not even covered, suggesting many were built after the flood. But many of these structures appear to be far away from the center of civilization as it started in Sumer. This also supports the idea that building of the cyclopean structures was going on after the initial 'Peleg'. Possibly they were built before Babel and when the earth was still in one piece and Babel was instigated to stop further divisions of people. That or the pyramids were still intact after Babel!

Why this is a problem is because one of the Peleg's, like the flood, stopped construction all around the earth in its tracks. No more building occurred using gigantic blocks of stone after the crystals capping the pyramids were destroyed. This was because they caused the separating the continents in such destructive fashion; stopping the building of the megalithic structures, and thus the decision to destroy the crystals. The order these things occurred can be deduced and then approximate dates attributed to each event.

The tower of Babel was meant as a reason to keep or lure all of mankind into a single area...something of great importance to man then. This conundrum very much suggests the tower of Babel occurred quite some time after the flood, and indeed the Sumerians have by some accounts continued on for as long as 1500 years. But this lengthy existence of the Sumerians seems incorrect because the Egyptians looked back on the Sumerians, and do not appear to consider them contemporaries. But if the Egyptians started 3100 BC as conventional dating puts them, then once again we see more problems in the timeline discussed in a previous chapter. We also see that Sumerian evidence is limited to a very small area and it is not spread out all over the world. Also if they survived to about 2000 BC they would have overlapped the Egyptians for centuries. Sumerian is the mother tongue from which all languages came, and Egyptian is a language that also stemmed from Sumerian. So they could not overlap because after the tower of Babel, Sumerian as a language ceased to exists, though the actual people continued on, in whatever form of language they took on. So the tower of Babel instigated the change which had to happen before the Egyptians came into existence. So the tower incident had to happen within 300 years of the flood. But by all clues, at least as I see them, the pyramid crystals had to have been destroyed before the Egyptians came to be as we know them. So although it seems the pyramids may have created the continents, they may have only been mildly destructive compared to the time of the exodus which caused all the extinctions likely caused by meteors hitting the earth and possible Mars and Venus dancing the jig with the earth.

WHAT WAS THE TOWER?

What exactly the tower was they were building has mystified many. Certainly these Sumerians were not stupid people to think they could build a tower to the heavens. Evolutionary thought would gladly allow that they were moronic enough to build a tower to the skies. Some misunderstanding in translation and description seems to be in place here. It's been speculated that this tower was a space station as how else could you get to, or reach the heavens? If it was a space station I'm not entirely sure how a space station would keep people localized. We haven't all migrated to Cape Canaveral have we? However there is a strange clue.

The Sumerians apparently worshipped moon gods. But this too seems bizarre. These were not morons. Sumerian drawings and sculpture depict Sumerians with BIG blue eyes shaped like moons...blue moons, and it's known they worshipped moon gods. How lame is that? Or are we missing something really wild! Nimrod by some accounts is the person responsible for building the tower. He was smart enough to build Babylon and Nineveh,(book 41) surely he knew one can't build a tower to heaven, and if he thought he could, why start in the plain of Shinar and not on top of a mountain? If Nimrod was involved, this also speaks of an early start to the tower...sometime before 300 years after the flood. That's assuming Nimrod IS responsible for starting Babylon AND Nineveh.

In the biblical narrative "tower" means tall building and could also be used to describe a pyramidal bed of flowers, suggesting this tower of Babel was a pyramid, and indeed there is a pyramid in the plain of Shinar made of brick. This pyramid seems like something of a Ziggurat. How is a brick buildings going to reach unto heaven, especially when you know the area of the base will limit the height of the tower, meaning the top is going to be at a finite and predetermined spot? Certainly the Sumerians knew their geometry.

Interesting the narrative gives a clue, saying the top may reach unto heaven. Some have suggested this was for a transmission tower, to contact people in heaven. (Book 38 pg. 108) All Ziggurats seem to have no peak, but are flat on top, like something is going to be there or was there. Apparently the Indian book Ramayana speaks of flying machines in the shape of pyramids, (book 10 pg 145 quoting his obviously complete copy of this ancient text) yet other ancient descriptions of flying machines appear to resemble the modern UFO's. Possibly this pyramid shaped flying machine, is a mix up, intended to mean they are associated with pyramids.

There is room at the top of the ziggurats for one to fit on, and it would seem nowhere else is there any indication flying machines looked like pyramids, unless some were actually triangular, and I suppose that is a possibility. Once again when we look at some of the clues we see that at the top of what might be pyramids or ziggurats are cones and a sun (UFO) on top of the cone. Furthermore something at the tops of these ziggurats, possibly these cones where these UFO's seem to be associated with, were likely able to fly to heaven. My guess is somehow these ziggurats make it possible or easier for these UFO's, which utilize earth powers to fly, to land and take off. I suppose it's even possible these cones are the crystals known to be on the top of pyramids.

Since UFOs appear to utilize electromagnetic forces and follow power lines today, these pyramids, shaped like magnetite, which have some peculiar cosmic forces associated with them, suggests there is likely a connection. And this might also work for spherical craft like the blue moon. Since there's no reason to think the ancient strung power lines all over the place, these ziggurats may have been used instead... though admittedly it does seem like something of a large and somewhat primitive structure to make for the sole purpose of landing Vimanas. But they may be very important for a blue moon, though I can't imagine why, unless a ziggurat somehow focuses earth energy in a way we don't understand.

The answer to what this 'tower of Babel' was still appears to be linked to the heavens, and quite possibly to these "Moon gods", since we have to equate the first people after the flood as the single tongued Sumerians who were intimately acquainted with these moon gods. So it stands to reason they may have been trying to duplicate something the gods could do.

One thing that also seems mysterious in all this, is what the Sumerians say about their gods. They say that all the Sumerian's goodness and what they have made they owe to their gods. Yet this is not a religious statement but it appears quite clear that they actually had physical help from them to make their marvels. Indeed some actual buildings are attributed to the gods making them. But since this is the dawn of time after the flood the only people on earth were supposed to be themselves...the direct and immediate descendants of Noah, and indeed Noah was still alive even at the time of Abraham...probably long after the Sumerians ceased to exist... at least as Sumerians. The Sumerians are assumed to have disappeared off the face of the planet for some unknown reason. But the answer or reason for their "disappearance" is simple.

The Sumerians never actually disappeared, but the language they spoke became confused, so Sumerian as a language disappeared, but the people that spoke it remained. They even remained in some of the buildings they lived in, which is why the Sumerians appear to have been around as long as 2000 years or more. So when was the language confused? Before or shortly after Peleg? This to my way of understanding is in question.

After this event the people then traversed the globe. The ancient legends around the world that speak of a time when all were one people of one language. This is not just a biblical story, other legends exist to corroborate this scripture. Akkadian, Mayan, Egyptian, Hindu and Buddhists legends speak of a time when all the earth spoke one language which was subsequently confused.

Mexican annals say Wodan (apparently the grandson of Noah) co-operated in the building of a great edifice undertaken to help men reach the skies. This project was interrupted, and each family from then on received a different language. (book 41 pg 134) I mean this is an incredibly valuable extra piece of corroborating historic evidence.

Some say the Sumerian language is not like any other language old or new on earth yet they also say all languages stem from one source. And that source has been identified as the Sumerian language (Book 17 page 418) So one Sumerian would have become an Egyptian, another a Chinese, and another a Assyrian and so on. This explains their "disappearance". Though before this incident all man on earth likely already had the racial characteristics from some previous genetic tinkering. This likely means genetic variation had been a key factor in how each individual after the tower of Babel incident became linguistically altered. The people with the same physical characteristics also ended up with the same language. Then they grouped and migrated together. So instead of the tower halting the dispersion of the people of earth, the tower of Babel served to hasten the dispersion.

WHO HELPED THE SUMERIANS?

As for who was helping the Sumerians and who their gods were, I do not suppose for a second that they were getting demons or angels to help build their houses. And God knows we can build our own stuff, as he created us with mental capacities for even the most primitive folks to be able to at least make grass huts, tents or mud huts. So God himself wasn't helping them build whatever it was they were building and indeed it states that God actually stopped them from building the tower. So who were the gods the Sumerians owed so much to?

It would seem the tower had something to do with the gods in heaven...moon gods. Mind you this is just deduced from what we know about the Sumerians, and we have to conclude that the people building the tower of Babel were indeed Sumerians, as it was from this language that all languages stem from, and it was this incident that caused the Sumerian language to cease to exist.

Now understand that the Sumerians only existed for a short period of time...until the tower of Babel. Though some sources suggest they were around for 1500-2000 years, this seem far too long and some overlapping or continuation of Sumerian and Babylonian cultures may be the reason for this long period attributed to the Sumerians. But it is simply IMPOSSIBLE for the Sumerians to overlap any other language or culture, because all cultures and languages stem from them. Then language was confused at the tower they built.

After this many languages came into play and the same people that were "Sumerians" now become, all other ancient peoples, and so all legends will lead back to that time, which is why there are so many common themes in so many religions and legends. Interestingly after a judgment on earth God is going to "turn the people to a pure language" Zephaniah 2 :9, probably when Christ returns.

Naturally after the tower fiasco there was likely still motivation to keep the tower going and lure people closer together so a fast effort to reunite all people by way of translation would have come into play. There exist tablets showing how the Sumerian language translates into many languages. So they were still clued in enough to be able to decipher what they had written when they were still "Sumerians" even after they no longer spoke the Sumerian language, and indeed were technically no longer Sumerians themselves. (I suppose it's possible the gods made the translations themselves) But the dispersion was already too far established to bring everyone back to finish the tower even after they had deciphered the old tongue into the new languages.

So the problem becomes when did they build the tower, and did the Sumerians build the megaliths seen around the world in that short period of time after the flood, up to the point where languages were confused. Or did the technology to build them still exist after Babel to continue building unexplained structures around the world. Keep in mind there was still much flooding evident when the Sumerian gods descended.

Sorry to warp your brains by repeating the same thing so many ways.

THERE DOES SEEM A LOGICAL ANSWER.

If before the tower but after Peleg, careful time shares of the pyramid power were utilized, the pyramids could have been used safely. However if, because of the confusion of language, incorrect orchestration of the use of the pyramids started to occur, it could have been the cause of one last massive lurch occurring in the continents. All subsequent lurches would have been because of planets and meteors.

CONSTRUCTION BY THE GODS AFTER BABEL AND PELEG?

The reason this all becomes a question is because all around the earth there are cities, buildings and structures that ceased to be built in one instant, and there seem to be only two reasons in history why construction could have halted all around the earth at the same time. One being the flood, and two being Peleg. But my guess is they were still being built AFTER the first Peleg with assistance, suggesting even a third incident caused a sudden halt to construction. So once again it seems deducible that the initial Peleg was just a short start to the drift of the continents. They might have continued building with carefully planned coordination for a while. Then after the tower incident and each group doing what they want with poor communication occurring between the new language groups, suddenly the pyramid grid became wildly over taxed. Then too much work all at once sent the continents flying, ending the pyramid use for good as after this the crystals were then destroyed.

Curiously all these cyclopean structures all around the earth were attributed to the gods making them. So it would seem that someone after the tower incident was continuing the construction. This once again suggest the pyramids were intact after the tower incident. Were the Sumerian gods helping man all around the earth build these other structures. I don't think so. But if they were not built by them, then what other gods made those buildings? This then tends to suggest a second group of gods, different from the Sumerian moon gods was in place.

Thus we see there is another possibility. It is possible that some of these cyclopean structures were being built by people or 'gods' other then the Sumerians with little or no link with them whatsoever. Though some of the 'gods' helped the Sumerians, it's possible some of the other 'gods' went elsewhere on the earth building these cities and at some point causing the second and most cataclysmic Peleg action. So why then would there be two classes of gods… who were the gods? Curiously again ancient histories seem to speak of more than one class of the gods.

A TELLING DEDUCTION: FOLLOW IT CAREFULLY

It would seem that these other gods learned from the gods of the Sumerians. That is man learned from the Sumerian gods and became 'gods' themselves. Here is the clue. If we realize that in the 600 or so years after the flood while man was declining, people of previous [pre-flood] statures were like gods to those of the current status. As the Sumerians learned to do what the moon gods could do, then they became like gods to those who came after them. But reason says they would merely be known as the forefathers. The reason these people appear to be like gods is because they appear out of nowhere in a state better than the current state of man on earth at the time of their arrival. Otherwise they would simply be known as the forefathers: But they often are not considered to be forefathers, but merely 'gods'. So where do they arrive from, and where did they go to sever this link in which they would be known to be simply our forefathers? Something is fishy man.

CALENDARS GIVE A CLUE TO SOME EVENT

Other than the more modern calendars like the current dated one starting with Christ and the Muslim calendar which starts in 622 AD as year one, many calendars start at around 3100 BC. We'll get back to them shortly.

The exception is the Jewish calendar which by my reckoning starts somewhere between 1421/353 years before the flood, depending on what age we decipher is correct. I suspect the start of the Jewish calendar is the date our moon began to move due to asteroids hitting it and moving it out of the night sky, initiating the "month". Or possibly this is the date when the fifth planet was destroyed. And we can see that it was after this point in time that God says the days of man will be 120 years and he tells Noah to build the ark. From this period time seems to have started and this seems to be the time where the Jewish Calendar starts. They say time starts from that point though they don't seem to know what happened at that particular time. And obviously creation took place somewhere between 235-1303 years before their calendar starts. So at what event or point does their calendar start?

In revelations another meteor hits the earth (Rev 8:11)and after it hits it is said that time ceases! (Rev 10:6) Yet we know that the antichrist rules for 7 years after this event (Rev 12) and afterwards Christ rules earth for a thousand years after that. So time as we know it obviously doesn't end, but time based on meteoric judgment destruction does, so it would seem that time is measured by the asteroids, as it is by the asteroids that so much of a cataclysmic nature occurs on earth. So if time appears to end when the last asteroid hits the earth it stands to reason time starts when the asteroids are created. It's by them that the flood occurred and the clock goes backward ten degrees and days stop and on and so on.

I've often looked at the planets as some sort of cosmic clock, and though this is something of an assumption, it appears the asteroids are a time factor. This beginning of this calendar is not to be confused with deciphering as to the length of the year. The year was changing its length right up to about 687 BC or so.

As we have seen the flood happened around 3400 BC, 300 years earlier than the start of so many of these calendars. Why would so many calendars such as Mayan, Indian, Egyptian and such start at about this time?

THOSE OTHER CALENDARS

Dendrochronolgy pretty much nails the flood to a specific date of somewhere around 3408 BC(+ or -). So this starting of so many calendars about 300 years later doesn't seem to be related to the flood or Peleg for that matter. It could be related to the tower of Babel incident but my guess is, these calendar's start when the 'gods' left earth's surface, probably with some sort of promise that they would return, so calendars began counting the years. Note this is also about the time when the Egyptians start and they say they were originally ruled by the gods.

This chronology is obviously up for debate. If tree ring dating is adding still more years than previously thought, (by years with two winters in it) and the flood actually occurs as late as 2342 BC, then this really throws a lot of things out of whack. Consequently my only guess could be pre-flood factors starting all these calendars, which seems highly unlikely. But if this is the case this would mean we would have the earliest date (Jewish) being the destruction of say some moons around Saturn. This started their rings and created some asteroids. The later calendars being started possibly by the subsequent destruction of the fifth planet or by the moon being hit and starting months as we know them. But one account says the moon of Saturn was destroyed by an asteroid, so the 5th planet had to be destroyed before that.

But any starting these calendars before the flood is a stretch even by my theories. Indeed some of the calendars do appear to be linked to the gods leaving…which happened long after the flood, and indeed 'gods' were not even spoken of until after the flood. Possibly different calendars start at different events or disasters but some complete reworking of timelines might be in order.

Clearly with so many calendars being worked back or starting at around 3100 BC means something happened at that point in time to start so many widely dispersed calendars)

Calendars start at some event, but as we can see knowing the event isn't always easy. The French after the revolution briefly started a new calendar making the death of Louis XVI year one. China's calendar current date is 5372 (3366 B.C.) So by my reckoning it starts at 44 years after the flood. I must admit a bit of confusion concerning this date, though I can think of two possibilities. Maybe their gods, the Blue mooners left first figuring out the danger the fastest, and left at this date…but this seems too soon. Or possibly this could be the time, through genetics, the birth of the first person with Asian features. ((2nd ed. Insert 2008) Are there two Chinese Calendars, or have I got this date incorrect? According to Kent Hovind apparently one Chinese calendar starts at 2700 BC with a certain Foo Hai. Similarly he speaks of the Jewish Calendar being three years out from what I figured starting at 350 before my age for the flood.)

India is at 5119 (3113 B.C.) 297 years after the flood and the Mayan calendar is at 5117 (3111 B.C.) or 299 years after the flood. As stated when people worked an Egyptian Calendar based on some clues they came up with the first dynasty starting around 3100 BC. It has also been deduced the first dynasty occurred after the reign of the 'gods'. It all fits.

The similarity of all these dates suggests something started or ended at that approximate time. One has to surmise that some major event occurred at 353 years before the flood (Jewish Calendar) , and about 300 years after the flood (or thereabouts). All these dates mean something and they can't be ignored when calculating the age of the earth, either by biblical or some other standard.

Two possible events could be linked with this commonality of so many calendars beginning at the same time. They may also differ simply because of how the years were calculated. If the year got longer some may have corrected this in different ways. This gives a possible date for the tower of Babel at around 3100 BC. That, or a possible final visit from the 'gods'. One such clue is the end of Krishna's time, which ends at 3101 BC. This appears to be either his death or when he leaves the earth. These calendar's start dates vary a little but I tend to lean toward them starting the last time the gods were in the neighborhood. With the varying starts of calendars it could have something to do with the varying 'gods' last visits. Wherever they came from and wherever they went.

Many geologists have determined some major upheavals occurred around 3100 B.C. My deduction suggest this is when the pyramids were used for the last time and consequently when the gods left the surface of the earth.

SENTIMENTAL DEDUCTIONS.

My guess is the gods heard about and talked to Noah and got prophecies from him regarding earth. Noah lived to 950 years and his lifetime continues well past the time of 3100 BC. So my speculative guess is somewhere around 3100 BC the blue mooners chatted with Noah, then the rest of their friends, left earth but said they would come back, in about 5000 years, this guess would be based on their understanding of things but it could also be a prophecy. It may have been based on prophesies of when God himself would rule the earth and fix things back to a pre-flood environment. But since no man knows the day or the hour of Christ's return neither do they.

Ok I'm being sentimental, by trying to bring Noah into the picture. Who knows what happened. Maybe they never met Noah, but they could have. After all he was the one God got to make the ark and save all of mankind and animals. Who wouldn't want to talk to him!? They sure would have known who he was. I can see the conversation as the gods come back to earth and start to make stuff and then find people still alive on the face of the earth "Hey I thought everyone would have died in that flood... how did you survive?" "Oh, good Old Noah saved us."

I'm of course only speculating they have these prophesies but the blue mooners may have said they were coming back in 5000 years as a guess but we took them to mean exactly so the date December 24 2011 still seems important to many. (remember this doesn't talk about the return of Christ as no man knows the day or the hour) They knew earth was no longer the same and they would die at a young age should they stay. But in the mean time they wander space waiting for the earth to be restored. They keep away from us as they really don't want much contact with surface dwellers at this time. We appear to be pretty barbaric and dull witted compared to them, and intelligent interaction with us is just not possible.

By way of comparison animals became afraid of man after the flood. It has been noticed that animals in the Dead Sea area are more docile. The Dead Sea is the lowest point on the earth in an area where there is another 1300-2000 feet of atmosphere above. If the animals of earth in this area are more docile than in other parts of the earth, that is, above sea level, and they are more belligerent due to reduced atmosphere above them, it seems logical that some sort similar effect is also in place for us.

The 'gods' know that they are men like us, but because of their more intact physiology, men on earth tend to worship them, or consider them gods or angels or something. Legends are full of "gods" that lived in an island in the sky, and it seems that this theory explains the existence of so many legends about gods coming down to earth. These are not to be confused with the angels that came to earth in the pre-flood period and bred with men to create giants, though the stories are incredibly similar and thus they have been confused as the same story. Even stories that are post flood speak of the gods mating with men or women of earth.

Similarly the warring planets and other confusing legends of the past such as who in one ancient legend is the same as whom in another. Apparently some confusion exist, in the same way there are so many differing flood legends; where some refer to the great flood and some refer to a more local flood as a result of the Peleg actions. I've managed to some extent separate these flood legends.

But deciphering who is who from one legend to another such as Osirus, Ra, Nimrod etc. is just too difficult for me to sink my teeth into. I get way too tired too fast trying to slog through any of that stuff. It's just too boring by my way of thinking. Someone more familiar with ancient texts and legends and the people of these legends and such might be able to do this. What I present here may in some way assist in making the particular people easier to define.

But there seem to be two or three classes or types of 'gods' and I have managed to figure them out to some degree...as this seems to be the difference between the classes of the gods.

Those that went back to heaven in the blue moon were the gods of the Sumerians, and those that went to under the earth or under the water to get away from the destructive nature of the sun and the C14 starting to appear in the atmosphere were the other gods, such as those of the Incas.

My guess is people after the flood, direct descendants of Noah, through their interactions with the gods of the Sumerians came to realize the earth was rapidly becoming hostile to longevity. They went underground and underwater to build safe places to live away from the now hostile surface life. Then came back to the surface to help those remaining on the surface. Then they were called home.

CLARIFICATIONS.

Reading this I see some clarifications are needed here. Here's the point of all this dithering and talking in circles: there has to have been two ages of the Gods, not one. We know that the Sumerian god Enki came to the earth and saw that there was much flooding and went to get seeds from the planet he came down on and they had to plant them in the higher ground away from flooded areas. So this is a time right after the flood. Whereas other gods seem to come later, like Thoth, Anubis, Indian and Mayan gods speak different languages and must have come to the earth later and caused the events of 3100 BC, and likely caused the further separation of the continents. This will create two classes of gods. Possibly the Sumerian gods stayed too long and became devolved and then trying to get back to the home star they were contaminated and would have devolved the gene pool, or they left and others figuring out the problem went for a safer place. We'll get back to this.

DOWN UNDER...WAAY UNDER.

(3rd ed. Insert 2016) Zecharia Sitchen deduces that when Enki came to the earth he needed gold and sent a crew to the underworld to get some from there while others searched for it on the surface. (Another example of the underworld being thought of as a place to go.) But what I thought particularly interesting was Sitchen's deduction of what they needed the gold for. "The metal, with its unique properties, was to be sent back home for a vital need, affecting the very survival of life on that planet; as best as we can make out, this vital need could have been for suspending the gold particles in Nibiru's waning atmosphere and thus shield it from critical dissipation." (Book 42 page 78) Based on his other deductions Nibiru appears to be what others call Elysia. Enki comes to the earth from Nibiru shortly after the flood as shown in a firsthand account "When I approached the earth there was much flooding." (book 42 page 77) and the first problem they see is the need for seeds for agriculture so they went to Nibiru to get them. But the earth was still covered with much water so they planted them in the, what are now, mountainous territory. (book 42 page 121) We know the Sumerians are famous for so many different seeds originating from there so this may be part or all of their origin. But if Nibiru is Elysia (the man made planet returning to earth after the flood), then Nibiru's atmosphere is fine, and the deduction could very well be meant for earth's atmosphere instead. (Or possibly Mars?) It makes some sense too as we've already seen with the water canopy collapsing onto the earth. It left our atmosphere to dissipate into space as is known to be happening, thus Enki may have been trying to come up with something that could stop this from happening more pronouncedly on earth, making earth safe to inhabit...that is if you want to live to 900 or so, thus an obvious necessity as they would have surmised the need for it immediately.

So this could well be confirmation that the 'gods' were aware of the problem even if those on earth might not have been. Those on earth would have had the dulling effect of the direct sun putting a 'veil' over the minds of men, so that when the 'gods' came down, they were not seen as equals but as above us. To get out of the sun one of the things Enki created was a "primitive worker". This is interpreted as creating mankind, thus probably the origin of this panspermia or seeding earth with life business. But though Sitchen falls into this same trap, he rightly deduced it as "Genetic manipulation". (book 42 page 104-105)

The gods don't want to be on the earth and its detrimental influences too much, so they make a worker class, and apparently it's a mix of man and ape...Similar to the Egyptian legends of apes helping with their work, and also likely confirming my deductions for Sasquatch origins. Could Neanderthals be included in this group?

Though I noted before that Neanderthals have been deduced to have been a man with rickets it seems more than one Neanderthal has been found and I presume rickets was not in all the examples. It's been noted the bones of Neanderthals were 50% thicker and thus they might have been a much stronger race. Interestingly between 2 and 4% of Europeans DNA is that of Neanderthal, yet no Neanderthals have surfaced in today's European population. Could this 2-4% of DNA have been used to create a worker class of man for the gods with Stronger bones? Though this bit of DNA, is common to Europeans, no genetically fully Neanderthal have arisen, though normal hereditary rules would mean some Neanderthals should surface regularly. The sample size of Europeans these tests were done on was about 25,000 so something is quirky with this result as several Neanderthal should have surfaced in this sample group. But they were all 2-4% Neanderthal, suggesting to me anyway that a snippet was used to create the stronger class of man for work. (See Atlantis Rising #118)

However some legends mention three 'cities in the sky' (3 manmade moons?). Maybe like the 'Death Star' of Star Wars fame, one moon or 'city' was damaged and gold would fix the sky of that manmade planet. Though some think Richard Hoagland is a flake, he's convinced Star Wars is at least partially disguised ancient history of our solar system and the people who did the Star Wars movies had some inside information on pre-flood technology. I have to admit I saw the connection too, and when the start of the movie says a long time ago in a galaxy far away, it really means 'before the flood in our solar system', but didn't want it to look like I was relying on movies for research...I mean, where would *that* lead? Richard Hoagland has studied many pictures of space comparing shots from different times and different angles of the same objects and thinks for example the moon of Saturn, Iapetus, might be such an artificial moon. He strongly suspects or has evidence that the entire solar system is a junk yard of technology scattered throughout the planets and moons of our system. I don't rule this out at all. Man before the flood was a super human genius and they have 1656 years of this technology, we can't even grasp, at their fingertips. I wouldn't rule this possibility out in the least.

THE GODS HAD TO GO SOMEWHERE

The second class of gods, under earth and under water 'gods' might have thought they were just going away for a short time because the surface world was starting to affect them and promised to return when the effect of surface life wore off.

OUR RULER IS FROM WAAAY UP THERE.

(3rd ed insert 2016) Herodotus mentions that they were "indeed" ruled by the gods, sometimes one, sometimes another who lived among them. Almost as if they stayed for a short while, then were replaced so as not to be too affected by the sun. The last one to rule Egypt was Horus. (Herodotus book 2:144) The Egyptians were ruled by the gods, but looked backwards through time on the Sumerians indicating two periods of the gods ruling.

We get a real clue when we look at the Mayan 'god' Quetzacoatal. He helps originate several species of corn and made coloured cotton grow naturally. These coloured cottons have been confirmed as existing in ancient Mayan history. We still haven't come up with cotton that grows in different colours. He was a breeder of many plants. And it would appear man had genetic skills to produce some of the plants he came up with.

Suddenly one day he realized he had to leave. He had tears in his eyes and when he left he was never seen again. He left "prophecies" but they appear to be based on knowledge rather than premonition. For example he said one day people would come from the east with beards. This would be an entirely guessable prophecy if he knew the physical nature of the earth and its inhabitants, though he might not have known when they would come. He then left and went into the sea, and he was never seen again. Where did he go?

Why was he crying? He said he would return and warned of some bad characters that might subvert their ways of life. This is also a clue that man's nature was becoming barbaric, though trainable, through good moral and civilization techniques being followed if taught by people whose physiology wasn't as affected by the surface worlds as others.

Well maybe he knew he wasn't coming back and he seems to have loved these people even as they loved him. Legends seem clear that he even had kids by the Mayans, and even studies of the Mayans shows a strain of a different race is in the line. So why did he leave? He loved these people but had to leave them never to return. It would seem he knew this but also knew there might be a way to return and said he would. It would seem to me that he understood that the earth was no longer the same, and if he stayed his life span would just be very much shortened. Or maybe at first he just thought some sort of build up due to surface life was affecting him in his dealings and in a time of maybe a few years was needed to return to normal. He may have been ordered to leave by his superiors, and my guess is he was not allowed to take his wife and kids with him, because they were genetically compromised. There appear to be several gods on earth at this time and even in the neighborhood with similar stories. Virachoca also had to leave, and said he would come back and never did.

There even seems to have been a time where many civilizations, possibly after the tower of Babel incident, when the 'gods' came to help restart civilization as the earthly inhabitants may have become more aggressive in nature due to the change in earth's environment. Before they left they may have bestowed gifts on the surface dwellers, and indeed this also seems a common thread in many legends. Things like Vril rods and levitation discs are said to be gifts from the 'gods'. Japan has some sort of gift from the gods still kept covered up until the time of their return. No one has seen it for centuries.

It's entirely possible some of their science was left in the hands of some peoples before they left. But some of these items of science eventually became abused in some people's hands, likely to retain power and influence over men. Take the Pharaoh's of Egypt and the men they had around them when Moses came to free the Israelites. As marvelous as the things that Moses did with his staff by the power of God were, the Pharaoh's sorcerers were able to do almost all the same things! Things like turning water into blood and the staff turning into a serpent are astounding abilities that science might be able to accomplish, though how, I'm at a complete loss to even guess. They were able to do all that Moses did except the turning of the ground into lice.

So through time these gifts from the 'gods' almost became as revered as the 'gods' were themselves. Even Moses' items were later idolized by the Israelites. (II kings 18:4) Maybe a world wide effort to help rebuild the earth with the new inhabitants was abandoned when it was concluded this would result in the devolving of the men helping in this project. So they went to a safer environment.

HOW DO YOU GET AWAY FROM THE SUN AND THE AIR?

Quetzacoatle is said to have gone into the sea. Other ancient histories speak of this reign of the gods. It would seem all around the earth they arrived to try and instill a saner approach to life. But it would also appear that the 'gods' themselves were becoming a bit strange apparently using weapons and fighting among themselves. When they realized the earth's new environment was starting to affect them as well, they went back to the pre flood space house "Elysia" or underground and under the sea to get away to a safe environment. They likely thought this was just a temporary affect and they would get back to normal eventually and they would return to the surface world for shorter terms so as to limit any negative effects on them. (Like Herodotus mentions)

They may have figured that a long break from the solar energy coming down to the earth would renew them. But then studies would have made it clear to them that the earth was not just affecting their more natural peaceful disposition, but also indicated that surface life was affecting their gene pool! When they realized this, they knew they could no longer live on the surface without becoming like the very people they were trying to help become more civilized.

Their only choice then was to live under the sea, land or in the safe pre-flood manmade planet. Then they had to break off all personal interactions with surface world people and they couldn't bring their kids with them either because they would degenerate the gene pool. Thus Quetzacoatle tears.

After this time only periodical checks and visits to the surface world were done. This might explain why they most often come at night, to keep out of the sun. Obviously even night time visits are no guarantee of safety from the harmful effects of the earth in its current state as the very air is filled with Carbon 14, possibly a contributing factor to shorter lives in some way.

GOOD BETTER BEST

One can take this line of reasoning further too. There seems to be a hierarchy in these places, based on the genetic soundness of the inhabitants. Ancient histories speak of people being banished from one realm to another. For example Ishtar seeks a banished loved one in the underworld. (book 17. pg. 123) If the underworld is depositing their rejects on the surface world, where are the Blue mooners banishing their rejects to? If we conclude that mixing the genes is not allowed as it would downgrade the gene pool of a realm, then if some mixed offspring do occur they would be banished to the next lowest (genetically speaking) realm and appear to equal gifts from the higher realm to the lower one. So if by chance an Elysian mates with an underground or underwater inhabitant then the offspring would become the property of the lower gene pool realm, and possibly the parent would be banished to that realm too, with possibly only visitation rights to the higher realm. There are constant references to UFO nauts mating with people of the earth. What becomes of the offspring? Are they banished then to the surface world?, left in front of orphanages or let loose out of caves? Or are they allowed to reach adulthood then left on the surface?

The Orkney and Hebride islanders say some of their family's ancestors are descendants of the silkies who occasionally come to the surface from the underwater world, and songs are sung about them. (Book 35 pg. 96). Where did Saint Germain come from anyway? I have found on occasion some people say they have been to the underworld freely welcomed and unmolested, and returned safe and their reports appear as fiction. Even I have sloughed off these tales and only in retrospect do I wonder if there was something to the stories. Some have suggested Colonel Fawcett found an underground civilization and opted to stay.

NOT FROM THE LUNATIC FRINGE.

(3rd ed. Insert 2016) Conventional archeology and anthropology tells us, the common man, the things we read in text books and hear on "science programs", like gradual evolution and increased complexity of man and his civilization have been a long steady upward process. The fact is it's long been understood that man in the past was more scientifically advanced than we are today. Furthermore, this highly advanced ancestor is known to have lived well before what we call "prehistoric man". It's known that they faced some sort of cataclysmic disaster, comparable to that facing us now. And consequently these highly civilized people built completely new civilizations deep beneath the surface of the earth. (Book: Alternative 3 page 99)

GENETICS SAY THE GODS OR THE UFO PILOTS ARE HUMAN

If this mating with so called "Venusians, Martians, space men, and UFOnauts is true, this confirms that these are in fact humans or of human lineage. Otherwise they simply could not mate with humans of the surface world.

Consider the lowly spider. There are at least 22,000 different species of spiders yet not one of these species can mate with any other species. Conversely there are hundreds of breeds of dogs and they can all in theory at least mate with each other because they are all dogs, that is one species with many 'races'.

This deduction that a period of gods lasted from sometime after the flood to about 300 years after the flood is also substantiated in the bible. Once again I refer to a verse in Joshua. Joshua 24:2) "... Your Fathers dwelt on the other side of the flood in old time, even Terah, the father of Abraham, and the father of Nachor [same as Nahor]: and they served other gods. 3) And I took your father Abraham from the other side of the flood,..." Terah was born 222 years after the flood, and Terah's father Nahor was born 163 years after the flood. We see that Terah and Nahor were living during the time of these other gods. Abraham was born 292 years after the flood and God first talked to him around the time he was 58. So one could deduce that after the gods had left and their influence waned to a mere longing for them to return, the one true God stepped in. Admittedly there's little or nothing to distinguish handmade gods in the form of carved statues and actual physical people as gods in the biblical verses. But I have to think man made these images originally to remember the actual gods by, which subsequently became equated with the gods as time went on. I can't see smart intelligent people at the beginning serving carved statues first. They had to represent real people originally and of course all evidence points to this fact, so I think it's safe to assume Abraham's forefathers were in fact serving the people, and not statues at this early point in time so soon after the flood.

UFO CATEGORIES

Other than basic designs, UFO's appear to fall into four categories; residents of space, under the ground and in the sea, demonic, and current but secret technology as I've found some of this fourth type after publishing. Though the undersea and the underground ones may be the same and communication between them may be the same as communication between us on land in different countries.

Erick Von Daniken makes the deduction that these ancient UFO's fall into three categories, the oldest come from space, and the later ones come from the sea or the caves. I concur with this deduction, though not so much by looking at the evidence so much as deducing it logically, and the evidence falls into line with the deduction...so indeed I think I am on the right track. Again I don't concur with Von Daniken's overall conclusions, but in this area it appears we agree on this particular.

Some credit spacemen with building these incredible half built cities seen at various places around the earth as though some overly bored aliens with nothing better to do would come a bazillion miles through space just to build half a city, and not live in it, and then leave. No they were built by us, and intended for us, and some event (Peleg) stopped the building as shown. These were not aliens, though they may have appeared as 'spacemen' or 'gods' to those living in the area.

When we realize there are three general states of man in various states of devolution or preservation, these classifications of UFO's start to make sense and fall into place. Ancient legends speak of the gods dividing up the living space amongst themselves, Jupiter retained the above the earth space, Poseidon went under water, Hades was given the domain "far below". (book 17 pg 54) Again eluding to three zones and places where UFO's seem to originate, and also giving indication that these 'gods' were undevolved or less devolved people. A Greek legend infers that after an interplanetary war, a stellar race retreated underground. Some gods had dominion or visited a part of the earth called "apsu" (the word we get 'abyss' from) which meant deep dark dangerous waters in which one can sink and disappear. (book 17 pg. 312) But it also equals the word "nikbu" which means literally and precisely a deep man made cutting or drilling into the ground. (Book 17 pg. 318) One has to deduce since the UFO's have been here for thousands of years they must be living somewhere around here. But not in some strange dimension as some would have us believe but in actual places we could visit were we so inclined.

UNDERGROUND / UNDERWORLD : THREE DIFFERENT PLACES

I guess we must establish that there are two VERY differing underworld places, apparently one on top of the other. But because there is confusion about this point, consequently we mix the two up. In fact there actually seems to be three places under the ground: one where man can live and below that, two in the spirit world, as we'll see.

When one reads about several descriptions of an underworld place, it becomes clear that there are in fact at least two places. The Bible and the Chaldean books of the dead seem to be aware of the two different places. The one is clearly not a place where one wants to go and it is the place where one can go after death. Proverbs 15:24 "The way of life is above to the wise, that he may depart from hell beneath." This is interesting because it suggests that hell is below our feet, but this is not the only place this is hinted at. Amos 9:2. In suggesting that if one were even able to dig even to hell such an attempt would be useless to escape God. (See also Isaiah 14:9) Jesus was said to have descended into the lower parts of the earth (Ephesians 4:9) The bible seems pretty clear that hell is an actual place and odd as it sounds, it appears to be inside the earth. So consequently we automatically associate the underworld with Hell.

However it also speaks of not worshipping those underground or in the earth, obviously a different faction, for who would worship someone in hell? (Exodus 20:4, Deut 5:8) Ezekiel 26:20 is something of a curious verse that suggests the people of old went to the lower parts of the earth, and a city would be put into a pit where these people went. Philippians 2:10 is somewhat clearer. It says every knee would bow down to the name of Jesus, those in heaven those on earth and those under the earth. The second use of the word earth in this verse is different and it means subterranean. Though this is assumed to mean departed spirits it could very well be simply those that live underground. Similarly Revelations 5:3 speaks of **men** in THREE places!, In heaven, in the earth and under the earth.

In 1988 a drilling team drilled a new record of 8 miles down for geological survey soundings and recorded sounds, but instead of the expected geologic or seismic sound one might expect, they heard sounds of tormented screams and voices as though someone was being tortured. Shaken up by this they pulled up and left. However I have lost the original article, though records do show that the deepest we have dug is 8 miles, but I could not find any mention anywhere of these mysterious voices as heard by this crew. (I read about this in a newspaper around 1988 and can still 'see' the article with the accompanying picture in my mind. Likely persistent digging through the archives would find this article. However I looked through all 24 1988 reels of the local newspaper microfilms with no success. I suppose I might have missed it but I get some sort of car sickness of vertigo watching page after page of stuff roll by. Then it might not even be from a local paper!)

Still as eerie as that sounds if we tentatively state that hell is 8+ miles down then that leaves a full seven plus miles of underground space left to inhabit. Interestingly all the deepest parts of the ocean in the trenches stop at seven miles. The bible seems to indicate there are at least three types of underground states, one for those that live and two for those that don't, though admittedly the one place for those that are physically alive is perhaps a little obscure.

Curiously when Saul goes to the woman of Endor to call up Samuel she sees "gods ascending out of the earth" (1st Samuel 28:13) and Samuel asks "Why hast thou disquieted me, to bring me up" (Verse 15) We know Samuel to have been a Godly man so why was he coming from below?! This would indicate there are even three places below. This actually does make sense. Deuteronomy speaks of a "lowest hell" as thought there are different levels.

Though some refer to Jesus' story of Lazarus and the rich man as a parable, (usually groups that try and extinguish the belief in the existence of Hell) others maintain that there is no reason to suggest this is a parable but an actual event. After the rich man and Lazarus die the rich man asks Abraham to let Lazarus come to him with a bit of water. They can see each other but there is a fixed gulf between them which they cannot cross. They appear to be in different areas of the same place within sight of each other somewhere deep within the earth.

There is actually a text in the Chaldean / Egyptian books of the dead that appears to be a confirmation of this area spoken of by Jesus in regards to the place of the rich man and Lazarus. Chapter LXIIIa is the chapter of drinking water and not being burnt by fire in the underworld. (book 61 pg. 208) Even the Mahabharata acknowledges the existence of Hell.

THE PLACE MEN CAN ACTUALLY LIVE

Ok this section about UFO's does not deal with this hellish area of the earth whether it be actual or allegorical in nature, but I merely mention it for reference to show there is a difference. The people in these flying saucers do not seem connected with this place but rather with an inhabitable place of mortals somewhere between this place and the surface.

The Book of the dead appears to indicate there is more to the underworld than a place where you can either be with water or with fire. One chapter in the book of the dead is called "The chapter of breathing the air and having dominion over the water in the underworld" (book 61 pg. 203) Though the chapter appears to be a memory verse to speak if you get there insuring safe passage, such a chapter named this way indicates a place with water and breathable air exists underground, that is to say, If you're breathing, you're alive.

Osirus setteth the khu[s] (similar to mummies) in the Taut and he is loved by others in the Taut. (Book 61 pg. 81-82) Taut is supposed to be some region not in heaven or upon the face of the earth, where the dead are and the place through which the sun (Ra?) passed through at night. (book 61 Pg. 16) Later Taut is also equated as underworld (pg. 83) "one does not want to go into the chamber of torture which is in the taut. (Book 61 pg 273) So "Taut" here seems to be their name for Hell.

Osirus is said to have ruled the world and Akert (A name of the underworld) (Book 61 pg. 19, 20) Also "...and An looked beautiful in countenance in Ta-tchesert" Another name for the underworld.

So we see Taut, Akert and Ta-tchesert are three different names or places in the underworld. Even if we presume one is hell, and one is across the Berlin wall from there, that still leaves a third place. Chapter XXXVIII speaks of breezes in the underworld (Book 61 pg 164) and Chapter LVII and LIX speak of mastery over water in the underworld and even tell of storms and floods there. (Pg 200) Chapter XVIII says "I have come unto you, o great and godlike sovereign rulers who dwell in heaven, and in earth and in the underworld". (Book 61 pg. 112) This speaks of three distinct places one could visit. This is definitely not the ways we would normally think of the underworld.

THE PHYSICAL EARTHY LIVING SPACE IN THE UNDERWORLD

The Indian Rig Veda which speaks of three earths all inside each other and some equate this with the inner core, the outer core and the mantle. I tend to suspect this refers to the surface world, the underworld and the lower divided place. Actually geologists really know very little about the inner earth and only have educated guesses based on cause and effect of the outer earth and it's lithosphere and magnetosphere. But even if they are correct, the upper 8 miles or so of the crust is insufficient to alter much the observable outer earth phenomena. There's no real insurmountable reason there couldn't be people down there.

1   There is said to be a subterranean people in a land called Agartha that has 8 million people. This is like a New York somewhere underground! They have attained the highest degree of knowledge living under the rule of the "master of the world". (book 22 pg 243 in reference to a book called "Beasts, men and Gods")

2. Many Buddhists are said to be absolutely certain Agharta, [different spelling but the same place] a super city with advanced science and technology exists where the "King of the world" rules in this subterranean city. (book 29 pg. 85)

3. The Ancient South American Chronicle of Akakor also speaks of the wonderful subterranean dwelling places.(book 10 pg. 114)

4. The Hopi Indians speak of underground civilizations and believe an entrance to this place is near the junction of the Grand Canyon and the Little Colorado. They say that they came from the underworld with a white brother named Bahana who had supernatural wisdom. Apparently he returned to the underworld and similar to Quetzacoatle he said he would return. Their ancestors Sipapu are said to have emerged from there.

5. India firmly believes in a city underground called city of the Nagas. (Book 11 pg. 117)

6. Scandinavians have histories of subterranean city of Asar. Russia calls a subterranean city Alberdi or

Afyana. Mexican call an underground city Tula. Celtic call an underground city Duat or Dananda and the Chinese refer to an underground city called Chivan.

7. A Greek legend infers that after an interplanetary war, a stellar race retreated underground. Tunnels to these places were lit with cold lights. (book 23 pg. 178-179)

8. (3rd ed. Insert 2016) Lewis and Clark discovered a Mandan legend about the underworld. They say they came from an underground village which was near a subterranean lake. But the legend says some larger women (giants?) when climbing the way to the surface broke the vine they climbed leaving some of them underground. (Atlantis I.Donnelly. Page 114) This legend meshes somewhat with Hopi legends and infers that some people remain below, for whatever reason.

Not only did the Navajo Indians say ancestors came from underground to teach them, then return, but they were driven underground in the first place by a flood (Tsunami type). Similarly the Pueblo Indians say their god's place of origin is somewhere underground and they came to the surface world via the North Pole. I guess they must know Santa! I wonder if there's a connection between Santa legend of being at the North Pole and these other folks that come from the inner earth via the same location: I suspect it's no coincidence.

PATHS TO UNDERWORLD DANGEROUS TO FIND.

(3rd ed. Insert 2016) Not only do the Hopi say there is an entrance to the underworld somewhere in or near the Grand Canyon, they apparently guard it. An underground passage was found by a Seth Tanner who was half Hopi. Thus being in the neighborhood on an ongoing basis he stumbled on the entrance and explored it. But because he went into the place, the Hopi blinded him with a potion thrown at his eyes, because no white man was allowed to see the place. He never spoke about the find after that. Normally people are killed if they find the place but because his mother was Hopi they didn't give him the full treatment.

David H. Childress stumbled on a very interesting newspaper clipping from the Phoenix Gazette from April 5 1909. He makes some quotes from the article and gives an online link to the article which I followed for more of the information to follow. Apparently someone from the Smithsonian (G.E. Kinkaid) found this entrance and he was not found out by the Hopi and the story got out. Just short of one mile down, a huge chamber was found which had scores of passages radiating out from the main chamber. Steel and copper weapons were found there. But the entrance is on Government property and there is a penalty if you're caught, but with him being part of an archeological expedition they were protected by the Government. Many mummies were found sitting cross legged with lilies or lotus' in their hands. Artistic vases, urns, cups of copper and gold were found. Graneries as well as several hundred rooms were found! It was deduced that 50,000 people could live in this underground citadel, and they figured that the local people may have been descendants of the people of this underground site, and indeed the article mentions the legends of the Hopi in connection with the site. The entire complex was not fully explored as some places smelled awful and / or were so dark they just passed up the opportunities. Some passages were explored but not to the ends. So whether this place had a passage to the underworld of course was not determined. This may have been sealed off from below and may have been meant specifically for local North American survivors. Apparently the Hopi were warned, and led to the place. This in fact might even explain the existence of other underground cities, like Derinkuyu.

Near the entrance to the underground site is an archeological site of a town called Unkar where the Unkar stream meets the Colorado, so the general area is known…if you're the daring sort. The artifacts seemed to be similar to Egyptian according to the gazette, but were also described as "…doubtless they had their origin in the Orient." (Though the article equated the Orient as interchangeable with Egyptian: so take your pick)

The finding of this place vindicates the Hopi legends of its existence completely. But by association it also means that the entire continent indeed was overrun by waves just as the Hopis stated as well. (See Atlantis Rising #75)

One legend suggests that if we continue on with our wars they may come to the surface world and make it a dessert. I guess the neighbours downstairs have complained before! They can turn dry land into ocean and cause mountains to disappear. (Book 43 pg. 230) We appear to have been aware of these legends of underground cities for a long time but we have ignored them, refused to believe them or thought them to be the same as, or allegorical, of death.

There appear to be a few races of people living inside the earth. They range in attitude toward surface man from friendly to virtual enemies. It is stated that there is a dark order in the underworld that is bent on the total destruction of surface men (book 12 pg. 117)

We must not however confuse these with such underground cities as Derinkuyu and Kaymakli. These are known underground places though not cities per se; they are underground facilities of as many as 13 floors deep. Surprisingly the air is quite fresh in these known places showing advanced ventilation. This underground system could hold 60,000 people. At least 14 underground 'cities' are known to exist in Turkey alone. Apparently as many as 1.2 million people were sustainable in these underground places for as long as a year. (book 10 pg. 281)

In Wattis Utah while working in a new branch of a coal mining tunnel, workers broke into a whole series of previously unknown tunnels with no known history linked to them. The Indians never built them or even knew of them. The coal found in them was so weathered it was useless. (book 7 pg. 218) These were obviously dug in some ancient era and it must have been quite the eerie feeling to walk through them wondering who dug them so long ago, and for what purpose. I don't know that I've come across too many references to the ancients burning coal, so it's not even certain they were coal mining tunnels, and indeed the coal was still there.

UNDERWORLD: *ANOTHER* ROUTE?

(3rd ed. Insert 2016) Egyptians claimed they could *get* to the underworld. They told Herodotus, Priests with newly woven special robes, led whoever to a road that leads to the temple of Demeter and leave him there, the person is soon escorted the rest of the way by two wolves. After they get there they played dice with Demeter for golden cloth. (Golden fleece?) Then the priests pick them up where they left them and then a festival is had after whoever returned from there. (Herodotus Book 2: 122)

HOLLOW EARTH?

There are many legends and proponents of what's termed the "hollow earth" theory. I don't think this theory of a "hollow earth" is the case. If the flood meteor smashed into a hollow earth there wouldn't be a crater or a Hudson's bay, there would be this huge hole in the planet where all the water would just keep pouring into...unless Hudson's Bay was like 7000 miles deep then people living in there would be all flooded anyway and this would be a pointless section. No I don't think the earth's hollow. But I'm convinced that it is inhabited underground.

There are supposedly huge tunnels all through the earth that people living underground use for travel, and it is said in some sources that there are eight paths from the surface that can lead to them but that these are guarded. Though legends don't seem to say who they are guarded by, them or us.

Other sources suggest there are far more than this number of entrance ways to the underworld. It is said that there are markings around the world that indicate tunnel entrances. (Arne Saknussemm→?) It would appear some of these markings are in the form of rock drawings. (book 12 pg. 112) Could there be an unsuspected meaning to some of the petroglyphs around the world? Many proponents of this underworld civilization keep suggesting some entrances exist at the polar regions. Now this might be a convenient place to pick for these entrances because so few people live in the polar regions: so who's to say?

The idea or theory of a race of people living inside the earth is not a new theory. Someone named Olaf

Jansen wrote a book published in 1908 about his trip into the interior of the earth. He met people that lived from 400-800 years long. They were highly advanced in science, have energy better than our electricity and are the creators of flying craft which operated on electromagnetism. ((2nd ed. Insert 2008) Keep in mind this was written 39 years before such craft are sighted and the description of their power source echoes later explanations of UFO's power systems.)All this meshes with this theory too. (Book 43 pg. 57 refers to this book)

Others have reached this conclusion as well. A Brazilian book by O.C. Huguenin published around 1957 called "From the Subterranean World to the Sky: Flying Saucers." is referred to by Bernard and excerpts from this book can be found online. Though he appears to have believed in a hollow earth theory he concludes that UFO's must come from the interior of the earth. Bernard presumes because of the UFO's flying ability there must be vast empty spaces in the interior of the earth for them to fly through, thus part of his reason for his acceptance of a hollow earth. But, as we've seen, UFO's may not need vast empty sky to fly in.

Bernard concludes that the subterranean dwellers may live so long because no solar radiation reaches them and no food poisoning occurs by eating wrong foods.(book 43 pg. 220) Though I agree with the radiation not diminishing their life spans I think the opposite in regards to food. More foods would be edible to them because of their more intact and less devolved state. I suppose the radiation coming to the surface of the earth is also affecting our food supply compounding our problem. As for UFO's supposedly needing flying space; they may be able to fly through dirt when in a state of phasing. Huguenin also equates UFO's with Vimanas.

A commander Strauss also concludes this subterranean dwelling space is the origin of UFO's. He notes that they could not be of Russian or USA origin or these countries wouldn't continually denounce their existence or still be building conventional planes (for defense). He concluded that there must be millions of inhabitants down there and that we on the surface must be, by comparison considered a race of barbarians (book 43 pg. 175) Continually in old histories and more recent deductions of the lower underworld people, they are constantly referred to as superior humans in every way. It all fits.

CURIOUS...EVIDENCE?

There is a tantalizing physical feature in Peru that makes one start to take this tunnel theory seriously. There is a pillar of rock that the Indian legends say one day was thrust upward. I believe it was called a tree that grew into heaven, which might be in Venezuela. [or Peru?] (I saw this on TV so I do not remember the exact location or name of this pillar, and can't find it on the internet.) It is an almost perfectly shaped cylinder of earth just jutting straight up out of the surrounding landscape. What makes this piece of earth so interesting is a feature in the pillar. There is a perfectly shaped tunnel section (like a "D" flat end down) right smack in the middle of it! Oddly the commentator completely ignored this feature. It's almost like it was a deliberate cross section of a tunnel pushed upward for whatever reason. If you look at that pillar, the "tunnel section" seen on it isn't all that deep. I mean it's deep enough to be able to get under most if not all construction that would require digging deep, but it isn't much deeper than that. (That's assuming the top of the pillar wasn't lopped off or hasn't eroded so much that it makes the tunnel section appear to be closer to the surface then it really is) One might even be able to hear such tunnels dug at that depth.

I remember once I was out early in the morning when there was just no traffic to be seen or heard, and I kept hearing a machine like regular knocky-grinding noise, but there were simply no machines around... and it sounded like it was coming from underground! I looked all around the neighborhood but could find nothing and it just kept sounding like it was coming from underground. I never cleared that mystery up. I forgot about it eventually and thought nothing more of it. Then one day I read that others have heard this same thing in their neck of the woods. An underground superhighway? Similar noises have been heard in Chalfont St. Giles in Great Britain and Anglesey Island of North Wales. UFO's and mysterious splintered windshields have also been reported in or near the areas where these undetermined sounds were heard. (book 47 pg 159-166)

Some time ago when the Dalai Lama was interviewed (date not given but appears to be in the late forties) he said he wanted to fly in an airplane and that in ancient times visitors to his land had flying machines and that now they were in Agharta (the underworld kingdom). When he was asked to describe these flying machines of old, an old book was brought to the interviewer which had drawings of them in it. It was an egg shaped device shown flying. Immediately the interviewer recognized the picture to be the same as a UFO as described after WWII. Also described were underground tunnels in Tibet that were linked to other places around the earth.(book 12 pg 113-114) Apparently maps of the underground tunnels exist (book 12 pg. 102)

Some of these tunnels appear to be in plain sight. One such tunnel runs between Spain and Morocco, and 30 miles of this tunnel has been explored. Thirty miles! There are places all over the world where mysterious tunnels of no known origin are found, some are blocked with debris. Some seem to run under oceans and some seem to lead nowhere or return to the surface with no apparent reason for their existence. (book 21 pg. 35) Some legends exist that after a great war after the flood people lived in tunnels. Maybe this started them thinking on maybe making the underground a permanent place to live, when they realized radiation was not something that was just going to disappear and its effects were extremely detrimental to longevity. These wars on earth, may have made them realize not only were the animals more belligerent, so too were men thus instigating the search for underworld dwelling places to get away from the effects of the sun.

THAT IS THE SUN, THAT'S THE MOON AND THOSE THINGS ARE CALLED STARS...THAT'S AN OCEAN...

In the light of this consider for example the green children. Actually when I read about the green children it took me a while to realize this event happened twice, but the accounts were so similar it took a while to realize I was reading about two separate events that occurred years apart, one in the 1100's and this one in 1887 in Banjo Spain. But the gist of both stories is quite similar.

The Spanish green children. One day two kids, a boy and a girl, were seen walking out of a cave. They were green, and they spoke a language no one could understand or trace, though it did bear some similarities to some known languages. They tried to rub off the green pigment from their skin but it was natural, Their skin really was green! Eventually the skin did slowly turn a more white with exposure to sun and the elements. Their features were sort of Negroid but with Asian type eyes. Their cloths were of a completely unknown type. The boy died about a month later and the girl lived for 5 more years. She also learned to speak some Spanish and she told their story. She said they lived in a land with no sun and were in a permanent twilight. On the other side of a river they said those people had sunlight. [possibly an artificial sun.] They were walking and a whirlwind shoved them upward and deposited them in the cave. (book 5 pg. 143-144, Book 50 pg. 120-122))

The English green children. Sometime during the twelfth century this event takes place and the reference says this story is recorded in at least three sources from this time period. During harvest time near Suffolk England several people were gathering when they saw emerge from the pits or caves nearby, two green children wearing unusually textured clothes which were also of unusual colour. Though starving, no food offered them seemed acceptable until they chanced upon some empty bean shells. Eventually they brought them some actual shelled beans and they went for them until after a few days they learned to eat bread. They both lived long enough to learn some English but again the boy died not too long after they were found. The girl actually lived to adulthood and married. They naturally were asked where they came from and they said they came from St Martin's land. (thought to mean Merlin's land, a subterranean world) They were feeding their fathers flock when they heard a great noise like bells and they were "rapt up in the spirit" and found themselves by the pits where they were discovered. Where they lived there was no open sunshine, nor did a sun rise and set. A land of light was nearby where they lived but they were separated from it by a wide stream. (Book 47 pg. 96-98) There are some real close similarities to these stories that there may be a common origin to them, but enough differences to possibly mean it happened twice. Since both stories regard a green race, the children may have had similar living conditions to account for the similarity of the stories. England and Spain are not too far away from each other, compared to say the USA so the region these green kids came from may have been closely associated.

UNDERWORLD INHABITABLE?

People suggest that it would simply be impossible to live underground because it's very hot or because air doesn't circulate and it would all go bad very soon and they would die. People have come to great deep caverns deep in the earth and found the air perfectly fine, and not been able to understand why. And a lot less is known about the interior of the earth then geologists are letting on. No doubt if air circulating was a problem the underworld dwellers overcame it.

For example let's say they have exits from the underworld that enter the sea somewhere and I don't doubt this for a minute. Water is just air and hydrogen. No doubt they could separated hydrogen from the water and leave oxygen and they could devise pumps to circulate that air. There are many natural vents around the planet and many natural intake caves. No doubt they've used these to their maximum advantage and may even have made giant fans or pumps to circulate the air. Though I don't know that they would want the radioactive carbon 14 from the surface world circulating in their atmosphere and no doubt filter this out.

What about light sources. Well as seen man in ancient history has been able to engineer lights that burn for centuries, apparently without consuming anything. Natural light even exists underground in the form of a moss called schistostega osmundacea which gives off an eerie cold light in European caves. This moss could be transplanted and cultivated to light vast caverns, though likely they would come up with more elaborate means to light their world and give energy to produce food.

Interviews with these red people seen through history have stated they live to be about 3-400 years old. OK not as long as pre-flood men but about as long as we were living on earth a couple hundred years after the flood. This suggests that these are Men descendant from this period with this amount of remaining intact genetics.

The idea of living underground is completely logical to get away from fallout. We have developed fully generated self sufficient ecosystems for taking below ground. (Life Feb 1989 Pg 91) Though these are said to be for living on Mars, there's no reason they couldn't be used by military or political personnel in the event of all out war. We now understand the perils of radiation. No doubt some people after the flood became cognizant of the perils of radiation that started to enter earth's atmosphere after the flood. If we can make underground spaces inhabitable, no doubt this was easy for them.

CURIOUS FINDS

On May 1 1954 a dazzling red half sphere was seen to come out of the ground by a motorists near Logan Utah. In tandem with this event was a tremendous sound heard over a space of 250 square miles but no earthquake was registered. (book 47 pg. 233)

One person had three craters appear on his farm within 300 feet of each other, each occurring on November 12 during three concurrent years(1966-1968). Each time this happened there was a loud report heard for in excess of 20 miles, but the explosion appeared to be too loud for the crater found. No cause of the noises or the craters was established.

June 7 1954 three German tourists parked and locked their car outside the huge Lamprecht cave in Austria. They entered the cave and were never found or seen again. It's very unusual for three, even amateur, spelunkers to just totally disappear. A cave to the underworld? Some mysterious lights have been noted to descend to ground level near limestone caverns. (Book 47 pg. 47) A white light has been seen to descend from the sky and enter the ground (Book 47 pg. 172)

In 1770 a labourer in Staffordshire England while digging a tunnel came across a large stone and behind it he heard the sounds of heavy machinery. He pried away the rock and found a stone stairway behind it leading deep into the ground. He went down the stairs thinking he had stumbled onto an ancient tomb that might be filled with treasure. He found himself in a large stone chamber with the sound of machinery now getting louder. Suddenly he notice a man with a baton like object in his raised arm fast approaching him. The labourer turned and ran back to the surface. (Book 35 pg. 146)

MORE MOLE MEN

(3rd ed insert 2016) A David Fellin and Henry Throne were caught in a Pennsylvania mine cave-in, in 1963. During this incident they claimed they saw a huge door open revealing beautiful marble steps and men clothed in "Weird outfits" staring at them. (Atlantis Rising #73)

In 1138 a black dwarf was captured in the cellar of a German monastery. He "spoke no language". Not knowing what to do with him they let him go to see what he would do. He returned to the cellar room in which he was found, lifted a stone and then slipped away into a tunnel underneath it. No one could follow him, so they sealed the tunnel access with a cross. (Book 5 pg. 153)

The Persian god Tages was said to be born out of the ground, and Mithra came from a cave. (Book 41 pg. 260)

Aztecs say their ancestors came out of seven caverns called Chicomoztec north of Mexico. This history is shared by the Red Indians, Quiches and the Incas. (book 23 pg. 145) The Andes are said to be laced with tunnels. A tunnel is said to exist going from Cusco to Lima, then turns and continues on to Bolivia, a total of 1280 miles. (book 23 pg. 177)

Navajo legends speak of ancestors that came from the underground to teach them and then they went back underground. (Book 35 pg. 138)

A Pueblo Indian god originates in an inner earth world with an entrance to that world somewhere in the north. (Book 35 pg. 138)

Peruvian legends say a god named Manco Capac came from the depths of the earth through one of 3 "splendid openings" located some 20 miles southwest of Cuzco in the hill called Tampu-Tocco. Manco Capac was somehow turned into stone, though his body has not been found. (Book 5 pg. 33) Maybe he's one of the statues.

Apparently in most legends peoples have gone underground to escape natural catastrophes or a "hidden death that exists in the life giving rays of our sun" (Book 35 pg. 136) We have for some time realized our sun emits radiation to the earth but we assume this is normal. Many countries have problems with nuclear waste and do not know what to do with it. Some dump it in the environment and say the radiations levels are under some maximum standard allowable. But the fact is ALL radiation is harmful to animals, humans and our environment. So that hidden death in our sun may be the radiation it emits which we think is of an acceptable level. It is... if you only want to live 70 years.

As early as 1945 a Richard Shaver claimed to have been to a vast underground civilization. Though his story was thought to be science fiction, he maintained it was factual. He said an elder race that once lived on the surface began to notice the sun harboured detrimental rays that were shortening the life spans and causing premature aging, so they went underground and began carving the fantastic subterranean kingdom, using ray guns that disintegrated rock, and they made an artificial sun that did not emit these harmful rays. (Book 35 pg. 139-140)

SAME TUNNELS, DIFFERENT SOURCE.

(3rd ed. Insert 2016) Some sources I initially stumbled on telling of the existence of tunnels almost appear like something told by the lunatic fringe, but when more and more sources tell of these tunnels, and they are all put together, the volume of stories, legends and such start to make one think they just might exist. When Pizarro was terrorizing the Incas for more gold, he heard rumours of a vast network of subterranean tunnels, presumably hiding places for all the gold, but these tunnels were thousands of years old, ran for miles including under the Incan capital. Officially the story is that some people who found the tunnels never returned. One person did return and had with him two bars of gold, but it was reported that he had gone mad, and so the tunnels were walled up. Apache Indians say their ancestors took refuge in these tunnels during a cataclysm on earth. I've determined this must be the cataclysm that was the moving of the continents so fast, that water overran North America wiping out many species and creating the massive fossil sites all along the western coast of North America. It appears not just Hopi but the Apaches also had some forewarning of this disaster and managed to avoid it in the same way by going underground, apparently wandering in the tunnels for years. What they ate and drank for that time I've not found out yet. Even so these stories do not mention the origin of the existence of these tunnels. I've also found that Aztec legends say Quetzalcoatl went to Mictlan, the name of the Aztec underworld, thus confirming my deduction that he went underground via the route of the sea, to get away from the harmful elements of the earth, like direct sunlight and higher radiation now on planet earth. (See Atlantis Rising mag #101 Creatures of the Underworld)

UNDERWATER

We seem to have another place that UFO's can go to. And it's supported even by the bible. It says do not worship those in the ground or those above the earth or those in the sea. Some have suggested this is referring to creatures, but it could very well be referring to people. These are not referring to angels or even demons, as when the bible refers to them they are very specific about that.

Living underwater is even more fantastic then living underground but this seems distinctly possible too, though it seems to me such a living place would be fairly readily discovered by surface dwellers at some point.

UNDERSEA DWELLERS DON'T WANT TO BE FOUND.

(3rd ed. Insert 2016) I've begun to wonder if the Sargasso Sea, an area in the Atlantic covered by weeds where UFO's are often spotted leaving and entering the sea, and an area where astronauts have seen lit up from space; I wonder if these weeds are not grown there deliberately by those that appear to live under the waves in this area? I found this little tidbit possibly related to this thought. In 1948 Professor Auguste Piccard's crew in a bathysphere had reached a depth of 4600 feet, in an area of the sea not noted in the source. When they surfaced they were elated at their success and the bathysphere received no damage from the dive. But it then dawned on them that their aluminum radar mast had been neatly removed "as if a skilled underwater mechanic had accomplished a clean theft" (Book 35 pg 97)

Jerry Decker in Atlantis Rising #116 notes that an email he once got told of NASA astronauts living under water for 6 months and breathing a "special mix of gasses". Living there darkened their hair, toned their bodies and reversed their ages by 15-30 years. Blood test showed rejuvenating proteins from above the heart. Even their wives complained to NASA about their husbands being a bit too …uh…spicy, as if they were in their 20's. I'm willing to bet the 'gasses' were pretty much ordinary air (maybe with a hint of some odour mixed in to veil the fact) as obscuring this was needed to make it look like some special gasses were used to hide the fact that just being under water away from negative attributes of the sun was what was rejuvenating the astronauts, and not some secret elixir of breathable air. After all this would confirm legends of some of the ancients going under water for this very reason. (Remember people before the flood were technically "underwater".)

Though lights have been seen in the Sargasso sea, even from space, could a city under all that seaweed escape detection even to the present day? Especially considering our fairly pervasive submarines patrolling the seas? I have read of rumors of divers stumbling across underwater domes but found nothing concrete to present here. The last lights seen on earth from Apollo 12 were in the waters of the Bahamas near the Sargasso sea. Lights were also seen here in 1492 by Columbus. (book 7 pg. 81) Nikola Tesla predicted he could light up the ocean at night.

A quick internet search showed some people believe that off worlders live under the sea and they know this to be true because dolphins have made this clear to them. Small wonder this theory is not taken seriously! Dolphins have told me all and, I am at one with the dolphins. Ommm...

It seems more likely that an entrance to the underworld exists in this area accessible from the sea, though I don't rule out an underwater city being invisible with residual light being a byproduct of the technology that renders them invisible, as is seen in the Sargasso sea. Keeping an underwater city powered and safe from the water may have something to do with the continuous magnetic interferences and losses in the Bermuda triangle area.

If Quetzacoatle and his sort were descendants of Noah and were not from a ship out in space that has remained in existence in space after the flood, then he may not have gone or returned there, even if he and his kind were aware of such a craft. Where did he go then if not there? Legends say he went into the sea.

Footprints have been found on the ocean floor but such reports are ridiculed. (book 35 pg. 127)

Several sea captains say they have spotted UFO's coming straight out of the ocean and flying straight up into space.(book 35 pg. 94) Is that a clue? Fishermen complained of UFO's entering and leaving the water in the Gulf Of Mexico in areas where the water appeared to be boiling in circular shapes. (Book 35 pg. 124) They have been seen coming from larger ships shaped like cigars.

(I repeat this bit) One UFO visible to people from the highway was seen hovering over a pond with the interior visible and normal looking occupants which appeared to be working on some repairs. When they realized they were being observed, one of the mechanics pulled two levers and the craft just disappeared. (book 35 pg 189) If they can do this on a small scale, quite likely they can do it for an entire underwater city.

THAT LOZENGE SHAPED TRIANGLE

The whole of the Bermuda Triangle is something of an intriguing series of mysteries. To be fair many losses in the Bermuda triangle area are in all likelihood due to careless small craft taking on a big ocean. The coast guard is not impressed with the supernatural explanations often attributed to Bermuda triangle disappearances, so this needs to be considered. Having said that, there are hundreds of underwater archeological sites in this region, as well as countless disappearances blamed on strange phenomena, accidental interfering, or paths being crossed by the underwater folks with that of us surface dwellers. Or do we just like to believe this as a form of escapism? There does seem to be enough evidence to suggest there is something to this. And the phenomena in the triangle area are often exactly like those when UFO's are encountered.

One sighting, considered to be one of the most credible eye witness reports of UFO's, occurred in 1956. A large group of military personal, 30 of which were pilots, were in a plane 50 miles Northeast of Gander Newfoundland when A UFO showed up. It was about 30 feet high and 350-400 feet long. When the witnesses were debriefed and asked to describe their experience some or all were shown a photograph of a UFO photographed over the Atlantic some time prior to this incident, which turned out to be the same type of UFO. (Book 46 pg. 100-102) This clearly shows that even though authorities apparently pooh-poohs UFO's, governments know the UFO's are real and have pictures far better than the general public has access too.

A large number of UFO's appear to be seen in the Atlantic off the coast of North America, and may be responsible for some losses of planes and ships in this area. One of these losses in the area is revealing. The legendary flight 19 and the last radio report sent by Lieutenant Taylor said "don't come after me.... they look like they are from outer space" (Book 7. pg 34, Book 8 pg. 80)

The Bermuda Triangle occasionally displays very unusual atmospheric disturbances in the area and occasionally the very elements seem to go haywire. The whole locale where one might be in starts to glow and become a white or greenish haze. Sky, water and horizon all seem to blend together, yet in ways that cannot possibly be accounted for as fog or some other "natural" weather condition. Often these events occur in an otherwise calm sea and clear sky.

One event seen from an airliner flying over the area appeared like the sea had a cauliflower looking shaped hill in it about a mile wide and half a mile high, as though some power in the area was convexing and boiling the water's surface.

One night in September 1972 A boat named the "Nightmare" in Biscayne bay had difficulty reaching land that was in sight. It's compass was out and although their motor was at full throttle they appeared to be moving backwards. They then noticed an area of the sky was blotting out the stars. They saw a single moving light enter the dark area of the sky, stay stationary for a moment then disappear, presumably inside whatever was blotting out the stars. Then the dark patch of sky disappeared. Immediately afterward the compass started working again and the boat began to function normally. (Book 7 pg 97) Similarly in 1957 another boat going to Freeport in the Bahamas at night, couldn't move forward with engines running. They saw part of the night sky blotted out and three moving lights enter the dark area and then disappear. (Book 7 pg. 97-98)

The Bermuda triangle is not the only ocean area where these things seem to reside. In the summer of 1942 a craft approximately 150 feet long with a bronze textured surface that had a beak and fins with a "Cheshire cat" insignia, suddenly appeared next to an Australian plane near Tasmania. It then abruptly turned away and flew into the Pacific in an area where often fishermen had seen mysterious lights in the sea. (book 47 pg 225-226) This Cheshire cat insignia is freaky. As you know the Cheshire cat in the story Alice in Wonderland could phase in and out and just disappear. Did they get that logo idea from us or did we get it from them?

A DATING METHOD SUGGESTS SOMEONE IS MINING THE SEA FLOOR

Calculating sediments in the ocean is one of the methods used to determine the age of the earth. This dating method is somewhat open to question. What is done, is the amount of sediments of a particular element at the bottom of the ocean is measured and the amount is calculated. Then the amount of this same element is calculated to be added to this amount every day through runoff in streams and rivers.

However this method of dating is no doubt flawed to the extreme because it assumes none of these elements were on the ocean floor at the start which of course is ludicrous, because there had to be an ocean floor to start with made up with some kind of elements. But this method of dating the earth is also poor because some elements are disproportionate to others by a wide margin. Here are some examples.

The amount of uranium at the bottom of the ocean in sediments suggest the earth is 10-100 thousand years old or by another calculation 500,000 years.

Sodium content, an element of salt, gives an age of 260,000,000 years.

Silicone deposits gives an age of 8000 years but potassium build up suggests and age of 11 million years.

Lead content suggests the ocean to be just 2000 years old.

So you can see some problems with even suggesting you can date the earth by deposits in the sea is difficult at best as it would seem varying factors have changed over the millennia on the surface of the earth to vary the amounts of a particular type of sediment reaching the ocean floor. That is to say, if the earth is 6-7000 years old this would suggest that at one time there was a whole lot more uranium on the earth surface than there is now to have so much down there as to make the earth appear this old.

The reason I mention all this is because one of the elements and it's accumulation give a strikingly low age for the earth. There is only enough aluminum in the sediments of the oceans floors of the earth to give the earth an apparent age of 100 years! (book 9 pg 154)

This I find very interesting and it suggests to me that some sort of gathering of this element is being done to give such a low apparent age. We are not mining aluminum (or lead for that matter) from the ocean so why is it not there? One can easily see the conclusion in this context. To be fair aluminum has only been used by man to any serious degree for about 100 years so there may be a connection. Even so, how do you account for the low date arrived at by the lead content? Do the underwater folks use these elements and somehow attract, extract and gather them from the ocean floor, possibly similar to how some have suggested scooping hydrogen from space to use as fuel for the rocket so as to be able to reach other stars? (Or like a whale scooping krill as it swims with its mouth open.)

UNDERWATER UFO'S OR MORE PROPERLY USO (UNIDENTIFIED SUBMERSED OBJECTS)

A pilot (Bruce Cathie) spotted on 12 March 1965 a type of unknown submarine 100 by 15 foot in 30 feet of water in Kaipara Harbor New Zealand. But this harbor is inaccessible to any known type of submarine craft. (book 35 pg. 99, Harmonic 33 Pg. 4)

July 30 1967 The Argentine steamer Naviero spotted an unknown type of cigar shaped submarine about 110 feet long with no superstructure 120 miles off the coast of Brazil.

In what was thought to be a naval exercise southeast of Puerto Rico in 1963, a submarine USO was tracked by the US Navy moving at 150 knots! It moved at depths of up to 27,000 feet. (book 7 pg. 238)

ANCIENT LEGENDS

Verses of the Ancient Greek represent Bacchus being overcome by his enemies and taking refuge in the depths of the ocean. Venus too is said to go into the waters to get away from Typhon. (book 41 pg. 142-143)

A Babylonian legend speaks of a fishman named Oannes that came from the Red Sea or Persian Gulf that taught civilization to the Babylonians, by teaching them arts, science politics and religion. (book 41 pg. 243) However for what it's worth, it is clear that Oannes was actually only dressed as a fish man. (book 17 pg. 287) He is said to have come to the surface world to teach by day and go back to the depths of the ocean at night as did others like him. (book 34 pg. 185)

Greek historians speak of divine fish-men coming ashore occasionally from the Erythrean sea (western Indian Ocean) Ishtar is said to have sought a chief navigator who left in a sunken boat. "USO"? (Book 17, pg. 287)

Hopi legends also say they once escaped destruction by living under the sea. (Book 37 pg. 132) I'm often wondering why some legends speak of civilizations underground still yet so many speak of coming out of the ground. As we see some went underground to escape the harmful effects of the environment, so why would they come back up? The Hopi legends appear to have an answer. They say during a time when the mountains were crumbling into the seas and the seas overran the land, the world spun through lifeless space. (presumably off it's normal orbit) Consequently life on earth (North America anyway) ended or was frozen into ice. (Ice age? Frozen mammoths?) The only people that survived were those that went underground. (book 37 pg. 200) Here we see corroboration of the Peleg disasters that overran the North American continent. Interesting how they were able to get out of the way of the disasters as they must have entered pre-made caves or tunnels or caverns to get out of the way in time. Possibly they were in them at the time of surface wars when the continents started to shift and then the mountains fell and the seawater overran the land. Hopi say that when want was excessive, wars broke out only to end when the continents sank and the sea and land changed places. (book 6 pg. 212-213 referring to the book of the Hopi)

In Revelations chapter 12, after a war in heaven and the accuser is cast down to earth it says in verse 12: "Therefore rejoice, ye heavens, and ye that dwell in them, woe to the inhabitants of the earth and of the sea! for the devil is come down to you..." Though one might argue the seas inhabitants must be sailors I suspect this is a direct reference to the dwellers of the sea. Curiously we see a beast of prophesy is to come out of the sea. Some suggest this is taken to mean to be the "sea of nations". Could this "out of the sea" be more literal then has been previously assumed?

SEA BEASTIES?

(3rd ed. Insert 2016) Perhaps as Gog and Magog (Germany and Russia) are prophesied to start large wars in the last days against Gods people (the Jews). I also mentioned that the beast would come out of the sea. The German scientist was supposedly approached by undersea people. One polychrome cave painting is said by a native to depict people who vanished under the sea but who had promised to return. (Book 31 pg11)

ABOVE THE EARTH

There are many legends of another planet or house in the sky that beings have come down from, but these all seem like science fiction. People have written books or theories about planet X and the 12th and 10th, or 17th planet or what-have-you. Added to this, is planet Elysia or as I've been calling it, the "Blue Moon".

Even the more conservative researcher Immanuel Velikovsky felt ancient texts clearly indicated that there was a wandering planet in the past that he presumed to be Venus. He felt Venus was a new planet that was spit out by Jupiter.

I don't think the wandering planet he deduced could possibly be Venus, as that would violate Bode's law which shows planets are in specific orbits at predetermined distances from the sun for a reason. So I don't think a new planet such as Venus as he prescribed coming out of Jupiter is possible. Because if it did happen every planet in the solar system would have had to jump one orbit to make room for Venus to fit where it is now and have the rest of the solar system fall into line with Bode's law. In addition the surface detail of Venus it too normal. That is to say, if a blob of mass shot out of Jupiter I have to think it would be less than a perfectly proportioned planet that Venus is. It looks far too normal, as far as a planet with 800 degree atmosphere could be I suppose. Interestingly Velikovsky did predict correctly many aspects about Venus.

Velikovsky's deduction of a planet coming from Jupiter could in fact be the pre-flood man made moon. If this deduction that man made a moonlike craft before the flood is correct, this could be what Velikovsky stumbled on to. Since to his way of thinking this could not possibly be a man made planet, he had to come up with a seemingly more plausible answer to his way of thinking to account for this ancient tidbit. This idea of a man made planet would still likely fit with ancient histories as he read and understood them.

Others have suggested huge orbits for this extra planet "X" which are just beyond our normal understanding of planetary orbits, and indeed possibly beyond the sun capacity to retain them in its orbit. (though some have suggested Sirius is a binary star companion to our sun) The orbits these people theorize are so extreme that it is likely this planet "X" would have escaped the sun's pull were it to have been as far away as some suggested…though I can't say that for sure as I don't know gravitational formulas.

Again in some books interesting bits arise that suggest maybe there is a planet that came in and out of the solar system with a really long orbit. But such orbits as far as I understand it, really are not plausible, suggesting such a planet if it existed or exists is artificially propelled and not an orbiting one at all. This stands to reason. If pre-flood men overcame gravity they could make a large manmade body not subject to the laws of gravity, as much as to their whims.

CURIOUS CLUES

Mention of another planet in our solar system seem to persist in several sources and, such has actually been seen as recently as 19th century, and further evidence seems to exist that it has been interpreted as existing in the 20th century!

For a long time Jupiter was thought to have just four moons until telescopes got better, then it was seen that Jupiter in fact had 12 moons. This was the state of affairs until the voyager found several more smaller moons orbiting around Jupiter in 1979. But during the time when it was well established that Jupiter had 12 moons, a 13th moon was sighted and was seen several times. Then it vanished.

Venus our next door neighbor has no moons, yet for some time there was seen a moon orbiting Venus. Then it too vanished.

At one time there was another planet found that orbited inside the orbit of Mercury, that is...very close to the sun.

We'll go into more detail on these sightings shortly. These extra globes were seen by more than one astronomer too. It would seem we have our pre-flood moon shaped ship after all. But then where is it now? Perhaps it's in a geosychronous orbit at the back of Jupiter, or maybe they've decided to orbit directly on the other side of the sun in the same orbits as Earth, or even further out to avoid detection. Actually the most obvious place for it to 'hide' would be Jupiter as that planet has 63 moons!

Perhaps they saw Voyager coming, they got out of its way, then went back to one of the outer planets to pretend to be a moon. They may even have a "cloaking device" that renders them invisible or a disguise device that makes them look like a regular moon. (A convenient cop out if there were no evidence to support this.) Well it may be that the people of this erratic "moon" are very well aware that surface man has once again achieved space travel and they do not want to be found by us yet.

They may be in constant contact with the under worlders and under water people to be kept abreast of events occurring on the surface world if they are not able or unwilling to ascertain these things on their own, possibly to refrain from being in the earth's environment.

It seems they would know that at one time the earth will be made whole again, because they are evidently still sticking around. We see in Revelations that once again mankind's life span will equal that of a tree, and we see that the animals will once more no longer be afraid of man. So this strongly suggests that the earth will once again have a water sphere and a fully restored atmosphere.

As we have prophecies to show these things to us, so too would the men of the pre-flood ship have some prophetic understandings as they are human and they too need hope for the future and even more importantly hope for eternity. I think they will come back to earth when the earth is restored to its former state.

THEIRS IS BLUE TOO.

(3rd ed. Insert 2016) I repeat this bit: The Hopis speaking of the last Great War say a Blue star (now invisible) will appear. (Book 35 page 214) This appears to be when Christ returns.

JUST TOO BIG TO HIDE HERE

Some of the UFO's seen are so huge there seems no way they could hide on earth or in the earth, though I suppose some of the "smaller" ones might be able to hide in the sea.

On January 7 1948 a chaser pilot was blasted out of the sky while in pursuit of a UFO. In his last radio report he said it was of "tremendous size". (Book 47 pg.118)

In 1949 one UFO encountered off the eastern coast of U.S.A. was computed at an air and naval base and calculated to be a mile long (book 47 pg. 118) Wow...a mile long piece of technology just floating around... in mid air.

Early in 1954 a man and wife see a space ship that looked like a large planet over Adelaide Australia between 2:30 and 3:15 AM. It went from a yellow white to a deep orange. (book 47 pg. 119)

In Australia near Geelong Victoria on April 28 1954 two railway men in a train are swooped by a gigantic flying saucer that made the trees 'look like matchsticks'. They guessed it to be a quarter mile wide. It was dark blue and was covered in a haze. (book 47 pg 124)

September 5th 1954 three amateur astronomers watching the moon through a 6 inch telescope saw a spherical object ascend from the Mare Humbolt area of the moon. They estimated its size at 2 1/2 miles. (book 47 pg. 240)

An object was seen late at night "near" Cedar Rapids in 1956 that appeared to be the size of the moon in the sky. It moved back and forth over the horizon erratically. Stations in Omaha, Cedar Rapids Iowa and Davenport tracked it and placed it at 3000 miles out from earth. They called it an erratic meteor. No kidding! Meteors travel in straight lines curved only by gravity of the sun and other bodies...but back and forth? I asked myself how big would this item be if it looked like the size of the moon from 3000 miles away from earth. If the moon is about 240,000 miles it was one eightieth the size of the moon (2160 miles) or about 27 miles across! The only thing I find odd is that if this was as big as this why didn't more places see this "meteor"? So something may be screwy here.

ELYSIA

What about that ship that may have existed in space before and at the time of the flood? Is there any reason to believe there is a large craft wandering in our solar system? As we've seen Immanuel Velikovsky searching ancient texts deduces a wandering planet existed in the ancient past but identified it as Venus.

The ancient term for planets is "wanderer", as they appear to wander in the sky whereas stars stay stationary. But there may be more to the term "wanderer" then previously thought.

Zachariah Sitchen claims the ancients knew of 12 planets. Granting exceptional telescopes one starts to count. 1)Mercury 2) Venus 3)Earth 4) earths moon is counted as a planet by the ancients) 5) Mars 6) the blown up planet now an asteroid belt 7) Jupiter, 8) Saturn 9) Uranus 10)Neptune 11) Pluto. What is the 12th? Could it be this wanderer called "Marduk" by Sitchen. (some "aliens" say there is a planet that will be discovered outside the orbit of Pluto, so this could be the twelfth. But even if this is the case we can't really count the blown up planet because it likely didn't exist when these histories were written. So what is the twelfth planet? Small planets have been found further than Pluto, though they've been classified as dwarfs along with Pluto now.

Interestingly Von Daniken felt the old texts and archaeological evidence suggested the ancients had spherical ships. (book 4 pg. 58)

Many very competent astronomers have seen a moon or planet where at least today there is none to be found. After the telescope was reinvented some fascinating sightings have been recorded. Here's a list of very interesting observations made by astronomers.

January 25 1672 Cassini sights a smaller object near Venus and watches it for ten minutes. (book 11 pg. 80)August 18 1686 Cassini sees it again appearing 1/4 the size of Venus. It showed phases, similar to our moon. (The division seen in the rings of Saturn is called the "Cassini division" named after this astronomer. By the way Venus does not have a moon.)

October 23 1740 A body near Venus was seen for an hour by James Short.

May 20 1759 A moon was seen near Venus by a German astronomer.

February 10, 11, and 12 1761 a Venusian satelite was seen by Joseph-Louis Lagrange of Marsielle

March 3, 4, 7, & 11 1761 a moon of Venus was seen by Jaques Montaigne. Originally he was sceptical of the existence of a Venusian moon existence.

March 15, 28, and 29 1761 a Moon was seen around Venus by French astronomers. Copenhagen astronomers saw it eight times in June, July and August of 1761 and again on January 3 1768, then it disappeared for about a century.

March 26 1859 a disk 1/17th the mass of Mercury was seen to transit the sun inside the orbit of Mercury. It was seen enough times to get a name as a new planet and was called Vulcan. Interestingly an object seen transiting the sun in 1859 is still unidentified. The author Andrew Tomas asks "was the Venusian moon a huge space city cruising the galaxy?" (book 11 pg. 83)

In 1878 the planet Vulcan was again seen by Professor James Watson and Lewis Swift from Michigan and Pikes Peak Colorado respectively. Then it disappeared.

Venus was seen to have a moon in 1886 by Houzeau.

August 13 1892 it was seen again by Edward Emerson Barnard (the discoverer of the 5th moon of Jupiter)

In 1905 William Henry Pickering discovered a tenth moon of Saturn (Themis) it hasn't been seen since.

The innermost of Jupiter's 12 major moons (not named) has an odd habit of disappearing and reappearing at unpredictable intervals and altering its orbit. (Book 8 pg.. 18) This is an older source but I presume it refers to the moon Io, a very volcanic moon, a factor which may have something to do with the peculiar orbits of this moon. But I suppose there could be some unseen artificial moon somehow interplaying with this moon, affecting its orbit, though I would have to think this would be an artificial moon with substantial gravity or it would have to have a means of pushing Io around. I suppose if the UFO's have neutralized gravity they can increase gravity too. All speculation of course. But if it could blow up a planet then there's no reason to think it couldn't affect the orbit of a small moon.

ANCIENT HISTORIES SPEAK OF THE SAME THING?

Sumerians and Babylonians speak of Mars as one of three planets which has caused thunderbolts, and caused the earth to shudder and "move off its hinges". (Book 19 pg. 172) Presumably this is in reference to those planets moving close enough to earth to interact gravitationally or even exchange matter with the earth and/or cause an electrical discharge when any of the three planets come close enough to the earth. But if that's the case what could be the third planet? Mars yes, and Venus maybe if we presume earth and Venus were both temporarily out of a normal orbit and we got close to each other and there appear to be legends of both these planets coming close to earth, but what could be the third planet? Mercury and Jupiter are just too far away as also would be the fifth planet (now the asteroid belt) and it would have been destroyed before the flood thus before the legend was inscribed, so what could the third planet be?

It's been suggested that it appears to be Jupiter, but this is simply impossible, unless the earth itself moved so far out of it's orbit to come close to Jupiter, but this has to be impossible too, or we would have the most bizarre orbit of any planet. Not to mention Jupiter mythology would be just rampant in ancient history. But the legend appears to be linked with Jupiter, so maybe something from Jupiter came here.

Velikovsky seemed to think, based on legends that, Venus was born out of Jupiter and wondered what the origin of Jupiter's red spot was, suggesting it to be a vestige of the place where Venus was shot out of. But as we've discussed this contradicts Venus's physical appearance and Bode's law. If this were so, Venus would likely be more like the moon Miranda that appears to have been blown apart. Then the gravity of the parts pulled itself back together. Also as mentioned it's just as likely a huge chunk of the 5th planet landed on Jupiter causing the red spot.

We do however see that an odd moon has been seen on occasion to orbit Jupiter and this may be this erratic moon's most common home, and this may be the mysterious third "planet" or wanderer that the Sumerians and Babylonians spoke of.

The Gobi Desert, once known to have been a sea, is said to have had an island (it did) inhabited by white people that descended from heaven and a great white star. (book 21 pg 57) Northwest Indian legends speak of an old chief living in a house in the sky. (book 23 pg. 106)

I found this next bit after I had come up with the theory of men in space at the time of the flood. Iroquois, Huron and Wyandotte Indian legends taught that the first people (Not gods) lived in the sky before the great turtle [Probably referring to "Turtle Island" a name for North America see chapter 6] created earth on the face of the waters. If we see that as a description of the time of the flood with Noah waiting for the dry land to appear and men in space not in the flood it fits pretty well, but it could very well refer to when the continents moved. But the point being, they too have the legend of people living in the sky, obviously in some sort of craft, planet or planetoid.

IS IT BLUE?

Chapter LIV of the Book of the dead, in light of this theory, is an interesting short chapter. It speaks of the great egg which is in Kenkenur (the great Cackler) suggesting the egg (UFO?) comes from a larger or bigger source or dwelling place.

Then comes the enigmatic sentence "Hail thou who makest sweet the seasons of the two earths, thou dweller among celestial food, thou dweller in the cerulean heights of heaven. (literally "dweller in lapis-lazuli").

This colour of lapis-lazuli is too deep a blue to be the colour of the sky though lapis does seem to be a star studded rock that looks like twilight. This may however give the approximate colour of the blue moon. Since it speaks of the dweller amongst the celestial food and dweller IN lapis-lazuli one can see this could mean another name of the blue moon is Kenkenur, the second earth which is lapis-lazuli in colour.

Interestingly this ties in with the Sumerians who worshipped moon gods. Sumerian statues have eyes the colour of Lapis-lazuli and the eyes are shaped very round as though to reflect the blue moon in their eyes. Did they see it in the sky and make these statues to record the astonishment in their eyes?

(3rd ed. Insert 2016) uh...I may have said this before. The Hopis speaking of the last Great War say a Blue star (now invisible, [too far from earth to see]) will appear. Could they also be talking about Elysia?

The third planet that caused earth quakes or at least thunderbolts could be this artificial moon and as we've seen it appears to exist. It would seem Jupiter is a favorite hangout of this artificial moon and this was known to the ancients which included it in their legends. This may be why this third planet is confused with or linked to Jupiter.

As we have seen the Tower of Babel was possibly a more special ziggurat and the top was to reach unto heaven. We've also seen pyramids were meant to mean or used as a ramp to the sky... if indeed all ziggurats were not meant for this or some similar purpose. Do they somehow aid in antigravity flight of particularly large craft? As shown UFO's are often sighted in magnetic faults. Maybe pyramids and or ziggurats create magnetic faults by focusing some earthly energy and were built at a time when the earth had no magnetic faults or at least the earth was not thought to have any as they might not have been discovered until sometime after Peleg, if indeed Peleg didn't create them.

As mentioned other descriptions of these ancient flying machines say they looked like pyramids, but this could be confusion of their appearance with their association with pyramids, as I seriously doubt the pyramids fly and I'm not aware of any UFO's that actually look like pyramids. I have heard of upside-down pyramids underneath the surface pyramids but these seem more like conjectures, or flights of fancy. It would seem just too fantastic to suggest the pyramids themselves are flying machines. We know among other things the pyramids do strange things to cosmic rays. (Not to mention they appear to make stones fly and rip continents apart)

WHEN THE GODS INTERACTED WITH MEN.

The Sumerian temple of Anu is the construction that was actually built by the gods of the Sumerians. It was called "the house for descending from heaven"(book 17 pg 91) My guess is the ziggurats were a place where the vimanas or even moonlike objects and such landed. The Ziggurats and Pyramids are often said to have tunnels and passages underneath them, and the link between the pyramids and the underworld is also very pervasive in legends as well. My guess is at some point the people that flew these ancient craft would land on or near ziggurats and say hello to the people, have some interaction and then go into the pyramids / ziggurats to the passages leading to the underworld. Obviously this is pure conjecture which assumes the pyramids have tunnels underneath them. They may not and these gods could have gotten to the underworld in other ways.

Still other legends speak of interior walls of pyramids being lifted by sound. Suggesting these visitors knew where they were and how to open them, since they and their kind probably made them and understood them, so they would know what to look for. Similar to us when we try to drive a different model of car, we basically know what's what even if we've never driven that kind of vehicle before, we can still make it go, whereas if we drove these cars in the heart of some primitive tribe they would have no idea how to make the car go.

It's even possible the moon like ship also landed on the pyramids or ziggurats, as the Sumerians were moon worshippers so they must have seen, if not *thee* moon, then *a* moon do something particularly interesting if just coming to earth wasn't interesting enough. The flying craft are spoken of as taking off vertically. This capability also seems to be something of a moon shaped craft may have done as is the case even in more recent sightings of these spherical craft. For example a luminous sphere was seen to approach Mont Rougemont Quebec on Sept 20 1972. It was estimated at over 350 feet in diameter. Its path seemed to follow a local fault line and it disrupted television reception in the area. (book 46)

My guess is since there seem to be various moon shaped craft in a variety of sizes, then the real full blue moon would stay in orbit, close enough to the earth to be seen as a marvelous Lapis lazuli sphere in the sky. Then smaller spheres, and we must assume 350 feet wide spheres are indeed smaller, landed on the ziggurats.

There had to be a time of the undergrounds initial construction to make the underworld inhabitable during which time access to all three domains may still have been in place for all three sectors of gods. The "blue moon men" with their advanced capabilities may even have helped in the development of these places and come periodically to trouble shoot. When it was decided that the gods would have dominion over certain sectors, some of the gods would have dominion over the underworld and some would have dominion of the sea, and some of course in the artificial moon in the heavens. A time had to exists when these places were initially made inhabitable with under surface construction. It's possible that during this time the people slated to live there had temporary residence in the off world moon shaped craft until these places were finished or at least until they reached a state where they could be lived in and would come to the earth on or near these ziggurats and then proceed underground to the work sites.

ANOTHER "ARK"?

The ancient Mayan Calendar is said to predict something is going to happen on December 24 2011, and that a new era would begin at that time. Are the people of a moon shaped craft supposed to come back to earth on that date…once in a blue moon? Interestingly the term blue moon is used when a second full moon occurs during the same month, suggesting some sort of connection when on the rare occasion in the past a second moon was seen in the sky…possibly a blue one.

Is an underwater craft supposed to come to the surface on that date as it would seem some of the North American ancient gods went underground and underwater when they left. Maybe the blue mooners or the underworlders said to the Mayans that they would return after about 5000 years. Similar calendars start at or near this date and some clues suggest they started at this date because of the gods themselves, for whatever reason. So I have to think the 5000 years was an estimate possibly based on understanding of the devolved human nature and possibly linked with prophesies they might be aware of. (Apparently lots of people misinterpret the meaning of the Mayan calendar so things like apocalyptic disaster movies get made. I didn't study it either, and just noted it in passing. So to someone well versed in Mayan history… this may all be off the beam)

I don't know how much stock people put in such a scenario. Possibly people await such an event as a few of the books I read think this is a particularly interesting date, though none seemed to really suggest this idea. But if this is the case and since these people in any such ship appear to be as human as you or I are, I have to think they haven't been left out of the picture as far as prophesies are concerned. It looks like this particular date might be too early for their supposed return so some people will no doubt be disappointed… unless someone from the underwater world is going to pull something like coming the surface world trying to rule humanity or something. Or is this when the war in heaven casts someone down to earth?

I suspect that if they were supposed to return on that date then they won't return until sometime after because the earth has not been restored to its pre-flood state, and it won't be restored until after the return of Christ which is supposed to happen 7 years after the beginning of a great worldwide tribulation. I don't think they are going to come back to earth to rule as one might think, at least not the people in the blue moon. I don't think they want to come to earth where it is dangerous to their genetics and life spans. Also I think they would want to come back to earth when they will be looked upon as peers and not as 'gods'.

That can only be when the earth is restored and mankind once again has long life spans and restored mental and physiological abilities.

(My notes say put insert 12 here. But you've read about the Hopi Blue star…you must recall it by now)

If the people on that moon ship were going to restore the water sphere and the earth's atmosphere they would have done it a long time ago, so clearly this has to be beyond their ability. I mean try steamrolling water into a section of a water sphere, it has to be as difficult as blowing square bubbles. The water would just want to return to a small spherical shape or it would conglomerate into larger ones instead of becoming part of a planet encompassing one. Restoring that water sphere may be a whole lot more difficult than just taking large amounts of water from the ocean and placing it in orbit, in hopes enough water could generate and form into a single earth protecting sphere. OK I'm rambling. (We mentioned that Enki needed gold to protect life on his planet…Elysia…or this one so it appears options were attempted.)

WHAT WAS STUMBLED ON TO?

A book by Dr. M.K. Jessup from the mid fifties is well known among UFO buffs. This was the first book to mention the Philadelphia experiment. Though I haven't been able to find a copy, it is often quoted, and not always for the content, but because of a specific copy that had notes written in the margins.

Around 1959 a copy of Jessup's book was sent anonymously to the Office of Naval Research in Washington with very interesting notes written in the margins. These notes were apparently written by three people, one person which was known. Though a hoax has not been ruled out, the Navy was VERY interested in this annotated copy and made a limited number of reproductions of this book which included the notes written in the margin to circulate among themselves. Apparently a few copies made it into the public and occasionally the notes are referred to by other researchers.

Often the notes speak directly to the text of the book, but on some occasions they seem completely unrelated to the text. Even if the margin scripts are deemed to be a hoax, the margin comments are still very interesting. One margin note speaks of a UFOnaut that was forced to walk and died from walking. (probably due to the gravity of earths effect on the person).

Reference by Jessup about space lights seen on the moon are followed with comments referring to a peace that had lasted 70 years so they could build there. Also they mention they would like to see the great port city which, as always, is underground. Later they also refer to a "vaulted city" under the sea.

One note not particularly connected with the writing in the book states that there are different species of UFOnauts and almost as an example later refers to the little men of Mu, but then the margin notes seem to be contradictory by saying walking on Terra [presumably earth] is a great strain, (presumably from the gravity) but not difficult under the sea (where gravity is technically greater, unless they are suggesting they are walking on the ocean floor and being buoyed up by the water. But then they would have to be able to breathe underwater and this seems illogical, and no indication ever suggests there are fish men. For them to do this, incredible suits able to withstand astounding pressures would have to exist, and what civilization would always live in a diving suit? They may have extremely sound scuba gear that allows them to walk on the ocean floor and not be crushed by the water pressure, but certainly this is not the way they always dress. I suppose certain gasses might replace or mix with oxygen to reduce the affect of the deep on the body, but I have to think this is just too 'out there'. They would be living in "vaulted cities' with normal air and thus normal (though slightly stronger) gravity, so I don't get this statement. More likely walking on the earth would be difficult if they were used to walking on the moon or in an environment where there is less gravity or none at all [except artificial gravity].

The most interesting of all the comments in my mind is when Jessup refers to a mysterious dark spot that astronomers had periodically noticed moving over the face of Jupiter. (I hadn't found this mentioned anywhere else) The note in regards to this comment are striking. The notes, referring to this dark spot or shadow say, "The great Ark" and suggest seeing this would humble and terrify any human. Then the note maker says he wished he could have seen it, "the greatest structure ever built by humanoids" (Book 30 pgs. 158-165) Calling it the "Great Ark" also suggests it's link to Noah's ark in that they both preserved man from the flood. Obviously I'm not suggesting Noah built a space ark, but after the flood this spherical ship may have been referred to as such by some. Another curious aspect to this comment is saying it was built by "humanoids". This might confirm my guessing that maybe, sons of Adam, the Nephil and Angels themselves may have worked jointly to build the thing. But this begs the question, if angels had a hand in building this thing, just how marvelous *is* this "Great Ark"?

Since we've already determined that Adams peers and great grandsons likely did have space travel and may even have caused the flood from an off earth craft, maybe one of the vessels responsible for guarding the earth against the resulting asteroids hurtling through space was still on guard when the flood happened...maybe even the same craft, though it seems more than one spherical crafts exists.

CLUES FALLING INTO PLACE

Interesting... I didn't make this connection until I wrote the above paragraph. I just used the terms 'guarding the earth' in relation to protecting it from asteroids in the pre-flood period. Maybe this is what was meant by 'guardians of the sky'. They may even have watched in horror as one asteroid got by them. Maybe they saw the asteroid smash into earth, and the earth became a water world as the water shell, the protector of life on earth, collapsed onto the face of the earth, becoming the destroyer of all life on the surface. They may even have filmed it.

I repeat a sentence from an earlier chapter. Ovaherero tribesmen say that long ago "the greats of the sky' let the sky fall on the earth." (book 14 pg 103-104) Now that sentence makes sense! Maybe they watched as Mars got next to the earth and saw the water spout leave earth along with some of our atmosphere and saw it settle onto Mars. Thinking the earth was done for but perhaps they could survive on Mars. Maybe some UFO's do come from Mars as a small colony from earth or the Blue moon. With all that earthly water there they could live under ground where the water has sub ducted to. They might not have known a thing about Noah.

Remember, even though Noah's ark was made of wood, this does not mean it was by any means a primitive "boat". It was a marvel of ingenuity to be able to build such an ark to withstand such a flood for such a period of time. It may still be the largest wooden boat to have ever been built! This is no small task!

As is often the case God chooses the humble and the poor and the weak to confound the wise, strong and rich. Man was confident he could stop the destruction of earth via destroying asteroids as they came to earth and probably made no plans to save the earthly creatures, though they probably have some animals on the blue moon. Noah not only was used to preserve life and animals, he may have been an example for the blue mooners to follow. Maybe the off worlders knew about Noah and they might have thought him doomed with the earth destroyed and completely under water. So perhaps at first it was Mars or nothing but just a long endless journey through space. Before they got too determined to survive on Mars they realized that this water spout from the earth was in fact making it possible for life to exist again on earth... but what sort of life? They appear to have found life still on the earth and visited it and started civilization in Ur and Sumer, not terribly far from Noah. It appears they found us in the plains of Shinar when we were all still "Sumerians".

When the Sumerians saw them come to earth in this big blue moon they thought of them as gods. Maybe the people in the ship tried to stop this adulation but because of their original intact physiological attributes they were still looked upon as above man, because by the time they got here we were already succumbing to the affects of the sun and radiation on man's physiology. The Blue mooners no doubt told them who they were and so the truth filters into the mythology, tales and records. But as time passes the story has been handed down in the form of legends which then in turn get interpreted with our limited understanding. At first the earth was still in fairly good shape allowing ages of 600 years but by the time only 300 years pass since the flood if not earlier, already the symptoms of decay became evident. As man's lifespan became shorter and shorter the blue mooners visited the surface less and less, for fear it would affect their gene pool as it had ours.

VISUALIZING THIS SHIP

OK if we allow that a ship was in space at the time of the flood then one speculates on the nature of that ship. I suppose if it was just a little itty bitty space craft built for two this goes nowhere. They die of starvation and come hurtling down to some planet or moon somewhere to become the cause of one more crater...end of story.

But it seems that if pre-flood man was as advanced as we've determined, he would also have accomplished space travel on a grand scale. If they made a ship it would have been a perfectly balanced biosphere completely independent of earth, made in a way so that it would be safe for them to live in. Meaning the environment of the ship would duplicate as best they could the nature of the earth. That sounds like no big deal, but remember, this biosphere is duplicating the nature of the earth BEFORE the flood. In fact it would have to be more protective than the earth itself as they would get close to the sun and Jupiter. This means a far more grand project then what we would call a space station.

In trying to think how they would make a complete self cleansing biosphere one has to see that it was probably a huge project, maybe even a small moon sized structure...and then there would be smaller craft capable of docking with this man made moon for specific missions. Maybe even smaller moons for short term projects. And this stands to the evidence as moon shaped craft of various sizes have been seen.

REINVENTING THE BUBBLE

Now I don't think it would have been a small duplicate of earth because you might not be able to steer a planet...well what am I saying, they'd have figured out a way. But another problem exists because they would have to make the water sphere first. (When water is set loose in a zero gravity environment it naturally goes to a perfect spherical shape. You can pump air or gas into a water sphere and the air will gravitate to the center of the sphere, thus making a sort of bubble or balloon.) But to make a ship with a water sphere on the outside would likely mean your ship will run into it...if the water sphere is moving one way and the ship is moving in another direction the ship bumps into the water shell and the water sphere just grabs onto the ship and collapses. Well maybe that's not correct either.

But if this is the case and they got too close to another planet or moon that body could steal the water sphere from them...and with them hanging around Jupiter and it's 63 moons that had to be pretty dicey with a water sphere to protect.

The air inside the water sphere gravitating toward the ship on the interior might act as a cushion and keep the water shell intact even as they steered... Hmm or it still might collapse, but there is another problem. Why would they put the water sphere on the outside of the ship anyway? It and the air or gas inside the sphere would likely get in the way of perfect visibility, something you don't want out there in space; but then if we had a water sphere and could see the stars, then so could they.

One also wonders what would happen to a water sphere if it got too close to the sun....would it insulate or evaporate...does water evaporate in space? (I'm confessing my ignorance here.) (3rd ed insert: Apparently if Mars had a 1% atmosphere compared to the earth, Water on the surface would have evaporated instantly, so I guess a water exterior would then be impossible) Possibly they may have built the ship like a sort of inside out earth, with a water sphere inside the ship, and an artificial sun inside the sphere, or more likely they simply utilized the suns energy from outside the ship, as they obviously had very efficient energy sources as we've seen. A little energy from the sun would have gone a long way. OH heck I don't know, since they overcame gravity, maybe they didn't even need a water sphere. I'm not sure a suspended water sphere inside the ship would work either, but what do I know? It is kind of fun to imagine what it would be like. You could just jump upward and float into the water and swim...though I don't know how you got out of the water...maybe with some ladders you reach 'up' to or you could just jump like a fish and float back to the shell of the ship.

Maybe the ship was so large it had enough gravity in its mass to not need any compensation. Well anyway details aside, it's a theory. My guess is this space craft from the pre-flood era was a fairly large moon shaped object and it was coloured blue, maybe to give a bit of the look of earth as after all the earth is also a big blue marble as some have called it. And the blueness may be due to water and air. When the earth is seen from a distance the details of the land become more difficult to distinguish and the whole earth takes on a more bluish hue due to the atmosphere. Could this be why this "humanoid" built planet is the colour of Lapis lazuli? (Though before the flood, the earth might have appeared green?)

HOW BIG IS THIS MANMADE MOON ANYWAY?

That a manmade object could cast a shadow large enough on Jupiter to be observed by telescopes on earth has me wondering...just how big is this thing?! I thought maybe a high albedo was making it more readily visible as a 13th moon of Jupiter or a moon of Venus, but a cast shadow on Jupiter is hard to see at the best of times. They also say this planet Vulcan inside the orbit of Mercury was one seventeenth the mass of Mercury. People were seeing phases of the moon of Venus through telescopes also suggesting a huge dimension for this spherical ship. If I remember my math correctly when a sphere is half the diameter of another sphere it is 1/4 the volume, so if it is 1/4 the diameter then it would be one sixteenth the volume... very close to the specified mass from this observation.

Mercury is 3100 miles in diameter, but this would make the blue moon, Elysia, or Vulcan or whatever you want to call it 775 miles in diameter! A manmade object 775 miles in diameter?! Can that be possible? In space there are almost no limits to how big you can build something...but 775 miles!?!? But how else could such an object be visible from earth unless it was just plain huge and built on this scale? So I decide just for fun to calculate one seventeenth the mass of Mercury.>oh joy... math!< (You may want to check my figures, I mean if you're bored silly...but then what does that say about me?)

The volume of Mercury is 4 Pi 3100cubed / divided by 3 or 124788248987 cubic miles thus Vulcan would be 7340485234 cubic miles. Now work backwards and we can find the diameter of Vulcan. I get a diameter of about 559.5 miles across! GET OUT! That's still monstrous! Ok maybe since Mercury is difficult to see at the best of times and this particular sighting was in 1859, some miscalculations could have been made. Also it appears this sighting was a transit of the sun by this object. The size of the object would vary depending on how far from the sun it was and it could have been nearer to the orbit of Mercury when sighted, not to mention they could have meant just one seventeenth the diameter.

But even this is mind boggling. One seventeenth of the diameter of Mercury is still 182 miles across! Perhaps it was meant that the disk was one 17th the area of the disc of Mercury. This is a bit easier to calculate; we get 7547676 square miles as the disc of Mercury, and thus Vulcan would have a disc area 141323 square miles. We know that the area of a circle is Pi r squared. So the radius of Vulcan is about 211 Miles. That's still means it's about 420 miles across! There's no getting away from it. This manmade object is huge! These numbers are just beyond belief! But if this is accurate this starts to give an indication as to just how advanced the pre-flood technology was! It just dwarfs our current efforts at space technology. And it could be bigger still...

Other comments regarding this object says this planet is one quarter the diameter of Venus. Venus' diameter is 7519 miles (12,104 km) A quarter of that would be 1880 miles (or 3026K.M) across. Though that would cast a shadow big enough on Jupiter to be seen from earth, could it really be *that* big?

At present we are building an international space station that is 240 feet in length and is 15,000 cubic feet of living space. This does serve to show that even as in the days of Noah so shall it be in the last days. We are making a permanent space station and man will always be at one time or another in space, regardless of what occurs on the surface. The only difference right now is that it is still moored or anchored to the planet by an orbit rather than just wandering the solar system like that huge manmade moon.

GOLDEN CITY IN THE SKY DIMENSIONS KNOWN

(3rd ed. Insert 2016) Earlier I noted that the earth's pole shifted 100 Yojanas which equals 500-900 miles. Well I found something I had missed the first time, probably because I was rolling my eyes when I read it the first time. Tibetan tales tell of a city in the sky called Sudarsoma which was 2,500 Yojanas in length and breadth. (book 34 page 72) That would make the city in the sky a minimum of 1,250,000 miles wide. OK I think that's ridiculously huge and visible in a kids toy telescope. However that they say it exists and is huge, does substantiate the fact that it must even exist, at the very minimum my estimates of it size. Clearly when I read this the first time, this seemed off the wall, now reading the source the second time I wonder how I missed it! But then maybe the conversion of the distance of a Yojana is incorrect too.

THOSE MOONS WE'VE HAD

(3rd ed. Insert 2016) I probably mentioned this but in going through the 45 or so copies of the magazine I've been advertizing this book in {Atlantis Rising}, I decided to go through them all looking for some tidbits that might be useful for the third edition of this book. While reading the article "Late Arrival" (issue #96) by Mark Andrew on theories that the Earth's moon was captured and is a recent addition to the earth, I kept rolling my eyes and saying "C'mon guys… it was part of creation… Give it up!" (I believe, as we found in chapter five, where the moon was found to have just 1/8th inch of dust rather than the expected 137 feet, they figured it was a young moon, thus maybe it was captured recently… if we believe the earth and universe to be 4.5 billion or 13.5 billion or however many years old they want to believe. But consider, Mars doesn't have this same 137 feet of dust either…so the whole solar system…at the very least…is the same age: young. So I presume this is why this trying to determine when the earth got our moon theorizing started. Nevertheless this next bit has some interesting possibilities, so bear with it.) He might have come to the conclusion that the moon is new based on the amount of dust on the moon: 1/8th inch instead of 137 feet theorized. But Mars doesn't have this 137 feet either, so a new moon theory seemed completely illogical. I could easily have skipped and gone to the next article, but I like Astronomical stuff and you never know what might be in such an article… especially since it had a picture of Velikovsy in it, so I keep reading. … Suddenly I felt like I had been looking for any lost coins with my face down, then suddenly looked up and saw a room filled with treasure everywhere! I had been reading along and the date 3100 BC kept cropping up and the fact that the earth had at that time undergone massive upheavals. I said OK that's likely Peleg. (Actually I'm now rereading the article as I go here and being shocked at what I missed, but take the journey with me…its fun and when you see what I finally clicked into here… I think you'll like it) OK… we proceed.

There's mention that the moon might be a space ship…Ok I'm still asleep and keep reading…but a moon shaped spaceship… you mean like Elysia? One eye is creeping open. He speaks of a time in mythology where there are multiple references to a time before the moon existed. HUH? I don't remember reading any such myths. Interesting…But that's not possible as the moon was created with the earth. So at first I don't see, and keep reading. One myth mentioned seems like one of those 'make it up to explain to the kids the mysteries of the universe we don't understand' myths. Not impressed. I keep reading. A Greek Myth by Aristotle about when the Hellenes came to the land, they had been living in it before the moon came. OK more silly stuff… something like Stomping Tom's Connors song about loving till the moon falls to the earth. Poetry…showmanship. I'm still not impressed. I read more.

Another myth about the Arcadians dwelling in the hills before the moon appeared. I've still got my head down still looking for a coin. Then Velikovsky is mentioned. OH good, now maybe we'll get to some good stuff. What? Velikovsky mentioned a time about the earth being without a Moon? Ok I obviously missed that or I had the same reaction when he suggested it…C'mon it was with the earth when it was created… Move on! Another Author (Henry Kroll) suggested that maybe the Anunnaki aliens of Zechariah Sitchen fame brought the moon to the earth. Still nothing…maybe a coin over here… He starts talking about a time that it is thought *when the earth had a much more elliptical orbit* and a newly arriving moon might have stabilized the earth's orbit. (I didn't know *others* thought the earth had a more elliptical orbit!) OK I'm waking up now. I like this idea as it does fit. In had determined Mars had a very elliptical orbit imposed upon it by asteroids and maybe the earth had one for a while too for the same reason, making interaction between Mars and the Earth more plausible. So now I'm reading with my eyes open…though I'm not getting this new moon bit, but there might be a coin in here yet. He speaks of a Romanian bowl with a full circle and two crescents on either side which might be the earth with two moons. OK fluke. I know the earth had two moons at one time but for goodness sake! It's a freaking bowl! It's a design! Stop reading too much into that! Then in the same paragraph he mentions legends of African bushmen that "…tell of a time when the earth once had two moons". Great! More proof of Elysia. What else yah got? I'm still dismissing the earth capturing a moon business, but I keep reading anyway… He's clearly got a few interesting tidbits indeed.

Then he starts to mention the date 3100 BC. This is the time he states all high Mesopotamian civilization appears simultaneously… and he adds Egypt being founded about 3100 BC as well. Then another interesting tidbit pops up. He mentions Menes being known as a "Thinite" with "Thinis being a mythical place in heaven". And a place called Upper Egypt which used to be called Khemennu, or land of the moon. Wow. I missed *that* the first time I read this. Another name for Elysia? and more evidence that people came down from that man made moon to earth, just as I've deduced.

He's unknowingly…or knowingly talking about the arrival of "The gods". But he's still thinking this Menes is linked with our moon…not Elysia. Menes is then linked in the article with the Cretan "Minos" which means moon being. He's still trying to link all this with the arrival of the moon and confusing our moon with Elysia, but this is good stuff anyway! (And I'm thinking now…maybe Menes is the origin of our name the "Moon" in the first place, as some authors have stated our moon doesn't even have a name… but maybe it's named after Menes!) Wow I'm really glad I'm rereading this article again…I can't believe how much I missed. He's only mentioned the date 3100 BC once to this point so I wouldn't have yet woken up completely. Like I say I'm reading this article again as I write this and picking most of this stuff up the second time around.

Now once again the date 3200 BC and 3150 BC pop up with dating techniques with ice cores, tree ring dating and volcanic activity and…. OK more Peleg evidence, but he still keeps linking it with this supposed arrival of the moon. Good grief. He tries to link the coming of the moon to the tilting of the earth's axis to its current position and speaks of Atlantis and inundations. OK as we've seen you don't need the moon to create the massive tsunamis we've spoken of, we've shown it's the pyramids and Mars that have done this. I'm STILL not getting this moon business and he's not seeing Elysia and the Gods…well not to the degree I've fixed, though he has come remarkably close.

I read some more now….evidence that around 3100 BC…there's that date again…that some polar lands emerging and water drifting to the equatorial regions as a result of the moon pulling it there. This guy is putting stuff together well as these are two different bits of evidence coming from two completely different sources… "Dunbavin" and H.S. Bellamy. A good argument… but still I can attribute this stuff to Peleg and the pyramids, so I'm still not with you. He mentions the date 3100 BC again, linking it with the worlds megalithic structures such as the temple of the moon, the Stonehenge, and the approximate date the moon goddess worship commences. Good stuff! As you can see all this confirms my stating that around this period the man made moon Elysia showed up after the flood and the megalithic structures were made then and were all suddenly stopped around this date. His material is paralleling mine on a completely different tack, but with the dogged determination to link it all to the arrival of the moon. I'm picking up coins all over the place as I read this a second time and you as the reader I'm sure see the significance of this material in relation to what I've shown so far. He links the date 3113 BC to the arrival of the moon. I had suggested this was linked with the gods going back to the moon Elysia because of cataclysms they caused. So CLOSE!!! He states that maybe Velikovsky misinterpreted the arrival of the moon as the arrival of Venus to the solar system. That's not a bad call…if this arrival of the moon wasn't silliness. I'm still at this point

414 UFO Origins: Who They are, What They are, and Where They Come From.

not getting how anyone could think the moon is new if it was present at creation. The article ends and I'm scratching my head and start to mull the stuff over.

Most of this moon coming to the earth business he suggested that some have dated to about 12,000 BC. I know with dating corrected if this arrival of the moon had any basis in reality, this date corrected would probably date to shortly after the flood. But I start to put a few things together....consider these bits.

The Earth has been blasted out of its normal orbit as has Mars, and the Earth and Mars interact on several occasions, causing earthquakes, taking some of our water and atmosphere and sending us a few mineral samples. I never considered the moon getting any serious impact except all those craters from the 5th planet which blasted it. I didn't find much in my research that suggested the moon changed except the possibility that it now started to move around the earth. Obviously I read something about an arriving moon as apparently Velikovsky mentioned it, but my preconceived biases firmly kept the moon in the sky. Any suggestion that the moon was new to the earth was just not possible in my mind, so if I did read any such "nonsense" I just passed it up as silly myths. I had also concluded that Mars was at one time so close to the earth, to take our water that it was likely well inside the orbit of the moon. But if the moon was present at creation it's always been there... right? Well this article got me to thinking after I finished it the first time. With the Earth knocked silly, and Mars orbit suddenly highly elliptical ...could the Earth's moon have temporarily been lost at the time of the flood? Maybe Mars took the moon with it when it also took our water. Then later Mars came back and cause havoc on the earth and gave us back our moon. But another possibility crops up. Given that the man made planet (Elysia) destroyed the fifth planet, thus obviously meaning Elysia is very powerful...could it take a lost moon and bring it back to earth? This could account for these legends. Richard Hoagland seems to think the ancient gods, whoever they might have been, COULD move moons about, though as I write this I haven't figured out why. (Rereading my 3rd edition inserts I see this Chinese legend... "the five planets went out of their courses. In the night, stars fell like rain. The earth shook." If he's aware of this or similar legends, this could explain his reasoning and deductions. What little I've heard of Richards theories are very interesting, particularly because we seem to have come to similar conclusion by some very different methods: me by researching down here, and him looking closely at the solar system ...up there. He seems to think the records that show his conclusions are missing or hidden, I've found this stuff by deductions of what we still have.

I was also recently surprised to find out that Ceres, the first "asteroid" ever discovered because of the fifth planet being predicted to exist through Bode's Law, in fact isn't an asteroid at all... it's a moon! It's a sphere! This Ceres is smaller than our Moon, but as noted in creation, the moon originally stayed in the night sky as a light for the night. It seems it didn't revolve around the earth. Could we (the fifth planet and the Earth) have switched moons? After the fifth planet's destruction, the fifth planet's moon would have wandered. Assuming Ceres was the fifth planets original moon and based on what the explosion did to Mars, it's a wonder this little moon Ceres wasn't destroyed. Could it have been pulled away before the 5th planet was destroyed to protect it? Could the moon we have, have originally belonged to the fifth planet and our moon gotten lost or switched with what we now call Ceres? I'm not saying this is the case, but suddenly I can't rule it out! Interesting indeed! More likely our moon could have fallen behind or moved so much out if earth's orbit as to be like a second planet in the same orbit, meaning certain destruction should the two ever collide. Could the Elysians have carefully nudged it back into orbit with Earth, causing even more stuff to happen on the planet...stuff I have for the most part attributed to the pyramids and Peleg? Or could the Elysians have switched Ceres (our original moon) with the moon without a planet wandering in the asteroid belt? Or maybe Mars took our little moon then it got flung or taken to the asteroid belts. Then the moon we now have, is suggested to have been brought back to the earth to alter the earth's orbit and tilt and tides to make our moon's interaction with the earth more pronounced, and to make life and weather here more robust and accommodating to compensate for the loss of our water shell. Somewhat speculative conclusions, but interesting that some have come up with this hypothesis. Interesting possibilities.

THE VOTES ARE IN AND UFO'S ARE...

My conclusion is some UFO's live underground and underwater away from harmful solar radiation and radioactive carbon 14 in the atmosphere and some live in our solar system in a fairly large permanent and substantial manmade globe with a self sustaining ecosystem as close to pre-flood environment as we can possibly imagine. This ship they live in is in all probability a large and guidable blue sphere somewhere from 182 to 775 miles in diameter...or more. In fact it probably has a better safer environment then the pre-flood earth to allow it to get close to the sun and Jupiter.

It is possible that not only did the people in this man made moon come to earth after the flood and help rebuild civilization alongside the Sumerians, they appear to have been responsible for some of the hitherto unexplained monolithic cities around the earth. When all these ancient cities started being built simultaneously they over taxed the earth's ability and created or disrupted the earth's continents and then they left while the getting was good and stayed in their moon ever since.

Others of their kind may have devolved in this period and went underground or underwater. They do not want us mingling with them as it would introduce our devolved genetics into their gene pool, down trending the viability of them all. They are probably still genetically sound enough to be able to marry their sisters. The reason they live underground and above the earth in their blue moon is because there are at least two classes of them (based on genetic soundness.)

One class is the pre-flood fully complete and sound, genetically speaking, humans which live on the blue moon. They are descendants of Adam but not of Noah. There may even still be descendants of the Nephil alive living with them.

The second (and third?) class of UFO pilot groups are the people that lived on earth after the flood but then upon realizing the harmful effects of the solar radiation then coming to earth after the flood, went underground out of harm's way. They are on speaking and visiting terms with the blue mooners as they would be the informants as to the goings on earth. They (the blue mooners, or blue star folk) would one day hope to come back to earth when the earth is renewed to a pre-flood condition.

The earth bound underground/underwater UFO's of course would still be miles ahead of us technologically and biologically but are inferior to the blue mooners. These are possibly sons of Noah and more likely even are some strains among them that are direct descendants of Adam (blue mooners) only mingled with descendants of Noah. These are not inferior enough to be repelled from visiting the blue moon men. But likely not allowed to stay. As mentioned we've found some sightings of UFO's leaving right out of the Bermuda Triangle water area and going straight up into space...to visit them, on Elysia, the moon or Mars or who knows where. Richard Hoagland, by studying many pictures of our solar systems planets, feels certain someone has messed with them, terraforming them; left ruins and artifacts on them, domed ruins, and even whole cities are out there...stuff Nasa is trying to hide. (And we've talked about the moon men and their flashlights)

All we know about these blue mooners, appears to be in legends and their space sphere appears to even be confused with heaven in some myths. The Biblical new Jerusalem is a 1500 mile square cube that comes out of space after the Judgment. It appears that some have come to feel the celestial city is this Elysian Blue spherical moon. They are talked about in legends as gods partly because they seem to live forever, but they in fact would only live similar life spans to those of the pre-flood era, about 900 plus years, or possibly a bit longer if some Nephil still reside in amongst them. This would seem like forever to earthbound humans with average life spans of a mere 120 years (as was the case about 1000 years after the flood) or our current 70-80 year life spans.

The UFO's that have Greys, apelike creatures, and small men are genetic crossbreeds of man and who knows what, used to investigate the surface world. These short men "of Mu" may be rebels from this function and have decided to live on their own away from their makers. Some may still be in good with them and still work for them.

Then of course there's the various disguised creatures made to look like aliens to throw us off but in fact are normal men. And what does one do with the possibility that some might be angels or even demons. If this is the case they would seem to be the minority. I have to think if angels are going to walk among men, as is suggested in the bible, they are not going to use UFO's to get here or even appear to us near them to prevent confusion. They do not usually want to draw attention to themselves so they would come using the supernatural abilities they possess and walk among us disguised as men. They seem content to appear among men and appear to be men, and who knows if you haven't entertained them at some time. Angels seem not only to be messengers for men, but messengers for God and some indications suggest they are like scouts reporting events on earth. So they may be here a whole lot more often than we think. Whether they use the chariots of God to get here is up for debate.

WHO'S WHO

Consider this. Before the flood "sons of God" came to earth to take women. We have to assume "sons of god" mean the same people who are later called angels and the word 'angel' really means messenger. Before the flood, men and angels were on a more even playing field. Men were created a little lower than the angels.

As entropy or devolution declined our species, our interaction with angels is more on a protection and messenger basis rather than an interaction basis. Something that is quite interesting is that before the first judges of Israel started to happen after Joshua died, an angel actually talks to all of Israel to castigate them for their backsliding from the word. So even at that point angels were still interacting with men, albeit in more of a big brother role then as a near equal.

I suppose one possibility does exist. That the angels that came to the earth before the flood became alienated from Heaven to some degree, and they built the blue moon. But then why would they come to earth later and build and then leave due to dangers from the sun and the damaged earth. And if they lived forever why would they care, so it again seems to indicate the people of the blue moon are indeed human people with reason to want to get away from the damaging nature of the earth to their genes and ultimately their longevity. Also we have to assume angels with a Godly nature are not going to destroy a planet, but men with a destructive "evil" nature obtained from eating the fruit would.

One could surmise or presume by some of the UFO reports that there may still be a more interactive relationship between angels and the less devolved men of the underworld, under sea or blue moon, at least that seems to be the sense I get, but this is somewhat speculative too.

It may be that based on some descriptions of UFO inhabitants, such as smelly and disgusting looking that some of the UFOnauts may in fact BE demons. Recall that there is supposedly an underground sector of individuals that despise the surface people. Is there a connection? That's not to say demons need UFO's to get around, but they may be useful to them for deception. It would appear that God turned Satan and his followers into unclean beasts. However it also mentions that Satan can turn himself into an angel of light. The point here is IF demons are using some type of UFO's then it would seem they may even have more visible interactions with the people of the underworld, the underwater people and the Blue mooners as well. This brings to mind the scripture where there is a battle in heaven and Satan is cast down to earth. What the nature of that battle might be is not certain, and presumably it is between angels and demons. But I suppose it could be between blue mooners and them. But that too is only speculative, and I think we have to be carefull putting too much humanness into some of the prophesies such as this one. Some things clearly were not meant for men to understand or know, for example when seven thunders speak John is told not to record what it said. (Rev. 10:4)

This term "guardians of the sky" comes to mind. Do demon UFO's have to pass the moon to get permission to go further? I doubt this. We do know they at present have access to Gods throne room as they went to God and talked about Job. Obviously we can't get too mixed up in trying to figure all this out and we can't presume all is on the physical plane as God is spirit. By the same token we can't presume that phasing and being invisible means you are a spirit. Man is flesh and blood and we do not comprehend all that is of spirit. With humans in UFO's it may be possible to view these demons at the phasing level of the material world.

MORE THAN ONE KIND.

(3rd ed. Insert 2016) As mentioned I felt that definitely some of the UFO's fall under the category of demons or demonic manifestations. I did my best to consider other possibilities and came to the conclusion that there were three origins and explanations for various UFO's: Ancient Underworlders, Pre-flood Elysians and Demons, but, as above notes appear to indicate, a fourth type appears to exist.

Though I did not mention it, I did briefly come across the odd UFO story that mentioned that some UFO's had Nazi markings. Since I knew the Nazi symbols originated from ancient times I assumed what was meant was the swastika, and that these UFO's were of ancient origin. But I later realized they were probably talking about the Balkenkreuz cross, *not* the swastika. Shortly after publishing the book I found out that there was reason to suspect that some of the UFO's were in fact of Nazi origin and were headquartered in Antarctica. As crazy as that sounds, that branch of UFO's could in fact merit another complete book all by itself, and some books exist on this topic. So I won't go into it in any depth here. The stuff I found supporting this possibility was riveting and fascinating…even sobering and frightening. I have many good reasons to suspect that this explanation for some UFO's is completely valid. It was a roller-coaster ride finding this stuff out. Surprisingly this possibility was completely washed over by most UFO books…as most UFO books want to promote the idea that we have aliens hanging out on our planet…and suggesting they are Nazis simply cannot possibly explain them all. So suggesting they are Nazi's might make them appear to be out on the lunatic fringe. Suffice it to say this is a fourth aspect of UFO's to be considered. They obviously don't all have these markings or a whole lot more would have been written concerning this possibility.

UFO'S SOME BE DEMONS?

(3rd ed. Insert 2016) As I showed previously, many UFO's may be of ancient origins, and in today's time line that means some come from either Elysia, the underwater world, or from under the earth. For the most part I didn't focus too much on the possible Demonic origins, though I may have been trying to be overly fair considering my stated original bias as to their origins, so I may have neglected this aspect more than I should have. So in this next section I deliberately look exclusively for evidence that might indicate that some UFO's and accompanying phenomena are demonic. Once I determined to do this I realized there was actually quite a bit that could fit into this category. If this seems a bit religiously slanted please excuse it… but I think this might have some definite validity.

EVIDENCE ALLOWED CREATING THE THEORY, OR A THEORY TO MAKE ALL EVIDENCE PROVE?

(3rd ed. Insert 2016) It seems that UFO researchers occasionally want to force the UFO's into a single explanation and thus, like explaining world history in terms of evolution, the logic or theories breaks down in places. Most UFO researchers, generally speaking, assume they are extra terrestrials, or the gods. UFO's plain and simply just don't fall into a single category, so trying to explain them all as one type or phenomena will do the researcher disservice and writer can appear to be closed to options in the attempt to force them all into one bag. I tried very hard to avoid this tendency and stated what my preconceived ideas were right at the start, and only eliminated information if it seemed superfluous. Though it was usually clear what other writers thought of them, I felt the evidence was clear enough to be able to see through and come to my own independent conclusions. But nowhere has slanted theorizing been more evident than in a book on UFO's I stumbled onto and read after publishing this book. It's called 'UFO's What on Earth is Happening? The Coming Invasion' by John Weldon and Zola Levitt.

Had I read this book on UFO's first and had it been the only UFO book I read, I might have been swayed or cemented in the idea or conclusion that UFO's were all demonic manifestations. But having read other people's works and research on UFO's prior to reading this work, I found this book typical of closed minded conclusions before the research sort of work. Come up with a theory then find evidence or interpret it in such a way that it supports your theory. It's surprising how often research takes this tack. I have to say that I discovered that Evolutionists are extreme in this manner, though there were exceptions, notably Immanuel Velikovsky.

You may have come across studies that theorize that such and such is explainable with such and such a conclusion, and then they focus their efforts on proving their theory and forcing all evidence to fit the theory. They often ignore or explain away pertinent information that might suggest their theory isn't wholly correct, and only present the evidence that supports their theory or they present or even twist the evidence to fit the theory. This comes from people that don't want to think they've wasted their time or are certain they are right despite any evidence to the contrary. So these works end up being inadequate or completely wrong theories which become perpetuated simply because SOME of the evidence could support the theory or has been forced into a mold the researcher has built for the evidence. The book mentioned above is such a book. I have to admit I had to resist this tendency on a few occasions during my research for this book.

With my previous research it was immediately clear to me that Weldon and Levitt were forcing all UFO sightings and phenomena into one single category: demons. It was very frustrating to read. I saw them speak of things I had read about but they slanted the information wholly to their point of view and overlooked evidences in those stories that could point in another direction. But because I too had concluded that *some* UFO are of demonic origin I stuck it out, as I wanted to see what they DID have that supported their point of view. It took half the book to get to it, but they eventually DID make their case. In fact they came up with stuff I had not come across, by some researchers I was familiar with. Though like I said, this book was frustrating and though they jammed all their evidence to support this one single categorical concept of UFO's, the book is still worth checking out. Since this is an older book and probably quite hard to find I will present here some of their more persuasive points. I will also elucidate…ooh nice word…more on why I deduce some of these UFO are indeed demonic or at least anti-biblical in philosophy, and this is to some extent echoed by this source.

SIGNS SIGNS EVERYWHERE A SIGNS, BLOCKING THE SCENERY AND BLOWING MY MIND.

(3rd ed. Insert 2016) As mentioned, the bible foretells there being in the last days signs in the heavens. We saw the rare triple conjunction of Mars, Jupiter and Venus on June 17 1991, (a perfect bright inverted equilateral triangle in the sky) which could be considered one of those signs in the heavens considering it only happens about once every 2000 years. But another heaven in which there have been signs, is our own atmosphere. Though there have been seen in the skies UFO's since the flood, they are acknowledged to be occurring at almost frightening frequency of late. The bible tells of a time when there is a war in heaven and Satan is cast down to earth. Could the rash or UFO's sightings since 1947 or possibly even more recently be the result of Satan being cast down to earth? I'm sure some might interpret it this way. With UFO's suddenly showing up to, apparently check nuclear activity, this would be a good 'cover' for demonic UFO's start showing up too.

Some…not all, but some of the UFO occupants have been described as hideous and smelling horrific. These authors of the book "UFO's What on earth is happening? The Coming Invasion'" note that UFO occupants seem to have loose morals, mating willy nilly with those of earth, or flying about with no apparent reason, or even scaring us as though it's just for fun. (though mating might be ongoing proof they are the same species) But then who says Spacemen or as I ascribe, underworlders are as pure as the driven snow either and not prone to enjoying their 'vimanas'. Heck if I had one I'd be having a bit of fun flying them myself. Now sure the tendency might be to ascribe such hideous creatures as aliens, but the bible also describes Satan and his helpers as unclean beasts...able to transform themselves into angels of light. So sure one could argue they are aliens, but they also fit demonic descriptions as well.

These authors suggest the possibility of these UFO pilots (coming out of the sea?) influencing world politics or outright taking over the world to 'help' mankind. But they always seem to have an agenda of getting rid of certain undesirable people. What Weldan and Levitt really keyed in on, that I only vaguely connected, was the constant connection between many UFO's and the Occult, or striking similarities between the way they act or operate and occult practices. What was even more surprising was that many well known UFO researchers had also made this connection, though oddly enough, it either wasn't in the few UFO sources I read or I somehow passed over them. I suspect that authors, keen on making the alien connection of UFO origins would naturally want to play down the occult aspect. I did of course see it myself on a few occasions and just lumped it into demonic classification of *some* UFO's. But it was clear that there were some definite evidences to strongly suggest some of the UFO's seen were indeed either Demonic, or flown by demons. Recall we see God has 20,000 chariots of Fire, so why wouldn't demons have a few as well?

SIMILAR MODIS OPERANDI'S

(3rd ed. Insert 2016) This little section is how I grasp the situation, but next section is how others more familiar with the subject get it. Bear with me...this section is short. Some researchers connecting the links between UFO's and Demons have become aware there are similarities between them and poltergeists. Poltergeists are often considered to be demons, and doing their bidding can lead to trouble. Curious...just like demons being cast out of people, these poltergeists have been known to stop their behavior when told in no uncertain terms to cease and desist. UFO 'pilots' have been linked to séances...which are considered to be demons being talked to, but they mimic the person the seeker is trying to contact. (After all demons roam the earth and know your history fairly well, so they could easily stand in and pretend to be someone else...they can become an angel of light) Similarly mediums often get messages from 'UFO' people in the same way they get messages from the 'dead'. Indeed sometimes these" "UFO" people attempt to direct their 'contacts' and take over their lives exactly like demons; but the "UFO" cover is there to make them seem more palatable, or to disguise the connection.

Psychics are considered to be receiving messages from spirits just as some receive messages from "UFO's". Psychics could be prone to hear a deceiving spirit (as it says to test the spirits) or demon and taking personal or 'whispered' ideas and promoting them as God's. Some UFOnauts have said they want to take over the world after certain key elements of society have been gotten rid of. Those 'elements' would be people who have their number, who fight against principalities in high places, and know who at least some of them are and what they represent. "Extra terrestrials" have been dubbed by some as "Spirit Guides"... again the link is clear.

I hear all and See All Evidence that some ufo-nauts can be of demonic origin: George King of England's Aetherius Society says in 1954 he was "accosted" by a Venusian who stated he had been chosen to be earth's spokesman for their universal brotherhood. Accepting this lofty position King states "I have been in contact with Bhuda, Jesus, Shri Krishna, and other great masters". Any person familiar with the bible would instantly identify this as bogus malarkey and these prophets of the "new age" as they call themselves are dangerous deceptive nonsense, as new age stuff systematically equates Jesus as just another of the "masters" or great teachers. (That might sound biased but Jesus said "I am the way the truth and the life, No man cometh to the father but by me". Meaning he's not just another one, he is thee one. He won't bow to the gods of this world) (Book 29 page 9-10)

OTHERS HAVE SEEN THE CONNECTION

(3rd ed. Insert 2016) If you don't like how I put it...consider what others have said. Brad Steiger is said to have linked UFO's to thirteen different areas of Occult-Psychic phenomena, "including, Telepathy, Clairvoyance, and heightened psychic abilities on the part of the contactees" [UFO's What on earth... Page 101] US Air Force research had also spotted the link and made a statement... "A Large part of the available UFO literature is closely linked with mysticism and the metaphysical. It deals with subjects like mental telepathy, automatic writing [temporary possession], and invisible entities, as well as phenomena like poltergeist manifestations and 'possession'...many popular press accounts allege incidents that are strikingly similar to demoniac possession and psychic phenomena which has long been known to theologians and parapsychologists". [ibid]

Needless to say one needs to consider these connections carefully when looking into UFO's if perchance you should come into contact with them.

Consider this seemingly innocent little bit. Patrolman Herbert Schirmer of Ashland, Nebraska saw a UFO on December 3rd 1967. It seemed like a short sighting, but persistent problems clued researchers in, and under hypnosis, he drew a symbol seen on the UFO pilot's chest which turned out to be a feathered serpent. (Book 29 pg. 169-190) I could be wrong, but my theory on this symbol seems to indicate a Garden of Eden origin. The serpent beguiled Eve into eating the fruit who in turn got Adam to eat it, then the fall of mankind and the dominion over creation was lost, passing lordship of the earth from man to Satan. So naturally the winged serpent would be a perfect symbol for them. After the conversation with Eve and Adam, God changed the serpent to forevermore crawl on the ground as we now see snakes do. Upon hearing that snakes had vestigial parts to indicate legs I took it at first as confirmation of this. But I've since found out these vestigial bits are needed for reproduction. (As are vestigial legs on whales actually for the same thing...and nothing to do with walking on land.) Nevertheless it still seems plausible that the feathered serpent might be what the serpent looked like before the change thus the often seen symbol associated with UFO's. This could be an idolization of the serpent as something that took dominion of the earth away from man and placed it in Satan's hand. Again this is a possible interpretation of this symbol, though my interpretation could possibly influenced by my own preference for Biblical history. Oddly enough, though Eric Norman author of this reference book was decidedly anti biblical in his entire work, he too came to this as a possible conclusion for this symbol!!! (book 29 pg 191)

IF THEY ARE DOING IT NOW...WOULDN'T THEY HAVE DONE IT IN THE PAST?

(3rd ed. Insert 2016) So we can reasonably assume that some UFO's, of a more demonic origin, are spreading strange psychobabble to 'space brothers' for the purpose of deception. If this is happening now and we see they existed in ancient history, then these same UFO's after the flood would be spreading similar nonsense back then. One place that seems very likely to me is India as that is the land of a "million gods". It seems many of these UFO's were known back then telling India residents things like Brahmin was 154 million, million years. This doesn't mean India didn't have vimanas, as I'm sure they did, but where did all the gods that India looks to come from?

Things like this are being adhered to by current researchers as evidence that 'see we aren't the first to suggest the earth is far older than the bible wants us to believe!'(The serpent's deception?) Mankind today seems to be falling for the same lines: the earth is far older and there are more gods...as though a single God couldn't do all the things attributed to him, and it had to take eons to make the place, so there must have been more gods...to help creation / evolution along, and feel slighted if their god isn't given equal billing as the creator. Often people ask what makes the God of the bible the only god? OR Jesus? Why not Krishna or Buddha, or whoever. But if there is only one God...which one is it? Searchers for this truth need to then ask themselves if this one isn't and this one is then that one must be pulling many people's legs. "Copycats", or as Lucifer said "I will be like the most high".

Raymond Drake constantly belittled the biblical narrative, yet when it suited him he refers to it to substantiate something seen somewhere else. Then goes right back and belittles the biblical record again as though it was old news when it was written, like a bunch of copycats. He is quite happy to accept Ancient India tales of many gods, Sumerian gods, and apparently older texts are better texts. The way it looks from my perspective, is man initially knew all at one time and didn't need writing to tell him how to do stuff, but after the flood devolution set in. When pre-flood man saw the deteriorating post-flood man, he gave him council to build and some recommendations for life. These are recorded in ancient Egypt, Sumerian and such. Abraham's fathers served the gods. Then later on after Abraham, Isaac and Jacob and the Israelites going through the wilderness 500 or so years later and now well deteriorated, they needed the law once again, but a perfect law handed down from God himself and not just one of the gods. Thus this explains why there are older traditions then the biblical ones, but that doesn't mean they are more correct. As a fog descends on the mind of man, and a veil hides his ability to see, things of essential importance had to be re-iterated to the man behind the foggy veils. I don't have a problem with ancient man before biblical records having older texts. Older science, older knowledge. Heck the people that said them were the "men that knew everything". But as man declined, he needed a written record of things good for him, and laws that would prolong his life, as our capacity to understand diminished. As others on the earth had the old stories slowly descend into incomprehensible stories, a record understandable and highly prized as something from God was needed, to show the way to the Israelites and by example to the rest of the world. It makes sense. But other's either jealous or wanting pre-eminence, belittle this book, or promote their favorites above it.

Ikky monsters.(3rd ed. Insert 2016) Norman notes that a high percentage of space men, such as a "monster from a saucer" landing in Flatwoods, West Virginia, Sept 12 1952 seen by Mrs. Kathleen May and several children, had a blood red face, glowing green eyes, terrible claws and a sickening odour like "sulfur". A reporter (?) A. Lee Stewart, from the Braxton W.V. "democrat"(?) arrived shortly after this appearance and a "sickening, irritating odor" was present that was unlike anything he had inhaled while in the air force. (book 29 pg 7)

The Dark trinity? Another clue to some possible Spirit connection with UFO's was stumbled upon by Brad Steiger. With him being a UFO researcher and trying to decipher what these things are with help from fellow researchers he was suddenly plagued by "Men in black" and poltergeist activity. Also voices cut in on phone conversations, until some of his associates couldn't take talking on the phone about UFO's, and would only talk in person. These interruptions ranged from quirky out-bursts by unknown people to accidental eavesdropping of these people by Steigers group. They began to realize their whereabouts were always known when making reservation or even when forgoing reservations in hopes of evading the … well whoever they were. Trips on trains had 3 men in black watching them, then apparently following them to their rented rooms. Cars driven by them had license plates that didn't match up with anything known.

One of the researchers was visited at 3:oo am, while working a night shift by strangers (his impression was they were from the government) who addressed him by name, and asked about a certain UFO case he was investigating. Saying he was closing the case, the men satisfied, left. Twenty seconds later he followed them and should have seen them in the long hallway but they were gone. He walked down the hall about ten feet and felt some sort of energy, which lasted in that specific spot for about half an hour, slowly dissipating. Furthermore, no one at the front desk had signed any visitors in that night.

One of his fellow researchers "Bill" was getting freaked out by the harassment: anonymous calls detailing his actions he thought were secret, books jumping off shelves, mysterious presences, mysterious shimmering, little people visiting him in the middle of the night trying to sell him on some scheme to work with the 'intergalactic traveling evangelist', and on and on. So Brad Steiger went to spend some time with "Bill" to discuss the going's on. Upon his arrival he was very welcome and they felt much better. But that night at 2AM just when they were about to retire, Bill's wife spotted peculiar zigzagging light actions out in the sky. Then more lights, and then the entire sky seemed full and they were surrounded by them… "…

like besieged settlers in a wagon train". They followed them and the sky was full of them, "...skitter[ing] across the sky the way waterbugs skim across the surface of a pond".

"About this time"...Steiger himself began to be plagued with curious happenings to his mail, and telephone. Correspondence went missing in the mail, mail to him appeared to be tampered with, or mysterious stuff appearing over night from long distance with no post marks. His fellow researcher expecting Steiger's arrival overheard on his phone when he picked it up two people talking about a trip Steiger was about to take, including the motel he was going to stay in. The researcher broke in asking who the hell was on his line. They shut up, a click, and suddenly the line was clear. The curious nonsense started to impinge on Brad's life, and he would smell foul odours (such as are often associated with poltergeistic occurrences) in his office. One night while Steiger was working on a deadline things started happening. He heard a heavy footstep at the top of the stairs, but a quick glance showed no one was there. While at his work his painting of Edgar Allen Poe fell onto the floor, which irritated Steiger. Then papers started rustling near him, and then one piece of paper became airborne. Well Brad had had enough, and did not want to be disturbed so he just yelled "Just cut it the hell out!", and suddenly it all stopped...complete silence. And it left him alone for good. Suddenly he clued in and his book takes an interesting analytic turn as just what UFO's and accompanying phenomena could be... something we allow and then let ruin our lives. He just commanded it to stop and it did. (Book 30 pgs 193-208)

The similarities of this to an exorcism are unmistakable. Others let the occurrences frighten them then control their lives and live in constant fear...or become embroiled in the 'brotherhood of the stars' and talk gobbledygook. And it would seem to be a twist or precursor to possession by spirits. Brad just told them to take a hike...and it worked...like an exorcism before it takes hold, while others start UFO cults, or have constant activities in their lives making their lives miserable.

I mentioned that this influx of UFO sightings since 1947 could be the fulfilling of a prophesy stating Satan would be cast to earth in the last days...and the above bits seem to suggest a confirmation of this deduction. I wonder. Brad Steiger in Alien meetings (Book 32 pg 110) quoting John A. Keel "The Menace [from men in black] is not in our skies, it's on the ground, and at this moment it is spreading like a disease across the country and the world." Later Quoting Michael Talbot about how eastern Mysticism entities called Brothers of the Shadow "...like the MIB, are known for threatening students of the occult whenever they get too close to lifting the veil of Isis. ... they are the "leading 'stars' on the great spiritual stage of materialization'"(Pg 114 IBID). Brad himself says...

"MIB activity seems to be increasing....maybe it is happening because of the social transformation which seems to be upon us." (pg 118 Ibid)(I suspect the two may be linked) And his observation a couple pages later is most telling "In the majority of MIB reports which I have received in the past few months, visits by the once ubiquitous three dark-garbed men have been largely supplanted by trance states, whispered commands prompting the afflicted to become "one of them", shouted expressions of desire for the percipients' actual physical bodies. In addition, stigmata like rashes and wounds have appeared on the percipients' flesh, often taking the form of letters of the alphabet or esoteric symbols. The percipients' normal facial expressions and the basic characters alter in front of friends, so that the percipients appear to be possessed." (Book 32 page 122)(Prophecy notes that in the last days many would be possessed with devils. Could this be one of the avenues to this end?)

Something suddenly dawned on me. It's known that Satan wants to be like God so he mimics many of his forms and formats. Abraham was met by three men whom he addressed as Lord. Could the "Men in Black" be Satan's counterpart of the three 'men' who spoke to Abraham concerning the destruction of Sodom and Gomorra? Steiger noted that through time men in contemporary black dress have come to people, and this new form of men in black suits took predominance at the same time as James Bond movie's Agents of SMERSH hit the scenes. Brad Steiger connects popular imagery with how these MIB appear as though we of the general population, UFO researchers, and popular choice of imagery is what the "MIB" use when contacting whom they zero in on as possibly receptive. Satan can assume the look of an angel of light…why not men in black? I have to admit, it could fit.

LOGIC BEHIND THE SIGNS IN THE HEAVENS

We can understand why UFO's might be visiting the surface world more regularly now, because we have become so destructive with the waste, weapons and wonders we have that they are simply keeping tabs on us…after all they live here too. It may even come to the point where we become so dangerous to ourselves that they take an active hand in steering men. Perhaps they will come out of the sea and start to lead men or native leaders of men at some point. (Keep in mind since they often appear just like us, once they come out of the sea, unless we actually saw them come out of the sea we might not know they came from there and have no ideas of their origins.)

UFO's reports are staggeringly common now, though this might be because of so much technology in our hands that everyone has video capabilities in their pocket phones. So the appearances may not be more common, just the ability to record their visits is more common. But it would seem there's more to the accelerated UFO's sighting numbers then just proliferation of video technology. With the danger we represent to ourselves and the earth, perhaps they are changing their laws to allow some subtle form of intervention with the surface world dwellers, thus the more frequent incidences of UFO activity. Some want to interfere or stop us in our tracks and some want to change the courses of history if left to our own devices or at least slow it down. Who can say where that might lead? And as mention Demonic types could be blending in with the others too.

ALTRUISTIC OR REALISTS?

(3rd ed. Insert 2016) Many have suggested the UFO's with their visits to nuclear sites around the globe are warning mankind of the dangers of nuclear technology to man, and are trying to guide us away from the use of nuclear technology. They sometimes spent a lot of time near Nuclear facilities that have been shut down due to problems. But the reason they do this might not be completely altruistic. If as I've concluded they live underground, then they just might be trying to determine surface world affect on the underworld. The last thing they would want would be a China syndrome coming down to the places where they live. They might be assessing whether they need to move to get away from under some of these plants.

For example from New Years eve 1974 to Feb. 4 '75, for four weeks, UFO's often visited and monitored five nuclear reactors in Pickering Ontario. Why? Well for 5 months reactor #3 had been shut down because they discovered it had been leaking heavy water from 19 of the 390 pressure tubes. Six of the craft stayed in the area on New Year's eve for two HOURS!!! One stayed over the plant for half an hour, and on one occasion UFO's hung around the area for almost 8 hours! If you think of them as Aliens from space this intense scrutiny doesn't make any sense, but if you go with the theory they live here, under the earth, this monitoring and obvious concern about these plants and the malfunctioning of them make perfect sense. (book 46 pages 115-117)

MORE NEPHIL?!

The Sumerians actually saw their gods as opposed to making them up and caving their imagination. We know they were not gods of wood, stone or silver. They were people because they taught the Sumerians many things such as making metals and specialized crops like barley, plus these gods built actual buildings. Greek gods are deciphered as being the same gods as those of the Sumerians and the Greeks knew that the gods were in fact men, men of great abilities and such, but men all the same. They even bred together with the descendants of Noah, creating a similar situation as that before the flood with giants making an encore appearance.

Curiously when the 'sons of God' came to earth before the flood the offspring were called Nephil, which means bully or tyrant. These were also referred to as men of renown or leaders.

Surprisingly often the term "Nephilim" is used by other authors in relation to the Sons of God, not their offspring, but this is an error. The term is specifically meant to denote the offspring of the sons of God and daughters of men. For example we saw there were offspring of angels.

A slight variation of this same word is used once more AFTER the flood in Numbers 13:33 when referring to the sons of Anak. They are called giants [Nephil] which came from the giants [Mighty men of larger or mighty stature or abilities.] The first word for giants in this phrase is basically the same as the pre-flood word used to describe the children of the sons of God and women. The second use of the word giant in this phrase is more related to the characteristics of these people.

But were not all the Nephil destroyed in the flood? Obviously not! So we see another clue that someone other than Noah either survived the flood or more specifically, was not in the flood. OR we have to conclude that more angels came to the earth after the flood, to make more Nephil. Or we could just say the word was used to describe the similarity to the pre-flood Nephil, but why call them Nephil then? The words chosen are very specific and precise when used in scriptures. Admittedly the two words are slightly different. One is Nephiyl and one is Nephil, and with my limited resources I do not know the meaning of the subtle difference, nor do I even know which one is used where, as the distinction is not clear. I only know they both mean approximately the same thing, so perhaps there is some flaw in this deductive reasoning. But it deserves mention for further work with someone who knows.

Nevertheless I thus suggest that these Nephil were descendants of the gods and it suggests some of the gods were Nephil. But for them to survive they would have to have been off the earth at the time of the flood or on the ark. Were the sons of Noah Nephil? Not likely as the lineage is clear back to Adam. A "son of god" descendant would not come from the lineage of Adam. But if they weren't then where did more Nephil come from? These Nephil were the sons of the giants. No mention of Noah or his sons being giants is stated either. We are therefore stuck in what seems an impossible situation and have to come up with an origin for these giants. No one, as far as I know, has bothered to do this.

((2nd ed. Insert 2008) However it has been noted that creatures were often bigger in the past, but they were in fact the same creatures we have now that just grew larger. We saw that dinosaurs existed because they never stop growing all their lives and beavers and other animals reached huge proportions. It's possible I suppose that when the bible refers to Giants in the pre-flood environment and perfect genetics that it was the environment that made them giants and not some sort of interbreeding with the sons of God or whatnot. So possibly the land that the sons of Anak were in was of such a quality that it fostered better than average growth in the people that lived there. But I tend to think that this would then have made the Israelites giants too, which it did not, so I have to think some other origin for these giants is probable such as I have mentioned above.)

Could these giants be the result of genetic tinkering? I don't thinks so. It seems to me genetic tinkering can only play with what is there. If gigantism isn't in the DNA can you add it, and if you can...where do you add it? Admittedly it would appear that giants may have been artificially produced BEFORE the sons of God came to earth before the flood, but these giants were not referred to as Nephil, only the children of the sons of God have this annotation. (if I was to make a guess as to where giants came from I would suppose some gene of the dinosaurs was input into the men that they would continue growing all their lives like reptiles do.) This does seem not out of the realm of possibility. Some giants mentioned were ridiculously tall...30 40 feet or more. If there are genuine remains, then mixing genes with reptiles just might have been the reason some giants existed, and might explain their attitude.

I suggest the second strain of giants are sons of the gods, but the gods were not Noah or the sons of Noah as far as we have established, so we therefore have to presume Noah's family were of normal stature and abilities as well. Thus we have to tentatively conclude some Nephil were on the "Great ark", "Elysia", or the "blue moon" at the time of the flood. After all the Nephil were also leaders and men of renown.

These two descriptions of the Nephil suggest some were bullies and tyrants and some were leaders and men of renown. So I'm saying not all Nephil had all these characteristics and some of them were on good terms with men and not lording it over them being bullies.

Do we consider bullies leaders? Perhaps some people do, but by and large we usually consider them as something less than this. Sons of Nephil, tyrant bullies or leaders, could also be one or the other, that is bullies or leaders. This is who I think these Nephil sons of Anak were...sons of the giants...which were not sons of Noah. No matter how much you wrangle with this it's not going to go away: there were giants *after* the flood, even up to the 19th century, and some may possibly exist today in some jungles.

Giant graves have been found in America with skeletons in them that were 10-12 feet tall. By giants I mean men of stature from 11 1/2-13 Feet(Goliath: six cubits and a span) to a possible height of 15-17 feet (Og: his bedstead was 9 cubits by 4 cubits or 16-18 feet long, so assuming one foot clearance he would be a little shorter than his bed) (I've decided to add the evidence of the existence of giants in the past in the third edition because I've realized it both gives an indication of devolution, and validates ancient histories that speak of them as well. So I placed it in Chapter 8)

Though the bible does say we were created a little lower than the angels, the word used for angels in that verse is not "messengers" but Elohiym, a plural word, the same word used for God in many instances. But I have to assume it means the sons of God, which would be a plural word. This same plurality is used when God comments on man after he eats from the fruit. He says, seemingly agreeing with the serpent, that man had become like one of us. (Genesis 3:22) This curious statement coupled with the Serpents words to Eve has tainted mans view of his betters and even of himself ever since.

Chapter 10 Part One

WHO WERE THE GODS

GOD ACKNOWLEDGES GODS

Though God clearly states there are no other Gods, he does acknowledge gods and that he will judge them (Psalm 82:1) (caps and lower case letters is the way the differences are noted: IE Lord, lord, and LORD) This lends more validity to the conclusion that there was a time when the gods reigned. Further on He says "I have said, ye are gods: all of you are children of the most high but ye shall die like men. (Psalm 82: 6-7) There is seen here equating normal men with the gods because we are all children of God. So these gods were mortals, and he even appears to be referring to us as gods or equating us with them. (Emphasis on the small 'g').

Furthermore, though God did not want us worshipping other gods, yet he said not to revile them, nor curse the rulers of the people. (Exodus 22:28) So these people were not to be worshipped but by the same token not to be abhorred should we meet them. In other words treat them like people, and respect them and give them due honor. Yet again he lets the title 'gods' stand when referring to them. This seems to indicate another class of men not necessarily of the surface of the earth, though indeed some people of the earth have been called gods, and indeed some indications suggest rulers were by their position also referred to as gods, or at least lumped in the same class as them, almost as though when the gods ruled at one time the term 'god' was equated with a ruler or leader. And sometimes these rulers were actual direct descendants of the gods.

The distinction of the small letter 'g' is usually always in place when referring to men as gods. But whenever men have been called God and allowed this title to stand or been presumptuous enough to accept something as a man that belongs to God, they have been chastised (Nebuchadnezzar), destroyed (Herod), or been purveyors of great wickedness (the antichrist). So this is clearly not a title meant for mortal men.

Obviously there are many shades too numerous to go into here, for example the Caesars, as I understand it, had the titles of gods and when the Christians did not bow down to them or acknowledge this 'godhood' status of the Caesars but rather gave that status to Jesus, they were persecuted. We also see that Herod was said to speak with the voice of a god (small 'g') and the angel destroyed him. (Acts 12) This is curious because small 'g' gods are acknowledged to exist by God himself, but this word god when used for Herod has some sort of shade of meaning in the title 'god' that was not acceptable. So I would conclude it is not wise in any way to call others by the term one of the gods, for it is better to err on the side of conservatism in this regard.

Furthermore when the angel was worshipped by John, the angel quickly stopped this, declaring himself as a fellow servant of John, his brothers and the prophets, and then told him to worship God. That is to say he equated himself, an angel, with John, a man, and that worship was meant only for God, something we will see later on is an important distinction. (Revelations 22:8,9) But this is important here too. The gods therefore were in all likelihood not angels either. If they won't accept worship, would they accept the title 'gods' and would they even rule? Not even the slightest clue ever suggests the angels ruled the earth. As close as it gets is when the angel led the Israelites and he was known to be an angel, and not a 'god'. So if the gods weren't angels, who were they?

THE RULING OF THE GODS NARROWS DOWN BABEL.

We know that there was a time in the past when the gods lived and ruled on the earth. Though I've actually given you most of the answer as to who the UFO's are, and that they seem equated with the gods, why they are actually mentioned in the bible may not have seemed as amazing as it should.

Abram was probably born in Ur, 8 years short of 300 years after the flood; about the time the gods left. We see that Sarah had an Egyptian handmaid who seems to have lived in this region with them around 368 years after the flood. This helps to narrow down the time when the languages were changed. Why? Because if Sarah had an Egyptian handmaid, then "Egyptians" as a people already existed at that point in time. We know Abram (Abraham) came from Ur (which means 'the region of light'.) They came from the east: in Mesopotamia, likely at the head of the Persian Gulf. Ur was of the Chaldees, that is, **a place of the descended**! It's felt by some that this was in a place where there is a temple known to be dedicated to the MOON! (Bible dictionary, Smith, Peloubet 1884)

Fantastic! I couldn't ask for better confirmation! I had thought maybe this 'Ur' place was in Sumer, though it is in the same general area. After finishing this work and proof reading I decided to look up and find out where Ur was and, for whatever reason, add the location of Ur here. I mean after all we know Abraham's fathers served the gods in Ur, so I figured I might as well determine where these gods were. It turned out to be in a region of brilliant light, and in a place of descending, likely in a place where there is a temple to the moon! Without knowing this, I had already deduced it or something very similar in the previous chapter!

I have to guess the blue moon descended there as well as in Sumer and it is these gods the fathers of Abraham served. It all fits. We know Abraham's fathers (Nahor and Terah) served these gods but it does not seem that Abraham did. Though Sitchen seems to think he may have, but he appears to have been born too late (8 years before they left) if my time line is correct. This to some degree helps place the rule of the gods in the timeline, and it matches the timeline of the Egyptian legends that say before the first dynasty the gods ruled. Which has been determined to be sometime before 3100 BC.

Nahor was born 193 years after the flood, and Terah was born 222 years after the flood. At this point after the flood life spans were still 4-600 years, so then Noah or the sons of Noah could not be the "gods" spoken of, for if they were the gods, their reign would have ended maybe 600 years after the flood, not 300. Shem the son of Noah died AFTER Terah and Nahor, so their great great great great great Grandfathers were outliving them! (we don't know when the other two [Ham, Japeth] died)

No one mentioned in the bible during this time appears to be the gods, yet they served them. But this is at the dawn of civilization. If the gods weren't Noah, and weren't any of his descendants, then who were the gods? Though you know the answer as seen in last chapter, now you can see why this is such a mystery.

MORE SUMERIAN STUFF FROM A MORE TRADITIONAL SOURCE.

(3rd ed. Insert 2016) Deductions of Ur's key place in history seem to be bearing out. Ur was the place of descending. Was that name a reference to the gods coming down there? To get away from the maverick researchers material, I looked in *Near Eastern Mythology* by John Gray and other sources to get the official conclusions on the Sumerians. It is concluded that the Sumerians built the tower of Babel. (and I quickly interject here: "All seem to have spoken one language, and to have lived in great peace, black men and white together." Atlantis by Donnelly pg. 176 quoting the Popul Vuh) These Sumerians are said to have mingled with the gods who came down. This seems inescapable. Thus the "place of descending" aka

Ur, is the place where the gods came down. This was immediately after the flood, presumably to renew civilization on earth. Thus Sumerian was the original language as deduced. It's said Oannes (half man half fish) presumably a man in fish costume, or diving gear, (though I don't rule out a genetically engineered man/fish), taught the Sumerians by day and by night went back into the sea. So I queried... thinking out loud... were the gods who came down, those we now refer to as Sumerians or did the Sumerians come to the area and meet the gods when they came down? We know Noah would have spread out from the mountains of Ararat which are nowhere near Ur. It would seem the Sumerian came to the area as they are said to have mingled with the gods...named the Annunak, or Anu. I think it is safe to assume this is who the sons of Anak (those referred to in the book of Joshua) are descended from. This has incredibly huge in ramifications. We seem to solve two mysteries, or problems with this one piece of ancient history. First we answer the problem of how there could be more giants after the flood, if they were all killed in the flood. AND we prove that the gods descended in Ur, like the name suggests, thus we show that indeed someone besides Noah survived the flood...because they were never in the flood or indeed even on the earth at the time.

PARALLELS. (SOME BIBLICAL INTROSPECTIONS)

(3rd ed. Insert 2016) As noted we know Abraham's fathers served the Gods, in the land of Ur, the place of descending. Sitchen asks the question who was Abraham?... meaning before the time when God calls him out of Ur. He deduces he is a Sumerian, but no average Sumerian. His father served the Gods, and these would be the ones who came down...and by being his son he would have had some of his powers. Later on Abraham does things not typical for average citizens, but of high conduct (not taking booty) associated with Pharos, makes treaties, led bands to stop kings, and deduces he is "...a personage of high standing skilled in negotiation and diplomacy." So there seems to be some interesting irony in God's choice of Abraham. His father's served the gods in Ur where they lived, the gods that are the origin of so many myths and I wouldn't be surprised if his father is part and parcel of those myths. Abram no doubt informs his house and says I am leaving to serve God. If Terah, his father received directions by speaking to the gods and knew what they were up to, it adds some irony when God says can we hide what we are about to do from Abraham concerning Sodom and Gomorrah. Though I don't know ancient languages and can't prove this, there are so many parallels between the gods and God, I have to think this is one too. Parallels? Consider...

Myths and legends show the gods fought wars on earth and man fought for his gods, but the gods used man for his purposes and many men who fought for the gods died. Jesus states he will return and fight the enemies of God and his servants.

The gods left the earth, abandoned it and said to the people who served them they would return though some of them left with tears and never returned. Jesus was watched leaving but said he too would return. Isis was said to have conceived without conception. Mary was a virgin giving birth. The gods descending apparently taught the Sumerians skills, and laws. God came down on a mountain gave laws to Moses. The gods moved massive weights, Jesus said we can move mountains. I have to think God is using the parallels deliberately.

Because of so many parallels, some have suggested God was just one of the gods, and since the gods came first they must have pre-eminence. Some have said the bible is using earlier sources and can't be relied on, choosing rather to rely on say Sumerian, ancient Indian, or Egyptian texts. As if more than one witness to an event and thus more than one source is not possible?! And as though people need to read 'earlier sources' to be able to tell the story accurately? But it appears, or could easily be interpreted as God using what man is familiar with and showing he is thee God and better than the other gods who used, abused, and let man down. And don't forget the parallels also exist because the god of this world (the devil) said I will be like the most high, so it could just as easily be argued that he is copying God! Not the other way around.

RULING "GODS" A NEWER PHENOMENA

There is no mention of pre-flood people serving other gods, and indeed before the flood, no other god is referred to other than God himself. Curiously the serpent says to Eve that she and Adam would be as gods if they ate of the fruit. You and I know that they were still men and they died like men. Could this title somehow have attached itself to these pre-flood men once they came back to the earth after the flood? Again I believe all the clues indicate some of the pre-flood men and women were in space at the time of the flood. Though one might think based on this assumption that many would have escaped because if they had flying saucers before the flood they could just hop in and get off the earth, which speaks of the incredible suddenness of the collapse of the water sphere to get every last one that was on the earth at the time.

This raises a fair question. If man had chariots of this type before the flood, why then have none of them been found in the clay layer of the earth? One possible explanation. The sons of God which were eternal beings occasionally went to God and were still welcomed in his presence had inside information. They took 20,000 chariots and left the earth making escape impossible. Admittedly a somewhat speculative explanation dependant on the theories presented here, though it is a possibility when we realize God does have this number of chariots.

As one might suspect there is reference to people from this pre-flood period actually being the gods of the post-flood era, once again indicating that somehow pre-flood men survived. This can only be in the ark of Noah or the off earth ship I have been calling the blue moon. We have seen already that the stature, physiology and abilities of the pre-flood men were far beyond the ability of the post-flood men, and this difference appears to be what was in place when the gods ruled on the earth. In other words it seems that pre-flood men came to the earth after the flood to help and settle on the earth again and found themselves ruling because their abilities were far above men born on the earth after the flood. I have to think they tired of this adulation and they were heartsick to see man physiology disintegrate before their eyes, and had to leave when it became unbearable and dangerous to them as well.

WHY WEREN'T THE GODS SUBMITTING TO THE ELEMENTS?

Before I go on, one might ask the question: well if the sun was affecting men after the flood, to diminish their capabilities, why wasn't it diminishing the gods capabilities as well, making them the equal to post flood men and not their superiors? What was in place to make this difference so apparent, that they were thus being considered gods?

First. If they were observed coming to earth in their blue moon or a smaller craft clearly with them originating from the blue moon, this would have superseded the fact that they were just men, as they were apparently superior men to be able to do this. Coming from the heavens like this would put anyone in awe. Even if they explained till they were blue in the face, with men already succumbing to the elements they still would be in awe.

Second, after the flood men would have simply continued on, possibly not fully cognizant of the subtle changes going on in their physiology. They would have declined gradually thinking they were for the most part normal, when in fact they were rapidly (at first) declining in cognitive and physical abilities. Men of the earth would only have this fact dawn on a few individuals when they came into contact with the pre-flood men and realized something was happening to them to cause this difference. Even if they understood what was happening, the difference would have been vast already. After all they were told that these people called gods were in fact men of pre-flood origin, so they would have wondered what happened.

The gods when they came back to earth may have immediately recognized potential problems before returning to the earth, or certainly after coming into contact with the Sumerians. They would have done tests to see if the earth's surface life would be a problem and took precautions before coming here. They may have used protective clothing and helmets, and limited their exposure to the environment.

This is why the gods are often drawn in peculiar clothing or have unusual skin colours. Anubis is blue skinned and he appears to have been wearing a helmet that looked like a dogs head, or at least that is one possible interpretation of this character. Though they may have had a different skin colour which was not exposed to the sun like ours similar to the green children, this different colour may also be like something of a protective measure against the sun. People not knowing this, might have thought these people were in fact red or blue skinned rather than red or blue tinted with something akin to our ultra violet sunscreen. If they appeared to have a different skin colour this may have further differentiated them as gods somehow different from men. But they may not have had a different skin colour at all! They may have been wearing some advanced formula of sun screen ointment that turned their skin the colour of the ointment. But this is purely speculation. Still if I had my druthers, I would hope they did have a green or blue skin...I think green and blue girls look pretty cool....but then maybe I've been reading too many comic books.

Of course we can't forget the Red men in history and the Green Children. Legends exist of Blue people as well. So coloured skin appears to have existed, whether genetic, race or result of not being born under the sun, Lion Men, Anubis, types and on...maybe the gods were mimicking animals, or genetically crossed or mimicking genetically some demons.

ON THE OTHER HAND...

On the other hand maybe the gods stayed too long and *were* affected by the earth's reduced or devolved environment. Remember the reproductive organs are the most susceptible to radiation. Their cognitive abilities might not have been reduced much or returned to normal when out of the effects of the devolving earth and the direct sun, back up on the Blue moon or Elysia. BUT when they got back there, they were examined and determined to be compromised and repulsed, or kicked out and given visitor status only. With their now faulty genes they were not allowed to mingle with the Elysians anymore and devolve the gene pool. Frosted at the rejection they attacked Elysia thus the many legends of wars in heaven. They lost and were cast down to the earth and divided the underworld between the groups. Thus Poseidon went under water, Hades was given the domain "far below". (book 17 pg 54) So we see an even more likely scenario for the war of the gods in the heavens and their retreat underground and into the sea.

A Greek legend infers that after an interplanetary war, a stellar race retreated underground. (book 23 pg. 178-179)

INDISTINGUISHABLE FROM MEN

This one is big...see if you catch it. The Ainu of Hokkaido Japan claim they are children of the gods that came from the skies. They say that these gods were the same people who live in the clouds and sent flying saucers to earth. A monument marks the spot where the first Ainu came to earth. (Book 4 pg 112, Nat. Geo. Feb 1967 Pg. 291, 292) I didn't make the connection until the last day of working on this 3rd edition! These "Ainu" have to be the same gods that mingled with the Sumerians! They were called Annunak or the Anu, and the giants that came from them, the Anakim from the land of Israel that God helped Joshua's army beat.

When Andrew Tomas (an author of some of my source material) went to India he was revered as a god. Though he tried to dissuade them, they didn't want to take any chance that he might be a sky being from the stars, pretending to be from Australia. (Book 11 pg. 173-174) This is a curious slant indeed. Here we see that the gods as known by those in India are men from the stars, or sky people, or as the bible might put it a Host of heaven, but on the other hand indistinguishable from people from Australia, or wherever. (Do they have green people in Australia?) It has been noted that not only do these UFOnauts look like us they often speak with an accent. (Book 43 pg. 198)

It is noted in many ancient ledgers, that after a great catastrophe the gods of Egypt, Greece, Rome, Scandinavia, and Mexico withdrew from the earth. These gods were not thunderbolts, the sun or the moon, or even spirits, but actual people usually described as men that came from the skies or the stars. (Book 43 pg. 235-236) But we also see they left after a catastrophe that in all likelihood changed the earth to a far more hostile environment. This suggests that the last Peleg attributable to the pyramids is around 300 years after the flood. And this ties in with the date 3100 B.C. when a world catastrophe is known to have happened, when all the calendars start, and the reason the gods left, because they caused it.

Ancient Greek histories speak of a time when the earth was ruled by gods, and one of their plays speaks of "god from the machine". One Greek poet in speaking of the gods said there was one race of gods and one race of men, both which came from a single mother. (Book 23 pg. 209) At one time long ago I had heard this and it didn't make any sense to me. This theory clears it up completely. If you didn't get it, Eve the mother of all bore the pre-flood race. Most died in the flood, some (Noah and sons survived and devolved into us men, and some of Eve's children didn't devolve as they were protected in the off world Blue moon craft, later to be considered gods by the descendants of Noah. Thus the gods and men were descendants of the same mother Eve. Again…it all fits.

The Egyptian Imhotep (same as the Greek god Imouthes) was promoted from "mortal" to a god.(Book 8 pg. 91) Admittedly this shows some of the gods were men descendants of Noah, but it also shows that mortal men were gods.

All UFO Pilots are humanoid and it has been deduced that a common biological origin is a serious possibility (Book 46 pg 55)

Though stated before, constantly the ancients speak of people being descendants of the gods. They had children by the gods which in turn had descendants, and some lines continue to this very day. I'm sure the gods knew what they were doing. This was proof they were human! They could not possibly have descendants from these marriages if they were not the same species as us! As mentioned there are 22,000 species of spiders and none can mate with another. Consider the mule. It is a cross between a donkey and a horse, different species. It's possible to cross some species, but Mules cannot have offspring. I'm sure genetics prove the gods therefore HAD to be humans. And they are thus descendant of Adam, if not Noah, as we have already deduced. So we come to the same conclusion two ways. The gods, though they came from space after the flood…were human. If evolutionists or panspermians want to somehow say by some bizarre fluke two human species by some incredible fluke evolved on two star systems and then met 400 million years ago so they could squash trilobites under foot with their sandals, they can go ahead and believe that. In my mind, it just can't possibly get any clearer; the gods were human and part of the same creation, sons and daughters of Adam and Eve and just happened to be in space at the time of the flood. They came back and thus the legends.

Teatihuacan is said to have been built by the gods who were white giants(Book 21 pg. 159) And when an Incan has kids of unusual fairness the people say they are descendants of the gods (Book 21 pg. 166)

The god Quetzalcoatl was in every regard human and came from the east. (book 21 pg 162)

When Columbus landed about 50 natives greeted him, kissing the members of his parties' hands and feet, begging them to be taken to their heavenly dwelling. Though Columbus's ships pale in comparison to the ships of our day, they must have seemed like veritable palaces to the Incas.

The natives of Ellis Island worshipped a god named John Thrum who came down from the skies bringing gifts. This god stayed for five years then left. But John Thrum was an American airman who flew to that island in 1941 during the war against Japan. (Book 34 pg. 199)

The only conclusion we can make when we ask the question "who were the gods' is that they were at least, for the most part either men and women which descended to the earth sometime after the flood in the blue moon. Some were men and women in safe areas of the earth away from the degenerative influences of the sun and the radiation building up on the earth since the flood. Some were simply heroes that seemed to later be given the status of gods.

WHO WERE THE GODS PART II

T his will be more of a social commentary than one that would continue on with the general themes as seen thus far. I speak plainly here.

Later on this becomes a religious commentary on some changes occurring in society, and speaks more to those who have accepted the bible as the word of God and attempt to live by the words spoken in them. I'll let you know when that starts so you can decide whether you want to continue reading.

HEROES IN A BOX: WHO ARE THE GODS OF TODAY?

We need to encourage different heroes. We have idiots on TV and many in society often follow their lead, when we should be encouraging people to seek knowledge, be inventive, innovative, and upright in character. While people argue that viewers don't copy what they see on TV, they forget that what you think about and meditate on, you end up emulating in some way. How many people do hair styles or dress like these heroes in the box or talk like them and say the same things. We are supposed to think about things that are good and pure but all we see are things that are anything but. Our society, though slightly behind the "standards" fostered on TV, it seems that clearly TV, movie, and singer personalities want to become the driving force that in many ways dictates society's moral standards. So to say people do not mimic what they see on TV, the theatre or the stage is ignoring the obvious. Now no doubt you're aware of the violence, sexual looseness and rebelliousness we normally blame on them, but I'm going to throw you a curve. They spout stuff like global warming and climate change and we follow like zombies lock step. Idiotic politicians and scare tactics blaming forest fires on climate change, not even looking at the real science, but following heroes that want people in jail if we don't believe their climate lies. They attack oil while driving cars and flying jets and expect us to be the ones to sacrifice. Sounds like how the gods took advantage of mankind. Boy nothing changes. We seem to be burying our heads in the sand in order to justify the abuses of these media to continue acting negatively on society.

EDWARD R MURROW'S FEARS REALIZED

On October 15 1958 Edward R Murrow passed out a well publicized speech commenting on the use of TV and radio. (This speech can be found on the internet) He was seized by a fear of what they were doing to society. He felt they were responsible for decadence, escapism and insulation from the realities of the world in which we live. [It appears he was afraid of something very similar to what Timothy predicted when he said men would be lovers of pleasure more than lovers of God. (II Timothy 3:4)]

He commented that news which had to be acceptable by sponsors to be used as news, isn't news. He showed concern about advertisers promoting shows that will reach the largest audiences just to sell their cola or whatever, thus the process of fostering escapism from reality and insulation would continue, to the detriment of that society. (exactly like happened to Quebec with targeted consumerism.) Indeed now the advertisers are further speeding up the degradation of society, by utilizing somewhat lude and immoral situations to promote their products; in effect catering to a society they to some degree helped create.

Some positive programming did come about because of Murrow's reproof. But swill still permeates the box. Naturally the problem becomes the multiple channels on radio and TV. Those who have distaste for learning things of value will simply change the channel. And this has trickled down to the children. If parents wanted to watch pablum, the children were subjected to this too, and when they were finally exposed to hard truths they often rejected them, in favor of what they grew up with.

These media need to be used as vehicles to illuminate and inspire. There should be a one or two hour slot every day on every station in broadcasting devoted to illuminating the mind rather than tickling the funny bone, increasing our tolerance to horror or lowering our moral standards. If people don't want to watch, listen and learn from quality programming, they can turn off the TV or the Radio and have some quality family time, and that is sorely needed too. But computers have made a mess of even that avenue.

School didn't end when we graduated grade twelve or college or University. Learning should be an ongoing process fostered by our media. Were this the case, maybe our children wouldn't be so allergic to learning when they go to school. These media need to teach that knowledge is better than gold (Proverbs 8:10) The ear of the wise seeks knowledge (Proverbs 18:15) and by a man of understanding and knowledge the state of things will be prolonged. (Proverbs 28:2)

Often specific groups are not allowed broadcasting privileges, for example I understand Christian radio programming is not allowed in British Columbia. Meanwhile Evolution based programming (an admitted religion) floods the airwaves unchecked.

These media have become methods of selling goods to the public and social engineering, rather than vehicles of informing. (To be fair there are still some good solid programs but sadly they are few and far between.)

Any information given on these media has to pass the biases of those selling merchandise, the bias' of the station and the bias' of the country and the bias' of the establishment. For example though there's little reason to believe anything promoted by the evolution theory, I've yet to see any program presenting material that uses devolution or creation as an logical basis when presenting archaeology, history or whatever, unless of course it is on a Christian Sunday service.

In fact people that support established "science" refuse to allow anyone presenting science that contradicts established theories, and they will even heckle and act completely antagonistic towards people doing so in whatever platform they *do* find to present their data. For example Henry Morris was persistently heckled in places he talked. Clearly this is anything but genuine scientific conduct and discipline. This is done, not because they think our material is worthless, otherwise they would hear out the material and if possible shoot sound holes in the material.

If there are holes in this theory I'll gladly hear alternative hypothesis out, for I'm more interested in the truth then being "right" or having the pre-eminent theory. Heck I've been shooting holes in some areas if the theory isn't bullet proof in some areas anyway. (In fact many of the theories in this book really are not new, so I can't really take a whole lot of credit for them. All I've done is assembled the clues and arranged them in a plausible way based on creation and devolution to enable logical solutions) Instead evolution scientists refuse to hear and won't let anyone else hear if they have their way. This is done for fear that their years invested in a wrong theory will make them look like terrible scientists that missed the blatantly obvious, for indeed much of the stuff that disproves aspects of evolution are very obvious indeed. (But that too is hardly new as all three kinds of evolution conclusively disprove the other two types of evolution theories.) For example it is plainly obvious to many observers of geological formations that these features happened in fast upheavals, rather then slowly over millions of years.

Do you think schools teach with a balanced outlook to their students? Guess again. Though the voting population of USA is spilt about 50 / 50 republican (Left) and democrat (Right), yet depending on the school of higher education be it college or university: of the teachers polled between .03% -5% to as high as 13% of teachers were identified as right of center.

Science and truth can only be the victims with this attitude and wrong theories being shoved down the audiences throats. These "sciences" actually inhibit and stop publication or presentation of any evidence that contradicts their theories. For example red shift interpretations and observations that contradict the big bang theory have been buried. This is not science. It's a power struggle and proponents of the big bang and evolution are afraid to lose their position and status. I mean if the big bang is wrong, so what! Come up with another theory if you don't like this one...as long as it takes all observed data into account. I think my theory does, but I could be wrong... I may have missed something. No crime, no shame, but at least I'm trying to be fair.

Murrow also noted that news was coming out in bites, not in comprehensive lots meant to duly inform the masses, and indeed radio news is anything but comprehensive. (In fact the few people who looked over some of this work repeatedly kept suggesting shorter sections to accommodate those with shorter attention spans so I have attempted to do this. If you don't think this is the case you should have seen it before!)

The media is in my opinion responsible for attention deficit disorders so rampant in our society. Information is usually presented in less than 5 minute 'bites'. In fact these 'bites' are becoming so short that people are starting to actually have seizures in front of their televisions. I've counted over one hundred scene changes in a 3 minute music video.

Often talk programs that are geared to make the star hosts look pompous and wise and their guests like buffoons ...unless the host is enamored of the guests views, then they exalt the guest as some sort of icon that could never do wrong. This engenders icon veneration. Fairness is almost nonexistent as an option when interviewing people with views counter to the established norms. This practice of course insulates society against realities and alternatives, and possibly unpleasant truths. Consequently society at large becomes increasingly unwilling to hear such opinions, because so much effort has been placed in countering those views.

Furthermore news only tells what happened, when it's too late to do anything about it, but rarely, if ever, does news tell what is going on in a way to show what *could* happen. Had a comprehensive public news service been in place all along maybe things would be different. People would understand how we affect other countries and societies and how they affect us. Meaning we might be just a little bit more respectful of the viewers of our programs in other countries. This was virtually Murrow's motto. We seem to think our view is the one and only right view, and like the scientists with their evolution theories shoving them down our throat, we shove our trash down domestic and foreign markets in the name of free speech.

Murrow went on to suggest the use of the media should also be used to "itch" the audiences instead of just tranquilizing it, but instead "we are protecting the mind of the ... public from any real contact with the menacing world that squeezes in upon us".

The powers that be seem to want to prevent the public at large from panic should situations become dire, like they are our nannies. We're grown up, we can take it. Murrow went on: "We have currently a built-in allergy to unpleasant and disturbing information." They want to protect us from information that would make us panic. Maybe a little panic is a good thing, as it lends support and the will to fight the things that cause the panic in the first place. Maybe a certain event on September 11 2001, might not have happened were the public made aware of how our so called freedom of speech is perceived by people of other groups around the world.

So soon has the general public forgotten the twin towers, and whine when wars are fought in defense of the freedoms we supposedly stand for and believe in. It would appear that the media has once again lulled us away from the realities pressing in on us from the world around us. The media when analyzing politicians that set aside funding for the same media, treat the darling politicians with kid gloves, analyzing style rather than content, but crucify non conformists.

These freedoms didn't come easy; we had to fight a terrible war in Europe to maintain them. We didn't whine when a LOT of our soldiers died in the fight to maintain those freedoms, for we understood how countries so far away can affect us here, though admittedly even back then they had to declare war on some of us in order to wake us up. Now apparently we don't value these freedoms as much because as soon as we stub our toes in say the Middle East, we want to run and let the world do its own thing.

If we don't care what powers run other countries we will eventually become victims of our own negligence and indifference, when these countries start to dictate policies here and how we live. This is what some would very much like to do. The forces of evil powers that rule the countries of our potential enemies are not in the least bit shy about forcing their domination on as many people as they can overcome, so we should be equally as "aggressive" in promoting justice and fairness in the countries others would rule and dictate.

If we don't objectively see our place and influences, be they negative or positive, on others in the world and judge ourselves accordingly, others will judge us and make it quite clear as to what they think of us, and they might do it in very violent ways. Of course if we let justice go by the wayside in our countries, what hope do countries in which we hope to promote these values have that look to us for leadership and help in these areas?

We take some of the freedoms we have for granted and abuse them in the name of freedom of speech. Freedom of speech? We whine when someone talks about politics or religion in our presence, but think nothing of pushing our potty mouths on the viewing public. Some say 'if you don't like it don't watch', but even the subtlest forms of psychological abuses are in the tamest of programs geared to wear away at the foundations of societies, such as programs that foster disrespect for parents or authority figures on the pretext of doing things that seem right. The ends does not justify the means; we should not promote things that are wrong to accomplish things that are right.

Pushing our TV programs and movies on other countries with the accompanying sex and violence and disrespect for authority figures is like a gang or deviate trying to lure our children away from us to have their way with them. We as parents would not in any way want such people around our children. Though we seemingly have desensitized ourselves to the extremes of our programming, the excesses do not go unnoticed in other countries. Though I don't condone these extremists and their methods, I can empathize with their concerns. Just as our programs over the years has eroded respect for authority and godly characteristics here in our heirs, so too has this started to happen in other countries. But this time some people in those countries are fighting mad that their "children" are being lured to our way of living.

Some people think freedom of speech means to be free to be loathsome and disrespectful to other people. We need to think of others before ourselves, and in this way we just might respect them more. If we make a practice of this among ourselves it will carry on into our media exports and in turn we'll regain some of the respect we once had.

Yes there are civil abuses in other countries that are horrendous. But how can we hope to positively affect people in those countries when their leaders equate our 'liberties' seen in our media and connected with religious freedom and loath what they see. They become unwilling to adopt some of our wiser practices simply because they see it all as part of the same society and somehow see them as all intertwined and mutually supportive. But then part of the problem is they fail to see and understand how freedom of religion or divergent opinions can co-exist with freedom of immorality in the same society, when they are used to top down populace control.

REALITY CHECKS NEEDED.

Our society has become dependent on governments to fix all that ails society. Rather than becoming part of the solution we have become part of the problem and burden. Many have become like whining children pestering their parents ranting and raving until the government gives them what they want. Rather than asking what we can do for our country we demand what our country can do for us. Governments have too often given in to the people rather than doing the right and the tough thing, and consequently so many countries are far more in debt in peacetime then they ever were in wartime, and indeed some countries teeter on collapse and bankruptcy.

Giveaways have given us false sense of security and blinded us to economic realities. I have actually heard a person give her child a reproach because he was going to go out and buy a loaf of bread! Her reasoning was that there is so much free bread out there that no one should have to buy any! If everyone did this who would make the bread, and why would they?

So few have learned to save and instead live in perpetual debt, to the extent that they accuse governments that manage to balance budgets and create a surplus of being stingy with the surpluses when these funds should be earmarked for paying off obligatory debts and investing in the future, and not pandering to some special interest groups. Rome promised free bread every day, but when they couldn't keep up, the population revolted, into unrest and riots, then dictatorship took over Rome. Governments around the world have promised their people too much and floating debt to do it, and that is about to collapse. I guess they have learned from history and are prepared for the riots. Several empty concentration camps all across North America are waiting for hundreds of thousands of new roomers. Tens of thousands of passenger trains have been built with 144 seats each, with each seat set up with nice comfortable shackles. Well at least that's what one internet site has mentioned.

FOUNDATIONS STILL REMAIN.

I'm not saying we are beyond hope. I still see many remnants of an honest society due to the Godly principles we usually held dear for so long, and the law and order structure that was in place so long, but even this is now eroding, with the mistaken idea that change is somehow an improvement. More often than not change is an erosion of what was already working fine.

Many people in the past put so much care into the work they did, as though it was a labor of love. Look at the old buildings and see the ornate time consuming work they lavished on their projects. Look at the old advertising and see the craftsmanship they put into the labels and the art. Look at the masters who spent months even years working on a single painting. Nowadays little time is spent on the work we crank out and in direct proportion little satisfaction is received when we finish the work. Consequently life itself is less satisfying, because so much of our livelihood is dependent on the wages we earn doing the work we do. Though doing a bang-up job takes longer, the contentment gained by a job well done exceeds the monetary profits we gain from the work.

MORE IS LESS?

We have so much yet the more we have the less satisfied we seem to be. One thing I have often noted is how content people are in countries with less; many a person has come back from some have-not country and been impacted by how content the people were in what was apparent want and need.

The people of these "poor" countries were so willing to share and give what little they had. Clearly our overabundance has instead of making us generous has often made us even stingier. We need to see those that have so little so we can be more appreciative of what we have. True many are cognizant of these differences and give generously of time and resources to help others and offset imbalances. If we lost half of everything we owned, in most cases we would still be richer than those in other countries who are considered rich by the standards of those countries. Our welfare recipients are often more well off than people with good jobs in other countries and often they receive more free in one month then people in other countries *earn* in a year.

SHAKESPEARE STILL TEACHES

We need to remember the child who has one toy and is content with it. There's a Shakespeare play that is applicable here, though I forget the title. I didn't get this play when I read it in grade nine, but I get it now. Though I forget the exact details, the play goes something like this...

A man is in a room and two people bring in a chair and they spend many minutes arranging this chair and finding the perfect place in the room for this chair. When they are satisfied with it placement the two people leave and presently bring in a desk. More minutes are spent arranging the desk in conjunction with the chair. Then the two leave and later on they bring in a table and a bit of time is spent arranging the three items, but they are soon satisfied with the arrangement.

Eventually many things have come into the room and the man just sits in the chair and tells them put the item over here or there and eventually he ignores them altogether as they constantly fill the room to overflowing. The more we have the less each thing means to us. We have too much and think more will fix the lack of satisfaction we receive from what we do have. This doesn't necessarily mean just material goods either.

Instead of constantly making our society more comfortable we need to look at those who have so little. For example I hear so much whining over a few potholes in the roads when some places in the world have no roads to put potholes in. It is in helping others that we find some wonderful satisfaction and meaning in life. Some of my most special times were found in helping people move. We need different priorities.

We need to place more value in the people around us and we need better heroes. We need these heroes to encourage others to follow suit. We need "Heroes" that overcome shortcomings rather than use the shortcomings as an excuse not to succeed or even try. We are going in the opposite direction, and allowing our children excuses not to try by saying they have "learning disabilities". This is a cop-out; we all have learning disabilities. This is why success is so difficult to achieve. But success is the continual striving towards a worthwhile goal.

Our heroes should be people that against all odds won battles with some seemingly insurmountable barriers, or that failed and failed time and again only to finally succeed in lifelong ambitions; particularly in our day and age. Too often we give up after trying something once. And I don't mean eating that fiftieth hotdog, or doing ridiculous things, but things of lasting value, that give a sense of personal lasting satisfaction and contentment with life itself.

Edison tried hundreds of light bulbs before he got one that worked. We need to highlight our inventors, and those who accomplished things without personal gain as a motive, but persevered merely to understand, counting the understanding as the reward. We should promote heroes that did the right thing even if it meant loss to themselves, because they counted the right thing more valuable than what they might have gained had they done the wrong thing.

Heroes that quit addictions and find purpose in life. Instead of idolizing those who get that fiftieth goal we should be idolizing those who make fuel go fifty times as far or make resources last fifty times as long by saving or reusing what might be considered waste by showing fifty ways to reuse it. These are the heroes we need. Heroes that limit entropy of our environment, rather than speed it up. Not phony environmentalists that spend tons of jet fuel that cost more than a normal year's driving fuel, going to conferences to get nothing done. Even green party reps realized these conferences were a waste of time and fuel. Heroes that show the races are all created equal rather than promoting segregation and classism. We need heroes like George Washington Carver(G.W.C) rather than the nameless multitudes that cavort on the screens promoting the senseless. Heroes that live on little and make it go far rather than the rich and the famous that throw their excess to the wind, for we will do like the heroes we have or promote.

I'm not saying any individual is a standard we should strive to mirror, except that person be God himself, and then we can never fully attain this standard though we should always try to. Through introspection and honest personal judgment of our own motives, we should strive to achieve the perfection we find in the creator. We can however see in good role models aspects of God worthy to perpetuate, such as patience, honesty, perseverance, inner peace and contentment in doing a job well, or overcoming an obstacle and so on. I found reading about G.W.C. an inspiration. We should chose inspiring heroes that urge us on to quality lives rather than idiots on TV that inspire rebellion and wasteful excesses.

PLUGGING THE LEAK

Even as a child I thought it wasteful to toss out empty cans as they were made of metal. That seemed like something worth saving, and I was so glad to see them finally being recycled. I've made things out of the metal in these cans, like hinges or shelf supports or whatever. I've even made chandeliers out of empty "disposable" lighters.

We shouldn't reprimand children for picking stuff off the ground, maybe we should encourage them and compliment them for finding a use for what someone thought was a piece of garbage; after they wash them of course. (If we could just get junkies to stop throwing needles away.)

As I write this I remember coming from a place that had loads of decent furniture sitting outside of their garbage bins and as I look outside I see a dozen pieces of furniture beside our own disposal bins. Even if not used as furniture again, even the wood and metal could be reused to make something or donated to places that distribute or sell such necessities to the poor.

Obviously society has to start grasping the importance of recycling and begin striving for such innovative ways to save and reuse trash. Not only should this be popular, but such should have been popular all along. I mean books could be written on the innumerable ways to reduce waste and they should be best sellers, not catching dust in the backs of craft stores or wherever one finds such books. We all could come up with some way to save some materials. They did it during the war when recycling was a necessity, but when peace came and we got prosperous, recycling fell out of favor, when it should have started an industry. You could actually run a furniture store and never have to buy a stick of furniture for stock. You could just go around the city at the end of every month with a truck picking up all the furniture you want at apartment block dumpsters....and probably have a pretty well stocked knickknack area to boot.

Cuba, since its being cut off from American imports, has become by necessity something of an example. They can no longer import American cars so the cars they had before the revolution have by necessity been made to continue on working all these years. Their streets are like walking into the past with all the vintage model cars all over the place. Though the cars are often more than fifty years old they still run well. This should give us pause to wonder why we have been so quick to throw away our old cars, when clearly were we to take care of them they would last all this time. Has fad and style become more important than preservation? What have all these extra unnecessary cars being made done to our environment? This disposable society is speeding up entropy at a terrible rate. We complain about the environment becoming like a greenhouse yet we trade in that two year old car for a new one. As if that isn't enough, manufacturers deliberately plan to make things obsolete or worse to fall apart. Car manufacturers in the '50's could have put a coating on mufflers/exhaust systems that would make them last the life of the car that cost just 8 or 12 cents but wouldn't do it so they could sell more mufflers.(check out Vance Packard's *The Waste Makers*) We are choking and drowning in our planned obsolescence, and stylistic consciousness.

BLURRED AND REVERSED

Obviously no society can be sustained by resource preservation measures alone unless those preservations also include intestinal fortitude and moral fiber, for indeed perseverance and high moral values also limit decay. Higher levels of these qualities can also be equated with the slowing of entropy. As we deteriorate in positive values we become more destructive to those around us. If we act in love toward our fellow man we will not do negative destructive things towards them.

Though one can't legislate, and completely eliminate immorality, one can make the rewards for it impossible to achieve and the penalties for it prohibitive to force this negative behavior back into the closets. It's not Utopia but society is really a series of struggles between the forces of good and wickedness.

The problems is we tend to want to justify doing wrong so it doesn't feel as bad if we do it. In principal we all want to be perceived as doing right and shame is a powerful motive for doing right. But even shame has been banished and crass boldness has taken its place. People fiercely defend their right to do wrong and they want what is wrong to be called right and thus force what is right to be called wrong. Indeed some would outlaw telling what is right because in their eyes with no absolutes, right and wrong are subjective. Corrective measures have to be taken to make what was wrong appear wrong again, and this means understanding why it actually is wrong. To do this we need to understand why what was perceived as wrong is indeed wrong.

All too often we balk and rebel at what we are told is right and immediately want to do what is therefore perceived as wrong. No one likes to be told they are doing wrong. But rather than reacting in a knee jerk manner we should ask ourselves why something that is wrong is wrong. It's amazing how study in trying to understand what makes something wrong, actually wrong, helps us appreciate what is right.

C h a p t e r   1 0   P a r t   T h r e e

WHO IS GOD & OLD SCHOOL CONSERVATIVE CONCEPTS.

I hope you feel to this point you got your money's worth out of this work. With 19 years of off and on work on this book and these theories, plus an additional dozen or so years of light research, this is a huge if somewhat poorly written work. Though I have tried to keep this book as affordable as possible with the restrictions of self publishing forcing costs up beyond normal big house published books, no doubt after looking at likely finished book prices this will have been an expensive book by any standard. Still I can say honestly you've got a bargain, with so many ancient mysteries potentially solved in this one work.

Mind you I think once creation is accepted and devolution takes the place of the theory of Evolution, and the clues are clumped in logical groups, many of these mysteries seem to solve themselves. Granted having a natural curiosity for these things, a reasonably high IQ, and a predisposition toward solving puzzles and this penchant for organizing similar materials together has made some of these things pop out to me whereas to others they may have remained indistinct and indecipherable. And of course I still can't be sure all of these theories are correct. For example the solution for what the ziggurats and pyramids were used for don't really jibe with what we understand in science to this point.

And sadly due to my poor writing skills some of the things expounded here may to some people not be expounded at all. Maybe one day I'll be able to afford a professional proof reading editor, but for now I recommend reading it twice. I've read this work about 16 times in its various completed stages and for about the first 6, I kept figuring out new stuff to include as I reread the work. Rereading the material often made it clearer each time I proofread it, and made more things become decipherable from the material presented. I'm pretty sure as you read it a second time things will make more sense.

These last few pages from now on become something of a religious work. Don't read any further if you don't feel like reading about old school conservative concepts.

If you decide to keep reading don't say I didn't warn you. I don't want you getting offended because of some views I present which would for the most part be spoken inside of bible believing churches where few people seem to want hang out these days. But since I figure this book will have secular and religious appeal, to this point I have tried to keep the religious rhetoric to a minimum. I don't want people feeling like they got tricked into buying religious material thinly disguised as scientific theories, though admittedly with acceptance of a creation / devolution theory, it's almost inescapable to have some religious views surface in expounding such theories.

But to be honest part of my hope in writing this book was to engender an acceptance of the bible and the views expressed within that book. So in reality I hope you do read it all. But fair warning, I talk about some very hard subjects. The world and the church are very far apart in some areas, and the gap is getting wider. So although to old school bible believers these thoughts may be quite indicative of their points of views, to people of the far more liberal elements of society at large, some of the views expressed from here on in will be extremely distasteful…but then to some the bible and God are distasteful too. You are forewarned.

CROSS SECTIONS SHOW WEEDS AND WHEAT

Most people that attack the bible have never read it or believe hearsay about it and take things written in it completely out of context. For example many say "money is the root of evil", when in fact the bible says "The love of money is the root of all evil". Many people say the bible is full of contradictions, yet every time I ask such a person to show me one they can't. I suspect they are merely seeing contradictions in how various religious people adhere to any given doctrine.

Sadly some people, who say they promote the bible, do it more harm than good by being pitiful examples of the standards they supposedly hold so high. Admittedly the standards are high indeed, so in reality we never reach them but we should always strive to. I often hear people talk more negatively about the proponents of the book, then the book itself, and will consequently base their opinion of the bible by someone's actions. This is likely why the Jews were so maligned. People assume all Jews were proponents of the old testament standards, because its contents are so tied with their history. People seem to equate Jews with being obsessive about making money. But I dare to suggest that because this is a people that has been blessed by God, this ability to make money is just an offshoot of this blessing. I suspect they just have a knack for making money that others are simply jealous of. I don't see them as some sort of scourge of society but rather a vehicle by which a whole nation is which they reside in becomes blessed merely by their presence within. ((2ⁿᵈ ed. Insert 2008) I stumbled onto this curious fact shortly after this was published. To further illustrate this deduction that Israel's people seem somehow blessed: one in a thousand people of the earth's population is Jewish, yet as I understand it, as of 2008, a full 25% of all Nobel Prize winners are Jewish.) If that's not enough, Several times the bible says something like Genesis 26 4 "…; and in thy seed shall all the nations of the earth be blessed;… "Similarly Christ equated Christians with salt and salt preserves meat from turning rotten. Indeed were all Christians to truly promote and adhere to the principles of the bible no doubt societies would be abundantly preserved and blessed and its individuals would want to follow suit. Some think the end justifies the means and will commit crimes thinking to do promote good. Jesus said they would kill the servants of God thinking to do God service.

Like any cross section of a population, we will find good and bad people. Assuming all Jews are bible believing and consequently examples of the standards of the values of the book, is like thinking that everyone in North America are Christian and judge them accordingly…which is in fact what is going on right now with this trend toward terrorism against some "Christian" countries. Some good and some bad individuals will be found in any cross section of a group, no matter how noble that group may appear to be. Even Jesus himself put forth the notion that fully half the believers of the bible would be rejected by him. (Parable of the ten virgins). Small wonder society as a whole rejects this sector of the population, due to a few rotten apples on the top of the box.

This state of affairs fosters decline and regression to occur. Due to some abuses and insincerities by some of the leaders in this faith, worldwide cultures and North American culture in particular are becoming more and more hostile toward this religious faith and consequently societies are becoming more regressive and belligerent in general. Society rots for want of salt.

Oddly, now this religion is blamed for many wars. True many wars are of a religious origin, but many people that pretend to adhere to this faith do not do so with their hearts, and can give this religion a bad name.

The bible also says people with feigned words would make merchandise of you, Christian and non Christian alike. How many false Christians have stolen money in the pretext of advancing good will and the gospel, when in fact they may have done more harm to it and civilization than the Crusades and the Inquisition?

Furthermore our movies, even the older ones, make people that believe in the bible look like pompous, overbearing, boozers, or crazy unreasoning zealots. Rarely do movies portray Protestants as level headed individuals. Though Catholics usually get a better portrayal, even they occasionally are made to look like monsters. Granted there are the odd kooks in every religion and sect, but by and large these are the exceptions.

People that focus on these aberrant examples and portray them as regularities in a given community do themselves and society a disservice. Often people that portray Christians in this "light" have an agenda and people watching these movies need to realize this. Furthermore people with hateful agendas toward this faith think nothing of vilifying innocent individuals of these faiths just to satisfy their own hatred. This completely mystifies me. Remember Jezebel.

The bible says don't steal, lie, be honest in everything and work with the best of your ability, be content with your wages, don't murder, or go after someone else's wife, etcetera. All these are good qualities for man to follow and in a society where these qualities are adhered to you will find a very calm sane and peaceful society, even if that society is not a Christian one per se'. ((2ⁿᵈ ed. Insert 2008) A dramatic example of this religion causing reduced crime occurred during the Welsh Revival around 1904-05. Police had little to do and went around singing to keep occupied. Judges had many days off due to the lack of cases to try, and when they did have work they often wore white gloves to signify no serious crimes were being tried that day. Many taverns had to close up due to lack of business, and the jails were virtually empty. If that isn't a good reason to promote biblical values I don't know what is. And a cursory look at our schools and society in general would suggest a good infusion of this principle is somewhat needed rather than fighting against it at all costs.) Indeed, where these exact same morals are cast aside by a society, in general it will be a society in extreme turmoil and a terror to its citizens. If the individuals of any given society live by godly principles, that society will reap the benefits, but so too will a society reaps the "rewards" of unrestrained rebellion against these values.

WOLVES IN SHEEP'S CLOTHING

There will always be people in any given community that will want to appear to be good people so they can operate freely in those communities. No thief wants to look like a thief, or he cannot be successful in his endeavors. No liar or embezzler wants his actions to appear obvious thus ruining his chances at doing the wickedness he would otherwise accomplish successfully. In fact often these people will make themselves look conspicuously hard working, pure or religious in order to be able to deceive the members of the communities they live in for the maximum amount of time. Take Eddie Randall, who was a very friendly kind helpful neighbor. Went to work and always was cheerful to whoever he met. But he had people on the lam coming to him in secret. Fine upstanding citizens like John Dillinger, Baby Face Nelson, The Barkers and Karpis would come a calling. He would set up 'jobs' for them to get travelling money, maps of best escape routes, safe houses, 'self defense' weapons and ammunition. A kinder gentler man was hard to find, till he got caught.

But it is these aberrations that so many focus on and present as representative of the religion of the society in which they live, giving all members of a religion a bad name by association. We are all individuals and accountable for our own actions. Sadly, no matter what organization a criminal is associated with in which he carries out his misdeeds, that organization will suffer loss of social favor when these criminals are found out. Be that person "religious", or a banker, lawyer, teacher, movie mogul, real estate agent or what have you. Similarly heroes of faith attract new adherents with the same or more enthusiasm.

Signs are starting to show that there has been a decline in man in recent years partly because of environmental reasons and partly because of religious moral decay. Television is accelerating this process abnormally fast, and in more ways than one. People get fed up with the television evangelists and think of all religious people in this light. Consequently moral decay accelerates in rebellion to the biblical based standards that held our societies strong. Thus people from other countries view the standard of morality, or lack of it, on our broadcasts and think of all of us in this light, and it excites them to be our enemies. And we wonder what we did to make them hate us and want to kill us all. Our broadcasts are even affecting what was normally a more moral based population in the countries where our enemies are from, making them hate us even more. Yet we fight for freedom of speech not realizing the very abuse of this freedom is probably going to cause our own demise.

TWO BULLS BY THE HORNS

If something has been called wrong for centuries and even millennia, which is suddenly being called right, we should stop and ask ourselves why they were called wrong in the first place. I have in this book undertaken to explain some of the mysteries of the past, but I would be remiss if I neglected to impart some understanding into some current areas of somewhat heated debate. At the risk of extreme vilification for daring to approach these subjects I will offer some understanding into these areas that I think need to be said.

Often what is right blurs what is wrong because what is wrong appears to be involved in what is right, when in fact wrong perceptions give incorrect conclusions. For example I have heard it suggested that Jesus was a proponent of gay behavior because John would lean on his bosom while Jesus talked, and John spoke of his love for the master.

The problem partly lies in how we perceive love and affection. I remember hearing women proponents of this behavior or "lifestyle" get completely irate because they could not seem to make people understand that they loved the receiver of their affections.

I remember it being almost taboo for one man to hug another man. Yet we need this affection from people of the same gender as ourselves. But former times looked down upon this behavior of a more demonstrative affection for members of our same gender, but rather tended to enforce a far more restrained exhibition of affection. This is really sad. I deduce this is part of the root of a couple problems, one being a fulfillment of the prophesy that states that the love of many would grow cold. And secondly, had people been allowed a more natural way in which to exhibit affections for members of the same gender, perhaps far fewer would have analyzed their realizations of love for a member of the same gender as something other than it was always meant to be.

I've never forgotten seeing two very young boys a long time ago holding hands as they walked each other home. It was a natural caring affection and nothing more. Sadly as we got older such exhibitions have been frowned upon and discouraged. When one looks at ancient texts one sees that this was a more accepted behavior among adults, but somewhere along the way this natural open affection has been so discouraged that people came to believe it was wrong of the people doing so and so it was concluded they were gay. And indeed it appears that some who have realized they had these affections for people of the same gender have thus themselves concluded they were of this persuasion. But since this love is natural and genuine they rightly refuse to say it's not, but they also feel forced to conclude by association of society's standards they are gay when in fact they are normal. This does not mean their conclusions that they are gay are correct or normal, but merely the love they have for one another is.

It seems people of the distant past understood all this and it was natural. As we can fall for the right woman or man so too can we find a deep love for people of our own gender. People seemed to somehow think this deep love for people of our own gender was inappropriate and thus could only manifest itself in incorrect affections or behavior. Our society restrained what was natural and so consequently a swing has taken place. When people realized they adored a person of the same gender they felt they should feel guilty and avoid contact with that person at all costs, when in fact the complete opposite was true.

Later on in our society this realization that one was in love with a person of the same gender made them think that they were somehow naturally gay, when in fact they were normal and natural in every way. For as David loved Jonathan, so too should we hope to find people of our own gender we can love every bit as much as we can love people of the opposite gender. The mistake we make is to think that since we love them so much, that somehow this should mean on a sexual level. The bible calls this error 'unnatural affections'.

((2nd ed. Insert 2008) People that refer to themselves as "polies" likely can grasp this higher level of caring, affection and love for those around us as seen when John leans on Jesus' bosom. Polies have a similar close bonding that occurs between themselves during the long winter months spent at the South Pole. From February 15-October 25 there is virtually no way to leave the continent due to the extreme weather conditions that occur on the southernmost continent. So the teams left at the pole just bond in their mutual isolation and interdependence. For example during their relaxation periods they will pile up to 5 on a couch and sit sideways in such a way as to be leaning on each other chests while they watch recorded movies. Also if a bunch of "Polies" are together as was seen when a group of them were happened upon at a cafe in McMurdo Antarctica, they were found sitting on each other's laps, male on male, female on female, simply because there weren't enough chairs. (Icebound page 110) There were no sexual connotations in this situation whatsoever. The interdependence and isolation turns the polies into something of a tribe and suddenly they are foisted into an environment where mutual respect, caring, and dependence are at a peak. This bonding seems to never leave them and they are never really at home again when they get back into the world.

Everything is strictly recycled down on the pole, and things like a mere lettuce leaf are seen as a luxury. Jerri Neilson was given three lettuce leaves during her birthday party and she felt she had never had a nicer present. When they get back to the world they see how wasteful and frivolous our lives in society have become, and just how much we have that we don't need, and how distant we are to each other. Their whole outlook seemingly changes forever, and no doubt they can grasp fully how much love has diminished over time when comparing our day to the biblical era.)

I have seen people of my own gender that made me want to be with them and hold them, embrace them, lean on them and yes even kiss them, but I have never thought this meant I was gay. It means in essence I have found someone I could love very deeply through natural attraction based on what makes us tick. We need husbands and wives but we also need friends of the same gender that we can love every bit as much. It is no shame to find someone like this and it is to be desired. Just as people of the opposite gender will meet each other's needs in some areas, so too will people of the same gender meet each other's needs in completely different ways. We were created male and female so each gender has something to offer members of each gender.

Though older studies have all but been buried, surveys and studies showed that people that exhibited this behavior more often than not came from homes where the woman was the dominant figure in the household over the man. Ignoring these surveys, attempts have been made to justify this behavior through science saying, people who exhibit this behavior have different chemical makeup's from the population at large. I don't doubt this in the slightest.

How we behave affects how our bodies function. If we live in constant fear we will have adrenalin constantly surging, if we act lazy our muscles will become weak, and so on. Our bodies react to how we act and think. Many people in more superstitious cultures or societies when told they were cursed by the witch doctors, so believed these curses that they died from natural causes believing that curse. Their bodies gave out because they believed they would. Almost like they frightened themselves to death. We can become slaves or prisoners to our desires or our fears, thus they can rule us and can affect our physical and biological make-up. It therefore comes as no surprise whatsoever that people of this persuasion will exhibit similar biology's to other people of the same persuasion, but different from those who do not.

Is it wrong? The bible speaks directly to these practices. Romans chapter one clearly speak against it and Leviticus Chapter 18 are the original laws regarding this lifestyle. Remember these Levitical laws were handed down by God himself. Though this lifestyle can be all encompassing and as hard to break as heroin addiction, it can be beat. But one needs that help that one gets from a commitment to God and his principals. But then one has to believe he exists in order to be able to be committed to him and his standards.

THE WOMAN FILLS IN FOR SHORTCOMINGS

One mark of our society today that is actually new under the sun is the emergence of women into roles formerly not considered for women. On one hand this doesn't bother me as some tasks are necessary and who cares who does them. Earlier I said there was one new thing under the sun. This is it. In Jeremiah 31:22 it says "How long wilt thou go about, O thou backsliding daughter? for the LORD hath created a new thing in the earth, a woman shall compass the man." Believe it or not men, this emerging of a directionally oriented women appears to be Gods doing! This verse means that a time will come that women will compass the man. Compass here means point the way, and surround, kind of like a wagon train that went into a circle to protect the people on the inside from the attack on the outside, or like some animals will do to protect others, not even of their own species.

One nature story I remember that probably has no application here but I found interesting all the same. A deer was being chased by a predator, it might have been a wolf, and was clearly starting to tire. The deer happened upon a field where many cattle were and somehow all the cattle knew the score. Remarkably the deer just stood there panting in the midst of them and the cattle surrounded the deer all facing outward. When the wolf came upon the deer surrounded by the cows, rather than taking on the large cows in rank formation to get at the deer, the wolf, realizing the futility, left. When it was safe the circle broke up and the deer went on its way.

Back to the touchy subject at hand. I'll get back to the compassing woman shortly.

Lines are being blurred and some women are becoming demanding of roles that were never meant for them to fill. Before one goes off half cocked, realize there are indeed sound reasons that women were never meant to fill in these roles, so allow me explain why and what role I refer to.

The role I refer to is spoken of in I Timothy 2:11, 12, and indeed people are starting to hate this section of the bible more and more. It reads this way. "11: Let the woman learn in silence with all subjection. 12 But I suffer not woman to teach, nor usurp authority over the man but to be in silence." This is speaking about the women's roles in the church. Why is this verse here?

Women now have been demanding the roles of minister and pastors in the church, in spite of this verse, and thus become rebellious to the very word they supposedly plan on promoting. This in itself should be enough to dissuade the women of the faith who seek these roles, but often it isn't and to my horror, certain women are even achieving these goals.

The first time I read this verse, around 1978, I was quite stunned to see it in the bible. I liked to listen to women talk, so I wondered why it would be there. I supposed then that there must be a good reason for this, but I was at a loss to understand what that reason might be. I figured there must be something fundamentally different with women and men that becomes apparent in the way women attempt to lecture or speak when compared to men.

So for at least twenty years I watched women for more than just the usual reason one might watch them for. I read studies and watched documentaries. I knew women were different than men, and who doesn't, but I wanted to find out why and in what ways other than the obvious. I slowly gathered clues, but in this journey I also found some very interesting differences in women, that seemingly had nothing to do with how they spoke.

One of the remarkable differences I found in women compared to men was this ability to multi task. I saw a research exercise comparing men and women in this area of multi tasking that was simply amazing. Though I forget the exact details about the experiment as shown on TV, it went something like this. Men and women were given a series of tasks to do all at the same time. These tasks included things that would be typical of a series of tasks around the house, like ironing, cooking a 3 course meal, doing the laundry, warming a bottle and a few other things. About 8 or ten tasks were to be done all at the same time, in a time limit. It was impossible to do the things one after the other because of the time limitation, so they had to be done somehow in overlapping time frames, which meant basically juggling tasks by doing several things at once.

Of all the men tested, only one was able to do these tasks reasonably well, whereas virtually all the women were able to do the tasks successfully without burning the meal or the things on the ironing board and whatnot. Here was an incredibly displayable difference in women and men, and I found this absolutely fascinating. I myself tend to fall to pieces when I try and do more than one or two tasks. I regularly burn my meals while working on some other project, and often only wondering what that burning smell is or that noise from the smoke detector is all about will I leave my project to find my slightly blacker meal awaiting me in the kitchen. But herein lies a clue to the mind of women compared to mind's of men, which actually confirmed some of my observations of women in how they talk and present ideas... and this is key. So put down your swords, and your rolling pins and your frying pans and listen here.

I have listened to women speak in church, even against my better judgment (meaning since Timothy said they ought not to teach that meant by the same token I ought not to listen), simply to try and understand the differences in how women and men present material and how they talk. In all my life I have only ever seen one woman that to a marked degree went against this trend. I have seen women I respected and loved fall into this same way of speaking, and no amount of respect can change the trend.

What I have noticed, similar to how women multi task, is how they also multi diversify in what they talk about. Men think and speak in what I term linear ways, whereas women speak in what I term [spider] web patterns. By linear I mean that men have a point they want to make and they go straight to that point, similar to how a ladder is built. They will go straight to the topic at hand and bring in pertinent information in from the wings as is necessary to further emphasize or pertain to the point they are trying to make. As they go along, the items they bring into the discourse relate directly to that point and these things they bring in serve to make the point clear, defined and understandable. Women rarely do this. They think they do, but following their conversations is like walking in a maze or following a spider web.

Women will have some sort of point, but how they arrived at that point in their own minds generally only makes sense to them. When they present ideas they will appear to be going straight towards something and appear to make sense then they take a sharp turn and you're suddenly lost as to how she got to what she is talking about now. I have listened to some women do this and never figured out how they arrived at the point they presented, or even what the point was! Women do this constantly and to other women somehow this makes perfect sense, but not even all women can follow all other women either. I've seen women get lost trying to follow other women and so constant conversation between the two or more women is the result. That's fine. This is how women's synapses work. There is nothing wrong with this... except when women approach the pulpit. This is why this verse is there in the bible.

The way women's minds work is an obstacle to clear teaching in this forum. This is not to say women can't teach, but there is some subtle and sometimes blatantly obvious problem with how women arrive at spiritual truths and then try to recite them. So to attempt to do so from the pulpit often becomes counterproductive.

This is also not saying women cannot be used of God. Take Deborah, the prophetess. The very fact she is mentioned shows God can and will use women, however the role of preaching in the church is one role they were simply not built to do. Teaching, I would think, in a more class like setting is probably ok because the people learning can ask questions for clarification, whereas asking questions during a sermon would become very distracting indeed.

Any role that utilizes similar speaking/teaching skills will have this limitation. I am not too fussy about women in politics partly for this reason, though I'm actually for women leading civic groups. There have been quality women politicians of course, but you will find they are just fewer in number because of this natural way in which women tend to convey information. I have listened to women spokespersons and I sometimes become frustrated in the tunnel vision they occasionally display in arguing a point. (not that some men don't have this problem too) Some will get a single point in their mind and by their way of thinking this point is a point of contention but they seem unable or unwilling to allow rebuttal points to alter how they perceive the point they are presenting. It's almost like you have to know or decipher the mazelike rout they took to arrive at their conclusion in order to dissuade them from those conclusions. And so consequently they occasionally end up looking obtuse and bullheaded, particularly if a interviewer knows the material well. It's like some are loath to admit that maybe they are wrong.

Though supposedly not politically correct, shows such as one of my favorites "Red Green" often still joke how the women in relationships seem to have to get the last word in, and ways are taught tongue in cheek how to live with this fact of life. I too have had girlfriends that just seem to have to get the last word in and always be right. (Mind you I had this same problem too and am still working on it.) Well maybe this can be worked around in relationships but this tendency can be very counterproductive when it comes to arguing points in government. However sometimes this can work to a women's advantage. I've been in a position where women have been spokespersons for causes I stood for. In negotiations they can be very focused and determined to get what they want. They miss some obvious points but what they drive for can be quite exasperating because they will whittle away at some peoples resolve to oppose.

Obviously women have different priorities and women's points of view need to be addressed and who better to understand and represent these needs then women themselves in these positions, so obviously women should not be excluded from positions of authority, but such should be able to elucidate points and views clearly and concisely.

NOT all women have these communication tendencies and indeed there are many women that have somehow overcome this web like communication pattern peculiar to women. But the number of women able to do so is about 1 in 7, so in theory there should be at least 7 times as many men in these positions as women.

Why do I choose the number 1 in 7? Because this seems to be the correct ratio. When IQ's are measured this ratio crops up. This ratio crops up with people in Mensa where the women seem to be about one seventh the number of men in the group. There are 7 times as many genius's and idiots among men as there are among women. Women are more stable in the intelligence departments than men which are all across the map.

Curiously it has also been noted that there are 7 times as many men mentioned in the bible as there are women mentioned in the bible. This was not done to belittle the women as some would suggest, but this ratio occurs simply because of natural things built into the population at large which determines what individuals will affect history and society.

Some women and indeed now some men seem to think women should be equally as evident in all positions in society as men, but something built into the physiologies of men and women means the equalization of men and women in society is simply not a realistic goal, and indeed it is a counterproductive pursuit to attempt to attain such a ratio. But then neither should a goal of 1 in seven be pursued either.

Certain jobs and professions will be strong suits for males or females. One shouldn't automatically suspect discrimination where unusual ratios of men to women occur, rather one should see strengths of genders capabilities instead and these ratios will reflect natural tendencies of the dominant gender in any position. In reality to try and change natural ratios that crop up in segments of society, is to deny the very natural tendencies of a gender.

Quotas should not be strived for either in race or gender when it comes to filling positions, but seeking out genuine qualifications of individuals to fill in those positions. Granted there should be no barriers that any person of any group can achieve their goals, but it must be realized that limitations in the abilities of the population itself will determine the actual ratios. If we force quotas on the workforce, the quality of the work being done at any job will become inferior.

One other difference about women that plays in this, is they tend to let how a person appears sway how they perceive the capabilities of the person in question and often will accept a person based on how they look or come across, or vote for a person for reasons that have nothing to do with the issues at hand. That's not saying men don't do this too. However it's been noted that because the women preferred Clinton over Dole because of how he looked Clinton got elected. Had only men voted in that election Dole would have won by a wide margin. (I'm not saying one or the other would have been a better choice, I merely note that because of the known way women tend to vote, politicians have altered how they feel they need to present themselves to the voting public, simply because women have different priorities as to what they perceive is important. I have heard women actually admit they vote for certain politicians because of how they look or come across and nothing do with the issues. Some have even jokingly said "what issues?". One women in my own family said she would "never vote for someone who talked out of the side of his mouth" (referring to the then prime minister of Canada Jean Cretian) Clearly how he said something, meant more to her then the substance of what he said. ALL of us need to guard against this trend in how we perceive politicians. We should stop voting for politicians based purely by what we see or what they say in rallies. In any race there should be extensive write ups of each politicians views and answers to questions put to them in newspapers prior to elections. This way people can get to "know" who they vote for rather than voting by appearances alone. Perhaps instead of, or on top of party pamphlets being delivered by individual politicians to the houses in their ridings; pamphlets that include answers to questions by each of the politicians running for that riding should be distributed so that each politician gets equal coverage and exposure. This would also bring down costs for elections. I sure get sidetracked sometimes…

WOMEN: THE FAILSAFE BUILT INTO CIVILIZATION

Back to the trend of women becoming more like rudders or "compasses" in our society. As this trend becomes more predominant in our society, women are taking on more "compass" like roles. As we've seen there is something of God's hand in this trend. So having said all of the above, it is now time for me to some extent appear to counter my own views. I read that verse once more and began to realize my views of women's more predominant role in society may be more incorrect then I originally believed.

In fact I started to ask myself "why God would change women's roles in society by allowing them to become compasses?" I started to see another aspect of women's character more crystallized, as though realizing God was allowing this freed me up to accept it and see what I had formerly overlooked. (Yeah old biases die hard don't they?)

Though I can't put my finger on it, there seems to be a void that women are filling with this compass like role they are coming into. It was quite normal in times not too far removed from the present where men were men and they led, and women followed quite happily where their man led. Whatever has happened to society, this area has somehow changed and women have become rudders of the ship the men formerly took complete control of. Too my surprise I found out that though women will do this, they usually prefer to be led by a strong man, and they find great comfort in such.

During the Second World War when the men were gone, the women almost took over the society completely at home and they ran it just fine…maybe with a few quirks peculiar to women, but they ran it and they ran it well, and why not; they are made in God's image too. It's just God put something in their hearts that they prefer to be led by men. Genesis 3:16 "…thy desire shall be to thy husband, and he shall rule over thee."

Before I am taken out to the woodshed for bringing that verse up, remember women were to be mans helpmate, not slave, and there is more than one way to "rule". Some chose to rule with an iron hand and be dictators, and some rule by the council of those they rule over and make decisions for the good of all. It is true for kings, rulers, prime ministers and presidents of countries and it works for husbands and wives as the home is the microcosm of the world itself. Indeed some rulers are ruled by Satan himself and some are led by God, be it over countries or over the limits of the land they own and the house a family dwells in. It is no coincidence that God is referred to as King of Kings *and* the Bridegroom of the church. The two roles are often very synonymous.

Women have simply begun to fill in the vacuum left by less motivated men. It appears this is something of a built in failsafe in women's physiologies. And like it or not men, this is Gods doing, God built this failsafe into women. This doesn't mean men have to now and forever be subservient to women, for by all appearances women long for a strong motivated man that can compass them. But when the chips are down and there is no one there to step up and take the reins, women will fill in when they feel the need, and they will do the best they can not to let the buggy go over the edge.

Having said this does not mean it the desired end. Proverbs 31:3, Isaiah 3:12 among other verses appear to speak against this trend. But because of the modern trends in society, women have found themselves more often forced into this compass like role. I can't help wonder if there isn't some natural cause related to devolution in all this.

WOMEN AND CHILDREN TODAY

Birthrates are plummeting and schools are turning into empty caverns. Curiously the New Testament equates women having children with being saved, (I Tim. 2:15) A curious statement indeed. Obviously when a child is in the picture the full load of care for that child brings out the best in a woman. Yeah I know it's old school, but some things were never meant to be tampered with.

Female role models on the screen have caused many a woman to be dissatisfied with what previously was considered a joy. Consequently careers are sought often at the sacrifice of what previously was held in the highest esteem, and sometimes when they are ready to partake of the joys of parenthood, they are ready for this task too late. They build up nests and suddenly realize there is no nest eggs.

Though not too related I've seen commercials encouraging grandparents to mortgage their homes so they have a little fun. But obviously if they pass on, there is a lean on the house that never should have been there in the first place and if the mortgagers don't repossess the house the inheritors will be saddled with a debt which probably has exorbitant interest rates and payments that they may not be able to afford, thus companies can steal the houses children should be inheriting for the price of a fling. But I digress.

It's almost as though kids are something to be avoided. Though in some ways this seems to me to be no surprise. With society disdaining and interfering with what once was normal disciplinary actions taken to insure kids maintained respect for authority, children become exceedingly difficult to raise within these enforced parameters. Those entering adulthood, considering children see these examples and fear to have any themselves. I've heard youths speaking of these fears and concerns and being very apprehensive about having kids of their own. Yet children trained in the way they should be brought up in their formative years will not waver from this path when they grow older.

Diligent parenting in these first few years will pay dividends in short order. Even young children can be observed to have very godly personalities. (consider Proverbs 20:11, 22:6)

Christ apparently anticipating this trend prophesied that one day the barren womb would be called 'blessed".

I don't necessarily mean that women must have children to be a good woman. What the bible seems to be indicating is that idleness, that is insufficient responsibilities and life challenges, is the problem. It may surprise you to know that even Sodom and Gomorrah were destroyed partly because they had too much idle time on their hands (Ezekiel 16:49). Obviously idleness is not just a female domain, men have been known to be pretty adept at avoiding constructive activities too.

MEDICAL RECOMMENDATIONS

You may think I'm basing my opinions and observations purely on the biblical model. Not so. People in the 1930's were starting to perceive a concerning trend in the population of the women in general. Remember these are conclusions of the time when this trend was just starting to crop up. We often try and find new reasons for the existence of certain problems or trends forgetting that when the problems first started to occur is often when the most clear picture of the cause was visible. Subsequent analysis often only blurs the truth rather than making it clearer.

People were noticing a growing dissatisfaction in women and their conventional status leading to an endless pursuit of more and more 'gains' for women, yet never satisfied with the gains they've achieved. An endless spiral, similar to competing with the Jones's. Consequently women were becoming more dissatisfied with life in general, because their focus was not one based on what they need, but rather on an endless competitive cycle of wanting something more for their gender or for themselves. (These were observations from the '40's to the 60's by men and women in magazine articles such as readers digest.)

In a medical book from this period, this concern is addressed. Keep in mind this is a summation of a period piece and not necessarily my opinion. I summarize. It notes that girls are being encouraged to be a variety of career women such as teachers, concert pianists, lawyers, doctors etcetera, [as might be seen in movies of the period]. It notes that motherhood isn't being held up as an ideal as it should be. Women are being taught to seek these glamorous professions and those that don't attain them but find themselves washing dishes at home thus become less satisfied with this and even can despise their work. Women who have some measure of a career, say, in being a typist for a lumber or vacuum company, might suggest they have more education to become these professions than a mother who supposedly needs less education. (Notice these professions mentioned are far less adventurous then professions women seek today. This says to me that this continual striving for bigger and better careers for women is still escalating from these more humble beginnings, but with parallel escalating dissatisfaction with achievements "gained".)

But it goes on to note that a mother must be a nurse, physician, teacher, legal advisor, cook, dietitian, a financial genius, a diplomat, an authority on child psychology and a hundred other skills. Other professions alluded to that are wrapped up in the mother inferred are linguist, social instructors, etiquette and manner instructor, anger management instructor, as well as a teacher that instills patriotism, political and religious understanding, and respect for truth and fellow men. This is no small task! Few if any man could qualify for this job! Men tend to be more abrupt and expect something to be understood by children which they never even bothered to explain. All this and motherhood was being looked upon as too lowly an ideal for some women of the day. Yet here we see a natural setting for the multitasking ability built into women.

It went on to mention a woman bacteriologist was envied by one mother as a woman who had obtained some measure of success. The narrator said she should be reminded that while the other woman grew bacteria in tubes, she was growing men and women at home. To be a dedicated mother is truly a career to be worth seeking. The book asked why this can't be a career to which girls can be steered toward with pride. (Modern Home Medical Advisor. Morris Fishbein M.D. 1934-1940 edition)

In all this the writer made no allusion to biblical or traditional roles, but felt this was a medical area for a well balanced and contented woman. His point seemed to be geared toward the physiological, psychological and sexual aspects of women, and not some nebulous concern about a series of so called traditional roles being abandoned or religious principles being shaken. His comments seemed to be geared in his understanding of the basic natures and psychological needs of women.

I guess a sort of parallel would be a person growing up in the countryside seeing things that come from the city then longing to live in the city to be where these things are. When they get there they feel out of place and never seem to be at peace within. They have what they wanted but somehow satisfaction eludes them. But since they were raised in the country their psyches are formed to be at peace in those surroundings. Being in the city thus upsets a natural setting. Though life might be exhilarating it is never really at peace. Thus begins an endless search for things that might recapture that wonderment of the city, only to have it elude them. I guess it's like that old saying you can take the boy out of the country but you can't take the country out of the boy.

This appears to have been this physicians concern. Have I got nothing better to do then read old medical books!

We tend to all think that if someone is getting more than us that we should have it too, even if it serves us no useful purpose. This trend to keep up with the Jones's simply takes away peace of mind and the heart. I've seen children demand exactly what a sibling got just because the sibling got it and they didn't. The parent knowing the child's gender or personality tried to persuade them they wouldn't want it, finally gave it to them. Subsequently the child looking at it then tossed it away.

This is not to suggest women ought not to have careers, but that they need to always have room in their lives to allow what medical doctors of old felt was a natural inclination not to be denied, for to do so was to deny oneself the very joys life has to offer.

I think society has given all of us a bum steer in making us feel we ought to be well off in order to have families. Contrary to what those adoption agencies and social services would have you believe, there is absolutely nothing wrong with being poor and having kids. Kids don't have to have the latest styles or hockey equipment to be content, indeed sometimes too much crap just spoils their inclination to be productive and inventive. In fact I would argue we should all go without at some point in our lives so we can more fully appreciate what we have, and maybe be a little more generous. After all, Joseph and Mary were very poor. We know this because they offered two turtle doves for a sin offering instead of a lamb and one turtle dove. (See Leviticus 12:6-8, and Luke 2:21-24)

THOSE MARKS

((2nd ed. Insert 2008) There is a trend that needs to be spoken to, as it appears to something of a softening up of the general population for a purpose. People of late have been getting tattoos at a very fast clip. My opinion probably doesn't count for much as to how they look. I figure if I want to look at a drawing I can go to the art gallery or draw one myself. The last place I want to see distracting designs or pictures is on some part of someone's anatomy. But no doubt, that is just personal taste. Even though the Leviticus laws told people not to make any cuttings or marks on their flesh, one could argue that is the old law. However when one considers tattoos in the light of prophesy one can't help but realize this current trend of getting tattoos on so many people is gearing up for a time when getting the mark will be mandatory. They'll say it's just another tattoo and it can be small…but it is the mark of the beast…you do not want it. There are six ways the mark can be gotten. We are probably all familiar with the six three score and six, that is, the number of the beast. But it can also be the mark (image?) of the beast or his name…and since it can be on your right hand or on your forehead that makes a total of six different possibilities. My recommendations are stay away from tattoos so you don't somehow justify in your mind getting just one more…one that dooms you if not removed.)

BACK TO THE GODS

With all the gods in the past, is it possible that one of them actually was God himself? It does stand to reason that if God created the heavens and the earth that he at some point would live among his creation. The angels know him and see him every day. Is it reasonable to assume God also came to earth to dwell with the people created here at some point too? We know he walked with Adam, so it appears his original intention was to be here with us like a father would be with his family. After all, we are called the sons of God, so it's perfectly feasible that he came here too. Did he come after Adam ate the fruit and man became "fallen"?

If we believe the biblical record, and hopefully I have given you reason to do so, then the bible which speaks so much about God might indicate if this happened or not. It does. Before we get to that, lets briefly speak about some characteristics of God himself.

Though as many know "God is love" this is not his foremost characteristic, but holiness is. This is not some airy fairy characteristic, it simply means pure, righteous, undefiled with no wickedness. This is important because this means God is not a liar. You knew that. If God made man and he wants to communicate with him he is not going to lie while doing it to trick us or lead us astray, he is going to tell it straight, and he is not going to use liars to tell his story. Some liars will try and pass themselves off as men of God but by their fruits you will know them.

What I'm trying to get at, is the bible is his word, and to prove it was his word to those he spoke it through, he gave prophesies by his spokespersons; some long term and some short term prophesies. The short term ones enabled hearers to test whether what the prophets were saying was true. If they said such and such would happen in a given amount of time because God told them it would happen then all they had to do was wait to see if it happened and when it did they could trust the rest of what they said and what they wrote.

Occasionally some "prophets" guessed right and God gave other measuring sticks by which to measure such people by, such as their character and actions and 'fruit'. Also the prophets never contradicted previous prophets but rather built upon their words.

Well, these people wrote of a time when God would come to the earth. In fact they spoke of two times he would come to earth, but to the hearers they thought that they were speaking about one time, so some of what they were hearing didn't quite add up. They spoke of a suffering visitation and a triumphant visitation. But it didn't seem possible God could suffer so things were never understood until He came and went. And indeed some still can't quite get this.

Oddly the bible says that God would become a man and come among us and be like us, so it stands to reason that someone at some point in the past was God that appeared to look like a man. And most certainly this is not an unreasonable conclusion, nor should we think this couldn't be done. Could not the creator also appear as a man to communicate with men? After all he says we were created in his image.

It's funny really. There were many men in the past and we elevated them to the status of gods. Jupiter, Apollo, Aphrodite, Athena, and on and on, all elevated to the status of gods, But when the one true God came to earth people do their best to say he was simply a man. He humbled himself and became one of us and even became a servant. This isn't what people expected from God so they think he just couldn't possibly be God. But the reason he came in this fashion was to be an example for us to follow.

Actually some religions are against the Christian religion because most Christians seem to think Jesus is God, though some sectors of this community believe he is Michael the archangel, or just some teacher.

Here's why I went into this God and his prophets won't lie business. Many people though they don't think Jesus is God, they do think him a prophet of God, and a prophet of God wouldn't lie now would he? So I'm going to use Jesus words and actions to show who he was, even though he never appears to have actually said who he was!

Biblical references as to what form God would take when he came to earth as a man clearly indicate who this was. We will see that the person, Jesus, was certainly Godlike by some small act he did.

Some say if this person was God, how could God be killed? He could be if he allowed it to happen. We've seen that Jesus was about to be thrown off a cliff but he walked through the midst of these people that would do him harm and went on his way because his time was not come. So he had power to take up his life. He also had power to lay it down.

If we cannot perceive of God dying as a man John 10 : 17, 18 Jesus says this. "...I lay down my life, that I might take it again. 18 No man taketh it from me, but I lay it down of myself, I have power to lay it down and I have power to take it again. This Commandment have I received of my father. "Though this doesn't necessarily mean Jesus was God, it does show that if he was, how he could be subject to death. However as we will see his death was not necessarily the result of his physical injuries.

JUST WHO OR WHAT WAS JESUS?

Now, one could choose to prove Jesus is God because Jesus says in Revelation 1:11 "I am the Alpha and Omega" and in Verse 17 he says that he is the "First and the Last" (which means the same thing) and then compare this to Isaiah 44:6 which shows the **LORD** saying "I am the first, and I am the last" (repeated in

Isaiah 48:12) And then when we compare all this to Revelation chapter 22 Verse 13 we see Jesus saying "I am Alpha and Omega, the beginning and the end, the first and the last."

Upon reading this we should see and accept that this proves that Jesus is God, as Jesus speaks these things in revelations after his resurrection. However I have found that some versions of the bible actually take out some of the verses in Revelations that make the narration clear that it is Jesus speaking in the quoted verses above. Consequently the people that adhere to these versions of the bible think these verses were added in other versions. But what this means is that someone in the distant past has tampered with the scriptures. Can we figure out which scriptures are correct? I think so.

For those who are content to live with the King James and related versions of the bible: when one reads the entire narration it is clear in these verses that it is Jesus speaking, so this should do for you. For those who have other versions of the bible, we have to dig a little deeper.

Before Jesus was crucified he said "Ye believe in God, believe also in me" (John 14:1) Take that for what it's worth. I don't know if all versions of the bible have this verse and I don't know that it clearly indicates in all peoples mind that Jesus is God anyway, so I have to turn elsewhere. Still it is an very interesting thing for Jesus to have said, so it deserves mention.

THE IMPORTANT DISTINCTION

When the wise men came to Jesus they worshipped him (Matthew 3:11). Jesus was just a child at the time so some might say he didn't know any different to stop them. A leper worships Jesus in Math 8:2 and Jesus just heals him. A ruler comes and worships him and then gets him to heal his daughter. In fact there are several instances in the bible where people worship Jesus, including the disciples, blind men, healed men and on and on. What does Jesus do when these people worshipped him? Nothing but allowed it. When the angel was worshipped he immediately stopped John from doing so, but Jesus allows it. THIS IS HUGE!

Some versions of the bible use the words "did obeisance" when it comes to the verses that speak of Jesus being worshipped in other translations. Doing obeisance to Jesus is just not the same as worship. So which translation is correct?

To find out we have to go to the original Greek. As a control verse we use the word translated to "worship" where John worships the angel because it is clear in this instance that this is only allowable for God. All translations translate the word used here as worship. We can also go to Matthew 4:10 because Jesus himself says to Satan who wanted Jesus to worship him "...thou shalt worship the lord thy God, and him only shalt thou serve" When we go to the Greek we see the same word is used in both instances. In both of these verses all translations use the word worship in these places.

Now when we go where some translate the word obeisance for when Jesus is worshipped in the King James, we see that the same word or root word is being used in these instances as was being used in the control verses. Whereas in some places a different word is translated as worship which mean things like awaiting the master; something like what a butler might do to his master waiting on him. These verses could rightly be translated "did Obeisance", but in all the cases where Jesus is "worshipped" it is the same word or the same root word used for something only allowable to be done to God. If Jesus was not to be worshipped, which really means to be adored and loved and kissed toward, and bowed down to, he would have stopped the people from doing this...but he didn't. He would have picked them up like the angel did and said to only worship God. But he doesn't, not once.

So in concluding it is ok to worship Jesus we can then deduce which bible versions have been tampered with. This tampering likely goes a long way back. Since I understand the Caesar's expected to be bowed down to, it's likely people loyal to the Caesar's surreptitiously made copies of the scriptures taking out the references to the deity of Christ, thus taking away their part of the book of life (Rev. 22: 19)

TWO GODS?

Can this be? Jesus refers to the Father, and though he says the "father and I are one" he doesn't actually say that he is the father, only that they are one...usually taken to mean of one mind and heart, in complete agreement in all things. They have and are of the same spirit. If Jesus speaks of the father as God yet he too is worshipped does this mean there are two Gods, seemingly a contradiction? Jesus is God's only Begotten son, but there are sons of God not to be worshipped, so there is something very different about Jesus that is not the same as the ordinary sons of God. If we go further into all this we see that Jesus is also the creator.

Curiously this is something groups that think Jesus shouldn't be worshiped actually acknowledge. Yeah! Some groups who believe in the bible and acknowledge that Jesus is the creator actually do not think he is God. I don't get this! Did God create the universe or not? It would seem to me that if Jesus created the universe, we should pay pretty close attention to what he says and does.

I have to admit some of this is pretty deep and deserves some sort of in depth study that really doesn't belong here. But Jesus said a few things that shed some sort of light on this peculiar business. Jesus said "I am the way, the truth, and the life: no man cometh unto the Father, but by me"(John 14:6). He's clearly talking about two people here, himself and the Father.

When addressing aspects of this problem to the Jews, he spoke of something David said. Math 22:44 "The LORD said unto my Lord, sit thou on my right hand, till I make thine enemies thy footstool." This verse shows that the Father is going to make Jesus' enemies his footstool, and other verses show Jesus will build his church so we see different roles attributed to the Father and the Son. Then he asks, if David calls him Lord, then how could he be David's son? Since we know he is talking about himself as the son of David, as his lineage clearly shows, we see that Jesus is eternal, for he also says "Before Abraham was, I am" (John 8:58).

The Jews got pretty hot when he said this because he said, in essence, he was older than Abraham. Also the Jews got ready to stone him, apparently because he used the term "I am" in regards to himself, because this was the term God used when speaking to Moses in reference to himself. (Exodus 3:14) In all this we also see David's Lord has a LORD too. This "Lord" Is Jesus, and the "LORD" is the father. That's about as clear as it gets.

It seems the angels and man are creations of God, but Jesus is the foremost son of GOD, like a first born with the rights that go to the firstborn. So what seems to be the case here is that God the Father had a son, presumably similar to how some cells divides and become two. Then the son creates the rest of the universe. I don't know how to present the argument for Jesus being equal to God any better than this. There are gods, and there is God and there is GOD (all Capitals). There are lords, there is the Lord and then there is the LORD. So no doubt there will always be some confusion. It seems that Jesus is the pre-eminent son of God and has inherited some of the aspects of God the father. The two of them are one and they are God...a plural situation. I can't say I get it completely, but since GOD approved of what Jesus said, we have to trust it's OK to worship him, because he has all the aspects of God the Father. Jesus said basically if you love him you love the father if you don't like him you don't like God. If you deny him you deny God. You can't do for one what you wouldn't do for the other. There is to be no distinction. If you love them you will do what they say.

THE WORD OF GOD?

One thing people tend to want to do is minimize the bible as just words written by men. True, man physically wrote the bible...often quoting what God said. But what is particularly interesting is that some of the things done, said and written about in the bible were actually done seemingly at the whim of the prophets.

Sure the records speaks of bad men and it makes it clear what they do is bad or ungodly or just something they wanted to do that wasn't bad or good, just part of something they wanted to do, and events happened because of or in spite of their actions. But there is a curious aspect to the prophets that I think is why some people can't accept that the bible is purely the word of God. That is because God seems to be on some occasions being led by men.

For example, God was going to destroy Sodom if 50 just men were not found in that city. Abraham bargains with God! He talks him down to sparing the city if just 10 just men are found there.

Furthermore God was furious with the Israelites for many things and at one point God had had it and told Moses to leave him so he could steam a little and then destroy the Israelites and make a people out of Moses. Moses calms God down, and gets him to think about what the people of the world would say if he did all this to take the Israelites out of Egypt, just to destroy them. Moses talks God out of destroying the Israelites!

It goes on. Joshua wanted more time to waste the Amorites and tells the sun to stay over Gibeon and the moon to stay in the valley Ajalon. It then says the LORD hearkened unto the voice of a man.

This whole concept of bargaining with God and having him do things we think are necessary seem strange to people. But this is because so many think of God as being high and detached from men and forcing his will on us and just being the tough hardnosed Boss.

People forget or seem completely unaware of this other aspect of God where he is a Bridegroom and a father and a friend. He will listen to the apple of his eye just as men will do what their wives or children ask. If we do what is right God just loves us to pieces. He knows that if we will do what is right and not be selfish, then what we want and do will be God's will. Yeah! That's the rub. Man can do Gods will even when doing things that seem like our own agendas, because if we have set our hearts to do the right we won't do wicked, destructive selfish things we are only doing righteous things. In our endeavors he is for us. Just like a father will help his kid, a friend can be called upon in time of need and a husband will do things for his wife. By wanting to do what is right in how we approach life we then become extensions of God's will.

People often ask what is Gods will for my life when they come to God and want to do right. The answer is amazingly simple. Do what is just and right as seen in God's word and then be the person that you are within those parameters. It's that simple. When you determine to be Godly, what you set your hands to do will be an extension of the will of God.

This of course doesn't mean you can do no wrong. We are human and subject to temptations so we constantly have to be on guard that we are not misled, and stray from what is right. We constantly have to be willing to judge ourselves in relation to God's word. If we start to think we can do no wrong, we tread in dangerous waters. We become proud, bossy, self righteous and haughty. Definitely not a characteristic of Godly people. We've all met people like this.

Jesus said that whatever we bind on earth would be bound in heaven and whatever we loosed on earth would be loosed in heaven. Yeah, men can determine eternal things! All through the bible there are incidences where God is influenced in his decisions and actions by his disciples and prophets.

In fact it speaks of him wanting someone to be a hedge between him and the people, that is to intercede for the people, hold back God's anger and tell the people what's what. A go between, an advocate, and intercessor. Many people can't seem to understand these curiously very 'human' traits that God seems to exhibit. But remember, we were made in God's image. He even asks us to "reason" with him. People don't understand how man could change Gods mind, intents and actions.

Part of it is how God has to keep himself away from iniquity. He is holy and can't have wickedness in his presence. He is so pure he has to have iniquity cast out or destroyed instantly should it dare to encroach into his presence. So why then does the earth continue on?

Seemingly in contradiction to all this, is God has very much patience and "longsuffering" towards mankind. He knows that we are the sons and daughters of Adam, and we are not responsible for Adams actions. So he cuts us some slack. But he can't be physically with us or the power of his purity will simply kill us. It's almost like a spontaneous action. So God has to have a hedge of purity around him. He won't kill or destroy what is pure and holy, so if he is surrounded by it, his power won't lash out. Ok, an oversimplification but that's the gist of it. So he sought men of God to surround him so to speak and be hedges for us beyond the hedge and to intercede on our behalf. Like a dam that holds back the water or a resister that holds back the power.

Yeah little itty bitty humans like us can touch God's heart on our behalf. Just like Job interceded for the three "comforter" friends of his who made life miserable for him during his time of trial. He takes the concerns of those who follow him to be his own concerns. Does God care that much about us? More! for he even knows the number of hairs we have on our head. All that power and he counts the hairs in our head. Most curious. He can love us so much he will dote over us and sing over us. Like a husband doting on his wife. If we follow him in spirit and in truth he will love us, but if we mock him or whatever else, he is indeed fearsome.

Now there is a double hedge. Now there is a permanent hedge and intercessor for mankind. That hedge is Jesus. Romans 8:34 "...*It is* Christ that died, yeah rather, that is risen again, who is even at the right hand of God, who also maketh intercession for us." As Moses pleaded for the Israelites, so too does Jesus plead for us, and in turn we can plead for others.

DID JESUS DIE OF HIS INJURIES?

The crucifixion was such a brutal death sentence that it has been said that many died from the beatings alone before they even reached the cross. I'm not entirely certain this deduction is correct, because Pilate marveled that Jesus was already dead and had to confirm it by asking the centurion if it were so. If it was common for some of the sentenced to die from the beatings why would Pilate marvel that Jesus was already dead? (Mark 15:44)

Once nailed to the cross, in order to breath, victims had to lift and support themselves. The pain from this action caused pain and convulsions driving the body back down, and to breath in more air the process had to be repeated, literally beating the person against the cross. The victims actually died of suffocation when they no longer had the strength to continue the actions necessary to continue breathing.

Being an immortal with no sin one still has to wonder how it was possible for Jesus to die. Due to a clue in the scriptures it seems he did not die a normal crucifixion death of suffocation, but it would appear he died of heart failure due to fluid in the sac around the heart! When the Roman soldier drove the spear into Jesus' side, water mingled with blood came out, something that only happens after a death of this sort. Heart failure?! How could Jesus die of heart failure? Jesus cried 'My God why hast thou forsaken me'. What? God forsook Jesus? Heart failure? What is going on here?

There are some interesting true stories that illustrate what happened here. For example. There were two brothers, one who did well and one who was more prone to get into trouble. One day the bad brother got in a real fix when he happened to kill a man. He fled home and changed his clothes and took off, but his actions were observed by his brother. He quickly understood what was going on and took the blood stained clothes that his brother took off and put them on. Shortly the police trailed the killer to the house and found the brother wearing the bloody clothes and presumed they had caught the killer. The brother said nothing, was tried, found guilty and was sentenced to death. To all it seemed that the good brother was guilty and they turned their backs on him and sentenced him to die.

After his death the guilty brother, so remorseful at causing the death of his innocent brother, went to the police and confessed his crime and demanded to be punished. The police, though acknowledging his confession, said the crime had been paid for. The brother took his place and paid for his crime. The guilty brother was free to go.

Jesus who knew no sin became the payment of sin for all mankind. Since God cannot allow sin in his presence he turned his back on Jesus and there was for the first time in all eternity a break in an unbreakable bond between the Father and the Son. This is why Jesus said 'My God why hast thou forsaken me'(Matthew 27:46, Mark 15: 34). With a separation, it broke Jesus heart. Jesus took our place and became identified with sin, that we could go free. This temporary break in the Godhead meant for the first time in all eternity Jesus was truly alone.

He died from the pain of a broken heart...too much for the body of flesh in which he lived.

Curiously and somewhat similarly man cannot see God and live because our hearts and bodies are too weak to sustain us in such a moment. I have to think this was an element in the difference between man and Jesus. It would seem because he was sinless his body and heart could withstand seeing or being in the presence of God, similar to how Adam before he ate the fruit could walk with God and not die, and we as sinful flesh are accustomed to broken hearts so we can stand heart break. Only occasionally do people appear to die of heartbreak. I admit this conclusion is somewhat conjecture.

The creator of all we survey came to earth and laid down his life for us. He took the punishment meant for us. I hope this gives you insight into just how much God thinks of us that he would do this for us. Can we take this lightly? Can we reject this? If we do there is nowhere else to turn. We then have to take the punishment for our misdeeds if we reject what Jesus did for us. Some men would die for a good man, but Jesus while we were still rebellious sinners treating him like dirt laid down his life for us that we might go free should we see what he did and turn our backs on the lifestyle that caused his death to be deemed necessary.

RAISED FROM THE DEAD

But rejoice for he arose on the third day from the dead. That might be hard for some to swallow. But again consider the evidence. The entire new testament written by several authors all confirm this statement that Jesus rose from the grave. In law when two or three witnesses agree on a point it is considered justification for believing the point to be true. Jesus resurrection was written about by many authors and indeed it's been noted that over 500 people witnessed him alive after the burial and resurrection.

Some said of the disciples that they hid the body afterwards to make it look like he was risen. Were this the case the elation of the followers would not be so complete. Originally the disciples after the death started to go back into their normal lifestyles. Peter went back to fishing. The lifestyles of them all would eventually return to normal... except this did not happen. Why? Because they saw him alive and went to tell everyone the good news.

As one might expect, back then as now, there were people who doubted this claim. Even one of the disciples refused to believe this. Then Jesus appeared to Thomas and he was convinced. But Jesus said to him you have seen me and believed, blessed are those who have not seen me and believe.

At some point we run out of evidence then we have to allow ourselves to accept the evidence and act accordingly. We are of such a mind that we can convince ourselves one way or another, for indeed we can seemingly convince ourselves that wrong is right and right is wrong. But at some point we have to just accept things and believe people, and the record they wrote.

We must allow ourselves to accept and from then on just continue accepting and believing, regardless of how we or others try and talk ourselves out of believing. The disciples wrote the record of the events. They had no reason to lie and indeed were so jubilant in the spirit that they had to tell the world. Because there is so much harmony in the testimonies of the various writers of the new testament books, were this a case for the courts, they would have to conclude that the record is true.

Strangely many people are willing to accept some parts of the biblical record, but think themselves wiser than what is written by the prophets, and pick and choose what they will believe. Some people who pick and choose from the biblical record as to what is good for them become people that actually work against God and his word, for they say it isn't all good, just bits, therefore calling God and his prophets liars.

Since this is something of a work that could always be added to, indeed if all the evidence were used to prove my arguments and theories, this book might never be finished. Indeed science is never truly finished until all is known, and do we ever know all?

Perhaps after this is published, some people will offer criticisms and some will offer further evidence that I've completely missed. If this is the case I hope to add comments, further evidence or even rebuttals as indeed some of this material may be in error and I don't want errors to stand if I find them, or they are pointed out to me after the first edition reached print. If I have presented any errors in this work my apologies and I will make every effort to correct them in future editions given the chance to do so.

I hope this was of some value to you who have bothered to read this book. Originally I just did some research to see if man really was more advanced in the past and started to realize that other people might find my research conclusions as interesting as I have. I hope you did. I hope some aspects of this work aroused curiosities enough to jumpstart a continued willingness to seek knowledge and question and prove or disprove what is taught.

The Thessalonians didn't just accept what the disciples taught, but "searched the scriptures daily" to see if what they were teaching was true. (Acts 17:11) Don't take my word for these things, but be willing to prove or disprove things I and others have presented as truth. Good luck in your searches.

WITHOUT SUBSTANCE

(3rd ed. insert. This next section was added in the second edition. Some flaws are still here, but the general gist is there so I leave it. For example Saturn appears to have been hit by an asteroid from the exploded planet, but here I get it reversed)

(2nd ed. Insert 2008) The first edition of this book doesn't have this section. After I wrote the book and published it I realized that it might be a good idea to give the reader an overview to put it all together just in case it wasn't clear to some. If your one of those people that cheat and read the last chapter first to see whodunit, well this will spoil the revelation of reading it as it comes. However it might make you want to read the book to see how I got to arrive at my conclusions, because what you're going to read will probably make you wonder what the heck this guy is on. I'm not going to give you the evidence as this is just a quick summation of all what is theorized in this book, just for clarification. This part is kind of like someone who tells you in conversation some factual conclusion but doesn't bother to prove it to you and expects you to take his word for it. So the challenge is really to see if you 'got it' before you read this. This is like that answers page at the back of the textbook. If you cheat in school you might get the right answer but you'll never know how you got it unless you work through the body of the book. OK enough trying to dissuade you; if you're going to read this part of the book first... I can't stop you now.

At a single instant around 5079 BC, all that is, was created and came into being. With creation, man was made so perfect that Adam cloned himself just out of curiosity. Possibly 2 or 3 hundred years after creation many of the angels moved in with man on the earth and had kids that lived over 1000 years. They eventually started building the blue "man-made" planet Elysia to stroll around the solar system in. They blew up a moon of Saturn and created the rings of that planet and played asteroids with the larger chunks that got lost around the solar system. Perhaps some of the Saturn asteroids got away and started smashing into planets. As time went on the planet between Mars and Jupiter became colonized. As man became more destructive over time, friction between this 5th planet and the earth and Elysia rose to a fever pitch and the people roaming the solar system in Elysia destroyed the fifth planet turning it into the asteroid belt. This started the "game" of asteroids in earnest. They realized they had made a bit of a blunder due to their blind evil nature that was creeping over mankind due to their getting further away from Godly principals and had to stay close to Earth to destroy the asteroids before they hit the earth. They became the guardians of earth as well as the explorers of the solar system. However a big one, about 500 miles across escaped their notice and it hit the earth, collapsing the water shell surrounding the earth and slamming into the earth so hard that the inner part of the earth pushed outward causing water to shoot out of the ground. That, combined with the earth's water shell draining onto the surface, meant the entire planet flooded so fast that no one could escape, not even in their flying saucers and few if anyone even had them as the angels, knowing what was coming, took 20,000 of them away. All on dry land perished except 8 people who had been told to build an ark.

The asteroids that destroyed the earth were also smashing into the planets all around the solar system actually knocking some planets out of kilter. Some planets such as Mars and possibly Earth and Venus were knocked out of their orbit and Mars came close to the earth on many occasions. After the flood it actually circled earth and the close proximity of the two planets caused them to exchange matter, and Mars took a lot of water and atmosphere from the earth. Mars in turn sent some of its material to earth causing some red layers of dust around the earth and the occasional Martian meteorite to hit the earth. This enabled the water on earth to get low enough for living condition to exist again.

As man started to rebuild civilization after the flood, the man made planet Elysia returned to the earth to see the results of the Earth-Martian matter exchange and found people on earth still alive, and started to help rebuild. But as they came to earth they appeared to the earth people as gods. Men including Abraham's forefathers willingly served them. They helped build worldwide megalithic structures with the worldwide antigravity grid that we call the pyramids. After the flood the earth's magnetic field was reduced in strength from the hit the earth took from an asteroid, so they had to beef up the system by building more pyramids. But during construction of some pyramids the earth grid was overtaxed and flipped the magnetic field causing the cracks in the earth caused by the 500 mile meteor to pull apart causing the continents to come into being. Afterwards they were a bit more careful and probably used time-shares with the pyramids to not over extend the system. At first they just moved large stones with the pyramids, but as the system expanded they started moving the quarries.

Sometime after the Elysians came down to earth, they soon realized that the Earth's atmosphere was more hostile to man and it was making man's mind fogged. Furthermore man was dying much quicker than before the flood, so they left the earth to stay in their homemade planet Elysia.

After the Elysians left, man wanted to become like them so they started a structure to keep all man together and start a new Elysia. For some reason a tower was needed to start the project. As they started to build this tower God himself realized that man with a more deteriorated and aggressive nature could be a serious danger to earth so he stopped the tower project by confusing and fogging their minds even more and this caused diversity of languages. After the incident at Babel communication about using the pyramid grid broke down. This inability to communicate caused a competition for the time-shares of the pyramid grid causing it once again to become overtaxed. Thus the earth power grid and the magnetic structure of the earth ripped apart causing the newly formed breaks in the land masses to rip apart at the fracture zones causing the further separation of the continents. With the earth already lubed up from the original break up into continental sections, the continents suddenly lurched so much that the water overran the land and some lands (MU as well as countless ancient cities) sunk permanently. The continental drift continued occasionally, caused by the meteors from the destroyed planet hitting the earth. After that planet was destroyed the skies were filled with comets and meteors and they fell to earth far more often. Many of which were still so huge they could cause havoc on a worldwide basis.

Occasionally the land moved so fast that one could actually watch mountains rise right before their eyes. Animals couldn't run fast enough to get away from the moving land. Thousands of animals were crushed together, and this created the many massive animal death zones all around the globe. These sites were subsequently washed over with seawater as it overran the land, and these zones turned into massive fossil sites. The dinosaurs also were caught in similar circumstances at the same time. With the animals crushed by the land, their blood flowed into rivers making the water of some rivers undrinkable and in fact some rivers were so filled with the blood of the animals, that the rivers actually appeared to be turned into blood. The very atmosphere of space descended freezing animals in an instant as the land moved about with the poles changing position or even flipping and the cold air from the poles moving so fast they instantly froze mammoths.

Realizing the pyramids had just made the earth a more hostile place to live, the survivors destroyed the crystals on the pyramids to never let this destructive thing happen again. Men's life spans were further reduced because of the destructive nature of the pyramids and the upheaval of the entire planet caused atmosphere to flee the planet. Mankind also became antagonistic towards technology and each other. Wars became more frequent but with man's still superior technological capabilities these wars were often nuclear wars, which even further deteriorated the earth's environment and some of these weapons were so strong they may have even further separated the landmasses. Some of the less mind-fogged of men realized something was seriously wrong and tried to flee to live with the Elysians. But because of their declining state, they were not allowed to live with the Elysians because now the gene pool was deteriorating as well. This would mean were they to live with the Elysians they would bring down the average life span from 950 years to about 4-800 years. Consequently being rejected by the Elysians, they dug underground to get away from the accelerating harmful radiation coming to the earth. The reduced atmosphere and the now hostile planet's environment made living on the surface a hazard to long life, and they have been living underground ever since. They still used advanced technology of non-winged flight in egg shaped and disc shaped craft. They could still visit the planet Elysia but were not allowed to live with the Elysians. For a while they would help the surface dwellers, but this soon stopped. They realized the earth's new environment was even affecting them after short terms, so they banished themselves to the underworld and would never allow themselves to live on the surface anymore, but would only occasionally visit the surface.

When man once again started to become more technologically advanced and blowing up nuclear weapons, the underworld civilizations were disturbed and since then have been monitoring mans technology, causing this current state of more UFO sightings going on worldwide.

Bibliography

Book 1 The Outer Space Connection by Alan and Sally Lansburg July 1975 Bantam books Paperback

Book 2 Chariot of the Gods? by Erich Von Daniken 1969 Souvenir Press Hard Cover.

Book 3 In Search of Ancient Gods by Erick Von Daniken 1972 Souvenir Press (Putnam)

Book 4 Gods From Outer Space by Erick Von Daniken 1968 / 1970 Bantam Paperback April 1972

Book 5 Extraterrestrial Visitations From Prehistoric Times to the Present by Jacques Bergier 1970/1973 Signet paperback July 1974

Book 6 Atlantis The Eighth Continent by Charles Berlitz. 1984 Fawcett Crest (Ballantine 1985)

Book 7 The Bermuda Triangle by Charles Berlitz 1974 Avon Paperback September 1975

Book 8 In Search of Ancient Mysteries by Alan and Sally Lansburg February 1974 Bantam paperback

Book 9 Scientific Creationism Edited by Dr. Henry M. Morris 1974 /1985 Master Books

Book 10 Von Daniken's Proof by Erick Von Daniken 1977 Bantam July 1978 paperback

Book 11 Book 11 We Are Not The First by Andrew Tomas 1971 Bantam Paperback April 1973 paperback

Book 12 The Secret Forces of the Pyramids by Warren Smith 1975 Zebra paperback Kensington Publishing Corp.

Book 13 Earth Magic by Francis Hitching 1976 Kangaroo Pocket Book 1978

Book 14 Worlds In Collision by Immanuel Velikovsky 1950 Dell Paperback November 1973

Book 15 Incredible by Kevin McFarland 1976 Signet paperback June 1977

Book 16 The Lost Continent of Mu by James Churchward 1931 Vail-Ballou press hardcover(June 1950)

Book 17 The 12th Planet by Zecharia Sitchin 1976 Avon Paperback July 1978

Book 18 Invisible Horizons by Vincent Gaddis 1965 Ace paperback

Book 19 We Are The Earthquake Generation by Jeffrey Goodman Ph.D. 1978 Berkley Paperback October 1979

Book 20 In Search Of Extraterrestrials by Alan Lansburg. 1976 Bantam paperback Jan. 1977

Book 21 Timeless Earth by Peter Kolosimo 1968/1973 Bantam paperback May 1975

Book 22 The Mysterious Unknown by Robert Charroux 1969 Corgi Paperback 1973

Book 23 Gods and Spacemen in the Ancient West by W. Raymond Drake 1974 Signet paperback 1974

Book 24? Without a Trace by Charles Berlitz 1977 Ballantine paperback Dec. 1987

Book 25 Ages in Chaos Immanuel Velikovsky 1952 Abacus paperback 1974

Book 26 Limbo of the Lost by John Wallace Spencer 1969 Bantam Paperback 1974

Book 27 Limbo of the Lost- Today by John Wallace Spencer 1969 Bantam Paperback 1975

Book 28 UFOs: Interplanetary Visitors by Raymond E. Fowler 1974 Bantam paperback 1979

Book 29 Gods, Demons and Space Chariots by Eric Norman 1970 Lancer paperback

Book 30 Mysteries of Time and Space by Brad Steiger 1974 Dell Paperback March 1976

Book 31 Secrets of Lost Atland by Robert Scrutton 1978 Sphere paperback 1979

Book 32 Alien Meetings by Brad Steiger 1978 Ace paperback

Book 33 The Ancient Engineers by L. Sprague De Camp 1960 Ballantine paperback Feb. 1974

Book 34 Gods and Spacemen in the Ancient East by W. Raymond Drake 1968 Signet paperback Dec. 1973

Book 35 Atlantis Rising by Brad Steiger 1973 Dell paperback Nov. 1975

Book 37 Mysteries From Forgotten Worlds by Charles Berlitz 1972 Granada Paperback 1983

Book 38 Did Genesis Man Conquer Space by Emil Gaverluk and Jack Hamm Nelson Paperback C. 1971

Book 41 The Two Babylons by Rev. Alexander Hislop Circa 1859, 1959 Loizeaux Bros. Hardcover.

Book42 The War of Gods and Men by Zecharia Sitchin 1985 Avon Paperback June 1985

Book 43 The Hollow Earth by Dr. Raymond Bernard 1969 Citadel paperback

Book 44 The evolution of Physics by Albert Einstein and Leopold Infeld 1938 Cambridge press 1961

Book 46 UFO Canada by Yurko Bondarchuk 1979 Signet paperback May 1981

Book 47 Flying Saucers Uncensored by Harold T. Wilkins 1955 Pyramid paperback Feb. 1975

Book 49 Entropy by Jeremy Rifkin 1980 Bantam paperback Oct. 1981

Book 50 Parallel Universe by Adi-Kent Thomas Jeffrey 1977 Warner Books Paperback June 1977

Book 51 Maps of the Ancient Sea Kings by Charles Hapgood

Book 52 Lightning in his Hand by Inez Hunt & Wanehaw Draper 1964 A biography about Nikola Tesla

Book 53 Earth in Upheaval by Immanuel Velikovsky 1955 Pocket Paperback Sept. 1977

Book 54 Evolution- The Fossils Say No! by Duane T. Gish Ph.D. 1978 Creation -Life Pub. Paperback

Book 56 Peter Freuchen's Book of the Eskimos 1961 World Pub. Comp. Hardcover

Book 57 Mysteries of the Unexplained by Readers Digest 1982

Book 58 Omni's Continuum 1982 Little Brown paperback 1st ed.

Book 61 The Book of the Dead translated by Sir E. A. Wallace Budge 1960

Book 62 Strange Worlds by Frank Edwards 1964 Ace paperback

Book 63 Understanding Physics: Light, Magnetism, and Electricity by Isaac Asimov 1966 Signet paperback April 1969 2nd ed.

Book 64 The Mystery of Atlantis by Charles Berlitz 1969 Tower paperback

Book 65 The Ramayana as translated By Aubrey Menen 1954

OTHER SOURCE MATERIAL

The Bible King James Version 1611

A Dictionary of the Bible by Smith and Peloubet Published by John C. Winston 1884 ed

Atlantis Rising magazine #35, 68-118 (most issues)

Book of the Hopi. Frank Waters.

CEN Technical Journal of August 2001

Discover Jan '89

Discover Feb '89

Discover, September 1989,

Discover Nov. 1989

Discover, April 1990

Encyclopaedia of Science and Technology, Volume 2, page 299, 1987 Ed.

1989 Guinness book of records

Harmonic 33 by Bruce Cathie 1968 Sphere paperback 1980

Icebound by DR. Jerri Nielson

Life magazine Feb 1989

Mahabarata

Mechanics Illustrated June 1964

Modern Home Medical Advisor. Morris Fishbein M.D. 1934-1940 edition

National Geographic Feb 1967

National Geographic June, 1973

National Geographic October 1974

National Geographic September 1976

National Geographic April 1979

National Geographic March 1980,

National Geographic Dec '84

National Geographic November 1985,

National Geographic Dec 1992

Time magazine, March 25, 1991,

Readers Digest March 1959

Readers Digest Aug. 1959

Realm of the Incas. Victor von Hagen

Science digest October 1982

Scientific American Sept. '75

Scientific American March 1989

Strange Stories, Amazing Facts. Readers Digest (Copyright 1975)

Strongs concordance (Copyright 1890)

World of Strange Phenomena

Printed in the United States
By Bookmasters